NEW ACRONYMS,
INITIALISMS, & ABBREVIATIONS
1981

OTHER GALE PUBLICATIONS

TRADE NAMES DICTIONARY—Second Edition. 2 volumes. Contains over 130,000 alphabetically arranged entries for consumer products and their manufacturers. Product entries give: trade name, brief description, name of manufacturer, and a code identifying the source of the information. Company entries provide company names and addresses. **NEW TRADE NAMES**, 1980 and 1981 supplements. **TRADE NAMES DIC-TIONARY: COMPANY INDEX**. Rearranges entries from *TND* alphabetically by firm, with separate name and address list of 30,000 companies.

ENCYCLOPEDIA OF ASSOCIATIONS—Fifteenth Edition. Volume 1, **NATIONAL ORGANIZATIONS OF THE U.S.**, contains over 14,000 entries in 17 categories. With index to organization names and keywords. Volume 2, **GEOGRAPHIC AND EXECUTIVE INDEX**. Volume 3, **NEW ASSOCIATIONS AND PROJECTS**, quarterly supplements to Volume 1. With cumulative alphabetical and keyword indexes.

DIRECTORY OF SPECIAL LIBRARIES AND INFORMATION CENTERS—Sixth Edition. Volume 1 contains information on over 14,000 special libraries, information centers, and documentation centers in the U.S. and Canada. Detailed subject index. Volume 2, **GEOGRAPHIC AND PERSONNEL INDEXES.** Volume 3, **NEW SPECIAL LIBRARIES,** a periodical supplement to Volume 1. Cumulatively indexed.

SUBJECT DIRECTORY OF SPECIAL LIBRARIES AND INFORMATION CENTERS—Sixth Edition. A subject arrangement of all entries in *Directory of Special Libraries*. Five volumes covering these major fields: Business and Law, Education and Information Science, Health Sciences, Social Sciences and Humanities, and Science and Technology.

RESEARCH CENTERS DIRECTORY—Sixth Edition. A guide to over 6,000 university-related and other nonprofit research organizations in the U.S. and Canada. With indexes of subjects, institutions, and research centers. **NEW RESEARCH CENTERS,** periodical supplements to *RCD*. Cumulatively indexed.

MANAGEMENT INFORMATION GUIDE SERIES. Authoritative, comprehensive, carefully indexed guides to the literature of such major business and governmental areas as Accounting, Commercial Law, Computers, Insurance, Communications, Transportation, Public Relations, and Economic and Business History.

TRAINING AND DEVELOPMENT ORGANIZATIONS DIRECTORY—Second Edition. Provides detailed profiles of the activities and specialties of hundreds of companies, institutes, and special consulting groups that conduct managerial and supervisory training courses for business firms and governmental agencies. Indexes.

DIRECTORY OF DIRECTORIES—First Edition. A cumulation of material found in the 1977-78 issues of *Directory Information Service*, this single clothbound volume contains updated and revised entries for nearly 4,000 directories listed in *DIS*, plus about 1,400 entries for directories not found in *DIS*. Covers business and industrial directories, professional and scientific rosters, and other lists and guides of all kinds. Detailed subject index and title index. **DIRECTORY INFORMATION SERVICE,** inter-edition supplements.

NEW ACRONYMS, INITIALISMS, & ABBREVIATIONS 1981

Volume 2 of
Acronyms, Initialisms, & Abbreviations Dictionary,
Seventh Edition

A Guide to Alphabetic Designations,
Contractions, Acronyms, Initialisms,
Abbreviations, and Similar Condensed Appellations

Covering: Aerospace, Associations, Biochemistry, Business and Trade,
Domestic and International Affairs, Education, Electronics, Genetics, Government,
Labor, Medicine, Military, Pharmacy, Physiology, Politics, Religion, Science, Societies,
Sports, Technical Drawings and Specifications, Transportation, and Other Fields

Edited by
Ellen T. Crowley

OTHER VOLUMES

GALE RESEARCH COMPANY • BOOK TOWER • DETROIT MICHIGAN 48226

Editor: Ellen T. Crowley

Associate Editor: Donna Wood
Assistant Editor: Helen E. Sheppard
Editorial Assistant: Prindle Parkhurst

Computerized photocomposition by
Computer Composition Corporation
Madison Heights, Michigan

This set consists of the following volumes:

Volume 1—Acronyms, Initialisms, and Abbreviations Dictionary
Volume 2—New Acronyms, Initialisms, and Abbreviations
(Two paperbound supplements published
between editions of Volume 1)
Volume 3—Reverse Acronyms, Initialisms, and Abbreviations Dictionary

ISBN 0-8103-0501-1
ISSN 0148-866X
Library of Congress Catalog Card Number 80-82871

CONTENTS

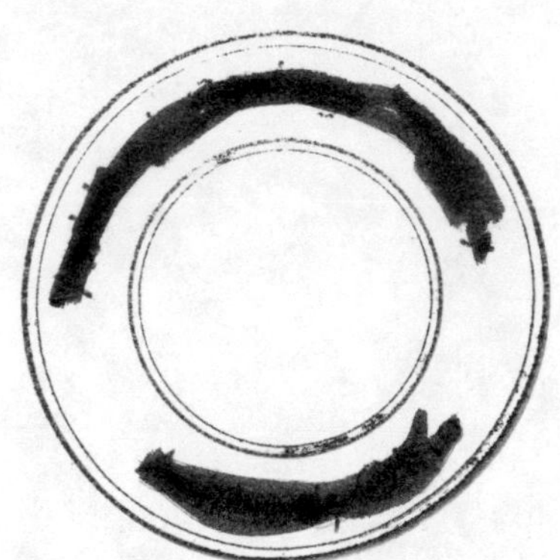

A WORD ABOUT
NEW ACRONYMS, INITIALISMS, AND ABBREVIATIONS

The publication of supplements to each edition of *Acronyms, Initialisms, and Abbreviations Dictionary (AIAD)* has proved helpful in making terms available while their currency is at a peak and in keeping users informed and up to date in a constantly changing and expanding field.

New Acronyms, Initialisms, and Abbreviations 1981 (NAIA-1981) is the first of two supplements to the seventh edition of *Acronyms, Initialisms, and Abbreviations Dictionary (AIAD).* It contains over 13,000 newly coined or newly found terms. The rationale for compiling this supplement and editorial practices followed in preparing it are the same as those that applied to the seventh edition, the preface to which is reprinted following this note.

New Fields Contribute Many Terms

It is safe to say that the more dynamic a field of endeavor is, the greater is the number of acronyms and initialisms emanating from it. *New Acronyms, Initialisms, and Abbreviations* reflects this trend; it is especially strong in terms from such forward-moving activities as science, medicine, data processing, aerospace technology, social welfare, education, military affairs, and various popular causes.

Current Events Well Represented

Current events are often the source of abbreviated designations intended as time- and space-savers or as catchy references to timely topics. Examples in the 1981 supplement include the automotive industry's J, K, and X cars; O & W (Oldest and Wisest), reporters' waggish nickname for President Ronald Reagan; and CC (Closed Captioned), a designation indicating that a television program has been specially captioned for the deaf.

The growing use of acronymic shorthand can be seen in many other phases of modern living. The medical field has shown increasing concern with TSS (Toxic Shock Syndrome) and PTSD (Post-Traumatic Stress Disorder), a psychiatric problem that is beginning to manifest itself in some Vietnam veterans. The popularizing of things "preppie" has resulted in more widespread use of such slang initialisms as KPOC (Key Prep on Campus), TTFW (Too Tacky for Words), and T & T (Tanqueray and Tonic). Hundreds of recently formed organizations vie for public attention to their causes. MM (Moral Majority), MERA (Mormons for ERA), and LCHA (Love Canal Homeowners Association) are only a few.

Modern technology promises a VAT soon (Voice-Activated Typewriter), modern music now includes a movement known as NW, or New Wave, and the New York Stock Exchange (NYSE) has given birth to the New York Futures Exchange (NYFE, pronounced "knife"). Not only does the world now know who shot JR on television's "Dallas" series, but also that the "JR" stands for John Ross Ewing, Jr.

Not All Terms Recent

Not all entries in *NAIA-81* are newly formed or even in common current use, but are included for their historical interest or to expand fields that have been covered in Volume 1 *(AIAD).* Users will find in this supplement greatly expanded coverage of periodical title abbreviations, broadcasting call letters, and airport codes. Also continuing is coverage of scientific and medical terminology, data processing terms, organization names, and other subject fields. There are brand names: ADIDAS and JARTRAN; rock music groups: MC5 (Motor City Five); and mnemonic guides to the notes on the treble clef (EGBDF), the nine planets (MVEMJSUNP), and early Cabinet departments (ST. WAPNIACL). A number of terms date to World War I, and several originated in the 19th century, including HOM (Heartless Old Man), a sobriquet for British Prime Minister William Gladstone.

Acknowledgments

The efforts of several persons were of considerable help in the compilation of the 1981 supplement. Mildred Hunt and Miriam M. Steinert, editorial consultants, continue to furnish many timely entries along with expanding our collection of science terms; Dr. Edwin B. Steen, Professor Emeritus of Biology, contributed a number of medical entries; and Leland G. Alkire, editor of *Periodical Title Abbreviations,* third edition, continues to add to our collection of such abbreviations. Charles Parsons, of the Translation Research Institute, contributed a number of terms; and valuable additions were also provided from the extensive personal collections of David Glagovsky, Jack Gordon, and Donald Weeks. Our appreciation is extended to Burroughs Corporation, for permission to include terms from their *Computer Acronyms and Abbreviations Handbook.*

Suggestions Are Welcome

Users of *NAIA* and *AIAD* can make unique and important contributions to future supplements and new editions by notifying the editor of subject fields that are not adequately covered, by suggesting sources for covering such fields, and even by sending individual terms they feel should be included. Suggestions and new material can be addressed:

> Ellen T. Crowley
> Gale Research Company
> Book Tower
> Detroit, Michigan 48226

PREFACE TO
THE SEVENTH EDITION

Acronyms and similar abbreviated terms have served as handy communication shortcuts for centuries. In ancient Rome SPQR stood for Senatus Populusque Romanus (Senate and People of Rome). A boastful inscription during the Middle Ages read AEIOU, one variation of which expanded to Austriae Est Imperare Orbi Universo, or, It Is Given to Austria to Rule the Whole World.

It has been in the fast-paced, technological atmosphere of the twentieth century, however, that these terms have thrived. The era of the New Deal produced an alphabet soup of agencies and programs—NRA (National Recovery Administration), WPA (Works Progress Administration), and so forth. World War II spawned new weapons, new codes, and a resulting population explosion of "initialese." It was during this period that the word "acronym" may have been coined, since it appears to have been used first in the February, 1943, issue of *American Notes and Queries*.

In modern times, breakneck progress in electronics, space exploration, and data processing brought new concepts, new projects, and new instruments. It also brought new acronymic forms to save precious inches of newsprint and precious seconds of broadcast time, to serve as cloaks of military secrecy and as spotlights on products, ideas, and programs that the public was expected to support, admire, or purchase.

Keeping Up with "Acronymizing"

The furious growth of this new "language" and the need to make it manageable for the public led to this book.

The first edition (1960) provided a compact collection of about 12,000 terms. That number increased nearly fourfold by the time the second edition was published a few years later, and, in an attempt to stay abreast of the proliferation of terms, yearly supplements have been issued between editions since 1968. With this seventh edition, the number of entries has climbed to over 211,000, and the editors detect no slackening in the pace at which this particularly modern language is growing.

Subject Range Varies Widely

An extensive variety of subjects is represented in *Acronyms, Initialisms, and Abbreviations Dictionary (AIAD)*. There are thousands of entries, of course, from the particularly acronym-oriented fields of data processing, the military, aerospace, and so forth. In addition, there are less-expected entries such as automobiles: MG (Morris Garage); religious orders: SJ (Societas Jesu, or, Society of Jesus); police terms: B & E (Breaking and Entering); and slang: TGIF (Thank God It's Friday).

There are alphabetical designations for songs and musical groups, films and television shows, clothing and food, authors and US Presidents.

Coverage Continues to Expand

Nearly every subject area covered by this dictionary is expanded to some extent with each new edition. Often, expansion efforts include the addition of entire new fields of terms not previously covered.

For the seventh edition, official aircraft nationality and registration marks are listed, as well as FAA designations for Canadian aircraft operators engaged in flight into United States airspace.

The coverage of abbreviations for periodical titles, greatly increased in the sixth edition, continues to expand, with over 2,500 added to the seventh edition. The information can be of great assistance to researchers and bibliographers, since abbreviations for periodicals have never been successfully standardized.

Many additional items appear in chemistry, biochemistry, endocrinology, immunology, and other scientific and medical specialties.

Library and Country-of-Publication Codes

Included for the first time in *AIAD-7* is the complete list of symbols for American and Canadian libraries, as compiled by the Library of Congress. Such symbols are widely used to briefly identify the institutions in union catalogs, bibliographies, and similar compilations.

Because Machine-Readable Cataloging (MARC) is so extensively used in the information industry, the alphabetic codes used to represent each country or place of publication in MARC records are included in *AIAD-7*.

Updating Continues

New editions of *AIAD* are prepared not only by adding thousands of previously unlisted terms, but by updating many entries from earlier editions as well. For instance, *AIAD-7* indicates that the familiar HEW (Department of Health, Education, and Welfare) is now the HHS (Department of Health and Human Services). The new Department of Education is not yet represented by an entry, since the initials DOE had already been claimed by the Department of Energy, and "DEd" seemed a less than desirable designation.

For *AIAD-7*, both New York and American Stock Exchange symbols have been extensively updated. Call letters for AM and FM radio stations, which are changed frequently, have also been updated for this edition. Many science terms or their identifying categories have been adjusted to reflect current spelling or usage.

Obsolete entries are not deleted, but merely noted or cross-referenced.

Expansion of Coverage—Expansion of Title

The increased popularity of abbreviated terms is evidenced not only in the accelerated growth of total entries, but also in the changing titles for this publication.

The first edition was called *Acronyms Dictionary*. Later editions, to indicate wider coverage and a finer distinction in terminology, were entitled *Acronyms and Initialisms Dictionary (AID)*. With the fifth edition, the title was expanded once more to reflect our broadened coverage: *Acronyms, Initialisms, and Abbreviations Dictionary (AIAD)*.

Slight Distinctions among Terms

Distinctions are not always made among the three terms used in the title, nor are distinctions always necessary, since in many ways the definitions overlap. But the most commonly accepted, if somewhat simplified, explanations are as follows:

> An *acronym* is composed of the initial letters or parts of a compound term.
> It is usually *read or spoken as a single word,* rather than letter by letter.

Examples include RADAR (Radio Detection and Ranging) and LASER
(Light Amplification by Stimulated Emission of Radiation).

An *initialism* is also composed of the initial letters or parts of a compound
term, but is generally *verbalized letter by letter,* rather than as a single
"word." Examples include PO (Post Office) and RPM (Revolutions per
Minute).

An *abbreviation* is a shortened form of a word or words that does not
follow the formation of either of the above. Examples include APR (April),
Ph D (Doctor of Philosophy), and DR (Doctor).

Also included in *AIAD* are many alphabetic *symbols,* in which the letters used do not always
correspond to the words that they represent. Included in this category are R, a missile launch
environment symbol for Ship, and T, representing Meridian Angle.

Trends in the Field

As the *AIAD* collection grows, varying trends in the field are noticed.

Acronym formation often follows what might be termed the "chicken or egg" syndrome. Recent
years have shown that in choosing a name or slogan, new organizations, ad hoc groups, or activist
movements frequently will select a colorful acronym first—one that they hope will spotlight their philosophy
and be associated easily in the public mind with their ideas or purposes. The catchy acronym will
then be fleshed out with more-or-less appropriate words. This back-formation is common with ecology-minded
groups, feminist organizations, consumer-protection interests, and countless other topical coali-
tions.

A few editions ago it was reported that there was a noticeable movement among corporations to
abbreviate names, often because merger or expansion had rendered the original names meaningless
or misleading. General American Transportation Corporation had become GATX Corporation, for
instance, and Missouri Beef Packers - Kansas Beef Industries changed to MBPXL Corporation.
Perhaps threatened with corporate anonymity, many firms have more recently begun a reversal of
the practice. J-S Industries has become American-Kitchen Foods and VWR United Corporation changed
to Univar. Although almost universally referred to as IBM, the International Business Machines
Corporation retains its full title officially.

Acronyms or initialisms as titles of films and television programs, or as informal references to them,
is another noted trend. It has resulted in LATER (Life and Times of Eddie Roberts), PTS
(Prime Time Sunday), and L & S (Laverne and Shirley), among others.

Twentieth-Century Living as Reflected in *AIAD*

The editors also find that the new entries compiled for each edition of *AIAD* offer a sort of
alphabetical sampling of current concerns of society, its social movements, its popular culture, its
political events and ideologies.

Among the new terms collected since the sixth edition are many that have been prominent in head-
lines of recent years—TMI (Three Mile Island), the Pennsylvania site of a nuclear reactor accident in
1979; ABSCAM (Arab Scam), the FBI's congressional "sting" operation; and FLAG (Family
Liaison Action Group), an organization of the families of American hostages in Iran. The state
of the economy has increased discussion of MMCs (Money Market Certificates) and GPM
(Graduated Payment Mortgage), while the energy crisis has forced the automotive industry to
strive for CAFE (Corporate Average Fuel Economy) and the construction industry to face
BEPS (Building Energy Performance Standards).

Not all the recent terms that have gained popularity deal with such grave matters. There are also the modern lifestyle POSSLQ (Persons of Opposite Sex Sharing Living Quarters) and the college fad game D & D (Dungeons and Dragons). Some cynics have labeled the high-level decision-making process in our country as BOGSAAT (A Bunch of Guys Sitting around a Table).

Several Thousand Foreign Terms Included

By far the largest proportion of terms in *Acronyms, Initialisms, and Abbreviations Dictionary* is made up of items that are specifically identified with the United States. Foreign terms are assuming an increasing importance, however, because of constantly closer association—politically, economically, and socially—between the United States and the rest of the world. The editors have therefore attempted to include as many as possible of the terms most likely to be encountered by the businessman, government official, student of political affairs, or interested citizen.

For example, the acronyms of international association names have been included because, since they are international, their activities are presumed to include Americans. Many terms, of course, have a military origin; and since World War II, which generated so many acronyms and initialisms, was the joint concern of several nations, many military terms from Great Britain and other countries appear. Foreign political parties, and their often-related labor unions, are also included, since the names and alphabetical designations of such organizations are commonly encountered by the reader of magazines and daily newspapers in the United States.

As a result, this edition contains in the aggregate several thousand acronyms, initialisms, and abbreviations based on Russian, French, German, Italian, Spanish, Japanese, and other major languages. In many cases, English translations are provided.

Voices of Dissent

There have been rumblings of discontent through the years because of the overuse or misuse of acronyms, initialisms, and abbreviations. In a lecture presented before the International Congress of Pharmaceutical Sciences, Dr. Anatole Sliosberg, of the International Federation of Translators, expressed his dismay over the abuses of "abbreviomania":

> . . . whenever you open a scientific, technical, or economic publication,
> or even a daily newspaper, you are immediately struck by the number
> of apparently meaningless letter or syllable combinations which the most
> knowledgeable reader cannot decipher without the aid of a dictionary
> or a keen sense of divination.

Dr. Sliosberg's was not a voice in the wilderness. He cited such impressive company as Seneca and Justinian I, who had spoken out against the abuse of abbreviations in manuscripts of their own day. He added that "the laws of France [since the 14th century] still forbid the use of abbreviations in legal documents, civil registers, and broker's books."

Need for a Guide Evident

The frustration of wrestling with inadequately identified designations or with the overuse of these terms is understandable. Yet, what H. L. Mencken called "the characteristic American habit of reducing complete concepts to starkest abbreviations" seems likely to continue unabated for some time. Despite the obvious drawbacks, the abbreviation of terms is convenient, speedy, and well-suited to the highly technical modern world.

Accordingly, the editors of *Acronyms, Initialisms, and Abbreviations Dictionary* will continue to guide *AIAD* users through this expanding maze of linguistic shorthand.

Although every effort is made to maintain accuracy, errors may occasionally occur; we will be grateful if these are called to our attention. Comments and suggestions will be welcome.

EDITORIAL POLICIES

Determining the subject areas to be covered in a book such as this is not nearly so difficult as deciding on the type of terms to be selected from each field. In other words, "Where should the line be drawn?"

The definitions of terms offered in the Preface immediately preceding this note are deliberately simplified, and some students of language may hold out for more precise or more limiting definitions. Strictly speaking, for instance, acronyms are words made from the tips of other words—but the question immediately arises, "How large a tip?" Some linguists insist on syllables and accept as acronyms only such terms as ARBOR from the virological term, *Arthropod Borne*. One of the most common uses of abbreviated terms, however, is in the shortening of designations by the use of only initial-letter "tips." AID (*Agency for International Development*), SRO (*Standing Room Only*), MP (*Military Police*), and thousands of similar terms are examples of this practice. Some refer to such terms, not as acronyms (even when they are pronounceable), but as initialisms or "abecedisms."

Thus, to some, the difference between terms is based solely on structure; to others, the important consideration is pronounceability. Many use "acronym" and "initialism" almost interchangeably, and the designation "abbreviation" is sometimes used as an umbrella-term for *all* types of alphabetical short-forms.

What Is Included?

Which of these points of view is linguistically correct is not important here; and, quite possibly, there is no single correct theory. The essential point that concerned the editors was that no user of the book should be disappointed because the term for which he sought an explanation was omitted on a technicality. It was decided, therefore, to include in *AIAD* all terms of the types described above and defined in the Preface, as well as terms that *appear* to be of those types and may be thought to be acronyms, initialisms, or abbreviations when encountered in reading or conversation.

Thus, one will find in *AIAD* some entries that might be considered alphabetical *symbols* rather than one of the terms in the title These include the Selective Service classifications such as 4-F and 1-H; the symbols for chemical elements, such as K for potassium; etc. There is an entry for ACTION, an independent government agency, because it is nearly always written in uppercase and appears to be an acronym. Actually, as the entry explains, the word is not an acronym and the letters do not represent other words.

Should Shortened Terms Be Pronounced?

On this point, the editors suggest that you let your conscience—and whatever common usage you know of—be your guide. Pronunciation is almost entirely a matter of choice. Some people pronounce alphabetical forms, whenever possible, as if they were complete words. Others prefer to rattle off the individual letters. As has been indicated, if one adheres strictly to the "acronyms are pronounceable" school of thought, the decision whether or not to pronounce as a word can be critical. The less structured viewpoint that the designations "acronym" and "initialism" are interchangeable to a great extent, is probably more manageable. It may also help to avoid ensnarement in this consideration: is COD (Cash on Delivery) rightfully an acronym because it *may* be pronounced as "cod," or correctly an initialism because it is *never* expressed except by each letter?

Occasionally, an initialism will acquire an unofficial stray letter or sound that never appears in print, but that renders the term pronounceable. SNCC (*S*tudent *N*ational [formerly, *N*onviolent] *C*oordinating *C*ommittee), for example, was widely pronounced "snick." For such cases as this, discreet and careful listening is essential.

To Capitalize or Not to Capitalize?

It is comparatively rare, and is becoming even less common, for acronyms and initialisms to be written any way other than in all-capital letters, without periods. There are occasional exceptions, especially in scientific or technical notation (names of chemical elements, for example), but it appears that the overwhelming tendency is toward the use of all capitals and the omission of all periods. The capitalization of abbreviations for common nouns, such as TV for Television, is typical.

The editors have speculated on the reasons for the tendency to use all capitals, without periods, and found no single answer. It seems significant, however, that the equipment that is more and more being used for records and/or for communication—such as Teletypes, computer printout units, punched cards, etc.—almost invariably has only uppercase letters, and, except for the Teletype, a relatively limited capacity for characters, punctuation, and spacing.

Therefore, the practice adopted in the first edition of writing terms uniformly in capitals without periods or space between letters has been, in general, followed for the subsequent editions.

The form of some widely used acronyms has evolved through the years until, in current usage, these terms are written as common nouns. "RADAR" became "Radar" and is now "radar." For consistency, such items are entered in *AIAD* in their original all-capital form. When used as a part of another entry (NGL—Neodymium Glass LASER), they are also entered in uppercase, to indicate to the uninitiated that they are acronyms and will be found as separate entries in their own alphabetical place in the dictionary.

The general rule of all-capital letters could not logically be applied to all entries, however. Unlike certain other types of terms that might be written in various ways, academic degrees, for example, often include both capital and lowercase letters. The degree of Bachelor of Science may be abbreviated BS, but it is also often used as B Sc, and it would not have been appropriate to apply the "all capital" rule to material of this type. T indicates "tablespoon" to a cook, and its lowercase form, t, indicates "teaspoon"; the difference could be critical in any recipe. Also, although conjunctions, prepositions, and articles are usually ignored in the formation of an initialism, they are occasionally found in such instances as C of C for Chamber of Commerce; obviously, this could not be written COFC.

Updating and Categorizing

As was indicated in the Preface, updating of entries is a continuing effort. Terms are updated as changes come to our attention, but obviously not all entries in the book can be kept constantly current.

Where possible, and if not already implied in the entry itself, a parenthetical category or identifier follows many terms. Examples are [*World War II*], [*Library of Congress*], [*Air Force*], and so forth. The purpose is to put as many entries as possible into some kind of context, since *AIAD* entries come from hundreds of different subject areas. These added identifiers may indicate that the entry is connected with or originated by the given category, or it may simply be an indication that the term is abbreviated in that particular way by the organization, group, or categorization used.

The identifier following an entry—such as [*FAA*] or [*Veterans Administration*]—is that current when the term was picked up for *AIAD*. The agency or organization used as an identifier may have since been altered in structure or dissolved; and while the entry for the agency itself may indicate the change, the identifiers in other related terms will not necessarily be altered.

For example, the Atomic Energy Commission (AEC) was dissolved and its functions transferred to two new agencies. The entry for AEC indicates this change:

> AEC . . . Atomic Energy Commission [*Functions divided, 1975, between Nuclear Regulatory Commission and Energy Research and Development Administration*]

There are, however, hundreds of other entries in the dictionary that are followed by the designation [*AEC*]. Some of these have been changed to indicate the term's ongoing connection with one of the new agencies. Others retain their [*AEC*] category, since it cannot be presumed that all designations for departments, processes, etc., are currently used by the superseding agencies.

Arrangement of Terms

Terms are arranged in alphabetical order, *according to the acronym*. If the same acronym has more than one meaning, the various translations are arranged alphabetically. Spacing within the acronym is not considered in alphabetizing, nor are symbols (hyphens, ampersands, etc.), or conjunctions and prepositions.

After this principal arrangement of terms will follow pluralized forms (usually indicated by *'s*) and then any forms of the entry using numerals. For example:

Straight forms of the term (including symbols, conjunctions and prepositions, etc.):	**MC** . . . . Magnetic Clearance
	M/C . . . . Maintenance Cycle
	M of C . . . . Master of Commerce
	MC . . . . Mine Cleaning
	M & C . . . . Morphine and Cocaine
	MC . . . . Munitions Command
Pluralized forms of the term:	**MC's** . . . . Military Characteristics
Forms of the term using numerals:	**MC1** . . . . . Medal for Cycling, First Place
	M2C . . . . Major of Two Cargoes

With respect to arrangement of terms and their meanings, it should be kept in mind that the point of view of the book, or the point of reference for the user, is an *acronym* rather than its meaning. Therefore, it is deliberate when there are two listings of, for example, the International Airline Stewards and Stewardesses Association under slightly different initialisms, both of which were encountered in one or another of the various sources used to compile this dictionary.

A

A .... Authority
AAA .... Anaa [*French Polynesia*] [*Airport symbol*]
AAAG .... Acting Assistant Adjutant-General [*Military*]
AAB .... Arrabury [*Australia*] [*Airport symbol*]
AAB .... Association of Applied Biologists
AABB .... American Association of Business Brokers
AABC .... American Association of Backgammon Clubs
AABGU ...... American Associates, Ben-Gurion University
AABP .... Association of Area Business Publications
AABPA ...... American Association for Budget and Program Analysis
AAC .... All Aluminum Conductor
AACC .... Affirmative Action Coordinating Center
AACD .... American Academy of Craniomandibular Disorders
AACM .... Association for Advancement of Creative Musicians
AACRC ..... American Association of Children's Residential Centers
AACT .... American Academy of Clinical Toxicology
AAE .... Annaba [*Algeria*] [*Airport symbol*]
AAED .... American Academy of Esthetic Dentistry
AAFDBI ..... American Association of Fitness Directors in Business
                and Industry
AAFLI .... Asian American Free Labor Institute
AAJ .... Association of American Jurists
AAL .... Aalborg [*Denmark*] [*Airport symbol*]
AAL .... Absolute Assembly Language [*Data processing*]
AALDEF .... Asian American Legal Defense and Education Fund
AAM .... American Academy of Mechanics
AAM .... American Agriculture Movement
AAMA ...... African American Museums Association
AAMD ...... American Academy of Medical Directors
AAMUC ..... Association of American Military Uniform Collectors
AAN .... American Academy of Nursing
AAO .... American Academy of Ophthalmology
AAO .... Anaco [*Venezuela*] [*Airport symbol*]
AAP .... American Academy of Psychoanalysis
AAPAA ..... Association of Asian/Pacific American Artists
AAR .... Aarhus [*Denmark*] [*Airport symbol*]
A/AR .... Aero/Acoustic Rotor
AAS .... Automated Accounting System
AASA .... Academy of the Arts and Sciences of the Americas
AASANA ... Administration de Aeropuertos y Servicios Auxiliares a la
                Nauegacion Aerea [*Bolivian airline*]
AASIR .... Afro-American Society for International Relations
AASM .... Association of Aviation and Space Museologists
AASP .... American Association of Swine Practitioners
AASWS ..... Antimassed Armor Strike Weapon System
AAT .... Australian Antarctic Territory
AAV .... Alah [*Philippines*] [*Airport symbol*]
AAWCJC ... American Association of Women in Community and
                Junior Colleges
AAWIPT .... Antiair Warfare Training in Port [*Navy*]
AAWPC ..... Asian-American Women's Political Caucus
AAW(R) ..... Antiair Warfare Reporting [*Navy*]
AAX .... Araxa [*Brazil*] [*Airport symbol*]
AB .... Ankina Breeders [*An organization*]
ABA .... Air New York, Inc. [*Albany, NY*] [*FAA designator*]
ABA .... American Beefalo Association
ABA .... American Book Awards [*Formerly, TABA*]
ABBS .... American Brittle Bone Society
ABC .... Advance Booking Charter [*Airline fare*]

ABC .... Alcobaca [*Brazil*] [*Airport symbol*]
ABD .... Abadan [*Iran*] [*Airport symbol*]
ABDS .... Accounting and Budget Distribution System [*Air Force*]
ABF .... Abaiang [*Kiribati*] [*Airport symbol*]
ABF .... Adaptive Beam Forming
ABF .... Americas Boychoir Federation
ABFS .... Auxiliary Building Filter System [*Nuclear energy*]
ABFSE ...... American Board of Funeral Service Education
ABG .... Abingdon [*Australia*] [*Airport symbol*]
ABG .... Arterial Blood Gasses
ABH .... Alpha [*Australia*] [*Airport symbol*]
ABI .... Abilene [*Texas*] [*Airport symbol*]
ABIT .... Aircraft Blast Interaction Tests
ABJ .... Abidjan [*Ivory Coast*] [*Airport symbol*]
ABL .... Ambler [*Alaska*] [*Airport symbol*]
ABLE .... Adult Basic Learning Examination
ABM .... Bamaga [*Australia*] [*Airport symbol*]
ABOS .... Advanced Banking On-Line System
ABP .... Actual Block Processor [*Data processing*]
ABPA .... American Backgammon Players Association
ABPA .... American Book Producers Association
ABPO .... American Board of Podiatric Orthopedics
ABQ .... Albuquerque [*New Mexico*] [*Airport symbol*]
ABR .... Aberdeen [*South Dakota*] [*Airport symbol*]
ABS .... Abu Simbel [*Egypyt*] [*Airport symbol*]
ABS .... American Biological Society
ABST .... Adult Basic Skill Training
ABT .... Automatic Bus Transfer
ABTD .... American Book Trade Directory [*A publication*]
ABV .... Absolute Value
ABX .... Albury [*Australia*] [*Airport symbol*]
ABY .... Albany [*Georgia*] [*Airport symbol*]
ABZ .... Aberdeen [*Scotland*] [*Airport symbol*]
AC .... Able Chief
AC .... Advisory Committee
AC .... Air Controller
AC .... Arch-Chancellor
AC .... Automatic Checkout
ACA .... American Council for the Arts
ACA .... Assignment Control Authority [*Military*]
ACA .... Association for Communication Administration
ACACP ..... Americans Concerned about Corporate Power [*An
                organization*]
ACAD .... Air Containment Atmosphere Dilution [*Nuclear energy*]
ACADS ..... Alarm Communications and Display Segment
ACAS .... Association of Concerned African Scholars
ACB .... Access Method Control Block [*Data processing*]
ACB .... Air Corps Board
ACBLT ..... Airlift Contingency Battalion Landing Team
ACC .... Accra [*Ghana*] [*Airport symbol*]
ACC .... Additives and Containments Committee [*British*]
ACC .... Alarm Control Center
ACC .... Anti-Communist Committee
ACC .... Approach Control Center
ACCESS ... American Coordinating Committee for Equality in Sport
                and Society
ACCESS ... Automated Computer Controlled Editing Sound System
AcChR ...... Acetylcholine Receptor [*Biochemistry*] [*Also, AChR*]
ACCP .... American College of Clinical Pharmacology

ACCPFF.... Anti-Communist Confederation of Polish Freedom Fighters in USA
ACD .... Acandi [*Colombia*] [*Airport symbol*]
ACD .... Anticoagulant Citrate Dextrose [*Hematology*]
ACE........... Arrecife [*Canary Islands*] [*Airport symbol*]
ACE........... Attorneys, Certified Public Accountants, and Enrolled Agents [*In "Operation ACE," IRS investigation of these occupations as sources of income tax evasion*]
ACE........... Automatic Calling Equipment
ACE........... Automatic Computer Evaluation
ACEBD..... Airborne and Communications-Electronics Board [*Army*]
ACES .... Automated Camera Effects System
ACF........... All-Craft Foundation
ACF........... Alternate Command Facility [*Navy*]
ACFNY..... Asthmatic Children's Foundation of New York
ACGS....... American-Canadian Genealogical Society
ACH .... Aircraft Hangar
ACHOBS... Assistant Chief Observer [*Navy*]
ACHP .... Advisory Council on Historic Preservation
AChR .... Acetylcholine Receptor [*Biochemistry*] [*Also, AcChR*]
ACI............ Alderney [*Channel Islands*] [*Airport symbol*]
ACI............ Amplifier-Control Intercommunications
ACI............ Assist Card International [*An organization*]
ACID .... Automatic Classification and Interpretation of Data
ACIS .... American Council on International Sports
ACIS .... Avionics, Control, and Information Systems
ACK .... Nantucket [*Massachusetts*] [*Airport symbol*]
ACL .... Air California [*Newport Beach, CA*] [*FAA designator*]
ACL........... Altimeter Check Location [*Aviation*]
ACL........... Applications Control Language [*Data processing*]
ACL........... Atlas Commercial Language [*Data processing*]
ACLP......... Above Core Load Pad [*Nuclear energy*]
ACM........... American Council on Marijuana and Other Psychoactive Drugs
ACME....... American Council on the Middle East
ACN .... American College of Nutrition
ACN .... TransCentral, Inc. [*Oklahoma City, OK*] [*FAA designator*]
ACO .... Armament Concepts Office [*Army*]
ACORN ..... Association of Community Organizations for Reform Now
ACOS........ Advanced Computer Oriented System
ACP........... American College of Psychiatrists
ACPDS...... Advisory Committee on Personal Dosimetry Services [*National Science Foundation*]
ACPR .... Advanced Core Performance Reactor
ACPS .... Alkaline Calcium Petroleum Sulfonate
ACR........... Aeroelastically Conformable Rotor
ACR........... Alternate CPU [*Central Processing Unit*] Recovery [*Data processing*]
ACR........... Araracuara [*Colombia*] [*Airport symbol*]
ACS........... Advanced Communications Systems [*Proposed communications network*] [*AT & T*]
ACS........... Assembly Control System
ACS........... Automated Communications Set
ACS........... Auxiliary Cooling System [*Nuclear energy*]
ACS........... Auxiliary Core Storage [*Data processing*]
ACSUS...... Association for Canadian Studies in the United States
ACT........... Advanced Concepts Team
ACT........... American Association of Agricultural Communicators of Tomorrow
ACT........... Waco [*Texas*] [*Airport symbol*]
ACTS .... American Christian Television Service [*Network*]
ACTS .... Association of Cable Television Suppliers
ACU .... Aircraft Control Unit
ACU .... Arithmetic and Control Unit
ACV........... Eureka/Arcata [*California*] [*Airport symbol*]
ACVT .... Armored Combat Vehicle Technology
ACWM....... Americans for Customary Weight and Measure [*An organization*]
ACY........... Atlantic City [*New Jersey*] [*Airport symbol*]
AD .... Armament Division [*Air Force Systems Command*]
AD .... Automatic Depositor
A/D .... Awaiting Delivery
ADA........... Adana [*Turkey*] [*Airport symbol*]
ADA........... Aiken Dynamic Algebra
ADAC........ Automatic Direct Analog Computer
ADAPS...... Automatic Display and Plotting System
ADC .... Anti-Drug Coalition
ADC .... Association of Diving Contractors
ADCA........ Aerospace Department Chairmen's Association

ADC-OA.... Air Defense Command - Office of Operations Analysis
ADCOM..... Advanced Cooperative Countermeasure
ADD .... Addis Ababa [*Ethiopia*] [*Airport symbol*]
ADD .... Attention Deficit Disorder [*Psychology*]
ADE........... Aden [*People's Democratic Republic of Yemen*] [*Airport symbol*]
ADE........... Apparent Digestible Energy [*Nutrition*]
ADEN/DEFA ... Armament Development Enfield/Direction Etude Fabrication [*Military*]
ADEX .... Air Defense Exercise
ADF .... Acid-Detergent Fiber [*Food analysis*]
ADF .... American Dance Festival
ADIDAS .... Adi Dassler [*Founder of German sporting goods company; acronym used as brand name of shoes manufactured by the firm*]
ADIS.......... Association for Development of Instructional Systems [*Later, ADCIS*]
ADK .... Adak Island [*Alaska*] [*Airport symbol*]
ADL .... Acid-Detergent Lignin [*Food analysis*]
ADL .... Adelaide [*Australia*] [*Airport symbol*]
ADM.......... Ardmore [*Oklahoma*] [*Airport symbol*]
ADM.......... Automatic Display Mode [*Data processing*]
ADMD .... Administrative Division [*Municipality*] [*Board on Geographic Names*]
ADMSPT ... Administrative Support
ADO.......... Andamooka [*Australia*] [*Airport symbol*]
ADQ .... Kodiak [*Alaska*] [*Airport symbol*]
ADR........... Address Register
ADR........... Adverse Drug Reaction [*Medicine*]
ADR........... Air Design Review
ADR........... Audit Discrepancy Report
ADRNDCK ... Adirondack [*National Weather Service*]
ADRS .... [*A*] Departmental Reporting System [*IBM Corp.*]
ADRSS..... Automated Data Reports Submission System
ADS........... Accelerated Declassification System
ADS........... Advanced Deep-Dive System
ADS........... Automated Data System
ADS........... Automatic Depressurization System [*Nuclear energy*]
ADSU .... Airstream Direction Sensing Unit
ADSU .... Albrecht Durer Study Unit
ADTDS...... Air Defense Tactical Data Systems [*Missile minder*]
ADU.......... Automatic Dialing Unit
ADVRY...... Advisory
ADVY....... Advisory
ADZ........... San Andres Island [*Colombia*] [*Airport symbol*]
AE .... Aerospace Environment
AE .... Arithmetic Element
AE .... Assault Echelon
AE .... Audit Entry
AEA........... Abemama [*Kiribati*] [*Airport symbol*]
AEA........... Air East Airlines [*Westfield, MA*] [*FAA designator*]
AEB........... Auxiliary Equipment Building [*Nuclear energy*]
AEI .... Acclimatization Experiences Institute
AEIOU....... Austria's Empire Is Obviously Upset [*Variation of 15th century inscription*]
AEK........... Aseki [*Papua New Guinea*] [*Airport symbol*]
AEM .... Automatic Environment Monitoring
AEMC....... Auger and Elevator Manufacturers Council
AEO.......... Aioun El Atrouss [*Mauritania*] [*Airport symbol*]
AEP .... Buenos Aires [*Argentina*] Jorge Newbery Airport [*Airport symbol*]
AER........... Adler/Sochi [*USSR*] [*Airport symbol*]
AERO .... Alternative Energy Resources Organization
AES........... Aalesund [*Norway*] [*Airport symbol*]
AES........... American Ecology Services
AET........... Aircrew Egress Trainer
AET........... Allakaket [*Alaska*] [*Airport symbol*]
AEX.......... Airway Express, Inc. [*Mesa, AZ*] [*FAA designator*]
AEY........... Akureyri [*Iceland*] [*Airport symbol*]
AF .... Firkin of Ale
AFA........... San Rafael [*Argentina*] [*Airport symbol*]
AFALD ...... Air Force Acquisition Logistics Division
AFAM........ Air Field Attack Munition
AFAR........ American Foundation for Aging Research
AFC........... Area Forecast Center
AFCAO..... Air Force Computer Acquisition Office
AFCOS..... Air Force Combat Operations Staff
AFCSP ...... Air Force Communications Security Pamphlet
AFD........... Airport/Facility Directory

AFDCS ...... Automatic Film Data Collection System
AFESC ...... Air Force Engineering and Services Center
AFESC/ESL ... Air Force Engineering and Services Center/ Engineering and Services Laboratory
AFETO ...... Air Force Engineering Technology Office
AFF .... Asociacion Filatelica Filipinas [*Philatelic Association of the Philippines*]
AFHPSP .... Air Force Health Professions Scholarship Program
AFHS .... American Family Heritage Society
AFID .... Alkali Flame Ionization Detector [*Instrumentation*]
AFIS .... Air Force Intelligence Service
AFL .... Animated Film Language
AFLC .... Air Force Logistics Center
AFLETS .... Air Force Law Enforcement Terminal System
AFMEA ...... Air Force Management Engineering Agency
AFMS .... Air Force Manpower Standards
AFOE .... Assault Follow-On Echelon
AFOLDS .... Air Force On-Line Data System
AFOSH ...... Air Force Occupational Safety and Health [*Standards*]
AFP .... Attached FORTRAN Processor [*Data processing*]
AFR .... Afore [*Papua New Guinea*] [*Airport symbol*]
AFSINC ..... Air Force Service Information and News Center
AFSIR .... Air Force Salary Impact Report
AFSO .... American Friends of Scottish Opera
AFSWB ...... American Friends of Scottish War Blinded
AFTFWC ... Air Force Tactical Fighter Weapons Center
AFV .... Alliance for Volunteerism
AG .... Air Ground
AG .... Americans for God [*An organization*]
AGA .... Agadir [*Morocco*] [*Airport symbol*]
AGA .... Association of Governmental Appraisers
AGC .... Ancient Gneiss Complex [*Geology*]
AGDS .... Auxiliary Deep Submergence Support Ship [*Navy*]
AGE .... Wangerooge [*West Germany*] [*Airport symbol*]
AGED .... Automated General Experimental Device [*Animal performance testing*]
AGF .... Agen [*France*] [*Airport symbol*]
AGFF .... Research Frigate [*Navy symbol*]
AGG .... American Groomer's Guild
AGG .... Angoram [*Papua New Guinea*] [*Airport symbol*]
AGH .... Angelholm/Helsingbord [*Sweden*] [*Airport symbol*]
AGJ .... Aguni [*Japan*] [*Airport symbol*]
AGL .... Wanigela [*Papua New Guinea*] [*Airport symbol*]
AGN .... Angoon [*Alaska*] [*Airport symbol*]
AGP .... Malaga [*Spain*] [*Airport symbol*]
AGPAM ..... American Guild of Patient Account Managers
AGR .... Agra [*India*] [*Airport symbol*]
Agr Spezia ... Agricoltura della Spezia [*A publication*]
Agr Tec ..... Agricultura Tecnica [*A publication*]
Agr Tec Mex ... Agricultura Tecnica en Mexico [*A publication*]
Agr Trop ... Agricultura Tropical [*A publication*]
Agr Venezie ... Agricoltura della Venezie [*A publication*]
Agr Vet Chem ... Agricultural and Veterinary Chemicals [*A publication*]
AGS .... Annulus Gas System [*Nuclear energy*]
Ag Sply Ind ... Agricultural Supply Industry [*A publication*]
AGSU .... Arbeiten zur Geschichte des Spaetjudentums und Urchristentums [*A publication*]
AGTS .... Advanced Gunnery Target Systems
AGV .... Acarigua [*Venezuela*] [*Airport symbol*]
Agway Coop ... Agway Cooperator [*A publication*]
AGZ .... Aggeneys [*South Africa*] [*Airport symbol*]
AHAWPK .. Aghandlungen der Heidelberger Akademie der Wissenschaften Philosophisch-Historische Klasse [*A publication*]
AHB .... Abha [*Saudi Arabia*] [*Airport symbol*]
AHCS .... American Historic and Cultural Society
AHD .... Ardmore [*Oklahoma*] [*Airport symbol*]
AHEAD ...... Army Help for Education and Development
AHFC .... American Hungarian Folklore Centrum
AHFR .... Argonne High Flux Reactor [*Argonne National Laboratory*]
AHH .... Association for Holistic Health
AHI .... Amahai [*Indonesia*] [*Airport symbol*]
AHIC .... Art Hazards Information Center
AHL .... Aishalton [*Guyana*] [*Airport symbol*]
AHN .... Athens [*Georgia*] [*Airport symbol*]
AHO .... Alghero [*Italy*] [*Airport symbol*]

AHRSJ ...... Americans for Human Rights and Social Justice [*An organization*]
AHSM .... Antiquarian Horological Society Monograph [*A publication*]
AHSSPPE ... Association of Handicapped Student Services Programs in Postsecondary Education
AHU .... Al Hoceima [*Morocco*] [*Airport symbol*]
AI .... Arrival Approved Request for IFR [*Instrument Flight Rules*] Flight [*Aviation*]
AI .... Automatic Input [*Data processing*]
AIA .... Acupuncture International Association
AIA .... Alliance [*Nebraska*] [*Airport symbol*]
AIASA ...... American Industrial Arts Student Association
AIBA .... Alpha-Aminoisobutyric Acid [*Organic chemistry*]
AIC .... Air Interception Control
AIChE Monogr Ser ... AIChE [*American Institute of Chemical Engineers*] Monograph Series [*A publication*]
AIChE Symp Ser ... AIChE [*American Institute of Chemical Engineers*] Symposium Series [*A publication*]
AICP .... Anthropological Index to Current Periodicals in the Library of the Royal Anthropological Institute [*A publication*]
AID .... Advanced Integrated Diagnostics
AID .... Algebraic Interpretive Dialogue
AID .... Automatic Implantable Defibrillator [*Medicine*]
AID Res Dev Abstr ... AID [*Agency for International Development*] Research and Development Abstracts [*A publication*]
AIDS .... Attitudinal Information Data System
AIDS .... Automatic Integrated Debugging System [*Data processing*]
AIE .... Aiome [*Papua New Guinea*] [*Airport symbol*]
AIFL .... America Israel Friendship League
AIGS .... Auxiliary Inerting Gas Subsystem [*Nuclear energy*]
AIHX .... Auxiliary Intermediate Heat Exchanger [*Nuclear energy*]
AIME Trans ... American Institute of Mining, Metallurgical, and Petroleum Engineers. Transactions [*A publication*]
AIMS .... Air-Launched Intercept Missile Record System
AIMS .... Assessment, Improvement, and Monitoring System [*School milk programs*]
AIMS .... Automated Information and Management Systems
AIN .... Wainwright [*Alaska*] [*Airport symbol*]
AIP .... Approval in Principle
AIPAD .... Association of International Photography Art Dealers
AIP Conf Proc ... AIP [*American Institute of Physics*] Conference Proceedings [*A publication*]
AIP Conf Proc Part Fields Subser ... AIP [*American Institute of Physics*] Conference Proceedings. Particles and Fields Subseries [*A publication*]
AIR .... Aircraft Inventory Record
AIR .... Airline Industrial Relations Conference
AIR .... American Indian Refugees [*An organization*]
AIREP .... Air Report
Air-Espace Tech ... Air-Espace Techniques [*A publication*]
AIRS .... Accident Information Retrieval System
AIRS .... Automatic Information Retrieval System
Air/Water Poll Rept ... Air/Water Pollution Report [*A publication*]
AIS .... Accounting Information System
AIS .... Aeronautical Information Specialist
AIS .... Alcohol Insoluble Solids [*Food analysis*]
AIS .... Arorae [*Kiribati*] [*Airport symbol*]
AISI .... Advanced International Studies Institute
AIS/MR ..... Alternative Intermediate Services for the Mentally Retarded
AIST .... Automatic Information Station
AIT .... Aitutaki [*Cook Islands*] [*Airport symbol*]
AITS .... Action Item Tracking System [*Radiation measurement*]
AIU .... Atiu [*Cook Islands*] [*Airport symbol*]
AIY .... Atlantic City [*New Jersey*] [*Airport symbol*]
AIZ .... Lake Of The Ozarks [*Missouri*] [*Airport symbol*]
AJ .... Applejack
AJA .... Ajaccio [*Corsica*] [*Airport symbol*]
AJAS .... Associated Japan-America Societies of the United States
AJDDA .... American Journal of Digestive Diseases [*A publication*]
AJER .... Alberta Journal of Educational Research [*A publication*]
AJF .... Jouf [*Saudi Arabia*] [*Airport symbol*]
AJMDA ..... American Journal of Mental Deficiency [*A publication*]
AJMNA ...... Australian Journal of Mental Retardation [*A publication*]
AJN .... Anjouan [*Comoro Islands*] [*Airport symbol*]

New Acronyms, Initialisms, & Abbreviations

AJNUA ...... American Journal of Nursing [*A publication*]
AJOGA ...... American Journal of Obstetrics and Gynecology [*A publication*]
AJOHA ...... American Journal of Orthodontics [*A publication*]
AJORA ...... American Journal of Orthopsychiatry [*A publication*]
AJOYA ...... American Journal of Optometry [*A publication*]
AJP .... American Journal of Psychiatry [*A publication*]
AJPCA ..... American Journal of Psychology [*A publication*]
AJPSA ...... American Journal of Psychiatry [*A publication*]
A J Psy ...... American Journal of Psychology [*A publication*]
AJSOA ...... American Journal of Sociology [*A publication*]
AJU .... Aracaju [*Brazil*] [*Airport symbol*]
Akad Nauk Armjan SSR Dokl ... Akademija Nauk Armjanskoi SSR. Doklady [*A publication*]
Akad Nauk Arm SSR Dokl ... Akademiya Nauk Armyanskoy SSR. Doklady [*A publication*]
Akad Nauk Azerbaidzan SSR Dokl ... Akademija Nauk Azerbaidzanskoi SSR. Doklady [*A publication*]
Akad Nauk Azerb SSR Dokl ... Akademiya Nauk Azerbaydzhanskoy SSR. Doklady [*A publication*]
Akad Nauk BSSR Dokl ... Akademiya Nauk BSSR. Doklady [*A publication*]
Akad Nauk Gruz SSR Geol Inst Tr ... Akademiya Nauk Gruzinskoy SSR. Geologicheskiy Institut. Trudy [*A publication*]
Akad Nauk Gruz SSR Soobshch ... Akademiya Nauk Gruzinskoy SSR. Soobshcheniya [*A publication*]
Akad Nauk Kaz SSR Izv Ser Geol ... Akademiya Nauk Kazakhskoy SSR. Izvestiya. Seriya Geologicheskaya [*A publication*]
Akad Nauk SSSR Dokl ... Akademiya Nauk SSSR. Doklady [*A publication*]
Akad Nauk SSSR Geol Inst Tr ... Akademiya Nauk SSSR. Geologicheskiy Institut. Trudy [*A publication*]
Akad Nauk SSSR Geol Inst Trudy ... Akademiya Nauk SSSR. Geologicheskiy Institut. Trudy [*A publication*]
Akad Nauk SSSR Izv Ser Fiz ... Akademiya Nauk SSSR. Izvestiya. Seriya Fizicheskaya [*A publication*]
Akad Nauk SSSR Izv Ser Geogr ... Akademiya Nauk SSSR. Izvestiya. Seriya Geograficheskaya [*A publication*]
Akad Nauk SSSR Izv Ser Geol ... Akademiya Nauk SSSR. Izvestiya. Seriya Geologicheskaya [*A publication*]
Akad Nauk SSSR Paleontol Inst Tr ... Akademiya Nauk SSSR. Paleontologicheskiy Institut Trudy [*A publication*]
Akad Nauk SSSR Vestn ... Akademiya Nauk SSSR. Vestnik [*A publication*]
Akad Nauk Tadzh SSR Dokl ... Akademiya Nauk Tadzhikskoy SSR. Doklady [*A publication*]
Akad Nauk Ukr RSR Dopov Ser B ... Akademiya Nauk Ukrainskoy RSR. Dopovidi. Seriya B. Geologiya, Geofizika, Khimiya, ta Biologiya [*A publication*]
Akad Nauk Ukr SSR Metallofiz ... Akademiya Nauk Ukrainskoi SSR. Metallofizika [*A publication*]
AKF .... Kufrah [*Libya*] [*Airport symbol*]
AKI .... Akiak [*Alaska*] [*Airport symbol*]
AKJ .... Asahigawa [*Japan*] [*Airport symbol*]
AKK .... Akhiok [*Alaska*] [*Airport symbol*]
AKL .... Auckland [*New Zealand*] [*Airport symbol*]
AKM .... Abhandlungen fuer die Kunde des Morgenlandes [*A publication*]
AKN .... King Salmon [*Alaska*] [*Airport symbol*]
AKONA ..... Archiv fuer Klinische und Experimentelle Ohren-Nasen- und Kehlkopfh- Kunde [*A publication*]
AKP .... Anaktuvuk Pass [*Alaska*] [*Airport symbol*]
AKS .... Association for Korean Studies
AKS .... Auki [*Solomon Islands*] [*Airport symbol*]
AKS .... Four Sons Flying Service [*Dodge City, KS*] [*FAA designator*]
Aktual Probl Inf & Dok ... Aktualne Problemy Informacji i Dokumentacji [*A publication*]
Aktuellt Lantbrukshogs ... Aktuellt fran Lantbrukshogskolan [*A publication*]
Aktuel Otorhinolaryngol ... Aktuelle Otorhinolaryngologie [*A publication*]
Aktuel Probl Chir ... Aktuelle Probleme in der Chirurgie [*A publication*]
Aktuel Probl Chir Orthop ... Aktuelle Probleme in Chirurgie und Orthopaedie [*A publication*]
Aktuel Probl Polym-Phys ... Aktuelle Probleme der Polymer-Physik [*A publication*]

Aktuel Urol ... Aktuelle Urologie [*A publication*]
Akush Ginekol (Sofia) ... Akusherstvo i Ginekologiya (Sofia) [*A publication*]
Akust Ul'trazvuk Tekh ... Akustika i Ul'trazvukovaya Tekhnika [*A publication*]
AKV .... Akulivik [*Canada*] [*Airport symbol*]
Akw Notes ... Akwesasne Notes [*A publication*]
AKY .... Akyab [*Burma*] [*Airport symbol*]
AL .... Action [*Indicator*] Level [*Radiation measurement*]
AL .... Analytical Limits
AL .... USAIR [*ICAO designator*]
ALA .... African Literature Association
ALA .... Alma-Ata [*USSR*] [*Airport symbol*]
ALA .... American Longevity Association
Ala Acad Sci Jour ... Alabama Academy of Science Journal [*A publication*]
Alabama Geol Soc Bull ... Alabama Geological Society. Bulletin [*A publication*]
Alabama Geol Survey Inf Ser ... Alabama. Geological Survey. Information Series [*A publication*]
Alabama Geol Survey Map ... Alabama. Geological Survey. Map [*A publication*]
Ala Corn Variety Rep ... Alabama Corn Variety Report [*A publication*]
Ala Geol Surv Atlas Ser ... Alabama. Geological Survey. Atlas Series [*A publication*]
Ala Geol Surv Geo-Petro Notes ... Alabama. Geological Survey. Geo-Petro Notes [*A publication*]
Ala Geol Surv Inf Ser ... Alabama. Geological Survey. Information Series [*A publication*]
Ala Geol Surv Map ... Alabama. Geological Survey. Map [*A publication*]
Ala G S ...... Alabama. Geological Survey [*A publication*]
Ala His S ... Alabama. Historical Society. Transactions [*A publication*]
Ala Ind Sc Soc Pr ... Alabama Industrial and Scientific Society. Proceedings [*A publication*]
Ala Nurse ... Alabama Nurse [*A publication*]
ALAP .... As Low as Practical
Alaska Med ... Alaska Medicine [*A publication*]
Alaska Sci Conf Proc ... Alaska Science Conference. Proceedings [*A publication*]
Alaska Univ Geophys Inst Rep ... Alaska University. Geophysical Institute. Report [*A publication*]
Alaska Univ School Mines Pub Bull ... Alaska University. School of Mines Publication. Bulletin [*A publication*]
ALAST ...... Advanced LASER Spot Tracker
ALATAS .... All Air Traffic [*Area*] Supervisors in Region
ALB .... Adyar Library Bulletin [*A publication*]
ALB .... Albany [*New York*]
ALB .... Albany [*New York*] [*Airport symbol*]
Albany Felt Guide ... Albany Felt Guidelines [*A publication*]
Albany Inst Pr ... Albany Institute. Proceedings [*A publication*]
Albany Inst Tr ... Albany Institute. Transactions [*A publication*]
Albany News Dig ... Albany International Weekly News Digest [*A publication*]
Alberta M L J ... Alberta Modern Language Journal [*A publication*]
Alberta Res Annu Rep ... Alberta Research. Annual Report [*A publication*]
Alberta Res Counc Bull ... Alberta Research Council. Bulletin [*A publication*]
Alberta Res Counc Inf Ser ... Alberta Research Council. Information Series [*A publication*]
Alberta Res Counc Rep ... Alberta Research Council. Report [*A publication*]
Alberta Research Council Bull ... Alberta Research Council. Bulletin [*A publication*]
Alberta Research Council Inf Ser ... Alberta Research Council. Information Series [*A publication*]
Alberta Research Council Mem ... Alberta Research Council. Memoir [*A publication*]
Alberta Research Council Mimeo Circ ... Alberta Research Council. Mimeographed Circular [*A publication*]
Alberta Research Council Rept ... Alberta Research Council. Report [*A publication*]
Alberta Res Econ Geol Rep ... Alberta Research. Economic Geology Report [*A publication*]
Alberta Res Rep ... Alberta Research. Report [*A publication*]
ALBS .... Air-Launched Balloon System
ALC .... Alicante [*Spain*] [*Airport symbol*]

Alcohol Health Res World ... Alcohol Health and Research World [*A publication*]
ALCP......... Area Local Control Panel
ALD .... Analog Line Driver
Alexandria J Agr Res ... Alexandria Journal of Agricultural Research [*A publication*]
Alex Dent J ... Alexandria Dental Journal [*A publication*]
ALF .... Alta [*Norway*] [*Airport symbol*]
ALF .... American Liver Foundation
ALFGL...... Automatic Low-Frequency Gain-Limiting Circuit
ALG .... Algiers [*Algeria*] [*Airport symbol*]
Alger Serv Geol Bull ... Algeria. Service Geologique. Bulletin [*A publication*]
ALGHNY ... Allegheny [*National Weather Service*]
Algoritmy i Algoritm Jazyki ... Algoritmy i Algoritmiceskie Jazyki [*A publication*]
Algot Holmbergs Arsb ... Algot Holmbergs Arsbok [*A publication*]
ALH .... Albany [*Australia*] [*Airport symbol*]
ALID .... Automated Library Issue Document
Aligarh Bull Math ... Aligarh Bulletin of Mathematics [*A publication*]
Aliment Vie ... Alimentation et la Vie [*A publication*]
ALIP .... Annular Linear Induction Pump [*Nuclear energy*]
ALJ .... Alexander Bay [*South Africa*] [*Airport symbol*]
Alkalmaz Mat Lapok ... Alkalmazott Matematikai Lapok [*A publication*]
ALL .... Airlifeline [*An organization*]
Allahabad Fmr ... Allahabad Farmer [*A publication*]
Allahabad Univ Studies ... Allahabad University Studies [*A publication*]
Allat Lapok ... Allatorvosi Lapok [*A publication*]
Allatteny ... Allattenyesztestani Tanszek [*A publication*]
Allegheny Ludlum Horiz ... Allegheny Ludlum Horizons [*A publication*]
Allerg Asthmaforsch ... Allergie und Asthmaforschung [*A publication*]
Allerg Immunol (Leipz) ... Allergie und Immunologie (Leipzig) [*A publication*]
Allergol Immunopathol (Madr) ... Allergologia et Immunopathologia (Madrid) [*A publication*]
Allg Deutsche Naturh Ztg ... Allgemeine Deutsche Naturhistorische Zeitung [*A publication*]
Allgem Berg- u Huettenm Ztg ... Allgemeine Berg- und Huettenmaennische Zeitung [*A publication*]
Allgemein Statist Arch ... Allgemeines Statistisches Archiv [*A publication*]
Allg Forst- u Jagdztg ... Allgemeine Forst- und Jagdzeitung [*A publication*]
Allg Forstzeitschr ... Allgemeine Forstzeitschrift [*A publication*]
Allg Papier-Rundschau ... Allgemeine Papier-Rundschau [*A publication*]
Allg Prakt Chem ... Allgemeine und Praktische Chemie [*A publication*]
Allg Wien Med Ztg ... Allgemeine Wiener Medizinische Zeitung [*A publication*]
Allg Ztschr Psychiat ... Allgemeine Zeitschrift fuer Psychiatrie und Psychisch-Gerichtliche Medicin [*A publication*]
Alliance Ind ... Alliance Industrielle [*A publication*]
Alliance Recd ... Alliance Record [*A publication*]
Allied Health & Behav Sci ... Allied Health and Behavioral Sciences [*A publication*]
Allis-Chalmers Eng Rev ... Allis-Chalmers Engineering Review [*A publication*]
Allm Sven Laekartidn ... Allmaenna Svenska Laekartidningen [*A publication*]
Alloy Dig ... Alloy Digest [*A publication*]
ALM .... Alamogordo [*New Mexico*] [*Airport symbol*]
Alma-Atin Gos Ped Inst Ucen Zap ... Alma-Atinskii Gosudarstvennyi Pedgogiceskii Institut im. Abaja. Ucenye Zapiski [*A publication*]
Almanak Agric Brasil ... Almanak Agricola Brasileiro [*A publication*]
ALMS .... Auxiliary Liquid Metal System [*Nuclear energy*]
ALO........... Automatic Lockon
ALO .... Waterloo [*Iowa*] [*Airport symbol*]
ALP .... Air-Launched Platform
ALP .... Aleppo [*Syria*] [*Airport symbol*]
ALPHGR.... Average Linear Planar Heat Generation Rate [*Nuclear energy*]
Alpine J..... Alpine Journal [*A publication*]
ALPS .... Associated Logic Parallel System

ALQ........... Alegrete [*Brazil*] [*Airport symbol*]
ALR .... Alexandra [*New Zealand*] [*Airport symbol*]
ALS .... Active LASER Seeker
ALS .... Alamosa [*Colorado*] [*Airport symbol*]
ALSA .... American Legal Studies Association
ALTAC ...... Algebraic Transistorized Automatic Computer Translator
Alta Freq Suppl ... Alta Frequenza. Supplemento [*A publication*]
Alt Energy ... Alternative Sources of Energy [*A publication*]
Alt Press Ind ... Alternative Press Index [*A publication*]
ALTS .... Aided LASER Tracking System
ALU .... Alula [*Somalia*] [*Airport symbol*]
Alumni Bull Sch Dent Indiana Univ ... Alumni Bulletin. School of Dentistry. Indiana University [*A publication*]
Alumni Bull Univ Mich Sch Dent ... Alumni Bulletin. University of Michigan. School of Dentistry [*A publication*]
Alum Rev .. Aluminum Review [*A publication*]
ALW .... Walla Walla [*Washington*] [*Airport symbol*]
ALWF .... Actual Wind Factor [*Meteorology*]
Alyum Splavy Sb Statej ... Alyuminievye Splavy Sbornik Statej [*A publication*]
ALZ .... Alitak [*Alaska*] [*Airport symbol*]
AMA .... Against Medical Advice
AMA .... Amarillo [*Texas*] [*Airport symbol*]
AMA .... Automatic Memory Allocation [*Data processing*]
AMAAA ..... Atti e Memorie dell Accademia di Storia dell Arte Sanitaria [*A publication*]
Am Alpine Jour ... American Alpine Journal [*A publication*]
Am Archivist ... American Archivist [*A publication*]
Am Arch Rehabil Ther ... American Archives of Rehabilitation Therapy [*A publication*]
AMAS....... Automatic Message Accounting System
Am As Museums Pr ... American Association of Museums. Proceedings [*A publication*]
Am As Petroleum G B ... American Association of Petroleum Geologists. Bulletin [*A publication*]
Am As Pr Mem ... American Association for the Advancement of Science. Proceedings. Memoirs [*A publication*]
AMASS ..... Amplitude Miss Distance Acoustical Scoring System
Am Assoc Adv Sci Symp ... American Association for the Advancement of Science. Symposium [*A publication*]
Am Assoc Pet Geol Repr Ser ... American Association of Petroleum Geologists. Reprint Series [*A publication*]
Am Assoc Petroleum Geologists Mem ... American Association of Petroleum Geologists. Memoir [*A publication*]
Am Astronaut Soc Publ Sci Technol ... American Astronautical Society. Publications. Science and Technology [*A publication*]
AMB .... AMB. Revista da Associacao Medica Brasileira [*A publication*]
AMB .... Ambilobe [*Madagascar*] [*Airport symbol*]
Am Baby ... American Baby [*A publication*]
Am Bank... American Banker [*A publication*]
AMBM....... Association of Men's Belt Manufacturers
Am Book Publ Recd ... American Book Publishing Record [*A publication*]
Am Bur Geog B ... American Bureau of Geography. Bulletin [*A publication*]
AMCA .... Antique Motorcycle Club of America
Am Cath His Rec ... American Catholic Historical Society. Records [*A publication*]
Am Ceramic Soc Jour ... American Ceramic Society. Journal [*A publication*]
Am Ceram Soc Bull ... American Ceramic Society. Bulletin [*A publication*]
AMCF....... Alkali Metal Cleaning Facility [*Nuclear energy*]
Am Chem Soc Div Fuel Chem Prepr ... American Chemical Society. Division of Fuel Chemistry. Preprints [*A publication*]
Am Chem Soc Mon ... American Chemical Society. Monograph [*A publication*]
Am Cin...... American Cinematographer [*A publication*]
Am Cinematog ... American Cinematographer [*A publication*]
AMCP........ Anhydrous Monocalcium Phosphate [*Inorganic chemistry*]
Am Cryst Assoc Trans ... American Crystallographic Association Polycrystal Book Service. Transactions [*A publication*]
AMD .... Ahmedabad [*India*] [*Airport symbol*]
AMD .... Association for Macular Diseases

AMDAPS... Automatic Meteorological Data Acquisition and Processing System
AMDEL Bull ... AMDEL [*Australian Mineral Development Laboratories*] Bulletin [*A publication*]
Am Dyest Rep ... American Dyestuff Reporter [*A publication*]
Am Dyestuff Reptr ... American Dyestuff Reporter [*A publication*]
AMEBA ..... Annales Medicinae Experimentalis et Biologiae Fenniae [*A publication*]
Am Educ... American Education [*A publication*]
Amer Arch Rehab Ther ... American Archives of Rehabilitation Therapy [*A publication*]
Amer Baker ... American Baker [*A publication*]
Amer Bee J ... American Bee Journal [*A publication*]
Amer Brewer ... American Brewer [*A publication*]
Amer Cattle Prod ... American Cattle Producer [*A publication*]
Amer Corp ... American Corporation [*A publication*]
Amer Correct Ther J ... American Corrective Therapy Journal [*A publication*]
Amer Dairy Rev ... American Dairy Review [*A publication*]
Amer Drug ... American Druggist [*A publication*]
Amer Economist ... American Economist [*A publication*]
Amer Econ R ... American Economic Review [*A publication*]
Amer Econ Rev ... American Economic Review [*A publication*]
Amer Industr Hyg Assoc J ... American Industrial Hygiene Association. Journal [*A publication*]
Amer J Agr Econ ... American Journal of Agricultural Economics [*A publication*]
Amer J Bot ... American Journal of Botany [*A publication*]
Amer J Clin Nutr ... American Journal of Clinical Nutrition [*A publication*]
Amer J Clin Pathol ... American Journal of Clinical Pathology [*A publication*]
Amer J Digest Dis ... American Journal of Digestive Diseases [*A publication*]
Amer J Dis Child ... American Journal of Diseases of Children [*A publication*]
Amer J Pathol ... American Journal of Pathology [*A publication*]
Amer J of Phys ... American Journal of Physics [*A publication*]
Amer J Physiol ... American Journal of Physiology [*A publication*]
Amer J Phys Med ... American Journal of Physical Medicine [*A publication*]
Amer J Sci Radiocarbon Suppl ... American Journal of Science. Radiocarbon Supplement [*A publication*]
Amer J Vet Res ... American Journal of Veterinary Research [*A publication*]
Amer Kenkyu ... America Kenkyu [*A publication*]
Amer Livestock J ... American Livestock Journal [*A publication*]
Amer Math Soc Transl ... American Mathematical Society. Translations [*A publication*]
Amer Midl Nat ... American Midland Naturalist [*A publication*]
Amer Miller Process ... American Miller and Processor [*A publication*]
Amer Nat .. American Naturalist [*A publication*]
Amer Nurserym ... American Nurseryman [*A publication*]
Amer Stat ... American Statistician [*A publication*]
Amer Stat Ind ... American Statistics Index [*A publication*]
Amer Veg Grower ... American Vegetable Grower [*A publication*]
Amer Woods US For Serv ... American Woods. US Forest Service [*A publication*]
AMEX........ AMEX-Canada [*A publication*]
AMF .... Ama [*Papua New Guinea*] [*Airport symbol*]
AMF .... Americans for Medical Freedom [*An organization*]
Am Forests ... American Forests [*A publication*]
Am Fox and Fur Farmer ... American Fox and Fur Farmer [*A publication*]
Am G......... American Geologist [*A publication*]
Am Game Bull Am Game Protect Ass ... American Game. Bulletin of the American Game Protective Association [*A publication*]
Am G As B ... American Geological Association. Bulletin [*A publication*]
Am Geog Soc ... American Geographical Society [*A publication*]
Am Geog Soc B J ... American Geographical Society. Bulletin. Journal [*A publication*]
Am Geog Soc Special Pub ... American Geographical Society. Special Publication [*A publication*]
Am Geog Stat Soc J ... American Geographical and Statistical Society. Journal [*A publication*]

Am Geol Inst Repr Ser ... American Geological Institute. Reprint Series [*A publication*]
Am Geol Inst Rept ... American Geological Institute. Report [*A publication*]
Am Health Care Assoc J ... American Health Care Association. Journal [*A publication*]
Am Her...... American Heritage [*A publication*]
Am His R... American Historical Review [*A publication*]
AMI .... Arginine Maturity Index [*For prediction of peanut harvest date*]
AMI .... Mataram [*Indonesia*] [*Airport symbol*]
AMIAA ...... American Imago [*A publication*]
Am I M Eng Tr B ... American Institute of Mining Engineers. Transactions. Bulletin [*A publication*]
Aminco Lab News ... Aminco Laboratory News [*A publication*]
Am Ind Hyg Assoc J ... American Industrial Hygiene Association. Journal [*A publication*]
Am Ink ...... American Inkmaker [*A publication*]
Am Inst Oral Biol Annu Meet ... American Institute of Oral Biology. Annual Meeting [*A publication*]
Am Irish His S J ... American Irish Historical Society. Journal [*A publication*]
AMIS .... Amis du Film et de la Television [*A publication*]
AMJ........... Almenara [*Brazil*] [*Airport symbol*]
Am J Agr... American Journal of Agriculture and Science [*A publication*]
AMJAMS... Automated Military Justice Analysis and Management System
Am J Art Ther ... American Journal of Art Therapy [*A publication*]
Am J Clin Hypn ... American Journal of Clinical Hypnosis [*A publication*]
Am J Community Psychol ... American Journal of Community Psychology [*A publication*]
Am J Conch ... American Journal of Conchology [*A publication*]
Am J Dis Child ... American Journal of Diseases of Children [*A publication*]
Am J Econ Sociol (New York) ... American Journal of Economics and Sociology (New York) [*A publication*]
Am J Epidemiol ... American Journal of Epidemiology [*A publication*]
Am Jew His ... American Jewish Historical Society. Publications [*A publication*]
Am J Gastroenterol ... American Journal of Gastroenterology [*A publication*]
Am J Health Plann ... American Journal of Health Planning [*A publication*]
Am J Hum Genet ... American Journal of Human Genetics [*A publication*]
Am J Hyg Monogr Ser ... American Journal of Hygiene. Monographic Series [*A publication*]
Am J Int L ... American Journal of International Law [*A publication*]
Am J Int L Supp ... American Journal of International Law. Supplement [*A publication*]
Am J IV Therapy ... American Journal of IV Therapy [*A publication*]
Am J Med Genet ... American Journal of Medical Genetics [*A publication*]
Am J Ment Defic ... American Journal of Mental Deficiency [*A publication*]
Am J Micr (NY) ... American Journal of Microscopy and Popular Science (New York) [*A publication*]
Am J Nursing ... American Journal of Nursing [*A publication*]
Am J Obstet Gynecol ... American Journal of Obstetrics and Gynecology [*A publication*]
Am J Occup Ther ... American Journal of Occupational Therapy [*A publication*]
Am J Optom & Physiol Opt ... American Journal of Optometry and Physiological Optics [*A publication*]
Am J Orthopsychiatr ... American Journal of Orthopsychiatry [*A publication*]
Am J Pharm ... American Journal of Pharmacy and the Sciences Supporting Public Health [*A publication*]
Am J Pharm Educ ... American Journal of Pharmaceutical Education [*A publication*]
Am J Phys Anthropol ... American Journal of Physical Anthropology [*A publication*]
Am J Phys Med ... American Journal of Physical Medicine [*A publication*]
Am J Pub Health ... American Journal of Public Health [*A publication*]
Am J Roentgenol ... American Journal of Roentgenology [*A publication*]

Am J Sc and Arts ... American Journal of Science and Arts [*A publication*]
Am J Sports Med ... American Journal of Sports Medicine [*A publication*]
Am J Surg Pathol ... American Journal of Surgical Pathology [*A publication*]
Am J Trop Dis (New Orleans) ... American Journal of Tropical Diseases and Preventive Medicine (New Orleans) [*A publication*]
Am J Vet Med ... American Journal of Veterinary Medicine [*A publication*]
Am J Vet Res ... American Journal of Veterinary Research [*A publication*]
AMK .... Antimisting Kerosene [*Aviation*]
AML .... Animated Movie Language
Am Lab ..... American Laboratory [*A publication*]
Am Laund Dig ... American Laundry Digest [*A publication*]
Am Libr (Chicago) ... American Libraries (Chicago) [*A publication*]
Am Libs .... American Libraries [*A publication*]
Am Lung Assoc Bull ... American Lung Association. Bulletin [*A publication*]
AMM .... Amman [*Jordan*] [*Airport symbol*]
AMM .... Army Mobility Model
Am Mach/Metalwork Manuf ... American Machinist/Metalworking Manufacturing [*A publication*]
Am Malacolog Union Ann Rept ... American Malacological Union. Annual Report [*A publication*]
Am Malacol Union Bull ... American Malacological Union. Bulletin [*A publication*]
Am Math Mon ... American Mathematical Monthly [*A publication*]
Am M Cong ... American Mining Congress [*A publication*]
Am Med .... American Medicine [*A publication*]
Am Med News ... American Medical News [*A publication*]
Am Meteorological J ... American Meteorological Journal [*A publication*]
Am Met Mark ... American Metal Market [*A publication*]
Am Micro Soc Pr ... American Microscopical Society. Proceedings [*A publication*]
Am Miner J ... American Mineralogical Journal [*A publication*]
AMMIS ...... Aircraft Maintenance Manpower Information System
Am Mtl Mkt ... American Metal Market [*A publication*]
Am Mus J ... American Museum Journal [*A publication*]
Am Mus Nat History Bull ... American Museum of Natural History. Bulletin [*A publication*]
Am Mus N H B Mem ... American Museum of Natural History. Bulletin. Memoirs [*A publication*]
Am Mus Novitates ... American Museum Novitates [*A publication*]
Am Nurse ... American Nurse [*A publication*]
AMP .... Agricultural Marketing Project
AMP .... American Majority Party
AMP .... Ampanihy [*Madagascar*] [*Airport symbol*]
AMP .... Associative Memory Processor [*Data processing*]
AMPA .... Adaptive Multibeam Phased Array [*RADAR*]
Am Paint ... American Paint Journal [*A publication*]
Am Paper Ind ... American Paper Industry [*A publication*]
Am Paper Inst ... American Paper Institute [*A publication*]
Am Paper Merch ... American Paper Merchant [*A publication*]
AMPCB ..... American Psychological Association. Proceedings of the Annual Convention [*A publication*]
Am Pharm ... American Pharmacy [*A publication*]
Am Photog ... American Photography [*A publication*]
Am Planning ... American Planning and Civic Planning [*A publication*]
AMPMA ..... Archives des Maladies Professionelles de Medicine du Travail et de Securite Sociale [*A publication*]
Am Poetry ... American Poetry Review [*A publication*]
Am Pressman Rept ... American Pressman Reports [*A publication*]
AMPS .... Advanced Mobile Phone Service [*Bell System*]
Am Pub Health Ass Rep ... American Public Health Association. Reports [*A publication*]
AMPYA ..... Annales Medico-Psychologiques [*A publication*]
AMQ .... Ambon [*Indonesia*] [*Airport symbol*]
Am Q J Agr ... American Quarterly Journal of Agriculture and Science [*A publication*]
Am Q Micro J ... American Quarterly Microscopical Journal [*A publication*]
AMR .... Automated Management Reports
AMR .... Automatic Message Routing
Am Rev Respir Dis ... American Review of Respiratory Disease [*A publication*]

AMS .... Access Method Service
AMS .... Alteration Management System
AMS .... Amsterdam [*Netherlands*] [*Airport symbol*]
Am Sch ..... American Scholar [*A publication*]
Am Schol ... American Scholar [*A publication*]
Am Soc Civ Eng Proc J Hydraul Div ... American Society of Civil Engineers. Proceedings. Journal of the Hydraulics Division [*A publication*]
Am Soc Civ Eng Proc Transp Eng J ... American Society of Civil Engineers. Proceedings. Transportation Engineering Journal [*A publication*]
Am Soc Civ Eng Trans ... American Society of Civil Engineers. Transactions [*A publication*]
Am Sociol Rev ... American Sociological Review [*A publication*]
Am Sociol S ... American Sociological Society. Publications [*A publication*]
Am Soc Mechanical Engineers Trans ... American Society of Mechanical Engineers. Transactions [*A publication*]
Am Soc Munic Imp ... American Society for Municipal Improvements. Proceedings [*A publication*]
Am Soc Photogramm Annu Meet Proc ... American Society of Photogrammetry. Annual Meeting. Proceedings [*A publication*]
Am Soc Photogramm Fall Conv Proc ... American Society of Photogrammetry. Fall Convention. Proceedings [*A publication*]
Am Soc Test Mater Spec Tech Publ ... American Society for Testing and Materials. Special Technical Publication [*A publication*]
Am Soc Trop Med Papers ... American Society of Tropical Medicine. Papers [*A publication*]
AMSOG ..... Army Molecular Sieve Oxygen Generator
Amsterdams Sociol Tijds ... Amsterdams Sociologisch Tijdsckrist [*A publication*]
Am Stockman ... American Stockman [*A publication*]
AMT .... Ammonium Metatungstate [*Inorganic chemistry*]
AMT .... AUTODIN [*Automatic Digital Network*] Multimedia Terminal
AMTE .... Adjusted Megaton Equivalent
Am Trust Rev Pacific ... American Trust Review of the Pacific [*A publication*]
AMU .... Amanab [*Papua New Guinea*] [*Airport symbol*]
Am Vet Rev ... American Veterinary Review [*A publication*]
Am Water Resour Assoc (Symp) Proc ... American Water Resources Association. (Symposium) Proceedings [*A publication*]
AMY .... Ambatomainty [*Madagascar*] [*Airport symbol*]
AMZ .... Ardmore [*New Zealand*] [*Airport symbol*]
AN .... Answer
A/N .... As Needed
ANA .... American Normande Association
An Acad Bras Cienc Supl ... Anais da Academia Brasileira de Ciencias. Suplemento [*A publication*]
ANA Clin Conf ... ANA [*American Nurses' Association*] Clinical Conferences [*A publication*]
ANA Clin Sess ... ANA [*American Nurses' Association*] Clinical Session [*A publication*]
Anaesthesiol Intensivmed Prax ... Anaethesiologische und Intensivmedizinische Praxis [*A publication*]
Anaesth Intensive Care ... Anaesthesia and Intensive Care [*A publication*]
Anais Esc Sup Agric "Luiz Queiroz" ... Anais da Escola Superior de Agricultura "Luiz De Queiroz" [*A publication*]
Anal .... Analyst [*A publication*]
Anal Abstr ... Analytical Abstracts [*A publication*]
Anal Adv ... Analytical Advances [*A publication*]
Anal Chem ... Analytical Chemistry [*A publication*]
Anal Chim Acta ... Analytica Chimica Acta [*A publication*]
Anal Chimica Acta ... Analytica Chimica Acta [*A publication*]
Anal Inst Cerc Agron ... Analele Institutului de Cercetari Agronomice al Academia Republicii Populare Romine [*A publication*]
Anal Instrum ... Analysis Instrumentation [*A publication*]
Anal Letters ... Analytical Letters [*A publication*]
Anal Math ... Analysis Mathematica [*A publication*]
Anal O .... Analecta Orientalia [*A publication*]
Anal Rev Tech Merlin Gerin ... Analyses. Revue Technique Merlin Gerin [*A publication*]

Anal Stiint Univ Cuza Iasi Chim ... Analele Stiintifice ale Universitatii. Al. I. Cuza. din Iasi. Sectia I-C. Chimie [*A publication*]

Anal Univ Buc Ser Stiint Nat Biol ... Analele Universitatii Bucuresti. Seria Stiintele Naturii. Biologie [*A publication*]

Analyt Abstr ... Analytical Abstracts [*A publication*]

ANA Nurs Res Conf ... American Nurses' Association. Nursing Research Conferences [*A publication*]

ANAPROP ... Anomalous Propagation

ANA Publ ... American Nurses' Association. Publications [*A publication*]

An Asoc Quim Argent ... Anales de la Asociacion Quimica. Argentina [*A publication*]

ANB .... Anniston [*Alabama*] [*Airport symbol*]

ANC .... Anchorage [*Alaska*] [*Airport symbol*]

An Chem ... Analytical Chemistry [*A publication*]

An Cient (Lima) ... Anales Cientificos (Lima) [*A publication*]

An Circ Med Argent ... Anales del Circa Medico Argentino [*A publication*]

ANCPCJ .... Alliance of NGOs on Crime Prevention and Criminal Justice

AND .... Anderson [*South Carolina*] [*Airport symbol*]

ANDFA ...... American Annals of the Deaf [*A publication*]

Andhra Agr J ... Andhra Agricultural Journal [*A publication*]

ANE .... Americans for Nuclear Energy [*An organization*]

An Esc Super Agr Luiz De Queiroz ... Anais da Escola Superior de Agricultura Luiz De Queiroz [*A publication*]

An Esp Pediatr ... Anales Espanoles de Pediatria [*A publication*]

Anesth Analg (Cleve) ... Anesthesia and Analgesia (Cleveland) [*A publication*]

Anesth Analg (Paris) ... Anesthesie Analgesie Reanimation (Paris) [*A publication*]

Anesthesiol Clin ... International Anesthesiology Clinics [*A publication*]

ANF .... Antofagasta [*Chile*] [*Airport symbol*]

An Fac Ci Univ Porto ... Anais de Faculdade de Ciencia. Universidade do Porto [*A publication*]

An Fac Med Lima ... Anales de la Facultad de Medicina de Lima [*A publication*]

An Fac Med (Montevideo) ... Anales de la Facultad de Medicina (Montevideo) [*A publication*]

An Fac Quim Farm (Santiago) ... Anales de la Facultad de Quimica y Farmacia. Universidad de Chile (Santiago) [*A publication*]

An Fis .... Anales de Fisica [*A publication*]

ANG .... Association of National Grasslands

An Geog .... Annales de Geographie [*A publication*]

Angew Chem Intern Ed ... Angewandte Chemie. International Edition in English [*A publication*]

Angew Elektron ... Angewandte Elektronik [*A publication*]

Angew Elektron Mess & Regeltech ... Angewandte Elektronik. Mess und Regeltechnik [*A publication*]

Angew Inf ... Angewandte Informatik [*A publication*]

Angew Makromol Chem ... Angewandte Makromolekulare Chemie [*A publication*]

Angew Met ... Angewandte Meteorologie [*A publication*]

Anglo-Ger Med Rev ... Anglo-German Medical Review [*A publication*]

An G Paleont ... Annales de Geologie et de Paleontologie [*A publication*]

ANI .... Aniak [*Alaska*] [*Airport symbol*]

Anim Breed Abstr ... Animal Breeding Abstracts [*A publication*]

Anim Husb ... Animal Husbandry [*A publication*]

Anim Husb Agric J ... Animal Husbandry and Agricultural Journal [*A publication*]

An Inst Agron (Lisbon) ... Anais do Instituto Superior de Agronomia (Lisbon) [*A publication*]

An Inst Biol (Mexico) ... Anales del Instituto de Biologia (Mexico) [*A publication*]

An Inst Biol Univ Mex ... Anales del Instituto de Biologia. Universidad Nacional Autonoma de Mexico [*A publication*]

An Inst Bot A J Cavanilles (Madrid) ... Anales del Instituto Botanico A. J. Cavanilles (Madrid) [*A publication*]

An Inst Hig Med Trop (Lisb) ... Anais do Instituto de Higiene e Medicina Tropical (Lisbon) [*A publication*]

An Inst Invest Vet (Madrid) ... Anales del Instituto de Investigaciones Veterinarias (Madrid) [*A publication*]

An In St Ma ... Annals of the Institute of Statistical Mathematics [*A publication*]

An Inst Med Nac ... Anales de Instituto Medico Nacional (Mexico) [*A publication*]

An Inst Med Trop ... Anais do Instituto de Medicina Tropical [*A publication*]

An Inst Super Agron (Lisboa) ... Anais do Instituto Superior dei Agronomia (Lisboa) [*A publication*]

ANL .... American National Standard Labels

Anleit Bienenzuechter ... Anleitungen Bienenzuechter [*A publication*]

Anls Prob ... Annals of Probability [*A publication*]

Anls Stat ... Annals of Statistics [*A publication*]

ANM .... Antalaha [*Madagascar*] [*Airport symbol*]

An Mag N H ... Annals and Magazine of Natural History [*A publication*]

An M Belgique ... Annales des Mines de Belgique [*A publication*]

An Mec Elect ... Anales de Mecanica y Electricidad [*A publication*]

An Mec & Electr ... Anales de Mecanica y Electricidad [*A publication*]

An Mex Cienc ... Anales Mexicanos de Ciencias [*A publication*]

An Mines ... Annales des Mines [*A publication*]

ANN .... Annette Island [*Alaska*] [*Airport symbol*]

Ann Acad Med (Singapore) ... Annals of the Academy of Medicine (Singapore) [*A publication*]

Ann Acad Sci Fenn A I ... Annales Academiae Scientiarum Fennicae. Series A-I (Mathematica) [*A publication*]

Ann Acad Sci Fenn A II ... Annales Academiae Scientiarum Fennicae. Series A-II (Chemica) [*A publication*]

Ann Acad Sci Fenn A VI ... Annales Academiae Scientiarum Fennicae. Series A-VI (Physica) [*A publication*]

Ann Acad Sci Fenn (Biol) ... Annales Academiae Scientiarum Fennicae. Series A-IV (Biologica) [*A publication*]

Ann Acad Sci Fenn (Med) ... Annales Academiae Scientiarum Fennicae. Series A-V (Medica) [*A publication*]

Ann Acad Sci Fenn Ser A I ... Annales Academiae Scientiarum Fennicae. Series A-I. Mathematica [*A publication*]

Ann Acad Sci Fenn Ser A II ... Annales Academiae Scientiarum Fennicae. Series A-II [*A publication*]

Ann Acad Sci Fenn Ser A III ... Annales Academiae Scientiarum Fennicae. Series A-III. Geologica-Geographica [*A publication*]

Ann Acad Sci Fenn Ser A IV ... Annales Academiae Scientiarum Fennicae. Series A-IV. Biologia [*A publication*]

Ann Acad Sci Fenn Ser A V ... Annales Academiae Scientiarum Fennicae. Series A-V. Medica [*A publication*]

Ann Acad Sci Fenn Ser A VI ... Annales Academiae Scientiarum Fennicae. Series A-VI. Physica [*A publication*]

Ann Agr Fenn ... Annales Agriculturae Fenniae [*A publication*]

Ann Agric Sci Univ A'in Shams ... Annals of Agricultural Science. University of A'in Shams [*A publication*]

Ann Agri Sci ... Annals of Agriculture Science [*A publication*]

Annali Fac Agr Portici ... Annali della Facolta di Agraria di Portici della Reale Universita di Napoli [*A publication*]

Annali Fac Agr Univ Bari ... Annali della Facolta di Agraria. Universita di Bari [*A publication*]

Annali Fac Agr Univ Perugia ... Annali della Facolta di Agraria della Universita degli Studi di Perugia [*A publication*]

Annali Geofisica ... Annali di Geofisica [*A publication*]

Annali Idrol ... Annali Idrologici [*A publication*]

Annali Microbiol ... Annali di Microbiologia (Ed Enzimologia) [*A publication*]

Annali Sper Agr ... Annali della Sperimentazione Agraria [*A publication*]

Annali Staz Chim Agr Sper Roma ... Annali della Reale Stazione Chimico-Agraria Sperimentale di Roma [*A publication*]

Annali Staz Sper Risicolt Vercelli ... Annali Stazione Sperimentale di Risicoltura e delle Colture Irrigue. Vercelli [*A publication*]

Annals KY Nat History ... Annals of Kentucky Natural History [*A publication*]

Annals and Mag Nat History ... Annals and Magazine of Natural History [*A publication*]

Ann Amelior Plantes ... Annales de l'Amelioration des Plantes [*A publication*]

Ann Anat Pathol (Paris) ... Annales d'Anatomie Pathologique (Paris) [*A publication*]

Ann Ass Amer Geogr ... Annals of the Association of American Geographers [*A publication*]

Ann Assoc Int Calcul Analogique ... Annales de l'Association Internationale pour le Calcul Analogique [*A publication*]

Ann Biochem Exp Med ... Annals of Biochemistry and Experimental Medicine [*A publication*]

Ann Biol Clin (Paris) ... Annales de Biologie Clinique (Paris) [*A publication*]
Ann Biomed Eng ... Annals of Biomedical Engineering [*A publication*]
Ann Bot ..... Annals of Botany [*A publication*]
Ann Clin Lab Sci ... Annals of Clinical and Laboratory Science [*A publication*]
Ann Clin Res ... Annals of Clinical Research [*A publication*]
Ann Dent .. Annals of Dentistry [*A publication*]
Ann Droit Int Med ... Annales de Droit International Medical [*A publication*]
Ann Ecole Nat Agr Alger ... Annales de l'Ecole Nationale d'Agriculture d'Alger [*A publication*]
Ann Ecole Nat Super Agron ... Annales de l'Ecole Nationale Superieure Agronomique [*A publication*]
Ann Ecole Nat Sup Mec (Nantes) ... Annales de l'Ecole Nationale Superieure de Mecanique (Nantes) [*A publication*]
Annee Afr ... Annee Africaine [*A publication*]
Annee Agr ... Annee Agricole [*A publication*]
Annee Sociol ... Annee Sociologique [*A publication*]
Annee Ther Clin Ophtalmol ... Annee Therapeutique et Clinique et Ophtalmologie [*A publication*]
Ann Endocrinol (Paris) ... Annales d'Endocrinologie (Paris) [*A publication*]
Ann Ent Fenn ... Annales Entomologici Fennici [*A publication*]
Ann Entomol Soc Am ... Annals of the Entomological Society of America [*A publication*]
Ann Ent Soc Am ... Annals of the Entomological Society of America [*A publication*]
Ann Epiphyt ... Annales des Epiphyties [*A publication*]
Ann Fac Agr (Perugia) ... Annali della Facolta di Agraria (Perugia) [*A publication*]
Ann Fac Agr Univ Pisa ... Annali della Facolta di Agraria Universita di Pisa [*A publication*]
Ann Fac Agr Univ Studii Perugia ... Annali della Facolta di Agraria Universita degli Studi di Perugia [*A publication*]
Ann Fac Med Chirurg ... Annali della Facolta di Medicina e Chirurgia [*A publication*]
Ann Fac Med S Paulo ... Annes de Faculdade de Medicina de Sao Paulo [*A publication*]
Ann Fac Med Vet Univ Studi Pisa ... Annali della Facolta di Medicina Veterinaria. Universita degli Studi di Pisa [*A publication*]
Ann Fac Med Vet Univ Torino ... Annali della Facolta di Medicina Veterinaria. Universita di Torino [*A publication*]
Ann Fac Sci Agr Univ Napoli Ser 3 ... Annali della Facolta di Science Agrarie della Universita di Napoli. Ser 3 [*A publication*]
Ann Fac Sci Agr Univ Torino ... Annali della Facolta di Science Agrarie della Universita degli Torino [*A publication*]
Ann Fac Sci Univ Toulouse ... Annales de la Faculte des Sciences de l'Universite de Toulouse [*A publication*]
Ann Falsif Expertise Chim ... Annales des Falsifications et de l'Expertise Chimique [*A publication*]
Ann Fitopatol ... Annali di Fitopatologia [*A publication*]
Ann Fr Chronom Micromec ... Annales Francaises de Chronometrie et de Micromecanique [*A publication*]
Ann Hum Genet ... Annals of Human Genetics [*A publication*]
Ann Hyg et Med Colon ... Annales Hygiene et de Medecine Coloniales [*A publication*]
Ann Hyg Pub et Med Legale ... Annales d'Hygiene Publique et de Medecine Legale [*A publication*]
Ann IA .... Annals of Iowa [*A publication*]
Ann Idrol ... Annali Idrologici [*A publication*]
Ann Ig ... Annali d'Igiene [*A publication*]
Ann Ig Sper ... Annali d'Igiene. Sperimentali [*A publication*]
Ann INSEE ... Annales de l'INSEE [*Institut National de la Statistique et des Etudes Economiques*] [*A publication*]
Ann Inst Henri Poincare A ... Annales de l'Institut Henri Poincare. Section A (Physique Theorique) [*A publication*]
Ann Inst Henri Poincare B ... Annales de l'Institut Henri Poincare. Section B (Calcul des Probabilities et Statistique) [*A publication*]
Ann Inst Henri Poincare Sect A ... Annales de l'Institut Henri Poincare. Section A (Physique Theorique) [*A publication*]
Ann Inst Nat Agron ... Annales de l'Institut National Agronomique [*A publication*]
Ann Inst Nat Rech For Tunis ... Annales de l'Institut National de Recherches Forestieres de Tunisie [*A publication*]

Ann Inst Poincare Sect A ... Annales de l'Institut Henri Poincare. Section A (Physique Theorique) [*A publication*]
Ann Inst Poincare Sect B ... Annales de l'Institut Henri Poincare. Section B (Calcul des Probabilities et Statistique) [*A publication*]
Anniv Bull Chuo Univ ... Anniversary Bulletin of Chuo University [*A publication*]
Ann Japan Assoc Philos Sci ... Annals of the Japan Association for Philosophy of Science [*A publication*]
Ann Laringol ... Annali di Laringologia, Otologia, Rinologia, Faringologia [*A publication*]
Ann Laringol Otol Rinol Faringol ... Annali di Laringologia, Otologia, Rinologia, Faringologia [*A publication*]
Annls Agric Fenn ... Annales Agriculturae Fenniae [*A publication*]
Annls Agron ... Annales Agronomiques [*A publication*]
Annls Cent Rech Agron Bambey ... Annales du Centre de Recherches Agronomiques de Bambey au Senegal [*A publication*]
Annls Epiphyt ... Annales des Epiphyties et de Phytogenetique [*A publication*]
Annls Gembloux ... Annales de Gembloux [*A publication*]
Annls Inst Natn Agron (Paris) ... Annales de l'Institut National Agronomique (Paris) [*A publication*]
Annls Inst Natn Rech Agron Tunisie ... Annales de l'Institut National de la Recherche Agronomique de Tunisie [*A publication*]
Annls Inst Pasteur (Paris) ... Annales de l'Institut Pasteur (Paris) [*A publication*]
Annls Inst Phytopath Benaki ... Annales de l'Institut Phytopathologique. Benaki [*A publication*]
Annls Mines Belg ... Annales des Mines de Belgique [*A publication*]
Annls Mines (Paris) ... Annales des Mines (Paris) [*A publication*]
Annls Physiol Veg (Brux) ... Annales de Physiologie Vegetale (Bruxelles) [*A publication*]
Annls Physiol Veg (Paris) ... Annales de Physiologie Vegetale (Paris) [*A publication*]
Annls SEITA ... Annales della Direction des Etudes et de l'Equipment. Service d'Exploitation Industrielle des Tabacs et des Allumettes [*A publication*]
Annls Univ Mariae Curie Sklodowska ... Annales Universitatis Mariae Curie-Sklodowska [*A publication*]
Ann Lyceum Nat Hist NY ... Annals of the Lyceum of Natural History. New York [*A publication*]
Ann and Mag Nat Hist ... Annals and Magazine of Natural History [*A publication*]
Ann Mag Natur Hist ... Annals and Magazine of Natural History [*A publication*]
Ann Math Logic ... Annals of Mathematical Logic [*A publication*]
Ann Math Stat ... Annals of Mathematical Statistics [*A publication*]
Ann Mat Pura Appl ... Annali di Matematica Pura ed Applicata [*A publication*]
Ann de Med Belge ... Annales de Medecine Belge et Etrangere [*A publication*]
Ann Med Belges ... Annales Medicales Belges [*A publication*]
Ann Med et Chir Inf ... Annales de Medecine et Chirurgie Infantiles [*A publication*]
Ann Med Nav e Colon ... Annali de Medicina Navale e Coloniale [*A publication*]
Ann Med et Pharm Colon ... Annales de Medecine et de Pharmacie Coloniales [*A publication*]
Ann Mines ... Annales des Mines [*A publication*]
Ann MO Bot Gdn ... Annals of the Missouri Botanical Garden [*A publication*]
Ann Neurol ... Annals of Neurology [*A publication*]
Ann Nucl Energy ... Annals of Nuclear Energy [*A publication*]
Ann Nucl Sci & Eng ... Annals of Nuclear Science and Engineering [*A publication*]
Ann Obs Besancon ... Annales de l'Observatoire de Besancon [*A publication*]
Ann Ocul (Paris) ... Annales d'Oculistique (Paris) [*A publication*]
Ann Oftalmol Clin Ocul ... Annali di Oftalmologia e Clinica Oculistica [*A publication*]
Ann Ostet Ginecol Med Perinat ... Annali di Ostetricia Ginecologia Medicina Perinatale [*A publication*]
Annot Bibliography of Econ Geology ... Annotated Bibliography of Economic Geology [*A publication*]
Ann Oto-Laryngol ... Annales d'Oto-Laryngologie [*A publication*]
Ann Otolaryngol Chir Cervicofac ... Annales d'Otolaryngologie et de Chirurgie Cervicofaciale [*A publication*]

Ann Otol Rhinol Laryngol Suppl ... Annals of Otology, Rhinology and Laryngology. Supplement [*A publication*]

Annot Zool Japon ... Annotationes Zoologicae Japonenses [*A publication*]

Ann Parasitol ... Annales de Parasitologie Humaine et Comparee [*A publication*]

Ann Paulist Med e Cirurg ... Annales Paulistas de Medicina e Cirurgia [*A publication*]

Ann Pediatr ... Annales de Pediatrie [*A publication*]

Ann Pharm Fr ... Annales Pharmaceutiques Francaises [*A publication*]

Ann Phys .. Annals of Physics [*A publication*]

Ann Phys (Germ) ... Annalen der Physik (Germany) [*A publication*]

Ann Physiol Veg ... Annales de Physiologie Vegetale [*A publication*]

Ann Phys (Leipzig) ... Annalen der Physik (Leipzig) [*A publication*]

Ann Phys (Paris) ... Annales de Physique (Paris) [*A publication*]

Ann Phytopath ... Annales de Phytopathologie [*A publication*]

Ann Phytopathol Soc Jap ... Annals of the Phytopathological Society of Japan [*A publication*]

Ann Plast Surg ... Annals of Plastic Surgery [*A publication*]

Ann Polon Math ... Annales Polonici Mathematici [*A publication*]

Ann Rech For Maroc ... Annales de la Recherche Forestiere au Maroc [*A publication*]

Ann Rept Progr Chem ... Annual Reports on the Progress of Chemistry [*A publication*]

Ann Rept Tokyo Univ Agr Technol ... Annual Report of Tokyo University of Agriculture and Technology [*A publication*]

Ann Rep United Fruit Co Med Dept ... Annual Report. United Fruit Company. Medical Department [*A publication*]

Ann Rev Biochem ... Annual Review of Biochemistry [*A publication*]

Ann Rev Ecol ... Annual Review of Ecology and Systematics [*A publication*]

Ann Rev Entomol ... Annual Review of Entomology [*A publication*]

Ann Rev Microbiol ... Annual Review of Microbiology [*A publication*]

Ann Rev Nuclear Sci ... Annual Review of Nuclear Science [*A publication*]

ANR ... Antwerp [*Belgium*] [*Airport symbol*]

ANRP ... Association for a National Recycling Policy

ANS ... Andahuaylas [*Peru*] [*Airport symbol*]

ANSA ... Advanced Network System Architecture

ANSC ... American National Standards (Institute) Committee

ANT ... Advanced Nosetip [*AEC*]

ANV ... Air Nevada Airlines, Inc. [*Las Vegas, NV*] [*FAA designator*]

ANV ... Anvik [*Alaska*] [*Airport symbol*]

ANX ... Andenes [*Norway*] [*Airport symbol*]

AO ... Abnormal Occurrence

A/O ... About or On

AO ... Aldehyde Oxidase [*An enzyme*]

AOD ... Automatic Overdrive

AOG ... Augmented Off-Gas System [*Nuclear energy*]

AOJ ... Aomori [*Japan*] [*Airport symbol*]

AOK ... Karpathos [*Greece*] [*Airport symbol*]

AOL ... Application Oriented Language [*Data processing*]

AOL ... Paso De Los Libres [*Argentina*] [*Airport symbol*]

AOM ... Active Oxygen Method [*Food fat stability test*]

AOMPS ... Automatic Outgoing Message Processor System

AOO ... Altoona [*Pennsylvania*] [*Airport symbol*]

AOR ... Alor Setar [*Malaysia*] [*Airport symbol*]

AORS ... Army Operations Research Symposia

AOS ... Active Optical Sensor

AOS ... Amook [*Alaska*] [*Airport symbol*]

AOTD ... Active Optical Target Detector

AOTH ... Active Optical Target Housing

AP ... Aluminum Perchlorate

AP ... Application Program [*Data processing*]

AP ... Array Processor [*Data processing*]

AP ... Associative Processor [*Data processing*]

AP ... Attached Processor [*Data processing*]

APA ... Air Patrol Area

APAM ... Array Processor Access Method [*Data processing*]

APAPA ... Association for the Preservation of Anti-Psychiatric Artifacts

APAR ... Automatic Program Analysis Report [*Data processing*]

APC ... Argon Purge Cart [*Nuclear energy*]

APDM ... Amended Program Decision Memorandum [*Navy*]

APDMS ... Axial Power Distribution Monitoring Systems [*Nuclear energy*]

APDS ... Advanced Personnel Data System

APE ... Annual Planning Estimate [*Navy*]

APF ... Authorized Program Facility [*Data processing*]

APF ... Naples [*Florida*] [*Airport symbol*]

API ... Application Program Interface [*Data processing*]

APIC ... Association for Practitioners in Infection Control

APICORP .. Arab Petroleum Investments Corporation [*Owned by the member countries of OPEC*]

APK ... Apataki [*French Polynesia*] [*Airport symbol*]

APL ... Associative Programing Language [*Data processing*]

APL ... Authorized Possession Limits [*Nuclear energy*]

APL ... Nampula [*Mozambique*] [*Airport symbol*]

APLSTATPACK ... Advanced Programing Language Statistical Package

APM ... American Prison Ministry [*An organization*]

APM ... [*A*] Permanent Malingerer [*Facetious translation of Assistant Provost Marshal initialism*]

APN ... Aircraft Procurement, Navy

APN ... Alpena [*Michigan*] [*Airport symbol*]

APO ... Apartado [*Colombia*] [*Airport symbol*]

APOCR ... Apocrypha

APP ... Acid Precipitated Protein [*Food analysis*]

APPLE-MD ... Age; Prior Service; Physical, Legal, Educational, and Marital Status; and Dependents [*Army recruiting questionnaire*]

APR ... Accredited in Public Relations

APR ... Acoustic Paramagnetic Resonance [*Physics*]

APR ... Advance Production Release

APR ... Ammunition Performance Report [*Military*]

APR ... Automatic Passbook Reader

APR ... Automatic Pressure Relief [*Nuclear energy*]

APRF ... American Parapsychological Research Foundation

APRM ... Average Power Range Monitor [*Nuclear energy*]

APRRE ... Association of Professors and Researchers in Religious Education

APS ... Altitude Proximity Sensor

APS ... American Purchasing Society

APS ... Appearance Potential Spectroscopy [*Physics*]

APS ... Association of Productivity Specialists

APS ... Auxiliary Program Storage [*Data processing*]

APSP ... Array Processor Subroutine Package [*Data processing*]

APSR ... Axial Power Shaping Rods [*Nuclear energy*]

APU ... Arithmetic Processing Unit [*Data processing*]

APV ... Apple Valley [*California*] [*Airport symbol*]

APVE ... Association of Professional Vocal Ensembles

APW ... Apia [*Western Samoa*] [*Airport symbol*]

APZ ... Air Patrol Zone

APZ ... Zapala [*Argentina*] [*Airport symbol*]

AQA ... Araraquara [*Brazil*] [*Airport symbol*]

AQD ... Additional Qualification Designator

AQI ... Qaisumah [*Saudi Arabia*] [*Airport symbol*]

AQJ ... Aqaba [*Jordan*] [*Airport symbol*]

AQP ... Arequipa [*Peru*] [*Airport symbol*]

AQQ ... Annual Qualifications Questionnaire [*Navy*]

AQS ... Saqani [*Fiji*] [*Airport symbol*]

AR ... Anna Regina [*Queen Anne*]

AR ... Automatic Resupply

A²R² ... Argonne Advanced Research Reactor

ARA ... Amsterdam, Rotterdam, Antwerp

ARA ... Arabic

ara-FC ... Arabinofuranosylfluorocytosine [*Antitumor compound*] [*Also, FCA*]

ARBA ... American Red Brangus Association

ARBOR ... Argonne Boiling Water Reactor

ARBRL ... Army Armament Research Ballistic Research Laboratory

ARC ... Afghanistan Relief Committee

ARC ... Alcohol Rehabilitation Center

ARC ... American Recreation Coalition

ARC ... Anthropology Resource Center

ARC ... Arctic Village [*Alaska*] [*Airport symbol*]

ARC ... Association for Research in Cosmecology

ARC ... Association for Retarded Citizens [*Formerly, NARC*]

ARC ... Audio Response Control

ARCSL ... Army Armament Research and Development Command Chemical Systems Laboratory

ARE ... Advanced Real-Time Executive

ARE ... Automated Responsive Environment

ARETS ... Armor Remoted Target System

ARFA ... Antirecession Fiscal Assistance

New Acronyms, Initialisms, & Abbreviations

ARG........... Argumento [*By an argument drawn from such a law*] [*Latin*]
ARGADS ... Army Gun Air Defense Systems
ARI .... Amaryllis Research Institute
ARI .... Arica [*Chile*] [*Airport symbol*]
ARI .... Arizona
ARM .... Adjustable Rate Mortgage
ARM .... Area Radiation Monitor
ARM .... Armidale [*Australia*] [*Airport symbol*]
ARN........... Stockholm [*Sweden*] Arlanda Airport [*Airport symbol*]
ARO........... Advanced Research Objective
ARO........... Aerial Refueling Operator
ARO........... Arboletas [*Colombia*] [*Airport symbol*]
AROW .... Apprenticeship, Referral, and Outreach for Women [*An organization*]
ARP .... Aragip [*Papua New Guinea*] [*Airport symbol*]
ARPA .... Archeological Resources Protection Act [*1979*]
ARPAD...... Army Armament Research and Development Command Product Assurance Directorate
ARPD .... Advanced Research Program Directive
ARPI .... Absolute Rod Position Indication [*Nuclear energy*]
ARQ........... Automatic Error Correction [*Aviation*]
ARR........... Alto Rio Senguerr [*Argentina*] [*Airport symbol*]
ARRA .... Asphalt Recycling and Reclaiming Association
ARS........... Airborne Relay Stations
ARS........... Aragarcas [*Brazil*] [*Airport symbol*]
ARSS .... Fellow of the Royal Society of Antiquaries [*British*]
ART .... Acoustic Reflex Test [*Audiology*]
ART .... Watertown [*New York*] [*Airport symbol*]
ARTIL....... Artillery
ARTIS....... Airborne Real-Time Instrumentation System
ARTSD ...... Army Armament Research and Development Command Technical Support Directorate
ARU........... Aracatuba [*Brazil*] [*Airport symbol*]
ARW.......... Arad [*Romania*] [*Airport symbol*]
ARX........... Asbury Park/Monmouth County [*New Jersey*] [*Airport symbol*]
ARY........... Ararat [*Australia*] [*Airport symbol*]
ARZ........... N'Zeto [*Angola*] [*Airport symbol*]
AS .... Alcuin Society
AS .... Assistant Secretary
AS .... Wait [*Morse telephony*]
ASA........... American Sportscasters Association
ASAE .... American Society for Aerospace Education
ASAIC....... Assistant Special Agent in Charge
ASAP .... Applied Systems and Personnel
ASB........... Army Science Board [*Formerly, ASAP*]
ASB........... Ashkhabad [*USSR*] [*Airport symbol*]
ASC........... Ally Sloper's Cavalry [*Facetious translation of Army Service Corps initialism, Ally Sloper being a comic-paper buffoon*] [*British*] [*World War I*]
ASC........... Ascension [*Bolivia*] [*Airport symbol*]
ASC........... Associative Structure Computer
ASC........... Asynchronous Communication Procedure
ASCC........ American Social Communications Conference
ASD........... Andros Town [*Bahamas*] [*Airport symbol*]
ASDA .... Accelerate/Stop Distance Available [*Aviation*]
ASE........... Armed Services Edition [*Publishing*] [*World War II*]
ASE........... Aspen [*Colorado*] [*Airport symbol*]
ASF .... Assist Ship's Force Funds [*Navy*]
ASGA .... American Sugarbeet Growers Association
ASHI .... American Society of Home Inspectors
ASHRM ..... American Society for Hospital Risk Management
ASI .... Agri-Silviculture Institute
ASI .... Aviation Safety Institute
ASID......... Address Space Identifier
ASIM .... Aircraft Stores Interface Manual
ASIP .... Avionic System Integration Plan
ASIR.......... Aeronautical Shipboard Installation Representative
ASIS .... Amphibious Support Information System
ASJ .... Amami O Shima [*Japan*] [*Airport symbol*]
ASK........... Yamoussoukro [*Ivory Coast*] [*Airport symbol*]
ASLAB ...... Atomic Safety and Licensing Appeal Board
ASLT......... Aerial Stores Lift Truck
ASM .... Antiship Missile
ASM .... Asmara [*Ethiopia*] [*Airport symbol*]
ASMC .... American Society of Music Copyists
ASO .... Atlantic Southeast Airlines, Inc. [*Hapeville, GA*] [*FAA designator*]

ASOP .... Automatic Scheduling and Operating Program
ASP .... ALCOA Smelting Process
ASP .... Alice Springs [*Australia*] [*Airport symbol*]
ASP .... Associative Structures Package
ASP........... [*A*] System for Programers
ASPC .... Association of Strategic Planning Consultants
ASPM........ Air Scatterable Antipersonnel Mine
ASQ .... Austin [*Nevada*] [*Airport symbol*]
ASR........... Accumulators Shift Right [*Data processing*]
ASR........... Kayseri [*Turkey*] [*Airport symbol*]
ASRAP...... Acoustic Sensor Range Prediction
ASRO .... Amateur Scientist Research Organization
ASS........... Association
ASSET ...... Automated System for Sequential Extraction and Tabulation
ASSFJ....... Aleksandr Solzhenitsyn Society for Freedom and Justice
ASSIST ..... Army System for Standardized Intelligence Support Terminals
ASSIST ..... [*A*] Simple Systematic Integration of Statistical Techniques
ASSIU .... Avionics Subsystem Interface Unit
ASST........ Antiship Surveillance and Targeting [*Navy*]
AST .... Astoria [*Oregon*] [*Airport symbol*]
ASTA .... American Sail Training Association
ASTD .... Antiship Torpedo Defense
ASTE........ Armament System Test Environment
ASTED ...... Association pour l'Avancement des Sciences et des Techniques de la Documentation [*Formerly, ACBLF. Acronym alone now used as organization's name*]
ASU........... Administrative Support Unit
ASU........... Approval for Service Use [*Military*]
ASU........... Asuncion [*Paraguay*] [*Airport symbol*]
ASU........... Automotive Study Unit
ASVIP .... American Standard Vocabulary for Information Processing
ASW.......... Aswan [*Egypt*] [*Airport symbol*]
ASWC .... Antisubmarine Warfare Coordinator [*Navy*]
ASX........... Ashland [*Wisconsin*] [*Airport symbol*]
AT .... Acceptance Tag
AT .... Arch-Treasurer
ATA........... Anta [*Peru*] [*Airport symbol*]
ATAC .... Airborne Tactical Air Coordinator [*Navy*]
ATACCO... Aviation Tactical Coordinator [*Navy*]
ATAWDS.... Advanced Terminal Aerial Weapon Delivery Simulation
ATAWS ..... Autonomous Tactical All-Weather Strike
ATB........... Atbara [*Sudan*] [*Airport symbol*]
ATC........... Artificial Top Component [*Virology*]
ATC........... Australian Trade Commission
ATCA .... American Transit Collectors' Association
ATCFAS..... Air Traffic Control Flight Advisory Service
ATCM........ Advanced Technology Cruise Missile
ATCS .... Air Traffic Communications Service
ATD........... Absolutely to Die [*Slang*]
ATD........... Armor Training Devices
ATEC .... Aviation Technician Education Council
ATESS ...... Automated Tactical Environmental System
ATF .... Automatic Tracking Feature
ATH .... Athens [*Greece*] [*Airport symbol*]
ATI .... Artigas [*Uruguay*] [*Airport symbol*]
ATLA........ Antiquarian Trade List Annual [*A publication*]
ATLS .... Advanced Trauma Life Support System
ATM........... Altamira [*Brazil*] [*Airport symbol*]
ATMR........ Advanced-Technology Medium-Range Transport
ATMS........ Advanced Text Management System [*Data processing*]
ATN........... Namatanai [*Papua New Guinea*] [*Airport symbol*]
ATO........... Army Tank Office
A & TP....... Assembly and Test Pit [*Nuclear energy*]
ATP........... Association of Tequila Producers
ATP........... Automated Test Plan
ATPG .... Automatic Test Program Generation
ATQ........... Amritsar [*India*] [*Airport symbol*]
ATR........... Atar [*Mauritania*] [*Airport symbol*]
ATRIS........ Air Transportation Research Information Service
ATS........... Air-to-Surface [*Missiles*]
ATSB........ Advanced Tactical Support Base [*Navy*]
ATSB........ Airborne Test Safety Board
ATSS........ Automatic Test Support Systems
ATT .... Atmautluak [*Alaska*] [*Airport symbol*]
ATTLA ...... Air Transportability Test Loading Agency

ATU .... American Technological University
ATW .... Appleton [*Wisconsin*] [*Airport symbol*]
ATWDDS ... Automated Terminal Weather Dissemination Display System
ATWS .... Anticipated Transients without Scram [*Physics*]
ATY .... Watertown [*South Dakota*] [*Airport symbol*]
AUC .... Arauca [*Colombia*] [*Airport symbol*]
AUD .... Augustus Downs [*Australia*] [*Airport symbol*]
AUDELCO ... Audience Development Committee [*Theatre*]
AUG .... Augusta [*Maine*] [*Airport symbol*]
AUH .... Abu Dhabi [*United Arab Emirates*] [*Airport symbol*]
AUI .... Aua [*Papua New Guinea*] [*Airport symbol*]
AUJ .... Ambunti [*Papua New Guinea*] [*Airport symbol*]
AUK .... Alakanuk [*Alaska*] [*Airport symbol*]
AUO .... Auburn/Opelika [*Alabama*] [*Airport symbol*]
AUP .... Aguan [*Papua New Guinea*] [*Airport symbol*]
AUQ .... Atuona [*Marquesas Islands*] [*Airport symbol*]
AUR .... Aurillac [*France*] [*Airport symbol*]
AUR .... Aurum [*Gold*] [*Latin*]
AUS .... Austin [*Texas*] [*Airport symbol*]
AUTDEX .... Author Index
AUU .... Aurukun Mission [*Australia*] [*Airport symbol*]
AUW .... Wausau [*Wisconsin*] [*Airport symbol*]
AUX .... Araguaina [*Brazil*] [*Airport symbol*]
AUY .... Aneityum [*Vanuata*] [*Airport symbol*]
AVANA ...... Altitude Reservation Void for Aircraft Not Airborne by______ [*Aviation*]
AVC .... All Very Cushy [*Facetious translation of Army Veterinary Corps initialism*] [*British*] [*World War I*]
AVFPNO .... Pilot Failed to Activate VFR/DVFR Flight Plan [*Aviation*]
AVISURS .. Aerospace Vehicle Inventory, Status, and Utilization Reporting System
AVL .... Asheville [*North Carolina*] [*Airport symbol*]
AVLIS .... Atomic Vapor LASER Isotope Separation
AVMS .... Annulus Vacuum Maintenance System [*Nuclear energy*]
AVNL .... Automatic Video Noise Leveling
AVOCON ... Automated Vocabulary Control [*Subsystem of PLIS*] [*Data processing*]

AVT .... All Volatile Treatment [*Nuclear energy*]
AVU .... Avuavu [*Solomon Islands*] [*Airport symbol*]
AVX .... Catalina Island [*California*] [*Airport symbol*]
AWA .... Away without Authorization
AWAC ...... Auto Workers Action Caucus
AWC .... Amphibians and Watercraft
AWC .... Association for Women in Computing
AWCAS .... Adverse Weather Close Air Support [*Military*]
AWDS ...... Automated Weather Distribution System
AWI .... Air Wisconsin [*Appleton, WI*] [*FAA designator*]
AWN .... Alton Downs [*Australia*] [*Airport symbol*]
AWPA .... American Word Processing Association
AWR .... Advanced Weather RADAR
AWR .... Automated Work Request
AWSC ...... Air Warfare Simulation Complex
AWSI .... Adaptive Wafer Scale Integration
AWU .... Association for the World University
AWW .... Above Water Warfare [*Navy*]
AWZ .... Ahwaz [*Iran*] [*Airport symbol*]
AXA .... Anguilla [*West Indies*] [*Airport symbol*]
AXAF .... Advanced X-Ray Astrophysics Facility
AXC .... Aramac [*Australia*] [*Airport symbol*]
AXD .... Alexandroupolis [*Greece*] [*Airport symbol*]
AXM .... Armenia [*Colombia*] [*Airport symbol*]
AXN .... Alexandria [*Minnesota*] [*Airport symbol*]
AXT .... Akita [*Japan*] [*Airport symbol*]
AXU .... Axum [*Ethiopia*] [*Airport symbol*]
AYG .... Yuguara [*Colombia*] [*Airport symbol*]
AYI .... Yari [*Colombia*] [*Airport symbol*]
AYP .... Ayacucho [*Peru*] [*Airport symbol*]
AYQ .... Ayers Rock [*Australia*] [*Airport symbol*]
AYT .... Antalya [*Turkey*] [*Airport symbol*]
AYU .... Aiyura [*Papua New Guinea*] [*Airport symbol*]
AZB .... Amazon Bay [*Papua New Guinea*] [*Airport symbol*]
AZD .... Yazd [*Iran*] [*Airport symbol*]
AZO .... Kalamazoo [*Michigan*] [*Airport symbol*]

B

B .... Baud [*Unit of data transmission speed*]
B .... Binary
B .... Blank
B² .... Brooks Brothers [*Clothing store*]
BAA .... Bialla [*Papua New Guinea*] [*Airport symbol*]
BAA .... BO-S-AIRE Airlines, Inc. [*Anderson, SC*] [*FAA designator*]
BACS .... Bay Area Cryonics Society
BADCT ...... Best Available Demonstrated Control Technology [*Environmental Protection Agency*]
BADSA ...... Backup Air Data Sensor Assembly
BAF .... Bioaccumulation Factor [*Nuclear energy*]
BAG .... Baguio [*Philippines*] [*Airport symbol*]
BAH .... Bahrain Islands [*Airport symbol*]
BAJ .... Bali [*Papua New Guinea*] [*Airport symbol*]
BAK .... Baku [*USSR*] [*Airport symbol*]
BALTO ..... Baltimore [*Maryland*]
BAM .... Basic Access Method [*Data processing*]
BAM .... Battle Mountain [*Nevada*] [*Airport symbol*]
BAMM ...... Balloon Altitude Mosaic Measurements
BAP .... Baibara [*Papua New Guinea*] [*Airport symbol*]
BAP .... Branch Arm Piping [*Nuclear energy*]
BAPE .... Branch Arm Piping Enclosure [*Nuclear energy*]
BAPG .... Business Applications Programming Guide
BAPN .... Beta-Aminopropionitrile [*Organic chemistry*]
BAPS .... Branch Arm Piping Shielding [*Nuclear energy*]
BAQ .... Barranquilla [*Colombia*] [*Airport symbol*]
BAR .... Base Address Register [*Data processing*]
BAS .... Balalae [*Solomon Islands*] [*Airport symbol*]
BASIC .... Basic Automatic Stored Instruction Computer
BASIS ...... Bank Automated Service Information System
BASIS ...... Burroughs Advanced Statistical Inquiry System [*Data processing*]
BAT .... Biological Abstracts on Tape
BATS .... Basic Additional Teleprocessing Support
BAU .... Bauru [*Brazil*] [*Airport symbol*]
BAV .... Baotou [*China*] [*Airport symbol*]
BAWA ...... Byelorussian-American Women Association
BAY .... Baia Mare [*Romania*] [*Airport symbol*]
BBA .... Balmaceda [*Chile*] [*Airport symbol*]
BBC .... Beam-to-Beam Correlation
BBG .... Butaritari [*Kiribati*] [*Airport symbol*]
BBI .... Bhubaneswar [*India*] [*Airport symbol*]
BBN .... Bario [*Malaysia*] [*Airport symbol*]
BBQ .... Barbuda [*West Indies*] [*Airport symbol*]
BBR .... Basse-Terre [*Guadeloupe*] [*Airport symbol*]
BBU .... Bucharest [*Romania*] Banesa Airport [*Airport symbol*]
BBX .... Blue Bell [*Pennsylvania*] [*Airport symbol*]
BBZ .... Zambezi [*Zambia*] [*Airport symbol*]
BCA .... Baracoa [*Cuba*] [*Airport symbol*]
BCA .... Broadcast Control Authority
BCC .... Bass Air Corp. [*Pine Bluff, AR*] [*FAA designator*]
BCC .... Budget Classification Code
BCD .... Bacolod [*Philippines*] [*Airport symbol*]
BCE .... Bovine Capillary Endothelial [*Cytology*]
BCG .... Bemichi [*Guyana*] [*Airport symbol*]
BCI .... Barcaldine [*Australia*] [*Airport symbol*]
BCK .... Bolworra [*Australia*] [*Airport symbol*]
BCL .... Burroughs Common Language [*Data processing*]

BCM .... Bacau [*Romania*] [*Airport symbol*]
BCM .... Basic Control Monitor
BCN .... Barcelona [*Spain*] [*Airport symbol*]
BCN .... Broadband Communication Network
BCS .... Biomedical Computing Society [*Later, SIGBIO*]
BCS .... Blood Cell Separator
BCSI .... Breast Cancer Screening Indicator
BCU .... Battery/Coolant Unit
BDA .... Bermuda [*Airport symbol*]
BDAM ...... Basic Direct Access Method [*Data processing*]
BDB .... Bundaberg [*Australia*] [*Airport symbol*]
BDH .... Bandar Lengeh [*Iran*] [*Airport symbol*]
BDI .... Bird Island [*Seychelles Islands*] [*Airport symbol*]
BDJ .... Banjarmasin [*Indonesia*] [*Airport symbol*]
BDK .... Bondoukou [*Ivory Coast*] [*Airport symbol*]
BDLC .... Burroughs Data Link Control [*Data processing*]
BDN .... Badana [*Saudi Arabia*] [*Airport symbol*]
BDN .... Bell Data Network [*Proposed*]
BDO .... Bandung [*Indonesia*] [*Airport symbol*]
BDP .... Bhadrapur [*Nepal*] [*Airport symbol*]
BDQ .... Vadodara [*India*] [*Airport symbol*]
BDR .... Bridgeport [*Connecticut*] [*Airport symbol*]
BDS .... Ballistics Dispensing System
BDS .... Brindisi [*Italy*] [*Airport symbol*]
BDT .... Bado Lite [*Zaire*] [*Airport symbol*]
BDU .... Bardufoss [*Norway*] [*Airport symbol*]
BE .... Best Estimate Model
BE .... Biplane Experimental [*Aircraft*] [*World War I*]
BEA .... Bereina [*Papua New Guinea*] [*Airport symbol*]
BEAM .... Burroughs Electronic Accounting Machine
BEB .... Benbecula [*Hebrides Islands*] [*Airport symbol*]
BEC .... Beginning of Equilibrium Cycle [*Nuclear energy*]
BECBSG ... Big Eight Council on Black Student Government
BEG .... Belgrade [*Yugoslavia*] [*Airport symbol*]
BEH .... Benton Harbor [*Michigan*] [*Airport symbol*]
BEJ .... Berau [*Indonesia*] [*Airport symbol*]
BEL .... Belem [*Brazil*] [*Airport symbol*]
BELA .... Black Entertainment Lawyers Association
BEMS .... Bioelectromagnetics Society
BEN .... Benghazi [*Libya*] [*Airport symbol*]
BEO .... Newcastle [*Australia*] Belmont Airport [*Airport symbol*]
BER .... Berlin [*West Germany*] [*Airport symbol*]
BERT .... BIT [*Binary Digit*] Error-Rate-Test [*Set*] [*Data processing*]
BES .... Brest [*France*] [*Airport symbol*]
BESM .... Bovine Embryo Skeletal Muscle
BET .... Bethel [*Alaska*] [*Airport symbol*]
BEU .... Bedourie [*Australia*] [*Airport symbol*]
BEV .... Beersheba [*Israel*] [*Airport symbol*]
BEW .... Beira [*Mozambique*] [*Airport symbol*]
BEY .... Beirut [*Lebanon*] [*Airport symbol*]
BEZ .... Beru [*Kiribati*] [*Airport symbol*]
BF .... Blast Furnace [*Ironmaking*]
BF .... Bristol Fighter [*Aircraft*] [*World War I*]
BFA .... Benzylfurylmethyl Alcohol [*Organic chemistry*]
BFCA .... Benzylfurancarboxylic Acid [*Organic chemistry*]
BFD .... Battery Firing Device
BFD .... Bradford [*Pennsylvania*] [*Airport symbol*]
BFF .... Scottsbluff [*Nebraska*] [*Airport symbol*]

BFJ............ Ba [*Fiji*] [*Airport symbol*]
BFL .... Bakersfield [*California*] [*Airport symbol*]
BFL .... Baptists for Life
BFN .... Bloemfontein [*South Africa*] [*Airport symbol*]
BFO .... Buffalo Range [*Zimbabwe*] [*Airport symbol*]
BFS .... Belfast [*Northern Ireland*] [*Airport symbol*]
BFT .... Beaufort [*South Carolina*] [*Airport symbol*]
BG .... British Gauge [*Metal industry*]
BGA .... Bucaramanga [*Colombia*] [*Airport symbol*]
BGB........... Booue [*Gabon*] [*Airport symbol*]
BGC .... Boat Group Commander [*Navy*]
BGC .... Braganca [*Portugal*] [*Airport symbol*]
BGF........... Bangui [*Central African Republic*] [*Airport symbol*]
BGI .... Barbados [*Airport symbol*]
BGJ .... Borgarfjordur [*Iceland*] [*Airport symbol*]
BGL........... Baglung [*Nepal*] [*Airport symbol*]
BGM.......... Binghamton [*New York*] [*Airport symbol*]
BGO .... Bergen [*Norway*] [*Airport symbol*]
BGR.......... Bangor [*Maine*] [*Airport symbol*]
BGW.......... Baghdad [*Iraq*] [*Airport symbol*]
BGX .... Bage [*Brazil*] [*Airport symbol*]
BH .... Binary to Hexadecimal
BHAS .... Burroughs Hospital Administrative System [*Data processing*]
BHB........... Bar Harbor [*Maine*] [*Airport symbol*]
BHCA .... Busy Hour Call Attempts [*Telephone technology*]
BHD.......... Beta-Hydroxysteroid Dehydrogenase [*An enzyme*]
BHE .... Blenheim [*New Zealand*] [*Airport symbol*]
BHH........... Bisha [*Saudi Arabia*] [*Airport symbol*]
BHI .... Bahia Blanca [*Argentina*] [*Airport symbol*]
BHI .... Bullet Hit Indicator
BHIBA .... Brain-Heart Infusion Blood Agar [*Microbiology*]
BHJ .... Bhuj [*India*] [*Airport symbol*]
BHK........... Bukhara [*USSR*] [*Airport symbol*]
BHNRC...... Beltsville Human Nutrition Research Center [*Department of Agriculture*]
BHO........... Bhopal [*India*] [*Airport symbol*]
BHP .... Bhojpur [*Nepal*] [*Airport symbol*]
BHQ .... Broken Hill [*Australia*] [*Airport symbol*]
BHR.......... Bharatpur [*Nepal*] [*Airport symbol*]
BHR.......... Block Handler Routine [*Data processing*]
BHS........... Bathurst [*Australia*] [*Airport symbol*]
BHU.......... Bhavnagar [*India*] [*Airport symbol*]
BHX .... Birmingham [*England*] [*Airport symbol*]
BHZ .... Belo Horizonte [*Brazil*] [*Airport symbol*]
BIA .... Bastia [*Corsica*] [*Airport symbol*]
BICS.......... Burroughs Inventory Control System [*Data processing*]
BID .... Block Island [*Rhode Island*] [*Airport symbol*]
BIF............ Basic in Flow
BIG .... Bicycle-Motocross Industrial Guild
BIG .... Blacks in Government
BIH .... Bishop [*California*] [*Airport symbol*]
BIHC........ Boat Inlet/High-Capacity [*Analytical combustion system*]
BIK .... Biak [*Indonesia*] [*Airport symbol*]
BIL............ Billings [*Montana*] [*Airport symbol*]
BIL............ Block Input Length [*Data processing*]
BIM........... Bimini [*Bahamas*] [*Airport symbol*]
BIMS .... Blade Inspection Method System
BIN .... Bamian [*Afghanistan*] [*Airport symbol*]
BINL .... Basic Inventory of Natural Language [*Test*]
BIO .... Bilbao [*Spain*] [*Airport symbol*]
BIP .... Bulimba [*Australia*] [*Airport symbol*]
BIPASS ..... Burroughs Inventory Planning Analysis and Simulation System [*Data processing*]
BIPS .... Banking Information Processing System
BIQ .... Biarritz [*France*] [*Airport symbol*]
BIR .... Biratnagar [*Nepal*] [*Airport symbol*]
BIS .... Bismarck [*North Dakota*] [*Airport symbol*]
BISC.......... Biscayan
BISS........... Base Intrusion Surveillance System
BIU .... Basic Information Unit
BIU .... Bildudalur [*Iceland*] [*Airport symbol*]
BJD .... Bakkafjordur [*Iceland*] [*Airport symbol*]
BJF............ Batsfjord [*Norway*] [*Airport symbol*]
BJH .... Bajhang [*Nepal*] [*Airport symbol*]
BJI............. Bemidji [*Minnesota*] [*Airport symbol*]
BJL........... Banjul [*Gambia*] [*Airport symbol*]
BJM........... Bujumbura [*Burundi*] [*Airport symbol*]
BJR .... Bahar Dar [*Ethiopia*] [*Airport symbol*]

BJZ............ Badajoz [*Spain*] [*Airport symbol*]
BK .... Bark
BK .... Break Signal [*Used to interrupt a transmission in progress*] [*Communications*]
BKC .... Buckland [*Alaska*] [*Airport symbol*]
BKI .... Kota Kinabalu [*Malaysia*] [*Airport symbol*]
BKK........... Bangkok [*Thailand*] [*Airport symbol*]
BKL .... Cleveland [*Ohio*] Burke Lakefront [*Airport symbol*]
BKM........... Bakalalan [*Malaysia*] [*Airport symbol*]
BKO .... Bamako [*Mali*] [*Airport symbol*]
BKQ .... Blackall [*Australia*] [*Airport symbol*]
BKS .... Bengkulu [*Indonesia*] [*Airport symbol*]
BKS .... Broadcast Keying Station
BKSP .... Backspace
BKU.......... Betioky [*Madagascar*] [*Airport symbol*]
BKW.......... Beckley [*West Virginia*] [*Airport symbol*]
BKX........... Brookings [*South Dakota*] [*Airport symbol*]
BKY........... Bukavu [*Zaire*] [*Airport symbol*]
BKZ........... Bukoba [*Tanzania*] [*Airport symbol*]
BL .... BLJ London [*Great Britain*] [*ICAO designator*]
BLA .... Barcelona [*Venezuela*] [*Airport symbol*]
BLA .... Brown Lung Association
BLCK .... Block
BLDUP ..... Buildup [*Meteorology*]
BLE .... Binary Logic Element [*Data processing*]
BLE .... Borlange [*Sweden*] [*Airport symbol*]
BLF .... Bluefield [*West Virginia*] [*Airport symbol*]
BLG .... Belaga [*Malaysia*] [*Airport symbol*]
BLH .... Blythe [*California*] [*Airport symbol*]
BLI .... Bellingham [*Washington*] [*Airport symbol*]
BLIS .... Baffle/Liner Interface Seal [*Nuclear energy*]
BLK .... Blackpool [*England*] [*Airport symbol*]
BLL .... Billund [*Denmark*] [*Airport symbol*]
BLM........... Basic Language Machine [*Data processing*]
BLM.......... Boundary Layer Model
BLO .... Blonduos [*Iceland*] [*Airport symbol*]
BLQ .... Bologna [*Italy*] [*Airport symbol*]
BLR .... Bangalore [*India*] [*Airport symbol*]
BLR .... Below Layer Range
BLR .... Blower
BLT .... Baltic Aviation, Inc. [*Denver, CO*] [*FAA designator*]
BLT .... Blackwater [*Australia*] [*Airport symbol*]
BLTC .... Bottom-Loading Transfer Cask [*Nuclear energy*]
BLU .... Basic Link Unit [*Data processing*]
BLWC....... Bread Loaf Writers Conference
BLZ .... Blantyre [*Malawi*] [*Airport symbol*]
BM............. Black Man
BM............. Black Muslim
BM............. Bubble Memory [*Data processing*]
BMA .... Stockholm [*Sweden*] Bromma Airport [*Airport symbol*]
BMB .... Bumba [*Zaire*] [*Airport symbol*]
BMC........... Bullnose Morris Club
BMD .... Belo [*Madagascar*] [*Airport symbol*]
BMDS........ Base Manager Data System
BMDS........ Base Manpower Data System
BME .... Broome [*Australia*] [*Airport symbol*]
BMEDS ..... Base Management Engineering Data System
BMG.......... Bloomington [*Indiana*] [*Airport symbol*]
BMI............ Bloomington [*Illinois*] [*Airport symbol*]
BMK.......... Borkum [*West Germany*] [*Airport symbol*]
BML........... Bulk Material Length
BMO .... Bhamo [*Burma*] [*Airport symbol*]
BMP .... Best Management Practice [*Environmental Protection Agency*]
BMP .... Brampton Island [*Australia*] [*Airport symbol*]
BMQ .... Bamburi [*Kenya*] [*Airport symbol*]
BMR .... Bearingless Main Rotor
BMS .... Business Management System
BMU .... Bima [*Indonesia*] [*Airport symbol*]
BMY .... Belep [*New Caledonia*] [*Airport symbol*]
BMZ .... Bamu [*Papua New Guinea*] [*Airport symbol*]
BNAC........ British-North American Committee
BNB........... Boende [*Zaire*] [*Airport symbol*]
BND.......... Bandar Abbas [*Iran*] [*Airport symbol*]
BNE .... Brisbane [*Australia*] [*Airport symbol*]
BNF........... Backus Normal Form [*Data processing*]
BNI........... Benin City [*Nigeria*] [*Airport symbol*]
BNKM .... Marine Bank [*Board on Geographic Names*]
BNM .... Bodinumu [*Papua New Guinea*] [*Airport symbol*]

BNN.......... Bronnoysund [*Norway*] [*Airport symbol*]
BNS.......... Barinas [*Venezuela*] [*Airport symbol*]
BNT.......... Bundi [*Papua New Guinea*] [*Airport symbol*]
BNY.......... Bellona Island [*Solomon Islands*] [*Airport symbol*]
BNZ.......... Banz [*Papua New Guinea*] [*Airport symbol*]
BO.............. Binary to Octal
BOB.......... Bora-Bora [*French Polynesia*] [*Airport symbol*]
BOB.......... Bureau of Biologics [*FDA*] [*Also, BB*]
BOC.......... Beginning of Cycle
BOC.......... Bottom of Conduit
BOC.......... Bureau of Customs [*Later, US Customs Service*] [*Department of the Treasury*]
BOD.......... Bordeaux [*France*] [*Airport symbol*]
BOG.......... Bogota [*Colombia*] [*Airport symbol*]
BOH.......... Bournemouth [*England*] [*Airport symbol*]
BOI.......... Boise [*Idaho*] [*Airport symbol*]
BOJ.......... Bourgas [*Bulgaria*] [*Airport symbol*]
BOLT........ Beam of Light Transmitter
BOM.......... Bombay [*India*] [*Airport symbol*]
BOMB....... British Overseas Media Bureau
BON.......... Bonaire [*Netherland Antilles*] [*Airport symbol*]
BON.......... Bonanza Airlines Co. [*Torrance, CA*] [*FAA designator*]
BONUS-CX ... Boiling Nuclear Superheat Critical Experiment
BOO.......... Bodo [*Norway*] [*Airport symbol*]
BOOST..... Broadened Opportunities for Officer Selection and Training [*Navy*]
BOP.......... Balance of Plant [*Nuclear energy*]
BOPS.......... Banking On-Line Package System
BOQ.......... Boku [*Papua New Guinea*] [*Airport symbol*]
BOR.......... Belfort [*France*] [*Airport symbol*]
BOS.......... Basic Oxygen Steel [*Metal industry*]
BOSS..... Business-Oriented Software System [*Data processing*]
BOST....... Boston [*Massachusetts*]
BOV.......... Boang [*Papua New Guinea*] [*Airport symbol*]
BOY.......... Bobo Dioulasso [*Upper Volta*] [*Airport symbol*]
BPC.......... Bonded Phase Chromatography
BPD.......... Basic Point Defense [*Military*]
BPD.......... Beach Party Division [*Navy*]
BPF.......... Blue Print Files
BPF.......... Buddhist Peace Fellowship
BPG.......... Beach Party Group [*Navy*]
BPG.......... Beach Party Guard [*Navy*]
BPH.......... Bislig [*Philippines*] [*Airport symbol*]
BPN.......... Balikpapan [*Indonesia*] [*Airport symbol*]
BPS.......... Basic Programing Support
BPS.......... Booklet Pane Society
BPS.......... Bytes per Second [*Data processing*]
BPS.......... Porto Seguro [*Brazil*] [*Airport symbol*]
BPT.......... Beach Party Team [*Navy*]
BPT.......... Beaumont/Port Arthur [*Texas*] [*Airport symbol*]
B + PV..... Boiler and Pressure Vessel [*Nuclear energy*]
BPY.......... Besalampy [*Madagascar*] [*Airport symbol*]
BQL.......... Basic Query Language [*Data processing*]
BQL.......... Boulia [*Australia*] [*Airport symbol*]
BQN.......... Aguadilla [*Puerto Rico*] [*Airport symbol*]
BQO.......... Bouna [*Ivory Coast*] [*Airport symbol*]
BQQ.......... Barra [*Brazil*] [*Airport symbol*]
BR.............. Banco Regis [*or Reginae*] [*The King's (or Queen's) Bench*]
BR.............. Bottom Reflection [*Navy*]
B & R........ Budget and Reporting
BRA.......... Barreiras [*Brazil*] [*Airport symbol*]
BRC.......... San Carlos De Bariloche [*Argentina*] [*Airport symbol*]
BRD.......... Brainerd [*Minnesota*] [*Airport symbol*]
BRE.......... Bremen [*West Germany*] [*Airport symbol*]
BRI.......... Bari [*Italy*] [*Airport symbol*]
BRIGAND ... Bistatic RADAR Intelligence Generation and Analysis System
BRL.......... Burlington [*Iowa*] [*Airport symbol*]
BRM.......... Barquisimeto [*Venezuela*] [*Airport symbol*]
BRN.......... Berne [*Switzerland*] [*Airport symbol*]
BRO.......... Brownsville [*Texas*] [*Airport symbol*]
BRP.......... Biaru [*Papua New Guinea*] [*Airport symbol*]
BRQ.......... Brno [*Czechoslovakia*] [*Airport symbol*]
BRR.......... Barra [*Hebrides Islands*] [*Airport symbol*]
BRR.......... Biological Research Resources
BRS.......... Boron Recycle System [*Nuclear energy*]
BRS.......... Bristol [*England*] [*Airport symbol*]
BRT.......... Bathurst Island [*Australia*] [*Airport symbol*]

BRT.......... Binary Run Tape [*Data processing*]
BRU.......... Brussels [*Belgium*] [*Airport symbol*]
BRUNCH ... Breakfast and Lunch [*Refers to a late morning or early afternoon meal*]
BRUNNEL ... Bridge-Tunnel [*Proposed English Channel link between Britain and France*]
BRV.......... Bremerhaven [*West Germany*] [*Airport symbol*]
BRW.......... Barrow [*Alaska*] [*Airport symbol*]
BS.............. Be Specific
BS.............. Bowel Sounds [*Medicine*]
BS.............. Burns and Schreiber Comedy Hour [*Television program*] [*Obsolete*]
BSA.......... Black Stuntmen's Association
BSA.......... Bosaso [*Somalia*] [*Airport symbol*]
BSB.......... Brasilia [*Brazil*] [*Airport symbol*]
BSC.......... Bahia Solano [*Colombia*] [*Airport symbol*]
BSCN....... BIT [*Binary Digit*] Scan [*Data processing*]
BSDC...... British Standard Data Code
BSE.......... Broadcasting Satellite Experimental
BSER........ Brainstem-Evoked Response [*Neurophysiology*]
BSF.......... Backspace File
BSJ.......... Bairnsdale [*Australia*] [*Airport symbol*]
BSL.......... Basel/Mulhouse [*Switzerland*] [*Airport symbol*]
BSM.......... Basic System Memory [*Data processing*]
BSN.......... Basin [*Board on Geographic Names*]
BSO.......... Basco [*Philippines*] [*Airport symbol*]
BSP.......... Burroughs Scientific Processor [*Data processing*]
BSS.......... Bram Stoker Society
BSU.......... Basankusu [*Zaire*] [*Airport symbol*]
BSUF........ British Schools and Universities Foundation
BSX.......... Bassein [*Burma*] [*Airport symbol*]
BT.............. Break Transmission
BT.............. Burnthrough
BT.............. Separative Sign [*Morse telephony*]
BTD.......... Binary to Decimal
BTDL........ Basic Transient Diode Logic [*Data processing*]
BTE.......... Better than Expected [*Politics*]
BTE.......... Bonthe [*Sierre Leone*] [*Airport symbol*]
BTI.......... Barter Island [*Alaska*] [*Airport symbol*]
BTJ.......... Banda Aceh [*Indonesia*] [*Airport symbol*]
BTK.......... Bratsk [*USSR*] [*Airport symbol*]
BTL.......... Battle Creek [*Michigan*] [*Airport symbol*]
BTL.......... Beginning Tape Label [*Data processing*]
BTM.......... Benzyltrimethylammonium Chloride [*Organic chemistry*] [*Also, TMBAC*]
BTM.......... Butte [*Montana*] [*Airport symbol*]
BTP.......... Branch Technical Position [*Nuclear energy*]
BTR.......... Baton Rouge [*Louisiana*] [*Airport symbol*]
BTS.......... Bratislava [*Czechoslovakia*] [*Airport symbol*]
BTSS........ Basic Time-Sharing System
BTT.......... Bettles [*Alaska*] [*Airport symbol*]
BTU.......... Bintulu [*Malaysia*] [*Airport symbol*]
BTV.......... Burlington [*Vermont*] [*Airport symbol*]
BTZ.......... Bursa [*Turkey*] [*Airport symbol*]
BUA.......... Buka Island [*Papua New Guinea*] [*Airport symbol*]
BUC.......... Burketown [*Australia*] [*Airport symbol*]
BUD.......... Budapest [*Hungary*] [*Airport symbol*]
BUE.......... Buenos Aires [*Argentina*] [*Airport symbol*]
BUG.......... Benguela [*Angola*] [*Airport symbol*]
BUH.......... Bucharest [*Romania*] [*Airport symbol*]
BUI.......... Bokoudini [*Indonesia*] [*Airport symbol*]
BUL.......... Bulolo [*Papua New Guinea*] [*Airport symbol*]
BUO.......... Burao [*Somalia*] [*Airport symbol*]
BUQ.......... Bulawayo [*Zimbabwe*] [*Airport symbol*]
BUR.......... Built-Up Roofing
BURDS...... Burroughs Distribution Scheduling System [*Data processing*]
BUS.......... Beilstein Unique Sequence [*Chemistry*]
BUSEN...... Beilstein Unique Sequence Number [*Chemistry*]
BUSH........ Bushel
BUW.......... Baubau [*Indonesia*] [*Airport symbol*]
BUX.......... Bunia [*Zaire*] [*Airport symbol*]
BUY.......... Bunbury [*Australia*] [*Airport symbol*]
BUZ.......... Bushehr [*Iran*] [*Airport symbol*]
BV.............. Carib Jet (Antigua) Ltd. [*Great Britain*] [*ICAO designator*]
BVB.......... Boa Vista [*Brazil*] [*Airport symbol*]
BVC.......... Boa Vista [*Cape Verde Islands*] [*Airport symbol*]
BVF.......... Bua [*Fiji*] [*Airport symbol*]
BVG.......... Berlevag [*Norway*] [*Airport symbol*]

BVI .... Birdsville [*Australia*] [*Airport symbol*]
BVM .... Belmonte [*Brazil*] [*Airport symbol*]
BVRM .... Beyond Visual Range Missile
BVZ .... Beverly Springs [*Australia*] [*Airport symbol*]
BWA .... Bhairawa [*Nepal*] [*Airport symbol*]
BWD .... Brownwood [*Texas*] [*Airport symbol*]
BWI .... Boating Writers International [*An organization*]
BWN .... Bandar Seri Begawan [*Brunei*] [*Airport symbol*]
BWP .... Bewani [*Papua New Guinea*] [*Airport symbol*]
BWST .... Borated Water Storage Tank [*Nuclear energy*]
BWSTx ..... Black Widow Spider Toxin
BWT .... Backward Wave Tube [*Physics*]
BWTS .... Base Wire and Telephone System [*Air Force*]
BXD .... Bade [*Indonesia*] [*Airport symbol*]
BXE .... Bakel [*Senegal*] [*Airport symbol*]
BXI .... Boundiali [*Ivory Coast*] [*Airport symbol*]

BXO .... Bissau [*Portuguese Guinea*] [*Airport symbol*]
BXS .... Borrego Springs [*California*] [*Airport symbol*]
BXU .... Butuan [*Philippines*] [*Airport symbol*]
BXV .... Breiddalsvik [*Iceland*] [*Airport symbol*]
BYC .... Yacuiba [*Bolivia*] [*Airport symbol*]
BYK .... Bouake [*Ivory Coast*] [*Airport symbol*]
BYM .... Bayamo [*Cuba*] [*Airport symbol*]
BYU .... Bayreuth [*West Germany*] [*Airport symbol*]
BYW .... Blakely Island [*Washington*] [*Airport symbol*]
BZE .... Belize City [*Belize*] [*Airport symbol*]
BZG .... Bydgoszcz [*Poland*] [*Airport symbol*]
BZN .... Bozeman [*Montana*] [*Airport symbol*]
BZP .... Bizant [*Australia*] [*Airport symbol*]
BZR .... Beziers [*France*] [*Airport symbol*]
BZV .... Brazzaville [*People's Republic of the Congo*] [*Airport symbol*]

C

C .... Character
C⁴ .... Command, Control, Communications, and Computer Systems
C-4 .... Computer-Controlled Catalytic Converter [*General Motors*]
CA.............. Census Agglomeration [*Canada*]
CA.............. Coast Alliance
CA.............. Commissioner of Accounts
CA.............. Commutator Assemblies [*SONAR*]
CA.............. Computers and Automation
CA.............. Construction Authorization
CA.............. Critical Assembly [*Nuclear energy*]
CAA .... Chinese for Affirmative Action
CAA .... Computer-Assisted Accounting
CAB........... Cabinda [*Angola*] [*Airport symbol*]
CAB........... Current Awareness Bulletin
CABL .... Consolidation above Battalion Level [*Army*]
CAC .... Cascavel [*Brazil*] [*Airport symbol*]
CAC .... Children's Advocacy Center
CAC .... Control and Analysis Centers [*ERADCOM*]
CACP .... Council for the Advancement of Consumer Policy
CACW .... Core Auxiliary Cooling Water [*Nuclear energy*]
CACWS..... Core Auxiliary Cooling Water System [*Nuclear energy*]
CAD .... Cartridge-Actuated Device [*Military*]
CAD .... Containment Atmosphere Dilution [*Nuclear energy*]
CADA .... Computer-Assisted Distribution and Assignment
CADENCE ... Computer-Aided Design and Numerical Control Effort [*General Motors*]
CADET ...... Can't Add, Doesn't Even Try [*Data processing*]
CAE........... Computer-Aided Education
CAE........... Computer-Assisted Estimating
CAE/MIS .. Computer-Assisted Estimating and Management Information Systems
CAEX .... Community Automatic Exchange [*Telephone*]
CAF........... Chemical Analysis Facility
CAFSU ...... Carrier and Field Service Unit
CAG .... Cagliari [*Italy*] [*Airport symbol*]
CAHE .... Core Auxiliary Heat Exchanger [*Nuclear energy*]
CAI............ Cairo [*Egypt*] [*Airport symbol*]
CAI............ Catalina Airlines, Incorporated [*Long Beach, CA*] [*FAA designator*]
CAI............ Civic Action Institute
CAI............ Consumer Alert, Incorporated
CAID .... Computer Aid
CAJ........... Canaima [*Venezuela*] [*Airport symbol*]
CAK .... Command Acknowledge
CAL........... Campbeltown [*Scotland*] [*Airport symbol*]
CAL........... Computer-Aided Learning
CALB .... Computer-Aided Line Balance
CALL........ Conservatives Against Liberal Legislation
CALM........ Custody Action for Lesbian Mothers [*An organization*]
CAM........... Camiri [*Bolivia*] [*Airport symbol*]
CAM........... Containment Atmospheric Monitoring [*Nuclear energy*]
CAM........... Continuous Air Monitor [*Nuclear energy*]
CAM......... Control Access Manager
CAMB .... Cambridge [*Municipal borough in England*]
CAMEL ..... Component and Material Evaluation Loop [*Nuclear energy*]

CAMIS ...... Computer-Assisted Makeup and Imaging Systems [*Data processing*]
CAMMIS ... Command Aerospace Maintenance Manpower Information System
CAMP........ Compiler for Automatic Machine Programing
CAMP........ Computer-Assisted Mathematics Program
CaMV .... Cauliflower Mosaic Virus [*Also, CLMV*]
CAN .... Guangzhou [*China*] [*Airport symbol*]
CAN Charlie Chan ... Coalition of Asians to Nix Charlie Chan
CANDE ..... Command and Edit Program [*Data processing*]
CANT .... Canticles [*Song of Solomon*] [*Old Testament book*]
CANTCO... Cannot Comply
CANTRAC ... Catalog of Navy Training Courses
CAOC........ Constant Axial Offset Control
CAOCI....... Commercially Available Organic Chemicals Index [*Data processing*] [*British*]
CAP........... Cap Haitien [*Haiti*] [*Airport symbol*]
CAP........... Capitulum [*Chapter*]
CAP........... Command Action Plan
CAP........... Communication Association of the Pacific
CAP........... Computer-Assisted Production
CAP........... Control Assembly Program
CAPCATS ... Capability Categories
CAPM........ Capital-Asset Pricing Model
CAPME ..... Committee of Americans for Peace in the Middle East
CAPS .... Cell Atmosphere Processing System [*Nuclear energy*]
CAPTIS ..... Computer-Assisted Prisoner Transportation Index Service [*National Sheriffs' Association*]
CAQ .... Caucasia [*Colombia*] [*Airport symbol*]
CAR........... Carat
CAR........... Computer-Assisted Research
CARA .... Classification and Rating Administration [*For movies*]
CARE .... Consolidated Assistance and Relocation Efforts
CARG .... Commander Amphibious Ready Group [*Navy*]
CARI......... Council of Air-Conditioning and Refrigeration Industry
CARP .... Cooperative Automotive Research Program [*Industry-government program*]
CARS .... Computerized Automotive Reporting Service
CAS........... Casablanca [*Morocco*] [*Airport symbol*]
CAS........... Connecticutensis Academiae Socius [*Fellow of the Connecticut Academy of Arts and Sciences*]
CASA .... Custom Automotive Sound Association
CASD .... Computer-Aided System Design
CASE .... Consolidated Aerospace Supplier Evaluation
CASI .... Chili Appreciation Society International
CAST .... Coordinated ASW [*Antisubmarine Warfare*] Services and Training [*Navy*]
CAT........... Communications Assist Team
CAT........... Compile and Test
CAT........... Computer-Assisted Testing
CAT........... Conditionally Accepted Tag
CAT........... Container Anchorage Terminal
CAT........... Credit Authorization Terminal
CATA .... Catalog
CATA .... Community Antenna Television Association
CATIES ..... Common Aperture Technique for Imaging Electro-Optical Sensors
CATLG ...... Catalog
CATRADA ... Combined Arms Training Developments Activity [*Army*]

CATX .... Climb and Cross [*Aviation*]
CAW .... Campos [*Brazil*] [*Airport symbol*]
CAWS ...... Computer-Aided Work Sampling
CAY .... Cayenne [*French Guiana*] [*Airport symbol*]
CAZ .... Cobar [*Australia*] [*Airport symbol*]
CAZ .... Cochise Airlines [*Tucson, AZ*] [*FAA designator*]
CB .... Containment Building [*Nuclear energy*]
CB .... Cyprair Tours Ltd. [*Cyprus*] [*ICAO designator*]
CBA .... Chemical Blowing Agent [*Plastics technology*]
CBB .... Cochabamba [*Bolivia*] [*Airport symbol*]
CBBK-FM ... Kingston, ON [*Broadcasting station call letters*]
CBBL-FM ... London, ON [*Broadcasting station call letters*]
CBC .... Couldn't Be Cuter [*Slang*]
CBCL-FM ... London, ON [*Broadcasting station call letters*]
CBCS-FM ... Sudbury, ON [*Broadcasting station call letters*]
CBD .... Current Bibliographic Directory of the Arts and Sciences [*A publication*]
CBDQ .... Wabush, NF [*Broadcasting station call letters*]
CBE .... Cumberland [*Maryland*] [*Airport symbol*]
CBEE-FM ... Chatham, ON [*Broadcasting station call letters*]
CBE-FM ... Windsor, ON [*Broadcasting station call letters*]
CBEG-FM ... Sarnia, ON [*Broadcasting station call letters*]
CBET .... Certified Biomedical Equipment Technician
CBF-FM .... Montreal, PQ [*Broadcasting station call letters*]
CBF-FM-1 ... Drummondville, PQ [*Broadcasting station call letters*]
CBFS .... Carbon Black Feedstock
CBG .... Cambridge [*England*] [*Airport symbol*]
CBG .... Committee to Bridge the Gap
CBGY .... Bonavista Bay, NF [*Broadcasting station call letters*]
CBI .... Charles Babbage Institute for the History of Information Processing
CBI-FM ..... Sydney, NS [*Broadcasting station call letters*]
CBIM-FM .. Iles De La Madeleine, PQ [*Broadcasting station call letters*]
CBJ-FM ..... Chicoutimi, PQ [*Broadcasting station call letters*]
CBL .... Ciudad Bolivar [*Venezuela*] [*Airport symbol*]
CBM .... Central Bank Money
CBM-FM .... Montreal, PQ [*Broadcasting station call letters*]
CBMI-FM .. Baie-Comeau, PQ [*Broadcasting station call letters*]
CBN .... Cubic Boron Nitride [*Cutting tool edges*]
CBN-FM .... St. John's, NF [*Broadcasting station call letters*]
CBO .... Cancel Back Order
CBO .... Cotabato [*Philippines*] [*Airport symbol*]
CBOF-FM ... Ottawa, ON [*Broadcasting station call letters*]
CBO-FM ... Ottawa, ON [*Broadcasting station call letters*]
CBON-FM ... Sudbury, ON [*Broadcasting station call letters*]
CBPOL ...... Consolidated Base Personnel Office Letter [*Air Force*]
CBPT .... CLIRA [*Closed-Loop In-Reactor Assembly*] Backup Plug Tool [*Nuclear energy*]
CBQ .... Calabar [*Nigeria*] [*Airport symbol*]
CBQ-FM .... Pickle Lake, ON [*Broadcasting station call letters*]
CBQL-FM ... Savant Lake, ON [*Broadcasting station call letters*]
CBQN-FM ... Osnaburgh, ON [*Broadcasting station call letters*]
CBQS-FM ... Sioux Narrows, ON [*Broadcasting station call letters*]
CBQX-FM ... Kenora, ON [*Broadcasting station call letters*]
CBR .... Canberra [*Australia*] [*Airport symbol*]
CBT .... Computer-Based Terminal
CBU-FM ... Vancouver, BC [*Broadcasting station call letters*]
CBUIVTF ... Concerned Broadcasters Using Inter-City Video Transmission Facilities
CBV-FM .... Quebec, PQ [*Broadcasting station call letters*]
CBW .... Continuous Butt-Weld [*Metal industry*]
CBW-FM ... Winnipeg, MB [*Broadcasting station call letters*]
CBX .... Condobolin [*Australia*] [*Airport symbol*]
CBX-FM .... Edmonton, AB [*Broadcasting station call letters*]
CBY .... Canobie [*Australia*] [*Airport symbol*]
CBZ-FM .... Fredericton, NB [*Broadcasting station call letters*]
CC .... Caribbeana Council
CC .... Closed Captioned [*Refers to captioning of television programs for the deaf*]
CC .... Coarse Control [*Nuclear energy*]
CC .... Control Cabin
CC .... Convoy Commodore [*Navy*]
CC .... Cursor Control [*Data processing*]
CC .... Cyclic Code
CC (TEST) ... Component Check Test [*Nuclear energy*]
CCA .... Chromated Copper Arsenate [*Wood preservative*]
CCA .... Current Cost Accounting
CCAP .... Commercial Commodity Acquisition Program [*DOD*]

CCATF ...... Commander, Combined Amphibious Task Force [*Military*]
CCB .... Command Control Block [*Data processing*]
CCC .... Cambodia Crisis Center
CCC .... Chlorocholine Chloride [*Organic chemistry*]
CCC .... Computer Command Control [*General Motors Corp.*]
CCC .... Computer Communications Converter
CCC .... Computer Control Communication
CCC .... Contract Carrier Conference
CCC .... Coordinate Conversion Computer
CCCC .... Charles County Community College [*Maryland*]
CCCEP ...... Commissary Civilian Career Enhancement Program [*Air Force*]
CCCL .... Complementary Constant Current Logic [*Data processing*]
CCCN .... Customs Cooperation Council Nomenclature [*Also, known as BTN*]
CCCS .... Core Component Cleaning System [*Nuclear energy*]
CCCS .... Core Component Conditioning Station [*Nuclear energy*]
CCD .... Camouflage, Concealment, and Deception
CCD .... Census County Division [*Bureau of Census*]
CCD .... Central Command Decoder
CCD .... Coarse Control Damper [*Nuclear energy*]
CCDN .... Corporate Consolidated Data Network [*IBM Corp.*]
CCE/SMHE ... Commercial Construction and Selected Materials Handling Equipment
CCF .... Carcassonne [*France*] [*Airport symbol*]
CCF .... Communications Control Field
CCF .... Congressional Clearinghouse on the Future
CCFT .... Controlled Current Feedback Transfer
CCI .... Center for Compliance Information
CCI .... Concordia [*Brazil*] [*Airport symbol*]
CCI .... Cost Control Item
CCJ .... Center for Community Justice
CCL .... Carbonate Compensation Level [*Oceanography*]
CCL .... Commodity Control List [*Office of Export Administration*]
CCL .... Communications Control Language
CCN .... Chakcharan [*Afghanistan*] [*Airport symbol*]
CC & NF .... Cell Culture and Nitrogen Fixation Laboratory [*Department of Agriculture*]
CCNWC .... Continuing Committee of the National Women's Conference
CCNYA ..... Campaign for the Creation of the National Youth Advisor
CCP .... Communication Control Program
CCP .... Concepcion [*Chile*] [*Airport symbol*]
CCP .... Core Component Pot [*Nuclear energy*]
CCPIT .... China Council for the Promotion of International Trade
CCRC .... Core Component Receiving Container [*Nuclear energy*]
CCS .... Caracas [*Venezuela*] [*Airport symbol*]
CCS .... Collective Consciousness Society [*Vocal and instrumental group*]
CCS .... Commitment Control System
CCS .... Computer Consulting Service
CCS .... Containment Cooling System [*Nuclear energy*]
CCSC .... Cemetery Consumer Service Council
CCSSA ..... Community College Social Science Association
CCSW .... Component Cooling Service Water [*Nuclear energy*]
CCT .... Coupler Cut-Through
CCTC-WAD ... Command and Control Technical Center WWMCCS [*Worldwide Military Command and Control System*] ADP [*Automatic Data Processing*] Directorate [*DOD*]
CCTL .... Core Component Test Loop [*Nuclear energy*]
CCU .... Calcutta [*India*] [*Airport symbol*]
CCV .... Craig Cove [*Vanuata*] [*Airport symbol*]
CCW .... Circulation Control Wing
CCW .... Component Cooling Water [*Nuclear energy*]
CCWS .... Component Cooling Water System [*Nuclear energy*]
CCX .... Caceres [*Brazil*] [*Airport symbol*]
CCZ .... Chub Cay [*Bahamas*] [*Airport symbol*]
CD .... Car Deck
CD .... Carrier Detector
CD .... Cash Dispenser
CD .... Clearance Delivery
CD .... Concept Definition
CD .... RADAR Cloud Detection Report [*Meteorology*]
CDA .... Core Disruptive Accident [*Nuclear energy*]
CDB .... Cold Bay [*Alaska*] [*Airport symbol*]
CDC .... Cedar City [*Utah*] [*Airport symbol*]
CDC .... Cell Division Cycle

CDC .... Combat Direction Center
CDE .... Certificate in Data Education
CDE .... Corporate Data Exchange [*An organization*]
CDEX .... Casual Disability Exclusion
CDF .... Combined Distribution Function
CDF .... Communications-Data Field
CDF .... Cumulative Damage Function [*Nuclear energy*]
CDFE .... Center for the Defense of Free Enterprise
CDG .... Paris [*France*] Charles De Gaulle Airport [*Airport symbol*]
CDH .... Camden [*Arkansas*] [*Airport symbol*]
CDI .... Capacitor Discharge Ignition
CDJ .... Conceicao Do Arguaia [*Brazil*] [*Airport symbol*]
CDK .... Communication Desk
CDL .... Computer Description Language
CDM .... Central Data Management
cDNA .... Deoxyribonucleic Acid, Cloned [*Biochemistry, genetics*]
CDP .... Center for Development Policy
CDPIR ...... Crash Detection Position Indication Recorder
CDPS .... Communications Data Processing System
CDQ .... Croydon [*Australia*] [*Airport symbol*]
CDR .... Cargo Drop Reel
CDR .... Chadron [*Nebraska*] [*Airport symbol*]
CDR .... Committee in Defense of the Revolution [*Cuba*]
CDR .... Conceptual Design Requirement
CDRS .... Container Design Retrieval System
CDS .... Command Disable System [*Air Force*]
CDS .... Component Disassembly Station [*Nuclear energy*]
CDS .... Computer Duplex System
CDS .... Congressional Descriptive Summaries
CDS .... Cord-Air [*Pavilion, NY*] [*FAA designator*]
CDT .... Cyclododecatriene [*Organic chemistry*]
CDTLBS ... Computer-Directed Training Lesson Building System
CDTS .... Computer-Directed Training System
CDU .... Call Director Unit
CDV .... Cordova [*Alaska*] [*Airport symbol*]
CDW .... Charge-Density Wave [*Physics*]
C/E .... Calculation/Experiment
CE .... Coal Equivalent
CEA .... Center for Early Adolescence
CEA .... Control Element Assembly [*Nuclear energy*]
CEB .... Cebu [*Philippines*] [*Airport symbol*]
CEBS .... Certified Employee Benefit Specialist
CEC .... Citizens Energy Corporation [*Nonprofit*]
CEC .... Crescent City [*California*] [*Airport symbol*]
CECO .... Cost Estimate Change Order
CECSET ... Committee for Enlisted Classification Selection and Testing [*Navy*]
CED .... Ceduna [*Australia*] [*Airport symbol*]
CED .... Center for Entrepreneurial Development [*Carnegie-Mellon University*]
CEEDO ...... Civil and Environmental Engineering Development Office [*Air Force*]
CEF .... Controlled Environmental Forestry
CEI .... Chiang Rai [*Thailand*] [*Airport symbol*]
CEL .... Celtic
CEM .... Center for Entrepreneurial Management
CEM .... Central [*Alaska*] [*Airport symbol*]
CEMAD ..... Coherent Echo Modulation and Detection
CEMC .... Counter Electromotive Cell
CEMF .... Counter Electromotive Force
CEN .... Ciudad Obregon [*Mexico*] [*Airport symbol*]
CEO .... Waco Kungo [*Angola*] [*Airport symbol*]
CEP .... Concepcion [*Bolivia*] [*Airport symbol*]
CEPA .... Coupled Electron Pair Approximation [*Physics*]
CER .... Cherbourg [*France*] [*Airport symbol*]
CER .... Critical Experiment Reactor
CERPS ...... Centralized Expenditure/Reimbursement Processing System
CERT .... Combined Environmental Reliability Testing [*Air Force*]
CERTIF ..... Certificate
CERTS .... Consolidated Eglin Real-Time System
CESD .... Composite External Symbol Dictionary
CESNEF .... Centro di Studi Nucleari Enrico Fermi [*Italy*]
CETA .... Civilian Electronics Technician Afloat [*Navy*]
CETS .... Control Element Test Stand [*Nuclear energy*]
CEVAR ...... Consumable-Electrode Vacuum-Arc Remelt [*Nuclear energy*]
CEY .... Murray [*Kentucky*] [*Airport symbol*]
CEZ .... Cortez [*Colorado*] [*Airport symbol*]

CF .... Confinement Factor [*Nuclear energy*]
CF .... Context Free
CFA .... Color Forming Ability [*Food technology*]
CFA .... Correspondence Factor Analysis
CFAK .... Fort Frances, ON [*Broadcasting station call letters*]
CFB .... Centrifugal Fluidized Bed [*Chemical engineering*]
CFBC-FM ... St. John, NB [*Broadcasting station call letters*]
CFBV .... Smithers, BC [*Broadcasting station call letters*]
CFCV-FM ... St. Andrews, NF [*Broadcasting station call letters*]
CFDC .... Canadian Film Development Corporation
CFDL-FM ... Deer Lake, NF [*Broadcasting station call letters*]
CFDS .... Congested Freeway Driving Schedule [*For vehicle emission measurements*]
CFE .... Clermont-Ferrand [*France*] [*Airport symbol*]
CFFR .... Cushman Foundation for Foraminiferal Research
CFG .... Cienfuegos [*Cuba*] [*Airport symbol*]
CFH .... Clifton Hills [*Australia*] [*Airport symbol*]
CFH .... Council on Family Health
CFIX .... Cornwall, ON [*Broadcasting station call letters*]
CFLC-FM ... Churchill Falls, NF [*Broadcasting station call letters*]
CFLG-FM ... Cornwall, ON [*Broadcasting station call letters*]
CFLP .... Rimouski, PQ [*Broadcasting station call letters*]
CFLY-FM .. Kingston, ON [*Broadcasting station call letters*]
CFM .... Covering Fire Mine
CFMX-FM ... Cobourg, ON [*Broadcasting station call letters*]
CFNI .... Port Hardy, BC [*Broadcasting station call letters*]
CFNN-FM ... St. Anthony, NF [*Broadcasting station call letters*]
CFOX-FM ... Vancouver, BC [*Broadcasting station call letters*]
CFOZ-FM ... Argentia, NF [*Broadcasting station call letters*]
CFPL-FM .. London, ON [*Broadcasting station call letters*]
CFPS .... Port Elgin, ON [*Broadcasting station call letters*]
CFQM-FM ... Moncton, NB [*Broadcasting station call letters*]
CFR .... Caen [*France*] [*Airport symbol*]
CFRC-FM ... Kingston, ON [*Broadcasting station call letters*]
CFRD-FM ... Richmond, BC [*Broadcasting station call letters*]
CFRP .... Forestville, PQ [*Broadcasting station call letters*]
CFRU-FM ... Guelph, ON [*Broadcasting station call letters*]
CFS .... Coffs Harbour [*Australia*] [*Airport symbol*]
CFSD .... Citizens for Space Demilitarization
CFTR .... Citizens for the Republic
CFU .... Color Forming Units [*Food technology*]
CFU .... Corfu [*Greece*] [*Airport symbol*]
CFVD .... Degelis, PQ [*Broadcasting station call letters*]
CFVM .... Amqui, PQ [*Broadcasting station call letters*]
CFYQ .... Gander, NF [*Broadcasting station call letters*]
CG .... Contrast Gate
CGA .... Clutter Gate Amplifier
CGA .... Craig [*Alaska*] [*Airport symbol*]
CGB .... Cuiaba [*Brazil*] [*Airport symbol*]
CGC .... Cape Gloucester [*Papua New Guinea*] [*Airport symbol*]
CGEL .... Cover Gas Evaluation Loop [*Nuclear energy*]
CGH .... Sao Paulo [*Brazil*] Congonhas Airport [*Airport symbol*]
CGI .... Cape Girardeau [*Missouri*] [*Airport symbol*]
CGIP .... Conference Group on Italian Politics
CGN .... Cologne/Bonn [*West Germany*] [*Airport symbol*]
CGO .... Zhengzhou [*China*] [*Airport symbol*]
CGP .... Chittagong [*Bangladesh*] [*Airport symbol*]
CGQ .... Changchun [*China*] [*Airport symbol*]
CGR .... Campo Grande [*Brazil*] [*Airport symbol*]
CGSEL ...... Common Ground Support Equipment List
CGSTN ...... Congestion [*Aviation*]
CGT .... Cheguitti [*Mauritania*] [*Airport symbol*]
CGTO .... Contracted Gaussian-Type Orbital [*Atomic physics*]
CGX .... Chicago [*Illinois*] Meigs Field [*Airport symbol*]
CGY .... Cagayan De Oro [*Philippines*] [*Airport symbol*]
CH .... Channel Continuity Check Transmission [*Communications*]
CH .... Character
CH .... Control Heading
CH .... Control Hole
CHA .... Christian Herald Association
CHAL .... Chaldron [*Unit of measure*] [*Obsolete*]
CHALD ...... Chaldea
CHAP .... Chapman [*One who sells in a cheaping or market*] [*Said to be origin of "chap," meaning "fellow"*]
CHAP/FAAR ... Chaparral/Forward Area Alert RADAR [*Military*]
CHAPGRU ... Cargo Handling and Port Group [*Navy*]
CHAS-FM ... Sault Ste. Marie, ON [*Broadcasting station call letters*]

CHAT .... CLIRA [*Closed-Loop In-Reactor Assembly*] Holddown Assembly Tool [*Nuclear energy*]
CHAY .... Barrie, ON [*Broadcasting station call letters*]
CHAY-FM ... Barrie, ON [*Broadcasting station call letters*]
CHC .... Channel Control
CHC .... Christchurch [*New Zealand*] [*Airport symbol*]
CHCH........ (Cyclohexenyl)cyclohexanone [*Organic chemistry*]
CHCR........ Montreal, PQ [*Broadcasting station call letters*]
CHE .... Channel End
CHES .... Chesapeake [*Bay*] [*Virginia and Maryland*]
CHESOP .. Charitable/Employee Stock Ownership Plan [*Tax plan*]
CHEZ-FM ... Ottawa, ON [*Broadcasting station call letters*]
CHF .... Coalition for Health Funding
CHGB-FM .. La Pocatiere, PQ [*Broadcasting station call letters*]
CHGG-FM .. Limestone, MB [*Broadcasting station call letters*]
CHI............ Chicago [*Illinois*] [*Airport symbol*]
CHI............ China
CHI............ Computer Human Interaction
CHIC .... Chicago [*Illinois*]
CHIM-FM .. Kelowna, BC [*Broadcasting station call letters*]
CHIN-FM ... Toronto, ON [*Broadcasting station call letters*]
CHIP.......... Chemical Hazard Information Profile [*Environmental Protection Agency*]
CHIPS .... Clearing House Interbank Payment System
CHKPT ...... Checkpoint
CHLG-FM-6 ... Brisay, PQ [*Broadcasting station call letters*]
CHLM-FM ... Rouyn-Noranda, PQ [*Broadcasting station call letters*]
CHLOREP ... Chlorine Emergency Plan [*Chlorine Institute*]
CHM .... Chimbote [*Peru*] [*Airport symbol*]
CHNL-1 ..... Clearwater, BC [*Broadcasting station call letters*]
CHNO........ Sudbury, ON [*Broadcasting station call letters*]
CHO .... Charlottesville [*Virginia*] [*Airport symbol*]
CHOI-FM.... Quebec, PQ [*Broadcasting station call letters*]
CHOMI...... Clearinghouse on Migration Issues [*Australia*]
CHOMPS .. Canine Home Protection Service [*Acronym is title of 1979 movie*]
CHOS-FM ... Rattling Brook, NF [*Broadcasting station call letters*]
CHOZ-FM ... St. John's, NF [*Broadcasting station call letters*]
CHP........... Circle Hot Springs [*Alaska*] [*Airport symbol*]
CHP........... Combined-Heat-and-Power Station [*Energy production*]
CHPR......... Hawkesville, ON [*Broadcasting station call letters*]
CHQ .... Chania [*Greece*] [*Airport symbol*]
CHQM-FM ... Vancouver, BC [*Broadcasting station call letters*]
CHR .... Character
CHRB .... High River, AB [*Broadcasting station call letters*]
CHRE-FM ... St. Catharines, ON [*Broadcasting station call letters*]
CHRS .... St. Jean, PQ [*Broadcasting station call letters*]
CHS........... Circular Hollow Section [*Metal industry*]
CHSC-FM ... St. Catharines, ON [*Broadcasting station call letters*]
CHUCK ..... Committee to Halt Useless College Killings
CHUM-FM ... Toronto, ON [*Broadcasting station call letters*]
CHY........... Choiseul Bay [*Solomon Islands*] [*Airport symbol*]
CHYQ........ Muskgravetown, NF [*Broadcasting station call letters*]
CHYR-7 ..... Leamington, ON [*Broadcasting station call letters*]
CI .... Card Input [*Data processing*]
CI .... Center Island [*Nuclear energy*]
C³I .... Command, Communications, Control, and Intelligence
CIA............ Catholic Irish Attorneys [*Fictional organization*]
CIA............ Containment Isolation A [*Nuclear energy*]
CIA............ Rome [*Italy*] Ciampino Airport [*Airport symbol*]
CIAB .... Coal Industry Advisory Board
CIB............ Catalina Island [*California*] Airport in the Sky [*Airport symbol*]
CIB............ Containment Isolation B [*Nuclear energy*]
CIBO .... Council of Industrial Boiler Owners
CIC............ Chico [*California*] [*Airport symbol*]
CIC............ Cicero [*Roman orator and author, 106-43 BC*]
CIC............ Communications Instructor Console
CIC............ Contemporary Issues Criticism [*A publication*]
CICOM...... Citizens for Informed Choices on Marijuana
CID............ Cedar Rapids/Iowa City [*Iowa*] [*Airport symbol*]
CID .... Commercial Item Drawing
CIDF.......... Control Interval Definition Field [*Data processing*]
CIDPL .... Commission for International Due Process of Law
CIDPS .... Continental Intelligence Data Processing System
CIEL-FM .... Montreal, PQ [*Broadcasting station call letters*]
CIEMS....... Catalog for Information Exchange and Message Standards
CIF .... Customer Information File

CIFFO .... Cost, Insurance, Freight, Free Out [*Business and trade*]
CIGB .... Trois-Rivieres, PQ [*Broadcasting station call letters*]
CIGL-FM... Belleville, ON [*Broadcasting station call letters*]
CIGM-FM ... Sudbury, ON [*Broadcasting station call letters*]
CII .... Computer-Integrated Instruction
CIJ............. Cobija [*Bolivia*] [*Airport symbol*]
CIK .... Chalkyitsik [*Alaska*] [*Airport symbol*]
CILA-FM.... Lethbridge, AB [*Broadcasting station call letters*]
CILC.......... California Iceberg Lettuce Commission
CILQ-FM... Toronto, ON [*Broadcasting station call letters*]
CIM .... Cimitarra [*Colombia*] [*Airport symbol*]
CIME-FM ... Ste. Adele, PQ [*Broadcasting station call letters*]
CIMF-FM... Ottawa-Hull, ON [*Broadcasting station call letters*]
CIMH-FM .. Sept-Iles/Port Cartier, PQ [*Broadcasting station call letters*]
CIMO-FM ... Sherbrooke, PQ [*Broadcasting station call letters*]
CIMP .... Controlled Impulse
CIN............ Cincinnati [*Ohio*]
CING-FM... Burlington, ON [*Broadcasting station call letters*]
CINQ-FM... Montreal, PQ [*Broadcasting station call letters*]
CINTEX..... Combined In-Port Tactical Exercise [*Navy*]
CIOCS....... Communications Input and Output Control System
CIOK-1...... Grande Centre, AB [*Broadcasting station call letters*]
CIP .... Chipata [*Zambia*] [*Airport symbol*]
CIP .... Coast-in-Point
C/IP........... Construction/Inspection Procedure
CIP .... Cryogenic Insulation Program
CIR .... Center for Investigative Reporting
CIR .... Collection Intelligence Requirements
CIR .... Committee on Changing International Realities
CIRB.......... Lac Ethemin, PQ [*Broadcasting station call letters*]
CIRC-FM... Rouyn, PQ [*Broadcasting station call letters*]
CIRIS........ Central Inertial Reference Instrumentation System
CIRK-FM... Edmonton, AB [*Broadcasting station call letters*]
CIS .... Containment Isolation System [*Nuclear energy*]
CIS .... Council for Inter-American Security
CISP.......... Commercial Item Support Program [*DOD*]
CITE-FM... Sherbrooke, PQ [*Broadcasting station call letters*]
CITI-FM..... Winnipeg, MB [*Broadcasting station call letters*]
CIU............ Community Information Utility
CIU .... Sault Ste. Marie [*Michigan*] [*Airport symbol*]
CIV .... Center Island Vessel [*Nuclear energy*]
CIX .... Chiclayo [*Peru*] [*Airport symbol*]
CIXX-FM ... London, ON [*Broadcasting station call letters*]
CIYQ .... Grand Falls, NF [*Broadcasting station call letters*]
CJ.............. Chapman-Jouquet [*Pressures*]
CJA .... Cajamarca [*Peru*] [*Airport symbol*]
CJAB-FM ... Chicoutimi-Jonquiere, PQ [*Broadcasting station call letters*]
CJAT-FM .. Trail, BC [*Broadcasting station call letters*]
CJAY-FM ... Calgary, AB [*Broadcasting station call letters*]
CJAZ-FM .. Vancouver, BC [*Broadcasting station call letters*]
CJB .... Coimbatore [*India*] [*Airport symbol*]
CJBQ-FM ... Belleville, ON [*Broadcasting station call letters*]
CJBR-FM .. Rimouski, PQ [*Broadcasting station call letters*]
CJBX-FM .. London, ON [*Broadcasting station call letters*]
CJC .... Calama [*Chile*] [*Airport symbol*]
CJC .... Colgan Airways Corp. [*Manassas, VA*] [*FAA designator*]
CJCB-FM ... Sydney, NS [*Broadcasting station call letters*]
CJCD.......... Yellowknife, NT [*Broadcasting station call letters*]
CJCH-FM .... Halifax, NS [*Broadcasting station call letters*]
CJCM-FM ... Brandon, MB [*Broadcasting station call letters*]
CJCW......... Sussex, NB [*Broadcasting station call letters*]
CJD .... Candilejas [*Colombia*] [*Airport symbol*]
CJET-FM .. Smiths Falls, ON [*Broadcasting station call letters*]
CJF .... Council of Jewish Federations [*Formerly, CJFWF*]
CJL............ Chitral [*Pakistan*] [*Airport symbol*]
CJLP.......... Disraeli, PQ [*Broadcasting station call letters*]
CJN .... El Cajon [*California*] [*Airport symbol*]
CJNS.......... Meadow Lake, SK [*Broadcasting station call letters*]
CJOA......... Consortium of Jazz Organizations and Artists
CJOX........ Yorkton, SK [*Broadcasting station call letters*]
CJOZ-FM ... Bonavista, NF [*Broadcasting station call letters*]
CJQM-FM ... Sault Ste. Marie, ON [*Broadcasting station call letters*]
CJQR-FM ... St. Catharines, ON [*Broadcasting station call letters*]
CJR .... Chaurjahari [*Nepal*] [*Airport symbol*]
CJRG......... Gaspe, PQ [*Broadcasting station call letters*]
CJS .... Ciudad Juarez [*Mexico*] [*Airport symbol*]
CJSL .... Yarmouth, NS [*Broadcasting station call letters*]

CJTN......... Trenton, ON [*Broadcasting station call letters*]
CJU........... Cheju [*South Korea*] [*Airport symbol*]
CJVA........ Caraquet, NB [*Broadcasting station call letters*]
CJWW....... Saskatoon, SK [*Broadcasting station call letters*]
CJXX........ Grande Prairie, AB [*Broadcasting station call letters*]
CJYQ........ St. John's, NF [*Broadcasting station call letters*]
CK............. Air Seychelles [*ICAO designator*]
CK............. Cytokinin [*Biochemistry*]
CKAL........ Vernon, BC [*Broadcasting station call letters*]
CKAN........ Newmarket, ON [*Broadcasting station call letters*]
CKAR........ Oshawa, ON [*Broadcasting station call letters*]
CKBH........ Baie Comeau, PQ [*Broadcasting station call letters*]
CKCH-FM ... Hull, PQ [*Broadcasting station call letters*]
CKCL-FM ... Truro, NS [*Broadcasting station call letters*]
CKDK........ Woodstock, ON [*Broadcasting station call letters*]
CKIG......... Dryden, ON [*Broadcasting station call letters*]
CKLW-FM ... Windsor, ON [*Broadcasting station call letters*]
CKMG....... Maniwaki, PQ [*Broadcasting station call letters*]
CKMS-FM ... Waterloo, ON [*Broadcasting station call letters*]
CKMV .... Grand Falls, NB [*Broadcasting station call letters*]
CKMW....... Toronto, ON [*Broadcasting station call letters*]
CKNX-FM ... Wingham, ON [*Broadcasting station call letters*]
CKO .... Pointe Claire, PQ [*Broadcasting station call letters*]
CKO-FM-1 ... Ottawa, ON [*Broadcasting station call letters*]
CKO-FM-2 ... Toronto, ON [*Broadcasting station call letters*]
CKO-FM-3 ... London, ON [*Broadcasting station call letters*]
CKO-FM-6 ... Edmonton, AB [*Broadcasting station call letters*]
CKOI-FM... Verdun, PQ [*Broadcasting station call letters*]
CKOR-FM ... Penticton, BC [*Broadcasting station call letters*]
CKOT-FM ... Tillsonburg, ON [*Broadcasting station call letters*]
CKOZ-FM ... Corner Brook, NF [*Broadcasting station call letters*]
CKPB .... Bagotville, PQ [*Broadcasting station call letters*]
CKPC-FM ... Brantford, ON [*Broadcasting station call letters*]
CKQM-FM ... Peterborough, ON [*Broadcasting station call letters*]
CKQT-FM ... Oshawa, ON [*Broadcasting station call letters*]
CKRA-FM ... Edmonton, AB [*Broadcasting station call letters*]
CKRD-FM ... Red Deer, AB [*Broadcasting station call letters*]
CKRM-FM ... Edmonton, AB [*Broadcasting station call letters*]
CKSJ........ St. Jovite, PQ [*Broadcasting station call letters*]
CKST .... Edmonton, AB [*Broadcasting station call letters*]
CKUA-FM ... Edmonton, AB [*Broadcasting station call letters*]
CKUA-FM-2 ... Lethbridge, AB [*Broadcasting station call letters*]
CKUA-FM-3 ... Medicine Hat, AB [*Broadcasting station call letters*]
CKUE .... Smiths Falls, ON [*Broadcasting station call letters*]
CKWG-FM ... Winnipeg, MB [*Broadcasting station call letters*]
CKXM-FM ... Edmonton, AB [*Broadcasting station call letters*]
CKYQ....... Grand Bank, NF [*Broadcasting station call letters*]
CKYR-1..... Grand Cache, AB [*Broadcasting station call letters*]
CL .... Chemiluminescence
CL .... Closing Station
CL .... Control Language [*Data processing*]
CLAW........ Close Air Support Weapon [*Military*]
CLBN .... Crash Locator Beacon [*Aviation*]
CLCGM..... Closed-Loop Cover Gas Monitor [*Nuclear energy*]
CLCIS .... Closed-Loop Control and Instrumentation System [*Nuclear energy*]
CLCV .... Cold Leg Check Valve [*Nuclear energy*]
C/LEC....... Citizen/Labor Energy Coalition
CLEM .... Closed-Loop Ex-Vessel Machine [*Formerly, EVHM*] [*Nuclear energy*]
CLF .... Christian Librarians' Fellowship
CLG........... Compile, Load, and Go [*Data processing*]
CLIRA .... Closed-Loop In-Reactor Assembly [*Nuclear energy*]
CLIV.......... Cold Leg Isolation Valve [*Nuclear energy*]
CLJA .... Closed-Loop Jumper Assembly [*Nuclear energy*]
CLKOB...... Clockwise Orbit [*Aviation*]
CLP .... Center on Law and Pacifism
CLPF......... Chlorine Pentafluoride [*Inorganic chemistry*]
CLR........... Clearance
CLR........... Cleared To
CLRIT........ Children's Legal Rights Information and Training [*An organization*]
CLRS......... Clear and Smooth [*Meteorology*]
CLS.......... Cask Loading Station [*Nuclear energy*]
CLS........... Close
CLS........... Closed-Loop System [*Nuclear energy*]
CLS........... Common Language System [*Data processing*]
CLS........... Concept Learning System [*Data processing*]

CLSMDA... Closed-Loop System Melt-Down Accident [*Nuclear energy*]
CLTR......... Center for Local Tax Research
CLV .... Clover Aero, Inc. [*Friendswood, TX*] [*FAA designator*]
CM .... Central Memory [*Data processing*]
CM .... Constant Misery [*Slang*]
CMA .... Cash Management Account [*Merrill Lynch*]
CMA......... Census Metropolitan Area [*Canada*]
CM/CCM .. Countermeasures/Counter Countermeasures [*Army*]
CMCS ...... Communications Monitoring and Control Subsystem
CMCS ...... COMSAT-Maritime Communications Satellite
CMDS ...... Command Manpower Data System
CMDS ...... Countermeasures Dispenser Set
CMF .... Central Maintenance Facility
CMFLPD... Core Maximum Fraction of Limiting Power Density [*Nuclear energy*]
CMG......... Chopped Meat Glucose [*Medium*] [*Microbiology*]
CMI .... Cash Management Institute
CMIO........ COMSEC [*Communications Security*] Material Issuing Office [*Military*]
CMIS......... Common Military Intelligence Skills
CMM .... Core Mechanical Mockup [*Nuclear energy*]
CMMF .... Component Maintenance and Mockup Facility [*Nuclear energy*]
CMMIO..... Communications Security Mobile Issuing Office [*Military*]
CMP .... CLEM [*Closed-Loop Ex-Vessel Machine*] Maintenance Pit [*Nuclear energy*]
CMR .... Center for Marxist Research
CMS .... Center for Management Systems
CMS .... Compiler Monitor System
CMS .... Computer Management System
CMS .... Corrective Maintenance System
CMSI .... Climatology Mission Success Indicators
CMSIO ...... Communications Security Material Sub-Issuing Office [*Military*]
CMSNA.... Chinese Music Society of North America
CMVIO ...... Communications Security Material Van-Issuing Office [*Military*]
CMW .... Campus Ministry Women [*An organization*]
C & N........ Communication and Navigation
CNAIP ...... Council for Native American Indian Progress
CNB .... Centrale Nucleaire Belge [*Nuclear reactor*]
CNCL .... Cancel
CNL........... Canal [*Board on Geographic Names*]
CNLI......... Irrigation Canal [*Board on Geographic Names*]
CNLN .... Navigation Canal [*Board on Geographic Names*]
CNNW ...... Coalition for a Non-Nuclear World
CNO .... Carbon-Nitrogen-Oxygen [*Galactic molecular formation cycle*]
CNOR....... Command Not Operationally Ready [*Navy*]
CNPD .... Candidate/Nominee Protective Division [*US Secret Service*]
CNPIC ...... China National Publications Import Corporation
CNTT .... Chief of Naval Technical Training
CNX.......... Cancel
CNY.......... Century Airlines [*Eureka, CA*] [*FAA designator*]
CO............ Chief Operator
CO........... Criminal Office
COBE .... Cosmic Background Explorer [*NASA*]
COC .... Coded Optical Character [*Data processing*]
COC .... Conventional Oxidation Catalysis [*of gasoline engine exhausts*]
COCHL ..... Cochleare [*Spoonful*] [*Pharmacy*]
CODAC ..... Collateral Duty Alcoholism Counselor [*Navy*]
CODEC ..... Coder-Decoders
COG .... Coke Oven Gas
COGENT... Cooperative Generic Technology [*Centers for cooperative government and industry work*]
COH .... Center for Occupational Hazards
COH .... Complex Overhaul
COIL......... Chemical Oxygen Iodine LASER
COJ........... Continental Jet, Inc. [*Palm Springs, CA*] [*FAA designator*]
COLPA...... Commission on Law and Public Affairs
COM......... Coal-Oil Mixture
COM........ Computer Output on Microfilm
COMAM ..... Continuous Motion Assembly Machine
COMD DSR ... Command Dental Service Report [*Air Force*]
COMEDS .. CONUS-Meteorological Data [*or Distribution*] System

COMEXAZ ... Comite de Mexico y Aztlan
COMNAVTELCOM ... Commander, Naval Telecommunications Command
COMP .... Composite Operational Mission Profiles
COMPACT ... Computer Planning and Control Technique
COMPASS ... Computer-Assigned Assignment System
COMPAY .. Computer Payroll
CONGL ..... Conglomerate
CONPLAN ... Concept Plan
CONVERSIONEX ... Contact Conversion Exercise [*Military*]
COOAL ..... Coordinated Activity List [*Navy*]
COP .... Coptic
COP .... Customer Order Processing
COPA .... Center Overage Pending Assignment
COPE .... Conference of Podiatry Executives
COPS .... Computer-Oriented Partial Sum
COPS .... Computerized Officer Planning System [*Navy*]
COR .... Command Operationally Ready [*Navy*]
CORSAC ... Council of Regional School Accrediting Commissions
COSCAA ... Council of State Community Affairs Agencies
COSMOS .. Computer-Oriented System for Management Order Synthesis
COSRIVRON ... Coastal River Squadron [*Navy*]
COSS .... Consules [*Consuls*]
COSSU ..... Coins on Stamps Unit
COST .... Coastal Offshore Stratigraphic Tests [*Geology*]
COSTAR ... Computer-Stored Ambulatory Record
COSWA ..... Committee on the Status of Women in Anthropology
COW .... Chlorinated Organics in Wastewater
CP .... Card Punch [*Data processing*]
CP .... Command Processor [*Data processing*]
CP .... General Call to Two or More Specified Stations [*Communications*]
CPA .... California Pistachio Association
CPA .... Canadian Psychiatric Association
CPA .... Coherent Potential Approximation [*Physics*]
CPA .... Control Purchasing Authority
CPB .... Career Planning Board [*Navy*]
CPC .... Cargo Processing Contract
CPC .... Certified Personnel Consultant [*Designation awarded by National Association of Personnel Consultants*]
CPC .... Computer Programing Concepts
CPC .... Consortium for Peaceful Coexistence
CPC .... Core Protection Computer [*Nuclear energy*]
CPCFA ..... Council of Pollution Control Financing Agencies
CPCI .... Computer Program Configured Item
CPCM .... Certification as Professional Contract Manager
CPCP .... Civilian Personnel Career Plan [*Air Force*]
CPCS .... Check Processing Control System
CPD .... Cards per Day [*Data processing*]
CPD .... Communications Planning and Development
CPDC .... Command Processor Distributor Control
CPDD .... Conceptual Project Design Description
CPE .... Central Planned Economy
CPEB .... Central Physical Evaluation Board [*Navy*]
CPF .... Control Program Facility
CPH .... Characters per Hour [*Data processing*]
CPI .... Cancer Potential Index
CPL .... Computer Program Library
CPMB .... Concrete Plant Manufacturers Bureau
CPMC .... (Chlorophenyl)methylcarbamate [*Organic chemistry*]
CPMIS .... Civilian Personnel Management Information System
CPO .... Concurrent Peripheral Operations
CPODA ..... Contention Priority-Oriented Demand Assignment [*Protocol*] [*Data processing*]
CPOL .... Communications Procedure-Oriented Language [*Data processing*]
CPP .... Card Punching Printer [*Data processing*]
CPP .... Center for Plutonium Production [*France*]
CPPD .... Calcium Pyrophosphate Dihydrate [*Inorganic chemistry*]
CPR .... Center for Parapsychological Research
CPR .... Center for Public Representation
CPR .... Critical Power Ratio [*Nuclear energy*]
CPS .... Conversion Program System
CPSCI .... Central Personnel Security Clearance Index [*Nuclear energy*]
CPWD .... Caucus for Producers, Writers, and Directors
CPY .... Copy
CQE .... Cognizant Quality Engineer

CR .... Card Reader [*Data processing*]
CR .... Chicago Reactor
CR .... Control Rod [*Nuclear reactor*]
CRA .... Community Reinvestment Act [*Requires banks to list credit facilities available to the communities they serve*]
CRA .... Control Rod Assembly [*Nuclear energy*]
CRANE ..... Cosmic Ray Nuclear Experiment
CRATT ..... Covered Radio Teletype
CRBC .... Chick Red Blood Cells
CRC .... Critical Reactor Component [*Nuclear energy*]
CRCTA ..... Composite Reactor Components Test Activity [*Nuclear energy*]
CRD .... Control Rod Driveline [*Nuclear energy*]
CRESS ..... Central Regulatory Electronic Stenographic System
CRF .... Correspondence Routing Form
CRG .... Center for Responsive Governance
CRI .... Constant Rate Injector [*Instrumentation*]
CRM .... Certified Records Manager
CRM .... Core Restraint Mechanism [*Nuclear energy*]
CRMA ...... City and Regional Magazine Association
CROS .... Contralateral Routing of Signal [*Audiometry*]
CRS .... Camp Sentinel RADAR [*Military*]
CRS .... Contract Repair Service
CRST .... Calcinosis Cutis Raynaud's Phenomenon, Sclerodactyly, and Teleangiectasia [*Medicine*]
CRT .... Count Reduction Technique [*Food bacteriology*]
CRTC .... Cold Regions Test Center [*Army*]
CS .... Card Station [*Data processing*]
CS .... Computer Science
CS .... Coupled States [*Physics*]
CS .... Cultural Survival [*An organization*]
CS .... Customer Service
CS .... Customer Support
CSA .... Caribbean Studies Association
CSA .... Center for Sustainable Agriculture
CSA .... Chimney Sweeps of America
CSA .... Clinical Sociology Association
CSA .... Common Service Area
CSA .... Computer System Analyst
CSAE .... Committee for the Study of the American Electorate
CSAVAP ... Child Sexual Assault Victim Assistance Project
CSBA .... Char-Swiss Breeders Association
CSC .... Centralized Supervisory and Control
CSCA .... Council of Scottish Clan Associations
CSCB .... Command Scheduling Control Block [*Data processing*]
CSCS .... Core Standby Cooling System [*Nuclear energy*]
CSD .... Coalition on Sexuality and Disability
CSDF .... Core Segment Development Facility [*Nuclear energy*]
CSDS .... Center for the Study of Democratic Societies
CSE .... Central State Airline [*Green Bay, WI*] [*FAA designator*]
CSEF .... Canadian Siberian Expeditionary Force
CSF .... Containment Support Fixture [*Nuclear energy*]
CSG .... Clean Sweep Generator
CSG .... Guided Missile Strike Cruiser [*Navy symbol*]
CSIS .... Center for Strategic and International Studies [*Georgetown University*]
CSITT .... Combat System Interface Test Tool
CSL .... Chemical Systems Laboratory [*Army*]
CSL .... Code Selection Language [*Data processing*]
CSL .... Computer Simulation Language [*Data processing*]
CSM .... Camouflage Signature Measurement [*Army*]
CSM .... Continuous Sheet Memory [*Data processing*]
CSM .... Continuous Slowing Down Models [*Physics*]
CSMG .... Center for the Study of Multiple Gestation
CSOT .... Combat Systems Operability Test
CSP .... Commercial Subroutine Package
CSP .... Control Switching Point
CSRT .... Combat Systems Readiness Test
CSS .... Cask Support Structure [*Nuclear energy*]
CSS .... Cinegraphic Scoring System
CSS .... Containment Spray System [*Nuclear energy*]
CSS .... Core Support Structure [*Nuclear energy*]
CSSA .... Control Stick Sensor Assembly
CSSU .... Converter Simulator Signal Unit
CSS-X-4 .... China Surface-to-Surface Experimental Number 4 [*Rocket*]
CST .... Classification on Science and Technology
CST .... Combat Systems Training

CSTP......... Crew Scheduling and Training Plan
CSTPA...... Council on Soil Testing and Plant Analysis
CSTU........ Combat System Training Unit
CSU........... Christmas Study Unit
CSW........... Channel Status Word
CSWAP..... Committee on the Status of Women in the Archival Profession
CSWD....... Center for the Survival of Western Democracies
CSWL....... Committee on the Status of Women in Linguistics
CSWS....... Committee on the Status of Women in Sociology
CT............. Chymotrypsin [*An enzyme*]
CT............. CLEM [*Closed-Loop Ex-Vessel Machine*] Transporter [*Nuclear energy*]
CT............. Connectivity Table [*Data processing*]
CT............. Controlled Temperature
CT............. Cycle Time
CTAK....... Cipher Text Auto Key [*Data processing*]
CTD........... Charged Tape Detection [*Fuel-failure monitor*] [*Nuclear energy*]
CTF........... Cask Tilting Fixture [*Nuclear energy*]
CTF........... [*The*] Following groups have been referred back to the originator for confirmation or correction [*Communications*]
CTG........... Control Techniques Guidelines [*Environmental Protection Agency*]
CTGY........ Category
CTJ........... Citizens for Tax Justice
CTM.......... Configuration and Tuning Module [*Data processing*]
CTMMA.... Central Technical Manual Management Activity [*Navy*]
CTP........... Construction Test Procedure
CTP........... Controlled Temperature Profile [*Vapor trap*] [*Nuclear energy*]
CTR........... Certified Test Results
CTS........... Clear to Send
CTS........... Computerized Tomography Society
CTS........... Contractor Technical Support
CTS........... Conversational Terminal System
CTT........... Combined Test Team
CTU.......... Captive Test Unit
CTU.......... Custom, Tradition, and Usage
CU............. Customer Premise
CUBS........ Center for Urban Black Studies
CUC.......... Cahiers Universitaires Catholiques [*A publication*]
CUE.......... Configuration Utilization Efficiency
CUES........ Center for Urban Environmental Studies
CUIUA....... Council of University Institutes for Urban Affairs
Cult Med Psychiatry ... Culture, Medicine, Psychiatry [*A publication*]
Cultura Med Mod ... Cultura Medica Moderna [*A publication*]
CULTURE ... Creative Use of Leisure Time under Restrictive Environments [*Federally funded prison program*]
Cum Comput Abstr ... Cumulative Computer Abstracts [*A publication*]
Curr Aff Bull ... Current Affairs Bulletin [*A publication*]
Curr Aus NZ Leg Lit Ind ... Current Australian and New Zealand Legal Literature Index [*A publication*]
Curr Bibl Aquatic Sci & Fish ... Current Bibliography for Aquatic Sciences and Fisheries [*A publication*]
Curr Dig Sov Press ... Current Digest of Soviet Press [*A publication*]
Curr Eng Pract ... Current Engineering Practice [*A publication*]
Current Adv Plant Sci ... Current Advances in Plant Science [*A publication*]
Current Chem Transl ... Current Chemical Translations [*A publication*]
Current Ind Rept ... Current Industrial Reports [*A publication*]
Current Math Publ ... Current Mathematical Publications [*A publication*]
Curr Hist ... Current History [*A publication*]
Curr Ind Commonw Leg Per ... Current Index to Commonwealth Legal Periodicals [*A publication*]

Curr Leather Lit ... Current Leather Literature [*A publication*]
Curr Leg Probl ... Current Legal Problems [*A publication*]
Curr Lit Blood ... Current Literature of Blood [*A publication*]
Curr Med Res Opin ... Current Medical Research and Opinion [*A publication*]
Curr Notes Int Aff ... Current Notes on International Affairs [*A publication*]
Curr Pap Phys ... Current Papers in Physics [*A publication*]
Curr Pract Orthop Surg ... Current Practice in Orthopaedic Surgery [*A publication*]
Curr Probl Cancer ... Current Problems in Cancer [*A publication*]
Curr Probl Cardiol ... Current Problems in Cardiology [*A publication*]
Curr Probl Dermatol ... Current Problems in Dermatology [*A publication*]
Curr Probl Pediatr ... Current Problems in Pediatrics [*A publication*]
Curr Probl Surg ... Current Problems in Surgery [*A publication*]
Curr Sci .... Current Science [*A publication*]
Curr Sci (India) ... Current Science (India) [*A publication*]
Curr Surg ... Current Surgery [*A publication*]
Curr Tit Electrochem ... Current Titles in Electrochemistry [*A publication*]
Curr Top Nutr Dis ... Current Topics in Nutrition and Disease [*A publication*]
Curr US Gov Per Mfiche ... Current US Government Periodicals on Microfiche [*A publication*]
C (US)....... Cinema (United States) [*A publication*]
Cushman Found Foram Research Contr ... Cushman Foundation for Foraminiferal Research. Contributions [*A publication*]
CUT.......... Control Unit Tester
CV............. Christian Voice [*An organization*]
CV............. Circular Vection [*Optics*]
CVA........... Corpus Vasorum Antiquorum [*A publication*]
CVC........... Committee for a Voluntary Census
CVCF........ Constant Voltage and Constant Frequency
CVCS........ Chemical and Volume Control System
CVF........... Central Visual Field [*Optics*]
CVFP......... Cancel VFR [*Visual Flight Rules*] Flight Plan [*Aviation*]
CVI............ Certified Vendor Information
CVIC......... Aircraft Carrier Intelligence Center
C Vind....... Commentationes Vindobonenses [*A publication*]
CVN.......... Aircraft Carrier, Nuclear Propulsion [*Navy symbol*]
CVP........... Cardiovascular and Pulmonary Technology. Journal [*A publication*]
CVT........... Color Video Tape
CVT........... Communication Vector Table
CW............ Air Continental Ltd. [*Great Britain*] [*ICAO designator*]
CW............ Cold-Worked [*Nuclear energy*]
CWA........... Clean Water Act [*Environmental Protection Agency*]
CWC.......... Comenius World Council
CWC.......... Composite Warfare Coordinator [*Military*]
CW/CBD... Chemical Warfare/Chemical Biological Defense
CWLTH..... Commonwealth
CWM.......... Cruciform Wing Module
CWO.......... Capital Work Order
CWP.......... Contractor Work Plan
CWPS....... Center for Women Policy Studies
CWS.......... Cooling Water System [*Nuclear energy*]
CWT.......... Cold Water Treatment [*Medicine*]
CWTI......... Civil War Times Illustrated [*A publication*]
Cyanamid Mag ... Cyanamid Magazine [*A publication*]
CYCIS....... Child and Youth Centered Information Systems
Cycl Anat and Physiol ... Cyclopaedia of Anatomy and Physiology [*A publication*]
CYTA .... California Yoga Teachers Association
CZ Chem-Tech ... CZ Chemie-Technik [*A publication*]
CZE........... Czech
Czech J Phys ... Czechoslovak Journal of Physics [*A publication*]
CZ-RSV..... Rous Sarcoma Virus, Carr-Zilber Strain

D

D .... Decimal
D .... [*Otto Erich*] Deutsch [*When used in identifying Schubert's compositions, refers to cataloging of his works by musicologist Deutsch*]
D .... Devonian Period [*Geology*]
D .... Dispenser
3-D .... Decapitation, Disembowelment, and Dismemberment [*Types of movies*]
DA .... Design Automation
DA .... Deutsches Archiv [*A publication*]
DA .... Direct Access
D & A .... International Defense and Aid Fund for Southern Africa
DAA .... Digital Automatic Acquisition
DAACA ..... Delegation for Afro-American and Caribbean Cultural Affairs
DABS .... Dynamic Air Blast Simulator
DAC .... Diamond Anvil Cell [*Spectrometry*]
DAC .... Downed Aircraft
DACL .... Dictionnaire d'Archeologie et de Liturgie [*A publication*]
DACT .... Dissimilar Air Combat Training
DAD .... Data Description Language [*Data processing*]
DADLE ..... [*D-Ala, D-Leu*] Enkephalin [*Biochemistry*]
DAE .... Defense Acquisition Executive
DAIM .... Dynamic Active Index Matrix
DAIR .... Dynamic Allocation Interface Routine [*Data processing*]
Dairy Sci Abstr ... Dairy Science Abstracts [*A publication*]
DAK .... Decision Acknowledge
DAL .... Data Access Line
Dal'Nevostocn Mat Sb ... Dal'Nevostocnyi Matematiceskii Sbornik [*A publication*]
DAM .... Direct Access Memory
Dance Mag ... Dance Magazine [*A publication*]
Danfoss J ... Danfoss Journal [*A publication*]
Dan Geol Unders Raekke 2 ... Danmarks Geologiske Undersoegelse. Raekke 2 [*A publication*]
Dan Geol Unders Raekke 3 ... Danmarks Geologiske Undersoegelse. Raekke 3 [*A publication*]
Dan Geol Unders Ser B ... Danmarks Geologiske Undersoegelse. Serie B [*A publication*]
Dan Kemi ... Dansk Kemi [*A publication*]
Danmarks Geol Undersoegelse ... Danmarks Geologiske Undersoegelse [*A publication*]
Dansk Audiol ... Dansk Audiologopaedi [*A publication*]
Danske Vid Selsk Mat Fys Medd ... Det Kongelige Danske Videnskabernes Selskab Matematisk-Fysiske Meddelelser [*A publication*]
Dansk Geol Foren Medd ... Dansk Geologisk Forening Meddelelser [*A publication*]
Dansk Geol Foren Meddel ... Dansk Geologisk Forening Meddelelser [*A publication*]
DAO .... Diamine Oxidase [*An enzyme*]
DAP .... Data Access Protocol
DAPA .... Drug and Alcohol Abuse Program Advisor [*Navy*]
DAPNA ...... Doklady Akademii Pedagogicheskikh Nauk RSRSR [*A publication*]
DARC .... Documentation and Automatization of Researches for Correlations [*For molecular structure*] [*Chemical physics*]

Dari Seama Sedint RPR Com Geol ... Dari de Seama ale Sedintelor. Republica Populara Romana Comitetul Geologic [*A publication*]
DARS .... Defense Acquisition Regulatory System [*DOD*]
Dartmouth Alumni Mag ... Dartmouth Alumni Magazine [*A publication*]
DARTS ...... Drug and Alcohol Rehabilitation Testing System [*Navy*]
DAS .... Dimethoxyanthracene Sulfonate [*Organic chemistry*]
DAS .... Directorate of Aerospace Studies [*Air Force*]
DASC .... Department of the Army System Coordinator
Das Chron ... Dasika Chronika [*A publication*]
DASDL ...... Data and Structure Definition Language [*Data processing*]
DAT .... Disconnect Actuating Tools [*Nuclear energy*]
DATA .... Direct Access Terminal Application [*Data processing*]
Data C .... Data Communications [*A publication*]
Data Process ... Data Processing Digest [*A publication*]
Data Process Educ ... Data Processing for Education [*A publication*]
Data Process Mag ... Data Processing Magazine [*A publication*]
Data Process Pract ... Data Processing Practitioner [*A publication*]
Data Rep ... Data Report [*A publication*]
DATC .... Development and Training Center [*Navy*]
DATC .... Direct Assistance and Training Command [*Navy*]
Dawe Dig .. Dawe Digest [*A publication*]
DBA .... Data Base Administration [*or Administrator*] [*Data processing*]
DBC .... Data Base Computer
DBD .... Data Base Description [*Data processing*]
DBDA .... Data Base Design Aid [*Data processing*]
DBDA .... Design Basis Depressurization Accident [*Nuclear energy*]
DBE .... Design Basis Earthquake [*Nuclear energy*]
DBF .... Design Basis Fault [*Nuclear energy*]
DBM .... Data Base Management [*or Manager*] [*Data processing*]
DBMS .... Data Base Management System [*Data processing*]
DBNA .... Dibutylnitrosamine [*Organic chemistry*] [*Also, DBN*]
DBNK .... Data Bank
DBO .... Dubbo [*Australia*] [*Airport symbol*]
DBoA .... Delayed Breeder or Alternative [*Nuclear energy*]
DBP .... Dichlorobenzophenone [*Organic chemistry*] [*Also, DCBP*]
DBQ .... Dubuque [*Iowa*] [*Airport symbol*]
DBT .... Design Basis Tornado [*Nuclear energy*]
DBTL .... Dibutyltin Dilaurate [*Organic chemistry*]
DBV .... Dubrovnik [*Yugoslavia*] [*Airport symbol*]
DBY .... Dalby [*Australia*] [*Airport symbol*]
DC .... Data Check
DC .... Data Communication
DC .... Data Concentrator [*Data processing*]
DC .... Design Contractor
DC .... Designs for Change [*An organization*]
DC .... Documentation Catholique [*A publication*]
DCA .... Dance Critics Association
DCA .... Distributed Communications Architecture
DCA .... Driver Control Area
DCA/MSO ... Defense Communications Agency/MILSATCOM Systems Office
DCARE ...... Driver Control Area Region Extension
DCBP .... Dichlorobenzophenone [*Organic chemistry*] [*Also, DBP*]
DCDD .... Dichlorodioxin [*Organic chemistry*]

DCE........... Data Circuit-Terminating Equipment [*Data processing*]
DCEC........ Defense Communications Engineering Center [*Army*]
DCEE .... Dichloroethyl Ether [*Organic chemistry*]
DCES .... Data Collection and Evaluation System
DCF........... Dispersion Coated Fabric [*Plastics technology*]
DCF........... Document Composition Facility [*IBM Corp.*]
DCF........... Dose Conversion Factor [*Radiation*]
D & C Ind .. Drug and Cosmetic Industry [*A publication*]
DCIPT .... Damage Control In-Port Training
DCM........... Deep Chlorophyll Maximum [*Oceanography*]
DCM .... Diagnostic Controlled MODEM [*Data processing*]
DCMS .... Deccan College Monograph Series [*A publication*]
DCNA .... Data Communication Network Architecture
DC Nurs Action ... District of Columbia Nursing Action [*A publication*]
DCP........... Data Communication Processor [*Data processing*]
DCP........... Dicalcium Phosphate [*Inorganic chemistry*]
DCP........... Dichlorophenol [*Organic chemistry*]
DCP........... Digital Computer Programing [*Data processing*]
DCPI........... Dichlorophenol-Indophenol [*Analytical reagent*] [*Also,
    DPIP*]
DCRN........ Dashpot Cup Retention Nut [*Nuclear energy*]
DCRZ .... Descend to and Cruise [*Aviation*]
DCS .... Data Control Services
DCS .... Deputy Clerk of Session [*British*]
DCS .... Digital Control Station [*Data processing*]
DCTA .... Diaminocyclohexanetetraacetic Acid [*Organic chemistry*]
    [*Also, OCTA*]
DCX........... Direct Current Experiments [*Nuclear energy*]
DD .... Data Definition
D & D .... Decontaminate and Decommission [*Nuclear energy*]
DD .... Delay Driver
D-D........... Deuterium-Deuterium Reaction [*Nuclear energy*]
DDA .... Dodecyldimethylamine [*or Dimethyldodecylamine*]
    [*Organic chemistry*]
DDC .... Digital Display Converter
DDC .... Dodge City [*Kansas*] [*Airport symbol*]
DDC .... Dopa Decarboxylase [*An enzyme*]
DDE .... Direct Data Entry [*Data processing*]
DDEL........ Dwight D. Eisenhower Library
DDH & DS ... Digital Data Handling and Display System
DDI .... Daydream Island [*Australia*] [*Airport symbol*]
DDI .... Direct Dial In
DDL .... Diode-Diode Logic [*Physics*]
DDM .... Dichlorodiphenylmethane [*Organic chemistry*]
DDMC .... Design and Drafting Management Council
DDN .... Delta Downs [*Australia*] [*Airport symbol*]
DDR........... Detector Dependent Response [*Measurement*]
DDT........... Data Description Table
DDT........... Design Data Transmittal
DDT........... Double Deflection Tube
DE .... Dextrose Equivalent [*Food technology*]
DE .... Division Entry
DEA........... Defense Exchange Agreement
DEAE .... (Diethylamino)ethanol [*Organic chemistry*]
Deafness Res & Train Cent ... Deafness Research and Training
    Center [*A publication*]
DEAS .... Data Entry Aboard Ship [*Navy*]
Death Educ ... Death Education [*A publication*]
DEB........... Downward Ejection Bomblet
DEBRA ...... Dystrophic Epidermolysis Bullosa Research Association
    of America
DEC........... Decatur [*Illinois*] [*Airport symbol*]
DECAA...... Dental Cadmos [*A publication*]
DECB .... Data Event Control Block [*Data processing*]
DECENT ... Distribution of Exact Classical Energy Transfer [*Physics*]
Dechema Monogr ... Dechema Monographien [*A publication*]
DEE........... Dixie Airways [*Nashville, TN*] [*FAA designator*]
Deep Sea Drill Proj Initial Rep ... Deep Sea Drilling Project. Initial
    Reports [*A publication*]
Deep Sea Res & Oceanogr Abstr ... Deep Sea Research and
    Oceanographic Abstracts [*A publication*]
Defektol .... Defektologija [*A publication*]
Defektosk ... Defektoskopiya [*A publication*]
Def Natl..... Defense Nationale [*A publication*]
DEG........... Diethylene Glycol [*Organic chemistry*]
DEHP .... Diethylhexyl Phthalate [*Organic chemistry*] [*Also, DOP*]
DEL........... Delhi [*India*] [*Airport symbol*]
Delaware Co Inst Sc Pr ... Delaware County Institute of Science.
    Proceedings [*A publication*]

Delft Prog Rep ... Delft Progress Report [*A publication*]
Delft Prog Rep Ser A ... Delft Progress Report. Series A. Chemistry
    and Physics. Chemical and Physical Engineering [*A
    publication*]
Delft Prog Rep Ser B ... Delft Progress Report. Series B. Electrical.
    Electronic and Information Engineering [*A
    publication*]
Delft Prog Rep Ser E ... Delft Progress Report. Series E. Geosciences
    [*A publication*]
Delft Prog Rep Ser F ... Delft Progress Report. Series F.
    Mathematical Engineering. Mathematics and
    Information Engineering [*A publication*]
Del Med J ... Delaware Medical Journal [*A publication*]
Del Nurs.... Delaware Nurse [*A publication*]
Deltion ...... Archaiologikon Deltion [*A publication*]
DEM .... Dembidollo [*Ethiopia*] [*Airport symbol*]
Demag Nachr ... Demag Nachrichten [*A publication*]
DEMAR ..... Data Element Management Accounting and Reporting
DENA .... Diethylnitrosamine [*Organic chemistry*] [*Also, DEN*]
DENEB...... Fog Dispersal Operations [*Aviation code*]
Denison Univ Sci Lab Jour ... Denison University. Scientific
    Laboratories. Journal [*A publication*]
Denison Univ Sc Lab B ... Denison University. Scientific Laboratories.
    Bulletin [*A publication*]
Dent Abstr ... Dental Abstracts [*A publication*]
Dent Assist ... Dental Assistant [*A publication*]
Dent Clin North Am ... Dental Clinics of North America [*A
    publication*]
Dent Ind .... Dental Literature Index [*A publication*]
Dent J .... Dental Journal [*A publication*]
Dent Radiogr Photogr ... Dental Radiography and Photography [*A
    publication*]
Denver Med Times ... Denver Medical Times [*A publication*]
DEP .... Design External Pressure
DEPLOC ... Daily Estimated Position Location [*Navy*]
Dept Bull US Dept Agric ... Department Bulletin. United States
    Department of Agriculture [*A publication*]
Derev Prom ... Derevoobrabatyvajuscaja Promyslennost [*A
    publication*]
Dermat Wohnschr ... Dermatologische Wochenschrift [*A publication*]
Derm Beruf Umwelt ... Dermatosen in Beruf und Umwelt [*A
    publication*]
Desarr Indoamer ... Desarrollo Indoamericano [*A publication*]
Des Eng (Toronto) ... Design Engineering (Toronto) [*A publication*]
Desert Mag ... Desert Magazine [*A publication*]
Des News ... Design News [*A publication*]
DESTA ...... Deutsche Stomatologie [*A publication*]
DET .... Detroit [*Michigan*] City Airport [*Airport symbol*]
DET .... Diethyltoluamide [*Insect repellant*] [*Organic chemistry*]
    [*Also, DETA*]
DETA .... Diethyltoluamide [*Insect repellant*] [*Organic chemistry*]
    [*Also, DET*]
Determ Org Struct Phys Methods ... Determination of Organic
    Structures by Physical Methods [*A publication*]
Detroit Rev Med and Pharm ... Detroit Review of Medicine and
    Pharmacy [*A publication*]
Deut Geog Blaetter ... Deutsche Geographische Blaetter [*A
    publication*]
Deut Oesterr Alpen-Ver Zs ... Deutscher und Oesterreichischer
    Alpen-Verein. Zeitschrift [*A publication*]
Deut Papierwirtsch ... Deutsche Papierwirtschaft [*A publication*]
Deut Rundschau ... Deutsche Rundschau [*A publication*]
Deutsche Aezte-Ztg ... Deutsche Aerztezeitung [*A publication*]
Deutsche Entom Ztschr "Iris" ... Deutsche Entomologische
    Zeitschrift "Iris" [*A publication*]
Deutsche Geol Gesell Zeitschr ... Deutsche Geologische
    Gesellschaft Zeitschrift [*A publication*]
Deutsche Keramische Gesell Ber ... Deutsche Keramische
    Gesellschaft. Berichte [*A publication*]
Deutsche Med Wochnschr ... Deutsche Medizinische. Wochenschrift
    [*A publication*]
Deutsche Med-Ztg ... Deutsche Medizinal-Zeitung [*A publication*]
Deutscher Geographentag Verh ... Deutscher Geographentag
    Verhandlungen [*A publication*]
Deutsches Arch Klin Med ... Deutsches Archiv fuer Klinische Medizin
    [*A publication*]
Deutsche Schlacht-u Viehhof-Ztg ... Deutsche Schlacht-und
    Viehhof-Zeitung [*A publication*]

New Acronyms, Initialisms, & Abbreviations

Deutsche Tieraerztl Wohnschr ... Deutsche Tieraerztliche Wochenschrift [*A publication*]

Deutsche Ztschr Chir ... Deutsche Zeitschrift fuer Chirurgie [*A publication*]

Deutsche Ztschr Nervenh ... Deutsche Zeitschrift fuer Nervenheilkunde [*A publication*]

Deutsch Gesell Geol Wiss Ber ... Deutschen Gesellschaft fuer Geologische Wissenschaften. Berichte [*A publication*]

Deutsch Kam ... Deutsche Kameramann [*A publication*]

Deutschoesterr Tieraerztl Wchnschr ... Deutschoesterreichische Tieraerztliche Wochenschrift [*A publication*]

Deutsch-Taschenb ... Deutsch-Taschenbuecher [*A publication*]

Dev Biochem ... Developments in Biochemistry [*A publication*]

Dev Comp Immunol ... Developmental and Comparative Immunology [*A publication*]

Dev Econ Geol ... Developments in Economic Geology [*A publication*]

Develop and Change ... Development and Change [*A publication*]

Develop Econ ... Developing Economies [*A publication*]

Dev Geotech Eng ... Developments in Geotechnical Engineering [*A publication*]

Dev Geotectonics ... Developments in Geotectonics [*A publication*]

Dev Growth Differ (Nagoya) ... Development, Growth and Differentiation (Nagoya) [*A publication*]

Dev Ind Sci ... Developpement Industriel et Scientifique [*A publication*]

Dev Mamm ... Development in Mammals [*A publication*]

DEVPA ...... Developmental Psychology [*A publication*]

Dev Sedimentol ... Developments in Sedimentology [*A publication*]

DEW Tech Ber ... DEW [*Deutsche Edelstahlwerke*] Technische Berichte [*A publication*]

DEZ .... Deir Ezzor [*Syria*] [*Airport symbol*]

DF .... Disk File [*Data processing*]

DF .... Duty Free [*Business and trade*]

DF .... I am connecting you to the station you request [*Communications*]

DFA .... Dance Films Association

DFB .... Dinitrofluorobenzene [*Organic chemistry*] [*Also, DNFB and FDNB*]

DFC .... Design Field Change

DFCS .... Distinguished Federal Civilian Service [*Award*]

DFFR .... Dynamic Forcing Function [*Information*] Report [*Nuclear energy*]

DFG Mitt ... DFG Mitteilungen. Deutsche Forschungsgemeinschaft [*A publication*]

DFH .... Dollars per Flight Hour

DFM .... Diesel Fuel, Marine

DFMO .... Difluoromethylornithine [*Organic chemistry*]

DFO .... Disk File Optimizer [*Data processing*]

DFP .... Demand Forecasting Program

DFWU .... Detroit Fast Food Workers' Union

DG .... Diesel Generator

DGA .... Dangriga [*Belize*] [*Airport symbol*]

DGDB .... Dipropylene Glycol Dibenzoate [*Organic chemistry*]

DGE .... Mudgee [*Australia*] [*Airport symbol*]

DGO .... Durango [*Mexico*] [*Airport symbol*]

DGT .... Dumaguete [*Philippines*] [*Airport symbol*]

DH .... Double Heterostructure [*Physics*]

DHA .... Dhahran [*Saudi Arabia*] [*Airport symbol*]

DHC .... Dehydrocholic Acid [*Organic chemistry*]

DHD .... Durham Downs [*Australia*] [*Airport symbol*]

DHEG .... Di(hydroxyethyl)glycine [*Organic chemistry*]

DHI .... Dhangarhi [*Nepal*] [*Airport symbol*]

DHN .... Dothan [*Alabama*] [*Airport symbol*]

DHPTA ...... Diaminohydroxypropanetetraacetic Acid [*Organic chemistry*] [*Also, DTA and DPTA*]

DHRS .... Decay Heat Removal System [*Nuclear energy*]

DHX .... Dump Heat Exchanger [*Nuclear energy*]

DHXCS ...... Dump Heat Exchanger Control System [*Nuclear energy*]

DI .... Dyskaryosis, Index of [*Cytopathology*]

DIA .... Documents Information Accessing

Diab Lit Ind ... Diabetes Literature Index [*A publication*]

Dial Ar .... Dialoghi di Archeologia [*A publication*]

Diamond Res ... Diamond Research [*A publication*]

Diario Of Minist Mar ... Diario Oficial del Ministerio de Marina [*A publication*]

Diatomic Research Bull ... Diatomic Research Bulletin [*A publication*]

DIB .... Dibrugarh [*India*] [*Airport symbol*]

DIBA .... Diisobutyl Adipate [*Organic chemistry*]

DIBA .... Diisobutylamine [*Organic chemistry*]

DIBHP .... Diisopropylbenzene Hydroperoxide [*Organic chemistry*]

DIBK .... Diisobutyl Ketone [*Organic chemistry*]

Dict Class Hist Nat ... Dictionnaire Classique d'Histoire Naturelle [*A publication*]

DIDA .... Diisodecyl Adipate [*Organic chemistry*]

DIDC .... Depository Institutions Deregulation Committee [*Congress*]

DIDOCS .... Device Independent Display Operator Console Support

DIDS .... Domestic Information Display System [*Data processing*]

DIE .... Diego Suarez [*Madagascar*] [*Airport symbol*]

Diecasting Met Moulding ... Diecasting and Metal Moulding [*A publication*]

Diehlektr Poluprovodn ... Diehlektriki i Poluprovodniki [*A publication*]

Diesel Gas Turb Prog Worldwide ... Diesel and Gas Turbine Progress Worldwide [*A publication*]

Dietsk Med ... Dietskaia Meditsina [*A publication*]

DIFA .... Difurfurylideneacetone [*Organic chemistry*]

DIFDEN ..... Duty in a Flying Status Not Involving Flying [*Air Force*]

Differ Equations ... Differential Equations [*A publication*]

Differ Uravn ... Differentsial'nye Uravneniya [*A publication*]

Differ Uravn Primen ... Differentsial'nye Uravneniya i ikh Primenenie [*A publication*]

Diffus Data ... Diffusion Data [*A publication*]

Diffus Defect Monogr Ser ... Diffusion and Defect Monograph Series [*A publication*]

DIFOPS ..... Duty in a Flying Status Involving Operational or Training Flights [*Air Force*]

DIFPRO ..... Duty in a Flying Status Involving Proficiency Flying [*Air Force*]

DIGISMAC ... Digital Scene Matching Area Correlator

Digit Process ... Digital Processes [*A publication*]

Dig Lit Dielec ... Digest of Literature on Dielectrics [*A publication*]

DIK .... Dickinson [*North Dakota*] [*Airport symbol*]

DIL .... Dili [*Indonesia*] [*Airport symbol*]

Dimens Health Serv ... Dimensions in Health Services [*A publication*]

Dimensions NBS ... Dimensions. National Bureau of Standards Technical News Bulletin [*A publication*]

DIMP .... Diisopropyl Methylphosphonate [*Organic chemistry*]

Din Sploshn Sredy ... Dinamika Sploshnoj Sredy [*A publication*]

DIOS .... Diisooctyl Sebacate [*Organic chemistry*]

DIP .... Design Internal Pressure [*Nuclear energy*]

DIP .... Diapaga [*Upper Volta*] [*Airport symbol*]

DIP .... Driver Improvement Program [*American Automobile Association*]

DIPA .... Diisopropanolamine [*Organic chemistry*]

DIR .... Dire Dawa [*Ethiopia*] [*Airport symbol*]

DIRC .... Defense Intelligence Relay Center

Direct Curr & Power Electron ... Direct Current and Power Electronics [*A publication*]

Direct Mkt ... Magazine of Direct Marketing [*A publication*]

DIS .... Distributed Intelligence System

DIS .... Drosophila Information Service [*Genetics*]

DISA Inf .... DISA [*Danske Industri Syndikat A/S*] Information [*A publication*]

DISAM ...... Defense Institute of Security Assistance Management

Discn Faraday Soc ... Discussions of the Faraday Society [*A publication*]

Discount M ... Discount Merchandiser [*A publication*]

DISI .... Door Insulating Systems Index

Diskret Analiz ... Diskretnyi Analiz. Sbornik Trudov [*A publication*]

DISOSS ..... Distributed Office Support System [*IBM Corp.*]

Dispos Intern ... Disposables International and Nonwoven Fabric Review [*A publication*]

Dissert Abs Internat ... Dissertation Abstracts International [*A publication*]

Dissert Abstr Int ... Dissertation Abstracts International [*A publication*]

Dissertationes Math (Rozprawy Mat) ... Dissertationes Mathematicae (Rozprawy Matematyczny) [*A publication*]

DIT .... Documentation Information Transmittal

DIY .... Diyarbakir [*Turkey*] [*Airport symbol*]

DJB .... Jambi [*Indonesia*] [*Airport symbol*]

DJC/JRI .... Detroit Jazz Center/Jazz Research Institute

DJE .... Djerba [*Tunisia*] [*Airport symbol*]

DJJ .... Jayapura [*Indonesia*] [*Airport symbol*]

DJO .... Daloa [*Ivory Coast*] [*Airport symbol*]

DKA .... Diketogulonic Acid [*Organic chemistry*]
DKI .... Dunk Island [*Australia*] [*Airport symbol*]
DKR .... Dakar [*Senegal*] [*Airport symbol*]
DL .... Dummy Load
DLA .... Douala [*Cameroon*] [*Airport symbol*]
DLC .... Dalien [*China*] [*Airport symbol*]
DLC .... Data Link Control [*Data processing*]
DLC .... Duplex Line Control
DLCF .... Data Link Control Field [*Data processing*]
DLCP .... Data Link Control Panel [*Data processing*]
DLE .... Dole [*France*] [*Airport symbol*]
DLG .... Dillingham [*Alaska*] [*Airport symbol*]
DLH .... Duluth [*Minnesota*] [*Airport symbol*]
DLMS .... Digital Land Mass Simulation
DLP .... Data Link Processor [*Data processing*]
DLR .... Data Link Receiver [*Data processing*]
DLS .... Direct Logistical Support
DLY .... Dillons Bay [*Vanuata*] [*Airport symbol*]
DM .... Dance Magazine [*A publication*]
DMAHTC... Defense Mapping Agency Hydrographic/Topographic Center [*Formerly, DMAHC, DMATC*]
DMAM .... Di(methylamyl) Maleate [*Organic chemistry*]
DMBA .... Dimethyl(butyl)amine [*Organic chemistry*]
DMBC .... Dimethylbenzylcarbinol [*Organic chemistry*]
DMBC .... Double Mark Blank Column
DMBCA ..... Dimethylbenzylcarbinol Acetate [*Organic chemistry*]
DMC .... Dull Men's Club
DMCA .... Direct Marketing Credit Association
DMCBAC .. Dimethylcetylbenzylammonium Chloride [*Antiseptic*] [*Organic chemistry*]
DMD .... Doomadgee Mission [*Australia*] [*Airport symbol*]
DME .... Dimethyl Ether [*Organic chemistry*]
DME .... Moscow [*USSR*] Domodedovo Airport [*Airport symbol*]
DMEV .... Distance Measuring Equipment-Collocated with VOR
DMH .... Department of Mental Health [*or Hygiene*]
DMMP .... Dimethyl Methylphosphonate [*Organic chemistry*]
DMO .... Sedalia [*Missouri*] [*Airport symbol*]
DMOS .... Depletion Metal-Oxide Semiconductor
DMP .... Dimercaptopropanol [*Detoxicant*] [*Organic chemistry*] [*Also, BAL: British Anti-Lewisite*]
DMPD .... Dimethylphenylenediamine [*Organic chemistry*]
DMPDT ..... Dimethylphosphorodithioate [*Organic chemistry*]
DMRP .... Dredged Material Research Program [*Waterways Experiment Station*] [*Army*]
DMS .... Dimercaptosuccinic Acid [*Organic chemistry*]
DMS .... Dimethyl Silicone [*Organic chemistry*]
DMS .... Dimethyl Sulfide [*Organic chemistry*]
DMT .... Dispersive Mechanism Test
DMTT .... Dimethyltetrahydrothiadiazinethione [*Pesticide*] [*Organic chemistry*]
DMU .... Digital Management Unit
DMU .... Dimapur [*India*] [*Airport symbol*]
DMU .... Dimethanolurea [*Organic chemistry*]
D & N .... Dekker & Nordemann [*Publisher*]
DNA .... DIMUS [*Digital Multibeam Steering*] Narrow-Band Accelerated
DNB .... Departure from Nucleate Boiling
DNB .... Dunbar [*Australia*] [*Airport symbol*]
DNBA .... Di-normal-butylamine [*Organic chemistry*]
DNBA .... Dinitrobenzoic Acid [*Organic chemistry*]
DNBR .... Departure from Nucleate Boiling Ratio
DND .... Do Not Duplicate
DND .... Dundee [*Scotland*] [*Airport symbol*]
DNM .... Delayed Neutron Monitor
DNM .... Denham [*Australia*] [*Airport symbol*]
DNNS .... Dinitronaphtholsulfonic Acid [*Organic chemistry*]
DNP .... Dang [*Nepal*] [*Airport symbol*]
DNPA .... Di-normal-propylamine [*Organic chemistry*]
DNPD .... Di(naphthyl)phenylenediamine [*Organic chemistry*]
DNQ .... Deniliquin [*Australia*] [*Airport symbol*]
DNR .... Dinard [*France*] [*Airport symbol*]
DNS .... Decentralized Data Processing Network System
DNV .... Danville [*Illinois*] [*Airport symbol*]
DOA .... Doany [*Madagascar*] [*Airport symbol*]
DOBP .... Dodecyloxyhydroxybenzophenone [*Organic chemistry*]
DOD .... Dihydroxydiphenyl [*Antioxidant*] [*Organic chemistry*]
DOD .... Dodoma [*Tanzania*] [*Airport symbol*]
DODMERB ... Department of Defense Medical Examination Review Board

DODS .... Different Orbitals for Different Spins [*Atomic physics*]
DOE .... Design of Experiments [*Conference*] [*Army*]
DOE/ET .... Department of Energy/Assistant Secretary for Energy Technology
DOF .... Dioctyl Fumarate [*Organic chemistry*]
DOG .... Dongola [*Sudan*] [*Airport symbol*]
DOH .... Doha [*Qatar*] [*Airport symbol*]
DOIP .... Dioctyl Isophthalate [*Organic chemistry*]
DOK .... Donetsk [*USSR*] [*Airport symbol*]
DOM .... Dominica [*West Indies*] [*Airport symbol*]
DOM .... Drawn over Mandrel [*Tubes*]
DONA .... Decentralized Open Network Architecture
DONO .... Dimethyloctadecanamine N-Oxide [*Organic chemistry*]
DOO .... Dorobisoro [*Papua New Guinea*] [*Airport symbol*]
DOP .... Dolpa [*Nepal*] [*Airport symbol*]
DOPMS ..... Defense Officer Personnel Management Study
DOR .... Dori [*Upper Volta*] [*Airport symbol*]
DOS .... Decision Outstanding
DOSS .... Decision-Oriented Scheduling System
DOSSU ..... Dogs on Stamps Unit
DOT .... Designating Optical Tracker
DOTG .... Di-ortho-toylguanidine [*Organic chemistry*]
DOU .... Dourados [*Brazil*] [*Airport symbol*]
DOV .... Discharged on Visit [*Psychiatry*]
DOVETT.... Double Velocity Transit Time [*Physics*]
DOX .... Dongara [*Australia*] [*Airport symbol*]
DP .... Dom Perignon [*Champagne*]
DPA .... Diphenylamine [*Organic chemistry*]
DPA .... Diphenylanthracene [*Organic chemistry*]
DPA .... Dipropylamine [*Organic chemistry*]
DPAE .... Director of Program Analysis and Evaluation
DPC .... Direct Program Control
DPC .... Dodecylpyridinium Chloride [*Organic chemistry*] [*Also, LPC*]
DPCCP ..... Defective Parts and Components Control Program
DPCSMA... Dry Process Ceramic and Steatite Manufacturers Association
DPD .... Dignitary Protective Division [*US Secret Service*]
DPE .... Demilitarization Protective Ensemble
DPE .... Development Project Engineer
DPE .... Dieppe [*France*] [*Airport symbol*]
DPE .... Diphenyltrichloroethane [*Organic chemistry*] [*AO DPT*]
DPL .... Dipolog [*Philippines*] [*Airport symbol*]
DPM .... Documents per Minute
DPNA .... Dipropylnitrosamine [*Organic chemistry*] [*Also, DPN and NDPA*]
DPO .... Devonport [*Tasmania*] [*Airport symbol*]
DPOC .... Dynamic Processor Overload Control [*Telephone technology*]
DPP .... Drip Pan Pot [*Closed-Loop Ex-Vessel Machine*] [*Nuclear energy*]
DPPC .... Diphenyl Phosphorochloridate [*or Diphenylphosphoric Acid Monochloride*] [*Organic chemistry*]
DPPG .... Defense Policy Planning Guidance
DPS .... Denpasar [*Indonesia*] [*Airport symbol*]
DPS .... Diphenyl Sulfone [*Organic chemistry*]
DPSR .... Data Processing Service Request
DPT .... Diphenyltrichloroethane [*Organic chemistry*] [*Also, DPE*]
DPTA .... Diaminopropanol Tetraacetic Acid [*Organic chemistry*] [*Also, DTA and DHPTA*]
DPTH .... Depth
DPTH .... Diphenylthiohydantoin [*Organic chemistry*]
DR .... D-Related [*Antigen*] [*Immunology*]
D-R .... Damp Rag [*Decontamination method*] [*Nuclear energy*]
DR .... Danish Reactor
DR .... Direct Reduction [*Iron ore*]
DR .... Double Reduced [*Tinplate*]
DRB .... Derby [*Australia*] [*Airport symbol*]
DRC .... Data Recording Controller [*Data processing*]
DRC .... Dutch Reformed Church
DRCTN ..... Direction
DRD .... Data Recording Device [*Data processing*]
DRD .... Dorunda Station [*Australia*] [*Airport symbol*]
D/RE .... Disassembly/Reassembly Equipment [*Nuclear energy*]
DRES .... Direct Reading Emission Spectrograph
DRET .... Direct Reentry Telemetry
DRG .... Deering [*Alaska*] [*Airport symbol*]
DRN .... Dirranbandi [*Australia*] [*Airport symbol*]
DRO .... Durango [*Colorado*] [*Airport symbol*]

DRP .... Drone Recovery Platform
DRR .... Document Release Record
DRR .... Dough Rate of Reaction [*Food science*]
DRR .... Durrie [*Australia*] [*Airport symbol*]
DRS .... Data Rate Selector
DRS .... Data Retrieval System [*Data processing*]
DRS .... Disassembly/Reassembly Station [*Nuclear energy*]
DRS .... Dresden [*East Germany*] [*Airport symbol*]
DRSG .... Division Restructuring Study Group [*TRADOC*] [*Army*]
DRT .... Del Rio [*Texas*] [*Airport symbol*]
DRW .... Darwin [*Australia*] [*Airport symbol*]
DS .... Data Scanning
DS .... Digit Select
DS .... Directionally Solidified [*Metallurgy*]
DS .... Discontinue
DSA .... Delay Study Analysis
DSA .... Digital Spectrum Analyzer
DSAMOS .. Diffusion Self-Aligned Metal-Oxide Semiconductor
DSAP .... Defense Security Assistance Program
DSB .... Device Status Byte [*Data processing*]
DSB .... Dictionary of Scientific Biography [*A publication*]
DSC .... Design Safety Criteria [*Nuclear energy*]
DSC .... Direct Satellite Communications
DSC .... Distant Station Connected [*Data processing*]
DSC .... Down's Syndrome Congress
DSD .... La Desirade [*Guadeloupe*] [*Airport symbol*]
DSDS .... Dataphone Switched Digital Service [*AT & T*]
DSE .... Data Set Extension [*Data processing*]
DSE .... Direct Support Element
DSE .... Distributed Systems Environment
DSHP .... Disodium Hydrophosphate [*Inorganic chemistry*] [*Also, DSP*]
DSK .... Dera Ismail Khan [*Pakistan*] [*Airport symbol*]
DSL .... Data Structures Language [*Data processing*]
DSL .... Drawing and Specification Listing
DSM .... Des Moines [*Iowa*] [*Airport symbol*]
DSMA .... Disodium Methyl Arsonate [*Herbicide*]
DSOPS ...... Direct Support Operations
DSP .... Desert Pacific Airlines [*Sedona, AZ*] [*FAA designator*]
DSPD .... Disalicylidenepropanediamine [*Organic chemistry*]
DSRS .... Deep Submergence Rescue System [*Navy*]
DSRT .... Desert [*Board on Geographic Names*]
DST .... Data Source Terminal
DSTE .... Defense System Terminal Equipment
DSU .... Data Service Unit
DT .... Deoxythymidine [*Organic chemistry*]
D/T .... Detection/Tracker
DTA .... Dental Therapy Assistant
DTA .... Diaminopropanoltetraacetic Acid [*Organic chemistry*] [*Also, DPTA and DHPTA*]
DTACCS ... Director/Telecommunications and Command and Control System
DTB .... Decimal to Binary [*Data processing*]

DTBHQ ...... Di-tert-butylhydroquinone [*Organic chemistry*]
DTCS .... Drone Target Control System
DTCS .... Drone Tracking and Control System
DTF .... Define the File [*Data processing*]
DTIC .... Defense Technical Information Center [*Formerly, DDC*]
DTL .... Detroit Lakes [*Minnesota*] [*Airport symbol*]
DTL .... Direct to Licensee
DTP .... Design to Price
DTR .... Document Transmittal Record
DTRF .... Data Transmittal and Routing Form
DTRS .... Development Test Requirement Specification
DTS .... Digital Tandem Switch
DTT .... Design Thermal Transient [*Nuclear energy*]
DTT .... Detroit [*Michigan*] [*Airport symbol*]
DU .... Chess Wing Ltd. [*Great Britain*] [*ICAO designator*]
DU .... Decision Unit [*Management*]
DUALEXTAC ... Dual Salvo Attack Tactic [*Navy*]
DUB .... Dublin [*City and county in Ireland*]
DUB .... Dublin [*Ireland*] [*Airport symbol*]
DUC .... Duncan [*Oklahoma*] [*Airport symbol*]
DUD .... Dunedin [*New Zealand*] [*Airport symbol*]
DUEL .... Data Update Edit Language [*Data processing*]
DUG .... Douglas [*Arizona*] [*Airport symbol*]
DUJ .... Du Bois [*Pennsylvania*] [*Airport symbol*]
DUP .... Democratic Unionist Party [*Ireland*]
DUP .... Diundecyl Phthalate [*Organic chemistry*]
DUQ .... Duncan/Quamichan Lake [*Canada*] [*Airport symbol*]
DUR .... Durban [*South Africa*] [*Airport symbol*]
DURA .... Durability
DUS .... Dockside Underway Replenishment Simulator [*Navy*]
DUS .... Dusseldorf [*West Germany*] [*Airport symbol*]
DUSD .... Deputy Under Secretary of Defense
DUT .... Dutch Harbor [*Alaska*] [*Airport symbol*]
DV .... Air Vendee [*France*] [*ICAO designator*]
DV .... Damage and Vulnerability
DV .... Demonstration and Validation
DVAB .... Defense Vocational Aptitude Battery [*Military*]
DVL .... Devils Lake [*North Dakota*] [*Airport symbol*]
DVO .... Davao [*Philippines*] [*Airport symbol*]
DVP .... Domestic Violence Project
DVV .... Downward Vertical Velocity [*Meteorology*]
DWB .... Soalala [*Madagascar*] [*Airport symbol*]
DWI .... Danish West Indies
DWS .... Development Work Statement
DWST .... Demineralized Water Storage Tank [*Nuclear energy*]
DXB .... Dubai [*United Arab Emirates*] [*Airport symbol*]
DXD .... Dixie [*Australia*] [*Airport symbol*]
DXR .... Danbury [*Connecticut*] [*Airport symbol*]
DYA .... Dysart [*Australia*] [*Airport symbol*]
DYNAMO .. Dynamic Model Continuous Time Simulation
DYU .... Dushanbe [*USSR*] [*Airport symbol*]
DZA .... Dzaoudzi [*Comoro Islands*] [*Airport symbol*]

E

E .... Error
E .... Experience
E .... Eye Disease [*Used by immigration officials*] [*Obsolete*]
EA .... Enrolled Agent [*IRS*]
EA .... Environmental Assessment
EAA .... Eagle [*Alaska*] [*Airport symbol*]
EAA .... Electric Auto Association
EAA .... Essential Amino Acids [*Nutrition*]
EAA .... Ethyl Acetoacetate [*Organic chemistry*]
EAB .... Abbse [*Yemen Arab Republic*] [*Airport symbol*]
EAB .... Exclusion Area Boundary [*Nuclear energy*]
EAC .... Echelon Above Corps [*Military*]
EACT .... Emergency Action Coordination Team [*Department of Energy*]
EAD .... Echelon Above Division [*Military*]
EAE .... Emae [*Vanuata*] [*Airport symbol*]
EAIC .... Electronic Air Inlet Controller
EAID .... Engine Air Intake Duct [*Hovercraft*]
EAL .... Equipment Air Lock [*Nuclear energy*]
EAM .... Nejran [*Saudi Arabia*] [*Airport symbol*]
EAP .... Experimental Activity Proposal [*Nuclear energy*]
EAR .... Experimental Alcoholic Rhabdomyolysis [*Medicine*]
EAR .... Kearney [*Nebraska*] [*Airport symbol*]
EAS .... Experiment Assurance System [*Nuclear energy*]
EAS .... San Sebastian [*Spain*] [*Airport symbol*]
EASI .... Estimate of Adversary Sequence Interruption [*Nuclear energy*]
EAT .... Expected Approach Time [*Aviation*]
EAT .... Wenatchee [*Washington*] [*Airport symbol*]
EATR .... Enroute Air Traffic Regulation
EAU .... Eau Claire [*Wisconsin*] [*Airport symbol*]
EB .... English Bible
EB .... Ethylbenzene [*Organic chemistry*]
EBA .... Elba Island [*Italy*] [*Airport symbol*]
EBA .... Ethyl Bromoacetate [*Organic chemistry*]
EBA .... Ethyl(butyl)amine [*Organic chemistry*]
EBB .... Entebbe/Kampala [*Uganda*] [*Airport symbol*]
EBBA .... (Ethoxybenylidene)butylaniline [*Organic chemistry*]
EBCA .... (Ethoxybenzylidene)cyanoaniline [*Organic chemistry*] [*Also, PEBAB*]
EBD .... El Obeid [*Sudan*] [*Airport symbol*]
EBG .... El Bagre [*Colombia*] [*Airport symbol*]
EBJ .... Esbjerg [*Denmark*] [*Airport symbol*]
EBONTA ... (Ethylenebis(oxyethylenenitrilo))tetraacetic Acid [*Organic chemistry*] [*Also, EGTA*]
EBRI .... Employee Benefit Research Institute
EBTF .... ECC [*Emergency Control Center*] Bypass Test Facility [*Nuclear energy*]
EBU .... St. Etienne [*France*] [*Airport symbol*]
EC .... Eddy Current [*Nuclear energy*]
EC .... Elder Craftsmen [*An organization*]
EC .... Electronic Calculator
EC .... Exchange Chromatography
EC .... Travelair GmbH & Co. KG [*West Germany*] [*ICAO designator*]
ECAP .... Energy Crisis Assistance Program [*Federal government*]
ECB .... Event Control Block [*Data processing*]
ECBA .... Eastern Coast Breweriana Association
ECC .... Error-Correcting Circuitry

ECCLUS ... Ecclesiasticus [*Old Testament book*]
ECFA .... Evangelical Council for Financial Accountability
ECFM .... Eddy Current Flow Meter [*Nuclear energy*]
ECHO .... Each Community Helps Others [*Environmental Protection Agency*]
ECI .... Eastern Carolina Aviation, Inc. [*Richlands, NC*] [*FAA designator*]
ECM .... Electronic Control Module [*Instrumentation*]
ECMO .... Electronic Countermeasures Officer [*Navy*]
ECMU .... Extended Core Memory Unit [*Data processing*]
ECN .... Ercan [*Cyprus*] [*Airport symbol*]
ECO .... English Chamber Orchestra
ECOS .... Experiment Computer Operating System
ECR .... Estimate Change Request
ECRF .... Externally Coupled Resonator Filter
ECRS .... Earthwork/Center for Rural Studies
ECS .... Environmental Control Shroud [*Nuclear energy*]
ECT .... Estimated Cloud Time [*Drinking slang*]
ECV .... Energy Conservation Vehicle [*British Leyland*]
Ed .... Department of Education [*Cabinet department*]
ED .... Electronic Development
ED .... Extraction Dialysis [*For separation of mixtures*]
EDB .... El Debba [*Sudan*] [*Airport symbol*]
EDC .... Emergency Decontamination Center [*Nuclear energy*]
EDC .... Ethyl(dimethylaminopropyl)carbodiimide [*Organic chemistry*]
EDD .... Extra Deep Drawing [*Metal industry*]
EDDA .... Ethylenediaminediacetic Acid [*Organic chemistry*]
EDDI .... Ethylenediamine Dihydriodide [*Organic chemistry*]
EDEN .... Emma Dorothy Eliza Nevitte Southworth [*American novelist, 1818-99*] [*Acronym used as pseudonym*]
EDG .... Emergency Diesel Generator
EDI .... Edinburgh [*Scotland*] [*Airport symbol*]
EDIS .... Environmental Data Information Service [*National Oceanic and Atmospheric Administration*]
EDL .... Eldoret [*Kenya*] [*Airport symbol*]
EDOS .... Extended Disk Operating System
EDR .... Edward River [*Australia*] [*Airport symbol*]
EDRAS ...... Economic Data Retrieval and Application System
EdReAn ..... Educational Research Analysts
EDS .... Ehlers-Danlos Syndrome [*Medicine*]
EDT .... Energy Dissipation Tests
EDTN .... Ethylenediaminetetraacetonitrile [*Organic chemistry*]
EDVAC ...... Electronic Discrete Variable Automatic Computer
EDW .... Edwards [*California*] [*Airport symbol*]
EEC .... End of Equilibrium Cycle [*Nuclear energy*]
EED .... Electronic Explosive Device
EEK .... Eek [*Alaska*] [*Airport symbol*]
EELS .... Electron Energy Loss Spectroscopy [*Also, ELS*]
EEN .... Keene [*New Hampshire*] [*Airport symbol*]
EES .... Energy Extension Service [*Department of Energy*]
EF .... Eglin Field [*Florida*] [*Air Force*]
EF .... Emitter Follower
EFA .... Editorial Freelancers Association
EFAPP ...... Enrico Fermi Atomic Power Plant [*Decommissioned*]
EFC .... Expeditionary Force Canteens [*Official supply organization*] [*British*] [*World War I*]
EFD .... Electrofluid Dynamic
EFD .... Engineering Flow Diagram

EFG .... Efogi [*Papua New Guinea*] [*Airport symbol*]
EFL .... Argostolion [*Greece*] [*Airport symbol*]
EFPM .... Effective Full Power Month
EFPZ .... Export Free Processing Zone
EFR .... Electro-Flux Remelting [*Metal industry*]
EG .... Ex Grege [*Among the Rest*] [*Latin*]
EGA .... Estimated Gestational Age
EGAP .... End Game Analysis Program
EGBDF ...... Every Good Boy Does Fine [*or Deserves Favor*]
       [*Mnemonic guide to notes on the treble clef*]
EGC .... Bergerac [*France*] [*Airport symbol*]
EGDF .... Embryonic Growth and Development Factor
       [*Biochemistry*]
EGL .... Equipment Guide List
EGM .... Sege [*Solomon Islands*] [*Airport symbol*]
EGN .... El Geneina [*Sudan*] [*Airport symbol*]
EGP .... Eagle Pass [*Texas*] [*Airport symbol*]
EGS .... Egilsstadir [*Iceland*] [*Airport symbol*]
EGX .... Egegik [*Alaska*] [*Airport symbol*]
EHA .... East Hampton Aire [*East Hampton, NY*] [*FAA designator*]
EHDP .... Ethanehydroxydiphosphonate [*or -diphosphonic Acid*]
       [*Organic chemistry*] [*Also, HEDP*]
EHI .... Electronic Height Indicator
EHL .... El Bolson [*Argentina*] [*Airport symbol*]
EHM .... Cape Newenham [*Alaska*] [*Airport symbol*]
EHP .... Electron-Hole Potential Method [*Physics*]
EI .... Electronic Interface
EI .... Emigrant Institute [*Sweden*]
EID .... Emitter Identification
EIN .... Eindhoven [*Netherlands*] [*Airport symbol*]
EIRT .... Executive Independent Review Team
EIS .... Effluent Inventory System [*Nuclear energy*]
EIS .... Tortola [*British Virgin Islands*] [*Airport symbol*]
EISB .... Electrical Industry Study Board
EISC .... Electronic Industry Show Corporation [*An organization*]
EITC .... Earned Income Tax Credit
EIY .... Ein Yahav [*Israel*] [*Airport symbol*]
EJA .... Barrancabermeja [*Colombia*] [*Airport symbol*]
EJC .... Owen Sound Air Services Ltd. [*Toronto, ON*] [*FAA
       designator*]
EJF .... Equal Justice Foundation
EJH .... Wedjh [*Saudi Arabia*] [*Airport symbol*]
EKA .... Eureka/Arcata [*California*] Murray Field [*Airport symbol*]
EKE .... Ekereku [*Guyana*] [*Airport symbol*]
EKG .... Effective Kilogram
EKI .... Elkhart [*Indiana*] [*Airport symbol*]
EKN .... Elkins [*West Virginia*] [*Airport symbol*]
EKO .... Elko [*Nevada*] [*Airport symbol*]
ELB .... El Banco [*Colombia*] [*Airport symbol*]
ELC .... Elcho Island [*Australia*] [*Airport symbol*]
ELD .... Economic Load Dispatching
ELD .... El Dorado [*Arkansas*] [*Airport symbol*]
ELDOR ...... Electron Electron Double Resonance [*Physics*]
ELF .... El Fasher [*Sudan*] [*Airport symbol*]
ELF .... Emergency Land Fund
ELGSS ...... Ev. Lutheran Good Samaritan Society
ELH .... North Eleuthera [*Bahamas*] [*Airport symbol*]
ELI .... Elim [*Alaska*] [*Airport symbol*]
ELITE .... Executive Level Interactive Terminal
ELJ .... El Recreo [*Colombia*] [*Airport symbol*]
ELM .... Elmira [*New York*] [*Airport symbol*]
ELSA .... Estonian Learned Society of America
EM .... Emergency Maintenance
EM .... Energy Maneuverability
EM .... Environmental Management
EM .... Evaluation Model
EMA .... Engineering Methods Analysis
EMBDD ..... Embedded [*Meteorology*]
EMC .... Emergency Message Changes
EMC .... Engineering Mockup Critical Experiment [*Nuclear
       energy*]
EMD .... Engine Monitor Display
EMGORS .. Electromyogram Sensors [*For control of artificial limbs*]
EML .... Equipment Modification List
EMOS .... Enhancement Metal-Oxide Semiconductor
EMPSKD ... Employment Schedule
EMQ .... Ethoxyquin [*Antioxidant*] [*Organic chemistry*]
EMR .... Executive Management Responsibility

EMRA .... Emergency Medicine Residents' Association
EMREL ...... Emission Release
EMS .... Earthquake Monitoring System
EMS .... Emergency Signal
EMSIB ...... Eastern Mediterranean Special Service Intelligence
       Bureau [*British*] [*World War I*]
EMTEDS ... Electromagnetic Test Environment Data System
EMW .... Electromagnetic Warfare
EN .... Enforcement Notification
ENCORE ... Encouragement, Normalcy, Counselling, Opportunity,
       Reaching Out, Energies Renewed [*for mastectomy
       patients*]
ENO .... English National Opera
ENRAT ...... En Route, Arrival at_______________ [*Military*]
ENSI .... Equivalent Noise Sideband Input
ENSYN ...... Electromagnetic Environment Synthesizer
EOA .... Exercise Operating Area
EOC .... End of Cycle
EOC .... Extended Overhaul Cycle
EOCC .... Engineering Operational Casualty Control
EOD .... Explosive Ordnance Detachment [*Army*]
EODN .... Explosive Ordnance Disposal, Nuclear
EOEC .... End of Equilibrium Cycle [*Nuclear energy*]
EOG .... Electroolfactogram
EOM .... End of Medium [*Data processing*]
EOP .... End of Push [*Spectroscopy*]
EOPS .... Equal Opportunity Program Specialist [*Navy*]
EOQI .... Equal Opportunity Quality Indicator [*Navy*]
EO/RR ...... Equal Opportunity/Race Relations [*Navy*]
EOS .... Eugene O'Neill Society
EOT .... End of Text [*Data processing*]
EOW .... Every Other Week
EP .... Economic Planning
EP .... Electrostatic Precipitator [*Also, ESP*]
EP .... Emergency Preparedness
EP .... Emulation Program
EP .... Entry Point
EPAD .... Enlisted Personnel Assignment Document [*Navy*]
EPB .... Ethylpyridinium Bromide [*Organic chemistry*]
EPC .... Ethyl Phenylcarbamate [*Plant regulator*] [*Organic
       chemistry*]
EPH .... Ephesians [*New Testament book*]
EPI .... Environmental Policy Institute
EPL .... Environmental Protection Limit
EPLF .... Eritrean People's Liberation Front
EPM .... Environmental Project Manager
EPMA .... Electron Probe Microanalysis [*Also, EPM*]
EPMAC .... Enlisted Personnel Management Center [*Navy*]
EPPC .... Ethics and Public Policy Center
EPR .... Elimination of Purchase Requirement [*Department of
       Agriculture*]
EPROM ..... Erasable Programable Read-Only Memory [*Data
       processing*]
EPRTCS .... Emergency Power Ride-Through Capability System
       [*Nuclear energy*]
EPS .... Event Processing System
EPS .... Expandable Polystyrene [*Plastics technology*]
EPS .... External Page Storage
EQ .... Engineering Quality
EQ .... Equipment
ER .... East River [*New York*]
ER .... Environmental Report
ER .... Error Recovery
ERA .... Equal Rights Advocates [*An organization*]
ERA .... Evoked Response Audiometry
ERADCOM/ASL ... Electronics Research and Development
       Command Atmospheric Sciences Laboratory [*Army*]
ERAM .... Extended Range Antitank Mine
ERC .... Emergency Relocation Center
ERC .... Engineering Research Council
ERCF .... Eglin RADAR Control Facility [*Air Force*]
ERCMIS .... Environmental Requirements/Capabilities Management
       Information System
EREP .... Environmental Recording, Editing, and Printing Program
ERH .... ERA Helicopter, Inc. [*Lake Charles, LA*] [*FAA designator*]
ERI .... Ear Research Institute
ERI .... Energy Research Institute
ERM .... Electrochemical Relaxation Methods
ERMA .... Extended Red Multialkali [*Cathode*]

ERP .... Elevated Release Point [*Nuclear energy*]
ERPC .... Eglin Refugee Processing Center [*Air Force*]
ERR .... Errata
ERT .... Environmental Research and Technology
ERW .... Enhanced-Radiation Weapon
ES .... Ejection Sound [*Cardiology*]
ES .... Emulsifying Salts [*Food technology*]
ESAS .... Engineered Safeguards Actuation System [*Nuclear energy*]
ESCA .... Exposition Service Contractors Association
ESCA .... Extended Source Calibration Area [*Nuclear energy*]
ESCAR ...... Experimental Superconducting Accelerating Ring [*Atomic physics*]
ESCWS ..... Essential Services Cooling Water Systems [*Nuclear energy*]
ESD .... Electrostatic Discharge
ESD .... Extension Shaft Disconnect [*Nuclear energy*]
ESDIAD ..... Electron-Stimulated Desorption Ion Angular Distribution [*For study of surfaces*]
ESF .... Engineered Safety Feature [*Nuclear energy*]
ESFAS ...... Engineered Safety Features Actuation System [*Nuclear energy*]
ESM .... Electrical Stimulation of the Midbrain
ESMC .... Eastern Space and Missile Center [*Air Force*]
ESO .... Emergency Support Organization
ESP .... Engineering Service Project
ESPOL ...... Executive System Problem-Oriented Language [*Data processing*]
ESR .... Early Site Review [*Nuclear energy*]
ESR .... Economic Subregion [*Bureau of Census*]
ESRP .... Environmental Standard Review Plan
ESRR .... Early Site Review Report [*Nuclear energy*]
ES & S ...... Engineering Services and Safety
ESS .... Explosive Safety Survey
ESSA .... Endangered Species Scientific Authority [*US Fish and Wildlife Service*]
ESSP .... Earliest Scram Set Point [*Nuclear energy*]
ESV .... Error Statistics by Volume
ESVR .... Examination Status Verification Report
ESW .... Error Status Word [*Data processing*]
ET .... Engineering Technology

ETAA .... Eelam Tamils Association of America
ETE .... Electromagnetic Test Environment
ETFIR .... Emergency Task Force for Indochinese Refugees
ETI .... Effectiveness Training, Incorporated
ETL .... Ending Tape Label [*Data processing*]
ETM .... Emery Testing Machine [*Nineteenth-century hydraulic testing machine*]
ETOS .... Extended Tape Operating System
ETP .... Engineering Thermoplastic [*Plastics technology*]
ETP .... Extended Term Plan
ETQAP ...... Education and Training in Quality Assurance Practices [*American Society for Quality Control*]
ETR .... Engine Transaction Report
ETS .... Environmental Technical Specifications
ETV .... Electric Test Vehicle [*Department of Energy*]
EUA .... Exchange Users Association
EUCC .... Employers' Unemployment Compensation Council
EUDAC ..... European Defense Analysis Center
EURIPA ..... European Information Providers Association
EVFM .... Ex-Vessel Flux Monitor [*Nuclear energy*]
EVHM .... Ex-Vessel Handling Machine [*Later, CLEM*] [*Nuclear energy*]
EVTM .... Ex-Vessel Transfer Machine [*Nuclear energy*]
EWA .... End Warning Area [*Data processing*]
EWIRC ...... Electronic Warfare Integrated Reprograming Concept
EWRS .... European Weed Research Society [*Formerly, EWRC*]
EWS .... Electronic Warfare System
EWSLA ..... East-West Sign Language Association
EX .... Exodus [*Old Testament book*]
EXCLV ...... Exclusive
EXECX ...... Executrix
EXON .... Exonia [*Exeter*] [*British*]
EXPOSE.... Ex-Partners of Servicemen (Women) for Equality [*An organization*]
EXTAC ...... Experimental Tactic
EXTORP.... Exercise Torpedo
EXTRN ...... External Reference
EXTSV ...... Extensive
EXWEP..... Exercise Weapon
EZ............. Ezra [*Old Testament book*]

F

F .... Fertility Factor [*Genetics*]
3 F's .... Fixity of Tenure, Fair Rents, and Free Sale [*Phrase used in Parliamentary discussions of Irish affairs, 1880-1882; opposition translated the initials as Fraud, Force, and Folly*]
F/A .... Fuel Assembly
FAA-AAF .. Federal Aviation Administration Airway Facilities Service
FAA-AAP .. Federal Aviation Administration Office of Airports Programs
FAA-AEE .. Federal Aviation Administration Office of Environment and Energy
FAA-AEM ... Federal Aviation Administration Office of Systems Engineering Management
FAA-AEQ ... Federal Aviation Administration Office of Environmental Quality
FAA-AF ..... Federal Aviation Administration Airway Facilities Service
FAA-AFS .. Federal Aviation Administration Flight Standards Service
FAA-AP ..... Federal Aviation Administration Office of Airports Programs
FAA-ARD ... Federal Aviation Administration Systems Research and Development Service
FAA/EE ..... Federal Aviation Administration Office of Environment and Energy
FAA-MS .... Federal Aviation Administration Office of Management Systems
FAA-NA .... Federal Aviation Administration National Aviation Facilities Experimental Center
FAA-NS ..... Federal Aviation Administration National Airspace System Program Office
FAAT .... First Article Acceptance Test
FAB .... Bradley Air Service [*Carp, ON*] [*FAA designator*]
FAB .... Fixed Action Button
FAC .... Fuel Adjustment Clause
FACAT ..... First Article Capability Assessment Test
FACE .... Federal Advertising Committee on Ethics
FACNHA ... Foundation of American College of Nursing Home Administrators
FACOSH ... Federal Advisory Committee on Occupational Safety and Health
FACS .... Flexible Accounting Control System
FACS .... Foundation for American Communications
FACTS ...... FLIR [*Forward-Looking Infrared RADAR*] Augmented Cobra TOW [*Tube-Launched, Optically-Tracked, Wire-Guided Weapon*] Sight
FAE .... Foundation for Accounting Education
FAF .... French-American Foundation
FAFR .... Fatal Accident Frequency Rate
FAG .... Forward Air Guide
FAHR .... Formosan Association for Human Rights
FAI .... Fail As-Is [*Nuclear energy*]
FAI .... Falcon Airways, Incorporated [*Addison, TX*] [*FAA designator*]
FAI .... Federal Acquisitions Institute [*Formerly, FPI*]
FAMS .... Forecasting and Modeling System
FANE .... Federation d'Action Nationale et Europeenne [*Federation for National and European Action*] [*Neo-Nazi organization*]
FANI .... Food, Agriculture, and Nutrition Inventory [*Federal government*]

FAP .... Fast Action Procedures
FAP .... (Furfurylamino)purine [*Plant hormone*] [*Organic chemistry*]
FAPA .... F-15 Adapted Place Atlas Program
FAR .... Foreign Affairs Research Documentation Center [*Department of State*]
FASD .... Flameless Alkali Sensitized Detector [*Instrumentation*]
FAST .... Facility for Analyzing Surface Texture [*National Bureau of Standards*]
FAST .... Fans Against the Strike
FAST .... Fast Acquisition Search and Track
FAST .... Fuel Assembly Stability Test
FASTAC .... Flame/Furnace Autosampling Technique with Automatic Calibration [*Spectroscopy*]
FASTEL .... Fast Economic Language [*Data processing*]
FAT .... Formula Assembler Translator [*Data processing*]
FAVC .... Flight Attendant Volunteer Corps
FBFS .... Fuel Building Filter System [*Nuclear energy*]
FBHL .... Force Beachhead Line [*Navy*]
FBR .... Feedback Report
FBSE .... Fellow of the Botanical Society of Edinburgh
FC .... Fail Closed [*Nuclear energy*]
FC .... File Conversion [*Data processing*]
FC .... Font Change
FC .... Fuel Cycle
FCA .... Fluorocytosine Arabinoside [*Antitumor compound*] [*Also, ara-FC*]
FCA .... Friendly Contacts Associates [*An organization*]
FCAP .... Fluor Chrome Arsenate Phenol [*Wood preservative*]
FCAP .... Foolscap
FCAS .... Frequency Control Analysis Subsystem
FCB .... File Control Block [*Data processing*]
FCD .... Fine Control Damper [*Nuclear energy*]
FCDA .... First Cavalry Division Association
FCDU .... Foreign Currency Deposit Units
FCES .... Flight Control Electronic Set
FCHGD ...... Feminist Center for Human Growth and Development
FCI .... Fuel Coolant Interaction [*Nuclear energy*]
FCL .... Feedback Control Loop [*Data processing*]
FCM .... Fellowship of Christian Magicians
FCOJ .... Frozen Concentrated Orange Juice
FCP .... File Control Processor [*Data processing*]
FCPRC ...... Federal Cultural Policy Review Committee [*Canada*]
FCPS .... Fellow of the Cambridge Philological Society [*British*]
FCREF ...... Free Congress Research and Education Foundation
FCT .... Fragment Connection Table [*Chemistry*]
FCTC .... Fleet Combat Training Center [*Navy*]
FCTT .... Fuel Cladding Transient Tester [*Nuclear energy*]
FD .... Floppy Disk [*Data processing*]
FDA .... Final Design Approval
FDC .... Functional Design Criteria
FDEC .... Forum for Death Education and Counseling
FDI .... Failure Detection and Isolation
FDM .... Freedom Airlines, Inc. [*Binghamton, NY*] [*FAA designator*]
FDNC .... Frequency Dependent Negative Conductance [*Physics*]
FDNR .... Frequency Dependent Negative Resistance [*Physics*]
FDR .... Functional Design Requirements
FDTE .... Final Development Test and Evaluation

FE .... Fecal Energy [*Nutrition*]
FEBA .... Federal Energy Bar Association
FECB .... File Extended Control Block [*Data processing*]
FED .... Foundation for Ethnic Dance
FED .... Fusion Engineering Device [*Nuclear energy*]
FEFPL .... Fuel Element Failure Propagation Loop [*Nuclear energy*]
FEICC .... Foundation for the Establishment of an International Criminal Court
FEMR .... Fleet Electromagnetic Radiation [*Team*] [*Navy*]
FEO .... Facility Emergency Organization [*Nuclear energy*]
FEORP ..... Federal Equal Opportunity Recruitment Program
FERD .... Fuel Element Rupture Detection [*Nuclear energy*]
FETS/SEA ... Federal Emission Test Sequence and Selective Enforcement Audit [*General Motors*]
FEWC .... Force Electronic Warfare Coordinator
FFBI .... Foundation for Blood Irradiation
FFBT .... Forward Fuel Ballast Tank
FFF .... Foundation for a Future
FFF .... Free Flight Facility
FFFFM ..... Full-Face Fire-Fighters' Mask
FFHR .... Fusion-Fission Hybrid Reactor
FFI .... Full Field Investigation
FFN .... Fleet Flash Net [*Navy*]
FFPLE .... Firm Fixed Price Letter [*Government contracting*]
FFR .... RADAR Picket Frigate [*Navy symbol*]
FG .... File Gap [*Data processing*]
FG .... Fission Gas
FG .... Frame Ground [*Data processing*]
FGLS .... Force Generation Levels [*Military*]
FGM .... Fission Gas Monitor
FHD .... Fixed-Head Disk [*Data processing*]
FH & RM .... Fuel Handling and Radioactive Maintenance
FHS .... Fellow of the Horticultural Society [*British*]
FHSR .... Final Hazards Summary Report [*Nuclear energy*]
FI .... Fail in Place [*Nuclear energy*]
FI .... Formaldehyde Institute
FI .... Icelandair [*Iceland*] [*ICAO designator*]
FIA .... Flow Injection Analyzer [*Chemical analyses*]
FIA .... Fluorescent Immunoassay [*Analytical biochemistry*]
FICE .... Federation Internationale des Choeurs d'Enfants [*International Federation of Children's Choirs*]
FID .... Free into Container Depot [*Business and trade*]
FIFP .... Filed IFR [*Instrument Flight Rules*] Flight Plan [*Aviation*]
FIGS .... Figures Shift [*Teleprinters*]
FIM .... Field Inspection Manual
FIMPACS ... Fashion Integrated Merchandising Planning and Control System
FIMS .... Facility Information Management System
FIOT .... Free In and Out and Trimmed [*Business and trade*]
FIP .... Field Inspection Procedure
FIR .... Finite Impulse Response
FIRA .... Furniture Industry Research Association
FIRAV .... Arrival Report Will Be Filed With [*Aviation*]
FIRST .... Futures Information Retrieval System [*Congressional Research Service*]
FIS .... Force Information Service [*Military*]
FITS .... Functional Individual Training System [*Navy*]
FITWING ... Fighter Wing [*Navy*]
FLA .... Air Florida [*Miami, FL*] [*FAA designator*]
FLAAR ...... Foundation for Latin American Anthropological Research
FLAC .... Florida Lime and Avocado Administrative Committee
FLECHT .... Full Length Emergency Cooling Heat Transfer [*Nuclear energy*]
FLEX .... Free Lance Exchange
FLF .... Fixed-Length Field [*Data processing*]
FLIPS .... Future Language Information Processing System
FLLS .... Waterfalls [*Board on Geographic Names*]
FLOC .... Farm Labor Organizing Committee
F/LP .... Freight/Luggage Panniers [*Hovercraft*]
FLPP/CWS ... Family Life and Population Program/Church World Service
FLRT .... Federal Librarians Round Table [*American Library Association*]
FLSS .... Flight Level Sensing Subsystems
FLTWO ..... Flight Watch Outlet
FM .... File Maintenance [*Data processing*]
FM .... Functional Manager
FMA .... Fluorescein Mercury Acetate [*Analytical chemistry*]
FMAG .... Fleet Maintenance Assistance Group [*Navy*]

FMCA .... [*The*] Forensic Medicine Consultant-Advisor [*Program*]
FMD .... Ferry Movement Directive [*Navy*]
FMIA .... Federal Meat Inspection Act
FMIRA ...... Fighter Multifunctional Inertial Reference Assembly
FMS .... Final Multiple Score
FMS .... Flux Monitoring System [*Nuclear energy*]
FN .... Fruitarian Network [*An organization*]
FNA .... Functional Name Addresses
FNI .... Foreign National Indirect
FNM .... Financial Network Manager
FO .... Fail Open [*Nuclear energy*]
FO .... Friends Outside [*An organization*]
FOA .... Forced Oil and Air
FOAM .... Fomenting Offensive Aerial Mine
FOB .... Full of Brooklyns [*Coined by baseball broadcaster Red Barber, initialism refers to bases loaded with Brooklyn Dodgers*] [*Obsolete*]
FOEB .... Fuel Oil Equivalent Barrel
FOFC .... Friends of Free China
FOH .... Friends of Haiti
FOL .... Facility Operating License [*Nuclear energy*]
FOL USA ... Friends of Libraries USA
FONCON .... Telephone Conversation
FOQCV ...... Fuel Oil Quick Closing Valve
FORDEX .... Formula Index [*Molecular formula indexing*]
FORECON ... Force Reconnaissance
FORECON ... Forward Reconnaissance
FORTE ...... File Organization Technique
FOS .... Fall of Shot
FOSS .... Family of Systems Studies [*Military*]
FOTA .... Fuels Open Test Assembly [*Nuclear energy*]
FOW .... Family of Weapons
FOXY .... Fraction-Optimizing X-Y Collector [*Spectroscopy*]
FP .... Fellowship in Prayer [*An organization*]
FP .... File Processor [*Data processing*]
FP .... Floating Point [*Data processing*]
FP .... Fluoropolymers [*Organic chemistry*]
FPCSTL .... Fission Product Control Screening Test Loop [*Nuclear energy*]
FPD .... Full Power Days [*Nuclear energy*]
FPDD .... Final Project Design Description
FPI .... Federal Procurement Institute [*Later, FAI*]
FPJPA .... Fully Proceduralized Job Performance Aid
FPL .... Forced-Choice Preferential Looking
FPM .... File Protect Memory [*Data processing*]
FPP .... Force Planning Package [*Military*]
FPS .... Financial Planning System [*IBM Corp.*]
FPSL .... Fission Product Screening Loop
FQS .... Flight Qualified System
FRAMATOME ... Societe Franco-Americaine de Constructions Atomiques
FRAP .... Fuel Rod Analysis Program [*Nuclear energy*]
FRAP-S ..... Fuel Rod Analysis Program - Steady-State [*Nuclear energy*]
FRAP-T ..... Fuel Rod Analysis Program - Transient [*Nuclear energy*]
FRCI .... Fibrous Refractory Composite Insulation
FRE .... French
FREE .... Feminist Resources on Energy and Ecology [*An organization*]
FREE .... Foundation for Rational Economics and Education
FREIR .... Federal Research on Biological and Health Effects of Ionizing Radiations
FRHistSoc ... Fellow of the Royal Historical Society [*British*]
FRP .... Fuel Reprocessing Plant [*Nuclear energy*]
FRR .... Functional Recovery Routine [*Data processing*]
FRRIO .... Fleet Replacement RADAR Intercept Officer [*Navy*]
FRS .... Frisian
FRSL .... Fellow of the Royal Society, London [*British*]
FRSSA ...... Fellow of the Royal Scottish Society of Arts
FRTEF .... Fast Reactor Thermal Engineering Facility [*Nuclear energy*]
FRWF .... Forecast Wind Factor [*Meteorology*]
F/S .... Film and Sheet [*Plastics technology*]
FS .... Frequency Shift
FSA .... Fellow of the Society of Arts [*British*]
FSAE .... Fellow of the Society of Antiquaries, Edinburgh
FSC .... Food Safety Council
FSC .... Full Systems Capable
FSCV .... Fire Support Combat Vehicle

FSED......... Full-Scale Engineering Development
FSGO .... Floating Spherical Gaussian Orbitals [*Atomic physics*]
FSI............. Family Suffering Index [*Economic measurement based on unemployment rate, plus costs of food, fuel, and housing*]
FSO .... Flight Safety Officer
FSPCT ...... Foundation for the Study of Presidential and Congressional Terms
FS & R .... Filling, Storage, and Remelt System [*Nuclear energy*]
FSR .... First Surrey Rifles [*Military unit*] [*British*]
FSRI .... Foreign Service Research Institute
FSS .... Floor Service Stations
FSSG .... Force Service Support Group [*Military*]
FSTK/SUP ... Friendly Strike or Support [*Military*]
FSV .... Fort St. Vrain [*Nuclear plant*]
FT.............. Flexible Trunk [*Hovercraft*]
FT............. Foundation of Thanatology
FTA .... Field Technical Authority
FTA .... Fur Takers of America [*An organization*]
FTD .... Field Training Detachment [*Program*] [*Air Force*]
FTDS......... Formal Training Data System
FTE .... FFTF [*Fast Flux Test Facility*] Test Engineering [*Nuclear energy*]
FT-FAM..... Fourier Transform-Faradic Admittance Measurements [*Spectrometry*]
FTL............ Full Term License [*For nuclear power plant*]
FTMS .... Federal Test Method Standards

FTO .... Field Test Office
FTP .... Falling to Pieces [*Slang*]
FTP .... Federal Test Procedure
FTP .... FFTF [*Fast Flux Test Facility*] Test Procedure [*Nuclear energy*]
FTP .... Fixed Term Plan
FTP .... Fuel Transfer Port
FTR .... Federal Travel Regulations
FTRC......... Federal Telecommunications Records Center
FTRIA........ Flow and Temperature Removable Instrument Assembly [*Nuclear energy*]
FTS .... Foreign Trade Statistics [*Bureau of Census*]
FTS .... Frequency Time Schedule
FTTS .... Flow-Through Tube Sampler [*Nuclear energy*]
FTW .... Fighter Tactical Wing
FUN .... Fractional and Unknown Nuclear [*Material in meteorites*]
FV.............. Floor Valve
FVA .... Cardinal/Air Virginia [*Lynchburg, VA*] [*FAA designator*]
FVA .... Fighting Vehicle Armament
FVA .... Floor Valve Adapter
FVS .... Fighting Vehicle Systems
FW............. Financial Weekly [*A publication*]
FWCC .... Friends of the World Council of Churches
FWG .... Feminist Writers' Guild
FWPCA ..... Federal Water Pollution Control Act [*1965*]
FWS/OBS ... Fish and Wildlife Service/Office of Biological Services [*Department of the Interior*]

G

G .... Gingival [*Dentistry*]
G .... Globulin
G .... Glucinum [*Old name for chemical element beryllium*] [*Also, Gl*]
G .... Goat [*Veterinary medicine*]
G .... Gold Inlay [*Dentistry*]
G .... Gonidial [*With reference to colonies of bacteria*]
G .... Greek
G .... [*Sir George*] Grove [*When used in identifying Beethoven's compositions, refers to cataloging of his works by musicologist Grove*]
GA .... Gingivoaxial [*Dentistry*]
GA .... Grapple Adapter [*Nuclear energy*]
GA .... Guessed Average
GAA .... Girls Athletic Association [*Local school affiliates of National Girls Athletic Association*] [*Defunct*]
GACI .... Geographic Area Code Index [*Bureau of Census*]
GACIAC .... Tactical Weapon Guidance and Control Information and Analysis Center [*DOD*]
GAD .... Gadsden [*Alabama*] [*Airport symbol*]
GAE........... Gallic Acid Equivalent [*Wine analysis*]
GAH .... Gayndah [*Australia*] [*Airport symbol*]
GAHF .... Grapple Adapter Handling Fixture [*Nuclear energy*]
GAJ .... Yamagata [*Japan*] [*Airport symbol*]
GAL .... Galena [*Alaska*] [*Airport symbol*]
GALA .... Graphic Arts Literature Abstracts [*A publication*]
GALV .... Galveston [*Texas*]
GAM.......... Gambell [*Alaska*] [*Airport symbol*]
GAM.......... Graphics Access Method
GAMA .... Graphics-Assisted Management Application
GANG........ Ganglion [*Medicine*]
GAO .... Guantanamo [*Cuba*] [*Airport symbol*]
GAO/CED ... General Accounting Office/Community and Economic Development Division
GAO/FGMSD ... General Accounting Office/Financial and General Management Studies Division
GAO/FPCD ... General Accounting Office/Federal Personnel and Compensation Division
GAO/LCD ... General Accounting Office/Logistics and Communications Division
GAO/PSAD ... General Accounting Office/Procurement and Systems Acquisition Division
GAP........... Gusap [*Papua New Guinea*] [*Airport symbol*]
GAPSAT ... Gap Filler Satellite
GAQ .... Gao [*Mali*] [*Airport symbol*]
GAR........... Garaina [*Papua New Guinea*] [*Airport symbol*]
GAR........... Growth Analysis and Review
GAS .... Glass Art Society
GAS .... Gun Aiming Sensor
GASP .... General Activity Simulation Program [*Data processing*]
GASP .... Graphic Applications Subroutine Package [*Data processing*]
GASTROC ... Gastrocnemius [*Muscle*] [*Anatomy*]
GAU .... Gauhati [*India*] [*Airport symbol*]
GAU .... Gun Automatic
GAUGE ..... General Automation Users Group Exchange
GAW.......... Gangaw [*Burma*] [*Airport symbol*]
GAX........... Gamba [*Gabon*] [*Airport symbol*]
GB .... Goofball [*Barbiturate pill*]

GBD .... Great Bend [*Kansas*] [*Airport symbol*]
GBE........... Gaborone [*Botswana*] [*Airport symbol*]
GBG .... Galesburg [*Illinois*] [*Airport symbol*]
GBJ .... Marie Galante [*French Antilles*] [*Airport symbol*]
GBK .... Gbangbatok [*Sierra Leone*] [*Airport symbol*]
GBL........... Goulburn Island [*Australia*] [*Airport symbol*]
GBS........... Ground Beacon System
GBV........... Gibb River [*Australia*] [*Airport symbol*]
GBZ........... Great Barrier Island [*Australia*] [*Airport symbol*]
GC .... Galvanized Corrugated [*Metal industry*]
GC .... Graham Center [*An organization*]
GC .... Grand Conductor
GC .... Guanine, Cytosine [*Type*] [*Biochemistry*]
GCA .... Guacamayas [*Colombia*] [*Airport symbol*]
GCB .... German Convention Bureau
GCC .... Gillette [*Wyoming*] [*Airport symbol*]
GCCG ...... German Colonies Collectors Group
GCI .... Guernsey [*Channel Islands*] [*Airport symbol*]
GCK .... Garden City [*Kansas*] [*Airport symbol*]
GCKP .... Grand Commander of the Knights of Saint Patrick
GCL........... Gas-Cooled Loop [*Nuclear energy*]
GCM .... Generator Coordinate Method [*Physics*]
GCM .... Grand Cayman [*West Indies*] [*Airport symbol*]
GCMAPA .. Gay Caucus of Members of the American Psychiatric Association
GCN .... Grand Canyon [*Arizona*] [*Airport symbol*]
GCR .... Group Coded Recording
GCRE .... Gas-Cooled Reactor Experiment
GCS .... Gifted Child Society
GDC .... General Design Criteria
GDG .... Generation Data Group [*Data processing*]
GDL........... Guadalajara [*Mexico*] [*Airport symbol*]
GDMS ...... Generalized Data Management System
GDN .... Gdansk [*Poland*] [*Airport symbol*]
GDO .... Guasdualito [*Venezuela*] [*Airport symbol*]
GDQ .... Gondar [*Ethiopia*] [*Airport symbol*]
GDT .... Grand Turk [*British West Indies*] [*Airport symbol*]
GDV .... Glendive [*Montana*] [*Airport symbol*]
GE .... Gnome Engine [*Hovercraft*]
GE .... Grand Encampment
GEA........... Noumea [*New Caledonia*] Magenta Airport [*Airport symbol*]
GEC .... Ground Environment Complex
GEF .... Gonadotrophin Enhancing Factor [*Endocrinology*]
GEG .... Spokane [*Washington*] [*Airport symbol*]
GEL .... Santo Angelo [*Brazil*] [*Airport symbol*]
GEMCOS .. Generalized Message Control System
GEMMSS ... Ground Emplaced Mine Scattering System
GEN........... Genealogy
GEN........... Oslo [*Norway*] Ardermoen Airport [*Airport symbol*]
GENET ...... Genetics
GEO .... Georgetown [*Guyana*] [*Airport symbol*]
GEODSS ... Ground-Based Electro-Optical Deep Space Surveillance [*Satellite-tracking network*]
GEOFILE ... Geographic File [*DOD*]
GEOGRAPHY ... George Emerson's Old Grandmother Rode a Pig Home Yesterday [*Mnemonic guide for spelling "geography"*]
GEORGE ... General Organizational Environment

GER .... Nueva Gerona [*Cuba*] [*Airport symbol*]
GERONTOL ... Gerontology
GES .... General Santos [*Philippines*] [*Airport symbol*]
GET .... Geraldton [*Australia*] [*Airport symbol*]
GEV .... Gallivare [*Sweden*] [*Airport symbol*]
GF .... Glass Factor [*Tissue culture*]
GFA .... Glial Fibrillary Acidic Protein [*Biochemistry*]
GFA .... Guitar Foundation of America
GFE & M .... Government-Furnished Equipment and Material
GFF .... Griffith [*Australia*] [*Airport symbol*]
GFK .... Grand Forks [*North Dakota*] [*Airport symbol*]
GFN .... Grafton [*Australia*] [*Airport symbol*]
GFO .... Bartica [*Guyana*] [*Airport symbol*]
GFP .... General Forecasting Program
GFY .... Grootfontein [*South-West Africa*] [*Airport symbol*]
GG .... Glycylglycine [*Organic chemistry*]
GGD .... Gregory Downs [*Australia*] [*Airport symbol*]
GGG .... Longview [*Texas*] [*Airport symbol*]
GGN .... Gagnoa [*Ivory Coast*] [*Airport symbol*]
GGO .... Guiglo [*Ivory Coast*] [*Airport symbol*]
GGS .... Gobernador Gregores [*Argentina*] [*Airport symbol*]
GGT .... George Town [*Bahamas*] [*Airport symbol*]
GGW .... Glasgow [*Montana*] [*Airport symbol*]
GHB .... Governors Harbour [*Bahamas*] [*Airport symbol*]
GHC .... Great Harbour Cay [*Bahamas*] [*Airport symbol*]
GHCI .... Guanidine Hydrochloride [*Organic chemistry*]
GHT .... Ghat [*Libya*] [*Airport symbol*]
GHU .... Gualeguaychu [*Argentina*] [*Airport symbol*]
GI .... Gold Institute
GI .... Growth-Inhibiting
GIB .... Gibraltar [*Gibraltar*] [*Airport symbol*]
GICC .... Government-Industry Coordinating Committee
GIE .... Glycerinisopropylidene Ether [*Organic chemistry*]
GIFT .... Gas-Insulated Flow Tube
GIG .... Rio De Janeiro [*Brazil*] [*Airport symbol*]
GIPS .... Government Imprinted Penalty Stationery Society
GIS .... Gisborne [*New Zealand*] [*Airport symbol*]
GIZ .... Gizan [*Saudi Arabia*] [*Airport symbol*]
GJR .... Gjogur [*Iceland*] [*Airport symbol*]
GJT .... Grand Junction [*Colorado*] [*Airport symbol*]
GKA .... Goroka [*Papua New Guinea*] [*Airport symbol*]
GKL .... Great Keppel Island [*Australia*] [*Airport symbol*]
GI .... Galvanized [*Metallurgy*]
GI .... Glucinum [*Old name for chemical element beryllium*] [*Also, G*]
G/L .... Grams per Liter
GL .... Greatest Length
GLA .... Gingivolinguoaxial [*Dentistry*]
GLA .... Glasgow [*Scotland*] [*Airport symbol*]
GLA .... Guadeloupe Liberation Army
GLAC .... Glacial
GLADIS ..... Ground LASER Attack Designator/Identification System
GLASS ...... Germanium-Lithium Argon Scanning System
GLC .... Glaucoma
GLD .... Goodland [*Kansas*] [*Airport symbol*]
GLD .... Ground-LASER Designators
GLF .... Golfito [*Costa Rica*] [*Airport symbol*]
GIFRP .... Glass-Fiber-Reinforced Plastic [*Also, GFRP*]
GLG .... Glengyle [*Australia*] [*Airport symbol*]
GLH .... Greenville [*Mississippi*] [*Airport symbol*]
GLI .... Glen Innes [*Australia*] [*Airport symbol*]
GLOB .... Globulin
GLS .... Galveston [*Texas*] [*Airport symbol*]
GLT .... Gladstone [*Australia*] [*Airport symbol*]
GITN .... Glomerulo-Tubulo-Nephritis [*Medicine*]
GLV .... Golovin [*Alaska*] [*Airport symbol*]
GLX .... Galela [*Indonesia*] [*Airport symbol*]
GLYC .... Glycerin
GM .... Grand Mal [*Epilepsy*]
GMA .... Gemena [*Zaire*] [*Airport symbol*]
GMB .... Gambela [*Ethiopia*] [*Airport symbol*]
GMF .... Ground Mobile Forces [*Military*]
GMF .... Ground Monitor Facility
GMI .... Gasmata [*Papua New Guinea*] [*Airport symbol*]
GMJSU ..... Gems, Minerals, and Jewelry Study Unit
GMR .... Gambier Island [*French Polynesia*] [*Airport symbol*]
GMR .... Gromer Aviation, Inc. [*Versailles, MO*] [*FAA designator*]
GMS .... General Maintenance System
GMT .... General Machine Test

GMT .... Green Mountain Airlines [*Barre, VT*] [*FAA designator*]
GMU .... George Mason University [*Virginia*]
GNATS ...... General Noise and Tonal System
GNB .... Grenoble [*France*] [*Airport symbol*]
GND .... Grenada [*Windward Islands*] [*Airport symbol*]
GNM .... Guanambi [*Brazil*] [*Airport symbol*]
GNU .... Goodnews Bay [*Alaska*] [*Airport symbol*]
GO .... Gaussian Orbitals [*Atomic physics*]
GO .... Glucose Oxidase [*An enzyme*] [*Also, GOD*]
GOA .... Genoa [*Italy*] [*Airport symbol*]
GOA .... Glacier-Ocean-Atmosphere [*Global system used for modelling*]
GOALS ...... Generalized Officer Assignment On-Line System [*Navy*]
GOD .... Glucose Oxidase [*An enzyme*] [*Also, GO*]
GOD-POD ... Glucose Oxidase-Peroxidase [*Enzyme mixture*] [*Also, PGO*]
GOM .... Goma [*Zaire*] [*Airport symbol*]
GON .... New London [*Connecticut*] [*Airport symbol*]
GOO .... Generalized Overhauser Orbitals [*Atomic physics*]
GOO .... Goondiwindi [*Australia*] [*Airport symbol*]
GOP .... General Outpost
GOP .... Gorakhpur [*India*] [*Airport symbol*]
GOQ .... Golmud [*China*] [*Airport symbol*]
GOR .... Gore [*Ethiopia*] [*Airport symbol*]
GOS .... Gosford [*Australia*] [*Airport symbol*]
GOT .... Gothenburg [*Sweden*] [*Airport symbol*]
GOU .... Garoua [*Cameroon*] [*Airport symbol*]
GOV .... Gove [*Australia*] [*Airport symbol*]
GOZ .... Gorna Orjachovica [*Bulgaria*] [*Airport symbol*]
GP .... Galvanized Plain [*Metal industry*]
GP .... General Product
GP .... Gutter Pair [*Philately*]
GPa .... Gigapascal [*SI unit of pressure*]
GPA .... Government Property Administration
GPB .... Glossopharyngeal Breathing
GPCL .... General Purpose Closed Loop [*Nuclear energy*]
GPD .... General Purpose Discipline [*IBM Corp.*]
G6PDH ...... Glucose-6-phosphate Dehydrogenase [*An enzyme*] [*Also, GPD, G6PD*]
GPFC .... General Purpose Function Code
GPI .... Guapi [*Colombia*] [*Airport symbol*]
GPIC .... General Purpose Intercomputer [*Test*]
GPL .... General Purpose Loop [*Nuclear energy*]
GPL .... Guapiles [*Costa Rica*] [*Airport symbol*]
GPLY .... Gingivoplasty [*Dentistry*]
GPM .... General Preventive Medicine
GPM .... Ground Potential Model [*Physics*]
GPN .... Garden Point [*Australia*] [*Airport symbol*]
GPO .... General Pico [*Argentina*] [*Airport symbol*]
GPS .... Galapagos Islands [*Ecuador*] [*Airport symbol*]
GPS .... Guinea Pig Spleen
GPT .... Gulfport/Biloxi [*Mississippi*] [*Airport symbol*]
GPZ .... Grand Rapids [*Minnesota*] [*Airport symbol*]
GQ & A ...... General's Branch, Quarter Master's Branch, and Adjutant's Branch [*Main divisions of Staff Duties*] [*Military*] [*British*]
GQQ .... Galion [*Ohio*] [*Airport symbol*]
GRA .... Great American Airways [*Reno, NV*] [*FAA designator*]
GRADS ...... Ground RADAR Aerial Delivery System
GRAV .... Gravid [*Pregnant*] [*Medicine*]
GRB .... Green Bay [*Wisconsin*] [*Airport symbol*]
GRC .... Global Reference Code [*Developed by Smithsonian Institution*]
GRC .... Grand Cess [*Liberia*] [*Airport symbol*]
GRD .... Greenwood [*South Carolina*] [*Airport symbol*]
GRDSR ...... Geographically Referenced Data Storage and Retrieval System [*Canada*]
GRFL .... Gerald R. Ford Library
GrFRP .... Graphite-Fiber-Reinforced Plastic [*Also, GFRP*]
GRGE .... Gorge [*Board on Geographic Names*]
GRH .... Garuahi [*Papua New Guinea*] [*Airport symbol*]
GRH .... Green Hills Aviation Ltd. [*Kirksville, MO*] [*FAA designator*]
GRI .... Grand Island [*Nebraska*] [*Airport symbol*]
GRJ .... George [*South Africa*] [*Airport symbol*]
GRQ .... Groningen [*Netherlands*] [*Airport symbol*]
GRR .... Grand Rapids [*Michigan*] [*Airport symbol*]
GRS .... Grid Reference Ship [*Navy*]
GRT .... General Reactor Technology [*Nuclear energy*]

GRX.......... Granada [*Spain*] [*Airport symbol*]
GRY.......... Grimsey [*Iceland*] [*Airport symbol*]
GRZ.......... Graz [*Austria*] [*Airport symbol*]
GS .... Glutamine Synthetase [*An enzyme*]
GSC .... Gas-Solid Chromatography
GSC .... Gascoyne Junction [*Australia*] [*Airport symbol*]
GSC .... Gravity Setting Culture
GSC .... Grid Spot Converter
GSH........... Glutathione-SH [*Reduced glutathione*] [*Biochemistry*]
GSI .... Grand Scale Integration
GSN .... Mount Gunson [*Australia*] [*Airport symbol*]
GSO .... General Spin Orbitals [*Atomic physics*]
GSR .... Gardo [*Somalia*] [*Airport symbol*]
GSR .... Generalized Schartzman Reaction [*Medicine*]
GSS........... Gamete Shedding Substance [*Endocrinology*]
GST .... Graphic Stress Teletethermometry [*Medicine*]
GST .... Gustavus [*Alaska*] [*Airport symbol*]
GSWA .... Gunshot Wound to the Abdomen
GT .... Genetic Therapy
G & T .... Gin and Tonic
GT .... Glycotyrosine [*Biochemistry*]
G/T........... Granulation Time
G/T........... Granulation Tissue
GT .... Green Thumb [*An organization*]
GT .... Green Thumbs [*National Weather Service and Department of Agriculture Extension Service telecommunication system*]
GTCP .... General Telephone Call Processing
GTE .... Groote Island [*Australia*] [*Airport symbol*]
GTED .... Gas-Turbine Engine-Driven [*Generator*]
GTF .... Great Falls [*Montana*] [*Airport symbol*]
GT-HTGR ... Gas-Turbine High-Temperature Gas-Cooled Reactor
GTN........... Glyceryl Trinitrate [*Explosive, vasodilator*] [*Also, NG and NTG*]
GTO .... Gaussian-Type Orbitals [*Atomic physics*]
GTO .... Gorontalo [*Indonesia*] [*Airport symbol*]
GTO's........ Girls Together Outrageously [*or Organically*] [*Rock music group*]
GTR........... Columbus [*Mississippi*] [*Airport symbol*]

GTSS .... General Time Sharing System [*Data processing*]
GTT .... Georgetown [*Australia*] [*Airport symbol*]
GTW .... Gottwaldov [*Czechoslovakia*] [*Airport symbol*]
GU .... Glycogenic Unit [*Medicine*]
GUA .... Guatemala City [*Guatemala*] [*Airport symbol*]
GUARD ..... Guaranteed Assignment Retention Detailing [*Navy*]
GUC .... Gunnison [*Colorado*] [*Airport symbol*]
GUD .... Goundam [*Mali*] [*Airport symbol*]
GUG .... Guari [*Papua New Guinea*] [*Airport symbol*]
GUH .... Gunnedah [*Australia*] [*Airport symbol*]
GUI .... Guiria [*Venezuela*] [*Airport symbol*]
GUM.......... Guam Island [*Mariana Islands*] [*Airport symbol*]
GUP........... Gallup [*New Mexico*] [*Airport symbol*]
GUQ .... Guanare [*Venezuela*] [*Airport symbol*]
GUR........... Alotau [*Papua New Guinea*] [*Airport symbol*]
GUS .... Group Unit Simulator
GUTS .... Guerilla Urban Traffic System [*Refers to driving in Boston*]
GUU .... Grundarfjordur [*Iceland*] [*Airport symbol*]
GV .... Guard Vessel [*Nuclear energy*]
GVA........... Geneva [*Switzerland*] [*Airport symbol*]
GVB........... Generalized Valence Bond [*Physics*]
GVI .... Green River [*Papua New Guinea*] [*Airport symbol*]
GVR........... Governador Valadares [*Brazil*] [*Airport symbol*]
GVTY .... Gingivectomy [*Dentistry*]
GVX........... Gavle [*Sweden*] [*Airport symbol*]
GWCSA..... Greater World Christian Spiritualist Association
GWD.......... Gwadar [*Pakistan*] [*Airport symbol*]
GWE.......... Gwelo [*Zimbabwe*] [*Airport symbol*]
GWL.......... Gwalior [*India*] [*Airport symbol*]
GWO .... Greenwood [*Mississippi*] [*Airport symbol*]
GWSRP ..... Gun Weapon System Replacement Program
GYA........... Guayaramerin [*Bolivia*] [*Airport symbol*]
GYE........... Guayaquil [*Ecuador*] [*Airport symbol*]
GYM.......... Guaymas [*Mexico*] [*Airport symbol*]
GYN........... Goiania [*Brazil*] [*Airport symbol*]
GZO .... Gizo [*Solomon Islands*] [*Airport symbol*]
GZT .... Gaziantep [*Turkey*] [*Airport symbol*]

H

H............... Heart Disease [*Used by immigration officials*] [*Obsolete*]
H............... Hexadecimal
H............... Hinged [*Philately*]
H............... [*Anthony von*] Hoboken [*When used in identifying Haydn's compositions, refers to cataloging of his works by musicologist Hoboken*]
H............... Holzknecht [*Unit*]
H............... Hyoscine [*Organic chemistry*]
H............... Hypermetropia
H............... Hypodermic
H²............. Hot and Heavy [*In reference to a romance*]
HA............. Absolute Hypermetropia
HA............. Headache
HABA........ (Hydrozybeneneazo)benzoic Acid [*Organic chemistry*]
HAC.......... Hachijo Jima Island [*Japan*] [*Airport symbol*]
HACL........ Harvard Air Cleaning Laboratory
HACLCS... Harpoon Aircraft Command and Launch Control Set [*Missiles*]
HACS........ Hyperactive Child Syndrome
HAD........... Halmstad [*Sweden*] [*Airport symbol*]
HAEM........ Haemolysis
HAEMAT... Haematocrit
HAEMATOL ... Haematology
HAEMORRH ... Haemorrhage
HAG.......... Helicopter Action Group
HAGG........ Hyperimmune Antivariola Gamma Globulin
HAH........... Moroni [*Comoro Islands*] Hahaia Airport [*Airport symbol*]
HAIRS....... High-Altitude Test and Evaluation of Infrared Sources
HAJ........... Hanover [*West Germany*] [*Airport symbol*]
HAK........... Haikou [*China*] [*Airport symbol*]
HALLUC.... Hallucination
HALP........ Husbands of Airline Pilots [*An organization*]
HALT......... Help Abolish Legal Tyranny [*In organization name HALT-ALR*]
HALT-ALR ... HALT - An Organization of Americans for Legal Reform
HAM.......... Hamburg [*West Germany*] [*Airport symbol*]
HAN........... Hanoi [*North Vietnam*] [*Airport symbol*]
HAOS........ Hydroxylamine-ortho-sulfonic Acid [*Organic chemistry*]
HAP........... Happy Bay [*Australia*] [*Airport symbol*]
HAP........... Health Alliance Plan
HAR........... Hover Agility Rotor
HARD........ Horizontal Acoustic Range Depiction
HAS........... Hail [*Saudi Arabia*] [*Airport symbol*]
HAS........... Highest Asymptomatic [*Dose*] [*Medicine*]
HASP........ High-Level Automatic Scheduling Program
HAT........... Heathlands [*Australia*] [*Airport symbol*]
HATR........ Hazardous Air Traffic Report
HAU........... Haugesund [*Norway*] [*Airport symbol*]
HAV........... Havana [*Cuba*] [*Airport symbol*]
HAWR....... Helicopter Attack Warning RADAR
HAZCON... Hazardous Condition
HB............. Horizontal Baffle
HBA........... Hobart [*Tasmania*] [*Airport symbol*]
HBB........... Hospital Blood Bank
HBC........... Hostage Bracelet Committee
HBF........... Hepatic Blood Flow
HbP........... Primitive [*Fetal*] Hemoglobin
HC............. Helicopter Command
HC............. High Conductivity [*Copper*]

HCA.......... Heart Cell Aggregate [*Cytology*]
HCA.......... Helicopter Club of America
HCA.......... Hexachloroacetone [*Organic chemistry*]
HCC.......... Hepatitis Contagiosa Canis [*Virus*]
HCD.......... Homologous Canine Distemper [*Antiserum*]
HCDD........ Hexachlorodioxin [*Organic chemistry*]
HCI........... Home Center Institute
HcIMP....... Hydrocolloid Impression [*Dentistry*]
HCLF........ Horizontal Cask Lifting Fixture [*Nuclear energy*]
HCM......... Hydraulic Core Mockup [*Nuclear energy*]
H & CP...... Hospital and Community Psychiatry
HCPAA..... Hungarian Catholic Priests' Association in America
HCQ.......... Halls Creek [*Australia*] [*Airport symbol*]
HCR........... Holy Cross [*Alaska*] [*Airport symbol*]
HCS.......... Human Cord Serum
HCSS........ Head Compartment Support Structure [*Nuclear energy*]
HCT........... Hydrochlorothiazide [*Drug*] [*Organic chemistry*] [*Also, HCTZ and HCZ*]
HCTZ........ Hydrochlorothiazide [*Drug*] [*Organic chemistry*] [*Also, HCT and HCZ*]
HCU.......... Helicopter Control Unit
HCU.......... Hydraulic Control Unit [*Nuclear energy*]
HCVIS....... High Clouds Visible [*Meteorology*]
HCZ........... Hydrochlorothiazide [*Drug*] [*Organic chemistry*] [*Also, HCT and HCTZ*]
HD............. Hoessel und Winkler GmbH Luftverkehragesellschaft [*West Germany*] [*ICAO designator*]
H-D............ Hypothetico-Deductive
HDD.......... Hyderabad [*Pakistan*] [*Airport symbol*]
HDLC........ High-Level Data Link Control
HDLW........ Distance at Which a Watch Is Heard with Left Ear [*Medicine*]
HDN........... Steamboat Springs [*Colorado*] [*Airport symbol*]
HDP........... Hydroxydimethylpyrimidine [*Organic chemistry*]
HDR........... Hot Dry Rock [*Geothermal science*]
HDRW....... Distance at Which a Watch Is Heard with Right Ear [*Medicine*]
HDU........... Hemodialysis Unit [*Medicine*]
HDW.......... High-Pressure Demineralized Water
HDY........... Haadyai [*Thailand*] [*Airport symbol*]
HE............. High Energy
HE............. Hoc Est [*That Is, or This Is*] [*Latin*]
HEA........... Herat [*Afghanistan*] [*Airport symbol*]
HEART...... Hydrometer Erosion and Recession Test
HEATH..... Higher Education and the Handicapped [*An organization*]
HEBBLE.... High-Energy Benthic Boundary Layer Experiment [*Oceanography*]
HECD........ Hall Electrolytic Conductivity Detector [*Analytical instrumentation*]
HEDP........ (Hydroxyethylidene)diphosphonic Acid [*Organic chemistry*] [*Also, EHDP*]
HEH........... Heho [*Burma*] [*Airport symbol*]
HEIDA....... (Hydroxyethyl)iminodiacetic Acid [*Organic chemistry*]
HEIFER..... High Frequency Relay
HEL........... Helsinki [*Finland*] [*Airport symbol*]
HEL........... Hen's Egg-White Lysozyme
HELCIS..... Helicopter Command Instrumentation System
HELCOS... High-Energy LASER Component Servicing
HELILEX... Helicopter Landing Exercise [*Amphibious*] [*Navy*]

HELP......... Hospital Equipment Loan Project
HELRATS ... High-Energy LASER RADAR Acquisition and Tracking System
HELSTF .... High-Energy LASER System Test Facility
HEM .... Heat Exchanger Method
HEMA .... Health Education Media Association
HEMP .... High-Altitude Electromagnetic Pulse
HEN.......... Holistic Education Network [*An organization*]
HEOY .... Handicapped Employe of the Year [*Award given to federal employees*]
HER .... Heraklion [*Greece*] [*Airport symbol*]
HERD .... High Explosives Research and Development
HERED ..... Heredity
HERO .... Home Economics Related Occupations
HERS........ Health Evaluation and Referral Service
HES.......... Hanford Engineering Service [*Nuclear energy*]
HET .... Hohhot [*China*] [*Airport symbol*]
HEZ .... Natchez [*Mississippi*] [*Airport symbol*]
HF............. Hard Filled [*Capsules*]
HF............. Hemorrhagic Factor
HFA .... Haifa [*Israel*] [*Airport symbol*]
HFCE........ HFIR [*High-Flux Isotope Reactor*] Critical Experiment
HFE .... Hefei [*China*] [*Airport symbol*]
HFET .... Highway Fuel Economy Test [*Environmental Protection Agency*]
HFI .... Hocker Federation International
HFN.......... Hofn [*Iceland*] [*Airport symbol*]
HFP .... Hexafluoropropylene [*Organic chemistry*]
HFR .... High Frequency of Recombination [*Medicine*]
HFT .... Hammerfest [*Norway*] [*Airport symbol*]
HGA .... Hargeisa [*Somalia*] [*Airport symbol*]
HGD .... Hughenden [*Australia*] [*Airport symbol*]
HGE .... Hydraulic Grade Elevations
HGH .... Hangzhou [*China*] [*Airport symbol*]
HGL.......... Helgoland [*West Germany*] [*Airport symbol*]
HGN .... Mae Hong Son [*Thailand*] [*Airport symbol*]
HGO .... Korhogo [*Ivory Coast*] [*Airport symbol*]
HGR.......... Hagerstown [*Maryland*] [*Airport symbol*]
HGS.......... Freetown [*Sierra Leone*] Hastings Airport [*Airport symbol*]
HGU .... Mount Hagen [*Papua New Guinea*] [*Airport symbol*]
HHH.......... Hilton Head Island [*South Carolina*] [*Airport symbol*]
HHLR........ Hand-Held LASER Range-Finder
HHPA .... Hexahydrophthalic Anhydride [*Organic chemistry*]
HHT........... Hereditary Hemorrhagic Telangiectasia [*Medicine*]
HI.............. Habitability Improvement
HI.............. Height Indicator
HIA .... Headwear Institute of America
HIB .... Hibbing [*Minnesota*] [*Airport symbol*]
HICAP....... High-Capacity Projectile
HICOMSEVONET ... High Command Secure Voice Network [*Navy*]
HIDAM ...... Hierarchical Indexed Direct Access Method [*Data processing*]
HiD/LoD.... High-Density/Low-Density Tariff
HIDM......... High Information Delta Modulation [*Data processing*]
HIFBS........ Heat-Inactivated Fetal Bovine Serum [*Immunology*]
HIJ............. Hiroshima [*Japan*] [*Airport symbol*]
HILAST ..... High Value Asset Control
HINT.......... Hinton [*Test*] [*Medicine*]
HIP .... Hydrostatic Indifference Point
HIPAC ...... High-Performance Aircraft Cannon
HIPE .... Hospital In-Patient Enquiry [*British*]
HIPP .... Hippocrates [*Greek physician, 460?-377? BC*]
HIPS .... Helmet Initiated Pointing System
HIPS .... High-Impact Polystyrene [*Plastics technology*]
HIR .... Honiara [*Guadalcanal*] [*Airport symbol*]
HIS .... Hayman Island [*Australia*] [*Airport symbol*]
HISAM....... Hierarchical Indexed Sequential Access Method [*Data processing*]
HISSG .... Hospital Information Systems Sharing Group
HITLS........ Hardware in the Loop Simulation [*Data processing*]
HJ.............. Halt and Jump [*Data processing*]
HJR .... Khajuraho [*India*] [*Airport symbol*]
H-K........... Hands to Knee [*Medicine*]
HK .... Hexokinase [*An enzyme*]
HKD.......... Hakodate [*Japan*] [*Airport symbol*]
HKG .... Hong Kong [*Hong Kong*] [*Airport symbol*]
HKK.......... Hokitika [*New Zealand*] [*Airport symbol*]
HKN.......... Hoskins [*Papua New Guinea*] [*Airport symbol*]

HKP.......... Kaanapali [*Hawaii*] [*Airport symbol*]
HKT.......... Phuket [*Thailand*] [*Airport symbol*]
HKY.......... Hickory [*North Carolina*] [*Airport symbol*]
HL............. Hyborean Legion [*An organization*]
H/L............ Hydrophile/Lipophile [*Followed by a number*]
HL............. Hypertrichosis Lanuginosa [*Medicine*]
HLA .... Heavy Lift Airship
HLA .... Homologous Leucocytic Antibodies
HLCV .... Hot Leg Check Valve [*Nuclear energy*]
HLF .... Hultsfred [*Sweden*] [*Airport symbol*]
HLIV .... Hot Leg Isolation Valve [*Nuclear energy*]
HLL .... Hill [*Board on Geographic Names*]
HLN .... Helena [*Montana*] [*Airport symbol*]
HLND .... Highlands [*Board on Geographic Names*]
HLP .... Jakarta [*Indonesia*] [*Airport symbol*]
HLSP .... Heitler-London-Slater-Pauling [*Method*] [*Physics*]
HLT .... Hamilton [*Australia*] [*Airport symbol*]
HLU .... Houailou [*New Caledonia*] [*Airport symbol*]
HLZ .... Hamilton [*New Zealand*] [*Airport symbol*]
Hm .... Manifest Hypermetropia [*Medicine*]
HMC .... Hydroxymethylcystosine [*Organic chemistry*]
HMC .... Hydroxypropyl(methyl)cellulose [*Synthetic food gum*] [*Organic chemistry*]
HMO .... Hermosillo [*Mexico*] [*Airport symbol*]
HMS .... Hanford Meteorology Surveys [*Nuclear energy*]
HMU .... Hydroxymethyluracil [*Organic chemistry*]
HN .... Host to Network [*Data processing*]
HN .... Station Open from Sunset to Sunrise [*ITU designation*]
HNA .... Hanamaki [*Japan*] [*Airport symbol*]
HNAB .... Hexanitroazobenzene [*Organic chemistry*]
HND .... Tokyo [*Japan*] Haneda Airport [*Airport symbol*]
HNG .... Hienghene [*New Caledonia*] [*Airport symbol*]
HNH.......... Hoonah [*Alaska*] [*Airport symbol*]
HNL .... Honolulu [*Hawaii*] [*Airport symbol*]
HNM .... Hana [*Hawaii*] [*Airport symbol*]
HNS .... Haines [*Alaska*] [*Airport symbol*]
HNW .... Heeresnachrichtenwesen [*Army Communications System*] [*German military - World War II*]
HOB.......... Hobbs [*New Mexico*] [*Airport symbol*]
HOD .... Hodeidah [*Yemen Arab Republic*] [*Airport symbol*]
HOD .... Hyperbaric Oxygen Drenching
HOE.......... Homing Overlay Experiment [*Ballistic Missile Defense*]
HOF .... Hafuf [*Saudi Arabia*] [*Airport symbol*]
HOFF......... Hoffman [*Reflex*] [*Medicine*]
HOG .... Holguin [*Cuba*] [*Airport symbol*]
HOI............ Hao Island [*French Polynesia*] [*Airport symbol*]
HOL........... Holiday and Leave [*Military*]
HOM.......... Heartless Old Man [*Alternative sobriquet for William Gladstone, 1809-98, British statesman and prime minister, who was known to admirers as GOM, which see*]
HOM.......... Homer [*Alaska*] [*Airport symbol*]
HON .... Huron [*South Dakota*] [*Airport symbol*]
HOP.......... HEDL [*Hanford Engineering Development Laboratory*] Overpower [*Nuclear energy*]
HOPT .... Hypoparathyroidism [*Endocrinology*]
HOQ .... Hof [*West Germany*] [*Airport symbol*]
HOR.......... Home of Record
HOR.......... Horta [*Faial Island*] [*Airport symbol*]
HORM .... Hybrid Orbital Rehybridization Method [*Atomic physics*]
HOT.......... Hot Springs [*Arkansas*] [*Airport symbol*]
HOV.......... Orsta/Volda [*Norway*] [*Airport symbol*]
HOY.......... Hoy Island [*Scotland*] [*Airport symbol*]
HP .... Hyperphoria
HPA .... Hypothalamic-Pituitary-Adrenocortical [*Endocrinology*]
HPA .... Lifuka [*Tonga Islands*] [*Airport symbol*]
HPB .... Hooper Bay [*Alaska*] [*Airport symbol*]
HPCI.......... High-Pressure Coolant Injection [*Nuclear energy*]
HPCS .... High-Pressure Core Spray [*Nuclear energy*]
H-PD .... Hough-Powell Digitizer
HPI .... High-Pressure Injection [*Nuclear energy*]
HPIS .... High-Pressure Injection System [*Nuclear energy*]
HPISS .... High-Power Illuminator Signal Source
HPL .... Human Parotid Lysozyme
HPN........... Hypertension [*Medicine*]
HPN........... White Plains [*New York*] [*Airport symbol*]
HPPLC ...... High-Performance Preparative Liquid Chromatography
HPS........... Hanford Plant Standard [*Nuclear energy*] [*Formerly, HWS*]

HPT .... Head per Track
HPV .... Princeville [*Hawaii*] [*Airport symbol*]
HQBP .... High Quality Bonus Point [*Advancement system*] [*Navy*]
H-R .... Hertzsprung-Russell [*Diagram*] [*Astronomy*]
HRA .... Heart Rate Audiometry
HRAI .... Human Rights Advocates International
HRAV .... Human Resources Availability
HRB .... Harbin [*Manchuria*] [*Airport symbol*]
HRC .... Horse Red Blood Cells [*Also, HRBC*]
HRE .... High-Resolution Electrocardiography
HRE .... Homogeneous Reactor Experiments
HRE .... Human Relations Education
HRG .... Hurghada [*Egypt*] [*Airport symbol*]
HRI .... High Resolution Image [*or Imager*] [*Astronomy*]
HRI .... Human Rights International [*An organization*]
HRK .... Kharkov [*USSR*] [*Airport symbol*]
HRL .... Harlingen [*Texas*] [*Airport symbol*]
HRO .... Harrison [*Arkansas*] [*Airport symbol*]
HS .... Hartman's Solution [*Dentistry*]
HS .... Headspace [*Above liquids*]
HS .... Homologous Serum
HSCLCS ... Harpoon Shipboard Command and Launch Control Set [*Missiles*]
HSCT .... High-Speed Compound Terminal [*Data processing*]
HSCU .... Helicopter Subcontrol Unit
HSI .... Hastings [*Nebraska*] [*Airport symbol*]
HSL .... Helicopter Antisubmarine Squadron Light
HSL .... Herpes Simplex Labialis
HSL .... Highway Safety Literature
HSL .... Huslia [*Alaska*] [*Airport symbol*]
HSM .... Horsham [*Australia*] [*Airport symbol*]
HSM-WA ... Hard Structure Munition Weaponization Analysis
HSS .... Historiae Societatis Socius [*Fellow of the Historical Society*]
HSTL .... Harry S Truman Library
H & T .... Hospitalization and Treatment
Ht .... Total Hypermetropia [*Medicine*]
HTA .... Herb Trade Association
HTB .... Howitzer Test Bed
HTCM .... Master Chief Hull Maintenance Technician [*Navy rating*] [*Formerly, SFCM*]
HTCS .... Senior Chief Hull Maintenance Technician [*Navy rating*] [*Formerly, SFCS*]
HTH .... Hawthorne [*Nevada*] [*Airport symbol*]
HTH .... Home Town Honey [*Slang*]
HTIS .... Heat Transfer Instrument System
HTL .... Heat Transfer Loop
HTO .... East Hampton [*New York*] [*Airport symbol*]
HTR .... Hanford Test Reactor
HTR .... Hateruma [*Japan*] [*Airport symbol*]

HTRI .... Heat Transfer Research Institute
HTS .... Huntington [*West Virginia*] [*Airport symbol*]
HTSF .... High-Temperature Sodium Facility [*Nuclear energy*]
HTZ .... Hato Corozal [*Colombia*] [*Airport symbol*]
HUC .... Humacao [*Puerto Rico*] [*Airport symbol*]
HUF .... Terre Haute [*Indiana*] [*Airport symbol*]
HUH .... Huahine [*French Polynesia*] [*Airport symbol*]
HUM .... Houma [*Louisiana*] [*Airport symbol*]
HUN .... Hualien [*Taiwan*] [*Airport symbol*]
HUPATS .... Heuristic Paper Trimming System
HUQ .... Houn [*Libya*] [*Airport symbol*]
HUS .... Hughes [*Alaska*] [*Airport symbol*]
HUT .... HEDL [*Hanford Engineering Development Laboratory*] Up Transient [*Nuclear energy*]
HUT .... Hutchinson [*Kansas*] [*Airport symbol*]
HUU .... Huanuco [*Peru*] [*Airport symbol*]
HUY .... Humberside [*England*] [*Airport symbol*]
HV .... His Verbis [*In These Words*] [*Latin*]
HV .... Hoc Verbum [*This Word*] [*Latin*]
HV .... Hyperventilation
HVA .... Analalava [*Madagascar*] [*Airport symbol*]
HVB .... Hervey Bay [*Australia*] [*Airport symbol*]
HVG .... Honningsvag [*Norway*] [*Airport symbol*]
HVK .... Holmavik [*Iceland*] [*Airport symbol*]
HVN .... New Haven [*Connecticut*] [*Airport symbol*]
HVP .... High Video Pass
HVR .... Havre [*Montana*] [*Airport symbol*]
HVT .... Half-Value Thickness
HVT .... High Value Target
HW .... Housewife
HWS .... Hanford Works Standard [*or Specification*] [*Nuclear energy*] [*Later, HPS*]
HWS .... Harpoon Weapons System
HWY .... Hundred Woman Years [*of Exposure*] [*Radiation*]
Hx .... Hypoxanthine
HXX .... Hay [*Australia*] [*Airport symbol*]
Hy .... Hypermetropia [*Medicine*]
HYA .... Hyannis [*Massachusetts*] [*Airport symbol*]
HYD .... Hyderabad [*India*] [*Airport symbol*]
HYF .... Hayfields [*Papua New Guinea*] [*Airport symbol*]
HYG .... Hydaburg [*Alaska*] [*Airport symbol*]
HYP .... Hyperresonance
HYP .... Hypertrophy
HYPN .... Hypertension
HYPNOT ... Hypnotism
HYR .... Hayward [*Wisconsin*] [*Airport symbol*]
HYS .... Hays [*Kansas*] [*Airport symbol*]
HYS .... Hysteria
HZK .... Husavik [*Iceland*] [*Airport symbol*]
HZL .... Hazleton [*Pennsylvania*] [*Airport symbol*]

I

i .... Incisor (Deciduous) [*Dentistry*]
I .... Induction
I .... Internal
I .... Internist [*Medicine*]
IA .... Initial Appearance
IABP .... International Association of Businessmen and
                 Professionals
IAC .... Interarray Communications
IAC .... Interim Acceptance Criteria
IACS .... Integrated Acoustic Communication System
IACS .... Integrated Avionics Control System
IACS .... International Academy of Cosmetic Surgery
IADS .... Integrated Air Defense System
IAF .... Initiative America Foundation
IAF .... Inter-American Foundation
IAFP .... Intergovernmental Affairs Fellowship Program
IAH .... Island Airlines Hawaii [*Honolulu, HI*] [*FAA designator*]
IAJS .... International Al Jolson Society
IAL .... International Algorithmic Language [*Data processing*]
IAL .... Investment Analysis Language [*Data processing*]
IAN .... Kiana [*Alaska*] [*Airport symbol*]
IAP .... Interarray Processor
IAP .... International Association of Parapsychologists
IAP .... Iranian Aircraft Program [*Military*]
IAPD .... International Association of Parents of the Deaf
IARM .... Interim Antiradiation Missile
IARP .... International Association for Religion and
                 Parapsychology
IAS .... Iasi [*Romania*] [*Airport symbol*]
IAS .... International Air Service Co. [*Napa, CA*] [*FAA
                 designator*]
IASC .... International Afroid Science Conference
IASCE .... International Association for the Study of Cooperation in
                 Education
IAT .... Information Assessment Team
IAT .... Iodine Azide Test [*Medicine*]
IATB .... International Aviation Theft Bureau
IATCS ...... International Air Traffic Communications System
IATP .... Individual Airplane Tracking Program
IB .... Immune Body
IBA .... Ibadan [*Nigeria*] [*Airport symbol*]
IBA .... Independent Bakers Association
IBA .... International Bocce Association
IBA .... Isobutylamine [*Organic chemistry*]
IBBBA .... International Bundle Branch Block Association
IBDU .... Isobutylidenediurea [*Organic chemistry*]
IBE .... Ibague [*Colombia*] [*Airport symbol*]
IBEA .... Industrial Base Engineering Activity
IBM .... Instant Big Mouth [*Martini*] [*Slang*]
IBMC .... International Buddhist Meditation Center
IBP .... Iron-Binding Protein
IBSSU .... Internal Bearing Stabilized Sighting Unit
IBT .... Isatin-beta-thiosemicarbazone [*Organic chemistry*]
IBYC .... Institute in Basic Youth Conflicts
IBZ .... Ibiza [*Spain*] [*Airport symbol*]
IC .... Implementation and Conversion
IC .... Inner Cabin
IC .... Intensive Care [*Medicine*]
IC .... Intercostal [*Between the ribs*] [*Medicine*]

ICA .... Icabaru [*Venezuela*] [*Airport symbol*]
ICA .... Independent Cost Assessment
ICA .... Inventors Club of America
ICA .... Item Control Area
ICAE .... Integrated Communications Adapter Extended
ICAFFH ..... International Committee for the Anthropology of Food
                 and Food Habits
ICAM .... Improved Cobra Agility and Maneuverability [*Military*]
ICAP .... Improved Cobra Armament Program [*Military*]
ICAP .... Integrated Criminal Apprehension Program
ICAPS ...... Integrated Carrier Acoustic Prediction System [*Navy*]
ICAR .... Interface Control Action Request
ICAS .... International Council of Air Shows
ICASSP .... International Conference on Acoustics, Speech, and
                 Signal Processing
ICAV .... Intracavity [*Dentistry*]
ICB .... Interface Control Board
ICBP .... Intracellular-Binding Proteins
ICC .... Independent Community Consultants [*An organization*]
ICCC .... International Concerns Committee for Children
ICCH .... International Conference on Computers and the
                 Humanities
ICCL .... International Committee for the Centennial of Light
ICCS .... Interim Command and Control System
ICCU .... Inter-Channel Comparison Unit [*Nuclear energy*]
ICD .... Interface Control Drawings
ICDFS .... Increased Capacity Drum Feed System
ICE .... Institute for Community Economics
ICF .... Inertial Confinement Fusion
ICF .... Intravascular Coagulation and Fibrinolysis Syndrome
                 [*Medicine*]
ICG .... Indochina Curriculum Group
ICG .... International Conference Group
ICH .... Ichthyology
ICI .... Cicia [*Fiji*] [*Airport symbol*]
ICI .... Interim Cargo Integrator
ICIC .... Interagency Committee on Intermodal Cargo
ICID .... Information Center for Individuals with Disabilities
ICIO .... Interim Cargo Integration Operations
ICK .... Nieuw Nickerie [*Surinam*] [*Airport symbol*]
ICKL .... International Council of Kinetography Laban
ICM .... Inner Cell Mass [*Embryology*]
ICOHEPANS ... International Conference on High Energy Physics and
                 Nuclear Structure
ICOI .... International Congress of Oral Implantologists
ICP .... Industrial Control Products
ICPMM ...... Incisors, Canines, Premolars, Molars [*Dentistry*]
ICR .... Industrial Cost Recovery [*Environmental Protection
                 Agency*]
ICR .... Nicaro [*Cuba*] [*Airport symbol*]
ICRM .... Institute of Certified Records Managers
ICRW .... International Center for Research on Women
ICS .... Institute for Contemporary Studies
ICS .... Interim Contractor Support
ICS .... International Cogeneration Society
ICS .... International Communications Sciences
ICSA .... In-Core Shim Assembly [*Nuclear energy*]
ICSB .... Interim Command Switchboard [*Navy*]

ICSEP .... International Center for the Solution of Environmental Problems
ICSG .... International Center for Social Gerontology
ICT .... Icterus [*Jaundice*] [*Medicine*]
ICT .... Incoming Trunk
ICT .... Intelligence Cycle Time
ICT .... Wichita [*Kansas*] [*Airport symbol*]
ICWS .... Institute of Civil War Studies
ID .... Atlantic Deutsche Luftverkehrs AG [*West Germany*] [*ICAO designator*]
ID .... [*The*] Ides
ID .... Independent Distributor [*Bookselling*]
ID .... Index of Discrimination
IDA .... Idaho Falls [*Idaho*] [*Airport symbol*]
IDAF .... International Defence and Aid Fund
IDAMST .... Integrated Digital Avionics for Medium STOL Transport
IDEP .... Interagency Data Exchange Program [*Later, GIDEP*]
IDIPS .... Intelligence Data Input Packages
IDO .... Santa Isabel Do Morro [*Brazil*] [*Airport symbol*]
IDP .... Individual Development Plan
IDR .... Indore [*India*] [*Airport symbol*]
IDS .... Interim Decay Storage [*Nuclear energy*]
IDT .... Interdigital Transducer [*Physics*]
IE .... Inspection and Enforcement
IE .... Intake (of a Unit of Food) Energy [*Nutrition*]
IEAR .... Instituto de Energia Atomica Reactor [*Brazil*]
IEC .... Injection Electrode Catheter
IEC .... Integrated Electronic Components
IECA .... Independent Educational Counselors Association
IED .... International Electronic Devices [*Conference*]
IEE .... Interim Expendable Emitter
IEEPA .... International Emergency Economic Powers Act [*1977*]
IEFUA .... International Electronic Facsimile Users Association
IEG .... Zielona Gora [*Poland*] [*Airport symbol*]
IEM .... Interim Examination and Maintenance [*Nuclear energy*]
IEMTF .... Interim Examination and Maintenance Training Facility [*Nuclear energy*]
IEP .... Independent Evaluation Plan
IEP .... Institute for Ecological Policies
IEPA .... Independent Electron Pair Approximation [*Physics*]
IERL .... Industrial Environmental Research Laboratory [*Environmental Protection Agency*]
IEV .... Kiev [*USSR*] [*Airport symbol*]
IFA .... Insulation Fabricators Association
IFA .... Integrated File Adapter [*Data processing*]
IFAC .... International Food Additives Council
IFCF .... Integrated Fuel Cycle Facilities [*Nuclear energy*]
IFDP .... Institute for Food and Development Policy
IFF .... Iffley [*Australia*] [*Airport symbol*]
IFF .... Iran Freedom Foundation
IFFC .... Integrated Flight and Fire Control
IFFH .... International Federation for Family Health
IFFLP .... International Federation for Family Life Promotion
IFHPMSM ... International Federation for Hygiene, Preventive Medicine, and Social Medicine
IFJ .... Isafjordur [*Iceland*] [*Airport symbol*]
IFN .... Interferon [*Biochemistry*] [*Also, IF*]
IFN .... Isfahan [*Iran*] [*Airport symbol*]
IFS .... Interchange File Separator [*Data processing*]
IFWTO .... International Federation of Women's Travel Organizations
IGA .... Inagua [*Bahamas*] [*Airport symbol*]
IGA .... Intergranular Attack [*Nuclear energy*]
IGE .... Iguela [*Gabon*] [*Airport symbol*]
IGF .... International Genetics Federation
IGFES .... Interactive Graphics Finite Element System
IGG .... Igiugig [*Alaska*] [*Airport symbol*]
IGL .... Izmir [*Turkey*] Cigli Airport [*Airport symbol*]
IGM .... Kingman [*Arizona*] [*Airport symbol*]
IGMC .... Independent Gasoline Marketers Council
IGN .... Iligan [*Philippines*] [*Airport symbol*]
IGO .... Chigorodo [*Colombia*] [*Airport symbol*]
IGPE .... International Guild of Professional Electrologists
IGR & P ..... Inert Gas Receiving and Processing
IGS .... Integrated Graphics System
IGS .... Interchange Group Separator [*Data processing*]
IHPVA .... International Human Powered Vehicle Association
IHR .... Institute for Historical Review
IHSS .... Idiopathic Hypertrophic Subaortic Stenosis [*Medicine*]

IHTS .... Intermediate Heat Transport System [*Nuclear energy*]
IHXGV .... Intermediate Heat Exchanger Guard Vessel [*Nuclear energy*]
II .... Interval International [*An organization*]
IIL .... Integrated Injection Logic [*Data processing*]
IIR .... Intelligence Information Report
IIS .... International Institute of Stress
IIS .... International Institutional Services [*An organization*]
IJCIC .... International Jewish Committee on Interreligious Consultations
IJP .... Inhibitory Junction Potential [*Neurophysiology*]
IJP .... Ink Jet Printing
IK .... Infusoria Killing [*Unit*] [*Medicine*]
IKRA .... International Kirlian Research Association
IL .... Idle
IL .... Intermediate Language [*Data processing*]
ILAAT .... Interlaboratory Air-to-Air Missile Technology
ILASS .... Integrated Light Attack Avionics System [*Navy*]
ILC .... Instruction Length Code [*Data processing*]
ILDP .... Interlook Dormant Period
ILIP .... In-Line Instrument Package [*Nuclear energy*]
ILIR .... In-House Laboratory Independent Research
ILLIAC ...... Illinois Integrator and Automatic Computer
ILo .... Iodine Lotion [*Medicine*]
ILP .... Intermediate Language Processor [*Data processing*]
ILS .... International Lilac Society
ILSG .... Interim Logistics Support Guide
ILTS .... Intermediate Level Test Station
IM .... Item Mark
IMAGES .... Instructional Material Adequacy Guide and Evaluation Standard
IMCC .... Interstate Mining Compact Commission
IMDT .... Immediate
IMF .... Impact Mechanical Fuze
IMHP .... Isopropyl Methyl Pyrimidinone [*Organic chemistry*]
IMI .... Institute on Money and Inflation
IMI .... Interrogation Sign [*Question mark*] [*Communications*]
IMIF .... International Maritime Industries Forum
IMMAT ...... Immature
IMMUN ...... Immunity
IMMUNOL ... Immunology
IMNB .... Isopropyl(methyl)nitrobenzene [*Organic chemistry*]
IMO .... International Mathematical Olympiad
IMP .... Important
IMPATT ..... Impact Ionization Avalanche Transit Time [*Solid state diodes*] [*Transistor technology*]
IMPGAC ..... Improved Guidance and Control
IMPIS .... Indirect Material Purchasing Information Standards
IMPX .... Impaction [*Dentistry*]
IMRB .... Improved Main Rotor Blade
IMT .... Induced Muscular Tension [*Physiology*]
In .... Insulin
INBSV .... Interim Narrow-Band Secure Voice
INC .... Incomplete
INC .... Inconclusive
INC .... Insertable Nuclear Components
INCA .... Integrated Numerical Control Approach
INCOR........ Incorporated
INCOT .... In-Core Test Facility [*Nuclear energy*]
INCSEA .... Incident at Sea [*Navy*]
IND .... Improvised Nuclear Device
IndMed ..... Index Medicus [*A publication*]
INEL .... Idaho Nuclear Engineering Laboratory
INFA .... International Nuclear Fuel Authority
INFO......... Information Network and File Organization
INH .... Inhalation
INICR .... Institute for Childhood Resources
INMARSAT ... International Maritime Satellite System [*Department of Commerce*]
INN .... Independent Network News [*Television*]
INNERV ..... Innervation [*Medicine*]
INO .... Iterative Natural Orbital [*Atomic physics*]
INPH.......... Iproniazid Phosphate [*Organic chemistry*]
INREM .... Internal REM [*Roentgen-Equivalent-Man*] [*Radiation dose*]
INSCOM.... Intelligence and Security Command [*Army*]
INSP .... Anspiration
INSURE ..... Industry Network for Social, Urban, and Rural Efforts
INT .... Intermediate

INT .... Intermittent
INT .... Interne [*Medicine*]
INT .... Internist [*Medicine*]
INT .... Intersection
INT .... Interstate Airlines, Inc. [*Ypsilanti, MI*] [*FAA designator*]
INTERALIS ... International Advanced Life Information System
INTEREX ... International Exchangors Association
INTERPRO ... International Probation Organization
INTEST ..... Intestinal
INTH .... Intrathecal [*Within a sheath*] [*Medicine*]
INTOX ...... Intoxication
INTSFY ..... Intensify [*Meteorology*]
INVOL .... Involuntary
INX .... Ion Exchange
IOI .... International Orphans, Incorporated
IOK .... International Order of Kabbalists
ION .... Ionic
IOP .... Initial Operating Production
IOP .... Inspection Operation Procedure
IOP .... Integrated Ordinance Package
IOP .... Interim Operating Procedure
IOR .... Index of Refraction
IOWE .... International Organization of Women Executives
I & P .... Inerting and Preheating [*Nuclear energy*]
IP .... Infection Prevention
IP .... Information Processing
IP .... Intellectual Property
IPA .... Information Process Analysis
IPA .... Interior Plantscape Association
IPA .... Isopropyl Alcohol [*Organic chemistry*]
IPADS ...... Interactive Processing and Display System
IPC .... Imaging Proportional Counter [*Astronomy*]
IPC .... Interconnections Packaging Circuitry
IPC .... Interprocessor Communication
IPD .... Instructional Program Development
IPDD .... Initial Project Design Description
IPG .... Isopropylthiogalactoside [*Organic chemistry*]
IPH .... Interphalangeal [*In reference to finger or toe joints*] [*Medicine*]
IPJ .... Institute for Peace and Justice
IPL .... Initial Program Load
IPN .... Instant Private Network
IPNA .... Isopropylnoradrenaline
IPOSA ...... International Photo Optical Show Association
IPP .... Integrated Plotting Package
IPPA .... Intercontinental Press Publishing Association
IPPB/I ...... Intermittent Positive Pressure Breathing/Inspiratory
IPPC .... Isopropyl N-phenylcarbamate [*Herbicide*] [*Also, INPC, IPC*]
IPPD .... Isopropyl(phenyl)para-phenylene Diamine [*Organic chemistry*]
IPPNW .... International Physicians for the Prevention of Nuclear War
IPPV .... Intermittent Positive Pressure Ventilation
IPS .... Interim Policy Statement
IPS .... Item Processing System
IPT .... Improved Programing Technologies
IPT .... Institute of Property Taxation
IPU .... Instruction Processing Unit
IPV .... Infectious Pustular Vaginitis [*Medicine*]
IPZP .... Iranian Peace Zebra Program [*Military*]
IQPF .... International Quick Printing Foundation
I-R .... Ito-Reenstierna [*Reaction*] [*Medicine*]
IRA .... Individual Retirement Arrangement
IRAC .... Indochina Refugee Action Center
IRAP .... Interagency Radiological Assistance Program
IRC .... International Record Carrier
IRCS .... Intersite Radio Communications System
IRCSI .... International Rabbinic Committee for the Safety of Israel
IRDO .... Intermediate Retention of Differential Overlap [*Physics*]
IRETS .... Infantry Remoted Target System
IRGI .... Immunoreactive Glucagon
IRGP .... Infrared Guided Projectile
IRH .... Institute for Research in History
IRL .... Institute on Religious Life
IRM .... Intermediate Range Monitor
IRMA .... International Rock 'n' Roll Music Association
IRO .... International Reception Operators [*An organization*]

IRODP .... International Registry of Organization Development Professionals
IROS .... Ipsilateral Routing of Signal
IRP .... Information Return Program [*IRS*]
IRPL .... Index to Religious Periodical Literature [*Data base*]
IRR .... Initial Rate of Return
IRRG .... Irrigation
IRRS .... Infrared Reconnaissance System
IRRTS .... Infrared Resolution Target System
IRS .... Interchange Record Separator [*Data processing*]
IRS .... Isoleucyl-tRNA Synthetase [*An enzyme*]
IRSCAN ..... Infrared Scanner
IRSU .... International Religious Studies Unit
IRT .... In Reference To
IRT .... In Reply To
IRT .... In Response To
IRW .... Indirect Reference Word
IS .... Immune Serum
IS .... Independent Sector [*An organization*]
IS .... Inside Sentinel [*Masonry*]
IS .... International Standard
ISA .... Institute for Scientific Analysis
ISA .... Integrated Support Area
ISAM .... Institute for Studies in American Music
ISASC ...... International Society of Antique Scale Collectors
ISB .... Intermediate Support Base [*Military*]
ISBA .... International Ships-in-Bottles Association
ISBD .... International Soap Box Derby, Inc.
ISC .... Integrated Storage Control
ISC .... International Society for Chronobiology
ISC .... Interstitial Cells [*Histology*]
ISCT .... Inner Seal Collar Tool [*Nuclear energy*]
ISD .... Isosorbide Dinitrate [*Organic chemistry*]
ISDF .... Impact Short Delay Fuze
ISDF .... Intermediate Sodium Disposal Facility [*Nuclear energy*]
ISDS .... Institute for Social Dance Studies
ISE .... Ion Selective Electrode [*Instrumentation*]
ISER .... Integral Systems Experimental Requirements
ISF .... Imperial Smelting Furnace [*Zinc and lead*]
ISFMS .... Indexed Sequential File Management System
ISFSI .... Independent Spent Fuel Storage Installation [*Nuclear energy*]
ISG .... Interfacial Surface Generation [*Instrumentation*]
ISGE .... International Society for Geothermal Engineering
ISHE .... International Society for Human Ethology
ISHOF .... International Swimming Hall of Fame
ISI .... In-Service Inspection
ISJ .... Institute for Social Justice
ISLS .... Islands [*Board on Geographic Names*]
ISMED .... International Society on Metabolic Eye Disease
ISOLN .... Isolation
ISOTAP ..... Interservice Occupational Task Analysis Program [*Military*]
ISP .... Imperial Smelting Process
ISP .... Industrial Security Plan [*Nuclear energy*]
ISP .... Intraspinal
ISP .... Isolated Safflower Protein [*Food technology*]
ISP .... Specific Impulse
ISR .... International Star Registry
ISR .... ISO Aero Service, Inc. [*Kingston, NC*] [*FAA designator*]
ISRA .... International Society for Research on Aggression
ISS .... International Society of Surgery
ISSA .... Institute of Social Services Alternatives
ISSMS .... Interim Surface-to-Surface Missile System
IST .... Information Science and Technology
IST .... Institute for Safety in Transportation
ISTS .... International Society for Twin Studies
ISU .... Interface Switching Unit
ISV .... Interval Service Value
ISY .... Intrasynovial [*Medicine*]
I & T .... Inspection and Test
IT .... Instrument Test [*or Tree*] [*Nuclear energy*]
IT .... Intelligent Terminal [*Data processing*]
IT .... Interval Training [*Physical fitness program*]
IT .... Intrathoracic [*Medicine*]
ITA .... International Trombone Association
ITA .... Itaconic Acid [*Organic chemistry*]
IT & AP ...... Inspection Test and Analysis Plan

ITAWDS .... Integrated Tactical Amphibious Warfare Data System [*Navy*]
ITB .... In the Business [*Refers to television and film industries*]
ITB .... Intermediate Transmission Block [*Data processing*]
ITC .... Interagency Testing Committee [*Toxicology*]
ITC .... International Teletraffic Congress
ITCI .... International Tree Crops Institute USA
ITDM .... Intelligent Time-Division Multiplexer
ITE .... In the Ear [*Hearing aid*]
ITF .... Interstitial Transfer Facility [*Nuclear energy*]
ITFTRIA ..... Instrument Tree Flow and Temperature Removal Instrument Assembly [*Nuclear energy*]
ITIP .... Improved Transtage Injector Program
ITMA .... Irradiation Test Management Activity
ITR .... Intratracheal [*Medicine*]
ITRIA .... Instrument Tree Removable Instrument Assembly [*Nuclear energy*]
ITRO .... Interservice Training Review Organization [*Military*]
ITS .... Idaho Test Station [*Nuclear energy*]
IT/SP .... Instrument Tree/Spool Piece [*Nuclear energy*]

ITX .... Independent Tour Excursion [*Airline fare*]
IU .... Intrauterine [*Medicine*]
IUC .... Immediate Unit Commander [*Navy*]
IUD .... Intrauterine Death [*Medicine*]
IUS .... Interchange Unit Separator [*Data processing*]
IV .... Intraventricular [*Cardiology*]
IVD .... Intervertebral Disc [*Medicine*]
IVHM .... In-Vessel Handling Machine [*Nuclear energy*]
IVHM-EM .. In-Vessel Handling Machine-Engineering Model [*Nuclear energy*]
IVO .... Improved Virtual Orbitals [*Atomic physics*]
IVS .... In-Vessel Storage [*Nuclear energy*]
IVSM .... In-Vessel Storage Module [*Nuclear energy*]
IWCA .... International Windsurfer Class Association
IWDM .... Intermediate Water Depth Mine
IWS/IT ...... Integrated Work Sequence/Inspection Traveler
IWTC .... International Women's Tribune Centre
IX .... Index
IZ .... Isolation Zone [*Nuclear energy*]

J

J (Cars)..... Designation for certain General Motors front-wheel-drive cars

JAB .... January Assumption Budget [*Budget based on economic forecasts available as of January*]

JACGUAR ... Johns and Call Girls United Against Repression

JADOR ...... Joint Advertising Directors of Recruiting [*Navy*]

JAFPUB .... Joint Army-Air Force Publication

JAM........... JUMPS [*Joint Uniform Military Pay System*] Action Memorandum

JARTRAN ... James A. Ryder Transportation [*Acronym is trade name of truck-rental firm*]

JASC......... Japan-American Student Conference

JASNA ...... Jane Austen Society of North America

JAUND ...... Jaundice [*Medicine*]

JAVA......... Jamming Amplitude Versus Azimuth

JBANC ...... Joint Baltic American National Committee

JC............. Jump on Condition [*Data processing*]

JCB .... Job Control Block [*Data processing*]

JCC........... Joint Communications Center

JCMHC ..... Joint Commission on Mental Health of Children

JEM........... Jet Engine Modulation

JET............ Job English Training

JEX .... Joint Exercise

JEZEX ...... Jezebel [*Sonobuoy*] Exercise [*Navy*]

JFCB .... Job File Control Block [*Data processing*]

JFKL .... John F. Kennedy Library

JFPH .... JUMPS [*Joint Uniform Military Pay System*] Field Procedures Handbook

JI .... Air Balear [*Spain*] [*ICAO designator*]

JIB............. Job Information Block [*Data processing*]

JJ .... Jaw Jerk [*Medicine*]

JK.............. Jishu Kanri [*Voluntary Management*] [*Japanese method for increasing productivity of industrial workers by involving them in planning*]

JMPP......... Joint Munitions Production Panel

JMS........... Jacob More Society

JMU........... James Madison University [*Virginia*]

JNA .... JerDon Air Service, Inc. [*Ardmore, OK*] [*FAA designator*]

JNO .... John [*New Testament book*]

JNY .... Jenney Beechcraft, Inc. [*East Bedford, MA*] [*FAA designator*]

JOCAS...... Job Order Cost Account System

JON .... Job Order Number

JONSDAP ... Joint North Sea Data Acquisition Program

Journ Annu Diabetol Hotel-Dieu ... Journees Annuelles de Diabetologie Hotel-Dieu [*A publication*]

JPAM .... Joint Program Assessment Memorandum

JPL Tech Memo ... JPL [*Jet Propulsion Laboratory*] Technical Memorandum [*A publication*]

JPL Tech Rep ... JPL [*Jet Propulsion Laboratory*] Technical Report [*A publication*]

JPSS .... Just, Participatory, and Sustainable Society [*World Council of Churches*]

JR.............. John Ross Ewing, Jr. [*Character in TV series ''Dallas''*]

JRNDEX .... Journal Index

JS............... Judean Society

JSATG ...... Joint Services Actions Task Group

JSCB......... Job Step Control Block [*Data processing*]

JSPD .... Joint Strategic Planning Document

JSR .... Jump to Subroutine [*Data processing*]

JSRT .... Joint Short Range Technology

JSSUP....... Japanese Space Shuttle Utilization Program

JTCG/MD ... Joint Technical Coordinating Group for Munitions Development [*Military*]

JTE............ Joint Technical Evaluation

JTN .... Jewish Television Network

JTR............ Santorini [*Thira Islands*] [*Airport symbol*]

JUB .... Juba [*Sudan*] [*Airport symbol*]

JUD .... Judith [*Old Testament book*]

Jugosl Ginekol Opstet ... Jugoslovenska Ginekologija i Opstetricija [*A publication*]

Jugosl Pedijatr ... Jugoslovenska Pediajatrija [*A publication*]

JUI............. Juist [*West Germany*] [*Airport symbol*]

JUJ............. Jujuy [*Argentina*] [*Airport symbol*]

JUL............ Juliaca [*Peru*] [*Airport symbol*]

JULIEX...... Julie [*Sonobuoy*] Exercise [*Navy*]

J Ultrastruct Res ... Journal of Ultrastructure Research [*A publication*]

J Ultrastruct Res Suppl ... Journal of Ultrastructure Research. Supplement [*A publication*]

JUM........... Jumla [*Nepal*] [*Airport symbol*]

J Univ Bombay ... Journal of the University of Bombay [*A publication*]

J Univ Gauhati ... Journal of the University of Gauhati [*A publication*]

J Univ Kuwait (Sci) ... Journal of the University of Kuwait (Science) [*A publication*]

J Univ Poona Sci Technol ... Journal of the University of Poona. Science and Technology [*A publication*]

J Univ Saugar ... Journal of the University of Saugar [*A publication*]

J Urol Nephrol ... Journal d'Urologie et de Nephrologie [*A publication*]

Justus Liebigs Ann Chem ... Justus Liebigs Annalen der Chemie [*A publication*]

JUVE .... Juvenile

JVA .... Ankavandra [*Madagascar*] [*Airport symbol*]

JVD .... Juris Utriusque Doctor [*Doctor of Both Laws; ie, Canon and Civil Law*]

J Verb Learn Verb Behav ... Journal of Verbal Learning and Verbal Behavior [*A publication*]

J Vet Anim Husb Res (India) ... Journal of Veterinary and Animal Husbandry Research (India) [*A publication*]

J Virol........ Journal of Virology [*A publication*]

J Vitaminol (Kyoto) ... Journal of Vitaminology (Kyoto) [*A publication*]

JVL............ Beloit/Janesville [*Wisconsin*] [*Airport symbol*]

J Wakayama Med Soc ... Journal of the Wakayama Medical Society [*A publication*]

J West Afr Inst Oil Palm Res ... Journal of the West African Institute for Oil Palm Research [*A publication*]

J West Afr Sci Assoc ... Journal of the West African Science Association [*A publication*]

J Wildl Dis ... Journal of Wildlife Diseases [*A publication*]

J Wildl Manage ... Journal of Wildlife Management [*A publication*]

JWKB........ Jordan-Wentzel-Kramers-Brillouin [*Physics*]

JWY........... Jet Way, Inc. [*Ypsilanti, MI*] [*FAA designator*]

JXN .... Jackson [*Michigan*] [*Airport symbol*]

JY .... Jersey European Airways [*Great Britain*] [*ICAO designator*]

J Yamagata Agric For Soc ... Journal of the Yamagata Agriculture and Forestry Society [*A publication*]

J Yonago Med Assoc ... Journal of the Yonago Medical Association [*A publication*]

JYV............ Jyvaskyla [*Finland*] [*Airport symbol*]

J Zoo Anim Med ... Journal of Zoo Animal Medicine [*A publication*]

J Zool Soc India ... Journal of the Zoological Society of India [*A publication*]

K

K .... Invitation to Transmit [*Communications*]

K .... [*Georg*] Kinsky [*When used in identifying Beethoven's compositions, refers to cataloging of his works by musicologist Kinsky*]

K .... [*Ralph*] Kirkpatrick [*When used in identifying D. Scarlatti's compositions, refers to cataloging of his works by musicologist Kirkpatrick*]

K .... [*Ludwig Ritter von*] Koechel [*When used in identifying Mozart's compositions, refers to cataloging of his works by musicologist Koechel*]

K (Cars) .... Designation for certain Chrysler front-wheel-drive cars [*Aries, Reliant*]

3 K's .... Kingsley, Kinsella, and Keeney [*Prominent citizens of Brooklyn; all three died within a year of each other, 1884-1885*]

K/A .... Ketogenic to Anti-Ketogenic [*Ratio*] [*In diets*]

KAA .... Kasama [*Zambia*] [*Airport symbol*]

KAAN .... Bethany, MO [*Broadcasting station call letters*]

KAB .... Kariba Dam [*Zimbabwe*] [*Airport symbol*]

KABE .... Orem, UT [*Broadcasting station call letters*]

KABK .... Augusta, AR [*Broadcasting station call letters*]

Kabul Univ Fac Agric Res Note ... Kabul University Faculty of Agriculture. Research Notes [*A publication*]

Kabul Univ Fac Agric Tech Bull ... Kabul University Faculty of Agriculture. Technical Bulletin [*A publication*]

KAC .... Kameshli [*Syria*] [*Airport symbol*]

K Acad Belg Jaarb ... Koninklijk Academie van Belgie Jaarboek [*A publication*]

KACJ .... Greenwood, AR [*Broadcasting station call letters*]

KACQ .... Hot Springs, AR [*Broadcasting station call letters*]

KACT-FM ... Andrews, TX [*Broadcasting station call letters*]

KAD .... Kaduna [*Nigeria*] [*Airport symbol*]

KADX .... Denver, CO [*Broadcasting station call letters*]

KAE .... Inglewood, CA [*Broadcasting station call letters*]

KAE .... Kake [*Alaska*] [*Airport symbol*]

KAER .... Sacramento, CA [*Broadcasting station call letters*]

KAGO-FM ... Klamath Falls, OR [*Broadcasting station call letters*]

KAI .... Kaieteur [*Guyana*] [*Airport symbol*]

KAI .... Keystone Aviation, Inc. [*New Cumberland, PA*] [*FAA designator*]

KAJ .... Kajaani [*Finland*] [*Airport symbol*]

KAJN-FM ... Crowley, LA [*Broadcasting station call letters*]

KAK .... Key-Auto-Key [*Data processing*]

KAKA .... Dermott, AR [*Broadcasting station call letters*]

KAKI .... Benton, AR [*Broadcasting station call letters*]

KAKZ .... Wichita, KS [*Broadcasting station call letters*]

KAL .... Kalendae [*The Kalends*] [*First day of the ancient Roman month*]

KAL .... Kaltag [*Alaska*] [*Airport symbol*]

KAMQ .... Carlsbad, NM [*Broadcasting station call letters*]

KAN .... Kano [*Nigeria*] [*Airport symbol*]

Kans Agric Exp Stn Bienn Rep Dir ... Kansas Agricultural Experiment Station. Biennial Report of the Director [*A publication*]

Kans Agric Exp Stn Bull ... Kansas Agricultural Experiment Station. Bulletin [*A publication*]

Kans Agric Exp Stn Circ ... Kansas Agricultural Experiment Station. Circular [*A publication*]

Kans Agric Exp Stn Res Publ ... Kansas Agricultural Experiment Station. Research Publication [*A publication*]

Kans Agric Exp Stn Tech Bull ... Kansas Agricultural Experiment Station. Technical Bulletin [*A publication*]

KANZ .... Garden City, KS [*Broadcasting station call letters*]

KAO .... Kuusamo [*Finland*] [*Airport symbol*]

KAOS .... Killer as an Organized Sport [*Campus game*]

KAPI-FM ... Pueblo, CO [*Broadcasting station call letters*]

KAR .... Kamarang [*Guyana*] [*Airport symbol*]

Kardiol Pol ... Kardiologia Polska [*A publication*]

Kariba Stud ... Kariba Studies [*A publication*]

Karnataka Med J ... Karnataka Medical Journal [*A publication*]

Karnatak Univ J Sci ... Karnatak University Journal of Science [*A publication*]

KARO .... Vancouver, WA [*Broadcasting station call letters*]

KARZ .... Phoenix, AZ [*Broadcasting station call letters*]

Kasetsart Univ Fish Res Bull ... Kasetsart University. Fishery Research Bulletin [*A publication*]

Kashmir Sci ... Kashmir Science [*A publication*]

Kasr El-Aini J Surg ... Kasr El-Aini Journal of Surgery [*A publication*]

KAT .... Kaitaia [*New Zealand*] [*Airport symbol*]

Kat Fauny Pol ... Katalog Fauny Polski [*A publication*]

KATQ .... Plentywood, MT [*Broadcasting station call letters*]

KATQ-FM ... Plentywood, MT [*Broadcasting station call letters*]

KATS .... Yakima, WA [*Broadcasting station call letters*]

KAU .... Keystation Adapter Unit [*Data processing*]

KAVV .... Benson, AZ [*Broadcasting station call letters*]

KAW .... Kawthaung [*Burma*] [*Airport symbol*]

Kawasaki Med J ... Kawasaki Medical Journal [*A publication*]

KAWS .... Hemphill, TX [*Broadcasting station call letters*]

KAX .... Kalbarri [*Australia*] [*Airport symbol*]

KAY .... Wakaya [*Fiji*] [*Airport symbol*]

KAYR .... Van Buren, AR [*Broadcasting station call letters*]

KAYY .... Fairbanks, AK [*Broadcasting station call letters*]

KAYZ .... El Dorado, AR [*Broadcasting station call letters*]

Kazan Med Zh ... Kazanskii Meditsinskii Zhurnal [*A publication*]

KAZI .... Austin, TX [*Broadcasting station call letters*]

KBA .... Kabala [*Sierra Leone*] [*Airport symbol*]

KBBI .... Homer, AK [*Broadcasting station call letters*]

KBBX .... Centerville, UT [*Broadcasting station call letters*]

KBC .... Birch Creek [*Alaska*] [*Airport symbol*]

KBCC .... Cuba, MO [*Broadcasting station call letters*]

KBCR-FM ... Steamboat Springs, CO [*Broadcasting station call letters*]

KBDG .... Turlock, CA [*Broadcasting station call letters*]

K Belg Inst Natuurwet Studiedoc ... Koninklijk Belgisch Instituut voor Natuurwetenschappen Studiedocumenten [*A publication*]

K Belg Inst Natuurwet Verh ... Koninklijk Belgisch Instituut voor Natuurwetenschappen Verhandelingen [*A publication*]

KBER .... Abilene, TX [*Broadcasting station call letters*]

KBFI .... Bonners Ferry, ID [*Broadcasting station call letters*]

KBGG-FM ... Merkel, TX [*Broadcasting station call letters*]

KBKR-FM ... Baker, OR [*Broadcasting station call letters*]

KBL .... Kabul [*Afghanistan*] [*Airport symbol*]

KBLL-FM .. Helena, MT [*Broadcasting station call letters*]

KBLS .... Santa Barbara, CA [*Broadcasting station call letters*]

KBLT .... Baxter Springs, KS [*Broadcasting station call letters*]

KBLX......... Berkeley, CA [*Broadcasting station call letters*]
KBON........ Lake Arrowhead, CA [*Broadcasting station call letters*]
KBP........... Kiev [*USSR*] Borispol Airport [*Airport symbol*]
KBR........... Kota Bharu [*Malaysia*] [*Airport symbol*]
KBS........... Bo [*Sierra Leone*] [*Airport symbol*]
KBSH........ Borrego Springs, CA [*Broadcasting station call letters*]
KBSQ........ Espanola, NM [*Broadcasting station call letters*]
KBTC-FM ... Houston, MO [*Broadcasting station call letters*]
KBWH .... Blair, NE [*Broadcasting station call letters*]
KBY........... Streaky Bay [*Australia*] [*Airport symbol*]
KBZN........ Bozeman, MT [*Broadcasting station call letters*]
KBZT......... San Diego, CA [*Broadcasting station call letters*]
KC............ Kathodal Closing [*Medicine*]
KC............ Kilocharacter
KCAN........ El Reno, OK [*Broadcasting station call letters*]
KCCW....... Terrell Hills, TX [*Broadcasting station call letters*]
KCCY........ Pueblo, CO [*Broadcasting station call letters*]
KCE........... Collinsville [*Australia*] [*Airport symbol*]
KCH........... Kuching [*Malaysia*] [*Airport symbol*]
KCI............ Aeromech Commuter Airlines [*Clarksburg, WV*] [*FAA designator*]
KCKO........ Spokane, WA [*Broadcasting station call letters*]
KCKS........ Concordia, KS [*Broadcasting station call letters*]
KCLB .... Santa Rosa, CA [*Broadcasting station call letters*]
KCLI.......... Clinton, OK [*Broadcasting station call letters*]
KCLY .... Clay Center, KS [*Broadcasting station call letters*]
KCLY .... Clay Center, KS [*Broadcasting station call letters*]
KCME .... Manitou Springs, CO [*Broadcasting station call letters*]
KCMI......... Terrytown, NE [*Broadcasting station call letters*]
KCMQ....... Columbia, MO [*Broadcasting station call letters*]
KCMR .... Mason City, IA [*Broadcasting station call letters*]
KCNB .... Waterloo, IA [*Broadcasting station call letters*]
KCPB .... Thousand Oaks, CA [*Broadcasting station call letters*]
KCPS .... Burlington, IA [*Broadcasting station call letters*]
KCRE .... Crescent City, CA [*Broadcasting station call letters*]
KCSD .... Chinle, AZ [*Broadcasting station call letters*]
KCSJ-FM ... Pueblo, CO [*Broadcasting station call letters*]
KCT.......... Kathodal Closing Tetanus [*Medicine*]
KCTB .... Flagstaff, AZ [*Broadcasting station call letters*]
KCTE .... Southwest City, MO [*Broadcasting station call letters*]
KCYN .... Pocahontas, AR [*Broadcasting station call letters*]
KCYX .... McMinnville, OR [*Broadcasting station call letters*]
KCZ........... Kochi [*Japan*] [*Airport symbol*]
KD............ Kathodal Duration [*Medicine*]
K Dan Vidensk Selsk Biol Skr ... Kongelige Danske Videnskabernes Selskab Biologiske Skrifter [*A publication*]
KDAO........ Marshalltown, IA [*Broadcasting station call letters*]
KDB........... Kambalda [*Australia*] [*Airport symbol*]
KDB........... Keller-Dorian, Berthon [*Method*] [*Photography*]
KDE........... Koroba [*Papua New Guinea*] [*Airport symbol*]
KDEM....... Deming, NM [*Broadcasting station call letters*]
KDEY .... Lufkin, TX [*Broadcasting station call letters*]
KDH........... Kandahar [*Afghanistan*] [*Airport symbol*]
KDI............ Kendari [*Indonesia*] [*Airport symbol*]
KDIG .... San Bernardino, CA [*Broadcasting station call letters*]
KDIQ .... Boise, ID [*Broadcasting station call letters*]
KDJQ .... Mesa, AZ [*Broadcasting station call letters*]
KDK .... Kodiak [*Alaska*] Municipal Airport [*Airport symbol*]
KDKQ .... Borger, TX [*Broadcasting station call letters*]
KDLN .... Dillon, MT [*Broadcasting station call letters*]
KDN .... N'Dende [*Gabon*] [*Airport symbol*]
KDOS .... Fremont, CA [*Broadcasting station call letters*]
KDP........... Kandep [*Papua New Guinea*] [*Airport symbol*]
KDQN-FM ... De Queen, AR [*Broadcasting station call letters*]
KDQQ........ Albuquerque, NM [*Broadcasting station call letters*]
KDR........... Kandrian [*Papua New Guinea*] [*Airport symbol*]
KDRK .... Spokane, WA [*Broadcasting station call letters*]
KDT........... Kathodal Duration Tetanus [*Medicine*]
KDUK .... Honolulu, HI [*Broadcasting station call letters*]
KDVL........ Devils Lake, ND [*Broadcasting station call letters*]
KDWT-FM ... Stamford, TX [*Broadcasting station call letters*]
KEAM....... Port Arthur, TX [*Broadcasting station call letters*]
KEAN .... Abilene, TX [*Broadcasting station call letters*]
KED.......... Kaedi [*Mauritania*] [*Airport symbol*]
KEDP .... Las Vegas, NV [*Broadcasting station call letters*]
KEF .... Reykjavik [*Iceland*] Keflavik Airport [*Airport symbol*]
KEI .... Kepi [*Indonesia*] [*Airport symbol*]
Keio J Med ... Keio Journal of Medicine [*A publication*]

KEIS.......... Kentucky Economic Information System [*Information service*]
KEJO......... Corvallis, OR [*Broadcasting station call letters*]
KEK .... Ekwok [*Alaska*] [*Airport symbol*]
KEKA .... Eureka, CA [*Broadcasting station call letters*]
KELC .... England, AR [*Broadcasting station call letters*]
KELN .... North Platte, NE [*Broadcasting station call letters*]
KEM .... Kemi [*Finland*] [*Airport symbol*]
KEMM-FM ... Marshfield, MO [*Broadcasting station call letters*]
KEN .... Kenema [*Sierra Leone*] [*Airport symbol*]
KENW-FM ... Portales, NM [*Broadcasting station call letters*]
Kenya Dep Agric Annu Rep ... Kenya Department of Agriculture. Annual Report [*A publication*]
KEO........... Odienne [*Ivory Coast*] [*Airport symbol*]
KEP........... Nepalganj [*Nepal*] [*Airport symbol*]
KEQ........... Kebar [*Indonesia*] [*Airport symbol*]
KER........... Kerman [*Iran*] [*Airport symbol*]
Kerala J Vet Sci ... Kerala Journal of Veterinary Science [*A publication*]
KESE......... Monterey, CA [*Broadcasting station call letters*]
KESP......... Eureka Springs, AR [*Broadcasting station call letters*]
KESY .... Omaha, NE [*Broadcasting station call letters*]
KESY-FM ... Omaha, NE [*Broadcasting station call letters*]
KET........... Kengtung [*Burma*] [*Airport symbol*]
Kew Bull ... Kew Bulletin [*A publication*]
Kew Bull Addit Ser ... Kew Bulletin. Additional Series [*A publication*]
KEWE........ Oroville, CA [*Broadcasting station call letters*]
KEX........... Kanabea [*Papua New Guinea*] [*Airport symbol*]
KEXL......... Norfolk, NE [*Broadcasting station call letters*]
KEXX......... Corpus Christi, TX [*Broadcasting station call letters*]
KEYE-FM ... Perryton, TX [*Broadcasting station call letters*]
KEYMAT ... Keying Material [*Data processing*]
KEZH......... Hastings, NE [*Broadcasting station call letters*]
KEZQ .... Jacksonville, AR [*Broadcasting station call letters*]
KEZS......... Liberal, KS [*Broadcasting station call letters*]
KFA........... Kiffa [*Mauritania*] [*Airport symbol*]
KFA........... Krishnamurti Foundation of America
KFAI.......... Minneapolis, MN [*Broadcasting station call letters*]
KFAN .... Fredericksburg, TX [*Broadcasting station call letters*]
KFBQ .... Cheyenne, WY [*Broadcasting station call letters*]
KFHM....... San Antonio, TX [*Broadcasting station call letters*]
KFIA......... Carmichael, CA [*Broadcasting station call letters*]
KFIM .... El Paso, TX [*Broadcasting station call letters*]
KFIO .... Ridgecrest, CA [*Broadcasting station call letters*]
KFKX........ Gregory, SD [*Broadcasting station call letters*]
KFLR .... Phoenix, AZ [*Broadcasting station call letters*]
KFLT .... Tucson, AZ [*Broadcasting station call letters*]
KFMT....... Moses Lake, WA [*Broadcasting station call letters*]
KFMX....... Minneapolis, MN [*Broadcasting station call letters*]
KFP........... False Pass [*Alaska*] [*Airport symbol*]
KFRN .... Long Beach, CA [*Broadcasting station call letters*]
KFRX........ Lincoln, NE [*Broadcasting station call letters*]
KFSH........ Hilo, HI [*Broadcasting station call letters*]
KFXY........ Morgan City, LA [*Broadcasting station call letters*]
K Fysiogr Sallsk Lund Arsb ... Kungliga Fysiografiska Sallskapets i Lund Arsbok [*A publication*]
K Fysiogr Sallsk Lund Forh ... Kungliga Fysiografiska Sallskapets i Lund Forhandlingar [*A publication*]
KFYZ-FM .. Bonham, TX [*Broadcasting station call letters*]
KG............ Orion Airways Ltd. [*Great Britain*] [*ICAO designator*]
KGA......... Kananga [*Zaire*] [*Airport symbol*]
KGAA .... Kirkland, WA [*Broadcasting station call letters*]
KGAM ...... Bakersfield, CA [*Broadcasting station call letters*]
KGAR........ Portland, OR [*Broadcasting station call letters*]
KGC .... Kingscote [*Australia*] [*Airport symbol*]
KGFJ......... Los Angeles, CA [*Broadcasting station call letters*]
KGFL........ Clinton, AR [*Broadcasting station call letters*]
KGG .... Kedougou [*Senegal*] [*Airport symbol*]
KGGI .... Riverside, CA [*Broadcasting station call letters*]
KGI .... Kalgoorlie [*Australia*] [*Airport symbol*]
KGIR .... Cape Girardeau, MO [*Broadcasting station call letters*]
KGJ .... Karonga [*Malawi*] [*Airport symbol*]
KGK .... Koliganek [*Alaska*] [*Airport symbol*]
KGL .... Kigali [*Rwanda*] [*Airport symbol*]
KGNR........ Sacramento, CA [*Broadcasting station call letters*]
KGOK....... Paul's Valley, OK [*Broadcasting station call letters*]
KGS .... Kos [*Greece*] [*Airport symbol*]
KGSU-FM ... Cedar City, UT [*Broadcasting station call letters*]
KGTL......... Homer, AK [*Broadcasting station call letters*]

KGU .... Keningau [*Malaysia*] [*Airport symbol*]
KGW .... Kagi [*Papua New Guinea*] [*Airport symbol*]
KGX .... Grayling [*Alaska*] [*Airport symbol*]
KGY .... Kingaroy [*Australia*] [*Airport symbol*]
KHAM .... Horseshoe Bend, AR [*Broadcasting station call letters*]
Kharchova Promst ... Kharchova Promyslovist [*A publication*]
KHDN-FM ... Hardin, MT [*Broadcasting station call letters*]
KHEI .... Kihei, HI [*Broadcasting station call letters*]
KHH .... Kaohsiung [*Taiwan*] [*Airport symbol*]
KHI .... Karachi [*Pakistan*] [*Airport symbol*]
Khig Zdraveopaz ... Khigiena i Zdraveopazane [*A publication*]
Khim-Farm Zh ... Khimiko-Farmatsevticheskii Zhurnal [*A publication*]
Khim Nauka Prom-st ... Khimicheskaya Nauka i Promyshlennost [*A publication*]
Khim Prir Soedin (Tashk) ... Khimiya Prirodnykh Soedinenii (Tashkent) [*A publication*]
Khim Sel'sk Khoz ... Khimiya v Sel'skom Khozaistve [*A publication*]
KHIP .... Hollister, CA [*Broadcasting station call letters*]
KHK .... Khark [*Iran*] [*Airport symbol*]
KHLB-FM ... Burnet, TX [*Broadcasting station call letters*]
KHM .... Khamtis [*Burma*] [*Airport symbol*]
KHN .... Nanchang [*China*] [*Airport symbol*]
KHOH .... Hoisington, KS [*Broadcasting station call letters*]
KHOL .... Beulah, ND [*Broadcasting station call letters*]
KHOW-FM ... Denver, CO [*Broadcasting station call letters*]
KHPR .... Honolulu, HI [*Broadcasting station call letters*]
KHT .... Khost [*Afghanistan*] [*Airport symbol*]
KHTZ .... Los Angeles, CA [*Broadcasting station call letters*]
KHUM .... Denver, CO [*Broadcasting station call letters*]
KHUT .... Hutchinson, KS [*Broadcasting station call letters*]
KHV .... Khabarovsk [*USSR*] [*Airport symbol*]
KHVN .... Anchorage, AK [*Broadcasting station call letters*]
KHYE .... Hemet, CA [*Broadcasting station call letters*]
KHYS .... Port Arthur, TX [*Broadcasting station call letters*]
KI .... Kings [*Old Testament book*]
KIA .... Kligler Iron Agar [*Medium*]
KIAE .... Aurora, NE [*Broadcasting station call letters*]
KIAL .... Unalaska, AK [*Broadcasting station call letters*]
KICR .... Coos Bay, OR [*Broadcasting station call letters*]
KICX-FM ... McCook, NE [*Broadcasting station call letters*]
KID .... Kristianstad [*Sweden*] [*Airport symbol*]
KID-FM ..... Idaho Falls, ID [*Broadcasting station call letters*]
Kidney Int Suppl ... Kidney International. Supplement [*A publication*]
KIDQ .... Boise, ID [*Broadcasting station call letters*]
KIDX .... Billings, MT [*Broadcasting station call letters*]
KIE .... Kieta [*Papua New Guinea*] [*Airport symbol*]
KIE .... Kinetic Isotope Effect [*Physical chemistry*]
Kiel Meeresforsch ... Kieler Meeresforschungen [*A publication*]
Kiel Milchwirtsch Forschungsber ... Kieler Milchwirtschaftliche Forschungsberichte [*A publication*]
KIFX .... Tulsa, OK [*Broadcasting station call letters*]
KIG .... Koingnaas [*South Africa*] [*Airport symbol*]
KIHR-FM ... Hood River, OR [*Broadcasting station call letters*]
KIIZ .... Killeen, TX [*Broadcasting station call letters*]
KIJ .... Niigata [*Japan*] [*Airport symbol*]
KIKC .... Forsyth, MT [*Broadcasting station call letters*]
KIM .... Kimberley [*South Africa*] [*Airport symbol*]
KIN .... Kingston [*Jamaica*] [*Airport symbol*]
Kinderaerztl Prax ... Kinderaerztliche Praxis [*A publication*]
Kinesither Sci ... Kinesitherapie Scientifique [*A publication*]
KINF .... Dodge City, KS [*Broadcasting station call letters*]
KINN-FM ... Alamogordo, NM [*Broadcasting station call letters*]
KIOB .... Coeur d'Alene, ID [*Broadcasting station call letters*]
KIOC .... Orange, TX [*Broadcasting station call letters*]
KIOK .... Richland, WA [*Broadcasting station call letters*]
KIOW .... Forest City, IA [*Broadcasting station call letters*]
KIQY .... Lebanon, OR [*Broadcasting station call letters*]
KIS .... Kisumu [*Kenya*] [*Airport symbol*]
KISZ .... Cortez, CO [*Broadcasting station call letters*]
KIT .... Kithira [*Greece*] [*Airport symbol*]
KITA .... Little Rock, AR [*Broadcasting station call letters*]
Kitakanto Med J ... Kitakanto Medical Journal [*A publication*]
Kitano Hosp J Med ... Kitano Hospital Journal of Medicine [*A publication*]
Kitasato Arch Exp Med ... Kitasato Archives of Experimental Medicine [*A publication*]
KIV .... Kishinev [*USSR*] [*Airport symbol*]
KIW .... Kitwe [*Zambia*] [*Airport symbol*]
KIXV .... Brady, TX [*Broadcasting station call letters*]

KIY .... Kilwa [*Tanzania*] [*Airport symbol*]
KIZZ .... Minot, ND [*Broadcasting station call letters*]
KJAB .... St. Paul, MN [*Broadcasting station call letters*]
KJAQ .... Gordonville, MO [*Broadcasting station call letters*]
KJCO .... Yuma, CO [*Broadcasting station call letters*]
KJEM .... Bentonville, AR [*Broadcasting station call letters*]
KJJR .... Whitefish, MT [*Broadcasting station call letters*]
KJKJ .... Logan, UT [*Broadcasting station call letters*]
KJLA .... Kansas City, MO [*Broadcasting station call letters*]
KJMC .... Richfield, UT [*Broadcasting station call letters*]
KJNO-FM ... Juneau, AK [*Broadcasting station call letters*]
KJOP .... Lemoore, CA [*Broadcasting station call letters*]
KJOT .... Boise, ID [*Broadcasting station call letters*]
KJQN .... Ogden, UT [*Broadcasting station call letters*]
KJQY .... San Diego, CA [*Broadcasting station call letters*]
KJSK-FM .. Columbus, NE [*Broadcasting station call letters*]
KJU .... Kamiraba [*Papua New Guinea*] [*Airport symbol*]
KK .... Arab International Aviation Co. [*Egypt*] [*ICAO designator*]
KK .... Knee Kick [*Medicine*]
KKA .... Koyuk [*Alaska*] [*Airport symbol*]
KKAL .... Arroyo Grande, CA [*Broadcasting station call letters*]
KKAQ .... Thief River Falls, MN [*Broadcasting station call letters*]
KKB .... Kitoi [*Alaska*] [*Airport symbol*]
KKBL .... Monett, MO [*Broadcasting station call letters*]
KKC .... Khon Kaen [*Thailand*] [*Airport symbol*]
KKCS .... Colorado Springs, CO [*Broadcasting station call letters*]
KKCS-FM ... Colorado Springs, CO [*Broadcasting station call letters*]
KKD .... Kokoda [*Papua New Guinea*] [*Airport symbol*]
KKDK-FM ... Morris, MN [*Broadcasting station call letters*]
KKE .... Kerikeri [*New Zealand*] [*Airport symbol*]
KKG .... Konawaruk [*Guyana*] [*Airport symbol*]
KKGO .... Los Angeles, CA [*Broadcasting station call letters*]
KKH .... Kongiganak [*Alaska*] [*Airport symbol*]
KKHJ .... Rapid City, SD [*Broadcasting station call letters*]
KKI .... Akiachak [*Alaska*] [*Airport symbol*]
KKIC .... Ashland, OR [*Broadcasting station call letters*]
KKJ .... Kita Kyushu [*Japan*] [*Airport symbol*]
KKJY .... Albuquerque, NM [*Broadcasting station call letters*]
KKJY-FM .. Albuquerque, NM [*Broadcasting station call letters*]
KKKX .... Ottawa, KS [*Broadcasting station call letters*]
KKLF .... Conway, AR [*Broadcasting station call letters*]
KKLR .... Edmond, OK [*Broadcasting station call letters*]
KKN .... Kirkenes [*Norway*] [*Airport symbol*]
KKO .... Kaikohe [*New Zealand*] [*Airport symbol*]
KKOK .... Morris, MN [*Broadcasting station call letters*]
KKOL .... El Paso, TX [*Broadcasting station call letters*]
KKOZ .... Billings, MT [*Broadcasting station call letters*]
KKQQ .... Clovis, NM [*Broadcasting station call letters*]
KKR .... Kaukura [*French Polynesia*] [*Airport symbol*]
KKRB .... Red Bluff, CA [*Broadcasting station call letters*]
KKRC .... Sioux Falls, SD [*Broadcasting station call letters*]
KKRK .... Douglas, AZ [*Broadcasting station call letters*]
KKRL .... Carrol, IA [*Broadcasting station call letters*]
KKU .... Ekuk [*Alaska*] [*Airport symbol*]
KKW .... Kikwit [*Zaire*] [*Airport symbol*]
KKX .... Kikaiga Shima [*Japan*] [*Airport symbol*]
KL .... Key Length [*Data processing*]
KLA .... Knight of [*the Order of*] Leopold of Austria
K Lantbruksakad Tidskr ... Kungliga Lantbruksakademiens Tidskrift [*A publication*]
K Lantbrukshogsk Ann ... Kungliga Lantbrukshogskolans Annaler [*A publication*]
KLAQ .... El Paso, TX [*Broadcasting station call letters*]
KLAT .... Houston, TX [*Broadcasting station call letters*]
KLB .... Kalabo [*Zambia*] [*Airport symbol*]
KLBA .... Albia, IA [*Broadcasting station call letters*]
KLBQ .... El Dorado, AR [*Broadcasting station call letters*]
KLDR .... Denver, CO [*Broadcasting station call letters*]
KLEH .... Anamosa, IA [*Broadcasting station call letters*]
KLEL .... San Jose, CA [*Broadcasting station call letters*]
KLER-FM .. Orofino, ID [*Broadcasting station call letters*]
KLG .... Kalskag [*Alaska*] [*Airport symbol*]
Klin Khir (Kiev) ... Klinicheskaya Khirurgiya (Kiev) [*A publication*]
Klin Med (Mosc) ... Klinicheskaya Meditsina (Moscow) [*A publication*]
Klin Monatsbl Augenheilkd ... Klinische Monatsblaetter fuer Augenheilkunde [*A publication*]
Klin Oczna ... Klinika Oczna [*A publication*]
Klin Paediatr ... Klinische Paediatrie [*A publication*]

Klin Rentgenol Resp Mezhved Sb ... Klinicheskoi Rentgenologii Respublikanshoi Mezhvedomstvennyi Sbornik [*A publication*]

Klin Wochenschr ... Klinische Wochenschrift [*A publication*]

KLIT .... Pomona, CA [*Broadcasting station call letters*]

KLKC-FM ... Parsons, KS [*Broadcasting station call letters*]

KLKE........ Del Rio, TX [*Broadcasting station call letters*]

KLL .... Levelock [*Alaska*] [*Airport symbol*]

KLLB .... Portland, OR [*Broadcasting station call letters*]

KLME .... Battle Mountain, NV [*Broadcasting station call letters*]

KLMF-FM ... Fabens, TX [*Broadcasting station call letters*]

KLN........... Larsen Bay [*Alaska*] [*Airport symbol*]

KLNG .... Council Bluffs, IA [*Broadcasting station call letters*]

KLO............ Kalibo [*Philippines*] [*Airport symbol*]

KLPL-FM .. Lake Providence, LA [*Broadcasting station call letters*]

KLPQ .... Little Rock, AR [*Broadcasting station call letters*]

KLR .... Columbus Air Transport, Inc. [*Columbus, OH*] [*FAA designator*]

KLR .... Kalmar [*Sweden*] [*Airport symbol*]

KLRR......... Leadville, AR [*Broadcasting station call letters*]

KLS .... Knotted List Structure

KLTC.......... Dickinson, ND [*Broadcasting station call letters*]

KLTE.......... Oklahoma City, OK [*Broadcasting station call letters*]

KLU............ Klagenfurt [*Austria*] [*Airport symbol*]

KLUA .... Lake Village, AR [*Broadcasting station call letters*]

KLV .... Karlovy Vary [*Czechoslovakia*] [*Airport symbol*]

KLVF.......... Las Vegas, NM [*Broadcasting station call letters*]

KLVR.......... Longview, WA [*Broadcasting station call letters*]

KLVV.......... Lompoc, CA [*Broadcasting station call letters*]

KLW .... Klawock [*Alaska*] [*Airport symbol*]

KLWJ .... Umatilla, OR [*Broadcasting station call letters*]

KLWT-FM ... Lebanon, MO [*Broadcasting station call letters*]

KLX .... Kalamata [*Greece*] [*Airport symbol*]

KLXL .... Dubuque, IA [*Broadcasting station call letters*]

KLYC .... Laurel, MT [*Broadcasting station call letters*]

KLZ .... Kleinzee [*South Africa*] [*Airport symbol*]

KLZR.......... Lawrence, KS [*Broadcasting station call letters*]

KMA.......... Kerema [*Papua New Guinea*] [*Airport symbol*]

KMAH .... Atherton, CA [*Broadcasting station call letters*]

KMAL .... Malden, MO [*Broadcasting station call letters*]

KMAV........ Mayville, ND [*Broadcasting station call letters*]

KMAV-FM ... Mayville, ND [*Broadcasting station call letters*]

KMAY........ Riverside, CA [*Broadcasting station call letters*]

KMAZ........ Beatrice, NE [*Broadcasting station call letters*]

KMCE .... Merced, CA [*Broadcasting station call letters*]

KMCK .... Siloam Springs, AR [*Broadcasting station call letters*]

KMCV .... Conroe, TX [*Broadcasting station call letters*]

KMDX........ Parker, AZ [*Broadcasting station call letters*]

KMFO........ Aptos-Capitola, CA [*Broadcasting station call letters*]

KMG.......... Kunming [*China*] [*Airport symbol*]

KMGN .... Bakersfield, CA [*Broadcasting station call letters*]

KMI .... Miyazaki [*Japan*] [*Airport symbol*]

KMJ............ Kumamoto [*Japan*] [*Airport symbol*]

KMJD .... Castle Rock, CO [*Broadcasting station call letters*]

KMJJ......... North Las Vegas, NV [*Broadcasting station call letters*]

KMJM........ St. Louis, MO [*Broadcasting station call letters*]

KML .... Kamileroi [*Australia*] [*Airport symbol*]

KMLE .... Chandler, AZ [*Broadcasting station call letters*]

KMM .... Kimam [*Indonesia*] [*Airport symbol*]

KMMR....... Malta, MT [*Broadcasting station call letters*]

KMMZ .... Greybull, WY [*Broadcasting station call letters*]

KMN........... Kamina [*Zaire*] [*Airport symbol*]

KMO........... Manokotak [*Alaska*] [*Airport symbol*]

KMOJ........ Minneapolis, MN [*Broadcasting station call letters*]

KMOO-FM ... Mineola, TX [*Broadcasting station call letters*]

KMOR .... Scottsbluff, NE [*Broadcasting station call letters*]

KMP .... Keetmanshoop [*South-West Africa*] [*Airport symbol*]

KMQ .... Komatsu [*Japan*] [*Airport symbol*]

KMR .... Karimui [*Papua New Guinea*] [*Airport symbol*]

KMS .... Kumasi [*Ghana*] [*Airport symbol*]

KMSC .... Sioux City, IA [*Broadcasting station call letters*]

KMTS........ Glenwood Springs, CO [*Broadcasting station call letters*]

KMU........... Kismayu [*Somalia*] [*Airport symbol*]

KMV........... Kalemyo [*Burma*] [*Airport symbol*]

KMVC........ Burley, ID [*Broadcasting station call letters*]

KMXU....... Manti, UT [*Broadcasting station call letters*]

KMY .... Moser Bay [*Alaska*] [*Airport symbol*]

KMZK........ Fort Worth, TX [*Broadcasting station call letters*]

KNAB-FM ... Burlington, CO [*Broadcasting station call letters*]

KNAK........ Delta, UT [*Broadcasting station call letters*]

KNAN........ Monroe, LA [*Broadcasting station call letters*]

KNAQ........ Rupert, ID [*Broadcasting station call letters*]

KNCO........ Grass Valley, CA [*Broadcasting station call letters*]

KNCW........ Grandcoulee, WA [*Broadcasting station call letters*]

KND .... Kindu [*Zaire*] [*Airport symbol*]

KNDA........ Yakima, WA [*Broadcasting station call letters*]

KNDE .... Tucson, AZ [*Broadcasting station call letters*]

KNDN........ Farmington, NM [*Broadcasting station call letters*]

K Ned Natuurhist Ver Uitg ... Koninklijke Nederlandse Natuurhistorische Vereniging Uitgave [*A publication*]

KNEK........ Washington, LA [*Broadcasting station call letters*]

KNEN........ Norfolk, NE [*Broadcasting station call letters*]

KNEU........ Roosevelt, UT [*Broadcasting station call letters*]

KNFO........ Waco, TX [*Broadcasting station call letters*]

KNG .... Kaimana [*Indonesia*] [*Airport symbol*]

KNOG........ Havre, MT [*Broadcasting station call letters*]

KNON........ Dallas, TX [*Broadcasting station call letters*]

K Nor Vidensk Selsk Forh ... Kongelige Norske Videnskabers Selskabs Forhandlinger [*A publication*]

K Nor Vidensk Selsk Mus Misc ... Kongelige Norske Videnskabers Selskabs Museet Miscellanea [*A publication*]

K Nor Vidensk Selsk Skr ... Kongelige Norske Videnskabers Selskabs Skrifter [*A publication*]

KNPR .... Las Vegas, NV [*Broadcasting station call letters*]

KNQ .... Kone [*New Caledonia*] [*Airport symbol*]

KNS........... King Island [*Tasmania*] [*Airport symbol*]

KNTB .... Bakersfield, CA [*Broadcasting station call letters*]

KNU .... Kanpur [*India*] [*Airport symbol*]

KNW.......... New Stuyahok [*Alaska*] [*Airport symbol*]

KNWR .... Bellingham, WA [*Broadcasting station call letters*]

KNX........... Kununurra [*Australia*] [*Airport symbol*]

KNYO........ Independence, CA [*Broadcasting station call letters*]

KNZ........... Kenieba [*Mali*] [*Airport symbol*]

KOA .... Kona [*Hawaii*] [*Airport symbol*]

KOAK-FM ... Red Oak, IA [*Broadcasting station call letters*]

KOB .... Koutaba [*Cameroon*] [*Airport symbol*]

Kobe J Med Sci ... Kobe Journal of Medical Science [*A publication*]

KOB-FM... Albuquerque, NM [*Broadcasting station call letters*]

KOBX........ Boonville, MO [*Broadcasting station call letters*]

KOC .... Koumac [*New Caledonia*] [*Airport symbol*]

KOCC........ Oklahoma City, OK [*Broadcasting station call letters*]

KODY-FM ... North Platte, NE [*Broadcasting station call letters*]

KOE .... Kupang [*Indonesia*] [*Airport symbol*]

Koedoe Monogr ... Koedoe Monograph [*A publication*]

KOH .... Koolatah [*Australia*] [*Airport symbol*]

KOHU-FM ... Hermiston, OR [*Broadcasting station call letters*]

KOI............ Kirkwall [*Orkney Islands*] [*Airport symbol*]

KOJ .... Kagoshima [*Japan*] [*Airport symbol*]

KOJC .... Cedar Rapids, IA [*Broadcasting station call letters*]

KOK .... Kokkola [*Finland*] [*Airport symbol*]

KOKL-FM ... Okmulgee, OK [*Broadcasting station call letters*]

KOKQ........ Seaside, CA [*Broadcasting station call letters*]

Koleopterol Rundsch ... Koleopterologische Rundschau [*A publication*]

Kolhospnyk Ukr ... Kolhospnyk Ukrainy [*A publication*]

KOLI.......... Coalinga, CA [*Broadcasting station call letters*]

KOLL-FM ... Gillette, WY [*Broadcasting station call letters*]

KOLM........ Rochester, MN [*Broadcasting station call letters*]

KOLM-FM ... Rochester, MN [*Broadcasting station call letters*]

KOM........... Komo-Manda [*Papua New Guinea*] [*Airport symbol*]

KOMB........ Ft. Scott, KS [*Broadcasting station call letters*]

KOMW-FM ... Omak, WA [*Broadcasting station call letters*]

Konservn Ovoshchesush Prom-st ... Konservnaya i Ovoshchesushil'naya Promyshlennest [*A publication*]

KOO .... Kongolo [*Zaire*] [*Airport symbol*]

KOOK-FM ... Billings, MT [*Broadcasting station call letters*]

KOP .... Nakhon Phanom [*Thailand*] [*Airport symbol*]

KOPA .... Scottsdale, AZ [*Broadcasting station call letters*]

KOPA-FM ... Scottsdale, AZ [*Broadcasting station call letters*]

KOR .... Kokoro [*Papua New Guinea*] [*Airport symbol*]

KORE .... Eugene, OR [*Broadcasting station call letters*]

KORE .... Kinetic Analysis Using Over-Relaxation [*FORTRAN computer program*] [*Physical chemistry*]

Korean Biochem J ... Korean Biochemical Journal [*A publication*]

Korean Cent J Med ... Korean Central Journal of Medicine [*A publication*]

Korean J Anim Sci ... Korean Journal of Animal Sciences [*A publication*]
Korean J Biochem ... Korean Journal of Biochemistry [*A publication*]
Korean J Bot ... Korean Journal of Botany [*A publication*]
Korean J Dermatol ... Korean Journal of Dermatology [*A publication*]
Korean J Entomol ... Korean Journal of Entomology [*A publication*]
Korean J Intern Med ... Korean Journal of Internal Medicine [*A publication*]
Korean J Microbiol ... Korean Journal of Microbiology [*A publication*]
Korean J Obstet Gynecol ... Korean Journal of Obstetrics and Gynecology [*A publication*]
Korean J Parasitol ... Korean Journal of Parasitology [*A publication*]
Korean J Pharmacogn ... Korean Journal of Pharmacognosy [*A publication*]
Korean J Pharmacol ... Korean Journal of Pharmacology [*A publication*]
Korean J Public Health ... Korean Journal of Public Health [*A publication*]
Korean J Zool ... Korean Journal of Zoology [*A publication*]
Korea Univ Med J ... Korea University Medical Journal [*A publication*]
KORS .... Miami, OK [*Broadcasting station call letters*]
KORT-FM ... Grangeville, ID [*Broadcasting station call letters*]
KOSI-FM... Aurora, CO [*Broadcasting station call letters*]
Kosm Biol Aviakosm Med ... Kosmicheskaya Biologiya i Aviakosmicheskaya Meditsina [*A publication*]
Kosm Biol Med ... Kosmicheskaya Biologiya i Meditsina [*A publication*]
Kosmos Ser A Biol (Warsaw) ... Kosmos. Seria A. Biologia (Warsaw) [*A publication*]
KOT........... Kotlik [*Alaska*] [*Airport symbol*]
KOVF-FM ... Kearney, NE [*Broadcasting station call letters*]
KOY .... Olga Bay [*Alaska*] [*Airport symbol*]
KOZZ .... Reno, NV [*Broadcasting station call letters*]
KP .... Keratitis Punctata [*Ophthalmology*]
KPBX-FM ... Spokane, WA [*Broadcasting station call letters*]
KPER........ Hobbs, NM [*Broadcasting station call letters*]
KPIG.......... Honolulu, HI [*Broadcasting station call letters*]
KPLV........ Pueblo, CO [*Broadcasting station call letters*]
KPLZ........ Seattle, WA [*Broadcasting station call letters*]
KPMO .... Mendocino, CA [*Broadcasting station call letters*]
KPNC-FM ... Ponca City, OK [*Broadcasting station call letters*]
KPOC .... Key Prep on Campus [*Slang*]
KPVU .... Prairie View, TX [*Broadcasting station call letters*]
KPYN .... Atlanta, TX [*Broadcasting station call letters*]
KQAC .... Glenwood, AR [*Broadcasting station call letters*]
KQID .... Alexandria, LA [*Broadcasting station call letters*]
KQIQ .... Lemoore, CA [*Broadcasting station call letters*]
KQIQ-FM .. Lemoore, CA [*Broadcasting station call letters*]
KQIV-FM... Corpus Christi, TX [*Broadcasting station call letters*]
KQKD....... Redfield, SD [*Broadcasting station call letters*]
KQKI .... Bayou Vista, LA [*Broadcasting station call letters*]
KQKK........ Manteca, CA [*Broadcasting station call letters*]
KQKY .... Kearney, NE [*Broadcasting station call letters*]
KQLA .... Tacoma, WA [*Broadcasting station call letters*]
KQNK .... Norton, KS [*Broadcasting station call letters*]
KQOK .... Soldotna, AK [*Broadcasting station call letters*]
KQPI......... Idaho Falls, ID [*Broadcasting station call letters*]
KQRN........ Mitchell, SD [*Broadcasting station call letters*]
KQSK .... Chadron, NE [*Broadcasting station call letters*]
KQTZ .... Hobart, OK [*Broadcasting station call letters*]
KQWI........ Clarinda, IA [*Broadcasting station call letters*]
KQXL .... New Roads, LA [*Broadcasting station call letters*]
KQYB .... Spring City, MN [*Broadcasting station call letters*]
KRCS .... Sturgis, SD [*Broadcasting station call letters*]
KRCT .... Ozona, TX [*Broadcasting station call letters*]
KRDF-FM ... Spearman, TX [*Broadcasting station call letters*]
KRDZ .... Wray, CO [*Broadcasting station call letters*]
KREK .... Bristow, OK [*Broadcasting station call letters*]
KREO .... Healdsburg, CA [*Broadcasting station call letters*]
KRFM........ Lake Havasu City, AZ [*Broadcasting station call letters*]
KRGO .... Granger, UT [*Broadcasting station call letters*]
KRHS .... Bullhead City, AZ [*Broadcasting station call letters*]
KRIZ.......... Roswell, NM [*Broadcasting station call letters*]
KRJH......... Hallettsville, TX [*Broadcasting station call letters*]
KRLB........ Lubbock, TX [*Broadcasting station call letters*]
KRM .... Kurzweil Reading Machine
Kroc Found Ser ... Kroc Foundation Series [*A publication*]
Kroc Found Symp ... Kroc Foundation Symposia [*A publication*]
KROI .... Sparks, NV [*Broadcasting station call letters*]

Krolikovod Zverovod ... Krolikovodstvo i Zverovodstvo [*A publication*]
KROY-FM ... Sacramento, CA [*Broadcasting station call letters*]
KRPC .... Owatonna, MN [*Broadcasting station call letters*]
KRPM........ Puyallup, WA [*Broadcasting station call letters*]
KRQK .... Lompoc, CA [*Broadcasting station call letters*]
Krs Jugosl Carsus Iugosl ... Krs Jugoslavije Carsus Iugoslaviae [*A publication*]
KRTM .... Temecula, CA [*Broadcasting station call letters*]
KRVD .... Cottonwood, AZ [*Broadcasting station call letters*]
KRWN .... Farmington, NM [*Broadcasting station call letters*]
KRWQ .... Gold Hill, OR [*Broadcasting station call letters*]
KRXV .... Yermo, CA [*Broadcasting station call letters*]
KRZJ........ Beloit, KS [*Broadcasting station call letters*]
KS .... Keyset [*Navy*]
KSAA .... Casa Grande, AZ [*Broadcasting station call letters*]
KSAS .... Liberty, MO [*Broadcasting station call letters*]
KSCC........ Berryville, AR [*Broadcasting station call letters*]
KSCF .... Florissant, MO [*Broadcasting station call letters*]
KSDM .... International Falls, MN [*Broadcasting station call letters*]
KSDW .... Sulphur, OK [*Broadcasting station call letters*]
KSDZ .... Gordon, NE [*Broadcasting station call letters*]
KSEM-FM ... Moses Lake, WA [*Broadcasting station call letters*]
KSGL .... Wichita, KS [*Broadcasting station call letters*]
KSHY .... Cheyenne, WY [*Broadcasting station call letters*]
KSJN .... St. Paul, MN [*Broadcasting station call letters*]
KSJU .... Collegeville, MN [*Broadcasting station call letters*]
KSJV .... Fresno, CA [*Broadcasting station call letters*]
KSKA .... Anchorage, AK [*Broadcasting station call letters*]
KSKD .... Salem, OR [*Broadcasting station call letters*]
KSKL-FM ... Sun Valley, ID [*Broadcasting station call letters*]
KSLE .... Seminole, OK [*Broadcasting station call letters*]
KSLS .... Liberal, KS [*Broadcasting station call letters*]
KSM & SG ... Knight of Saint Michael and Saint George [*Ionian Islands*]
KSNR .... Red Bluff, CA [*Broadcasting station call letters*]
KSPA .... Hot Springs, AR [*Broadcasting station call letters*]
KSPB .... Pebble Beach, CA [*Broadcasting station call letters*]
KSRA-FM ... Salmon, ID [*Broadcasting station call letters*]
KSRH .... San Rafael, CA [*Broadcasting station call letters*]
KSSK .... Honolulu, HI [*Broadcasting station call letters*]
KSSN .... Little Rock, AR [*Broadcasting station call letters*]
KSTI.......... Springfield, SD [*Broadcasting station call letters*]
K Sven Vetenskapsakad Handl ... Kunglica Svenska Vetenskapsakademiens Handlingar [*A publication*]
Ktavim Rec Agric Res Stn ... Ktavim Records of the Agricultural Research Station [*A publication*]
KTED .... Fowler, CA [*Broadcasting station call letters*]
KTIG-FM... Pequot Lakes, MN [*Broadcasting station call letters*]
KTJJ.......... Farmington, MO [*Broadcasting station call letters*]
KTKT-FM ... Tucson, AZ [*Broadcasting station call letters*]
KTLE .... Tooele, UT [*Broadcasting station call letters*]
KTLQ-FM ... Tahlequah, OK [*Broadcasting station call letters*]
KTLR-FM .. Terrell, TX [*Broadcasting station call letters*]
KTLS......... Oklahoma City, OK [*Broadcasting station call letters*]
KTMP .... Spanish Fork, UT [*Broadcasting station call letters*]
KTQQ .... Sulphur, LA [*Broadcasting station call letters*]
KTRI-FM ... Mansfield, MO [*Broadcasting station call letters*]
KTRX .... Tarkio, MO [*Broadcasting station call letters*]
KTTI.......... Yuma, AZ [*Broadcasting station call letters*]
KTTN-FM ... Trenton, MO [*Broadcasting station call letters*]
KTUF......... Terrill Hills, TX [*Broadcasting station call letters*]
KTWN-FM ... Anoka, MN [*Broadcasting station call letters*]
KTXQ .... Fort Worth, TX [*Broadcasting station call letters*]
KTYL-FM ... Tyler, TX [*Broadcasting station call letters*]
KUB.......... Kidney and Upper Bladder
KUBO........ Chualar, CA [*Broadcasting station call letters*]
Kuehn-Arch ... Kuehn-Archiv [*A publication*]
KUFO .... Odessa, TX [*Broadcasting station call letters*]
KUGN-FM ... Eugene, OR [*Broadcasting station call letters*]
KUIN .... Vernal, UT [*Broadcasting station call letters*]
Kulturpflanze Beih ... Kulturpflanze Beiheft [*A publication*]
KUMA-FM ... Pendleton, OR [*Broadcasting station call letters*]
Kumamoto J Sci Biol ... Kumamoto Journal of Science. Biology [*A publication*]
Kumamoto J Sci Geol ... Kumamoto Journal of Science. Geology [*A publication*]
Kumamoto J Sci Ser B Sect 2 Biol ... Kumamoto Journal of Science. Series B. Section 2. Biology [*A publication*]

Kumamoto Med J ... Kumamoto Medical Journal [*A publication*]
KUMS........ Roosevelt, UT [*Broadcasting station call letters*]
Kurme Med J ... Kurme Medical Journal [*A publication*]
KURY-FM ... Brookings, OR [*Broadcasting station call letters*]
KUUY .... Cheyenne, WY [*Broadcasting station call letters*]
KUXX .... Palmdale, CA [*Broadcasting station call letters*]
KVAA .... Volga, SD [*Broadcasting station call letters*]
KVAR .... San Antonio, TX [*Broadcasting station call letters*]
KVBA .... Kanamycin-Vancomycin Blood Agar [*Microbiology*]
KVCM .... Montgomery City, MO [*Broadcasting station call letters*]
KVEG .... Henderson, NV [*Broadcasting station call letters*]
K Vetenskapssamh Uppsala Arsb ... Kungliga
    Vetenskapssamhaellets i Uppsala Arsbok [*A
    publication*]
K Vetensk-Soc Arsb ... Kungliga Vetenskaps-Societetens Arsbok [*A
    publication*]
K Vet-Landbohojsk Arsskr ... Kongelige Veterinaer-og
    Landbohojskole Arsskrift [*A publication*]
KVGM .... Yakima, WA [*Broadcasting station call letters*]
KVLBA ...... Kanamycin-Vancomycin Labeled Blood Agar
    [*Microbiology*]
KVLY .... Edinburg, TX [*Broadcasting station call letters*]
KVMR .... Nevada City, CA [*Broadcasting station call letters*]
KVNF .... Paonia, CO [*Broadcasting station call letters*]
KVRD .... Cottonwood, AZ [*Broadcasting station call letters*]
KVVQ .... Victoriaville, CA [*Broadcasting station call letters*]
KW .... Kiloword
KWBJ .... Payette, ID [*Broadcasting station call letters*]
KWCB .... Floresville, TX [*Broadcasting station call letters*]
KWJM .... Farmersville, LA [*Broadcasting station call letters*]
KWK .... St. Louis, MO [*Broadcasting station call letters*]
KWLC .... Decorah, IA [*Broadcasting station call letters*]
KWLF .... Oakdale, CA [*Broadcasting station call letters*]
KWNE .... Ukiah, CA [*Broadcasting station call letters*]
KWRO-FM ... Coquille, OR [*Broadcasting station call letters*]
KWTY-FM ... Salinas, CA [*Broadcasting station call letters*]
KWUR .... Clayton, MO [*Broadcasting station call letters*]
KWWA ...... Bremerton, WA [*Broadcasting station call letters*]
KWYK .... Aztec, NM [*Broadcasting station call letters*]
KXDD .... Richland, WA [*Broadcasting station call letters*]
KXEG .... Tolleson, AZ [*Broadcasting station call letters*]
KXES .... Salinas, CA [*Broadcasting station call letters*]
KXEZ .... Yuba City, CA [*Broadcasting station call letters*]
KXKS .... Albuquerque, NM [*Broadcasting station call letters*]
KXL-FM .... Portland, OR [*Broadcasting station call letters*]
KXMS .... Alice, TX [*Broadcasting station call letters*]
KXOA-FM ... Sacramento, CA [*Broadcasting station call letters*]
KXPR .... Sacramento, CA [*Broadcasting station call letters*]
KXRT .... Taos, NM [*Broadcasting station call letters*]
KXTC .... Phoenix, AZ [*Broadcasting station call letters*]
KXVQ .... Pawhuska, OK [*Broadcasting station call letters*]
KXVR .... Mountain Pass, CA [*Broadcasting station call letters*]

KXXE......... Forsyth, MT [*Broadcasting station call letters*]
KYA-FM .... San Francisco, CA [*Broadcasting station call letters*]
KY Agric Exp Stn Annu Rep ... Kentucky Agricultural Experiment
    Station. Annual Report [*A publication*]
KY Agric Exp Stn Bull ... Kentucky Agricultural Experiment Station.
    Bulletin [*A publication*]
KY Agric Exp Stn Misc Pubs ... Kentucky Agricultural Experiment
    Station. Miscellaneous Publications [*A publication*]
KY Agric Exp Stn Prog Rep ... Kentucky Agricultural Experiment
    Station. Progress Report [*A publication*]
KY Agric Exp Stn Regul Bull ... Kentucky Agricultural Experiment
    Station. Regulatory Bulletin [*A publication*]
KY Agric Exp Stn Results Res ... Kentucky Agricultural Experiment
    Station. Results of Research [*A publication*]
KYBO .... Yakima, WA [*Broadcasting station call letters*]
KY Dep Fish Wildl Resour Fish Bull ... Kentucky Department of Fish
    and Wildlife Resources. Fisheries Bulletin [*A
    publication*]
KYDS .... Sacramento, CA [*Broadcasting station call letters*]
KY Farm Home Sci ... Kentucky Farm and Home Science [*A
    publication*]
KYFR .... Shenandoah, IA [*Broadcasting station call letters*]
KYGO .... Denver, CO [*Broadcasting station call letters*]
KYKK .... Humble City, NM [*Broadcasting station call letters*]
KYKS .... Lufkin, TX [*Broadcasting station call letters*]
KYNG-FM ... Coos Bay, OR [*Broadcasting station call letters*]
KYNN-FM ... Omaha, NE [*Broadcasting station call letters*]
KYNR .... Pueblo, CO [*Broadcasting station call letters*]
KYOO .... Bolivar, MO [*Broadcasting station call letters*]
KYOT .... Refugio, TX [*Broadcasting station call letters*]
KYRY-FM ... Brookings, OR [*Broadcasting station call letters*]
KYTX......... Amarillo, TX [*Broadcasting station call letters*]
Kyungpook Univ Med J ... Kyungpook University Medical Journal [*A
    publication*]
Kyushu J Med Sci ... Kyushu Journal of Medical Science [*A
    publication*]
KY Warbler ... Kentucky Warbler [*A publication*]
KZ .... Trans Europe Air [*France*] [*ICAO designator*]
KZAN .... Ogden, UT [*Broadcasting station call letters*]
KZED .... Wellington, KS [*Broadcasting station call letters*]
KZEV......... Clear Lake, IA [*Broadcasting station call letters*]
KZIO.......... Superior, WI [*Broadcasting station call letters*]
KZIQ-FM... Ridgecrest, CA [*Broadcasting station call letters*]
KZLA .... Los Angeles, CA [*Broadcasting station call letters*]
KZLA-FM ... Los Angeles, CA [*Broadcasting station call letters*]
KZOM........ Orange, TX [*Broadcasting station call letters*]
KZRI.......... Helena, AR [*Broadcasting station call letters*]
KZUM........ Lincoln, NE [*Broadcasting station call letters*]
KZZL .... Le Mars, IA [*Broadcasting station call letters*]
KZZP .... Mesa, AZ [*Broadcasting station call letters*]
KZZP-FM ... Mesa, AZ [*Broadcasting station call letters*]

L

L .... Lactobacillus
L .... Lameness [*Used by immigration officials*] [*Obsolete*]
L .... Lanthanum [*Chemical element; symbol is La*]
L .... Lethal
L .... Licensed to Practice [*Medicine*]
L .... Light Sense
L .... Lilac
L .... Lime
L .... [*Alessandro*] Longo [*When used in identifying D. Scarlatti's compositions, refers to cataloging of his works by musicologist Longo*]
L .... Loyalty
LAADS ...... Low-Altitude Air Dropped Stores
LAAG .... Latin American Anthropology Group
LA Agric.... Louisiana Agriculture [*A publication*]
LA Agric Exp Stn Bull ... Louisiana Agricultural Experiment Station. Bulletin [*A publication*]
LAAM .... Low-Cost Antiarmor Weapon System
LAAW .... Local Antiair Warfare
Lab Anim .. Laboratory Animals [*A publication*]
Lab Anim Care ... Laboratory Animal Care [*A publication*]
Lab Anim Handb ... Laboratory Animal Handbooks [*A publication*]
Lab Anim Sci ... Laboratory Animal Science [*A publication*]
Lab Anim Symp ... Laboratory Animal Symposia [*A publication*]
Lab Delo ... Laboratornoe Delo [*A publication*]
Labdev J Sci Technol ... Labdev Journal of Science and Technology [*A publication*]
Lab Dig ..... Laboratory Digest [*A publication*]
Lab Invest ... Laboratory Investigation [*A publication*]
Lab Manage ... Laboratory Management [*A publication*]
Lab Res Methods Biol Med ... Laboratory and Research Methods in Biology and Medicine [*A publication*]
LABS .... Laboratory Admission Baseline Studies
LAC .... Licentiate of the Apothecaries' Company [*British*]
LACV .... Lighter Air-Cushion Vehicle [*Usually used in combination with numerals*]
LAD .... Lactate Dehydrogenase [*An enzyme*] [*Also, LD, LDH*]
LAD .... LASER Acquisition Device
LAD .... Logical Aptitude Device
LAER .... Lowest Achievable Emission Rate [*Environmental Protection Agency*]
LAF .... Landscape Architecture Foundation
LAG .... Load and Go
LAGN .... Lagoon [*Board on Geographic Names*]
LAI .... Load Address Immediate
LAIA .... Latin American Integration Association [*Formerly, LAFTA*]
LAL .... Limulus Amebocyte Lysate
LALM .... Limulus Amebocyte Lysate Method
LAMC .... Lima Army Modification Center
LAND .... League Against Nuclear Danger
Landbauforsch Voelkenrode ... Landbauforschung Voelkenrode [*A publication*]
Landbouwkd Tijdschr ... Landbouwkundig Tijdschrift [*A publication*]
Landbouwproefstn Suriname Bull ... Landbouwproefstation Suriname Bulletin [*A publication*]
Landbouwproefstn Suriname Meded ... Landbouwproefstation Suriname Mededeling [*A publication*]
LANDFAE ... Large Area Nozzle Delivery of Fuel Air Explosive

Landwirtsch Forsch ... Landwirtschaftliche Forschung [*A publication*]
Landwirtsch Jahrb Schweiz ... Landwirtschaftliches Jahrbuch der Schweiz [*A publication*]
Langenbecks Arch Chir ... Langenbecks Archiv fuer Chirurgie [*A publication*]
Lantbrukshogsk Ann ... Lantbrukshogskolans Annaler [*A publication*]
Lantbrukshogsk Medd Ser A ... Lantbrukshogskolans Meddelanden. Series A [*A publication*]
Lantbrukshogsk Medd Ser B ... Lantbrukshogskolans Meddelanden. Series B [*A publication*]
LAO .... Licentiate of the Art of Obstetrics [*British*]
LAP .... Laparotomy [*Medicine*]
LAP .... Leukocyte Alkaline Phosphatase [*An enzyme*]
LAPPES ... Large Power Plant Effluent Study
LAPS .... Low-Altitude Proximity Sensor
LAR .... Left Arm Reclining [*or Recumbent*] [*Medicine*]
LARIS .... Low-Altitude RADAR Interface System
Laryngol Rhinol Otol ... Laryngologie, Rhinologie, Otologie [*A publication*]
Laryngol Rhinol Otol Ihre Grenzeb ... Laryngologie, Rhinologie, Otologie, und Ihre Grenzebiete [*A publication*]
LAS .... Laboratory Automation System
LAS .... Lord Advocate of Scotland
LASER ...... League for the Advancement of States' Equal Rights
LASS .... Large Area Sky Survey
LAST .... Low-Altitude Supersonic Target
LA State Dep Conserv Geol Bull ... Louisiana State Department of Conservation. Geological Bulletin [*A publication*]
LA State Univ Proc Annu For Symp ... Louisiana State University. Proceedings of the Annual Forestry Symposium [*A publication*]
LA State Univ Stud Biol Sci Ser ... Louisiana State University Studies. Biological Science Series [*A publication*]
Latv Lauksaimn Akad Raktsi ... Latvijas Lauksaimniecibas Akademijas Raktsi [*A publication*]
Latv Psr Zinat Akad Vestis ... Latvijas Psr Zinatnu Akademijas Vestis [*A publication*]
LATWING ... Light Attack Wing [*Navy*]
LAVA .... Low-Frequency Acoustic Vernier Analyzer
Laval Med ... Laval Medical [*A publication*]
Laval Univ For Res Found Contrib ... Laval University Forest Research Foundation. Contributions [*A publication*]
Lav Um ...... Lavoro Umano [*A publication*]
LAWB .... Los Alamos Water Boiler [*Nuclear reactor*]
LAWS .... Low-Altitude Warning System
LB .... Lady Boss
L & B .... Left and Below [*Medicine*]
LB .... Low Back [*Disorder*] [*Medicine*]
LBJL .... Lyndon B. Johnson Library
LBR .... LASER Beam Rider
LC .... Local Control
LC .... Locus Ceruleus [*Anatomy*]
LCBO .... Linear Combination of [*Semi-localized*] Band Orbitals [*Atomic physics*]
LCCN .... Library of Congress Catalog-Card Number
LCCS .... Low Cervical Caesarean Section
LCDT .... London Contemporary Dance Theatre
LCEWS ..... Low-Cost Electronic Warfare Suite

New Acronyms, Initialisms, & Abbreviations

LCF .... Level Control Function [*Data processing*]
LCGO .... Linear Combination of Gaussian Orbitals [*Atomic physics*]
LCHA .... Love Canal Homeowners Association
LCHS .... Large Component Handling System [*Nuclear energy*]
LCIGS .... Low-Cost Inertial Guidance Subsystem
LCL .... Linkage Control Language [*Data processing*]
LCO .... Launch Control Operation
LCO .... Limiting Conditions for Operation [*Nuclear energy*]
LCOM .... Logistics Composite Model
LCP .... Language Conversion Program [*Data processing*]
LCP .... Large Coil Program [*Physics*]
LCP .... Lower Cost Processor
LCQ .... Logical Channel Queue [*Data processing*]
LCR .... Log Count Rate [*Nuclear energy*]
LCRO .... Linear Combination of Rydberg Orbitals [*Atomic physics*]
LCS .... Loop Control System [*Nuclear energy*]
LCSR(L) .... Landing Craft Swimmer Recovery (Light) [*Navy symbol*]
LCTI .... Large Components Test Installation [*Nuclear energy*]
LCVIP .... Licensee Contractor Vendor Inspection Report
LCWSL ...... Large Caliber Weapon Systems Laboratory [*ARRADCOM*]
LD .... Lactate Dehydrogenase [*An enzyme*] [*Also, LAD, LDH*]
LD .... Long Days [*Botany*]
LDA .... Landing Distance Available [*Aviation*]
LDCC .... Large Diameter Component Cask [*Nuclear energy*]
LDH .... Lactate Dehydrogenase [*An enzyme*] [*Also, LAD, LD*]
LDM .... Limited-Distance MODEM
LDMS .... LASER Desorption Mass Spectrometry
LDP .... Lordship [*British*]
LDS .... Layered Defense System
LDT .... Long Distance Transmission
LDV .... League of Disabled Voters
LDWSS ..... LASER Designator Weapon System Simulation
Le .... Leonard [*Unit for cathode rays*]
LE .... Lower Extremity [*Medicine*]
LEAF .... Liberal Education for Adoptive Families [*An organization*]
Leafl West Bot ... Leaflets of Western Botany [*A publication*]
Leban Med J ... Lebanese Medical Journal [*A publication*]
Lebensm-Wiss Technol ... Lebensmittel-Wissenschaft Technologie [*A publication*]
Lebensversicher Med ... Lebensversicherungs Medizin [*A publication*]
Leben Umwelt (Aarau) ... Leben und Umwelt (Aarau) [*A publication*]
Leben Umwelt (Wiesb) ... Leben und Umwelt (Wiesbaden) [*A publication*]
LEC .... Limited Editions Club
LEC .... Liquid Encapsulation [*Semiconductor technology*]
Lect Math Life Sci ... Lectures on Mathematics in the Life Sciences [*A publication*]
Lect Notes Biomath ... Lecture Notes in Biomathematics [*A publication*]
LED .... Logistics Engineering Directorate [*ARRCOM*]
LEDR .... Light-Emitting Diode Recorder
LEEP .... Law Enforcement Explorer Post [*Boy Scouts*]
Lehrb Anthropol ... Lehrbuch der Anthropologie [*A publication*]
LEIS .... Low-Energy Ion Scattering [*For study of surfaces*]
Lek Pr .... Lekarske Prace [*A publication*]
LEL .... Large Engineering Loop [*NASA*]
LEMS .... Linear Econometric Modeling System
LEP .... List of Effective Pages
Lepr India ... Leprosy in India [*A publication*]
Lepr Rev ... Leprosy Review [*A publication*]
Lept .... Leptospira [*Genus of bacteria*]
LER .... Licensee Event Report [*Nuclear energy*]
LERP .... Labor Education and Research Project
LES .... Launch Environmental Simulator
LES .... Limited Early Site [*Nuclear energy*]
Lesn Khoz ... Lesnof Khozyaistvo [*A publication*]
Lesn Pr ..... Lesnicka Prace [*A publication*]
LESR .... Limited Early Site Review [*Nuclear energy*]
L/ESS .... Loads/Environmental Spectra Survey
LET .... Launch Effects Trainer
LEV .... Leibovitz-Emory Medium for Viral Cultures
Levende Nat ... Levende Natuur [*A publication*]
Leyte-Samar Stud ... Leyte-Samar Studies [*A publication*]
LF .... Lifting Fan [*Hovercraft*]
LF .... Logical File [*Data processing*]
LFAI .... Lifting Fair Air Intake [*Hovercraft*]

LFI .... Lifting Fan Intake [*Hovercraft*]
LFL .... Libertarians for Life
LFSC .... Lesbian-Feminist Study Clearinghouse
LG .... Leucylglycine [*Organic chemistry*]
LGN .... Logical Group Number
LGPIM .... Lesbian and Gay People in Medicine [*An organization*]
LGRS .... Light-Water-Cooled, Graphite-Moderated Reactors
LH .... Lightly Hinged [*Philately*]
LHGR .... Linear Heat Generation Rate [*Nuclear energy*]
LHM .... Loop Handling Machine [*Nuclear energy*]
LHRT .... Library History Round Table [*American Library Association*]
LHS .... Left Heart Strain [*Medicine*]
LHS .... Loop Handling System [*Nuclear energy*]
LHU .... Lake Havasu City [*Arizona*] [*Airport symbol*]
LHW .... Lanzhou [*China*] [*Airport symbol*]
Libyan J Agric ... Libyan Journal of Agriculture [*A publication*]
Libyan J Sci ... Libyan Journal of Science [*A publication*]
LIC .... LASER-Induced Chemistry
LIC .... Loop Insertion Cell [*Nuclear energy*]
LID .... Library Issue Document
LIE .... Libenge [*Zaire*] [*Airport symbol*]
LIF .... Lifu [*Loyalty Islands*] [*Airport symbol*]
Life Sci Res Rep ... Life Sciences Research Reports [*A publication*]
LIG .... Ligament [*or Ligamentum*]
LIG .... Limoges [*France*] [*Airport symbol*]
LIGG .... Ligaments [*or Ligamenti*]
LIH .... Lihue [*Hawaii*] [*Airport symbol*]
LII .... Mulia [*Indonesia*] [*Airport symbol*]
Lijec Vjesn ... Lijecnicki Vjesnik [*A publication*]
LIL .... Lille [*France*] [*Airport symbol*]
Lille Chir ... Lille Chirurgical [*A publication*]
Lille Med Actual ... Lille Medical Actualities [*A publication*]
LIM .... Lima [*Peru*] [*Airport symbol*]
LIM .... Line Interface Module
LIMAC .... Large Integrated Monolithic Array Computer
LIMIT .... Lot-Size Inventory Management Interpolation Technique
Limnol Donau ... Limnologie der Donau [*A publication*]
Limnol Oceanogr ... Limnology and Oceanography [*A publication*]
LIN .... Milan [*Italy*] Forlanini-Linate [*Airport symbol*]
LINIM .... Liniment
Linn Belg ... Linneana Belgica [*A publication*]
Linn Soc Symp Ser ... Linnean Society Symposium Series [*A publication*]
LINS .... LASER Inertial Navigation System
LIO .... Limon [*Costa Rica*] [*Airport symbol*]
Liofilizzazione Criobiol Appl Criog ... Liofilizzazione Criobiologia Applicazioni Criogeniche [*A publication*]
LIOP .... Limited Initial Operating Production
LIPAS .... LASER-Induced Photoacoustic Spectroscopy
Lippincott's Med Sci ... Lippincott's Medical Science [*A publication*]
LIQ .... Lisala [*Zaire*] [*Airport symbol*]
LIR .... Liberia [*Costa Rica*] [*Airport symbol*]
LIRBM .... Liver, Iron, Red Bone Marrow
LIRE .... Lincoln Institute for Research and Education
LIS .... Link Information Sciences
LIS .... Lisbon [*Portugal*] [*Airport symbol*]
LIS .... Lobular Insitu [*Medicine*]
LISC .... Local Initiatives Support Corporation
LIT .... Little Rock [*Arkansas*] [*Airport symbol*]
LITE .... Let's Improve Today's Education [*Newsletter*]
LIU .... Line Interface Unit
Liverp Manch Geol J ... Liverpool and Manchester Geological Journal [*A publication*]
Livest Prod Sci ... Livestock Production Science [*A publication*]
Living Mus ... Living Museum [*A publication*]
LIW .... Loikaw [*Burma*] [*Airport symbol*]
LJA .... Lodja [*Zaire*] [*Airport symbol*]
LJN .... Lake Jackson [*Texas*] [*Airport symbol*]
LJU .... Ljubljana [*Yugoslavia*] [*Airport symbol*]
LKB .... Lakeba [*Fiji*] [*Airport symbol*]
LKL .... Lakselv [*Norway*] [*Airport symbol*]
LKN .... Leknes [*Norway*] [*Airport symbol*]
LK-NDV .... Newcastle Disease Virus, L-Kansas Strain
LKO .... Lucknow [*India*] [*Airport symbol*]
LL .... Aero Lloyd [*West Germany*] [*ICAO designator*]
LLA .... Lulea [*Sweden*] [*Airport symbol*]
LLDEF .... Lambda Legal Defense and Education Fund
LLDPE .... Linear Low-Density Polyethylene [*Plastics technology*]

New Acronyms, Initialisms, & Abbreviations

LLFM......... Low-Level Flux Monitor [*Nuclear energy*]
LLG........... Chillagoe [*Australia*] [*Airport symbol*]
LLI............. Lalibella [*Ethiopia*] [*Airport symbol*]
LLM........... Localized Leukocyte Mobilization
LLW........... Lilongwe [*Malawi*] [*Airport symbol*]
LLW........... Low-Level Waste [*Nuclear energy*]
LLWSAS ... Low-Level Wind Sheer Alert System [*Meteorology*]
LM............. Lipid Mobilizing Hormone [*Endocrinology*]
LMA........... Lake Minchumina [*Alaska*] [*Airport symbol*]
LMB........... Laurence-Moon-Biedl [*Medicine*]
LMC........... Lamacarena [*Colombia*] [*Airport symbol*]
LMCC....... Low-Mintage Coin Club
LMHX....... Liquid Metal Heat Exchanger
LMI............. Lumi [*Papua New Guinea*] [*Airport symbol*]
LML........... Left Mediolateral [*Episiotomy*] [*Obstetrics*]
LMN........... Limbang [*Malaysia*] [*Airport symbol*]
LMP........... Lampedusa [*Italy*] [*Airport symbol*]
LMP........... Lumbar Puncture [*Medicine*]
LMT........... Klamath Falls [*Oregon*] [*Airport symbol*]
LMT........... Leadership and Management Training [*Navy*]
LMT........... Left Mentotransverse [*A fetal position*] [*Obstetrics*]
LMTO....... Linear Combination of Muffin Tin Orbitals [*Atomic physics*]
LNB........... Lamen Bay [*Vanuata*] [*Airport symbol*]
LND........... Hawaii Landair [*Honolulu, HI*] [*FAA designator*]
LNE........... Lonorore [*Vanuata*] [*Airport symbol*]
LNG........... Lese [*Papua New Guinea*] [*Airport symbol*]
LNK........... Lincoln [*Nebraska*] [*Airport symbol*]
LNM.......... Langimar [*Papua New Guinea*] [*Airport symbol*]
LNO........... Leonora [*Australia*] [*Airport symbol*]
LNS........... Lancaster [*Pennsylvania*] [*Airport symbol*]
LNV........... Londolovit [*Papua New Guinea*] [*Airport symbol*]
LNY........... Lanai City [*Hawaii*] [*Airport symbol*]
LNYV........ Lettuce Necrotic Yellows Virus
LNZ........... Linz [*Austria*] [*Airport symbol*]
LO............. Connect Me to a Perforator Receiver [*Communications*]
LO............. Line Occupancy
LO............. Love Object
LOA........... Lorraine [*Australia*] [*Airport symbol*]
LOAD......... Low-Altitude Defense
LOCE......... Loss-of-Coolant Experiment
LOCF......... Loss-of-Coolant Flow [*Nuclear energy*]
LOCOS..... Local Oxidation of Silicon [*Transistor technology*]
LOCP........ Loss-of-Coolant Protection [*Nuclear energy*]
LOCS .... Logic and Control Simulator [*Data processing*]
LOD........... Longana [*Vanuata*] [*Airport symbol*]
LOE........... Light-Off Examination [*Navy*]
LOE........... Loei [*Thailand*] [*Airport symbol*]
LOEC .... List of Effective Cards
LOEP........ List of Effective Pages
LOF........... Loss of Flow [*Nuclear energy*]
LOFA......... Loss of Flow Accident [*Nuclear energy*]
LOGHELO ... Logistics Helicopter
LOH........... Loja [*Ecuador*] [*Airport symbol*]
LOI............. Laboratory Operating Instructions
LOL........... Left Occipitolateral [*A fetal position*] [*Obstetrics*]
LOL........... Lovelock [*Nevada*] [*Airport symbol*]
LON........... London [*England*] [*Airport symbol*]
Long Ashton Res Stn Rep ... Long Ashton Research Station. Report [*A publication*]
Long Point Bird Obs Annu Rep ... Long Point Bird Observatory. Annual Report [*A publication*]
LOP........... Loss of Offsite Power [*Nuclear energy*]
LOPI.......... Loss of Pipe Integrity [*Nuclear energy*]
LORA .... Long-Range Addition
LORD .... List of Required Documents
LORD .... Lordosis [*Medicine*]
LORDS...... Licensing On-Line Retrieval Data System
LOS........... Lagos [*Nigeria*] [*Airport symbol*]
Los Ang Cty Mus Contrib Sci ... Los Angeles County Museum. Contributions in Science [*A publication*]
LOSP........ Loss of System Pressure [*Nuclear energy*]
LOTE......... Lesser of Two Evils [*Politics*]
Lotta Tuberc ... Lotta Contro la Tubercolosi [*A publication*]
Lotta Tuberc Mal Polm Soc ... Lotta Contro la Tubercolosi e le Malattie Polmonari Sociali [*A publication*]
Louv Med ... Louvain Medical [*A publication*]
Low Temp Res Stn Camb Annu Rep ... Low Temperature Research Station. Cambridge. Annual Report [*A publication*]

Low Temp Sci Ser B Biol Sci ... Low Temperature Science. Series B. Biological Sciences [*A publication*]
LOZ........... London [*Kentucky*] [*Airport symbol*]
L/P............ Lactate/Pyruvate [*Ratio*]
LP.............. List Processor [*Data processing*]
LP.............. Load Point
LP.............. Long Provost
LPA........... Las Palmas [*Canary Islands*] [*Airport symbol*]
LPB........... La Paz [*Bolivia*] [*Airport symbol*]
LPC........... Laurylpyridinium Chloride [*Organic chemistry*] [*Also, DPC*]
LPC........... Loop Preparation Cask [*Nuclear energy*]
LPCI.......... Low-Pressure Coolant Injection [*Nuclear energy*]
LPCS........ Low-Pressure Core Spray System [*Nuclear energy*]
LPD........... La Pedrera [*Colombia*] [*Airport symbol*]
LPD........... Language Processing and Debugging [*Data processing*]
LPD........... Linear Power Density [*Nuclear energy*]
LPE........... Loop Preparation Equipment [*Nuclear energy*]
LPG........... La Plata [*Argentina*] [*Airport symbol*]
LPGS........ Liquid Pathway Generic Study [*Nuclear energy*]
LPI............. Linkoeping [*Sweden*] [*Airport symbol*]
LPI............. Low-Power Injection [*Nuclear energy*]
LPID.......... Logical Page Identifier
LPIS........... Low-Pressure Injection System [*Nuclear energy*]
LPISS........ Low-Power Illuminator Signal Source
LPL........... Linear Programing Language [*Data processing*]
LPL........... Liverpool [*England*] [*Airport symbol*]
LPM........... Lamap [*Vanuata*] [*Airport symbol*]
LPM........... Licensing Project Manager [*Nuclear energy*]
LPN........... Logical Page Number
LPO........... La Porte [*Indiana*] [*Airport symbol*]
LPP........... Lappeenranta [*Finland*] [*Airport symbol*]
LPRB........ Loaded Program Request Block [*Data processing*]
LPRCO..... Logistics Planning and Reporting Code [*Military*]
LPRM........ Low-Power Range Monitor [*Nuclear energy*]
LPS........... Lopez Island [*Washington*] [*Airport symbol*]
LPSW........ Low-Pressure Service Water [*Nuclear energy*]
LPT............ Lampang [*Thailand*] [*Airport symbol*]
LPU........... Lions Philatelic Unit
LPZ........... Low Population Zone
LQ............. Lowest Quadrant
LQM........... Puerto Leguizamo [*Colombia*] [*Airport symbol*]
LQN........... Qala-Nau [*Afghanistan*] [*Airport symbol*]
LR.............. Loading Ramp
LRA........... Larissa [*Greece*] [*Airport symbol*]
LRCP........ Laboratory Research Cooperative Program [*Scientific Services Program*] [*Army*]
LRD........... Laredo [*Texas*] [*Airport symbol*]
LRE........... Longreach [*Australia*] [*Airport symbol*]
LRF........... Latex and Resorcinol Formaldehyde
LRG........... Land Resources Group
LRH........... La Rochelle [*France*] [*Airport symbol*]
LRIP.......... Low-Rate Initial Production
LRNBA...... La Raza National Bar Association
LRP........... Limited Range Production
LRP........... Long-Range Plans
LRT........... Lorient [*France*] [*Airport symbol*]
LRTNF....... Long-Range Theater Nuclear Force [*Military*]
LRUPS...... Line Replaceable Unit Power Supply
LS.............. Express Air Service (C.I.) Ltd. [*Great Britain*] [*ICAO designator*]
LSA........... Lichen Sclerosis et Atrophicus [*Dermatology*]
LSA........... Losuia [*Papua New Guinea*] [*Airport symbol*]
LSB........... Logistic Support Base
LSC........... Liquid Solid Chromatography
LScA......... Left Scapuloanterior [*A fetal position*] [*Obstetrics*]
LScP......... Left Scapuloposterior [*A fetal position*] [*Obstetrics*]
LSD........... Line-Sharing Device
LSD........... Line Signal Detector
LSD........... Local Spin Density [*Physics*]
LSDF......... Large Sodium Disposal Facility [*Nuclear energy*]
LSE.......... La Crosse [*Wisconsin*]/Winona [*Minnesota*] [*Airport symbol*]
LSE........... Large Scale Equipment
LSH........... Lashio [*Burma*] [*Airport symbol*]
LSI............. Lerwick [*Scotland*] [*Airport symbol*]
LSL............ Left Sacrolateral [*A fetal position*] [*Obstetrics*]
LSL............ Los Chiles [*Costa Rica*] [*Airport symbol*]
LSM........... Long Semado [*Malaysia*] [*Airport symbol*]

LSM........... Lysergic Acid Morpholide
LSO........... Lateral Superior Olive [*Brain anatomy*]
LSP .... Las Piedras [*Venezuela*] [*Airport symbol*]
LSp .... Life Span
LSP .... Lucas-Sargent Proposition [*Economics*]
LSQA .... Local System Queue Area [*Data processing*]
LSRA........ Logistic Support Requirement Analysis
LSS .... Les Saintes [*Guadeloupe*] [*Airport symbol*]
LSSD........ Level Sensitive Scan Design
LSSP.......... Latest Scram Set Point
LSSS........ Limiting Safety System Setting [*Nuclear energy*]
LST .... Last
LST .... Launceston [*Tasmania*] [*Airport symbol*]
LST .... Left Sacrotransverse [*A fetal position*] [*Obstetrics*]
LSU .... Lighthouse Study Unit
LSU .... Long Sukang [*Malaysia*] [*Airport symbol*]
LSY .... Lismore [*Australia*] [*Airport symbol*]
LTA .... Tzaneen [*South Africa*] [*Airport symbol*]
LTB .... Laryngo-Tracheal Bronchitis
LTC .... Long-Term Care [*Medicine*]
LTD .... Ghadames [*Libya*] [*Airport symbol*]
LTDSS ...... LASER Target Designator Scoring System
LTH .... Low-Temperature Holding
LTH .... Luteotrophic Hormone [*Endocrinology*]
LTK .... Latakia [*Syria*] [*Airport symbol*]
LTL............ Lastourville [*Gabon*] [*Airport symbol*]
LTLT .... Long Time Low Temperature [*Food processing*]
LTM........... Lethem [*Guyana*] [*Airport symbol*]
LTN .... Luton [*England*] [*Airport symbol*]
LTO .... Loreto [*Mexico*] [*Airport symbol*]
LTPP .... Lipothiamide-Pyrophosphate
LTQ .... Le Touquet [*France*] [*Airport symbol*]
LTQ .... Local Track Quality
L-TR .... Licensing Technical Review [*Nuclear energy*]
LTRC.......... Landing Traffic [*Aviation*]
LTRS........ Letters Shift [*Teleprinters*]
LTS .... LASER Target Simulator
LTSM .... Long-Range Tactical Strike Missile
LTU .... Long Ton Unit
LTV .... Large Test Vessel [*Nuclear energy*]
LUA .... Lukla [*Nepal*] [*Airport symbol*]
Lucr Gradinii Bot Bucur ... Lucrarile Gradinii Botanice din Bucuresti [*A publication*]
Lucr Inst Cercet Aliment ... Lucrarile Institutului de Cercetari Alimentaire [*A publication*]
Lucr Stiint Inst Cercet Zootech ... Lucrarile Stiintifice ale Institutului de Cercetari Zootechnice [*A publication*]
Lucr Stiint Inst Patol Ig Anim ... Lucrarile Stiintifice ale Institutului de Patologie si Igiena Animala [*A publication*]
LUD .... Luderitz [*South-West Africa*] [*Airport symbol*]

LUG........... Lugano [*Switzerland*] [*Airport symbol*]
LUI .... La Union [*Honduras*] [*Airport symbol*]
LUN .... Lusaka [*Zambia*] [*Airport symbol*]
LUNK .... Line/Trunk
LUO .... Luena [*Angola*] [*Airport symbol*]
LUP .... Kalaupapa [*Hawaii*] [*Airport symbol*]
LUQ........... San Luis [*Argentina*] [*Airport symbol*]
LUR .... Cape Lisburne [*Alaska*] [*Airport symbol*]
LUT .... Laura Station [*Australia*] [*Airport symbol*]
LUT .... Line Unit [*Data processing*]
LUU .... Illumination Unit
LUU .... Laura [*Australia*] [*Airport symbol*]
LUV .... Langgur [*Indonesia*] [*Airport symbol*]
LUW .... Luwuk [*Indonesia*] [*Airport symbol*]
LUX .... Luxembourg [*Luxembourg*] [*Airport symbol*]
LVB .... Livramento [*Brazil*] [*Airport symbol*]
LVED........ Left Ventricular End Diastolic [*Medicine*]
LVI............ Livingstone [*Zambia*] [*Airport symbol*]
LVN .... Licensed Visiting Nurse
LVO .... Laverton [*Australia*] [*Airport symbol*]
LW .... Lauda Air [*Austria*] [*ICAO designator*]
LWB .... Greenbrier [*West Virginia*] [*Airport symbol*]
LWC .... Lawrence [*Kansas*] [*Airport symbol*]
LWH .... Lawn Hill [*Australia*] [*Airport symbol*]
LWK .... Lerwick [*Scotland*] Tingwall Airport [*Airport symbol*]
LWL........ Wells [*Nevada*] [*Airport symbol*]
LWO .... Lwow [*USSR*] [*Airport symbol*]
LWS .... Lewiston [*Idaho*] [*Airport symbol*]
LWT .... Lewistown [*Montana*] [*Airport symbol*]
LWV .... Lawrenceville [*Illinois*] [*Airport symbol*]
LWY .... Lawas [*Malaysia*] [*Airport symbol*]
LWYACC .. Lithuanian World Youth Association Communications Center
LX............. Cross Air [*Switzerland*] [*ICAO designator*]
LXA .... Lhasa [*China*] [*Airport symbol*]
LXR .... Luxor [*Egypt*] [*Airport symbol*]
LXS .... Lemnos [*Greece*] [*Airport symbol*]
LY.............. Langley [*Unit of sun's heat*]
LYB .... Little Cayman [*West Indies*] [*Airport symbol*]
LYH .... Lynchburg [*Virginia*] [*Airport symbol*]
Lying-In J Reprod Med ... Lying-In Journal of Reproductive Medicine [*A publication*]
LYM........... Lymphocyte
LYMPH...... Lymphocyte
Lynx Suppl (Prague) ... Lynx Supplementum (Prague) [*A publication*]
LYP .... Faisalabad [*Pakistan*] [*Airport symbol*]
LYPW .... League of Young Polish Women
LYR .... Longyear [*Norway*] [*Airport symbol*]
LYS .... Lyon [*France*] [*Airport symbol*]
LZR .... Lizard Island [*Australia*] [*Airport symbol*]

M

M .... Mature
M .... Memory
M .... Mentum [*Chin*]
M .... Metabolite
M .... Micrococcus [*Genus of bacteria*]
M .... Mitosis [*Cytology*]
M .... Monkey
M .... Motivational Ability
M .... Murmur [*Heart*] [*Medicine*]
MA............ Marketing Assistance
MA............ Mentum Anterior [*In reference to the chin*]
MA............ Miscellaneous at Anchor [*Navy*]
MA............ Modified Atmosphere [*Food technology*]
MAA .... Madras [*India*] [*Airport symbol*]
MAA .... Material Access Area [*Nuclear energy*]
Maandbl Pieper ... Maandblad de Pieper [*A publication*]
MAARM .... Memory-Aided Antiradiation Missile
Maataloustiet Aikak ... Maataloustieteellinen Aikakauskiria [*A publication*]
MAB .... Maraba [*Brazil*] [*Airport symbol*]
MAC .... Medical Alert Center
MAC .... Monthly Availability Charge
MACC .... Maccabees [*Old Testament book*]
MACCT ..... Multiple Assembly Cooling Cask Test [*Nuclear energy*]
MACED ..... Macedonian
Mach Agric Trop ... Machinisme Agricole Tropical [*A publication*]
Macromol Rev ... Macromolecular Reviews [*A publication*]
MAD .... Madrid [*Spain*] [*Airport symbol*]
MAD .... Master Accession Document
MAD .... Mutual Ability for Defense [*Pentagon defense policy*]
MADC .... Machine-Assisted Detection and Classification
MADO .... Mulliken Approximation for Differential Overlap [*Physics*]
Madoqua Ser I ... Madoqua. Series I [*A publication*]
Madoqua Ser II ... Modoqua. Series II [*A publication*]
Madras Agric J ... Madras Agricultural Journal [*A publication*]
Madras Med J ... Madras Medical Journal [*A publication*]
MAF .... Midland/Odessa [*Texas*] [*Airport symbol*]
MAF .... Multiple Access Facility [*Data processing*]
MAFFEX.... Marine Amphibious Force Field Exercise [*Military*]
MAFLEX.... Marine Amphibious Force Landing Exercise [*Military*]
MAG .... Madang [*Papua New Guinea*] [*Airport symbol*]
MAG .... Magnification
MAGLAD... Marksmanship Gunnery LASER Device
MAGTF ..... Marine Air Ground Task Force
Magy Allatorv Lapja ... Magyar Allatorvosok Lapja [*A publication*]
Magy All Foldt Intez Evi Jel ... Magyar Allami Foldtani Intezet Evi Jelentese [*A publication*]
Magy All Foldt Intez Evk ... Magyar Allami Foldtani Intezet Evkonyve [*A publication*]
Magyarorsz Allatvilaga ... Magyarorszag Allatvilaga [*A publication*]
Magy Kem Foly ... Magyar Kemiai Folyoirat [*A publication*]
Magy Kulturfloraja ... Magyarorszag Kulturfloraja [*A publication*]
MAH .... Mahon [*Spain*] [*Airport symbol*]
MAID/MILES ... Magnetic Anti-Intrusion/Magnetic Intrusion Line Sensor
Maine Agric Exp Stn Bull ... Maine Agricultural Experiment Station. Bulletin [*A publication*]
Maine Agric Exp Stn Misc Publ ... Maine Agricultural Experiment Station. Miscellaneous Publication [*A publication*]

Maine Agric Exp Stn Misc Rep ... Maine Agricultural Experiment Station. Miscellaneous Report [*A publication*]
Maine Farm Res ... Maine Farm Research [*A publication*]
Maine Field Nat ... Maine Field Naturalist [*A publication*]
Maine Life Sci Agric Exp Stn Bull ... Maine Life Sciences and Agriculture Experiment Station. Bulletin [*A publication*]
MAJ........... Majuro [*Marshall Islands*] [*Airport symbol*]
MAJAC ..... Monitor Antijam and Control
Major Probl Clin Pediatr ... Major Problems in Clinical Pediatrics [*A publication*]
Major Probl Clin Surg ... Major Problems in Clinical Surgery [*A publication*]
MAK .... Malakal [*Sudan*] [*Airport symbol*]
Makerere Med J ... Makerere Medical Journal [*A publication*]
Makromol Chem ... Makromolekulare Chemie [*A publication*]
MAL .... Macroassembly Language [*Data processing*]
MAL .... Man and LASER
Malacol Rev ... Malacological Review [*A publication*]
Malakol Abh (Dres) ... Malakologische Abhandlungen (Dresden) [*A publication*]
Malawi Annu Rep Dep Agric ... Malawi Annual Report of the Department of Agriculture [*A publication*]
Malawi For Res Inst Res Rec ... Malawi Forest Research Institute. Research Record [*A publication*]
Malaya Dep Agric Bull ... Malaya Department of Agriculture. Bulletin [*A publication*]
Malayan Agric J ... Malayan Agricultural Journal [*A publication*]
Malay For ... Malayan Forester [*A publication*]
Malay For Rec ... Malayan Forest Records [*A publication*]
Malay Nat J ... Malayan Nature Journal [*A publication*]
Malay Rep For Admin ... Malay Report on Forest Administration [*A publication*]
Malays Agric J ... Malaysian Agricultural Journal [*A publication*]
Malays For ... Malaysian Forester [*A publication*]
Malays Inst Med Res Annu Rep ... Malaysia Institute for Medical Research. Annual Report [*A publication*]
Malays J Sci ... Malaysian Journal of Science [*A publication*]
Malays Minist Agric Fish Bull ... Malaysia Ministry of Agriculture and Fisheries. Bulletin [*A publication*]
Malays Rep For Admin West Malaysia ... Malaysia Report on Forest Administration in West Malaysia [*A publication*]
Malays Vet J ... Malaysian Veterinary Journal [*A publication*]
Mal Cardiovasc ... Malattie Cardiovascolari [*A publication*]
MAM .... Management and Administration Manual
MAM .... Matamoros [*Mexico*] [*Airport symbol*]
Mammal Rev ... Mammal Review [*A publication*]
Mamm Depicta ... Mammalia Depicta [*A publication*]
Mamm Species ... Mammalian Species [*A publication*]
MAMS .... Medical Administrative Management System
MAN .... Manchester [*England*] [*Airport symbol*]
MAND .... Mandible
Mandschr Kindergeneeskd ... Mandschrift voor Kindergeneeskunde [*A publication*]
Man His Environ ... Man and His Environment [*A publication*]
Manit Entomol ... Manitoba Entomologist [*A publication*]
Manit Nat ... Manitoba Nature [*A publication*]
Mankind Monogr ... Mankind Monographs [*A publication*]
Mankind Q ... Mankind Quarterly [*A publication*]

Man Mon Rec Anthropol Sci ... Man. A Monthly Record of Anthropological Science [*A publication*]

Man Nat .... Man Nature [*A publication*]

Manuf Milk Prod J ... Manufactured Milk Products Journal [*A publication*]

MAO.......... Manaus [*Brazil*] [*Airport symbol*]

MAOF....... Mexican-American Opportunity Foundation

MAP .... Mamai [*Papua New Guinea*] [*Airport symbol*]

MAP .... Modular Application System [*Data processing*]

MAPLHGR ... Maximum Average Planar Linear Heat-Generation Rate [*Nuclear energy*]

MAPS........ Muhammad Ali Professional Sports [*Commercial firm*]

MAR .... Management Assessment Review

MAR .... Maracaibo [*Venezuela*] [*Airport symbol*]

Marathwada Univ J Sci ... Marathwada University Journal of Science [*A publication*]

Mar Behav Physiol ... Marine Behaviour and Physiology [*A publication*]

Mar Biol (Berl) ... Marine Biology (Berlin) [*A publication*]

Mar Biol (NY) ... Marine Biology (New York) [*A publication*]

MARCH..... Marchioness

Mar Chem ... Marine Chemistry [*A publication*]

MARDAC .. Manpower Research and Data Analysis Center [*DOD*]

MARED ..... Materiel Acquisition and Readiness Executive Development [*Program*] [*Army*]

MAREMIC ... Maintenance Repair and Minor Construction [*Program*] [*Air Force*]

Mar Geotechnol ... Marine Geotechnology [*A publication*]

Mar Invertebr Scand ... Marine Invertebrates of Scandinavia [*A publication*]

Marit Sediments ... Maritime Sediments [*A publication*]

Mark Grow J ... Market Grower's Journal [*A publication*]

Mar Micropaleontol ... Marine Micropaleontology [*A publication*]

Maroc Med ... Maroc Medical [*A publication*]

Mar Pollut Bull ... Marine Pollution Bulletin [*A publication*]

MARRCS... Manpower Requirements and Resources Control System [*Navy*]

Mar Res Dep Agric Fish Scotl ... Marine Research. Department of Agriculture and Fisheries for Scotland [*A publication*]

Mar Res Indones ... Marine Research in Indonesia [*A publication*]

Mar Res Ser Scott Home Dep ... Marine Research Series. Scottish Home Department [*A publication*]

Mars Chir ... Marseille Chirurgical [*A publication*]

Mar Sci (NY) ... Marine Science (New York) [*A publication*]

Mar Technol Soc Annu Conf Prepr ... Marine Technology Society. Annual Conference Preprints [*A publication*]

Mar Zool ... Marine Zoologist [*A publication*]

MAS .... Manus [*Papua New Guinea*] [*Airport symbol*]

MAS .... Maritime Air Superiority

MASAP ..... Michigan Association of Single Adoptive Parents

MASEX ..... Maritime Air Superiority Exercise

MASS........ Monitor and Assembly System

MASS........ Multiple Access Sequential Selection

Mass Agric Exp Stn Bull ... Massachusetts Agricultural Experiment Station. Bulletin [*A publication*]

Mass Agric Exp Stn Monogr Ser ... Massachusetts Agricultural Experiment Station. Monograph Series [*A publication*]

Massey Agric Coll Dairyfarm Annu ... Massey Agricultural College. Dairyfarming Annual [*A publication*]

Massey Agric Coll Sheepfarm Annu ... Massey Agricultural College. Sheepfarming Annual [*A publication*]

MAST........ Military Assistance to Safety and Traffic

MAT .... Master Account Title [*Office of Management and Budget*]

MAT .... Matadi [*Zaire*] [*Airport symbol*]

MATC........ Maximum Acceptable Toxicant Concentration

Mater Floryst Geobot ... Materialy Florystyczne i Geobotaniczne [*A publication*]

Mater Istor Zemled SSSR ... Materialy po Istorii Zemledeliya SSSR [*A publication*]

Mater Leve Geobot Suisse ... Materiaux pour le Leve Geobotanique de la Suisse [*A publication*]

Mater Med Pol ... Material Medica Polona [*A publication*]

Matern Infanc ... Maternidade e Infancia [*A publication*]

Mater Org (Berl) ... Material und Organismen (Berlin) [*A publication*]

Mater Pr Antropol ... Materialy i Prace Antropologiczne [*A publication*]

Mater Ther ... Materia Therapeutica [*A publication*]

Math Biosci ... Mathematical Biosciences [*A publication*]

MATWING ... Medium Attack Wing

MATYC J .. MATYC [*Mathematics Association of Two-Year Colleges*] Journal [*A publication*]

MAU .... Maupiti [*French Polynesia*] [*Airport symbol*]

Mauritius Dep Agric Annu Rep ... Mauritius Department of Agriculture. Annual Report [*A publication*]

Mauritius Dep Agric Bull ... Mauritius Department of Agriculture. Bulletin [*A publication*]

Mauritius Inst Bull ... Mauritius Institute Bulletin [*A publication*]

Mauritius Sugar Ind Res Inst Leafl ... Mauritius Sugar Industry Research Institute. Leaflet [*A publication*]

MAV .... Chaparral Aviation, Inc. [*Reno, NV*] [*FAA designator*]

MAV .... Maximum Allowable Variation [*Net weight labeling*]

Mawdsley Mem ... Mawdsley Memoir [*A publication*]

MAX .... Matam [*Senegal*] [*Airport symbol*]

MAX .... Maxilla [*Jawbone*]

Max-Planck-Ges Jahrb ... Max-Planck-Gesellschaft Jahrbuch [*A publication*]

MAY .... Mangrove Cay [*Bahamas*] [*Airport symbol*]

Mayo Clin Proc ... Mayo Clinic Proceedings [*A publication*]

MAZ .... Mayaguez [*Puerto Rico*] [*Airport symbol*]

MB............. Mark of the Beast [*Disparaging term for clerical waistcoats. So called because, when first worn by Protestant clergymen about 1830, they were said to indicate a Roman Catholic tendency*]

MB............. Marsh-Bender [*Factor*] [*Muscle tissue*]

MB............. Microelectronics Bibliography [*A publication*]

MB............. Million Bytes [*Data processing*]

MBA .... Mombasa [*Kenya*] [*Airport symbol*]

MBB .... Marble Bar [*Australia*] [*Airport symbol*]

MBC .... M'Bigou [*Gabon*] [*Airport symbol*]

MBDA........ Minority Business Development Agency [*Formerly, OMBE*] [*Department of Commerce*]

MBE .... Monbetsu [*Japan*] [*Airport symbol*]

MBH .... Maryborough [*Australia*] [*Airport symbol*]

MBI............ Mbeya [*Tanzania*] [*Airport symbol*]

MBI............ MBI. Medico-Biologic Information [*A publication*]

MBIC .... Michigan Bigfoot Information Center

MBJ........... Montego Bay [*Jamaica*] [*Airport symbol*]

MBL .... Manistee [*Michigan*] [*Airport symbol*]

MBP .... Melitensis, Bovine, Porcine

MBPT .... Many-Body Perturbation Theory [*Physics*]

MBR .... Methylene Blue Reduced

MBRT .... Methylene Blue Reduction Time

MBTS........ Mercaptobenzothiazole Disulfide [*Organic chemistry*]

MBU .... MIRA [*Multifunctional Inertial Reference Assembly*] Basic Unit [*Air Force*]

MBUMR..... MIRA [*Multifunctional Inertial Reference Assembly*] Basic Unit Mounting Rack [*Air Force*]

MC .... Machine Cancellation [*Philately*]

MC .... Main Cabin

MC .... Mission Computer

MC .... Momentary Contact

MC .... Monitor and Control

MC5........... Motor City Five [*Rock music group*]

MCA .... Management and Command Ashore

MCA .... Management Control Authority

MCA .... Material Control and Accountability

MCA .... Maximum Credible Accident [*Nuclear energy*]

MCA .... Monetary Compensatory Amount

MCAR .... Machine Check Analysis and Recording

McB........... McBurney's [*Point*] [*Medicine*]

MCC......... Management Control Center

MCC......... Multiple-Chip Carrier [*Computer technology*]

MCC......... Multiple Communications Control

MCD .... Median Control Death

mcD .... Millicurie-Destroyed

MCD .... Minor Civil Division [*Bureau of Census*]

MCDD .... Monochlorodioxin [*Organic chemistry*]

MCDR .... Multichannel DIFAR [*Directional Frequency Analysis and Recording System*] Relay

MCG .... Millimeter-Wave Contrast Guidance

MCH .... March

mch.......... Millicurie Hour

MCHFR ..... Minimum Critical Heat Flux Rates [*Nuclear energy*]

MCI .... Machine Check Interruption

MCIS .... Materials Compatibility in Sodium [*Nuclear energy*]

MCN.......... American Journal of Maternal Child Nursing [*A publication*]

MCN.......... Maintenance Communications Net

MCOM....... Missile Command [*Army*]

MCP.......... Metacarpal Phalangeal

MCP.......... Mission Concept Paper

MCPESCF ... Multiconfiguration Paired Excitation Self-Consistent Field [*Physics*]

MCPR........ Maximum Critical Power Ratio [*Nuclear energy*]

MCR.......... Magnetic Character Recognition [*Data processing*]

MCR.......... Metabolic Clearance Rate

MCS.......... Medical Computer System

MCS.......... Message Control System

MCV.......... Movable Closure Valve

MCVQ Med Coll VA Q ... MCVQ. Medical College of Virginia Quarterly [*A publication*]

MCZDO..... Multicenter Zero Differential Overlap [*Physics*]

MD.......... Magnetic Disk [*Data processing*]

MD.......... Measured Discard

MD.......... Monitor Displays

MD.......... Multiple Dissemination

MDA.......... Muscular Dystrophy Association

MD Agric Exp Stn Bull ... Maryland Agricultural Experiment Station. Bulletin [*A publication*]

MD Agric Exp Stn MP ... Maryland Agricultural Experiment Station. MP [*A publication*]

MDC.......... Maximum Dependable Capacity [*Nuclear energy*]

MDC.......... Mechanically Deboned Chicken [*Food technology*]

MD Conserv ... Maryland Conservationist [*A publication*]

MDC/SS ... Microwave Multiple Drone Control Strike

MDCT........ Mechanical Draft Cooling Tower [*Nuclear energy*]

MDD.......... Maintenance Due Date

MDE.......... Magnetic Decision Element [*Data processing*]

MDE.......... Modular Design of Electronics

MDF.......... Myocardial Depressant Factor

MDG.......... Multipurpose Display Group

MDI.......... Manic Depressive Illness

MDL.......... Macro Description Language [*Data processing*]

MDL.......... Maintenance Diagnostic Logic [*Data processing*]

MDLRC..... Mental Disability Legal Resource Center

MD Nat...... Maryland Naturalist [*A publication*]

MDNB....... Meta-Dinitrobenzene [*Organic chemistry*]

MDPN........ Midshipman

MDR.......... Median Detection Range

MDRC....... Manual Data Relay Center

MDRI......... Multipurpose Display Repeater Indicator

MDS.......... Multiple Dataset System

MDSS-PCT ... Multidimensional Switching System-Packed Column Trap [*Instrumentation*]

MD State Med J ... Maryland State Medical Journal [*A publication*]

MDT.......... Mobile Data Terminal

MDV.......... Marek's Disease Virus

MDZ.......... Missile Danger Zone

M & E........ Material and Equipment [*Nuclear energy*]

ME............. Middle Ear

MEA.......... Monoethylamine [*Organic chemistry*]

MEA.......... Multiple Endocrine Adenomas

MEBU........ Maschinengewehr-Eisenbeton-Unterstand [*Machine-Gun-Iron-Concrete-Emplacement*] [*German "pill box," battlefield redoubts*] [*World War I*]

MEC.......... Main Evaluation Center

Mech Ageing Dev ... Mechanisms of Ageing and Development [*A publication*]

MED.......... Minimum Engineering Development

MEDA........ (Mercaptoethyl)dimethylammonium Chloride [*Organic chemistry*]

Med Actuelle ... Medecine Actuelle [*A publication*]

Med Afr Noire ... Medecine d'Afrique Noire [*A publication*]

Med Ann DC ... Medical Annals of the District of Columbia [*A publication*]

Med Arhiv ... Medicinski Arhiv [*A publication*]

Med Armees ... Medecine et Armees [*A publication*]

Med Biol Eng ... Medical and Biological Engineering [*A publication*]

Med Biol Eng Comput ... Medical and Biological Engineering and Computing [*A publication*]

Med Biol Illus ... Medical and Biological Illustration [*A publication*]

Med Bull Exxon Corp Affil Co ... Medical Bulletin. Exxon Corporation and Affiliated Companies [*A publication*]

Med Bull Fukuoka Univ ... Medical Bulletin of Fukuoka University [*A publication*]

Med Chem Ser Monogr ... Medicinal Chemistry. A Series of Monographs [*A publication*]

Med Chem Ser Rev ... Medicinal Chemistry. A Series of Reviews [*A publication*]

Med Chir Dig ... Medecine et Chirurgie Digestives [*A publication*]

Med Cir..... Medicina y Cirurgia [*A publication*]

Med Cir Farm ... Medicina Cirurgia Farmacia [*A publication*]

Med Clin ... Medicina Clinica [*A publication*]

Med Clin N Am ... Medical Clinics of North America [*A publication*]

Med Clin Sper ... Medicina Clinica e Sperimentale [*A publication*]

Med Colon (Madr) ... Medicina Colonial (Madrid) [*A publication*]

Med Contemp ... Medicina Contemporanea [*A publication*]

Med Cult... Medicina e Cultura [*A publication*]

Med Cutanea ... Medicina Cutanea [*A publication*]

Medd Dan Fisk Havunders ... Meddelelser fra Danmarks Fiskfri-og Havundersogelser [*A publication*]

Medd Dan Geol Foren ... Meddelelser Dansk Geologisk Forening [*A publication*]

Medd Gronl ... Meddelelser om Gronland [*A publication*]

Medd Havsfiskelab Lysekil ... Meddelande fran Havsfiskelaboratoriet Lysekil [*A publication*]

Medd Inst Maltdrycksforsk ... Meddelande fran Institutet foer Maltdrycksforskning [*A publication*]

Medd Kvismare Fagelstn ... Meddelande fran Kvismare Fagelstation [*A publication*]

Medd Nor Farm Selsk ... Meddelelser fra Norsk Farmaceutisk Selskap [*A publication*]

Medd Nor Inst Skogforsk ... Meddelelser fra Norsk Institute foer Skogforskning [*A publication*]

Medd Nor Skogforsoksves ... Meddelelser fra det Norske Skogforsoksvesen [*A publication*]

Med Dosw Mikrobiol ... Medycyna Doswiadczalna i Mikrobiologia [*A publication*]

Med Dosw Mikrobiol (Transl) ... Medycyna Doswiadczalna i Mikrobiologia (Translation) [*A publication*]

Medd Statens Skogsforskningsinst ... Meddelanden fran Statens Skogsforskningsinstitut [*A publication*]

Medd Statens Viltunders ... Meddelelser fra Statens Viltundersokelser [*A publication*]

Meded Geol Sticht ... Mededelingen van de Geologische Stichting [*A publication*]

Meded Landbouwhogesch Wageningen ... Mededelingen Landbouwhogeschool Wageningen [*A publication*]

Meded Rijksfac Landbouwwet Gent ... Mededelingen van de Rijksfaculteit Landbouwwetenschappen te Gent [*A publication*]

Med Electron Biol Eng ... Medical Electronics and Biological Engineering [*A publication*]

Med Electron Data ... Medical Electronics and Data [*A publication*]

Med Ernaehr ... Medizin und Ernaehrung [*A publication*]

Med Esp.... Medicina Espanola [*A publication*]

Med Esporte ... Medicina do Esporte [*A publication*]

Med Exp ... Medicina Experimentalis [*A publication*]

Med Fis Rehabil ... Medicina Fisica y Rehabilitacion [*A publication*]

Med Glas .. Medicinski Glasnik [*A publication*]

Med Gynaecol Androl Sociol ... Medical Gynaecology, Andrology, and Sociology [*A publication*]

Med Gynaecol Sociol ... Medical Gynaecology and Sociology [*A publication*]

Med Hist ... Medical History [*A publication*]

Med Hoje .. Medicina de Hoje [*A publication*]

Med Hyg ... Medecine et Hygiene [*A publication*]

Med Hypotheses ... Medical Hypotheses [*A publication*]

Medicamenta (Ed Farm) ... Medicamenta (Edicion para el Farmaceutico) [*A publication*]

Med Imaging ... Medical Imaging [*A publication*]

Med Infant ... Medecine Infantile [*A publication*]

Med Interna (Buchar) ... Medicina Interna (Bucharest) [*A publication*]

Med Istraz ... Medicinska Istrazivanja [*A publication*]

Med Istraz Suppl ... Medicinska Istrazivanja. Supplementum [*A publication*]

Mediterr Med ... Mediterranee Medicale [*A publication*]

Med J Armed Forces (India) ... Medical Journal. Armed Forces (India) [*A publication*]

Med J (Engl Transl Lijec Vjesn) ... Medical Journal (English Translation of Lijecnicki Vjesnik) [*A publication*]

Med J Kagoshima Univ ... Medical Journal of Kagoshima University [*A publication*]

Med J Kobe Univ ... Medical Journal of Kobe University [*A publication*]

Med J Malaysia ... Medical Journal of Malaysia [*A publication*]

Med J Osaka Univ ... Medical Journal of Osaka University [*A publication*]

Med J Shinshu Univ ... Medical Journal of Shinshu University [*A publication*]

Med J Zambia ... Medical Journal of Zambia [*A publication*]

Med Lab Sci ... Medical Laboratory Sciences [*A publication*]

Med Lab Technol ... Medical Laboratory Technology [*A publication*]

Med Lav .... Medicina del Lavoro [*A publication*]

Med Leg Dommage Corpor ... Medecine Legale et Dommage Corporel [*A publication*]

MEDList .... Master Enumeration District List [*Bureau of Census*]

Med Microbiol Immunol ... Medical Microbiology and Immunology [*A publication*]

Med Monatsschr ... Medizinische Monatsschrift [*A publication*]

Med Nucl Radiobiol Lat ... Medicina Nucleare Radiobiologica Latina [*A publication*]

Med Nutr ... Medecine et Nutrition [*A publication*]

MEDO .... Multipole Expansion of Diatomic Overlap [*Physics*]

Med Paedogog Jugendkd ... Medizinische und Paedogogische Jugendkunde [*A publication*]

Med Parazitol Parazit Bolezni ... Meditsinskaya Parazitologiya i Parazitarnye Bolezni [*A publication*]

Med Pediatr Oncol ... Medical and Pediatric Oncology [*A publication*]

Med Pharmacol Exp ... Medicina et Pharmacologia Experimentalis [*A publication*]

Med Phys ... Medical Physics [*A publication*]

Med Podmladak ... Medicinski Podmladak [*A publication*]

Med Pregl ... Medicinski Pregled [*A publication*]

Med Prisma ... Medizinische Prisma [*A publication*]

Med Prom-st SSSR ... Meditsinskaya Promyshlennost SSSR [*A publication*]

Med Psicosom ... Medicina Psicosomatica [*A publication*]

Med Radiogr Photogr ... Medical Radiography and Photography [*A publication*]

Med Radiol ... Meditsinskaya Radiologiya [*A publication*]

Med Razgledi ... Medicinski Razgledi [*A publication*]

Med Rec Ann ... Medical Record and Annals [*A publication*]

Med Res Cent (Nairobi) Annu Rep ... Medical Research Centre (Nairobi) Annual Report [*A publication*]

Med Res Counc (GB) Annu Rep ... Medical Research Council (Great Britain) Annual Report [*A publication*]

Med Res Counc (GB) Memo ... Medical Research Council (Great Britain) Memorandum [*A publication*]

Med Res Counc (GB) Monit Rep ... Medical Research Council (Great Britain) Monitoring Report [*A publication*]

Med Res Counc (GB) Spec Rep Ser ... Medical Research Council (Great Britain) Special Report Series [*A publication*]

Med Res Photosensit Dyes ... Medical Researches for Photosensitizing Dyes [*A publication*]

Med Res Ser Monogr ... Medicinal Research. A Series of Monographs [*A publication*]

Med Rev (Belgr) ... Medicinska Revija (Belgrade) [*A publication*]

Med Rev Mex ... Medicina Revista Mexicana [*A publication*]

Med Sci ..... Medical Science [*A publication*]

Med Sci Sports ... Medicine and Science in Sports [*A publication*]

Med Secoli ... Medicina nei Secoli [*A publication*]

Med Segur Trab (Madr) ... Medicina y Seguridad del Trabajo (Madrid) [*A publication*]

Med Serv J Can ... Medical Services Journal Canada [*A publication*]

Med Sestra ... Meditsinskaya Sestra [*A publication*]

Med Sport ... Medecine du Sport [*A publication*]

Med Sport (Basel) ... Medicine and Sport (Basel) [*A publication*]

Med Sport (Berlin) ... Medizin und Sport (Berlin) [*A publication*]

Med Sport (Turin) ... Medicina dello Sport (Turin) [*A publication*]

Med Surg ... Medicine and Surgery [*A publication*]

Med Technol Ser ... Medical Technology Series [*A publication*]

Med Tekh ... Meditsinskaya Tekhnika [*A publication*]

Med Thorac ... Medicina Thoracalis [*A publication*]

Med Treat (Tokyo) ... Medical Treatment (Tokyo) [*A publication*]

Med Trop ... Medecine Tropicale [*A publication*]

Med Ultrasound ... Medical Ultrasound [*A publication*]

Med Vet Hell ... Medecine Veterinaire Hellenique [*A publication*]

Med Welt .. Medizinische Welt [*A publication*]

Med Weter ... Medycyna Weterynaryjna [*A publication*]

Med Zh Uzb ... Meditsinskii Zhurnal Uzbekistana [*A publication*]

MEE .... Methyl Ethyl Ether [*Organic chemistry*]

MEEP .... Management and Equipment Evaluation Program

Meet Place J R Ont Mus ... Meeting Place Journal of the Royal Ontario Museum [*A publication*]

MEFV .... Maintenance Equipment Floor Valve

MEG .... Message Entry Generator

MEGG .... Merging [*Meteorology*]

MEGHP ..... Most Excellent Grand High Priest

Meijeritiet Aikak ... Meijeritieteellinen Aikakauskirja [*A publication*]

Meld Nor Landbrukshogsk ... Meldinger fra Norges Landbrukshogskole [*A publication*]

Melsheimer Entomol Ser ... Melsheimer Entomological Series [*A publication*]

Mem Acad Cienc Lisb Cl Cienc ... Memorias da Academia das Ciencias de Lisboa. Classe de Ciencias [*A publication*]

Mem Acad Malgache ... Memoires de l'Academie Malgache [*A publication*]

Mem Acad R Med Belg ... Memoires de l'Academie Royale de Medecine de Belgique [*A publication*]

Mem Am Acad Arts Sci ... Memoirs of the American Academy of Arts and Sciences [*A publication*]

Mem Am Entomol Inst (Ann Arbor) ... Memoirs of the American Entomological Institute (Ann Arbor) [*A publication*]

Mem Am Entomol Soc ... Memoirs of the American Entomological Society [*A publication*]

Mem Am Philos Soc ... Memoirs of the American Philosophical Society [*A publication*]

Mem Biol Mar Oceanogr ... Memorie di Biologia Marina e di Oceanografia [*A publication*]

Mem Botan Surv S Afr ... Memoirs of the Botanical Survey of South Africa [*A publication*]

Mem Bot Opname S-Afr ... Memoirs van die Botaniese Opname van Suid-Afrika [*A publication*]

Mem Cognition ... Memory and Cognition [*A publication*]

Mem Coll Agric Ehime Univ ... Memoirs of the College of Agriculture. Ehime University [*A publication*]

Mem Coll Agric Kyoto Univ ... Memoirs of the College of Agriculture. Kyoto University [*A publication*]

Mem Coll Agric Natl Taiwan Univ ... Memoirs of the College of Agriculture. National Taiwan University [*A publication*]

Mem Congr Nac Med Vet Zootec ... Memorias Congreso Nacional de Medicina Veterinaria y Zootecnia [*A publication*]

Mem Conn Acad Arts Sci ... Memoirs of the Connecticut Academy of Arts and Sciences [*A publication*]

Mem Ehime Univ Sect 6 (Agric) ... Memoirs of the Ehime University. Section 6 (Agriculture) [*A publication*]

Mem Ehime Univ Sect II Nat Sci ... Memoirs of the Ehime University. Section II. Natural Science [*A publication*]

Mem Entomol Soc Can ... Memoirs of the Entomological Society of Canada [*A publication*]

Mem Entomol Soc Que ... Memoirs of the Entomological Society of Quebec [*A publication*]

Mem Entomol Soc South Afr ... Memoirs of the Entomological Society of Southern Africa [*A publication*]

Mem Estud Mus Zool Univ Coimbra ... Memorias e Estudos do Museu Zoologica da Universidade de Coimbra [*A publication*]

Mem Fac Agric Hokkaido Univ ... Memoirs of the Faculty of Agriculture. Hokkaido University [*A publication*]

Mem Fac Agric Kagawa Univ ... Memoirs of the Faculty of Agriculture. Kagawa University [*A publication*]

Mem Fac Agric Kagoshima Univ ... Memoirs of the Faculty of Agriculture. Kagoshima University [*A publication*]

Mem Fac Agric Kinki Univ ... Memoirs of the Faculty of Agriculture. Kinki University [*A publication*]

Mem Fac Agric Kochi Univ ... Memoirs of the Faculty of Agriculture. Kochi University [*A publication*]

Mem Fac Agric Niigata Univ ... Memoirs of the Faculty of Agriculture. Niigata University [*A publication*]

Mem Fac Agric Univ Miyazaki ... Memoirs of the Faculty of Agriculture. University of Miyazaki [*A publication*]

Mem Fac Educ Niigata Univ ... Memoirs of the Faculty of Education. Niigata University [*A publication*]

Mem Fac Educ Shiga Univ Nat Sci ... Memoirs of the Faculty of Education. Shiga University. Natural Science [*A publication*]

Mem Fac Fish Hokkaido Univ ... Memoirs of the Faculty of Fisheries. Hokkaido University [*A publication*]

Mem Fac Fish Kagoshima Univ ... Memoirs of the Faculty of Fisheries. Kagoshima University [*A publication*]

Mem Fac Sci Kyoto Univ Ser Biol ... Memoirs of the Faculty of Science. Kyoto University. Series of Biology [*A publication*]

Mem Geopaleontol Univ Ferrara ... Memorie Geopaleontologiche dell'Universita de Ferrara [*A publication*]

Mem Hourglass Cruises ... Memoirs of the Hourglass Cruises [*A publication*]

Mem Hyogo Univ Agric ... Memoirs of the Hyogo University of Agriculture [*A publication*]

Mem Indian Bot Soc ... Memoirs of the Indian Botanical Society [*A publication*]

Mem Indian Mus ... Memoirs of the Indian Museum [*A publication*]

Mem Inst Butantan (Sao Paulo) ... Memorias do Instituto Butantan (Sao Paulo) [*A publication*]

Mem Inst Egypt ... Memoires Institut d'Egypt [*A publication*]

Mem Inst Geol Univ Louv ... Memoires de l'Institut Geologique de l'Universite de Louvain [*A publication*]

Mem Inst Oceanogr (Monaco) ... Memoires de l'Institut Oceanographique (Monaco) [*A publication*]

Mem Inst Oswaldo Cruz (Rio De J) ... Memorias do Instituto Oswaldo Cruz (Rio De Janeiro) [*A publication*]

Mem Ist Geol Minerol Univ Padova ... Memorie degli Istituti de Geologia e Minerologia dell'Universita de Padova [*A publication*]

Mem Junta Invest Ultramar Ser II ... Memorias Junta de Investagacoes do Ultramar. Serie II [*A publication*]

Mem Konan Univ Sci Ser ... Memoirs of the Konan University. Science Series [*A publication*]

Mem Mus Civ Stor Nat Verona ... Memorie del Museo Civico di Storia Naturale di Verona [*A publication*]

Mem Mus Dr Alvaro De Castro ... Memorias do Museu Dr. Alvaro De Castro [*A publication*]

Mem Mus Hist Nat "Javier Prado" ... Memorias del Museo de Historia Natural "Javier Prado" [*A publication*]

Mem Mus Natl Hist Nat ... Memoires du Museum National d'Histoire Naturelle [*A publication*]

Mem Mus Natl Hist Nat Ser A Zool ... Memoires du Museum National d'Histoire Naturelle. Serie A. Zoologie [*A publication*]

Mem Mus Natl Hist Nat Ser B Bot ... Memoires du Museum National d'Histoire Naturelle. Serie B. Botanique [*A publication*]

Mem Mus Tridentino Sci Nat ... Memorie del Museo Tridentino di Scienze Naturali [*A publication*]

Mem Nas Mus Bloemfontein ... Memoirs van die Nasionale Museum Bloemfontein [*A publication*]

Mem Nat Cult Res San-In Reg ... Memoirs of Natural and Cultural Researches of the San-In Region [*A publication*]

Mem Natl Mus Victoria ... Memoirs of the National Museum of Victoria [*A publication*]

Mem Natl Sci Mus (Tokyo) ... Memoirs of the National Science Museum (Tokyo) [*A publication*]

Mem NY Bot Gard ... Memoirs of the New York Botanical Gardens [*A publication*]

Memorabilia Zool ... Memorabilia Zoologica [*A publication*]

Mem ORSTOM ... Memoires ORSTOM [*Office de la Recherche Scientifique et Technique d'Outre-Mer*] [*A publication*]

Memo Soc Fauna Flora Fenn ... Memoranda Societatis pro Fauna et Flora Fennica [*A publication*]

Mem Pac Coast Entomol Soc ... Memoirs of the Pacific Coast Entomological Society [*A publication*]

Memphis Mid-South Med J ... Memphis and Mid-South Medical Journal [*A publication*]

Mem Queensl Mus ... Memoirs of the Queensland Museum [*A publication*]

Mem R Acad Cienc Artes Barc ... Memorias de la Real Academia de Ciencias y Artes de Barcelona [*A publication*]

Mem Res Inst Food Sci Kyoto Univ ... Memoirs of the Research Institute for Food Science Kyoto University [*A publication*]

Mem Soc Bot Fr ... Memoires Societe Botanique de France [*A publication*]

Mem Soc Broteriana ... Memorias da Sociedade Broteriana [*A publication*]

Mem Soc Cienc Nat La Salle ... Memoria de la Sociedad de Ciencias Naturelles La Salle [*A publication*]

Mem Soc Endocrinol ... Memoirs of the Society for Endocrinology [*A publication*]

Mem Soc Entomol Ital ... Memorie della Societa Entomologica Italiana [*A publication*]

Mem Soc Entomol Que ... Memoires de la Societe Entomologique du Quebec [*A publication*]

Mem Soc Geol Fr ... Memoires de la Societe Geologique de France [*A publication*]

Mem Soc Geol Mineral Bretagne ... Memoires de la Societe Geologique et Mineralogique de Bretagne [*A publication*]

Mem Soc Helv Sci Nat ... Memoires de la Societe Helvetique des Sciences Naturelles [*A publication*]

Mem Soc Hist Nat Afr Nord ... Memoires de la Societe d'Histoire Naturelle de l'Afrique du Nord [*A publication*]

Mem Soc Neuchatel Sci Nat ... Memoires de la Societe Neuchateloise des Sciences Naturelles [*A publication*]

Mem Soc R Belge Entomol ... Memoires de la Societe Royale Belge d'Entomologie [*A publication*]

Mem Soc R Bot Belg ... Memoires de la Societe Royale de Botanique de Belgique [*A publication*]

Mem Soc R Can ... Memoires de la Societe Royale du Canada [*A publication*]

Mem Soc Sci Nat Phys Maroc Bot ... Memoires de la Societe des Sciences Naturelles et Physiques du Maroc. Botanique [*A publication*]

Mem Soc Sci Nat Phys Maroc Zool ... Memoires de la Societe des Sciences Naturelles et Physiques du Maroc. Zoologie [*A publication*]

Mem Soc Vaudoise Sci Nat ... Memoires de la Societe Vaudoise des Sciences Naturelles [*A publication*]

Mem Soc Zool Fr ... Memoires Societe Zoologique de France [*A publication*]

Mem South Calif Acad Sci ... Memoirs of the Southern California Academy of Sciences [*A publication*]

Mem Tokyo Univ Agric ... Memoirs of the Tokyo University of Agriculture [*A publication*]

Mem Torrey Bot Club ... Memoirs of the Torrey Botanical Club [*A publication*]

MENT .... Mental

Ment Health Program Rep ... Mental Health Program Reports [*A publication*]

Ment Health Soc ... Mental Health and Society [*A publication*]

MEPM .... Medium-Term Energy Policy Model

MERA .... Mormons for ERA

Merentutkimuslaitoksen Julk ... Merentutkimuslaitoksen Julkaisu [*A publication*]

Merrill-Palmer Q ... Merrill-Palmer Quarterly [*A publication*]

MES .... Monitoring Energy Systems

MESA NY Bight Atlas Monogr ... MESA [*Marine Ecosystems Analysis*] New York. Bight Atlas Monograph [*A publication*]

MESC .... Mescaline

MESH .... Multiple Electronically Synopsing Hierarchy

MESL .... Mission Essential Subsystems List

MESOP ..... Mesopotamia

MET .... Metaphysics

METAB ...... Metabolism

Metab Clin Exp ... Metabolism Clinical and Experimental [*A publication*]

Metab Ophthalmol ... Metabolic Ophthalmology [*A publication*]

METAR ...... Aviation Routine Weather Report [*Aviation code*]

METAS ...... Metastasize [*Medicine*]

Met Bull .... Metal Bulletin [*A publication*]

METEOR ... Marine Environmental Testing and Electro-Optical Radiation

Meteor Forschungsergeb Reihe D Biol ... Meteor Forschungsergebnisse Reihe D. Biologie [*A publication*]

Meteor Gidrol Inf Byull ... Meteorologiya i Gidrologiya Informatsionnyi Byulleten [*A publication*]

Meteorol Gidrol ... Meteorologiya i Gidrologiya [*A publication*]

Meth Membrane Biol ... Methods in Membrane Biology [*A publication*]

Meth Mol Biol ... Methods in Molecular Biology [*A publication*]

Method Inf Med ... Methodik der Information in der Medizin [*A publication*]

Methodol Dev Biochem ... Methodological Developments in Biochemistry [*A publication*]

Methods Achiev Exp Pathol ... Methods and Achievements in Experimental Pathology [*A publication*]

Methods Anim Exp ... Methods of Animal Experimentation [*A publication*]

Methods Biochem Anal ... Methods of Biochemical Analysis [*A publication*]

Methods Cancer Res ... Methods in Cancer Research [*A publication*]

Methods Carbohydr Chem ... Methods in Carbohydrate Chemistry [*A publication*]

Methods Cell Biol ... Methods in Cell Biology [*A publication*]

Methods Enzymol ... Methods in Enzymology [*A publication*]

Methods Immunol Immunochem ... Methods in Immunology and Immunochemistry [*A publication*]

Methods Inf Med ... Methods of Information in Medicine [*A publication*]

Methods Med Res ... Methods in Medical Research [*A publication*]

Methods Pharmacol ... Methods in Pharmacology [*A publication*]

Metod Mater Nauchn Soobshch ... Metodicheskie Materialy i Nauchnye Soobshcheniya [*A publication*]

Metod Prirucky Exp Bot ... Metodicke Prirucky Experimentalni Botaniky [*A publication*]

Metrop Detroit Sci Rev ... Metropolitan Detroit Science Review [*A publication*]

Metsantutkumuslaitoksen Julk ... Metsantutkumuslaitoksen Julkaisuja [*A publication*]

Mezhdunar S-kh Zh ... Mezhdunarodnyi Sel'skokhozyaistvennyi Zhurnal [*A publication*]

MF ... Merthiolate-Formaldehyde [*Solution*]

Mf ... Microfilariae

MF ... Microscopic Factor

MF ... Myelin Figure [*Medicine*]

MFA ... Malfunction Alert

MFA ... Methyl Fluoracetate [*Organic chemistry*]

MFBF ... Main Feed Booster Pump

MFCI ... Molten Fuel Coolant Interaction

MFCM ... Multifunction Card Machine

MFD ... Multifunction Display

MFHBMA ... Mean Flight Hours between Maintenance Action

MFID ... Multiple-Electrode Flame Ionization Detector

MF-IFGR ... Michael Fund - International Foundation for Genetic Research

MFP ... Main Feed Pump

MFP ... Main Force Patrol [*In movie "Mad Max"*]

MFS ... Manufactures

MFS ... Message Format Service

MFT ... Multiprograming with Fixed Number of Tasks [*Data processing*]

MFTHBA ... Missouri Fox Trotting Horse Breed Association

MFU ... MIRA [*Multifunctional Inertial Reference Assembly*] Fighter [*Air Force*]

MFUMR ... MIRA [*Multifunctional Inertial Reference Assembly*] Fighter Unit Mounting Rack [*Air Force*]

MFV ... Maintenance Floor Valve

MFW ... Ms Foundation for Women

MGFEL ... Master Government-Furnished Equipment List

MGG ... Musik in Geschichte und Gegenwart [*A publication*]

MGL ... Matrix Generator Language [*Data processing*]

MGWS ... Modular Guided Weapon System

MH ... Mobile High-Power [*Reactor*] [*Proposed*]

MHDPA ... Monohexadecylphosphoric Acid [*Organic chemistry*]

MHE ... Munitions Handling Equipment

MHFR ... Maximum Hypothetical Fission Product Release [*Nuclear energy*]

MHLP ... Mental Health Law Project

MHS ... Member of the Historical Society

MHS ... Methylhydrazine Sulfate [*Organic chemistry*]

MHTS ... Main Heat Transport System [*Nuclear energy*]

MI ... Major Issue

MI ... Menstrual Induction [*Medicine*]

MI ... Meso-Inositol [*or Myoinositol*] [*Organic chemistry*]

MI ... Migration Inhibition [*Cytology*]

MI ... Mineral Insulated [*Cables*]

MIA ... Monoiodoacetic Acid [*Organic chemistry*]

MIAK ... Methyl Isoamyl Ketone [*Organic chemistry*]

Miami Winter Symp ... Miami Winter Symposium [*A publication*]

MIBT ... Methyl Isatin-beta-thiosemicarbazone

MIC ... Masonry Industry Committee

MIC ... Message Identification Code

MIC ... Microscopy

MICAP ... Mission Capability

Mich Acad ... Michigan Academician [*A publication*]

Mich Agric Exp Stn Annu Rep ... Michigan Agricultural Experiment Station. Annual Report [*A publication*]

Mich Agric Exp Stn Q Bull ... Michigan Agricultural Experiment Station. Quarterly Bulletin [*A publication*]

Mich Audubon Newsl ... Michigan Audubon Newsletter [*A publication*]

Mich Bot ... Michigan Botanist [*A publication*]

Mich Dep Conserv Game Div Rep ... Michigan Department of Conservation. Game Division Report [*A publication*]

Mich Entomol ... Michigan Entomologist [*A publication*]

Michoacan Mex Com For Bol Ser Tec ... Michoacan Mexico Comision Forestal. Boletin Serie Tecnica [*A publication*]

Mich State Coll Vet ... Michigan State College Veterinarian [*A publication*]

Micol Ital ... Micologia Italiana [*A publication*]

Microb Ecol ... Microbial Ecology [*A publication*]

Microb Genet Bull ... Microbial Genetics Bulletin [*A publication*]

MICROBIOL ... Microbiology

Microbiol Esp ... Microbiologia Espanola [*A publication*]

Microbios Lett ... Microbios Letters [*A publication*]

Microorg Infect Dis ... Microorganisms and Infectious Diseases [*A publication*]

Microsc Acta ... Microscopica Acta [*A publication*]

Microsc J Quekett Microsc Club ... Microscopy. Journal of the Quekett Microscopical Club [*A publication*]

Microvasc Res ... Microvascular Research [*A publication*]

MICVS ... Mechanized Infantry Combat Vehicle Systems [*Army*]

MID ... Meat Inspection Division [*Department of Agriculture*]

MID ... Midway Airlines, Inc. [*Chicago, IL*] [*FAA designator*]

MID ... Mortgage Interest Differential

Mid-Am Spectrosc Symp Proc ... Mid-America Spectroscopy Symposium Proceedings [*A publication*]

Mid-Cont Lepid Ser ... Mid-Continent Lepidoptera Series [*A publication*]

MIDS ... Management Information and Data Systems

MIDS ... Multifunctional Information Distribution System

Mie Med J ... Mie Medical Journal [*A publication*]

MIF ... Merthiolate-Iodine-Formaldehyde [*Technique*]

MIFG ... Shallow Fog

Mikol Fitopatol ... Mikologiya i Fitopatologiya [*A publication*]

Mikrobiol Sint Sb Inf Mater ... Mikrobiologicheskii Sintez Sbornik Informatsii Materialov [*A publication*]

Mikrobiol Zh (Kiev) ... Mikrobiolohichnyi Zhurnal (Kiev) [*A publication*]

Mikrobiyol Bul ... Mikrobiyoloji Bulteni [*A publication*]

Mikrobiyol Bul Suppl ... Mikrobiyoloji Bulteni. Supplement [*A publication*]

Mikrochim Acta ... Mikrochimica Acta [*A publication*]

Mikrochim Ichnoanal Acta ... Mikrochimica et Ichnoanalytica Acta [*A publication*]

Mikroelem Sib Inf Byull ... Mikroelementy Sibiri Informatsionnyi Byulleten [*A publication*]

Milbank Mem Fund Annu Rep ... Milbank Memorial Fund Annual Report [*A publication*]

Milbank Mem Fund Q ... Milbank Memorial Fund Quarterly [*A publication*]

Milchforsch-Milchprax ... Milchforschung-Milchpraxis [*A publication*]

Miles Int Symp Ser ... Miles International Symposium Series [*A publication*]

Milk Plant Mon ... Milk Plant Monthly [*A publication*]

Milk Prod J ... Milk Products Journal [*A publication*]

Milk Sci Int ... Milk Science International [*A publication*]

Mil Med ... Military Medicine [*A publication*]

MILSATCOM ... Military Satellite Communications [*Systems*]

Milw Public Mus Contrib Biol Geol ... Milwaukee Public Museum. Contributions in Biology and Geology [*A publication*]

MIMS ... Monthly Index of Medical Specialties [*A publication*]

MIMS ... Multiple Independently Maneuvering Submunitions

MIN ... Mineral

MIN ... Minim

MIND ... Method in Natural Development [*Mental diet plan*]

Minerva Aerosp ... Minerva Aerospaziale [*A publication*]

Minerva Anestesiol ... Minerva Anestesiologica [*A publication*]
Minerva Bioepistemol ... Minerva Bioepistemologica [*A publication*]
Minerva Biol ... Minerva Biologica [*A publication*]
Minerva Cardioangiol ... Minerva Cardioangiologica [*A publication*]
Minerva Chir ... Minerva Chirurgica [*A publication*]
Minerva Dietol ... Minerva Dietologica [*A publication*]
Minerva Farm ... Minerva Farmaceutica [*A publication*]
Minerva Gastroenterol ... Minerva Gastroenterologica [*A publication*]
Minerva Ginecol ... Minerva Ginecologica [*A publication*]
Minerva Med ... Minerva Medica [*A publication*]
Minerva Med Eur Med ... Minerva Medica. Europa Medica [*A publication*]
Minerva Med Guiliana ... Minerva Medica. Guiliana [*A publication*]
Minerva Med Sicil ... Minerva Medica Siciliana [*A publication*]
Minerva Nefrol ... Minerva Nefrologica [*A publication*]
Minerva Neurochir ... Minerva Neurochirurgica [*A publication*]
Minerva Nipiol ... Minerva Nipiologica [*A publication*]
Minerva Otorinolaringol ... Minerva Otorinolaringologica [*A publication*]
Minerva Pediatr ... Minerva Pediatrica [*A publication*]
Minerva Pneumol ... Minerva Pneumologica [*A publication*]
Minerva Psichiatr Psicol ... Minerva Psichiatrica e Psicologica [*A publication*]
Minerva Stomatol ... Minerva Stomatologica [*A publication*]
Minerva Urol ... Minerva Urologica [*A publication*]
Minist Ind Commer Que Rapp Annu ... Ministere de l'Industrie et du Commerce du Quebec. Rapport Annuel [*A publication*]
Minist Mar Merc Mem ... Ministero della Marina Mercantile Memoria [*A publication*]
Minn Agric Exp Stn Bull ... Minnesota Agricultural Experiment Station. Bulletin [*A publication*]
Minn Agric Exp Stn Misc Rep ... Minnesota Agricultural Experiment Station. Miscellaneous Report [*A publication*]
Minn Agric Exp Stn Stn Bull ... Minnesota Agricultural Experiment Station. Station Bulletin [*A publication*]
Minn Agric Exp Stn Tech Bull ... Minnesota Agricultural Experiment Station. Technical Bulletin [*A publication*]
Minn Dep Conserv Tech Bull ... Minnesota Department of Conservation. Technical Bulletin [*A publication*]
Minn Farm Home Sci ... Minnesota Farm and Home Science [*A publication*]
Minn Fish Game Invest Fish Ser ... Minnesota Fish and Game Investigations. Fish Series [*A publication*]
Minn Fish Invest ... Minnesota Fisheries Investigations [*A publication*]
Minn For Notes ... Minnesota Forestry Notes [*A publication*]
Minn For Res Notes ... Minnesota Forestry Research Notes [*A publication*]
Minn Geol Surv Spec Publ Ser ... Minnesota Geological Survey. Special Publication Series [*A publication*]
Minn Sci ... Minnesota Science [*A publication*]
Minn Symp Child Psychol ... Minnesota Symposia on Child Psychology [*A publication*]
MIOP .... Multiplexing Input-Output Processor [*Data processing*]
MIP .... Machine Instruction Processor [*Data processing*]
MIP .... Matrix Inversion Program [*Data processing*]
MIP .... Modest Improvement Program [*Military*]
MIPA .... Monoisopropylamine [*Organic chemistry*]
MIPS .... Missile Information Processing System
MIRBM ...... Medium Intermediate-Range Ballistic Missile
MIS .... Manufacturing Information System
MIS .... Medical Information Science
MIS .... Modified in Situ [*Experimental technique for converting shale into oil*]
Misc Bryol Lichenol ... Miscellanea Bryologica et Lichenologica [*A publication*]
Misc Inf Tokyo Univ For ... Miscellaneous Information. Tokyo University Forests [*A publication*]
Misc Pap Landbouwhogesch Wageningen ... Miscellaneous Papers. Landbouwhogeschool Wageningen [*A publication*]
Misc Publ Entomol Soc Am ... Miscellaneous Publications of the Entomological Society of America [*A publication*]
Misc Publ Genet Soc Can ... Miscellaneous Publications of the Genetics Society of Canada [*A publication*]
Misc Publ Mus Zool Univ Mich ... Miscellaneous Publications. Museum of Zoology. University of Michigan [*A publication*]
Misc Rep Yamashina Inst Ornithol ... Miscellaneous Reports of the Yamashina Institute for Ornithology [*A publication*]

Misc Zool ... Miscelanea Zoologica [*A publication*]
MISED .... Machine Independent Systems Effectiveness Data System
MISP .... Medical Information Systems Program
MISS .... Microwave Imager Sensor Study
MIT .... Miles in Trail [*Aviation*]
MITF .... Musser International Turfgrass Foundation
MIT Press Res Monogr ... MIT [*Massachusetts Institute of Technology*] Press Research Monograph [*A publication*]
Mitt Anthropol Ges Wien ... Mitteilungen der Anthropologischen Gesellschaft in Wien [*A publication*]
Mitt Bot Gart Mus Berl-Dahlem ... Mitteilungen aus dem Botanischen Garten und Museum Berlin-Dahlem [*A publication*]
Mitt Bot Staatssamml Muench ... Mitteilungen der Botanischen Staatssammlung Muenchen [*A publication*]
Mitt Dtsch Dendrol Ges ... Mitteilungen der Deutschen Dendrologischen Gesellschaft [*A publication*]
Mitt Dtsch Entomol Ges ... Mitteilungen der Deutschen Entomologischen Gesellschaft [*A publication*]
Mitt Dtsch Pharm Ges ... Mitteilungen der Deutschen Pharmazeutischen Gesellschaft [*A publication*]
Mitt Entomol Ges Basel ... Mitteilungen der Entomologische Gesellschaft Basel [*A publication*]
Mitt Entomol Ges BRD ... Mitteilungen der Entomologischen Gesellschaft in der BRD [*A publication*]
Mitt Florist-Soziol Arbeitsgem ... Mitteilungen der Floristisch-Soziologischen Arbeitsgemeinschaft [*A publication*]
Mitt Geb Lebensmittelunters Hyg ... Mitteilungen aus dem Gebiete der Lebensmitteluntersuchung und Hygiene [*A publication*]
Mitt Geogr Ges Hamb ... Mitteilungen der Geographischen Gesellschaft in Hamburg [*A publication*]
Mitt Geol Ges Wien ... Mitteilungen der Geologischen Gesellschaft in Wien [*A publication*]
Mitt Geol Staatsinst Hamb ... Mitteilungen aus dem Geologischen Staatsinstitut in Hamburg [*A publication*]
Mitt Hamb Zool Mus Inst ... Mitteilungen aus dem Hamburgischen Zoologischen Museum und Institut [*A publication*]
Mitt Int Moor-Torf-Ges ... Mitteilungen der Internationalen Moor-und Torf-Gesellschaft [*A publication*]
Mitt Int Ver Saatgutpruefung ... Mitteilungen der Internationalen Vereinigung fuer Saatgutpruefung [*A publication*]
Mitt Int Ver Theor Angew Limnol ... Mitteilungen Internationale Vereinigung fuer Theoretische und Angewandte Limnologie [*A publication*]
Mitt Muench Entomol Ges ... Mitteilungen Muenchener Entomologischen Gesellschaft [*A publication*]
Mitt Naturforsch Ges Bern ... Mitteilungen der Naturforschenden Gesellschaft in Bern [*A publication*]
Mitt Naturwiss Ver Steiermark ... Mitteilungen des Naturwissenschaftlichen Vereines fuer Steiermark [*A publication*]
Mitt Schweiz Entomol Ges ... Mitteilungen der Schweizerischen Entomologischen Gesellschaft [*A publication*]
Mitt Staatsinst Allg Bot Hamb ... Mitteilungen aus dem Staatsinstitut fuer Allgemeine Botanik Hamburg [*A publication*]
Mitt Tieraerztl Fak Reichsuniv Gent ... Mitteilungen der Tieraerztlichen Fakultaet der Reichsuniversitaet Gent [*A publication*]
Mitt Zool Mus Berl ... Mitteilungen aus dem Zoologischen Museum in Berlin [*A publication*]
MIU .... Multistation Interface Unit [*Data processing*]
MIVA .... Missionary Vehicle Association
MJ .... Marijuana
MJB .... Master Jet Base [*Navy*]
MJI .... Masters and Johnson Institute
MJU .... Multijunction Unit
MK .... Mebyon Kernow [*Sons of Cornwall*] [*National liberation party*]
MKCT .... Make Check Turn [*Aviation*]
MKH .... Million of Kilowatt Hours
MKK .... Morgan, Keenan, Kellman [*System*] [*Astronomy*]
ML .... Midline
ML .... Mobile Low-Power [*Reactor*]
MLA .... Mento-Laeval Anterior [*A fetal position*] [*Obstetrics*]
MLB .... Monaural Loudness Balance [*Audiology*]
MLC .... Multiline Control
MLD .... Missile Launch Detector

MLIS .... Molecular LASER Isotope Separation
MLP-USA ... Marxist-Leninist Party of the USA
MLRS .... Multiple Launch Rocket System
MLS .... Median Longitudinal Section
MLS .... Medium Life Span
MLTA .... Multiple Line Terminal Adapter [*Data processing*]
MLTLVL .... Melting Level [*Meteorology*]
MM .... Modified Mercalli [*Nuclear energy*]
MM .... Moral Majority [*An organization*]
MMA .... Monomethylamine [*Organic chemistry*]
MMC .... Man-Machine Communication [*Data processing*]
MMD .... Material, Maintenance, and Distribution
MMDA ...... Mass Merchandising Distributors' Association
MME .... Methylmethacrylate [*Organic chemistry*]
MMF .... Maximum Midexpiratory Flow [*Medicine*]
MMG .... Motor-Motor Generator [*Nuclear energy*]
MMI .... Macrophage Migration Inhibition [*Cytology*]
MMMM ...... Connect to Stations [*Communications*]
MMO .... Maio [*Cape Verde Islands*] [*Airport symbol*]
MMP .... Maintenance Monitor Panel
MMP .... Mompos [*Colombia*] [*Airport symbol*]
mmpp .... Millimeters Partial Pressure
MMR .... Monomethylolrutin [*Organic chemistry*]
MMS .... Master of Medical Science
MMS .... Money Management System
MMT .... Manual Muscle Test
MMTP .... Methyl(methylthio)phenol [*Organic chemistry*]
MMV .... Mast Mount Visionics
MMVS ...... Mast Mount Visionics System
MMY .... Miyako Jima [*Japan*] [*Airport symbol*]
MMZ .... Maimana [*Afghanistan*] [*Airport symbol*]
mN .... Millinormal [*One one-thousandth of normal*]
MNA .... Melanguane [*Indonesia*] [*Airport symbol*]
MNA .... Meta-Nitroaniline [*Organic chemistry*]
MNA .... Multishare Network Architecture
MNB .... Moanda [*Zaire*] [*Airport symbol*]
MNBA .... Mono-normal-butylamine [*Organic chemistry*]
MND .... Ministry of National Defense [*British*]
MNF .... Mana [*Fiji*] [*Airport symbol*]
MNG .... Maningrida [*Australia*] [*Airport symbol*]
MNI .... Montserrat [*Airport symbol*]
MNJ .... Mananjary [*Madagascar*] [*Airport symbol*]
MNK .... Maiana [*Kiribati*] [*Airport symbol*]
MNL .... Manila [*Philippines*] [*Airport symbol*]
MNM .... Menominee [*Michigan*] [*Airport symbol*]
MNMT ...... Monument [*Board on Geographic Names*]
MNN .... Madness Network News [*An organization*]
MNO .... Manono [*Zaire*] [*Airport symbol*]
MNPA .... Mono-normal-propylamine [*Organic chemistry*]
MNPT .... Meta-Nitro-para-toluidine [*Organic chemistry*]
MNQ .... Methylnaphthoquinone [*Organic chemistry*]
MNQ .... Monto [*Australia*] [*Airport symbol*]
MNR .... Mongu [*Zambia*] [*Airport symbol*]
MNS .... Mansa [*Zambia*] [*Airport symbol*]
MNT .... Minto [*Alaska*] [*Airport symbol*]
MNU .... Moulmein [*Burma*] [*Airport symbol*]
MNY .... Mono Island [*Solomon Islands*] [*Airport symbol*]
MNZ .... Manassas [*Virginia*] [*Airport symbol*]
MO .... Air Mindanao Corp. [*Philippines*] [*ICAO designator*]
MO .... Mineral Oil
MO .... Minute Output [*Of heart*]
MO .... Mouth
MOA .... Moa [*Cuba*] [*Airport symbol*]
MO Acad Sci Occas Pap ... Missouri Academy of Science. Occasional Paper [*A publication*]
MO Agric Exp Stn Res Bull ... Missouri Agricultural Experiment Station. Research Bulletin [*A publication*]
MO Agric Exp Stn Spec Rep ... Missouri Agricultural Experiment Station. Special Report [*A publication*]
MOBIL .... Mobility
MOC .... Montes Claros [*Brazil*] [*Airport symbol*]
MOCIC ...... Molecular Orbital Constraint of Interaction Coordinates [*Atomic physics*]
MO Conserv ... Missouri Conservationist [*A publication*]
MOD .... Moderate [*Used to qualify icing, turbulence, interference, or static reports*] [*Aviation*]
MOD .... Modesto [*California*] [*Airport symbol*]
Mod Brew Age ... Modern Brewery Age [*A publication*]

MODCAR .. Modified Owners and Drivers Corporation for the Advancement of Racing
MO Dep Conserv Terr Ser ... Missouri Department of Conservation. Terrestrial Series [*A publication*]
MODIGSI ... Modular Digital Simulation
Mod Med Asia ... Modern Medicine of Asia [*A publication*]
Mod Perspect Psychiatry ... Modern Perspectives in Psychiatry [*A publication*]
MODPOT ... Model Potential [*Physics*]
Mod Probl Ophthalmol ... Modern Problems in Ophthalmology [*A publication*]
Mod Probl Paediatr ... Modern Problems in Paediatrics [*A publication*]
Mod Probl Pharmacopsychiatry ... Modern Problems of Pharmacopsychiatry [*A publication*]
MODREFTRA ... Modified Refresher Training [*Navy*]
MODS .... Medically Oriented Data System
Mod Treat ... Modern Treatment [*A publication*]
Mod Vet Pract ... Modern Veterinary Practice [*A publication*]
MOE .... Momeik [*Burma*] [*Airport symbol*]
MOF .... Marine Oxidation/Fermentation
MOF .... Maumere [*Indonesia*] [*Airport symbol*]
MOG .... Monghsat [*Burma*] [*Airport symbol*]
MOI .... Mitiaro [*Cook Islands*] [*Airport symbol*]
MOIP .... Mandatory Oil Import Program
MOL .... Maximum Operating Level
MOL .... Maximum Output Level
MOL .... Molde [*Norway*] [*Airport symbol*]
Mol Aspects Med ... Molecular Aspects of Medicine [*A publication*]
Mol Biol Biochem Biophys ... Molecular Biology, Biochemistry, and Biophysics [*A publication*]
Mol Biol (Mosc) ... Molekulyarnaya Biologiya (Moscow) [*A publication*]
Mol Biol Rep ... Molecular Biology Reports [*A publication*]
Mol Cell Biochem ... Molecular and Cellular Biochemistry [*A publication*]
Mol Cell Endocr ... Molecular and Cellular Endocrinology [*A publication*]
Mol Cryst ... Molecular Crystals [*A publication*]
Mol Gen Genet ... Molecular and General Genetics [*A publication*]
Molochn Prom-st ... Molochnaya Promyshlennost [*A publication*]
Mol Pharmacol ... Molecular Pharmacology [*A publication*]
Mol Photochem ... Molecular Photochemistry [*A publication*]
MOLY .... Molecular Analysis [*by a computer graphics system*] [*Chemistry*]
MON .... Monocyte
MON .... Mount Cook [*New Zealand*] [*Airport symbol*]
Monatsber Dtsch Akad Wiss Berl ... Monatsberichte der Deutschen Akademie der Wissenschaft zu Berlin [*A publication*]
Monatsh Chem ... Monatshefte fuer Chemie [*A publication*]
Monatsh Veterinaermed ... Monatshefte fuer Veterinaermedizin [*A publication*]
Monatskurse Aerztl Fortbild ... Monatskurse fuer die Aerztliche Fortbildung [*A publication*]
Monatsschr Brau ... Monatsschrift fuer Brauerei [*A publication*]
Monatsschr Kinderheilkd ... Monatsschrift fuer Kinderheilkunde [*A publication*]
Monatsschr Lungenkr Tuberk-Bekaempf ... Monatsschrift fuer Lungenkrankheiten und Tuberkulose-Bekaempfung [*A publication*]
Monatsschr Psychiatr Neurol ... Monatsschrift fuer Psychiatrie und Neurologie [*A publication*]
Monatsschr Unfallheilkd ... Monatsschrift fuer Unfallheilkunde [*A publication*]
Mon Bull Coffee Board Kenya ... Monthly Bulletin. Coffee Board of Kenya [*A publication*]
Monde Plant ... Monde des Plantes [*A publication*]
Monit Farm Ter ... Monitor de la Farmacia y de la Terapeutica [*A publication*]
Monit Zool Ital ... Monitore Zoologico Italiano [*A publication*]
Monit Zool Ital Monogr ... Monitore Zoologico Italiano. Monografia [*A publication*]
Monit Zool Ital Suppl ... Monitore Zoologico Italiano. Supplemento [*A publication*]
Monogr Acad Nat Sci Phila ... Monographs of the Academy of Natural Sciences of Philadelphia [*A publication*]
Monogr Allergy ... Monographs in Allergy [*A publication*]
Monogr Anaesthesiol ... Monographs in Anaesthesiology [*A publication*]

Monogr Angew Entomol ... Monographien zur Angewandten Entomologie [*A publication*]

Monogr Ann Radiol ... Monographies des Annales de Radiologie [*A publication*]

Monogr Annu Soc Fr Biol Clin ... Monographie Annuelle de la Societe Francaise de Biologie Clinique [*A publication*]

Monogr Atheroscler ... Monographs on Atherosclerosis [*A publication*]

Monogr Biol ... Monographiae Biologicae [*A publication*]

Monogr Bot ... Monographiae Botanicae [*A publication*]

Monogr Clin Cytol ... Monographs in Clinical Cytology [*A publication*]

Monogr Dev Biol ... Monographs in Developmental Biology [*A publication*]

Monogr Dev Pediatr ... Monographs in Developmental Pediatrics [*A publication*]

Monogr Drugs ... Monographs on Drugs [*A publication*]

Monogr Endocrinol ... Monographs on Endocrinology [*A publication*]

Monogr Fauny Pol ... Monografie Fauny Polski [*A publication*]

Monogr Gesamtgeb Neurol Psychiatr ... Monographien aus dem Gesamtgebiete der Neurologie und Psychiatrie [*A publication*]

Monogr Groupe Etude Main ... Monographies du Groupe d'Etude de la Main [*A publication*]

Monogr Hum Genet ... Monographs in Human Genetics [*A publication*]

Monogr INIA ... Monografias INIA [*Instituto Nacional de Investigaciones Agrarias*] [*A publication*]

Monogr Inst Butantan Sao Paulo ... Monografias do Instituto Butantan Sao Paulo [*A publication*]

Monogr Inst Oswaldo Cruz Rio De J ... Monografias do Instituto Oswaldo Cruz Rio De Janeiro [*A publication*]

Monogr Ned Entomol Ver ... Monografieen van de Nederlandse Entomologische Vereniging [*A publication*]

Monogr Neural Sci ... Monographs in Neural Sciences [*A publication*]

Monogr Nucl Med Biol Ser ... Monographs on Nuclear Medicine and Biology Series [*A publication*]

Monogr Oceanogr Methodol ... Monographs on Oceanographic Methodology [*A publication*]

Monogr Oral Sci ... Monographs in Oral Science [*A publication*]

Monogr Paediatr ... Monographs in Paediatrics [*A publication*]

Monogr Parazytol ... Monografie Parazytologiczne [*A publication*]

Monogr Pathol ... Monographs in Pathology [*A publication*]

Monogr Pharmacol Physiol ... Monographs in Pharmacology and Physiology [*A publication*]

Monogr Physiol Causale ... Monographie de Physiologie Causale [*A publication*]

Monogr Physiol Soc ... Monographs of the Physiological Society [*A publication*]

Monogr Physiol Veg ... Monographies de Physiologie Vegetale [*A publication*]

Monogr Popul Biol ... Monographs in Population Biology [*A publication*]

Monogr Rutgers Cent Alcohol Stud ... Monographs of the Rutgers Center of Alcohol Studies [*A publication*]

Monogr Soc Res Child Dev ... Monographs of the Society for Research in Child Development [*A publication*]

Monogr Theor Appl Genet ... Monographs on Theoretical and Applied Genetics [*A publication*]

Monogr Virol ... Monographs in Virology [*A publication*]

Monogr West Found Vertebr Zool ... Monographs of the Western Foundation of Vertebrate Zoology [*A publication*]

Mont Agric Exp Stn Bull ... Montana Agricultural Experiment Station. Bulletin [*A publication*]

Mont For Conserv Exp Stn Bull ... Montana Forest and Conservation Experiment Station. Bulletin [*A publication*]

Mont For Conserv Exp Stn Note ... Montana Forest and Conservation Experiment Station. Note [*A publication*]

Mont For Conserv Exp Stn Res Note ... Montana Forest and Conservation Experiment Station. Research Note [*A publication*]

Mont Wool Grow ... Montana Wool Growers [*A publication*]

MOO .... Moomba [*Australia*] [*Airport symbol*]

MOPPE ..... Modified Operational Propulsion Plan Examination [*Navy*]

MOQ .... Morondava [*Madagascar*] [*Airport symbol*]

Morfol Norm Patol (Buchar) ... Morfologia Normala si Patologica (Bucharest) [*A publication*]

Morris Arbor Bull ... Morris Arboretum Bulletin [*A publication*]

MOS .... Modular Operating System

MOS .... Months

Mosc Univ Biol Sci Bull ... Moscow University Biological Sciences Bulletin [*A publication*]

Mosc Univ Soil Sci Bull ... Moscow University Soil Science Bulletin [*A publication*]

Mosk Kolkhozn ... Moskovskii Kolkhoznik [*A publication*]

Mosq News ... Mosquito News [*A publication*]

Mosq Syst ... Mosquito Systematics [*A publication*]

Mosq Syst News Lett ... Mosquito Systematics. News Letter [*A publication*]

MOSS .... Market Oversight Surveillance System

MOT .... Minot [*North Dakota*] [*Airport symbol*]

MOTA .... Materials Open-Test Assembly [*Nuclear energy*]

MOU .... Mountain Village [*Alaska*] [*Airport symbol*]

MOUT .... Military Operations on Urban Terrain

MOV .... Moranbah [*Australia*] [*Airport symbol*]

MOV .... Motor-Operated Valve

MOW .... Moscow [*USSR*] [*Airport symbol*]

MOZ .... Moorea Island [*French Polynesia*] [*Airport symbol*]

M & P .... Mansfield Park [*Novel by Jane Austen*]

MP .... Maturity Phase

MP .... Media Processor

MP .... Member of Police

MP .... Mentum Posterior

MP .... Metacarpal-Phalangeal

MP .... Multiple Processor

MPA .... Medroxyprogesterone Acetate [*Endocrinology*] [*Also, MAP*]

MPA .... Metroplex Airlines, Inc. [*Fort Worth, TX*] [*FAA designator*]

MPB .... Male-Pattern Baldness

MPB .... Miami [*Florida*] Public Seaplane Base [*Airport symbol*]

MPBME ..... Munitions Production Base Modernization, Expansion

MPC .... Metals Properties Council

MPC .... Motion Picture Camera

MPCC .... Multiprotocol Communications Controller

MPCO .... Military Police Commanding Officer

MPCU .... Maximum Permissible Concentration of Unidentified Radionuclides in Water

MPI .... Maximum Point of Impulse

MPL .... Maxillofacial Prosthesis Laboratory [*WRAMC*]

MPL .... Mechanical Properties Loop [*Nuclear energy*]

MPL .... Montpellier [*France*] [*Airport symbol*]

MPL .... Multischedule Private Line

MPM .... Maputo [*Mozambique*] [*Airport symbol*]

MPM .... Maximum Permitted Mileage [*Airlines*]

MPM .... Message Processing Modules

MPO .... Manufacturing Production Order

MPO .... Mobile Post Office

MPP .... Mailer's Postmark Permit

M & PP ...... Materials and Plant Protection [*Nuclear energy*]

MPRS .... Microform Personnel Records System

MPS .... Manpower System

MPS .... Mathematical Programming Society

MPS .... Message Processing System

MPS .... Mount Pleasant [*Texas*] [*Airport symbol*]

MPS .... Movement-Produced Stimuli

MPU .... Mapua [*Papua New Guinea*] [*Airport symbol*]

MPV .... Montpelier [*Vermont*] [*Airport symbol*]

MQL .... Mildura [*Australia*] [*Airport symbol*]

MQS .... Motion to Quash Subpoena

MQT .... Marquette [*Michigan*] [*Airport symbol*]

MQU .... Mariquita [*Colombia*] [*Airport symbol*]

MQX .... Makale [*Ethiopia*] [*Airport symbol*]

MRA .... Misurata [*Libya*] [*Airport symbol*]

MRASM .... Medium-Range Air-to-Surface Missile

MRC .... Methylrosaniline Chloride [*A dye*] [*Also, GV*]

MRCC .... Member of the Royal College of Chemistry [*British*]

MRCP .... Member of the Royal College of Preceptors [*British*]

MRD .... Merida [*Venezuela*] [*Airport symbol*]

mrd .... Millirutherford

MRD .... Multireference Double Excitation [*Physics*]

MRE .... Mara Lodges [*Kenya*] [*Airport symbol*]

MRF .... Mankind Research Foundation

MRGL .... Marginal

MRGS .... Member of the Royal Geographical Society [*British*]

mrhm .... Milliroentgen per Hour at One Meter

MRI............ Material Receiving Instruction [*Nuclear energy*]
MR, Inc...... Men's Rights, Incorporated
MRINDO.... Modified Rydberg Intermediate Neglect of Differential Overlap [*Physics*]
MRK .... Marco Island [*Florida*] [*Airport symbol*]
MRL........... Maximum Recording Level
MRM.......... Manari [*Papua New Guinea*] [*Airport symbol*]
MROC .... Mobile Range Operation Center
MRP .... Maintenance Real Property
MRP .... Marla [*Australia*] [*Airport symbol*]
MRP .... Minimum Reaction Posture
MRQ .... Marinduque [*Philippines*] [*Airport symbol*]
MRR .... Macara [*Ecuador*] [*Airport symbol*]
MRS .... Marseille [*France*] [*Airport symbol*]
MRU .... Mauritius [*Airport symbol*]
MRU .... Multifunction Reference Unit
MRV .... Mineral Nyye Vody [*USSR*] [*Airport symbol*]
MRY .... Monterey [*California*] [*Airport symbol*]
MRZ .... Moree [*Australia*] [*Airport symbol*]
MS .... Management Science
MS .... Mandala Society
MS .... Matched Set [*Philately*]
MS .... Molar Solution [*Dentistry*]
MS .... Musculactive Substance [*Medicine*]
MSA .... Marigold Society of America
MSA .... Material Surveillance Assembly [*Nuclear energy*]
MSC .... Chief Mess Management Specialist [*Navy rating*] [*Formerly, CSC, CST, SDC*]
MSC .... Macro Selection Compiler [*Data processing*]
MSC .... Main Storage Control [*Data processing*]
MSC .... Mass Storage Control [*Data processing*]
MSC .... Mesa [*Arizona*] [*Airport symbol*]
MSC .... Micronesia Support Committee
MSCI........ Molten Steel Coolant Interaction
MSCM....... Master Chief Mess Management Specialist [*Navy rating*] [*Formerly, SDCM*]
MSCS........ Multiservice Communications Systems
MSCS........ Senior Chief Mess Management Specialist [*Navy rating*] [*Formerly, CSCS, SDCS*]
MSD .... Molecular Structures and Dimensions [*A publication*]
MSDC .... Maintenance Signal Data Converter
MSDF........ Maritime Self-Defense Force [*Japan*]
MSDR........ Maintenance Signal Data Recorder
MSDS........ Material Safety Data Sheets [*DOD*]
MSE .... Military Specification Exception
MSF .... Master Source File [*Data processing*]
MSG........... Modular Steam Generator
MSH........... Men of the Sacred Hearts [*An organization*]
MSI............ Mission Success Indicator
MSIV .... Main Steam Isolation Valves [*Nuclear energy*]
MSIVLCS ... Main Steam Isolation Valve Leakage Control System [*Nuclear energy*]
MSJ........... Misawa [*Japan*] [*Airport symbol*]
MSL........... Manpower Source Listing
MSL........... Muscle Shoals [*Alabama*] [*Airport symbol*]
MSLD........ Mass Spectrometer Leak Detector
MSLO........ Medical Service Liaison Officer [*Air Force*]
MSM.......... Mass Scatterable Mine
MSM.......... Modified Source Multiplication
MSMA....... Monosodium Methyl Arsonate [*Herbicide*]
MSN .... Madison [*Wisconsin*] [*Airport symbol*]
MSN .... Mobil Showcase Network [*Television*]
MSNF........ Milk Solids-Not Fat [*Food industry*]
MSO.......... Medial Superior Olive [*Brain anatomy*]
MSO.......... Missoula [*Montana*] [*Airport symbol*]
MSOS .... Mass Storage Operating System
MSP .... Master Simulator Program
MSP .... Monosodium Orthophosphate [*Inorganic chemistry*]
MSPLT...... Master Source Program Library Tape [*Data processing*]
MSQ.......... Minsk [*USSR*] [*Airport symbol*]
MSR .... Mark Sheet Reader [*Data processing*]
MSR .... Material Status Report [*Nuclear energy*]
MSR .... Mobile Sea Range
MSR .... Munster [*West Germany*] [*Airport symbol*]
MSRG........ Moated Sites Research Group
MSS .... Main Support Structure
MSS .... Massena [*New York*] [*Airport symbol*]
MSS .... Master Switching Station
MSS .... Meter Stamp Society

MSSC........ Mass Storage System Control [*Data processing*]
MSSU........ Meteorology on Stamps Study Unit
MST .... Maastricht [*Netherlands*] [*Airport symbol*]
MST .... Mean Swell Time [*Botulism test*] [*Food analysis*]
MST .... Mobile Support Team
MSTh .... Mesothorium [*Radioelement*]
MSU .... Maseru [*Lesotho*] [*Airport symbol*]
MSU .... Monosodium Urate [*Organic chemistry*]
MSV .... Catskills/Sullivan County [*New York*] [*Airport symbol*]
MSV .... Mass Stimulated Vehicles
MSV .... Mean Square Voltage
MSVC........ Mass Storage Volume Control [*Data processing*]
MSW .... Massawa [*Ethiopia*] [*Airport symbol*]
MSZ .... Mossamedes [*Angola*] [*Airport symbol*]
MT .... Measured Time
MT .... Membrana Tympani [*Anatomy*]
MT .... Metatarsal [*Anatomy*]
MT .... Mitral Valve [*Medicine*]
MT .... MUX [*Multiplex*] Terminal
MTA .... Desert Air Service [*Mesa, AZ*] [*FAA designator*]
MTAT........ Mean Turn-Around Time [*Quality control*]
MTC .... Marcus Tullius Cicero [*Roman orator and author, 106-43 BC*]
MTCS........ Minimal Terminal Communications System
MTD .... Midwife Teacher's Diploma [*British*]
MTD .... Multiple Target Deception
MTF........... Mizan Teferi [*Ethiopia*] [*Airport symbol*]
MTG .... Methanol-to-Gasoline [*Process*] [*Mobil Oil Corp.*]
MTG .... Methoxytriglycol [*Organic chemistry*]
MTH .... Marathon [*Florida*] [*Airport symbol*]
MTI .... Mosteiros [*Cape Verde Islands*] [*Airport symbol*]
MTJ .... Montrose [*Colorado*] [*Airport symbol*]
MTK .... Makin [*Kiribati*] [*Airport symbol*]
MTL .... Maitland [*Australia*] [*Airport symbol*]
MTL .... Mobiltherm Light
MTLS .... Munitions Transfer and Loading System
MTLS .... Munitions Transporter/Loader System
MTM .... Modified Thayer-Martin [*Medium*] [*Microbiology*]
MTO .... Mattoon [*Illinois*] [*Airport symbol*]
MTOS........ Magnetic Tape Operations System
MTP........... Manufacturing Technology Program [*Aviation Systems Command*]
MTP........... Montauk Point [*New York*] [*Airport symbol*]
MTPF......... Maximum Total Peaking Factor [*Nuclear energy*]
MTQ .... Mitchell [*Australia*] [*Airport symbol*]
MTR .... Metroflight, Inc. [*Houston, TX*] [*FAA designator*]
MTR .... Monitor
MTR .... Monteria [*Colombia*] [*Airport symbol*]
MTRY .... Momentary
MTS .... Manzini [*Swaziland*] [*Airport symbol*]
MTS .... Module Tracking System
MTS .... Mountains [*Board on Geographic Names*]
Mt Sinai J Med ... Mount Sinai Journal of Medicine [*A publication*]
MTT........... Minatitlan [*Mexico*] [*Airport symbol*]
MTT........... Munitions Transfer Truck
MTTD .... Mean Time to Diagnosis [*Quality control*]
MTU .... Metric Ton Unit
MTU .... MIRA [*Multifunctional Inertial Reference Assembly*] Transport Unit [*Air Force*]
MTUMR..... MIRA [*Multifunctional Inertial Reference Assembly*] Transport Unit Mounting Rack [*Air Force*]
MTV .... Mota Lava [*Vanuata*] [*Airport symbol*]
MTV .... Motor Transport Volunteers [*Military unit*] [*British*]
MTV .... Munitions Tow Vehicle
MTW .... Manitowoc [*Wisconsin*] [*Airport symbol*]
MTX .... Fairbanks [*Alaska*] Metro Field [*Airport symbol*]
MTY .... Monterrey [*Mexico*] [*Airport symbol*]
MUA .... Munda [*Solomon Islands*] [*Airport symbol*]
MUB .... Maun [*Botswana*] [*Airport symbol*]
MUC .... Munich [*West Germany*] [*Airport symbol*]
MUE .... Kamuela [*Hawaii*] [*Airport symbol*]
Muench Med Wochenschr ... Muenchener Medizinische Wochenschrift [*A publication*]
MUF .... Muting [*Indonesia*] [*Airport symbol*]
MUG.......... Mulege [*Mexico*] [*Airport symbol*]
MUGA .... Multiple-Gated Acquisition [*Nuclear medicine*]
MUIG........ Minicomputer Users Interest Group
MUJ........... Mui [*Ethiopia*] [*Airport symbol*]
MUK .... Mauke [*Cook Islands*] [*Airport symbol*]

MULDEX ... Multipoint Cross-Reference Index
Multivar Behav Res ... Multivariate Behavioral Research [*A publication*]
Multivar Behav Res Monogr ... Multivariate Behavioral Research. Monographs [*A publication*]
MULTOTS ... Multiple Units Link 11 Test and Operational Training System [*Navy*]
MUM .... Methodology for Unmanned Manufacture
MUM .... Mumias [*Kenya*] [*Airport symbol*]
MUMS ...... Multiple Unguided Mine System
MUN .... Maturin [*Venezuela*] [*Airport symbol*]
MUP .... Mouvement d'Unite Populaire [*Tunisia*]
MUR .... Management Update and Retrieval System
MUR .... Marudi [*Malaysia*] [*Airport symbol*]
MUS .... Multiutility System
MUSC .... Muscles [*or Muscular*]
Mushroom Sci ... Mushroom Science [*A publication*]
Mus Mem (Salisbury) ... Museum Memoir (Salisbury) [*A publication*]
Mus Nac Hist Nat Bol (Santiago) ... Museo Nacional de Historia Natural. Boletin (Santiago) [*A publication*]
Mus Natl Hist Nat: Not Syst ... Museum National d'Histoire Naturelle. Notulae Systematicae [*A publication*]
Mus North Ariz Bull ... Museum of Northern Arizona. Bulletin [*A publication*]
MUV .... Middle Ultraviolet
MUX .... Multan [*Pakistan*] [*Airport symbol*]
MUZ .... Musoma [*Tanzania*] [*Airport symbol*]
MVA .... Myvatn [*Iceland*] [*Airport symbol*]
MVB .... Mvengue [*Gabon*] [*Airport symbol*]
MVD .... Montevideo [*Uruguay*] [*Airport symbol*]
MVEMJSUNP ... My Very Excellent Mother Just Served Us Nine Pies [*Mnemonic guide to the nine planets: Mercury, Venus, Earth, Mars, Jupiter, Saturn, Uranus, Neptune, Pluto*]
MVJ .... Mandeville [*Jamaica*] [*Airport symbol*]
MVK .... Mulka [*Australia*] [*Airport symbol*]
MVN .... Mount Vernon [*Illinois*] [*Airport symbol*]
MVP .... Mitu [*Colombia*] [*Airport symbol*]
MVR .... Maroua [*Cameroon*] [*Airport symbol*]
MVR .... Mechanical Vapor Recompression [*For evaporators*]
MVS .... Multiple Virtual Systems [*Data processing*]
MVT .... Mataiva [*French Polynesia*] [*Airport symbol*]
MVU .... Musgrave [*Australia*] [*Airport symbol*]
MVW .... Mount Vernon [*Washington*] [*Airport symbol*]
MVX .... Minvoul [*Gabon*] [*Airport symbol*]
MVY .... Martha's Vineyard [*Massachusetts*] [*Airport symbol*]
MWA .... Marion [*Illinois*] [*Airport symbol*]
MWA .... Mayflower Warehousemen's Association
MWCS ...... Millimeter Wave Contrast Seeker
MWE .... Merowe [*Sudan*] [*Airport symbol*]
MWGCP .... Most Worthy Grand Chief Patriarch
MWH .... Moses Lake [*Washington*] [*Airport symbol*]

MWHS .... Marine Wing Headquarters Squadron
MWJ .... Matthews Ridge [*Guyana*] [*Airport symbol*]
MWQ .... Magwe [*Burma*] [*Airport symbol*]
MWR .... Morale, Welfare, and Recreation [*Air Force*]
MWRC .... Maintain Well to Right of Course [*Aviation*]
MWS .... Management Work Station
MWT .... Moolawatana [*Australia*] [*Airport symbol*]
MWU .... Mussau [*Papua New Guinea*] [*Airport symbol*]
MWY .... Miranda Downs [*Australia*] [*Airport symbol*]
MWZ .... Mwanza [*Tanzania*] [*Airport symbol*]
MX .... Matrix
MXB .... Masamba [*Indonesia*] [*Airport symbol*]
MXL .... Mexicali [*Mexico*] [*Airport symbol*]
MXM .... Morombe [*Madagascar*] [*Airport symbol*]
MXN .... Morlaix [*France*] [*Airport symbol*]
MXP .... Milan [*Italy*] Malpensa Airport [*Airport symbol*]
MXT .... Maintirano [*Madagascar*] [*Airport symbol*]
MXU .... Mullewa [*Australia*] [*Airport symbol*]
MXX .... Mora [*Sweden*] [*Airport symbol*]
my .... Mayer [*A unit of heat capacity*]
MY .... Myopia
MYB .... Mayoumba [*Gabon*] [*Airport symbol*]
MYC .... Maracay [*Venezuela*] [*Airport symbol*]
MYCO .... Mycobacterium
Mycol Mem ... Mycologia Memoir [*A publication*]
Mycopathol Mycol Appl ... Mycopathologia et Mycologia Applicata [*A publication*]
MYD .... Malindi [*Kenya*] [*Airport symbol*]
MYE .... Miyake Jima [*Japan*] [*Airport symbol*]
MYEL .... Myelocyte
MYF .... San Diego [*California*] Montgomery Field [*Airport symbol*]
MYG .... Mayaguana [*Bahamas*] [*Airport symbol*]
MYI .... Magical Youths International
MYJ .... Matsuyama [*Japan*] [*Airport symbol*]
Mykol Sb ... Mykologicky Sbornik [*A publication*]
MYM .... Monkey Mountain [*Guyana*] [*Airport symbol*]
MYN .... Mareb [*Yemen Arab Republic*] [*Airport symbol*]
MYR .... Myrtle Beach [*South Carolina*] Myrtle Air Force Base [*Airport symbol*]
Mysore Agric J ... Mysore Agricultural Journal [*A publication*]
Mysore J Agric Sci ... Mysore Journal of Agricultural Sciences [*A publication*]
MYT .... Myitkyina [*Burma*] [*Airport symbol*]
MYU .... Mekoryuk [*Alaska*] [*Airport symbol*]
MYW .... Mtwara [*Tanzania*] [*Airport symbol*]
MYX .... Menyamya [*Papua New Guinea*] [*Airport symbol*]
MYY .... Miri [*Malaysia*] [*Airport symbol*]
MZC .... Mitzic [*Gabon*] [*Airport symbol*]
MZFR .... Mehrzweck Forschungs [*Reactor*] [*West Germany*]
MZG .... Makung [*Taiwan*] [*Airport symbol*]

N

N .... Neurology
N .... Nicotinamide [*Vitamin*] [*Also, NAA*]
N .... Nonmalignant [*Of tumors*] [*Medicine*]
N .... Nonne [*Globulin test*]
NA .... Nomina Anatomica [*System of anatomical terminology*]
NA .... Numerical Analysis [*Data processing*]
NAA .... Nicotinic Acid Amide [*Also, N*]
NAAP .... N-Acetylaminophenazone [*Organic chemistry*]
NAARPR ... National Alliance Against Racist and Political Repression
NABE .... National Association of Boards of Education
NABF .... National Alliance of Black Feminists
NABL .... National Association of Bond Lawyers
NABSTP .... Navy Adult Basic Skills Training Program
NABSW .... National Association of Black Social Workers
NAC .... Naples Alcofuel Club
NAC .... Naval Avionics Center
NAC .... Network Advisory Committee [*to Library of Congress and Council on Library Resources*]
NACAA ..... National Assembly of Community Arts Agencies
NACS .... National Association of Computer Stores
NACSARS ... National Association of Companion Sitter Agencies and Referral Services
NADEO ..... National Association of Diocesan Ecumenical Officers
NADUG ..... North American Datamanager Users Group
NAFE .... National Association for Free Enterprise
NAFL .... National Alliance for Family Life
NAFMIS .... Nonappropriated Funds Management Information System
NAFPA ...... National Alcohol Fuels Producers Association
Nagasaki Med J ... Nagasaki Medical Journal [*A publication*]
Nagoya J Med Sci ... Nagoya Journal of Medical Science [*A publication*]
Nagoya Med J ... Nagoya Medical Journal [*A publication*]
Nagpur Coll Agric Mag ... Nagpur College of Agriculture Magazine [*A publication*]
NAHIS .... National Arts and Handicapped Information Service
NAIMSAL ... National Anti-Imperialist Movement in Solidarity with African Liberation
NAIS .... Navy Attitudinal Information System
NAITP .... National Association of Income Tax Practitioners
NAJA .... National Association of Junior Auxiliaries
NAK .... Negative Acknowledgement
Na,K-ATPase ... Adenosinetriphosphatase (Na, K-Activated) [*An enzyme*]
NALC .... Naval Aviation Logistics Center
NALTS ...... National Advertising Lead Tracking System [*Navy*]
NAM .... Nonaligned Movement
NAMAD ..... National Association of Minority Automobile Dealers
N Am Bird Bander ... North American Bird Bander [*A publication*]
NAMDEX ... Name Index
N Am Fauna ... North American Fauna [*A publication*]
N Am Flora ... North American Flora [*A publication*]
N Am Flora Ser II ... North American Flora. Series II [*A publication*]
NAMIS .... Nitride-Barrier Avalanche Injection Missile
NAMPS ...... Navy Manpower Planning System
N Am Vet .. North American Veterinarian [*A publication*]
NANS .... National Association for Neighborhood Schools
NAP .... Napoleon [*or Napoleonic*]
NAP .... Nonnuclear Armament Plan

NAP .... Nucleic Acid Phosphorus [*Biochemistry*]
NAPA .... N-Acetyl-p-aminophenol [*Organic chemistry*]
NAPAC ..... National Association of Paper and Advertising Collectors
NAPP .... National Association of Printing Purchasers
NAPSS ..... National Association of Professional Secretarial Services
NAPTS ...... National Association of Public Television Stations
NAR .... No Action Required
NARDAC .... Navy Regional Data Automation Center
NARIC .... National Rehabilitation Information Center
NARP .... Nonaqueous Reversed Phase [*Chromatography*]
NARS .... National Association of Rehabilitation Secretaries
NAS .... Nasal
NAS .... No Added Salt [*Medicine*]
NAS .... Numerical Analysis Subroutines [*Data processing*]
NASA .... North Atlantic Seafood Association
NASA Contract Rep ... NASA [*National Aeronautics and Space Administration*] Contractor Report [*A publication*]
NASA Tech Brief ... NASA [*National Aeronautics and Space Administration*] Technical Brief [*A publication*]
NASA Tech Memo ... NASA [*National Aeronautics and Space Administration*] Technical Memorandum [*A publication*]
NASA Tech Note ... NASA [*National Aeronautics and Space Administration*] Technical Note [*A publication*]
NASA Tech Rep ... NASA [*National Aeronautics and Space Administration*] Technical Report [*A publication*]
NASA Tech Transl ... NASA [*National Aeronautics and Space Administration*] Technical Translation [*A publication*]
NASB .... National Association of Spanish Broadcasters
NASCP ...... National Association of Sports for Cerebral Palsied
NASILP ..... National Association of Self-Instructional Language Programs
Nas Mus Bloemfontein Jaarversl ... Nasionale Museum Bloemfontein Jaarverslag [*A publication*]
NAS-NRC Nucl Sci Ser Rep ... National Academy of Sciences-National Research Council. Nuclear Sciences Series Report [*A publication*]
NAS-NRC Publ ... National Academy of Sciences-National Research Council. Publication [*A publication*]
NAT .... Not ARTS [*Automated RADAR Terminal System*] Tracked
Nat Appl Sci Bull ... Natural and Applied Science Bulletin [*A publication*]
Nat Belg .... Naturalistes Belges [*A publication*]
Nat Cambs ... Nature in Cambridgeshire [*A publication*]
Nat Conserv Branch Transvaal Bull ... Nature Conservation Branch. Transvaal Bulletin [*A publication*]
NATF .... New Arrivals Task Force
Nat Heimat ... Natur und Heimat [*A publication*]
Nat Hist Bull Siam Soc ... Natural History Bulletin of the Siam Society [*A publication*]
Nat Hist Misc (Chic) ... Natural History Miscellanae (Chicago) [*A publication*]
Nat Jutlandica ... Natur Jutlandica [*A publication*]
Natl Acad Sci India Annu Number ... National Academy of Sciences (India) Annual Number [*A publication*]
Nat Land ... Natur und Land [*A publication*]
Nat Landschaft ... Natur und Landschaft [*A publication*]

Nat Landschap ... Natuur en Landschap Tijdschrift van de Contact Commissie voor Natuur-en Landschapsebescherming [*A publication*]

Natl Bot Gard Lucknow Annu Rep ... National Botanic Gardens. Lucknow Annual Report [*A publication*]

Natl Cactus Succulent J ... National Cactus and Succulent Journal [*A publication*]

Natl Cancer Conf Proc ... National Cancer Conference. Proceedings [*A publication*]

Natl Cancer Inst Monogr ... National Cancer Institute. Monograph [*A publication*]

Natl Clgh Poison Control Cent Bull ... National Clearinghouse for Poison Control Centers. Bulletin [*A publication*]

Natl Eclectic Med Q ... National Eclectic Medical Quarterly [*A publication*]

Natl Hortic Mag ... National Horticultural Magazine [*A publication*]

Nat Life Southeast Asia ... Nature and Life in Southeast Asia [*A publication*]

Natl Inst Anim Health Q ... National Institute of Animal Health. Quarterly [*A publication*]

Natl Inst Genet (Mishima) Annu Rep ... National Institute of Genetics (Mishima) Annual Report [*A publication*]

Natl Inst Nutr Annu Rep ... National Institute of Nutrition. Annual Report [*A publication*]

Natl Inst Res Dairy Rep (Engl) ... National Institute for Research in Dairying. Report (England) [*A publication*]

Natl Mus Bloemfontein Annu Rep ... National Museum Bloemfontein. Annual Report [*A publication*]

Natl Mus Bloemfontein Res Mem ... National Museum Bloemfontein. Researches Memoir [*A publication*]

Natl Mus Can Bull ... National Museum of Canada. Bulletin [*A publication*]

Natl Mus Can Nat Hist Pap ... National Museum of Canada. Natural History Papers [*A publication*]

Natl Mus NZ Misc Ser ... National Museum of New Zealand. Miscellaneous Series [*A publication*]

Natl Mus NZ Rec ... National Museum of New Zealand. Records [*A publication*]

Natl Parks Conserv Mag ... National Parks and Conservation Magazine [*A publication*]

Natl Parks Mag ... National Parks Magazine [*A publication*]

Natl Res Counc Philipp Bull ... National Research Council of the Philippines. Bulletin [*A publication*]

Natl Res Counc Rev ... National Research Council. Review [*A publication*]

Natl Sci Found Annu Rep ... National Science Foundation. Annual Report [*A publication*]

Natl Sci Found Sci Manpower Bull ... National Science Foundation. Scientific Manpower Bulletin [*A publication*]

Natl Shade Tree Conf Proc ... National Shade Tree Conference. Proceedings [*A publication*]

Natl Swed Inst Plant Prot ... National Swedish Institute for Plant Protection [*A publication*]

Natl Vitamin Found Annu Rep ... National Vitamin Foundation. Annual Report [*A publication*]

Natl Wildl ... National Wildlife [*A publication*]

Natl Wool Grow ... National Wool Grower [*A publication*]

Nat Malgache ... Naturaliste Malgache [*A publication*]

Nat Monspeliensia Ser Bot ... Naturalia Monspeliensia. Serie Botanique [*A publication*]

Nat Mus .... Natur und Museum [*A publication*]

Nat New Biol ... Nature New Biology [*A publication*]

Nat Resour ... Nature and Resources [*A publication*]

Nat Resour Res (Paris) ... Natural Resources Research (Paris) [*A publication*]

Nat Study ... Nature Study [*A publication*]

NATSU ...... Naval Air Technical Services Unit

Naturhist Mus Stadt Bern Jahrb ... Naturhistorisches Museum der Stadt Bern. Jahrbuch [*A publication*]

Naturwiss Med ... Naturwissenschaft und Medizin [*A publication*]

Naturwiss Rundsch ... Naturwissenschaftliche Rundschau [*A publication*]

Natuurhist Maandbl ... Natuurhistorisch Maandblad [*A publication*]

Natuurwet Tijdschr ... Natuurwetenschappelijk Tijdschrift [*A publication*]

Nat Verden ... Naturens Verden [*A publication*]

Nat Vivante ... Nature Vivante [*A publication*]

Nat Volk (Frankf) ... Natur und Volk (Frankfurt) [*A publication*]

NATwA ...... North American Tiddlywinks Association

NATWF ..... North American Tug of War Federation

NAU .... Network Address Unit [*Data processing*]

Nauchn Dokl Vyssh Shk Biol Nauki ... Nauchnye Doklady Vysshei Shkoly Biologicheskie Nauki [*A publication*]

Nauchn Issled Klin Lab ... Nauchnye Issledovaniva v Klinikakh I V Laboratoriyakh [*A publication*]

Nauchno-Tekh Byull Agron Fiz ... Nauchno-Tekhnicheskii Byulleten' po Agronomicheskoi Fizike [*A publication*]

Nauchn Rab Vrach Mord SSSR ... Nauchnye Raboty Vrachei Mordovskoi SSSR [*A publication*]

Nauchn Tr Akad Kommunal'n Khoz ... Nauchnye Trudy Akademii Kommunal'nogo Khozyaistva [*A publication*]

Nauchn Tr Bashk Gos Med Inst ... Nauchnye Trudy Bashkirskogo Gosudarstvennogo Meditsinskogo Instituta [*A publication*]

Nauchn Tr Irkutsk Med Inst ... Nauchnye Trudy Irkutskii Meditsinskii Institut [*A publication*]

Nauchn Tr Kazan Med Inst ... Nauchnye Trudy Kazanskogo Meditsinskogo Instituta [*A publication*]

Nauchn Tr Khar'k S-kh Inst ... Nauchnye Trudy Khar'kovskogo Sel'skohozyaistvenogo Instituta [*A publication*]

Nauchn Tr Kirg Med Inst ... Nauchnye Trudy Kirgizskogo Meditsinskogo Instituta [*A publication*]

Nauchn Tr Kuban Gos Med Inst ... Nauchnye Trudy Kubanskogo Gosudarstvennogo Meditsinskogo Instituta [*A publication*]

Nauchn Tr Kurgan S-kh Inst ... Nauchnye Trudy Kurganskogo Sel'skohozyaistvennogo Instituta [*A publication*]

Nauchn Tr Leningr Lesotekh Akad ... Nauchnye Trudy Leningradskoi Lesotekhnicheskoi Akademii [*A publication*]

Nauchn Tr Litov S-kh Akad ... Nauchnye Trudy Litovskoi Sel'skokhozyaistvennoi Akademii [*A publication*]

Nauchn Tr L'vov Lesotekh Inst ... Nauchnye Trudy L'vovskogo Lesotekhnicheskogo Instituta [*A publication*]

Nauchn Tr Mosk Gor Klin Bol'n N 52 ... Nauchnye Trudy Moskovskoi Gorodskoi Kliniceskci Bol'nitsy. N 52 [*A publication*]

Nauchn Tr Novosib Med Inst ... Nauchnye Trudy Novosibirskogo Meditsinskogo Instituta [*A publication*]

Nauchn Tr Omsk Med Inst ... Nauchnye Trudy Omskii Meditsinskii Institut [*A publication*]

Nauchn Tr Omsk S-kh Inst ... Nauchnye Trudy Omskogo Sel'skokhozyaistvennogo Instituta [*A publication*]

Nauchn Tr Omsk Vet Inst ... Nauchnye Trudy Omskogo Veterinarnogo Instituta [*A publication*]

Nauchn Tr Permsk Farm Inst ... Nauchnye Trudy Permskogo Farmatsevticheskogo Instituta [*A publication*]

Nauchn Tr Ryazan Med Inst ... Nauchnye Trudy Ryazanskii Meditsinskii Institut [*A publication*]

Nauchn Tr Samark Gos Univ ... Nauchnye Trudy Samarkandskogo Gosudarstvennogo Universiteta [*A publication*]

Nauchn Tr Samark Med Inst ... Nauchnye Trudy Samarkandskogo Meditsinskogo Instituta [*A publication*]

Nauchn Tr Stavrop S-kh Inst ... Nauchnye Trudy Stavropol'skogo Sel'skokhozyaistvennogo Instituta [*A publication*]

Nauchn Tr Sverdl Gos Pedagog Inst ... Nauchnye Trudy Sverdlovskii Gosudarstvennyi Pedagogicheskii Institut [*A publication*]

Nauchn Tr Taskh Gos Univ ... Nauchnye Trudy Taskhentskogo Gosudarstvennogo Universiteta [*A publication*]

Nauchn Tr Tul Gos Pedagog Inst ... Nauchnye Trudy Tulskogo Gosudarstvennogo Pedagogicheskogo Instituta [*A publication*]

Nauchn Tr Uch Prakt Vrachei Uzb ... Nauchnye Trudy Uchenykh i Prakticheskikh Vrachei Uzbekistana [*A publication*]

NAUFMA ... National Association of Urban Flood Management Agencies

NAVAVNLOGCEN ... Naval Aviation Logistics Center

NAVCHAPGRU ... Navy Cargo Handling and Port Group

NAVCON ... Navigation Control Systems

NAVENVPREDRSCHFAC ... Naval Environmental Prediction Research Facility

NAVFORSTAT ... Naval Force Status Report

NAVHLTHRSCHC ... Naval Health Research Center

NAVMACS ... Naval Modular Automated Communications System

NAVMMAC ... Naval Manpower and Material Analysis Center

NAVNET .... Navigation Network

Navorsinge Nas Mus (Bloemfontein) ... Navorsinge van die Nasionale Museum (Bloemfontein) [*A publication*]

NAVSSES ... Naval Ship Systems Engineering Station

New Acronyms, Initialisms, & Abbreviations

NAVSUPACT ... Naval Support Activity
NAVTACSUPPACT ... Navy Tactical Support Activity
NAWP .... National Association for Widowed People
NAWRSRF ... New Age World Religious and Scientific Research Foundation
NB .... Newborn
NB .... Nominal Bore [*Tubing*]
NBCDL ...... National Board for Certification of Dental Laboratories
NBGS .... New Bedford Glass Society
NBI .... Nonbattle Injuries
NBI .... Nothing but Initials [*Initialism is name of commercial word processor firm*]
NBM .... Nothing by Mouth
NB Mus Monogr Ser ... New Brunswick Museum. Monographic Series [*A publication*]
NBPP .... National Black Political Party
NBTA .... National Board of Trial Advocacy
NC .... Network Connect
NC .... Nonconformist [*Indicating religious preference*] [*Military*] [*British*]
NCA .... N-Chloroethylnorapomorphine [*Organic chemistry, biochemistry*]
NCA .... National Certification Agency for Medical Lab Personnel
NCA .... Nurse Consultants Association
NCAA .... National Center for the Arts and Aging
NCAA .... Nonnuclear Consumable Annual Analysis
NCADV ..... National Commission Against Domestic Violence
NC Agric Exp Stn Bull ... North Carolina Agricultural Experiment Station. Bulletin [*A publication*]
NC Agric Exp Stn Tech Bull ... North Carolina Agricultural Experiment Station. Technical Bulletin [*A publication*]
NC Agric Ext Serv Ext Circ ... North Carolina Agricultural Extension Service. Extension Circular [*A publication*]
NC Agric Ext Serv Ext Folder ... North Carolina Agricultural Extension Service. Extension Folder [*A publication*]
NC Agric Ext Serv Leafl ... North Carolina Agricultural Extension Service. Leaflet [*A publication*]
NCAH .... National Committee, Arts for the Handicapped
NCAT .... Naval College Aptitude Test
NCBA .... National Center on Black Aged
NCBG .... National Coalition of Black Gays
NCCBMI .... National Consortium for Computer Based Music Instruction
NCCC .... National Cambodia Crisis Committee
NCCDS ..... National Cooperative Crohn's Disease Study
NCCPA ..... National Commission on Certification of Physician's Assistants
NCD .... National Council on Drugs
NCDM .... Numerically Controlled Drafting Machine
NCDTO ..... National Council of Dance Teacher Organizations
NCEA .... National Center for Economic Alternatives
NCEB .... National Council for Environmental Balance
NCEC .... National Construction Employers Council
NCEE .... National Congress for Educational Excellence
NCEFT ...... National Commission on Electronic Fund Transfers
NCF .... Nuclear Capable Forces
NCFA .... Naval Campus for Achievement
NCHCT ..... National Center for Health Care Technology [*US Congress agency*]
NCHFCI .... National Committee to Honor the Fourteenth Centennial of Islam
NCHMHHSO ... National Coalition of Hispanic Mental Health and Human Services Organizations
NCI .... Naphthalene Creosote, Iodoform [*Powder for lice*]
NCIMS ...... Negative Chemical Ionization Mass Spectra
NCJD .... National Coalition for a Just Draft
NCJJ .... National Center for Juvenile Justice
NCLC .... Nineteenth Century Literature Criticism [*A publication*]
NCMDLRJO ... National Council of Marriage and Divorce Law Reform and Justice Organizations
NCMET ..... Nonclosed Shell Many Electron Theory [*Physics*]
NCNEVAW ... National Communications Network for the Elimination of Violence Against Women
NCNW .... National Congress of Neighborhood Women
NCP .... Network Control Program [*Data processing*]
NCPA .... National Conservation Policy Act [*1979*]
NCPAG ..... National CPA Group

NCPTCAN ... National Center for the Prevention and Treatment of Child Abuse and Neglect
NCR .... Nonconformance Report [*Nuclear energy*]
NCR .... Notification of Change Report
NCRP Rep ... NCRP [*National Council on Radiation Protection and Measurements*] Reports [*A publication*]
NCRWS ..... National Campaign for Radioactive Waste Safety
NCSAG ..... Nuclear Cross Section Advisory Group
NCSBI ...... National Council for Small Business Innovation
NCSC .... Naval Coastal Systems Center
NCSFP ...... National Council on Synthetic Fuels Production
NCSL .... National Center for Service-Learning [*Part of ACTION*]
NCSSM ..... North Carolina School of Science and Mathematics [*Free, residential public high school for gifted students*]
NCWTM .... National Council on Wholistic Therapeutics and Medicine
NCWW ...... National Commission on Working Women
ND .... I am not able to deliver message addressed to aircraft [*Communications*]
N-D .... N-Dimensional
ND .... Negative Declaration
Nd .... Number of Dissimilar [*Matches*]
NDCCC ..... National Defense Communications Control Center
NDCT .... Natural Draft Cooling Tower [*Nuclear energy*]
NDE .... Nondestructive Examination
NDF .... Neutral Detergent Fiber [*Food analysis*]
ND Hist ..... North Dakota History [*A publication*]
NDI .... Nephrogenic Diabetes Insipidus [*Endocrinology*]
NDPA .... Nitrosodipropylamine [*Organic chemistry*] [*Also, DPN and DPNA*]
NDS .... Navy Director System
NDSS .... National Down Syndrome Society
NDT .... Net Data Throughout
NE .... Nerve Excitability [*Test*]
NEA .... New England Airlines, Inc. [*Westerly, RI*] [*FAA designator*]
NEAS .... Newsletter of Engineering Analysis Software [*A publication*]
NEB .... Nonenzymatic Maillard Browning [*Food technology*]
NEC .... National Education Center for Paraprofessionals in Mental Health
NEC .... Nuclear Energy Center
NECSS ...... Nuclear Energy Center Site Survey
NEDS .... New Enlisted Distribution System
NEFI .... New England Fuel Institute
NEH .... I am connecting you to a station which will accept traffic for the station you request [*Communications*]
NEIS .... National Engineering Information System
NEMA .... Nematode [*Threadworm*]
NEMO .... Nonempirical Molecular Orbitals [*Atomic physics*]
NEMVAC ... Noncombatant Emergency and Evacuation Plan
NEO .... Neoarsphenamine [*or Neosalvarsan*] [*Medicine*]
NEOCS ...... Navy Enlisted Occupational Classification System
NERV .... Nervous [*Medicine*]
NES .... News Election Service [*Vote-counting consortium of the major TV networks and two wire services*]
NESEA ...... Naval Electronic Systems Engineering Activity
NESO .... Navy Environmental Support Office
NET .... Nimbus Experiment Team [*NASA*]
NETA .... National Environmental Training Association
NETA .... Northeast Test Area [*Military*]
NETC .... Naval Education and Training Center
NEVE .... Nonempirical Valence-Electron [*Physics*]
NEW .... Native Egg White
NEWPOSITREP ... New [*Corrected*] Position Report
NEXRAD ... Next Generation Weather RADAR [*National Weather Service*]
NF .... Negro Female
NFA .... National Forensic Association
NFC .... National Fenestration Council
NFC .... No Further Consequences
NFCA .... Nonfuel Core Array [*Nuclear energy*]
NFDM .... Nonfat Dry Milk
NFEA .... Non-Fleet Experienced Aviator
NFEW .... National Forum for Executive Women
NFFC .... National Family Farm Coalition
NFID .... National Foundation for Infectious Diseases
NFIE .... National Foundation for the Improvement of Education

NFL .... Northaire Freight Lines Ltd. [*Davisburg, MI*] [*FAA designator*]
NFP .... National Federation of Parents for Drug-Free Youth
NFPI .... National Frozen Pizza Institute
NFPRHA .... National Family Planning and Reproductive Health Association
NFT .... Neurofibrillary Tangle [*Brain anatomy*]
NG .... New Granada
NG .... Noble Grand
NGFEX ...... Naval Gunfire Exercise
NGOCD ..... Non-Governmental Organization Committee on Disarmament
NGPA .... National Gas Policy Act [*1978*]
NGR .... Narrow Gauze Roll [*Medicine*]
NGSF .... Noble Gas Storage Facility
NH .... New Haven [*Connecticut*]
NHA .... Nonhydrogen Atom [*Chemistry*]
NHC .... N-Hexylcarborane [*Rocket fuel*]
NHCP .... Nonhistone Chromosomal Protein [*Genetics*]
NI .... Numerical Index
NICOA .... National Indian Council on Aging
NICUFO .... National Investigations Committee on Unidentified Flying Objects
NIHR .... National Institute of Handicapped Research [*Department of Health and Human Services*]
NIL .... I have nothing to send to you [*Communications*]
NIPA .... Notice of Initiation of Procurement Action
NIPGM ...... National Institute on Parks and Grounds Management
NIRS .... Nuclear Information and Resource Service
NIRSA .... National Intramural-Recreational Sports Association
NIS .... National Information System
NITRAS ..... Navy Integrated Training Resources and Administration System
NIWC .... Naval Inshore Warfare Command
NLCPI .... National Legal Center for the Public Interest
NLHRSA .... National Left-Handers Racquet Sports Association
NLP .... National Land for People [*An organization*]
NLP .... Neurolinguistic Programing
NM .... Navy Mines
NM .... Negro Male
NM .... New Measurement
NMBR .... Number
NMC .... National Maritime Council
NMC .... Naval Memorandum Correction
NMC .... Network Management Center [*Data processing*]
NMC .... Not Mission Capable
NMCC .... Navy-Marine Corps Council
NMDRP ..... National Military Discharge Review Project
NMHF .... National Manufactured Housing Federation
NMIA .... National Military Intelligence Association
NMIS .... Nuclear Materials Inventory System
NMLS .... National Microwave Landing System
NMMSS ..... Nuclear Materials Management and Safeguards System
NMOA .... National Mail Order Association
NMP .... National Meter Programing
NMP .... Navy Manning Plan
NMPC .... National Moratorium on Prison Construction
NMPD .... Nitromethylpropanediol [*Organic chemistry*]
NMR .... No Maintenance Requirement
NMRS .... Navy Manpower Requirements System
NMU .... Nitrosomethylurethane [*Organic chemistry*]
NN .... Nerves
NNFF .... National Neurofibromatosis Foundation
NNNDO ..... Neglect of Non-Neighbor Differential Overlap [*Physics*]
NNP .... Nerve Net Pulse [*Neurobiology*]
NNPA .... Nuclear Nonproliferation Act
NNYAB ...... National Network of Youth Advisory Boards
NO .... Narcotics Officer
NOBLE ...... National Organization of Black Law Enforcement Executives
NOC .... Naval Operations Center
NOHS .... National Organization of Human Services
NOKD .... Not Our Kind, Dear [*Slang*]
NOLEO ...... Notice to Law Enforcement Officials
NOMb .... Nitric Oxide Myoglobin [*Food technology*]
NONUM ..... Notional Number
NOP .... Nuclear Ordnance Platoon [*Marine Corps*]
NOR .... Nonoperational Ready
NORC .... Nuclear Ordnance Record Card

NORLEU .... Norleucine [*An amino acid*]
NORM .... Nonoperational Ready Maintenance
NORPI .... No Pilot Balloon Observation Will Be Filed Next Collection Unless Weather Changes Significantly [*National Weather Service*]
NORVAL ... Norvaline
NOSIH ... Naval Ordnance Station, Indian Head
NOSS .... National Ocean Survey System [*Cooperative program of governmental agencies*]
NOSS .... National Oceanic Satellite System
NOT .... Nucleus of the Optic Tract [*Eye anatomy*]
NOTA .... None of the Above [*Politics*]
NOTAEI .... National Old Timers' Association of the Energy Industry
NOTAP ...... Navy Occupational Task Analysis Program
NOTMAR ... Notice to Mariner
NOX .... Nitrous Oxide [*or NOx*] [*Laughing gas*]
NOXA .... Naphthoxyacetic Acid [*Organic chemistry*]
NP .... No Prospect [*In sports*]
NPA .... N-Propylamine [*Organic chemistry*]
NPAS .... Normalized Photoacoustic Signal [*Instrumentation*]
NPBE .... Nitrophenyl Butyl Ether [*Organic chemistry*]
NPC .... National Philatelic Collections [*Smithsonian Institution*]
NPDDE ..... Nitrophenyl Dodecyl Ether [*Organic chemistry*]
NPF .... National Pharmaceutical Foundation
NPF .... Nuclear Power Facility
NPG .... [*The*] Nuclear Power Group [*British*]
NPHE .... Nitrophenyl Hexyl Ether [*Organic chemistry*]
NPHOE ...... Nitrophenyl Hydroxyoctyl Ether [*Organic chemistry*]
NPLG .... Night Plane Landing Guard
NPO .... Neighborhood Patrol Officer
NPO .... Not Pickled Ordinary [*Metal industry*]
NPOE .... Nitrophenyl Octyl Ether [*Organic chemistry*]
NPOST ...... Nonperturbative Open-Shell Theory [*Physics*]
NPPE .... Nitrophenyl Pentyl Ether [*Organic chemistry*]
NPPRE ..... Nitrophenyl Propyl Ether [*Organic chemistry*]
NPR .... North Polar Region
NPRDS ..... Nuclear Plant Reliability Data System
NPS .... National Periodicals System
NPS .... Numerical Plotting System
NPSO .... Nonpaired Spatial Orbitals [*Atomic physics*]
NPTF .... Nuclear Proof Test Facility [*Proposed, but never built*]
NQ .... Northwest Territorial Airlines [*Canada*] [*ICAO designator*]
NR .... CSE Aviation Ltd. [*Great Britain*] [*ICAO designator*]
NR .... Neutral Red [*An indicator*]
NR .... Non-Rebreathing
NR .... Normal Range
NR .... North River [*New York and New Jersey*]
NR .... Nutritive Ratio
NRC .... National Rural Center
NRCMC ..... National Resource Center for Minority Contractors
NRF .... National Roofing Foundation
NRF .... Naval Reserve Force
NRH .... Natural Rate Hypothesis [*Economics*]
NRL .... Normal Response Level
NRL/SVIC ... Naval Research Laboratory Shock and Vibration Information Center [*ONR*]
NRM .... National Revolutionary Movement [*France*]
NRMC .... Naval Regional Medical Center
NRP .... National Religious Party [*Israel*]
NRRC .... Northern Regional Research Center [*Department of Agriculture*] [*Formerly, NRRL*]
NRSC .... National Radio Systems Committee
NRTS .... National Reactor Test Station [*INEL*]
NRW .... Narrow
NRZ1 .... Nonreturn to Zero Change on One
NS .... Nylon Suture [*Medicine*]
NSA .... Normal Serum Albumin [*Clinical chemistry*]
NSCC .... Naval Sea Cadet Corps
NSD .... Next Most Significant Digit [*Data processing*]
NSDAJ ...... National Space Development Agency of Japan
NSDSA ...... Naval Sea Data Support Activity
NS & E ...... Nuclear Science and Engineering [*A publication*]
NSG .... Neurosecretory Granules
NSHRC ..... National Self-Help Resource Center
NSIEE .... National Society for Internships and Experiential Education
NSLP .... National School Lunch Program [*Department of Agriculture*]

NSLRS ...... National School Labor Relations Service
NSM .... National Socialist Movement
Nsn .... Number of Similar Negative [*Matches*]
NSO .... National Symphony Orchestra
Nsp .... Number of Similar Positive [*Matches*]
NSPS .... National Society of Professional Sanitarians
NSSFA ...... National Single Service Food Association
NSURG ...... Neurosurgery
NSV .... Net Sales Value
NT .... Naso-Tracheal [*Medicine*]
NT .... Naturalization Test
NT .... Neotetrazolium
NT .... Nevada Territory [*Prior to statehood*]
NT .... No Test
NT .... Nuclear Technology [*A publication*]
NTA .... Net Technical Assessment
NTB .... No Talent Bum [*Slang*]
NTC .... Naturally Occurring Top Component [*Virology*]
NTC .... No Traffic Reported [*Aviation*]
NTE/IOTE ... Navy Technical Evaluation/Initial Operational Test and
          Evaluation
NTFND ...... No Trouble Found
NTICED ..... National Training Institute for Community Economic
          Development
NTN .... New Trade Names [*A publication*]
NTO .... Natural Transition Orbitals [*Atomic physics*]
NTP .... Naval Tactical Publication
NTP .... Naval Telecommunications Procedures
NTP .... Naval Telecommunications Publication
NTP .... Navy Training Plan
NTPA .... Naval Technical Proficiency Assist
NTPF .... Number of Terminals per Failure [*Data processing*]
NTS .... Nucleus Tractus Solitarii [*Brain anatomy*]

NTULC ...... Negro Trade Union Leadership Council
NUBA .... National UHF Broadcasting Association
NUC .... Nucleated
NUCL .... Nucleus
NUCLIT ..... Nucleare Italiana [*Government corporation*] [*Italy*]
NUCMUN .. Nuclear Munitions
NUDET ...... Nuclear Detection
NUDET ...... Nuclear Detonation Evaluation Technique
NUIS .... Navy Unit Identification System
NUMERALS ... Numerical Analysis System
NUMS .... Nuclear Materials Security
NUWAX ...... Nuclear Weapons Accident Exercises
NUWES ..... Naval Undersea Warfare Engineering Station
NV .... Naked Vision
NV .... Nonvaccinated
NV .... Nonveteran
NVII .... Navy Vocational Interest Inventory
NVOCC ...... Nonvessel Operating Common Carrier [*Shipping*]
NW .... New Wave [*Style of music*]
NWA .... New World Alliance
NWDA ...... National Wine Distributors' Association
NWEE .... National Women's Employment and Education [*An
          organization*]
NWEF .... New World Education Fund
NWPL .... Naval Warfare Publications Library
NWRA .... National Women's Rowing Association
NWSA ...... National Women's Studies Association
NWSC .... Naval Weapons Support Center
NWW .... New Ways To Work [*An organization*]
NYFE .... New York Futures Exchange [*Acronym pronounced
          "knife"*]
NYLG .... New York Law Group

O

O	Occiput [*Medicine*]
O	Octal [*Number system with a base of eight*] [*Data processing*]
O	Operator
O	Operon [*Genetics*]
O	Output
OA	Occiput Anterior [*Medicine*]
OA	Old Age
OA	Open Annealed [*Metal industry*]
OA	Opera America [*An organization*]
OA	Overspenders Anonymous
OAAD	Ovarian Ascorbic Acid Depletion [*Test*]
OAAT	Ortho-Aminoazotoluene [*A dye*] [*Organic chemistry*]
OACT	Officer, Airman, Civilian, and Total
OAD	Oxford American Dictionary [*A publication*]
OADC	Oleic Acid, Albumin, Dextrose, Catalase
OAF	Open Air Factor
OARS	On-Line Automated Reference Service [*Library science*]
OAS	Oasis [*Board on Geographic Names*]
OASD/IL	Office of the Assistant Secretary of Defense, Installations, and Logistics
OASN(M/RA/L)	Office of the Assistant Secretary of the Navy (Manpower, Reserve Affairs, and Logistics)
OATP	Operational Acceptance Test Procedure
OATUU	Organization of African Trade Union Unity [*Formerly, AATUF and ATUC*]
OB	Octal to Binary [*Data processing*]
OBA	Off Boresight Angle
OBBO	Observation Balloon
OBD	Organic Brain Disease
OBE	Operating Basis Earthquake [*Nuclear reactor*]
OBG	Obstetrics-Gynecology [*Medicine*]
OBOF	Old Buffer over Forty [*Elderly recruits*] [*British*] [*World War I*]
OBR	Outboard Recorder
OBS	Observatory
OBSH	Oxybis(benzenesulfonylhydrazine) [*Organic chemistry*]
OBTVR	Office for Battlefield Technical Vulnerability Reduction [*Army*]
OBU	Offshore Banking Unit
OBV	On-Balance Volume [*Measurement devised by stock market technician Joseph Granville*]
OC	Occlusocervical [*Medicine*]
OC	On Call
OC	Operating Curve
OCA	Oral Contraceptive Agent [*Endocrinology*]
OCA	Organization of Chinese Americans
OCAC	Officer Commanding Administrative Centre [*British*] [*World War I*]
OCAW	Organization of Chinese American Women
OCC	Occlusion
OCC	Operator Control Command
OCCBP	Organization for Collectors of Covered Bridge Postcards
OCD	Ovarian Cholesterol Depletion [*Test*]
OCDD	Octachlorodioxin [*Organic chemistry*]
OCDF	Operations Control and Display Facility [*Military*]
OCI	Oxide Control and Indication
OCL	Operation Control Language [*Data processing*]
OCPNA	Ortho-Chloro-para-nitroaniline [*Organic chemistry*]
OCPO	Office of Civilian Personnel Operations [*Air Force*]
OCS	Optical Communicator System
OCSOT	Overall Combat Systems Operability Test
OCT	Optical Contract Seeker
OCTA	Ortho-Cyclohexanediaminetetraacetic Acid [*Organic chemistry*] [*Also, DCTA*]
OCTG	Oil Country Tubular Goods [*Metal industry*]
OD	Octal to Decimal [*Data processing*]
OD	Open Drop
OD	Original Dirac [*Vacuum model*] [*Physics*]
ODC	Ordinary Decent Criminal [*British prison slang for other than a political prisoner*]
ODDS	Optional Delivery Dispenser System
ODE	Optical Designation Evaluation
ODL	Officer Deficiency Letter [*Navy*]
ODM	Outboard Data Manager
ODMR	Optical Detection of Magnetic Resonance [*Physics*]
ODONT	Odontology
ODP	Octyl Isodecyl Phthalate [*Organic chemistry*]
ODP	Open Data Path
ODS	Oxide Dispersion Strengthened [*Metallurgy*]
ODW	Office of Drinking Water [*Environmental Protection Agency*]
OE	Oil Equivalent
OE	Operating Engineer
OECON	Offshore Engineering Conference
OEE	Outer Enamel Epithelium [*Dentistry*]
OEET	Office of Environmental Engineering and Technology [*Environmental Protection Agency*]
OEF	Optical Evaluation Facility
OEHL	Occupational and Environmental Health Laboratory [*Air Force*]
OESOPH	Oesophagus
OF	Occipital-Frontal [*Diameter of head*]
OF	Official Files
O & F	Organizations and Functions
OFP	Occluded Frontal Passage [*Meteorology*]
OFR	Officer Fitness Report [*Navy*]
OFT	Observed Fire Trainer [*Military*]
OG	Orange Green [*Stain*] [*Medicine*]
OGST	Overthread Guide Sleeve Tool [*Nuclear energy*]
OHBC	Oregon Highland Bentgrass Commission
OHC	Outer Hair Cells
OHU	Overseas Homeparted Units [*Navy*]
OI	Opsonic Index [*Medicine*]
OI	Organizational/Intermediate
OIC	On-Line Instrument and Control Program [*Data processing*]
OINT	Ointment
OIP	Operating Internal Pressure [*Nuclear energy*]
OIU	Operator Interface Unit [*Data processing*]
OJARS	Office of Justice Assistance, Research, and Statistics [*Department of Justice*]
OJCC	Occupied Japan Collectors Club
OJJDP	Office of Juvenile Justice and Delinquency Prevention [*Department of Justice*]
OLF	Oromo Liberation Front
OLI	Out-of-Line Interrupter
OLIP	On-Line Instrument Package [*Data processing*]

OLP .... Oxygen Lime Powder [*Steelmaking process*]
OLTS .... On-Line Test System [*Data processing*]
OLU .... Columbus [*Nebraska*] [*Airport symbol*]
OLUG .... Office Landscape Users Group
OM .... Occipitomental [*Diameter of head*]
OM .... Otitis Media [*Medicine*]
OM .... Out for Maintenance
O/M .... Oxygen-to-Metal [*Ratio*]
OMA .... Operation and Maintenance, Army
OMA .... Operational Maintenance Activity
OMB .... Omboue [*Gabon*] [*Airport symbol*]
OME .... Nome [*Alaska*] [*Airport symbol*]
OMH .... Omaha Aviation, Inc. [*Omaha, NE*] [*FAA designator*]
OMH .... Orumieh [*Iran*] [*Airport symbol*]
OML .... Organizational Maintenance Level
O & MNR ... Operation and Maintenance, Naval Reserve
OMR .... Orad [*Romania*] [*Airport symbol*]
OMS .... Omsk [*USSR*] [*Airport symbol*]
OMT .... Office of Manufacturing Technology [*DARCOM*] [*Army*]
OMT .... Oleoyl Methyl Taurate [*Organic chemistry*]
OMTNS ..... Over Mountains [*Meteorology*]
OND .... Orthopaedic Nursing Diploma [*British*]
ONDE .... Office of Naval Disability Evaluation
ONE .... Onepusu [*Solomon Islands*] [*Airport symbol*]
ONG .... Mornington Island [*Australia*] [*Airport symbol*]
ONH .... Oneonta [*New York*] [*Airport symbol*]
ONI .... Moanamani [*Indonesia*] [*Airport symbol*]
ONP .... Newport [*Oregon*] [*Airport symbol*]
ONS .... Onslow [*Australia*] [*Airport symbol*]
ONU .... Ono-I-Lau [*Fiji*] [*Airport symbol*]
ONWI .... Office of Nuclear Waste Isolation
OOA .... Out of Area
OOALC ..... Ogden Air Logistics Center
OOC .... Out of Commission
OOC .... Out of Control [*Slang*]
OOK .... Toksook [*Alaska*] [*Airport symbol*]
OOL .... Gold Coast [*Australia*] [*Airport symbol*]
OOM .... Cooma [*Australia*] [*Airport symbol*]
OOP .... Out of Print [*Also, OP*]
OOS .... Out of Service
OOT .... Onotoa [*Kiribati*] [*Airport symbol*]
OP .... Occiput Posterior [*Medicine*]
OP .... Operations Order
OP .... Orbital Probe [*NASA*]
OP .... Osmotic Pressure
OP .... Other than Psychotic
OP .... Outpatient [*Medicine*]
OPA .... Kopasker [*Iceland*] [*Airport symbol*]
OPAAW ..... Organization of Pan Asian-American Women
OPACT ...... Organization of Professional Acting Coaches and Teachers
OPB .... Open Bay [*Papua New Guinea*] [*Airport symbol*]
OPC .... Operator Position Controller [*Communications*]
OPC .... Outer Passenger Cabin
OP-CAL .... Operation California [*An organization*]
OPCOMCTR ... Operational Command Center [*Navy*]
OPDEC ..... Operational Deception [*Navy*]
OPEN .... Origin of Plasma in Earth's Neighborhood
OPFM .... Outlet Plenum Feature Model [*Nuclear energy*]
OPH .... Ophthalmology
OPHF .... Orbital Polarized Hartree-Fock [*Atomic physics*]
OPMA .... Open Pit Mining Association
OPMARV ... Operational Maneuvering Reentry Vehicle
OPMET ..... Operational Meteorological Information
OPO .... Oporto [*Portugal*] [*Airport symbol*]
OPOSS ...... Office of Personnel Operations Standards and Systems Office [*Army*]
OPP .... Oriented Polypropylene [*Plastics technology*]
OPPE .... Operational Propulsion Plant Examination [*Navy*]
OPR .... Off-Site Procurement Request
OPS .... Offshore Power Systems
OPS .... Operation and Support
OPS .... Operational Protection System [*Nuclear energy*]
OPS .... Oriented Polystyrene [*Plastics technology*]
OPSCOMM ... Operations Communications
OPTI .... Office of Productivity, Technology, and Innovation [*Department of Commerce*]
OPTIM .... Order Point Technique for Inventory Management
OPU .... Balimo [*Papua New Guinea*] [*Airport symbol*]

OPX .... Off Premise Extension
OR .... Oil Retention [*Enema*] [*Medicine*]
OR .... Optical Reader [*Data processing*]
ORA .... Opportunity Resources for the Arts [*An organization*]
ORACLE ... Online Retrieval and Computational Language for Economists
ORB .... Orebro [*Sweden*] [*Airport symbol*]
ORC .... On-Line Reactivity Computers [*Data processing*]
ORD .... Orderly
ORDSER ... Ordnance Support Element Review
ORE .... Occupational Radiation Exposure
ORF .... Norfolk/Virginia Beach [*Virginia*] [*Airport symbol*]
ORFM .... Outlet Region Feature Model
ORG .... Paramaribo [*Surinam*] Zorg En Hoop Airport [*Airport symbol*]
ORH .... Worcester [*Massachusetts*] [*Airport symbol*]
ORI .... Port Lions [*Alaska*] [*Airport symbol*]
ORIF .... Open Reduction with Internal Fixation [*Medicine*]
OrJ .... Orange Juice
ORJ .... Orinduik [*Guyana*] [*Airport symbol*]
ORJETS .... Online Remote Job Entry Terminal System [*Data processing*]
ORK .... Cork [*Ireland*] [*Airport symbol*]
ORL .... Otorhinolaryngology [*Medicine*]
ORN .... Oran [*Algeria*] [*Airport symbol*]
ORP .... Orapa [*Botswana*] [*Airport symbol*]
ORR .... Oak Ridge Research Reactor [*ORNL*]
ORS .... Orthopedic Surgeon
ORV .... Noorvik [*Alaska*] [*Airport symbol*]
ORY .... Paris [*France*] Orly Airport [*Airport symbol*]
ORZ .... Orange Walk [*Belize*] [*Airport symbol*]
OS .... Opening Snaps [*Cardiology*]
OS .... Operating System
OSA .... Osaka [*Japan*] [*Airport symbol*]
OSAI .... Office of Systems Analysis and Information [*Department of Transportation*]
OSB .... Osage Beach [*Missouri*] [*Airport symbol*]
OSD .... Ostersund [*Sweden*] [*Airport symbol*]
OSH .... Oshkosh [*Wisconsin*] [*Airport symbol*]
OSI .... Open Systems Interconnections [*Data processing*]
OSI .... Osijek [*Yugoslavia*] [*Airport symbol*]
OSK .... Oskarshamn [*Sweden*] [*Airport symbol*]
OSL .... Oslo [*Norway*] [*Airport symbol*]
OSM .... Osmotic
OSP .... Slupsk [*Poland*] [*Airport symbol*]
OSR .... Ostrava [*Czechoslovakia*] [*Airport symbol*]
OST .... Ostend [*Belgium*] [*Airport symbol*]
OSTEO ..... Osteomyelitis [*Medicine*]
OSWS ...... Operating System Workstation [*Data processing*]
OSY .... Namsos [*Norway*] [*Airport symbol*]
OSZ .... Koszalin [*Poland*] [*Airport symbol*]
OT .... Linhas Aereas de S Tome e Principe [*Portugal*] [*ICAO designator*]
OT .... Oregon Territory [*Prior to statehood*]
OT .... Overlap Telling
OTA .... Open Test Assembly [*Nuclear energy*]
OTAS .... On Top and Smooth [*Meteorology*]
OTC .... Once-Through Cooling [*Nuclear energy*]
OTC .... Oxytetracycline [*Antibiotic*]
OTF .... Orbital Test Flight
OTG .... Worthington [*Minnesota*] [*Airport symbol*]
OTH .... North Bend [*Oregon*] [*Airport symbol*]
OTHDC & T ... Over the Horizon Detection, Classification, and Targeting
OTM .... Ortho-Tolidine Manganese Sulphate
OTM .... Other than Mexican [*Term applied by US Border Patrol to certain illegal immigrants*]
OTM .... Ottumwa [*Iowa*] [*Airport symbol*]
OTMS .... Operational Technical Managerial System
OTO .... Otology [*Medicine*]
OTPEC ...... Officer Training Program Examining Center [*Air Force*]
OTSG .... Once-Through Steam Generator [*Nuclear energy*]
OTT .... Operational Training Test
OTTE .... Operational Testing, Training, and Evaluation
OTU .... Otu [*Colombia*] [*Airport symbol*]
OTW .... Off the Wall [*Slang*]
OTY .... Oria [*Papua New Guinea*] [*Airport symbol*]
OTZ .... Kotzebue [*Alaska*] [*Airport symbol*]
OUA .... Ouagadougou [*Upper Volta*] [*Airport symbol*]

OUD .... Oujda [*Morocco*] [*Airport symbol*]
OUH .... Oudtshoorn [*South Africa*] [*Airport symbol*]
OUL........... Oulu [*Finland*] [*Airport symbol*]
OUS .... Ourinhos [*Brazil*] [*Airport symbol*]
OUZ........... Zouerate [*Mauritania*] [*Airport symbol*]
OVA........... Bekily [*Madagascar*] [*Airport symbol*]
OVB........... Novosibirsk [*USSR*] [*Airport symbol*]
OVD .... Oviedo [*Spain*] [*Airport symbol*]
OVONIC .... Ovshinsky and Electronic [*Excitation processing term formed by combining name of Stanford Ovshinsky, energy researcher, and "electronic"*]
O & W .... Oldest and Wisest [*Nickname for President Ronald Reagan*]
OW .... Options for Women [*An organization*]
O-W........... Ordinary Wave

OWASU..... Old World Archaeological Study Unit
OWB.......... Owensboro [*Kentucky*] [*Airport symbol*]
OWD.......... On-Line Wholesale Distribution System [*Data processing*]
OWU.......... Overload Warning Unit
OX .... Oxymel [*Honey, water, vinegar*] [*Medicine*]
OXF........... Oxford [*England*]
OXR........... Oxnard [*California*] [*Airport symbol*]
OYA........... Goya [*Argentina*] [*Airport symbol*]
OYE........... Oyem [*Gabon*] [*Airport symbol*]
OYO .... Tres Arroyos [*Argentina*] [*Airport symbol*]
OYS........... Yosemite National Park [*California*] [*Airport symbol*]
OZC........... Ozamis City [*Philippines*] [*Airport symbol*]
OZH........... Zaporozh'ye [*USSR*] [*Airport symbol*]
OZZ........... Ouarzazate [*Morocco*] [*Airport symbol*]

P

P .... Papilla [*Optic*] [*Medicine*]
P .... Pasteurella [*Genus of bacteria*]
P .... Percentile
P .... Perceptual
P .... Percussion
P .... Peyote
P .... Phenolphthalein [*Chemical indicator*]
P .... Pink
P .... Plasma
P .... Porcelain
P .... Postpartum [*Medicine*]
P .... Presbyopia [*Ophthalmology*]
P .... Primitive
P .... Product
P .... Psychiatry
P3 .... Portable Plotting Package
5 P's .... Poet, Printer, Publisher, Publican, and Player [*Nickname given to William Oxberry (fl. 1784-1824)*]
PA .... Paper Advance
PA .... Pills Anonymous [*An organization*]
PA .... Polyacetal [*Organic chemistry*]
PA .... Posterior Anterior [*Medicine*]
PA .... Precision Approach
PA .... Protected Area
PA .... Pulpoaxial [*Dentistry*]
PAA .... Pa-An [*Burma*] [*Airport symbol*]
PAA .... Pyridineacetic Acid [*Organic chemistry*]
PAAT .... Personnel and Administrative Assistance Team [*Navy*]
PAAWWW ... Pacific Asian American Women Writers West [*An organization*]
PAB .... Program Advisory Board
PABS .... Para-Aminobenzensulfonamide [*Antibiotic*]
PAC........... Panama City [*Panama*] Paitilla Airport [*Airport symbol*]
PAC........... Powdered Activated Carbon [*Adsorbent*]
PAC........... Prime [*or Principal*] Associate Contractor
PACE .... Performing Arts, Culture, and Entertainment [*Proposed cable television system*]
PACE .... Planetary Association for Clean Energy
PACE .... Plant Acquisition and Construction Equipment
PACE .... Program for Afloat College Education [*Navy*]
PACER...... Prescriptive Analysis for Curriculum Evaluation [*Vocational guidance*]
PACFLAP ... Pacific Fleet Augmentation Plan [*Navy*]
PACS .... Physics and Astronomy Classification Scheme
PAD........... Packet Assembler/Disassembler
PAD........... Paderborn [*West Germany*] [*Airport symbol*]
PADA .... (Pyridylazo)dimethylaniline [*Organic chemistry*]
PAF .... Pulmonary Arteriovenous Fistula [*Medicine*]
PAFVA ...... Polish Air Force Veterans Association
PAG........... Pagadian [*Philippines*] [*Airport symbol*]
PAH........... Paducah [*Kentucky*] [*Airport symbol*]
PAH........... Panorama Air Tour, Inc. [*Honolulu, HI*] [*FAA designator*]
PAI .... Polyamide-Imide [*Organic chemistry*]
PAIC......... Public Address Intercom System
PAIP .... Public Affairs and Information Program [*Atomic Industrial Forum*]
PAK........... Program Attention Key [*Data processing*]
PAL .... Paleontology
PAL .... Pectin Acid Lyase [*An enzyme*]

PAL .... Present Atmospheric Level
PAL .... Programer Assistance and Liaison [*Data processing*]
PAL .... Prototype Application Loop [*Nuclear energy*]
PALP........ Palpable [*Medicine*]
PALPI....... Palpitation [*Medicine*]
PAM .... Post-Accident Monitoring [*Nuclear energy*]
PAM .... Primary Amebic Meningitis [*Medicine*]
PAM-A ...... Payload Assist Module - Atlas Class
PAMA........ Professional Aviation Maintenance Association
PAM-D ...... Payload Assist Module - Delta Class
PAMPUS ... Photons for Atomic and Molecular Processes and Universal Studies [*Physics*]
PAMS........ Procurement Action Management System
PAN........... Pattani [*Thailand*] [*Airport symbol*]
pap............ Papilla [*Medicine*]
PAP .... Phenolphthalein in Paraffin [*Emulsion*]
PAP .... Platelet Alkaline Phosphatase [*An enzyme*]
PAP .... Port Au Prince [*Haiti*] [*Airport symbol*]
PAP .... Primary Atypical Pneumonia [*Medicine*]
PAPS........ Periodic Armaments Planning System
PAR........... Paris [*France*] [*Airport symbol*]
PAR........... Performance Appraisal Report
PAR........... Problem Analysis and Resolution
PAR........... Professional Abstracts Registries [*Database Innovations, Inc.*]
PAR........... Program Assessment Report [*or Review*]
PAR........... Purchasing Approval Request
PAR........... (Pyridylazo)resorcinol [*Organic chemistry*]
PARAPSYCH ... Parapsychology
PARENT.... Parenteral
PARLY ...... Parliamentary
PAROSS ... Passive/Active Reporting Ocean Surveillance System [*Navy*]
PAROX ...... Paroxysmal [*Medicine*]
PARS........ Procurement Accounting and Reporting System [*Navy*]
PAS .... Privacy Act Statement
PAS........... Progressive Accumulated Stress [*Psychiatry*]
PASGT...... Personnel Armor System for Ground Troops
PAST........ Pasteurella [*Genus of bacteria*]
PASU........ Provisional Approval for Service Use [*Navy*]
PAT .... Patna [*India*] [*Airport symbol*]
PAU........... Pauk [*Burma*] [*Airport symbol*]
PAV .... Paulo Afonso [*Brazil*] [*Airport symbol*]
PAW .... Pambwa [*Papua New Guinea*] [*Airport symbol*]
PAW .... People for the American Way [*An organization*]
PAY .... Pamol [*Malaysia*] [*Airport symbol*]
PAZ .... Poza Rica [*Mexico*] [*Airport symbol*]
PB .... Bachelor of Philosophy
PB .... Philosophiae Baccalaureus [*Bachelor of Philosophy*]
PB .... Plate Block [*Philately*]
Pb .... Presbyopia [*Ophthalmology*]
PB .... Primitive Baptist
PBA .... Physical Blowing Agent [*Plastics technology*]
PBA .... Pressure Breathing Assistor [*Medicine*]
PBAC .... Pacific Bantam Austin Club
PBB .... Paranaiba [*Brazil*] [*Airport symbol*]
PBD........... Plenum Bleed Duct [*Hovercraft*]
PBD........... Polybutadiene [*Organic chemistry*]
PBD .... Porbandar [*India*] [*Airport symbol*]

PBE .... Perlsucht Bacillen Emulsion
PBE .... Prompt Burst Experiments [*Nuclear energy*]
PBE .... Puerto Berrio [*Colombia*] [*Airport symbol*]
PBF .... Pine Bluff [*Arkansas*] [*Airport symbol*]
PBFWR..... Presiding Bishop's Fund for World Relief
PB and J.... Peanut Butter and Jelly
PBL .... Puerto Cabello [*Venezuela*] [*Airport symbol*]
PBM .... Paramaribo [*Surinam*] [*Airport symbol*]
PBM .... Peripheral Blood Mononuclear [*Cells*] [*Hematology*]
PBN .... Porto Amboin [*Angola*] [*Airport symbol*]
PBO .... Paraburdoo [*Australia*] [*Airport symbol*]
PBPE .... Population Biology/Physiological Ecology
PBS .... Pressure Boundary Subsystem [*Nuclear energy*]
PBS .... Project Breakdown Structure [*Nuclear energy*]
PBU .... Putao [*Burma*] [*Airport symbol*]
PBW .... Particle Beam Weapon
PBW .... Posterior Bite Wing [*Dentistry*]
PBZ .... Plettenberg [*South Africa*] [*Airport symbol*]
PC .... Paper Chromatography
PC .... Peripheral Control
PC .... Plug Compatible
PC .... Polar Crane [*Nuclear energy*]
PCA.......... Patriotic Catholic Association [*Name given to nationalized Catholic Church in China*]
PCA.......... Portage Creek [*Alaska*] [*Airport symbol*]
PCA.......... Principal Component Analysis
PCAS .... Primary Central Alarm Station [*Nuclear energy*]
PCB.......... Program Control Block [*Data processing*]
PCc .... Periscopic Concave [*Ophthalmology*]
PCCH....... Pentachlorocyclohexene [*Organic chemistry*]
PCD.......... Power Control Device [*Nuclear energy*]
PCDD .... Pentachlorodioxin [*Organic chemistry*]
PCF .... Parents Choice Foundation
PCF .... Pharyngoconjunctival Fever [*Medicine*]
PCGVB..... Pairwise Correlated Generalized Valence Bond [*Physics*]
PCIS......... Production Control Information System
PCL .... Permissible Contamination Limits [*Nuclear energy*]
PCL .... Pucallpa [*Peru*] [*Airport symbol*]
PCLD........ Dependent Political Entity [*Board on Geographic Names*]
PCLDI .... Prototype Closed-Loop Development Installation [*Nuclear energy*]
PCLI .... Independent Political Entity [*Board on Geographic Names*]
PCLS........ Prototype Closed-Loop System [*Nuclear energy*]
PCLT........ Prototype Closed-Loop Test [*Nuclear energy*]
PCLX........ Section of Independent Political Entity [*Board on Geographic Names*]
PCM .... Post Column Method [*Chromatography*]
PCMA....... Phenylcyclopropanemethylamine [*Organic chemistry*]
PCMC .... Para-Chloro-meta-cresol [*Organic chemistry*]
PCMS....... Production Control Monitoring System
PCON........ Para-Chloro-ortho-nitroaniline [*Organic chemistry*] [*Also, PCONA*]
PCONA ..... Para-Chloro-ortho-nitroaniline [*Organic chemistry*] [*Also, PCON*]
PCP.......... Post-Construction Permit
PCPT........ Perception
PCR.......... Puerto Carreno [*Colombia*] [*Airport symbol*]
PCR.......... Punched Card Reader [*Data processing*]
PCS.......... Preconscious
PCS.......... Print Contrast System
PCS.......... Production Control System
PCT .... Princeton [*New Jersey*] [*Airport symbol*]
PCT .... Project Control Tool
PCx .... Periscopic Convex [*Ophthalmology*]
PCX.......... Plasma Confinement Experiment [*Physics*]
PD .... Doctor of Philosophy
PD .... Ipec Aviation Pty. Ltd. [*Australia*] [*ICAO designator*]
pd .... Papilla Diameter [*Medicine*]
PD .... Parkinsonism Dementia [*Medicine*]
PD .... Pars Distalis [*Medicine*]
PD .... Partner Air Services A/S [*Norway*] [*ICAO designator*]
PD .... Pediatric [*or Pediatrics*]
PD .... Performance Demonstration
PD .... Peripheral Device
PD .... Phenyldichlorarsine [*A war gas*]
PD .... Philosophiae Doctor [*Doctor of Philosophy*]
PD .... Presidential Directive
PD .... Pressor Dose [*Medicine*]

PD .... Projected Decision Date
PD .... Protective Device
pd............ Pupillary Distance [*Medicine*]
PDA.......... Pediatric Allergy
PDA.......... Predocketed Application
PDA.......... Preliminary Design Approval [*or Authorization*]
PDA.......... Puerto Inirida [*Colombia*] [*Airport symbol*]
PDAP .... Programable Digital Autopilot
PDAR........ Preferential Arrival/Departure Route [*Aviation*]
PDC.......... Mueo [*New Caledonia*] [*Airport symbol*]
PDD.......... Prospective Decision Date
PDE .... Pandie Pandie [*Australia*] [*Airport symbol*]
PDES........ Preliminary Draft Environmental Statement
PDF .... Plant Design Factor [*Nuclear energy*]
PDG.......... Padang [*Indonesia*] [*Airport symbol*]
P-DIOL ...... Pregnanediol
PDIS......... Product Description Information Standards [*or System*]
PD/JV ...... Project Definition/Joint Validation
PDK.......... Atlanta [*Georgia*] De Kalb/Peachtree Airport [*Airport symbol*]
PDL .... Ponta Delgada [*Portugal*] [*Airport symbol*]
PDL .... Procedure Definition Language [*Data processing*]
PDO.......... Printer Direction Optimizer
PDP .... Punta Del Este [*Uruguay*] [*Airport symbol*]
PDQ.......... PDQ Air Charter, Inc. [*Pontiac, MI*] [*FAA designator*]
PDR.......... Program Design Review
PDR.......... Program Document Requirement
PDR.......... Public Document Room
PDRP........ Program Data Requirement Plan
PDS.......... Passive Detection System
PDS.......... Perimeter Defense System
PDS.......... Plasma Display
PDS.......... Portable Data System
PDS.......... Predocketed Special Project
PDS.......... Probability Distribution Subprogram [*Data processing*]
PDS.......... Program Data Source
PDS.......... Program Distribution System
PDT .... Pendleton [*Oregon*] [*Airport symbol*]
PDU.......... Paysandu [*Uruguay*] [*Airport symbol*]
PDZ.......... Pedernales [*Venezuela*] [*Airport symbol*]
Pe............ Pressure on Expiration [*Medicine*]
PE............ Proteus Engine [*Hovercraft*]
PE............ Pulmonary Embolism [*Medicine*]
PEA .... Penneshaw [*Australia*] [*Airport symbol*]
PEA .... Phenethyl Alcohol [*Organic chemistry*]
PEA .... Poly(ethyl Acrylate) [*Organic chemistry*]
PEART ...... Passive Electronic Advanced Receiver
PEB .... Propulsion Examining Board [*Navy*]
PEBAB ..... Para-(Ethoxybenzylidene)aminobenzonitrile [*Organic chemistry*] [*Also, EBCA*]
PEC .... Pelican [*Alaska*] [*Airport symbol*]
PEd .... Physical Education
PEDS........ Protective Equipment Decontamination Section [*Nuclear energy*]
PEG.......... Pneumoencephalogram [*Medicine*]
PEH .... Pehuajo [*Argentina*] [*Airport symbol*]
PEI............ Pereira [*Colombia*] [*Airport symbol*]
PEK.......... Beijing [*China*] [*Airport symbol*]
PEM .... Puerto Maldonado [*Peru*] [*Airport symbol*]
PEMS .... Propulsion Energy Management Study
PEN.......... Penang [*Malaysia*] [*Airport symbol*]
PENIC .... Penicillin
PEO.......... Patrol Emergency Officer
PEP .... Partitioned Emulation Program [*Data processing*]
PEP .... Personnel Exchange Program [*Navy*]
PEP .... Positron Electron Proton [*Physics*]
PEP .... Power Extension Plant
PEP .... Pre-Ejection Period [*Cardiology*]
PEPE........ Parallel Element Processing Ensemble
PER .... Perth [*Australia*] [*Airport symbol*]
PER .... Planning, Evaluation, and Reporting [*Education-improvement system*]
PERDEX .... Permuted Formula Index [*Molecular formula indexing*]
PERI .... Perigee
PERIAP ..... Periapical [*Dentistry*]
PERLA....... Pupils Equal, React to Light and Accommodation [*Medicine*]
PERMIC .... Personnel Management Information Center [*Navy*]

PERRLA .... Pupils Equal, Round, React to Light and Accommodation [*Medicine*]
PERT .... Pertussis [*Whooping cough*]
PERUV ...... Peruvian
PET .... Pelotas [*Brazil*] [*Airport symbol*]
PET .... Pentaerythritol Tetranitrate [*Explosive, vasodilator*] [*Also, PETN*]
PET .... Peripheral Equipment Tester
PET .... Petrine [*Of, or relating to, Peter the Apostle or Peter the Great*]
PET .... Pierre Elliott Trudeau [*Canadian prime minister*] [*Acronymic designation considered derogatory*]
PET .... Positron-Emission Tomography
PETROL .... Petroleum
PEW .... Peshawar [*Pakistan*] [*Airport symbol*]
PEWS .... Platoon Early Warning System
PF .... Page Footing
PF .... Peanut Flour
Pf .... Pfeifferella [*Genus of bacteria*]
PF .... Pulmonary Factor [*Medicine*]
PF .... Punch Off [*Data processing*]
PFA .... Para-Fluorophenylalanine [*Biochemistry*]
PFA .... Prison Families Anonymous
PFB .... Passo Fundo [*Brazil*] [*Airport symbol*]
PFCS .... Primary Flow Control System [*Nuclear energy*]
PFD .... Primary Flash Distillate [*Chemical technology*]
PFE .... Plenum Fill Experiment [*Nuclear energy*]
PFEP .... Programable Front-End Processor [*Data processing*]
PFJ .... Patreksfjordur [*Iceland*] [*Airport symbol*]
P/FM .... Pylon/Fin Movement
PFMR .... Project Funds Management Record
PFN .... Panama City [*Florida*] [*Airport symbol*]
PFO .... Patent Foramen Ovale [*Medicine*]
PFOD .... Presumed Finding of Death [*DOD*]
PFPI .... Pentafluoropropionyl Imidazole [*Organic chemistry*]
PFPM .... Production Flight Procedures Manual
PFR .... Peak Flow Rate [*or Reading*] [*Medicine*]
PFR .... Pike Fry Rhabdovirus
PFRA .... Professional Football Researchers Association
PFS .... Peripheral Fixed Shim [*Nuclear energy*]
PFT .... Page Frame Table
PFV .... Physiological Full Value
PG .... Phosphogluconate [*Biochemistry*]
PG .... Polygalacturonase [*An enzyme*]
PG .... Pregnanediol Glucuronide
PG .... Propyl Gallate [*Antioxidant*] [*Organic chemistry*]
PGA .... Page [*Arizona*] [*Airport symbol*]
P-GABA .... Phenyl-gamma-aminobutryic Acid [*Organic chemistry*]
PGCRA ...... Professional Golf Club Repairmen's Association
PGD .... Punta Gorda [*Florida*] [*Airport symbol*]
PGDB .... Propylene Glycol Dibenzoate [*Organic chemistry*]
PG & E ...... Pacific Gas and Electric [*Rock music group*]
PGF .... Perpignan [*France*] [*Airport symbol*]
PGI .... Chitato [*Angola*] [*Airport symbol*]
PGK .... Pangkalpinang [*Indonesia*] [*Airport symbol*]
PGL .... Polyglutaraldehyde [*Organic chemistry*]
PGM .... Platinum Group Metal
PGMA .... Poly(glyceryl Methacrylate) [*Organic chemistry*]
PGO .... Peroxidase-Glucose Oxidase [*Enzyme mixture*] [*Also, GOD-POD*]
PGV .... Greenville [*North Carolina*] [*Airport symbol*]
PH .... Page Heading
P of H .... Patron of Husbandry
Ph .... Pharmacopoeia
PH .... Phiala [*Bottle*] [*Pharmacy*]
Ph .... Phosphate
PH .... Probability of Hit
PharC .... Pharmaceutical Chemist [*British*]
Ph B .... Bachelor of Philosophy
Ph B .... Philosophiae Baccalaureus [*Bachelor of Philosophy*]
PHC .... Port Harcourt [*Nigeria*] [*Airport symbol*]
Ph D .... Doctor of Philosophy
Ph D .... Philosophiae Doctor [*Doctor of Philosophy*]
PHE .... Port Hedland [*Australia*] [*Airport symbol*]
PHF .... Newport News [*Virginia*] [*Airport symbol*]
PHF .... Plug Handling Fixture
Phgly .... Phenylglycine [*An amino acid*]
PHIBSKDN ... Amphibious Ship Shakedown Cruise [*Navy*]
PHIL .... Philadelphia [*Pennsylvania*]

PHIL .... Philemon [*New Testament book*]
PHIL .... Philippians [*New Testament book*]
PHILEM ..... Philemon [*New Testament book*]
PHITAR ..... Predesignated High Interest Tactical Area [*Navy*]
PHK .... Postmortem Human Kidney [*Cells*]
PHO .... Point Hope [*Alaska*] [*Airport symbol*]
PHOPT ...... Pseudohypoparathyroidism [*Endocrinology*]
PHQ .... Postal Headquarters [*British*]
PHR .... Pacific Harbour [*Fiji*] [*Airport symbol*]
PHS .... Phitsanuloke [*Thailand*] [*Airport symbol*]
PHSPS ...... Preservation, Handling, Storage, Packaging, and Shipping
PHTS .... Primary Heat Transport System [*Nuclear energy*]
PHW .... Phalaborwa [*South Africa*] [*Airport symbol*]
PHX .... Phoenix [*Arizona*] [*Airport symbol*]
PI .... Pansophic Institute
PI .... Parallel Input [*Data processing*]
P & I .... Piping and Instrumentation [*Nuclear energy*]
Pi .... Pressure of Inspiration [*Medicine*]
PI .... Program Instruction [*Data processing*]
PI .... Programed Introduction
PI .... Prolactin Inhibitor [*Endocrinology*]
PI .... Pulmonary Incompetence [*Medicine*]
PIA .... Peoria [*Illinois*] [*Airport symbol*]
PIAC .... Permanent International Altaistic Conference
PIB .... Laurel/Hattiesburg [*Mississippi*] [*Airport symbol*]
PIC .... Payload Integration Contractor
PIC .... Pine Cay [*British West Indies*] [*Airport symbol*]
PICADAD ... Place Identification/Characteristics and Area/Distance and Direction [*Bureau of Census*]
PICKFAIR ... [*Mary*] Pickford and [*Douglas*] Fairbanks [*Acronym is name of estate once owned by these early film stars*]
PICOST ..... Probability of Incurring Estimated Costs
PICS .... Productivity Improvement and Control System
P & ID .... Piping and Instrumentation Diagram [*Nuclear energy*]
PID .... Prolapsed Intervertebral Disc [*Medicine*]
PIE .... Parallel Instruction Execution [*Data processing*]
PIE .... Post-Irradiation Examination
PIE .... St. Petersburg [*Florida*] [*Airport symbol*]
PIES .... Project Independence Evaluation System [*Energy policy*]
PIF .... Personnel Identification Feature [*Navy*]
PIH .... Pocatello [*Idaho*] [*Airport symbol*]
PIK .... Glasgow [*Scotland*] Prestwick Airport [*Airport symbol*]
PILOT .... Paton Lyall Tosh [*Rock music group*]
PINS .... Political Information System [*Data bank of political strategist Richard Wirthlin*]
PIO .... Palestine Information Office
PIOCS .... Physical Input-Output Control System [*Data processing*]
PIOTA .... Post Irradiation Open Test Assembly
PIOTA .... Proximity Instrumented Open Test Assembly [*Nuclear energy*]
PIP .... Photo Interpretive Program
PIP .... Pilot Point [*Alaska*] [*Airport symbol*]
PIP .... Problem Input Preparation [*Data processing*]
PIP .... Product Improvement Proposal
PIP .... Program in Process [*Data processing*]
PIP .... Proposal Instruction Package
PIP .... Prototypic Inlet Piping [*Nuclear energy*]
PIR .... Pierre [*South Dakota*] [*Airport symbol*]
PIS .... Poitiers [*France*] [*Airport symbol*]
PISE .... No Pilot Balloon Observation Due to Unfavorable Sea Conditions [*National Weather Service*]
PIU .... Path Information Unit [*Data processing*]
PIU .... Process Input Unit [*Data processing*]
PIWI .... No Pilot Balloon Observation Due to High, or Gusty, Surface Wind [*National Weather Service*]
PL .... Pectate Lyase [*An enzyme*]
PL .... Piping Loads [*Nuclear energy*]
PL .... Portable Low-Power [*Reactor*]
PLA .... Phase Locked Arrays [*Physics*]
PLACE ...... Post-LANDSAT Advanced Concept Evaluation
PLANCODE ... Planning, Control, and Decision Evaluation System [*IBM Corp.*]
PLAT .... Plateau [*Board on Geographic Names*]
PLC .... Programable Logic Control [*Data processing*]
PLCAA ...... Professional Lawn Care Association of America
PLCLAS .... Propagation Loss Classification System [*Navy*]
PLD .... Precision LASER Designator
PLH .... Palaemontes-Lightening Hormone

PLIS .... Preclinical Literature Information System [*Data processing*]
PLNN .... Planning
PLOB .... Place of Birth
PLOCAP .... Post Loss-of-Coolant Accident Protection [*Nuclear energy*]
PLP .... Partners for Livable Places
pLRF .... Placental Luteinizing Hormone-Releasing Factor [*Endocrinology*]
PLRV .... Potato Leafroll Virus
PLT .... Photoluminescent Thermometer
PLUPF .... Pluperfect [*Grammar*]
PLX .... Plexus [*Medicine*]
PM .... Passed Midshipman
PM .... Petit Mal [*Epilepsy*]
PM .... Portable Medium-Power [*Reactor*]
PM .... Power Module
PM .... Precious Metal
PMA .... Pyridylmercuric Acetate [*Fungicide*] [*Organic chemistry*]
PMAG .... Program Manager Assistance Group [*Military*]
PMC .... Partial Mission Capable
PMC .... Pro Maria Committee
PMC .... Procurement Committee
PMC .... Programable Machine Controller
PMC .... Pseudo Machine Code [*Data processing*]
PMC .... Public Media Center
PMDP .... Project Manager Development Program [*Army*]
PMDT .... Pentamethyldiethylenetriamine [*Organic chemistry*]
PME .... Process and Manufacturing Engineering
PMF .... Probable Maximum Flood
PMG .... Polymethylgalacturonase [*An enzyme*]
PMH .... Probable Maximum Hurricane
PMHP .... Para-Menthane Hydroperoxide [*Organic chemistry*]
PMI .... Preliminary Maintenance Inspection
PMI .... Present Medical Illness
PMI .... Programable Machine Interface
PMIC .... Payload Mission Integration Contract
PMIS .... Precision Mechanisms in Sodium
PMN .... Polymorphonuclear Neutrophilic [*Hematology*]
PMNP .... Platform-Mounted Nuclear Plant
PMP .... Persistent Mentoposterior [*A fetal position*] [*Obstetrics*]
PMP .... Probable Maximum Precipitation
PMPEA ..... Professional Motion Picture Equipment Association
PMRT .... Program Management Responsibility Transfer
PMS .... Picturephone Meeting Service [*Bell System*]
PMS .... Poor Miserable Soul [*Medical slang*]
PMS .... Probable Maximum Surge [*Nuclear energy*]
PM TRADE ... Office of the Project Manager for Training Devices [*Military*]
PMX .... Packet Multiplexer
PN .... Preliminary Notification
PN .... Psychoneurologist
PNA .... Para-Nitroaniline [*Organic chemistry*]
PNA .... Peanut Agglutin
PNA .... Processing Terminal Network Architecture [*Data processing*]
PNBAS ..... ((Para-Nitrophenyl)azo)salicylic Acid [*A dye*] [*Organic chemistry*]
PNBT .... Para-Nitroblue Tetrazolium
PNC .... Penicillin
PNCB .... Para-Nitrochlorobenzene [*Organic chemistry*]
PNDO .... Partial Neglect of Differential Overlap [*Physics*]
PNed .... Pharmacopeia Nederlandsche
PNEUG ...... Pneumatic Pressure Generator
PNOA .... Para-Nitro-ortho-anisidine [*Organic chemistry*]
PNO-CI ..... Pair Natural Orbital Configuration Interaction [*Atomic physics*]
PNOT .... Para-Nitro-ortho-toluidine [*Organic chemistry*]
PNR .... Peninsula Airlines, Inc. [*Port Angeles, WA*] [*FAA designator*]
PNT .... Para-Nitrotoluene [*Organic chemistry*]
PNTOS ...... Para-Nitrotoluene-ortho-sulfonic Acid [*Organic chemistry*]
PNX .... Pneumothorax
PO .... Parallel Output [*Data processing*]
PO .... Polyolefin [*Organic chemistry*]
PO .... Procurement Objective
POA .... Phenoxyacetic Acid [*Organic chemistry*]
POA & M ... Plan of Action and Milestones

POB .... Penicillin, Oil, Beeswax [*Medicine*]
POD .... Peroxidase [*An enzyme*]
POE .... Projected Operational Environment
POEA .... Protection of Offshore Energy Assets [*Navy*]
POET .... Petty Officer Enroute Training [*Navy*]
POIS .... Prototype On-Line Instrument Systems [*Data processing*]
POL .... Pair Orthogonalized Lowdin [*Physics*]
POL .... Paul Otchakovsky-Laurens [*Publishing imprint, named for imprint editor*]
POLGEN ... Problem-Oriented Language Generator [*Data processing*]
POM .... Particulate Organic Matter [*Environmental chemistry*]
POMP .... Principal Outer Membrane Protein
POP .... Plasma Osmotic Pressure [*Medicine*]
POPAE ...... Protons on Protons and Electrons [*Physics*]
POPS .... Pyrotechnic Optical Plume Simulator
POQ .... Push Off Quickly [*i.e., Be quick about it*] [*British*]
POR .... Portuguese
POR .... Price on Request
PORSE ...... Post Overhaul Reaction Safeguard Examination [*Navy*]
PORT .... Prescriptive Objective Reference Testing [*Vocational guidance*]
POS .... Plant Operating System [*Nuclear energy*]
POS .... Polycystic Ovarian Syndrome [*Endocrinology*]
POSA .... Preliminary Operating Safety Analysis [*Nuclear energy*]
POST .... Passive Optical Scan Tracker
POT & I ..... Preoverhaul Tests and Inspections [*Navy*]
POTMC ..... Protective Outfit Toxicological Microclimate Controlled
POTS .... Preoverhaul Tests [*Navy*]
POTWS ..... Publicly Owned Treatment Works [*Environmental Protection Agency*]
POWWER ... Power of World Wide Energy Resources [*In organization name "Natural POWWER"*]
PP .... Descent through Cloud [*Procedure*] [*Aviation code*]
PP .... Page Printer
P & P .... Pride and Prejudice [*Novel by Jane Austen*]
PP .... Princess Pat's [*Princess Patricia of Connaught's Light Infantry*] [*Military unit*] [*Canada*]
PP .... Print-Punch [*Data processing*]
PP .... Producer Price
PP .... Propeller Pitch
PP & A ...... Palpation, Percussion, and Auscultation [*Medicine*]
PPA .... Phenylpropanolamine [*Organic chemistry*]
PPCH .... People-to-People Committee for the Handicapped
PPCLI .... Princess Patricia of Connaught's Light Infantry [*Military unit*] [*Canada*]
PPD .... Presidential Protective Division [*US Secret Service*]
PPDB .... Point-Positioning Data Base [*Cartography*]
PPDD .... Preliminary Project Design Description
PPF .... Plasma Protein Fraction [*Hematology*]
PPFA .... Plastic Pipe and Fittings Association
PPH .... Paid Personal Holiday
PPHOPT .... Pseudo-Pseudohypoparathyroidism [*Endocrinology*]
PPI .... Patient Package Insert [*Proposed instructional leaflet to be distributed with certain prescription drugs*]
PPIRO .... Planned Position Indicator Readout
PPL .... Peter Peregrinus Limited [*Publisher*]
PPL .... Populated Place [*Board on Geographic Names*]
PPLX .... Section of Populated Place [*Board on Geographic Names*]
PPP .... Progressive People's Party [*Liberia*]
PPP .... Purchasing Power Parity [*Economics*]
PPQ .... Abandoned Police Post [*Board on Geographic Names*]
PPR .... Polish People's Republic
PPR .... Price's Precipitation Reaction [*Medicine*]
PPRS .... Promotions and Placements Referral System
PPS .... Plant Protection System [*Nuclear energy*]
PPS .... Primary Power System
PPU .... Professional Psychics United
PPV .... Preprogramed Vehicles
P-Q .... Porphyrin-Quinone [*Photochemistry*]
PQA .... Protected Queue Area [*Data processing*]
PQAD .... Plant Quality Assurance Director [*Nuclear energy*]
PQLI .... Physical Quality of Life Index
PR .... Patient Relations [*Medicine*]
PR .... Pattern Recognition
PR .... Per
PR .... Phenol Red

PR .... Philippine Reactor
P & R .... Picture and Resume [*Theatre slang*]
PR .... Prefix
PR .... Prism
PR .... Proctologist
PR .... Program Register [*Data processing*]
PRBSG ...... Pseudo-Random Binary Sequence Generator [*Data processing*]
PRC .... Population Resource Center
PRCA .... Palamino Rabbit Co-Breeders Association
PRDDO ...... Partial Retention of Diatomic Differential Overlap [*Physics*]
PRE .... Precision Airlines [*North Springfield, VT*] [*FAA designator*]
PRE .... Processing Refabrication Experiment
PREP .... Purchasing, Receiving, and Payable System
PRF .... Partial Reinforcement [*Training*]
PRF .... Plymouth Rock Foundation
PRF .... Protein Rich Fraction [*Food analysis*]
PRIDE .... Parent Resources and Information on Drug Education [*An organization*]
PRIM & R ... Public Responsibility in Medicine and Research
PRISE .... Page Reader Input System with Editing
PRISM .... Personnel Requirements Information System Methodology
PRIZM .... Potential Rating Index by ZIP [*Zone Improvement Plan*] Market [*Advertising*]
PRM .... Process Radiation Monitor
Proc Int Congr Protozool ... Proceedings of the International Congress on Protozoology [*A publication*]
Proc Int Congr Psychother ... Proceedings of the International Congress of Psychotherapy [*A publication*]
Proc Int Hortic Congr ... Proceedings of the International Horticultural Congress [*A publication*]
Proc Int Meet Biol Stand ... Proceedings of the International Meeting of Biological Standardization [*A publication*]
Proc Int Ornithol Congr ... Proceedings. International Ornithological Congress [*A publication*]
Proc Int Pharmacol Meet ... Proceedings of the International Pharmacological Meeting [*A publication*]
Proc Int Seaweed Symp ... Proceedings of the International Seaweed Symposium [*A publication*]
Proc Int Seed Test Assoc ... Proceedings of the International Seed Testing Association [*A publication*]
Proc Int Soc Sugar Cane Technol ... Proceedings of the International Society of Sugar Cane Technologists [*A publication*]
Proc Int Water Qual Symp ... Proceedings of the International Water Quality Symposium [*A publication*]
Proc Iowa Acad Sci ... Proceedings of the Iowa Academy of Science [*A publication*]
Proc Iraqi Sci Soc ... Proceedings of the Iraqi Scientific Societies [*A publication*]
Proc Jpn Acad ... Proceedings of the Japan Academy [*A publication*]
Proc LA Acad Sci ... Proceedings of the Louisiana Academy of Sciences [*A publication*]
Proc Leucocyte Cult Conf ... Proceedings of the Leucocyte Culture Conference [*A publication*]
Proc Linn Soc Lond ... Proceedings of the Linnean Society of London [*A publication*]
Proc Linn Soc NSW ... Proceedings of the Linnean Society of New South Wales [*A publication*]
Proc Linn Soc NY ... Proceedings of the Linnean Society of New York [*A publication*]
Proc Malacol Soc Lond ... Proceedings of the Malacological Society of London [*A publication*]
Proc Microsc Soc Can ... Proceedings of the Microscopical Society of Canada [*A publication*]
Proc Minn Acad Sci ... Proceedings of the Minnesota Academy of Sciences [*A publication*]
Proc Mont Acad Sci ... Proceedings of the Montana Academy of Sciences [*A publication*]
Proc Natl Acad Sci USA ... Proceedings of the National Academy of Sciences of the United States of America [*A publication*]
Proc Natl Shellfish Assoc ... Proceedings of the National Shellfisheries Association [*A publication*]
Proc ND Acad Sci ... Proceedings of the North Dakota Academy of Sciences [*A publication*]

Proc Nebr Acad Sci Affil Soc ... Proceedings of the Nebraska Academy of Sciences and Affiliated Societies [*A publication*]
Proc NJ Mosq Control Assoc ... Proceedings of the New Jersey Mosquito Control Association [*A publication*]
Proc Northeast Weed Contr Conf ... Proceedings of the Northeastern Weed Control Conference [*A publication*]
Proc Northeast Weed Sci Soc ... Proceedings of the Northeastern Weed Science Society [*A publication*]
Proc NS Inst Sci ... Proceedings of the Nova Scotian Institute of Science [*A publication*]
Proc Nutr Soc ... Proceedings of the Nutrition Society [*A publication*]
Proc NZ Soc Anim Proc ... Proceedings of the New Zealand Society of Animal Production [*A publication*]
Proc Ohio State Hortic Soc ... Proceedings of the Ohio State Horticulture Society [*A publication*]
Proc Okla Acad Sci ... Proceedings of the Oklahoma Academy of Science [*A publication*]
Proc Oreg Acad Sci ... Proceedings of the Oregon Academy of Science [*A publication*]
Proc PA Acad Sci ... Proceedings of the Pennsylvania Academy of Science [*A publication*]
Proc Pak Acad Sci ... Proceedings of the Pakistan Academy of Sciences [*A publication*]
Proc Pak Sci Conf ... Proceedings of the Pakistan Science Conference [*A publication*]
Proc Peoria Acad Sci ... Proceedings of the Peoria Academy of Science [*A publication*]
Proc Phytochem Soc ... Proceedings of the Phytochemical Society [*A publication*]
Proc Rajasthan Acad Sci ... Proceedings of the Rajasthan Academy of Sciences [*A publication*]
Proc R Ir Acad Sect B ... Proceedings of the Royal Irish Academy. Section B [*A publication*]
Proc Rochester Acad Sci ... Proceedings of the Rochester Academy of Science [*A publication*]
Proc R Physiogr Soc Lund ... Proceedings of the Royal Physiograph Society at Lund [*A publication*]
Proc R Soc Lond B Biol Sci ... Proceedings of the Royal Society of London. Section B. Biological Sciences [*A publication*]
Proc R Soc Med ... Proceedings of the Royal Society of Medicine [*A publication*]
Proc R Soc NZ ... Proceedings of the Royal Society of New Zealand [*A publication*]
Proc R Soc Queensl ... Proceedings of the Royal Society of Queensland [*A publication*]
Proc R Zool Soc NSW ... Proceedings of the Royal Zoological Society of New South Wales [*A publication*]
Proc S Afr Soc Anim Prod ... Proceedings of the South African Society of Animal Production [*A publication*]
Proc Sci Assoc Nigeria ... Proceedings of the Science Association of Nigeria [*A publication*]
Proc Sci Sect Toilet Goods Assoc ... Proceedings of the Scientific Section of the Toilet Goods Association [*A publication*]
Proc SD Acad Sci ... Proceedings of the South Dakota Academy of Science [*A publication*]
Proc Silvic Conf ... Proceedings of the Silviculture Conference [*A publication*]
Proc Soc Am For ... Proceedings of the Society of American Foresters [*A publication*]
Proc Soc Appl Bacteriol ... Proceedings of the Society for Applied Bacteriology [*A publication*]
Proc Soc Exp Biol Med ... Proceedings of the Society for Experimental Biology and Medicine [*A publication*]
Proc Soc Ind Microbiol ... Proceedings of the Society for Industrial Microbiology [*A publication*]
Proc South For Tree Improv Conf ... Proceedings of the Southern Forest Tree Improvement Conference [*A publication*]
Proc South Weed Sci Soc ... Proceedings of the Southern Weed Science Society [*A publication*]
Proc Staff Meetings Mayo Clin ... Proceedings of the Staff Meetings of the Mayo Clinic [*A publication*]
Proc Sugar Beet Res Assoc ... Proceedings of the Sugar Beet Research Association [*A publication*]
Proc Symp Chem Physiol Pathol ... Proceedings of the Symposium on Chemical Physiology and Pathology [*A publication*]

PROCT ...... Proctology
Proc Tall Timbers Fire Ecol Conf ... Proceedings of the Tall Timbers Fire Ecology Conference [*A publication*]
Proc Tex Water Util Short Sch ... Proceedings of the Texas Water Utilities Short School [*A publication*]
Proc Trans Rhod Sci Assoc ... Proceedings and Transactions of the Rhodesia Scientific Association [*A publication*]
Proc UNESCO Conf Radioisot Sci Res ... Proceedings of the UNESCO Conference on Radioisotopes in Scientific Research [*A publication*]
PRODVAL ... Product Validation
Prog Agric Ariz ... Progressive Agriculture in Arizona [*A publication*]
Prog Allergy ... Progress in Allergy [*A publication*]
Prog At Med ... Progress in Atomic Medicine [*A publication*]
Prog Biochem Pharmacol ... Progress in Biochemical Pharmacology [*A publication*]
Prog Biol Sci Relat Dermatol ... Progress in the Biological Sciences in Relation to Dermatology [*A publication*]
Prog Bioorg Chem ... Progress in Bioorganic Chemistry [*A publication*]
Prog Biophys Biophys Chem ... Progress in Biophysics and Biophysical Chemistry [*A publication*]
Prog Biophys Mol Biol ... Progress in Biophysics and Molecular Biology [*A publication*]
Prog Bot.... Progress in Botany [*A publication*]
Prog Brain Res ... Progress in Brain Research [*A publication*]
Prog Cancer Res Ther ... Progress in Cancer Research and Therapy [*A publication*]
Prog Cardiol ... Progress in Cardiology [*A publication*]
Prog Cardiovasc Dis ... Progress in Cardiovascular Diseases [*A publication*]
Prog Chem Fats Other Lipids ... Progress in the Chemistry of Fats and Other Lipids [*A publication*]
Prog Chem Fibrinolysis Thrombolysis ... Progress in Chemical Fibrinolysis and Thrombolysis [*A publication*]
Prog Chem Toxicol ... Progress in Chemical Toxicology [*A publication*]
Prog Clin Biol Res ... Progress in Clinical and Biological Research [*A publication*]
Prog Clin Pathol ... Progress in Clinical Pathology [*A publication*]
Prog Drug Metab ... Progress in Drug Metabolism [*A publication*]
Prog Drug Res ... Progress in Drug Research [*A publication*]
Prog Explor Tuberc ... Progres de l'Exploration de la Tuberculose [*A publication*]
Prog Exp Pers Res ... Progress in Experimental Personality Research [*A publication*]
Prog Exp Tumor Res ... Progress in Experimental Tumor Research [*A publication*]
Prog Fish-Cult ... Progressive Fish-Culturist [*A publication*]
Prog Food Nutr Sci ... Progress in Food and Nutrition Science [*A publication*]
Prog Gastroenterol ... Progress in Gastroenterology [*A publication*]
Prog Hematol ... Progress in Hematology [*A publication*]
Prog Hemostasis Thromb ... Progress in Hemostasis and Thrombosis [*A publication*]
Prog Histochem Cytochem ... Progress in Histochemistry and Cytochemistry [*A publication*]
Prog Hortic ... Progressive Horticulture [*A publication*]
Prog Immunobiol Stand ... Progress in Immunobiological Standardization [*A publication*]
Prog Ind Microbiol ... Progress in Industrial Microbiology [*A publication*]
Prog Learn Disabil ... Progress in Learning Disabilities [*A publication*]
Prog Liver Dis ... Progress in Liver Diseases [*A publication*]
Prog Med ... Progres Medical [*A publication*]
Prog Med Chem ... Progress in Medicinal Chemistry [*A publication*]
Prog Med Genet ... Progress in Medical Genetics [*A publication*]
Prog Med Parasitol Jpn ... Progress in Medical Parasitology in Japan [*A publication*]
Prog Med Psychosom ... Progres en Medecine Psychosomatique [*A publication*]
Prog Med Virol ... Progress in Medical Virology [*A publication*]
Prog Mol Subcell Biol ... Progress in Molecular and Subcellular Biology [*A publication*]
Prog Neurobiol (NY) ... Progress in Neurobiology (New York) [*A publication*]
Prog Neurobiol (Oxf) ... Progress in Neurobiology (Oxford) [*A publication*]

Prog Neurol Psychiatry ... Progress in Neurology and Psychiatry [*A publication*]
Prog Neurol Surg ... Progress in Neurological Surgery [*A publication*]
Prog Neuropathol ... Progress in Neuropathology [*A publication*]
Prog Nucleic Acid Res ... Progress in Nucleic Acid Research [*A publication*]
Prog Nucleic Acid Res Mol Biol ... Progress in Nucleic Acid Research and Molecular Biology [*A publication*]
Prog Nucl Energy Ser VII Med Sci ... Progress in Nuclear Energy. Series VII. Medical Sciences [*A publication*]
Prog Nucl Med ... Progress in Nuclear Medicine [*A publication*]
Prog Obstet Gynecol ... Progres en Obstetrique et Gynecologie [*A publication*]
Prog Oceanogr ... Progress in Oceanography [*A publication*]
Prog Ophtalmol ... Progres en Ophtalmologie [*A publication*]
Prog Org Chem ... Progress in Organic Chemistry [*A publication*]
Prog Oto-Rhino-Laryncol ... Progres en Oto-Rhino-Laryncologie [*A publication*]
Prog Pediatr Pueric ... Progresos de Pediatria y Puericultura [*A publication*]
Prog Pediatr Surg ... Progress in Pediatric Surgery [*A publication*]
Prog Physiol Psychol ... Progress in Physiological Psychology [*A publication*]
Prog Phytochem ... Progress in Phytochemistry [*A publication*]
Prog Psychobiol Physiol Psychol ... Progress in Psychobiology and Physiological Psychology [*A publication*]
Prog React Kinet ... Progress in Reaction Kinetics [*A publication*]
Prog Rech Cancer ... Progres dans les Recherches sur le Cancer [*A publication*]
Prog Rech Exp Tumeurs ... Progres de la Recherche Experimentale des Tumeurs [*A publication*]
Prog Rech Pharm ... Progres des Recherches Pharmaceutiques [*A publication*]
Prog Reprod Biol ... Progress in Reproductive Biology [*A publication*]
Prog Respir Res ... Progress in Respiration Research [*A publication*]
Prog Sep Purif ... Progress in Separation and Purification [*A publication*]
Prog Surf Membr Sci ... Progress in Surface and Membrane Science [*A publication*]
Prog Theor Biol ... Progress in Theoretical Biology [*A publication*]
Prog Virol Med ... Progres en Virologie Medicale [*A publication*]
Prog Water Technol ... Progress in Water Technology [*A publication*]
PROMPT ... Production, Reviewing, Organizing, and Monitoring of Performance Techniques
PRON .... Pronation
PROP .... Performance Review for Operating Programs
PROPH ...... Prophylactic
PROPLOSS ... Propagation Loss
PROS .... Prostrate
Pro Soc Water Treat Exam ... Proceedings of the Society for Water Treatment and Examination [*A publication*]
PROSTH .... Prosthesis
PROT .... Protein
Protein Synth Ser Adv ... Protein Syntheses. A Series of Advances [*A publication*]
PROTHROM ... Prothrombin [*Hematology*]
Protok Fischereitech ... Protokolle zur Fischereitechnik [*A publication*]
Prot Vitae ... Protectio Vitae [*A publication*]
Proyecto Desarrollo Pesq Publ ... Proyecto de Desarrollo Pesquero. Publicacion [*A publication*]
PRP .... Prepare
PRR .... Passenger Reservation Request
PRR .... Puerto Rico Reactor
PR-RSV ..... Rous Sarcoma Virus, Prague Strain
PRS .... Process Radiation Sampler
PRSNT ...... Present
Pr Statneho Geol Ustavu (Bratisl) ... Prace Statneho Geologickeho Ustavu (Bratislava) [*A publication*]
PRT .... Prompt Relief Trip
PRTM .... Printing Response-Time Monitor
PRTRNS.... Programable Transformer Converter
Przegl Antropol ... Przeglad Antropologiczny [*A publication*]
Przegl Dermatol ... Przeglad Dermatologiczny [*A publication*]
Przegl Epidemiol ... Przeglad Epidemiologiczny [*A publication*]
Przegl Lek ... Przeglad Lekarski [*A publication*]
Przem Ferment Rolny ... Przemysl Fermentacyjny i Rolny [*A publication*]
PS .... Physical Status [*Medicine*]

PSA .... Professional Stringers Association
PSB .... Philatelic Sales Branch [*US Postal Service*]
PSBT .... Pilot Self-Briefing Terminal
PSD .... Photon Stimulated Desorption [*For analysis of surfaces*]
PSD .... Power Spectral Density
PSD .... Pressure-Sensitive Devices
PSDA .... Partial Source Data Automation
PSDD .... Preliminary System Design Description
PSE .... Packet-Switching Exchange
PSEBM ...... Proceedings of the Society for Experimental Biology and Medicine [*A publication*]
PSES .... Pretreatment Standards for Existing Sources [*Environmental Protection Agency*]
PSF .... Passive Solar Foundation
PSG .... Pacific Seabird Group
PSG .... Parachute Study Group
PSI .... Pollutant Standards Index
PSI .... Programed School Input
PSI .... Project Starlight International
PSIC .... Production Scheduling and Inventory Control
PSID .... Preliminary Safety Information Document [*Nuclear energy*]
PSIR Bull Monogr ... PSIR [*Pakistan Council of Scientific and Industrial Research*] Bulletin Monograph [*A publication*]
PSISIG ...... Psychic Science International Special Interest Group
PSK .... Program Selection Key [*Data processing*]
PSM .... Past Savio Movement
PSMA .... Pyrotechnic Signal Manufacturers Association
PSN .... Public Switched Network
PSNS .... Pretreatment Standards for New Indirect Sources [*Environmental Protection Agency*]
PSO .... Polysulfone [*Organic chemistry*] [*Also, PS*]
PSP .... Primary Sodium Pump [*Nuclear energy*]
PSPGV ...... Primary Sodium Pump Guard Vessel [*Nuclear energy*]
PSR .... Pennsylvania State University Reactor
PSR .... Peripheral Shim Rods [*Nuclear energy*]
PSR .... Procurement Status Report
PST .... Primary Surge Tank [*Nuclear energy*]
PSTF .... Proximity Sensor Test Facility [*Nuclear energy*]
PSTF .... Pump Seal Test Facility [*Nuclear energy*]
PSTM .... Persistent Standoff Target Marker
PSV .... Psychological, Social, and Vocational [*Adjustment factors*]
Psychiatr Ann ... Psychiatric Annals [*A publication*]
Psychiatr Clin ... Psychiatria Clinica [*A publication*]
Psychiatr Fenn ... Psychiatria Fennica [*A publication*]
Psychiatr J Univ Ottawa ... Psychiatric Journal of the University of Ottawa [*A publication*]
Psychiatr Neurol ... Psychiatria et Neurologia [*A publication*]
Psychiatr Neurol Jpn ... Psychiatria et Neurologia Japonica [*A publication*]
Psychiatr Neurol Med Psychol ... Psychiatrie Neurologie und Medizinische Psychologie [*A publication*]
Psychiatr Neurol Neurochir ... Psychiatria Neurologia Neurochirurgia [*A publication*]
Psychiatr Pol ... Psychiatria Polska [*A publication*]
Psychiatr Prax ... Psychiatrische Praxis [*A publication*]
Psychiatr Q ... Psychiatric Quarterly [*A publication*]
Psychiatr Res Rep ... Psychiatric Research Reports [*A publication*]
Psychiatr Soc ... Psychiatrie Sociale [*A publication*]
Psychiatry Med ... Psychiatry in Medicine [*A publication*]
Psychoanal Rev ... Psychoanalytic Review [*A publication*]
Psychoanal Study Child ... Psychoanalytic Study of the Child [*A publication*]
Psychoanal Study Child Monogr Ser ... Psychoanalytic Study of the Child. Monograph Series [*A publication*]
Psychol Afr Monogr Suppl ... Psychologie Africana. Monograph and Supplement [*A publication*]
Psychol Beitr ... Psychologische Beitraege [*A publication*]
Psychol Belg ... Psychologica Belgica [*A publication*]
Psychol Bull ... Psychological Bulletin [*A publication*]
Psychol Can ... Psychologie Canadienne [*A publication*]
Psychol Forsch ... Psychologische Forschung [*A publication*]
Psychol Issues Monogr ... Psychological Issues Monographs [*A publication*]
Psychol Med ... Psychologie Medicale [*A publication*]
Psychol Monogr (Gen Appl) ... Psychological Monographs (General and Applied) [*A publication*]

Psychol Prax ... Psychologische Praxis [*A publication*]
Psychopathol Afr ... Psychopathologie Africaine [*A publication*]
Psychopathol Pict Expression ... Psychopathology and Pictorial Expression [*A publication*]
Psychopharmacol Bull ... Psychopharmacology Bulletin [*A publication*]
Psychopharmacol Commun ... Psychopharmacology Communications [*A publication*]
Psychopharmacol Suppl Encephale ... Psychopharmacologie. Supplement de l'Encephale [*A publication*]
Psychosom Med ... Psychosomatic Medicine [*A publication*]
Psychother Psychosom ... Psychotherapy and Psychosomatics [*A publication*]
Psychother Theory Res Pract ... Psychotherapy Theory Research and Practice [*A publication*]
PsyD .... Doctor of Psychology
PT .... Penetrant Test
P-T .... Plasma Thermocouple Reactor [*Nuclear energy*]
PT .... Plastics Technology [*A publication*]
PTA .... Percutaneous Transluminal Angioplasty [*Medicine*]
PTA .... Phosphotransacetylase [*An enzyme*]
PTA .... Point of Total Assumption
PTA .... Purchase Transaction Analysis
PTC .... Phase Transfer Catalysis [*Physical chemistry*]
PTC .... Programed Transmission Control
PTC .... Prothrombin Complex [*Hematology*]
PTCP .... Positive Turnaround Control Point
PTDU .... Pointing and Tracking Demonstration Unit
PTH .... Peak Tanning Hours [*Supposedly occurring between 10am and 2pm*] [*See also BROTS and SROTS*]
PTI .... Plugging Temperature Indicator [*Nuclear energy*]
PTMS .... Para-Toluidine-meta-sulfonic Acid [*Organic chemistry*] [*Also, PTMSA*]
PTMSA ...... Para-Toluidine-meta-sulfonic Acid [*Organic chemistry*] [*Also, PTMS*]
PTP .... Proximity Test Plug [*Nuclear energy*]
PTR .... Professional Tennis Registry, USA
PTS .... People's Translation Service
PTS .... Photothermal Spectroscopy
PTSD .... Post-Traumatic Stress Disorder [*Psychiatry*]
PT/SP .... Pressure Tube to Spool Piece [*Nuclear energy*]
PTV .... Prototype Test Vehicle
P-TWP .... Post-Township
PU .... Participating Unit
PUB .... Publisher
Pubbl Stn Zool Napoli ... Pubblicazioni della Stazione Zoologica di Napoli [*A publication*]
Publ Am Inst Biol Sci ... Publication. American Institute of Biological Sciences [*A publication*]
Publ Avulsas Mus Nac (Rio De J) ... Publicacoes Avulsas do Museu Nacional (Rio De Janeiro) [*A publication*]
Publ Cent Estud Entomol Univ Chile ... Publicaciones del Centro de Estudios Entomologicos. Universidad de Chile [*A publication*]
Publ Cent Estud Leprol ... Publicacoes do Centro de Estudos Leprologicos [*A publication*]
Publ Cent Natl Geol Houillere ... Publication du Centre National de Geologie Houillere [*A publication*]
Publ Cent Stud Citogenet Veg CNR ... Pubblicazioni del Centro di Studio per la Citogenetica Vegetale del Consiglio Nazionale delle Richerche [*A publication*]
Publ Cult Cia Diamantes Angola ... Publicacoes Culturais da Companhia de Diamantes Angola [*A publication*]
Publ Diverses Mus Natl Hist Nat ... Publications diverses du Museum National d'Histoire Naturelle [*A publication*]
Publ Fac Agron Univ Teheran ... Publications de la Faculte d'Agronomie. Universite de Teheran [*A publication*]
Publ Gulf Coast Res Lab Mus ... Publications of the Gulf Coast Research Laboratory Museum [*A publication*]
Publ Health Lab ... Public Health Laboratory [*A publication*]
Public Health Eng Abstr ... Public Health Engineering Abstracts [*A publication*]
Public Health Monogr ... Public Health Monograph [*A publication*]
Public Health Rep ... Public Health Reports [*A publication*]
Public Health Rev ... Public Health Reviews [*A publication*]
Publ Inst Antart Argent (B Aires) ... Publicacion del Instituto Antartico Argentino (Buenos Aires) [*A publication*]
Publ Inst Biol Apl Barc ... Publicaciones del Instituto de Biologia Aplicada Barcelona [*A publication*]

Publ Inst Mar Sci Univ Tex ... Publications of the Institute of Marine Science. University of Texas [*A publication*]

Publ Inst Pesqui Mar ... Publicacao do Instituto de Pesquisas da Marinha [*A publication*]

Publ Inst Suflos Agrotec (B Aires) ... Publicacion del Instituto de Suflos y Agrotecnia (Buenos Aires) [*A publication*]

Publ Inst Zootec (Rio De J) ... Publicacao do Instituto de Zootecnia (Rio De Janeiro) [*A publication*]

Publ Mar Biol Stn Al Ghardaqa ... Publications of the Marine Biological Station. Al Ghardaqa [*A publication*]

Publ Mar Lab Busan Fish Coll ... Publications of the Marine Laboratory. Busan Fisheries College [*A publication*]

Publ Mus Mich State Univ Biol Ser ... Publications of the Museum. Michigan State University Biological Series [*A publication*]

Publ Natuurhist Genoot Limburg ... Publicaties van het Natuurhistorisch Genootschap in Limburg [*A publication*]

Publ S Afr Inst Med Res ... Publications of the South African Institute for Medical Research [*A publication*]

Publ Serv Geol Luxemb ... Publications du Service Geologique de Luxembourg [*A publication*]

Publ Serv Piscic Ser I-C ... Publicacao Servico de Piscicultura. Serie I-C [*A publication*]

Publ SETO Mar Biol Lab ... Publications of SETO Marine Biological Laboratory [*A publication*]

Publ Tec Inst Patol Veg (B Aires) ... Publicacion Tecnica. Instituto de Patologia Vegetal (Buenos Aires) [*A publication*]

Publ Univ Joensuu Ser B-II ... Publications of the University of Joensuu. Series B-II [*A publication*]

PUBS .... Publications

Pudoc Annu Rep ... Pudoc Annual Report [*A publication*]

PUM .... Prepare a New Perforated Tape for Message [*Communications*]

Punjab Med J ... Punjab Medical Journal [*A publication*]

Punjabrao Krishi Vidyapeeth Res J ... Punjabrao Krishi Vidyapeeth Research Journal [*A publication*]

PUO .... Placed under Observation [*Medicine*]

PUP .... Plutonium Utilization Program

PV .... [*The*] People's Voice [*Pre-World War II publication of Adam Clayton Powell, Jr., and Charlie Buchanan*]

PV .... Playback Verifier

PV .... Private Varnish [*Privately owned railroad cars*]

PVAE .... Poly(vinyl Acetate) [*Organic chemistry*]

PVD .... Protective Vehicle Division [*US Secret Service*]

PVF .... Peripheral Visual Field [*Optics*]

P-V Seances Soc Sci Phys Nat Bord ... Proces-Verbaux des Seances de la Societe des Sciences Physiques et Naturelles de Bordeaux [*A publication*]

PVT .... Product Verification Test

PVTI .... Piping and Valve Test Insert [*Nuclear energy*]

PW .... Prime Western [*Zinc*]

PWA .... Performance Warehouse Association

PWM .... Planar Wing Module

PWU .... Political World Union

PYRS .... Pyramids [*Board on Geographic Names*]

Q

QAC .... Quadrant Aimable Charge Warhead
QAC .... Quality Assurance Checklist
QAI .... Quality Assurance Instruction
QAPI .... Quality Assurance Program Index
QAPP .... Quality Assurance Program Plan
QAR .... Quality Assurance Requirements
Q-BOP ...... Quick Basic Oxygen Process [*Steelmaking*]
QC .... Quality Circle [*Labor-management team organized to increase industrial productivity*]
QCDPA ..... Quality Chekd Dairy Products Association
QCE .... Quality Control and Evaluation
QDM .... Magnetic Heading (Zero Wind) [*Aviation code*]
QDMBPT ... Quasi-Degenerate Many-Body Perturbation Theory [*Physics*]
QDR .... Magnetic Bearing [*Aviation code*]
QF .... Quality Form
QFE .... Atmospheric Pressure at Aerodrome Elevation [*or Runway Threshold*] [*Aviation code*]

QFR .... Quarterly Force Revision [*Military*]
QFU .... Magnetic Orientation of Runway [*Aviation code*]
QHR .... Quality History Records
QND .... Quantum Nondemolition [*Method of measurement*]
QNH .... Altimeter Subscale Setting to Obtain Elevation When on the Ground [*Aviation code*]
QP .... Quadratic Programing [*Data processing*]
QPM .... Quality Program Manager
QRS .... Quantum Readout System [*Method of measurement*]
QSI .... Quality Service Indicator
QSR .... Quarterly Statistical Report
QT .... Questioned Trade [*on a stock exchange*]
QTE .... True Bearing [*Aviation code*]
QTP .... Quality Test Plan
QU .... Uganda Airlines Corp. [*ICAO designator*]
QW .... Inter-Island Air Services Ltd. [*Great Britain*] [*ICAO designator*]
QWL .... Quality of Work Life

R

RA .... Radio Antenna
RA .... Ready Alert [*Navy*]
RABVAL.... RADAR Bomb Evaluation
RAC........... Radiometric Area Correlator
RAC........... Repair, Alignment, and Calibration
RACD .... Royal Army Clothing Department [*British*]
RACS .... Recruit Allocation Control System [*Navy*]
RACT .... Reasonable Available Control Technology
        [*Environmental Protection Agency*]
RAD........... Random Access Data
RAD........... Random Access Device
RAD........... Rapid Access Drive
RADC .... RADAR Countermeasures and Deception [*Military*]
RADREF.... RADAR Refraction
RADS .... Radiation and Dosimetry Services
RAF .... Racial Awareness Facilitator [*School*] [*Navy*]
RAG........... Ragged
RAID.......... River Assault Interdiction Division [*Navy*]
RAIP.......... Requester's Approval in Principle
RAIS.......... Reflection-Absorption Infrared Spectroscopy
RALSA .... Restraint and Lifesupport Assembly
RAM .... Repeater Amplitude Modulation
RAMC .... Rats after Mouldy Cheese [*Facetious translation of Royal Army Medical Corps initialism*] [*British*] [*World War I*]
RAMC .... Rob All My Comrades [*Facetious translation of Royal Army Medical Corps initialism*] [*British*] [*World War I*]
RAMC .... Run Away, Matron's Coming! [*Facetious translation of Royal Army Medical Corps Initialism*] [*British*] [*World War I*]
RAMPART ... Route to Airlift Mobility through Partnership
RAMS........ Remotely Accessible Management Systems [*Data processing*]
RAPCC...... RADAR Approach Control Center
RAPS........ RADAR Absorbing Primary Structure
RAPS........ Radioactive Argon Processing System
RAR........... Request RADAR Blip Identification Message [*Communications*]
RARE......... Roadless Area Resource Evaluation
RAREF ...... Radiation and Repair Engineering Facility
RAS........... RADAR Augmentation System
RAS........... Reactor Analysis and Safety [*Nuclear energy*]
RASS .... Ruggedized Airborne Seeker Simulator
RASSW ..... Radical Alliance of Social Service Workers
RAV........... Cravo Norte [*Colombia*] [*Airport symbol*]
RAW .... Rifleman's Assault Weapon
RAW .... Rural American Women [*An organization*]
RAX........... Rosenbalm Aviation, Inc. [*Ypsilanti, MI*] [*FAA designator*]
RBA........... Rabat [*Morocco*] [*Airport symbol*]
RBI .... Rabi [*Fiji*] [*Airport symbol*]
RBJ .... Rebun [*Japan*] [*Airport symbol*]
RBM........... Rod-Block Monitor [*Nuclear energy*]
RBP........... Raba Raba [*Papua New Guinea*] [*Airport symbol*]
RBQ........... Rurrenabaque [*Bolivia*] [*Airport symbol*]
RBR........... Rio Branco [*Brazil*] [*Airport symbol*]
RBS........... Rutherford Backscattering [*For study of surfaces*]
RBT .... Rational Behavior Therapy
RBTA......... Road Builders Training Association
RBY........... Ruby [*Alaska*] [*Airport symbol*]

RC .... Rear Commodore [*Navy*]
RC .... Relay Computer
RC .... Republic Airlines, Inc. [*ICAO designator*]
RC .... Rescriptum [*Counterpart*] [*Latin*]
RCA........... RADAR Controlled Approach
RCA........... Radiological Control Area
RCA........... Rate Change Authorization
RCAC........ Radio Corporation of America Communications
RCAC........ Remote Computer Access Communications Service
RCB........... Reactor Containment Building [*Nuclear energy*]
RCB........... Region Control Block [*Data processing*]
RCB........... Richards Bay [*South Africa*] [*Airport symbol*]
RCC .... Radiochemical Centre [*United Kingdom*]
RCC .... Relative Casein Content [*Food analysis*]
RCC .... Rod Cluster Control [*Nuclear energy*]
RCC/MG... Range Commanders Council Meteorological Group [*White Sands Missile Range*]
RCD........... Receiver-Carrier Detector
RCGM .... Reactor Cover Gas Monitor [*Nuclear energy*]
RCH........... Riohacha [*Colombia*] [*Airport symbol*]
RCIC.......... Reactor Core Isolation Cooling [*Nuclear energy*]
RCL........... Redcliff [*Vanuata*] [*Airport symbol*]
RCM........... Richmond [*Australia*] [*Airport symbol*]
RCN........... Air Ventures, Inc. [*Madison, CT*] [*FAA designator*]
RCP........... Radiological Control Program
RCPB......... Reactor Coolant Pressure Boundary [*Nuclear energy*]
RCQ .... Reconquista [*Argentina*] [*Airport symbol*]
RCS........... Reactor Coolant System [*Nuclear energy*]
RCS........... Remote Computing Service
RCS........... Request for Consultation Service
RCT........... Region Control Task [*Data processing*]
RCT........... Remote Control [*Systems*]
RCT........... Rework/Completion Tag
RCU........... Rio Cuarto [*Argentina*] [*Airport symbol*]
RCV........... Reversed Circular Vection [*Optics*]
RD .... Rear Door
RDC........... Remote Data Concentrator
RDD........... Redding [*California*] [*Airport symbol*]
RDDM........ Reactor Deck Development Mockup [*Nuclear energy*]
RDF........... Record Definition Field [*Data processing*]
RDG .... Reading [*Pennsylvania*] [*Airport symbol*]
RDM .... Redmond [*Oregon*] [*Airport symbol*]
RDP........... Reactor Development Program [*Nuclear energy*]
RDSS .... Rapid Deployable Surveillance Systems [*Military*]
RDT........... Richard-Toll [*Senegal*] [*Airport symbol*]
RDV........... Recoverable Drop Vehicle
RDV........... Red Devil [*Alaska*] [*Airport symbol*]
RDWND..... RADAR Dome Wind [*Meteorology*]
RDZ........... Rodez [*France*] [*Airport symbol*]
RE .... Risk Exercise
REARM ..... Underway Rearming [*Navy*]
REC........... Recife [*Brazil*] [*Airport symbol*]
REC........... Recorder
REC........... Recurring
REC........... Regional Evaluation Center
RECO .... Remote Command and Control
RECON ..... Resources Conservation
RECSAT.... Reconnaissance Satellite
RECT......... Rector

REES........ Reactive Electronic Equipment Simulator
REF .... Reformation
REG.......... Reggio Calabria [*Italy*] [*Airport symbol*]
REGAL ...... Remotely Guided Autonomous Lightweight Torpedo
REK .... Reykjavik [*Iceland*] [*Airport symbol*]
REL .... Radiation Evaluation Loops
REL .... Trelew [*Argentina*] [*Airport symbol*]
REM .... C & M Aviation, Inc. [*Inyokern, CA*] [*FAA designator*]
REMIS ...... Real Estate Management Information System
REP .... Reporter
REP .... Research Project
REQSTD ... Requested
RES .... Resistencia [*Argentina*] [*Airport symbol*]
RESAR ...... Reference Safety Analysis Report [*Nuclear energy*]
RET .... Ring Emitter Transistor
RET .... Rost [*Norway*] [*Airport symbol*]
RETO .... Review of Education and Training for Officers
REU .... Reus [*Spain*] [*Airport symbol*]
REX .... Reynosa [*Mexico*] [*Airport symbol*]
REY .... Reyes [*Bolivia*] [*Airport symbol*]
RFD .... Rockford [*Illinois*] [*Airport symbol*]
RFF .... Ready for Ferry [*Navy*]
RFF .... Remote Fiber Fluorometer [*Instrumentation*]
RFN .... Raufarhofn [*Iceland*] [*Airport symbol*]
RFNCC ...... Regional Nuclear Fuel Cycle Centers
RFP .... Raiatea [*French Polynesia*] [*Airport symbol*]
RFR .... Rio Frio [*Costa Rica*] [*Airport symbol*]
RG .... Regulatory Guide
RGA.......... Rio Grande [*Argentina*] [*Airport symbol*]
RGE.......... Porgera [*Papua New Guinea*] [*Airport symbol*]
RGI .... Rangiroa [*French Polynesia*] [*Airport symbol*]
RGL .... Rio Gallegos [*Argentina*] [*Airport symbol*]
RGN .... Rangoon [*Burma*] [*Airport symbol*]
RGT.......... Rengat [*Indonesia*] [*Airport symbol*]
RH .... Report Heading
RH .... Request-Response Header [*Data processing*]
RHA.......... Reykholar [*Iceland*] [*Airport symbol*]
RHA.......... Rose Hybridizers Association
RHE.......... Reims [*France*] [*Airport symbol*]
RHI .... Rhinelander [*Wisconsin*] [*Airport symbol*]
RHO.......... Rhodes Island [*Greece*] [*Airport symbol*]
RHR.......... Residual Heat Removal [*Nuclear energy*]
RHRP........ Residual Heat Removal Pump [*Nuclear energy*]
RHS.......... Rectangular Hollow Section [*Metal industry*]
RHTS........ Reactor Heat Transport System [*Nuclear energy*]
R & I.......... Radical and Intense [*Extremely great*] [*Slang*]
RI............... Radio Inertial
RI............... Radio Interference
RI............... Range Instrumentation
RI............... Refugees International [*An organization*]
R & I.......... Removal and Installation
RIA .... Reactivity Initiated Accident [*Nuclear energy*]
RIA .... Removable Instrument Assembly [*Nuclear energy*]
RIA .... Santa Maria [*Brazil*] [*Airport symbol*]
RIB .... Riberalta [*Bolivia*] [*Airport symbol*]
RIC .... Reconstructed Ion Chromatogram
RIDP........ RADAR-IFF Data Processor
RIDS........ Range Information Display System
RIDS........ Receiving Inspection Data Status [*Report*]
RIE .... Rice Lake [*Wisconsin*] [*Airport symbol*]
RIEI .... Roofing Industry Educational Institute
RIF............ Rate Input Form
RIG .... Rio Grande [*Brazil*] [*Airport symbol*]
RII............ Receiving Inspection Instructions
RIIES .... Research Institute on Immigration and Ethnic Studies
      [*Smithsonian Institution*]
RIJ............ Rioja [*Peru*] [*Airport symbol*]
RIN .... Ringi Cove [*Solomon Islands*] [*Airport symbol*]
RIO .... Rio De Janeiro [*Brazil*] [*Airport symbol*]
RIP .... Receiving Inspection Plan
RIP .... Report on Individual Personnel
RIR .... RADAR Interface Recorder
RIRMS...... Remote Information Retrieval and Management System
RIS .... Reblooming Iris Society
RIS .... Retail Information System
RIS .... Rishiri [*Japan*] [*Airport symbol*]
RIT .... Rate of Information Throughput [*Data processing*]
RIT .... Relative Ignition Temperature
RIW .... Riverton [*Wyoming*] [*Airport symbol*]

RIX .... Riga [*USSR*] [*Airport symbol*]
RJB .... Rajbiraj [*Nepal*] [*Airport symbol*]
RJETS....... Remote Job Entry Terminal System [*Data processing*]
RJK .... Rijeka [*Yugoslavia*] [*Airport symbol*]
RJT........... Rejection Message [*Communications*]
RKD......... Rockland [*Maine*] [*Airport symbol*]
RKS......... Rock Springs [*Wyoming*] [*Airport symbol*]
RKT.......... Ras Al Khaymah [*United Arab Emirates*] [*Airport symbol*]
RKU......... Yule Island [*Papua New Guinea*] [*Airport symbol*]
RKY......... Rokeby [*Australia*] [*Airport symbol*]
RL............ Reactor Licensing [*Nuclear energy*]
RL............ Ring Level
RLC .... Report Landing Completed [*Aviation*]
RLD .... Richland [*Washington*] [*Airport symbol*]
RLD .... Run Length Discriminator
RLI .... Right/Left Indicator
RLIN .... Research Libraries Information Network [*Formerly,*
      BALLOTS]
RLOP........ Reactor Licensing Operating Procedure [*Nuclear energy*]
RLP .... Rosella Plains [*Australia*] [*Airport symbol*]
RLSA........ Republican Law Students Association of New York
RLSD........ Received Line Signal Detector
RLW .... Real West Airlines [*Fargo, ND*] [*FAA designator*]
RM............ Record Mark
RMA .... Roma [*Australia*] [*Airport symbol*]
RMAAS ..... Reactivity Monitoring and Alarm System [*Nuclear*
      energy]
RM & C...... Reactor Monitoring and Control [*Nuclear energy*]
RMC .... Reduced Material Condition
RMG .... Rome [*Georgia*] [*Airport symbol*]
RMK .... Renmark [*Australia*] [*Airport symbol*]
RML.......... Remote Measurements Laboratory
RMP .... Rampart [*Alaska*] [*Airport symbol*]
RMP .... Range Maintenance Plan
RMRS....... Remote Meter Resetting System [*Postage meter*]
RMS .... Regulatory Manpower System
RMS .... Regulatory Monitoring System
RMS .... Rheometrics Mechanical Spectrometer
RMS .... Root Mean Square
RMSS....... Range Meteorological Sounding System
RMT .... Resource Management Team
RMTH....... River Mouth [*Board on Geographic Names*]
RNAS .... Really Not a Sailor [*Facetious translation of Royal Naval*
      Air Service initialism] [*British*] [*World War I*]
RNB.......... Ronneby [*Sweden*] [*Airport symbol*]
RNE.......... Roanne [*France*] [*Airport symbol*]
RNJ .... Yoron-Jima [*Japan*] [*Airport symbol*]
RNL .... Rennell Island [*Solomon Islands*] [*Airport symbol*]
RNN.......... Ronne [*Denmark*] [*Airport symbol*]
RNO .... Reno [*Nevada*] [*Airport symbol*]
RNR.......... Robinson River [*Papua New Guinea*] [*Airport symbol*]
RNS.......... Rennes [*France*] [*Airport symbol*]
RNU.......... Ranau [*Malaysia*] [*Airport symbol*]
RO .... Reportable Occurrence [*Nuclear energy*]
Ro.............. Rhodium [*Chemical element*] [*Correct symbol is Rh*]
ROB.......... Monrovia [*Liberia*] Roberts International Airport [*Airport*
      symbol]
ROC .... Rochester [*New York*] [*Airport symbol*]
ROCC........ Range Operations Control Center
ROCK....... Rocket
ROD .... Release Order Directive [*Later, ERO*]
ROH.......... Robinhood [*Australia*] [*Airport symbol*]
ROJ .... Range of Jamming
ROK .... Rockhampton [*Australia*] [*Airport symbol*]
ROM .... Romans [*New Testament book*]
ROM ...... Rome [*Italy*] [*Airport symbol*]
ROMAC..... Range Operations Monitor Analysis Center
RON .... Rondon [*Colombia*] [*Airport symbol*]
RONA....... Return on Net Assets
ROO .... Rondonopolis [*Brazil*] [*Airport symbol*]
ROP........ Record of Purchase
ROP........ Rota [*Mariana Islands*] [*Airport symbol*]
ROR.......... Koror [*Palau Islands*] [*Airport symbol*]
ROR.......... Rate of Return
ROS.......... Rosario [*Argentina*] [*Airport symbol*]
ROSAT..... RADAR Ocean Surveillance Satellite
ROT.......... Rotorua [*New Zealand*] [*Airport symbol*]
ROU.......... Russe [*Bulgaria*] [*Airport symbol*]
ROV.......... Rostov [*USSR*] [*Airport symbol*]

ROW .... Roswell [*New Mexico*] [*Airport symbol*]
ROWPU ..... Reverse Osmosis Water Purification Unit [*Army*]
ROY .... Rio Mayo [*Argentina*] [*Airport symbol*]
RP .... Remote Printer
RPC .... Refugee Processing Center
RPC .... Registered Protective Circuit
RPCS .... Reactor Plant Control System [*Nuclear energy*]
RPD .... Reactor Plant Designer [*Nuclear energy*]
RPD .... Retired Pay Defense
RPE .... Resource Planning and Evaluation
RP HPLC ... Reversed-Phase High-Performance Chromatography
RPI .... Retail Prices Index
RPI .... Rod Position Indicator [*Nuclear energy*]
RPIE .... Replacement of Photography Imagery Equipment
RPL .... Repetitive Flight Plan [*Aviation*]
RPL .... Request Parameter List [*Data processing*]
RPM .... Relaxation Potential Model [*Physics*]
RPN .... Rosh-Pina [*Israel*] [*Airport symbol*]
RPPI .... Remote Plan Position Indicator
RPR .... Raipur [*India*] [*Airport symbol*]
RPS .... Reactor Protection Systems [*Nuclear energy*]
RPS .... Regulatory Performance Summary [*Report*] [*Nuclear energy*]
RPS .... Remote Processing Service
RPSA .... Rudder Pedal Sensor Assembly
RPT .... Recirculation Pump Trip [*Nuclear energy*]
RPV .... Reactor Pressure Vessel [*Nuclear energy*]
RR .... RADAR Range Station
RR .... Religious Roundtable [*An organization*]
RRDU .... Recreation Research Demonstration Unit
RRE .... Marree [*Australia*] [*Airport symbol*]
R & RE ...... Radiation and Repair Engineering [*Nuclear energy*]
RRG .... Requirements Review Group [*Air Staff*] [*Air Force*]
RRG .... Rodrigues Island [*Mauritius*] [*Airport symbol*]
RRIM .... Reinforced Reaction Injection Molding [*Plastics technology*]
RRP .... Reactor Refueling Plug [*Nuclear energy*]
RRPI .... Relative Rod Position Indication [*Nuclear energy*]
RRPI .... Rotary Relative Position Indicator [*Nuclear energy*]
RRR .... Rum, Romanism, and Rebellion [*Phrase coined during the Presidential campaign of 1884 to describe the Democratic party*]
RRS .... Reactor Refueling System [*Nuclear energy*]
RRS .... Readiness Reportable Status
RRS .... Roros [*Norway*] [*Airport symbol*]
RS .... RADAR Scanner
RS .... RADAR Selector
RS .... Reader Stop [*Data processing*]
RS .... Reconstitution Site
RS .... Relocation Site
RS .... Responsus [*To Answer*] [*Latin*]
RS .... Rocket System
RSA .... Royal Society of Antiquaries
RSA .... Santa Rosa [*Argentina*] [*Airport symbol*]
RSB .... Reactor Service Building [*Nuclear energy*]
RSB .... Roseberth [*Australia*] [*Airport symbol*]
RSC .... Riga [*USSR*] Skulte Airport [*Airport symbol*]
RSC .... Royal Society of Chemistry [*Formerly, CS, RIC*]
RSCS .... Rod Sequence Control System [*Nuclear energy*]
RSCW ...... Research Reactor, State College of Washington
RSD .... Responsible System Designer
RSD .... Rock Sound [*Bahamas*] [*Airport symbol*]
RSH .... Russian Mission [*Alaska*] [*Airport symbol*]
RSI .... Reactor Siting Index [*Nuclear energy*]
RSIM .... Retrospective Single Ion Monitoring [*Analytical chemistry*]

RSM .... Response Surface Methodology
RSP .... Reactivity Surveillance Procedures [*Nuclear energy*]
RSP .... Respirable Suspended Particulate[*s*]
RSP .... Rotating Shield Plug
RSPT .... Real Storage Page Table [*Data processing*]
RSRM .... Reduced Smoke Rocket Motor
RSS .... Reactor Shutdown System [*Nuclear energy*]
RSS .... Roseires [*Sudan*] [*Airport symbol*]
RSSU .... Remote Site Simulation Unit
RST .... Rochester [*Minnesota*] [*Airport symbol*]
RSTN .... Radio Solar Telescope Network
RSU .... Runway Supervisory Unit [*Aviation*]
RSV .... Reservoir [*Board on Geographic Names*]
RSVC .... Resident Supervisor Call
RT .... Radiographic Test
RTAM .... Remote Terminal Access Method [*Data processing*]
RTB .... Response/Throughput Bias [*Data processing*]
RTB .... Roatan [*Honduras*] [*Airport symbol*]
RTC .... Removable Top Closure
RTC .... Resort Timesharing Council
RTD .... Delayed [*Indicates delayed meteorological message*]
RTDAP ...... RADAR Target Data Analog Processor
RTE .... Residual Total Elongation [*Nuclear energy*]
RTIP .... Remote Terminal Interactive Processor
RTL .... Radioisotope Transport Loop [*Nuclear energy*]
RTL .... Research and Technology Laboratories [*Army*]
RTL .... Resistor Transistor Logic [*Data processing*]
RTM .... Rotterdam [*Netherlands*] [*Airport symbol*]
RTP .... Recruitment and Training Program
RTP .... Rutland Plains [*Australia*] [*Airport symbol*]
RTS .... Reactor Trip System [*Nuclear energy*]
RTS .... Readiness Training Squadron [*Military*]
RTS .... Request to Send
RTS .... Rottnest Island [*Australia*] [*Airport symbol*]
RTSP .... Real-Time Signal Processor
RTY .... Merty [*Australia*] [*Airport symbol*]
RU .... Request-Response Unit [*Data processing*]
RUH .... Riyadh [*Saudi Arabia*] [*Airport symbol*]
RUM .... Rumjartar [*Nepal*] [*Airport symbol*]
RUN .... Reunion Island [*Airport symbol*]
RUR .... Rurutu Island [*French Polynesia*] [*Airport symbol*]
RUS .... Marau [*Solomon Islands*] [*Airport symbol*]
RUSSWO .. Revised Uniform Summary of Surveyed Weather Observations
RUT .... Rutland [*Vermont*] [*Airport symbol*]
RUT .... Standard Regional Route Transmitting Frequencies [*Communications*]
RV .... Reactor Venezolano [*Nuclear reactor*] [*Venezuela*]
RVA .... Farafangana [*Madagascar*] [*Airport symbol*]
RVE .... Saravena [*Colombia*] [*Airport symbol*]
RVIS .... Reactor and Vessel Instrumentation System [*Nuclear energy*]
RVN .... Rovaniemi [*Finland*] [*Airport symbol*]
RVY .... Rivera [*Uruguay*] [*Airport symbol*]
RWCU ...... Reactor Water Cleanup [*Nuclear energy*]
RWI .... Rocky Mount [*North Carolina*] [*Airport symbol*]
RWP .... Radiation Work Permit
RWP .... Rawalpindi/Islamabad [*Pakistan*] [*Airport symbol*]
RWRS .... RADAR Warning System
RWS .... Radioactive Waste System
Rx .... Recipe [*Used as a symbol for medical prescriptions*]
RXS .... Roxas City [*Philippines*] [*Airport symbol*]
RYN .... Ryan Aviation Corp. [*Wichita, KS*] [*FAA designator*]
RYO .... Rio Turbio [*Argentina*] [*Airport symbol*]
RZA .... Santa Cruz [*Argentina*] [*Airport symbol*]
RZE .... Rzeszow [*Poland*] [*Airport symbol*]

S

S .... [*Wolfgang*] Schmieder [*When used in identifying J. S. Bach's compositions, refers to cataloging of his works by musicologist Schmieder*]
S .... Synthesis [*Phase in mitosis*] [*Cytology*]
SA .... Safety Analysis [*Nuclear energy*]
SA .... Scoliosis Association
SA .... Selected Ammunition
S & A .... Sickness and Accident [*Insurance*]
SA .... Situation Audit
SA .... Staphylococcus aureus [*Microbiology*]
SA .... Station Address [*Data processing*]
SA .... Surveillance Approach
SAA .... Sunflower Association of America
SAB .... Saba [*Netherlands Antilles*] [*Airport symbol*]
SAB .... Sabouraud Dextrose Agar [*Microbiology*]
SAC .... Senate Appropriations Committee
SAC .... Spiritual Advisory Council
SACS .... SONAR Accuracy Check Site
SAD .... Safety Analysis Diagram
SAD .... Safety Assurance Diagram
SADARM... Sense and Destroy Armor [*Missile system*]
SADR .... Secure Acoustic Data Relay
SADS .... Social Avoidance and Distress Scale [*Psychology*]
SADSAC ... Small Acoustic Device Simulating Aircraft Carrier
SAEC .... South American Explorers Club
SAF .... Santa Fe [*New Mexico*] [*Airport symbol*]
SAF .... Second Amendment Foundation
SAF .... Single Action [*Maintenance*] Form
SAFE .... Self-Acceptance, Faulty Information, Effectiveness Counselling or Training [*Sex therapy*]
SAFE .... Society for the Application of Free Energy
SAFE .... Spectronix Automatic Fire Extinguishing [*System*] [*For armored vehicles*]
SAG .... Semiautogenous Grinding System [*Ore-crushing process*]
SAGMI ...... Surface Attack Guided Missile
SAH .... Sanaa [*Yemen Arab Republic*] [*Airport symbol*]
SAHA .... Society of American Historical Artists
SAI .... Shoplifters Anonymous International [*An organization*]
SAI .... Surveillance Aided Intercept
SAIB .... Sucrose Acetate Isobutyrate [*Organic chemistry*]
SAIC .... Special Agent in Charge
SAID .... Safety Analysis Input Data
SAIP .... Spares Acquisition Integrated with Production
SAJ .... Golden Eagle Aviation [*Bedford, MA*] [*FAA designator*]
SAK .... Saudarkrokur [*Iceland*] [*Airport symbol*]
SAL .... San Salvador [*El Salvador*] [*Airport symbol*]
SAL-GP ..... Semiactive LASER-Guided Projectile
SALP .... Sodium Aluminum Phosphate [*Inorganic chemistry*]
SAM .... Salamo [*Papua New Guinea*] [*Airport symbol*]
SAM .... Shared Appreciation Mortgage
SAM .... Strela Antiaircraft Missiles
SAM .... Student Achievement Monitoring [*Vocational guidance*]
SAM .... Subject Activity Monitor [*Device used in biological research*]
SAM-DC ... S-Adenosylmethionine Decarboxylase [*An enzyme*]
SAMF .... Ship's Air Maintenance Facility [*Navy*]
SAMICS .... Systems Applications of Millimeter Wave Contact Seeker
SAMO .... Simulated Ab Initio Molecular Orbitals [*Atomic physics*]

SAMPAM .. System for Automation of Material Plans for Army Material
SAMS........ Sandia Air Force Material Study
SAN........... San Diego [*California*] [*Airport symbol*]
SANA .... Soycrafters Association of North America
SANSC...... Sanscrit
SAO .... Sao Paulo [*Brazil*] [*Airport symbol*]
SAP........... ASAP Air, Inc. [*Fort Worth, TX*] [*FAA designator*]
SAP........... San Pedro Sula [*Honduras*] [*Airport symbol*]
SAPHE....... Semi-Armor-Piercing High Explosive [*Projectile*]
SAQ .... San Andros [*Bahamas*] [*Airport symbol*]
SAR........... Service Aptitude Rating [*Military*]
SAR........... South African Railways
SAR........... Study and Review [*Reports*]
SAR........... Successive Approximation Register [*Data processing*]
SARD .... Sardinia
SARI.......... Standby Altitude Reference Indicator
SARS .... Simulated Airborne RADAR System
SAS........... Secondary Alarm Station
SAS........... Security Agency Study
SAS........... Societatis Antiquariorum Socius [*Fellow of the Society of Antiquaries*] [*British*]
SAS........... Special Ammunition Storage
SAS........... Statistical Analysis System
SAS........... System Application Software [*Data processing*]
SASG .... Smoke/Aerosol Steering Group [*DARCOM*]
SASP .... Science and Application Space Platform
SASRS ...... Satellite-Aided Search and Rescue System
SAT........... Standard Area of Tinplate [*100,000 square inches*]
SAT........... System Alignment Test
SATCAMS ... Semiautomatic Tactical Control and Airspace Management System
SATH .... Society for the Advancement of Travel for the Handicapped
SATS......... Simulated Airborne Transpondent System
SAV .... Savannah [*Georgia*] [*Airport symbol*]
SAW .... Subantarctic Water
SAW .... Submerged Arc Weld
SAWGUS .. Standoff/Attack Weapons Guidance Utility Study
SAWID ..... Shipboard Acoustic Warfare Integrated Defense
SAY .... Salisbury [*Zimbabwe*] [*Airport symbol*]
SAZ .... Sasstown [*Liberia*] [*Airport symbol*]
SB .... Society for Biomaterials
SBA .... Santa Barbara [*California*] [*Airport symbol*]
SBBT........ Short Basic Battery Test
SBC.......... Small Business Computer
SBCCI....... Southern Building Code Congress, International
SBD........... Sunbird Airlines, Inc. [*Maiden, NC*] [*FAA designator*]
SBE........... Selebi-Pikwe [*Botswana*] [*Airport symbol*]
SBGT .... Standby Gas Treatment System
SBH........... St. Barthelemy [*Leeward Islands*] [*Airport symbol*]
SBK........... St. Brieuc [*France*] [*Airport symbol*]
SBL........... Santa Ana [*Bolivia*] [*Airport symbol*]
SBM .... System Balance Measure
SBN........... South Bend [*Indiana*] [*Airport symbol*]
SBP........... San Luis Obispo [*California*] [*Airport symbol*]
SBR .... Segment Base Register
SBR .... Signal to Background Ratio [*Instrumentation*]
SBS........... Sensor Based System

SBS .... Steamboat Springs [*Colorado*] [*Airport symbol*]
SBT .... Side Buoyancy Tank
SBU .... Springbok [*South Africa*] [*Airport symbol*]
SBV .... Sabah [*Papua New Guinea*] [*Airport symbol*]
SBW .... Sibu [*Malaysia*] [*Airport symbol*]
SC .... Side Cabin
SCA .... Simulated Core Assembly [*Nuclear energy*]
SCA .... Standard Consolidated Area [*Bureau of Census*]
SCA .... Subcarrier Channel [*Telecommunications*]
SCAFEDS ... Space Construction Automated Fabrication Experiment
    Definition Study
SCAM .... Strike Camera
SCAN .... Stock Control and Analysis
SCAS .... Stability Control Augmentation System
SCB .... Session Control Block [*Data processing*]
SCC .... Satellite Communications Controller
SCC .... Self-Contained Canister
SCC .... Sequential Control Counter [*Data processing*]
SCC .... Specialized Common Carrier
SCDS .... Sensor Communication and Display System
SCE .... Society of Christian Engineers
SCEL .... Small Components Evaluation Loop
SCEPS ...... Solar Cell Electric Power System
SCF .... SNAP [*Systems for Nuclear Auxiliary Power*] Critical
    Facility
SCF .... Sodium Cleaning Facility
SCHLSHIP ... Schoolship [*Navy*]
SCHOL ...... Scholium [*A note*]
SCHS .... Small Component Handling System
SCI .... Special Customs Invoice
SCI .... Spinal Cord Injury [*Medicine*]
Sci Agric... Science in Agriculture [*A publication*]
Sci Agron Rennes ... Sciences Agronomiques Rennes [*A publication*]
Sci Alaska Proc Alaskan Sci Conf ... Science in Alaska. Proceedings.
    Alaskan Science Conference [*A publication*]
Sci Aliment ... Scienza dell'Alimentazione [*A publication*]
Sci Basis Med Annu Rev ... Scientific Basis of Medical Annual
    Reviews [*A publication*]
Sci Biol J... Science of Biology Journal [*A publication*]
Sci Biol Ser ... Science of Biology Series [*A publication*]
Sci Bull Cotton Res Inst Sindos ... Science Bulletin. Cotton Research
    Institute Sindos [*A publication*]
Sci Bull Fac Agric Kyushu Univ ... Science Bulletin of the Faculty of
    Agriculture. Kyushu University [*A publication*]
Sci Chron (Karachi) ... Science Chronicle (Karachi) [*A publication*]
Sci Couns ... Science Counselor [*A publication*]
Sci Cult..... Science and Culture [*A publication*]
Sci Dimens ... Science Dimension [*A publication*]
Sci Educ ... Science Education [*A publication*]
Sci Farmer ... Science for the Farmer [*A publication*]
Sci Geol Sin ... Scientia Geologica Sinica [*A publication*]
Sci Hortic ... Scientia Horticulturae [*A publication*]
Sci Hum Life ... Science of Human Life [*A publication*]
SCII .... Strong-Campbell Interest Inventory [*Vocational
    guidance*]
Sci Icel ...... Science in Iceland [*A publication*]
Sci Ind (Karachi) ... Science and Industry (Karachi) [*A publication*]
Sci March ... Science on the March [*A publication*]
Sci Nat ...... Science et Nature [*A publication*]
Sci New Guinea ... Science in New Guinea [*A publication*]
Sci Nourishment ... Science of Nourishment [*A publication*]
Sci Peche ... Science et Peche [*A publication*]
Sci Pest Control ... Scientific Pest Control [*A publication*]
Sci Pharm ... Scientia Pharmaceutica [*A publication*]
Sci Proc R Dublin Soc ... Scientific Proceedings of the Royal Dublin
    Society [*A publication*]
Sci Proc R Dublin Soc Ser A ... Scientific Proceedings of the Royal
    Dublin Society. Series A [*A publication*]
Sci Proc R Dublin Soc Ser B ... Scientific Proceedings of the Royal
    Dublin Society. Series B [*A publication*]
Sci Prog Decouverte ... Science Progres Decouverte [*A publication*]
Sci Prog Nat (Paris) ... Science Progres la Natur (Paris) [*A
    publication*]
Sci Psychoanal ... Science and Psychoanalysis [*A publication*]
Sci Publ Sci Mus Minn ... Scientific Publications of the Science
    Museum of Minnesota [*A publication*]
Sci Publ Sci Mus (St Paul) ... Scientific Publications of the Science
    Museum (St. Paul, Minnesota) [*A publication*]

Sci Rep Agric Coll Norway ... Scientific Reports from the Agricultural
    College of Norway [*A publication*]
Sci Rep Cent Res Inst Kasauli ... Scientific Report of the Central
    Research Institute. Kasauli [*A publication*]
Sci Rep Coll Gen Educ Osaka Univ ... Science Reports. College of
    General Education. Osaka University (Japan) [*A
    publication*]
Sci Rep Fac Agric Ibaraki Univ ... Scientific Reports of the Faculty of
    Agriculture. Ibaraki University [*A publication*]
Sci Rep Fac Agric Kobe Univ ... Science Reports of the Faculty of
    Agriculture. Kobe University [*A publication*]
Sci Rep Fac Agric Meijo Univ ... Scientific Reports of the Faculty of
    Agriculture. Meijo University [*A publication*]
Sci Rep Fac Educ Gunma Univ ... Science Reports of the Faculty of
    Education. Gunma University [*A publication*]
Sci Rep Fac Sci Ege Univ ... Scientific Reports of the Faculty of
    Science. Ege University [*A publication*]
Sci Rep Hirosaki Univ ... Science Reports of the Hirosaki University
    [*A publication*]
Sci Rep Hokkaido Fish Exp Stn ... Scientific Reports of the Hokkaido
    Fisheries Experimental Station [*A publication*]
Sci Rep Hokkaido Salmon Hatchery ... Scientific Reports of the
    Hokkaido Salmon Hatchery [*A publication*]
Sci Rep Indian Agric Res Inst ... Scientific Reports of the Indian
    Agricultural Research Institute [*A publication*]
Sci Rep Kagoshima Univ ... Science Reports of Kagoshima University
    [*A publication*]
Sci Rep Kanazawa Univ ... Science Reports of Kanazawa University
    [*A publication*]
Sci Rep Kyoto Prefect Univ Agric ... Scientific Reports of the Kyoto
    Prefectural University. Agriculture [*A publication*]
Sci Rep Meiji Seika Kaisha ... Scientific Reports of Meiji Seika Kaisha
    [*A publication*]
Sci Rep Niigata Univ Ser D Biol ... Science Reports of Niigata
    University. Series D. Biology [*A publication*]
Sci Rep Shima Marinel ... Science Report of Shima Marineland [*A
    publication*]
Sci Rep Whales Res Inst (Tokyo) ... Scientific Reports of the Whales
    Research Institute (Tokyo) [*A publication*]
Sci Rep Yamaguchi Univ ... Science Reports of the Yamaguchi
    University [*A publication*]
Sci Rep Yokosuka City Mus ... Science Report of the Yokosuka City
    Museum [*A publication*]
Sci Res Br Univ Coll ... Scientific Research in British Universities and
    Colleges [*A publication*]
Sci Res (NY) ... Scientific Research (New York) [*A publication*]
Sci Rev ...... Scienca Revuo [*A publication*]
Sci Rev (Manila) ... Science Review (Manila) [*A publication*]
Sci Silvae ... Scientia Silvae [*A publication*]
Sci Sin ...... Scientia Sinica [*A publication*]
Sci Sol ...... Science du Sol [*A publication*]
Sci Stud St Bonaventure Univ ... Science Studies. St. Bonaventure
    University [*A publication*]
Sci Technol ... Science and Technology [*A publication*]
Sci Tools... Science Tools [*A publication*]
Sci Total Environ ... Science of the Total Environment [*A publication*]
Sci Vie ...... Science et Vie [*A publication*]
Sci Yearb Vet Fac Thessalonica ... Scientific Yearbook of the
    Veterinary Faculty. Thessalonica [*A publication*]
SCK .... Studiecentrum voor Kernenergie [*Belgium*] [*Also known
    as CEEN or NERC*]
SCL .... System Command Language [*Data processing*]
SCM .... Simulated Core Mockup [*or Model*] [*Nuclear energy*]
SCOL .... School
SCOR .... Small Cycle Observation Recording
Scotl Dep Agric Fish Mar Res ... Scotland Department of Agriculture
    and Fisheries. Marine Research [*A publication*]
Scotl Dep Agric Fish Tech Bull ... Scotland Department of
    Agriculture and Fisheries. Technical Bulletin [*A
    publication*]
Scott Agric ... Scottish Agriculture [*A publication*]
Scott Birds ... Scottish Birds [*A publication*]
Scott Fish Bull ... Scottish Fisheries Bulletin [*A publication*]
Scott Fish Res Rep ... Scottish Fisheries Research Report [*A
    publication*]
Scott For... Scottish Forestry [*A publication*]
Scott Geogr Mag ... Scottish Geographical Magazine [*A publication*]
Scott J Geol ... Scottish Journal of Geology [*A publication*]

Scott Mar Biol Assoc Annu Rep ... Scottish Marine Biological Association. Annual Report [*A publication*]

Scott Med J ... Scottish Medical Journal [*A publication*]

Scott Nat .. Scottish Naturalist [*A publication*]

SCP.......... Symbolic Conversion Program

SCPT......... Self-Consistent Perturbation Theory [*Physics*]

SCR.......... Skin Conductance Response

SC Resour Cent Tech Rep ... South Carolina Marine Resources Center. Technical Report [*A publication*]

Scr Geobot ... Scripta Geobotanica [*A publication*]

SCRI.......... Science Court and Research Institute

SCRIP .... Scripture

Scr Med (Brno) ... Scripta Medica (Brno) [*A publication*]

Scr Sci Med Annu Sci Pap ... Scripta Scientifica Medica. Annual Scientific Papers [*A publication*]

SCS.......... Sea Control Ship [*Navy*]

SCS.......... Single Control Support

SCS.......... Sodium Cellulose Sulfate [*Organic chemistry*]

SCS.......... Sodium Characterization System

SCSL......... Standing Lenticular Stratocumulus [*Meteorology*]

SCSO........ Superconducting Cavity Stabilized Oscillator [*For clocks*]

SCTF......... Sodium Chemical Technology Facility

SCULP ...... Sculpsit [*He, or She, Engraved It*] [*Latin*]

SCV.......... Side Control Valves

SD .... Short Days [*Botany*]

SD .... Side Deck

SD .... Skin Destruction [*Medicine*]

SD .... Sound [*Board on Geographic Names*]

SDA.......... Source Data Acquisition

SDA.......... Stepwise Discriminant Analysis

SDA.......... Sulfadiazine [*Antibiotic*]

SDA.......... Supplier Data Approval

SD Agric Exp Stn Bull ... South Dakota Agricultural Experiment Station Bulletin [*A publication*]

SDAP .... Systems Development and Acquisition Plan

SD Bird Notes ... South Dakota Bird Notes [*A publication*]

SDC .... Space Defense Center

SDC .... Sundance Airlines, Inc. [*Temecula, CA*] [*FAA designator*]

SDCC........ Small-Diameter Component Cask [*Nuclear energy*]

SDD........... System Design Description

SDDC........ Sodium Dimethyldithiocarbamate [*Organic chemistry*]

SDDS .... Secondary Data Display System

SDE .... Steam Distillation Extracton

SD Farm Home Res ... South Dakota Farm and Home Research [*A publication*]

SD Geol Surv Rep Invest ... South Dakota Geological Survey. Report of Investigations [*A publication*]

SDIHD .... Sudden-Death Ischemic Heart Disease

SD J Med .. South Dakota Journal of Medicine [*A publication*]

SD J Med Pharm ... South Dakota Journal of Medicine and Pharmacy [*A publication*]

SDL .... System Directory List [*Data processing*]

SDM .... Space Division Multiplexing [*Physics*]

SDO .... Shielded Diatomic Orbitals [*Atomic physics*]

SDRS .... Signal Data Recording Set

SDRW .... SONAR Dome Rubber Window

SDSAM ..... Specifically Designated Special Air Mission [*Aircraft*] [*Air Force*]

SDSD .... Single Disk Storage Device [*Data processing*]

SE .... Safety Evaluation

SEA .... Sea Echelon Area [*Navy*]

SEACOM .. Southeast Asia Communications

Sea Fish Res Stn Haifa Bull ... Sea Fisheries Research Station. Haifa. Bulletin [*A publication*]

SEAL......... Standard Electronic Accounting Language [*Data processing*]

SEALITE ... Systematic Evaluation and Analysis of a LASER in a Test Environment

Seara Med ... Seara Medica [*A publication*]

Seara Med Neurocir ... Seara Medica Neurocirurgica [*A publication*]

Search Agric (Geneva, NY) ... Search Agriculture (Geneva, New York) [*A publication*]

SEATO Med Res Monogr ... Southeast Asia Treaty Organization. Medical Research Monograph [*A publication*]

SEB .... Selective Enlistment Bonus [*Navy*]

SEC.......... Submarine Element Coordinator

SECAS...... Ship Equipment Configuration Accounting System

SECC .... Safe Energy Communications Council

SECC .... Scientific and Engineering Computing Council

SECP .... State Energy Conservation Program

SECS .... Simulation and Evaluation of Chemical Synthesis [*Data processing*]

SED.......... Shipper's Export Declaration

SED.......... Students for Economic Democracy

Sediment Geol ... Sedimentary Geology [*A publication*]

SEDR .... System Effective Data Rate

SEDSCAF ... Standard ELINT Data System Codes and Format

SEE .... Senior Environmental Employment Program [*Environmental Protection Agency*]

Seed Res (New Delhi) ... Seed Research (New Delhi) [*A publication*]

Seed Sci Technol ... Seed Science and Technology [*A publication*]

SEGD .... Society of Environmental Graphics Designers

SEIA.......... Solar Energy Institute of America

SEIT .... System Evaluation, Integration, and Test

SEITA Ann Dir Etud Equip Sect 2 ... SEITA [*Service d'Exploitation Industrielle des Tabacs et des Allumettes*] Annales de la Direction des Etudes de l'Equipement. Section 2 [*A publication*]

SEL .... Selected Equipment List

Sel Bibliogr Algae ... Selected Bibliography on Algae [*A publication*]

SELGEM ... Self-Generating Master [*Information management system*] [*Data processing*]

Sel Khoz Turkmen ... Sel'skoe Khozyaistvo Turkmenistana [*A publication*]

SELREFTRA ... Selected Refresher Training [*Navy*]

SELRFT..... Selected Refresher Training [*Navy*]

Sel Semenovod (Mosc) ... Selekstsiya i Semenovodstvo (Moscow) [*A publication*]

Sel'sk Khoz ... Sel'skoe Khozyaistvo [*A publication*]

Sel'sk Khoz Kaz ... Sel'skoe Khozyaistvo Kazakhstana [*A publication*]

Sel'sk Khoz Kirg ... Sel'skoe Khozyaistvo Kirgizii [*A publication*]

Sel'sk Khoz Tatar ... Sel'skoe Khozyaistvo Tatarii [*A publication*]

Selskostop Nauka ... Selskostopanska Nauka [*A publication*]

SEM .... Semble [*It Seems*]

SEMA .... Special Electronic Mission Aircraft

SEMCIP .... Shipboard Electromagnetic Capability Improvement Program [*Navy*]

Sem Hop Paris ... Semaine des Hopitaux de Paris [*A publication*]

SEMI .... Special Electromagnetic Interference

Semin Arthritis Rheum ... Seminars in Arthritis and Rheumatism [*A publication*]

Semin Drug Treat ... Seminars in Drug Treatment [*A publication*]

Semin Hematol ... Seminars in Hematology [*A publication*]

Semin Nucl Med ... Seminars in Nuclear Medicine [*A publication*]

Semin Psychiatry ... Seminars in Psychiatry [*A publication*]

Semin Roentgenol ... Seminars in Roentgenology [*A publication*]

Semin Thromb Hemostasis ... Seminars in Thrombosis and Hemostasis [*A publication*]

Sem Med .. Semana Medica [*A publication*]

Senckenb Biol ... Senckenbergiana Biologica [*A publication*]

Senckenb Lethaea ... Senckenbergiana Lethaea [*A publication*]

Senckenb Marit ... Senckenbergiana Maritima [*A publication*]

SEO .... State Energy Office

SEON .... Solar Electro-Optical Network

Seoul J Med ... Seoul Journal of Medicine [*A publication*]

Seoul Univ J Biol Agric Ser (B) ... Seoul University Journal. Biology and Agriculture. Series (B) [*A publication*]

SEOW .... Society of Engineering Office Workers

SEP .... SOSUS [*Sound Surveillance System*] Estimated Position

Sep Purif Methods ... Separation and Purification Methods [*A publication*]

SEPS......... Solar Electronic Propulsion System

Sep Sci ..... Separation Science [*A publication*]

SEPTAR .... Seaborne Powered Target [*Navy*]

SEQOPT .... Sequential Optimization

SER .... Safety Evaluation Report

SER .... Shore Establishment Realignment [*Navy*]

SER .... System Environment Recording

SERENDIP ... Search for Extraterrestrial Radio Emission from Nearby Developed Intelligent Populations

Serengeti Res Inst Annu Rep ... Serengeti Research Institute. Annual Report [*A publication*]

Ser Entomol (The Hague) ... Series Entomologica (The Hague) [*A publication*]

Ser Haematol ... Series Haematologica [*A publication*]

Ser Monogr Inst Zootec ... Serie Monografias. Instituto de Zootecnia [*A publication*]

Serol Mus Bull ... Serological Museum Bulletin [*A publication*]

Ser Paedopsychiatr ... Series Paedopsychiatrica [*A publication*]
SERS......... Surface-Enhanced Raman Spectroscopy
Serv Can Faune Cah Biol ... Service Canadien de la Faune. Cahiers de Biologie [*A publication*]
Serv Shell Agric Ser A ... Servicio Shell para el Agricultor. Serie A [*A publication*]
SESDA...... Small Engine Servicing Dealers Association
SESMI....... Systems Engineering Support and Management Integration
SETAD...... Secure Transmission of Acoustic Data
SETTA...... Southeastern Test and Training Area [*Military*]
Sewage Ind Wastes ... Sewage and Industrial Wastes [*A publication*]
SEWPS..... Safety Weather Probability Study
SEXAFS.... Surface-Extended X-Ray Absorption Fine Structure
Seychelles Dep Agric Annu Rep ... Seychelles Department of Agriculture. Annual Report [*A publication*]
SFA.......... Sempervivum Fanciers Association
SFA.......... Single Failure Analysis
SFA.......... Stopped-Flow Analyzer [*Chemical analysis*]
SFC.......... Synthetic Fuels Corporation [*Sponsored by the federal government*]
SFCS....... Secondary Flow Control System [*Nuclear energy*]
SFDI......... Solar Facility Design Integration
SFE.......... Solar-Flare Effect [*Physics*]
SFEL........ Standard Facility Equipment List
SFF.......... Self-Forging Fragment
SFO.......... Secular Franciscan Order [*Roman Catholic religious order*] [*Formerly, TOSF*]
SFP.......... Spent Fuel Pit [*Nuclear energy*]
SFSP........ Spent Fuel Storage Pool [*Nuclear energy*]
SFTWR..... Software [*Data processing*]
SF/USA .... Stopped-Flow/Unsegmented Storage Analyzer [*Chemical analysis*]
SG............ Safety Guide
SG............ Signal Ground
SG............ Sort Generator
SG............ Spheroidal Graphite [*Ductile iron*]
SGAE....... Studiengesellschaft fuer Atomenergie [*Implements Austria's nuclear program*]
SGAS....... Society for German-American Studies
SGC......... Standard Geographical Classification [*Canada*]
SGHW...... Steam-Generating, Heavy-Water [*Reactor*] [*British*]
SGHWR..... Steam-Generating, Heavy-Water Reactor [*British*]
SGO......... Sydney Godolphin Osborne [*Literary signature of 19th-century British writer*]
SGPM....... Saint-Gobain-Pont-A-Mousson [*French industrial giant*]
SGR.......... Self-Generation Reactor
SGSI........ Stabilized Glide Slope Indicator
SH............ Sexual Harassment
SH............ Stationary High-Power [*Reactor*]
SH............ Stored Heading
SHAWL..... Special Hard Target Assault Weapon Lightweight
SHB.......... Sodium Hydroxybutyrate [*Organic chemistry*]
SHDI......... Supraoptic-Hypophyseal Diabetes Insipidus [*Endocrinology*]
Sheepfarming Annu ... Sheepfarming Annual [*A publication*]
SHF.......... Storage-Handling Facility [*Nuclear energy*]
SHG......... Special High Grade [*Zinc metal*]
Shhh........ Self-Help for Hard of Hearing People [*An organization*]
Shikoku Acta Med ... Shikoku Acta Medica [*A publication*]
SHL.......... Sacred Heart League
SHMD....... Shore Manning Document [*Navy*]
SHMP....... Sodium Hexametaphosphate [*Inorganic chemistry*]
SHOPAT ... Shore Patrol [*Navy*]
SHS.......... Societatis Historiae Socius [*Fellow of the Historical Society*]
SHS.......... Sodium Hexadecyl Sulfate [*Organic chemistry*]
SHS.......... Square Hollow Section [*Metal industry*]
SHTL........ Small Heat-Transfer Loop [*Nuclear energy*]
SHUSA...... Scottish Heritage USA
SIA.......... Semiconductor Industry Association
SIA.......... Service in Informatics and Analysis
SIAC........ Southeastern Intercollegiate Athletic Association
SIAM........ Separate Index Access Method [*Data processing*]
Sib Geogr Sb ... Sibirskii Geograficheskii Sbornik [*A publication*]
SIBMAS.... Section Internationale des Bibliotheques et Musees des Arts du Spectacle [*International Association of Libraries and Museums of the Performing Arts*]
SIC........... SONAR Information Center

SICAC....... Society of Inter-Celtic Arts and Culture
SICL......... Self-Interview Checklist [*Navy*]
SID........... Sodium Ionization Detector [*Nuclear energy*]
Sida Contrib Bot ... Sida Contributions to Botany [*A publication*]
Side Eff Drugs Annu ... Side Effects of Drugs Annual [*A publication*]
SIDS......... Satellite Imagery Dissemination System
SIDTS ...... Single Integrated Development Test Cycle
SIE........... Sierra Express [*Reno, NV*] [*FAA designator*]
Sierra Leone Fish Div Tech Pap ... Sierra Leone Fisheries Division. Technical Paper [*A publication*]
SIF............ Security and Intelligence Fund
SII............. Special Interest Items
Silkworm Inf Bull ... Silkworm Information Bulletin [*A publication*]
Silliman J ... Silliman Journal [*A publication*]
Silvae Genet ... Silvae Genetica [*A publication*]
Silva Fenn ... Silva Fennica [*A publication*]
Silvic Sao Paulo ... Silvicultura em Sao Paulo [*A publication*]
SIMP .... Satellite Information Message Protocol
SIMPO....... Simulation of Personnel Operations [*Army Research Institute for the Behavioral and Social Sciences*]
SIMSIN...... Simulated Strapdown Inertial Navigation
Sind Univ Res J (Sci Ser) ... Sind University Research Journal (Science Series) [*A publication*]
Singapore J Primary Ind ... Singapore Journal of Primary Industries [*A publication*]
Singapore Med J ... Singapore Medical Journal [*A publication*]
SIP .... Sodium Iron Pyrophosphate [*Inorganic chemistry*]
SIP .... Strain Isolator Pad [*Aerospace*]
SIP .... Symbolic Input Program [*Data processing*]
SIR .... Search, Inspection, and Recovery
SIRA.......... Social Issues Research Associates
SIRA.......... Stable Isotope Ratio Analysis
Siraraj Hosp Gaz ... Siriraj Hospital Gazette [*A publication*]
SIS .... Safety Injection System
SIS .... Special Information System
S & IS .... Survey and Investigation Staff [*Navy*]
SISAM...... Spectrometer with Interference Selective Amplitude Modulation [*Physics*]
SISI .... Surveillance and In-Service Inspection [*Nuclear energy*]
Sist Nerv ... Sistema Nervoso [*A publication*]
Sistole Rev Urug Cardiol ... Sistole. Revista Uruguaya de Cardiologia [*A publication*]
SIT .... Systems Interface Test
SITA .... System International Tinplate Area
SITE .... Shipboard Information, Training, and Education [*System*] [*Navy*]
Sitzungsber Finn Acad Wiss ... Sitzungsberichte der Finnischen Akademie der Wissenschaften [*A publication*]
SIUSA .... Survival International USA [*An organization*]
SIV .... Silicon Videcon [*TV system*]
SJAE .... Steam Jet Air Ejector
SJLAC....... Soviet Jewry Legal Advocacy Center
S-kh Biol ... Sel'skohozyaistvennaya Biologiya [*A publication*]
S-kh Proizvod Urala ... Sel'skohozyaistvennoe Proizvodstvo Urala [*A publication*]
S-kh Rub Rastenievod ... Sel'skohozyaistvo za Rubezhom Rastenievodstvo [*A publication*]
Skin Res ... Skin Research [*A publication*]
SKP.......... Skip
SKR.......... Saturn Kilometer-Wave Radiation [*Planetary science*]
Skr Udgivet Univ Zool Mus Kbh ... Skrifter Udgivet af Universitetets Zoologiske Museum. Kobenhavan [*A publication*]
SL............. Safety Limit
SL............. Scanning Slit
SL............. Simulation Language [*Data processing*]
SL............. Source Language [*Data processing*]
SL............. Stationary Low-Power [*Reactor*] [*Dismantled*]
SL............. Synchronous Line Medium Speed
SLAC .... Straight-Line (Linear) Accelerator [*Nuclear energy*]
SLAM .... Sea-Launched Air Missile
SLAMS..... Surface Look-Alike Mine System
SLAR........ Steerable LASER Radiometer
SLASC...... St. Louis Area Support Center [*Military*]
SLC.......... Single Line Control
SLC.......... Sonobuoy Launch Container
SLC.......... Standard Location Codes
SLC.......... Synchronous Line Medium Speed with Clock
SLCP........ Ship's Loading Characteristics Pamphlet [*Navy*]

SLCRS ...... Supplementary Leak Collection and Release System [*Nuclear energy*]
SLCS .... Standby Liquid Control System [*Nuclear energy*]
SLD .... Solid Logic Dense
SLEEP ...... Silent, Lightweight, Electric Energy Plant
SLF .... System Library File [*Data processing*]
SLG .... Synchronous Line Group
SLI .... Spacelab Integration
SLI .... Steam Line Isolation [*Nuclear energy*]
SLI .... Suppress Length Indication
SLIV .... Steam Line Isolation Valve [*Nuclear energy*]
SLLL .... Synchronous Line, Low, Load
SLOT .... Submarine-Launched One-Way Tactical [*Buoy*]
SLP .... Source Language Processor [*Data processing*]
SLP .... Surface Launch Platform
SLRS .... Satellite LASER Ranging System
SLS .... Sodium Lauryl Sulfate [*Organic chemistry*] [*Also, SDS*]
SM .... Secondary Memory [*Data processing*]
SM .... Set Mode
SM .... Shared Memory [*Data processing*]
S & M ...... Structures and Materials
SM .... Systems Memory [*Data processing*]
Small Mamm Newsl ... Small Mammal Newsletters [*A publication*]
Small Stock Mag ... Small Stock Magazine [*A publication*]
SMART ..... Structural Maintenance and Repair Team
SMAW .... Shoulder-Launched Multipurpose Assault Weapon
SMC .... Segmented Maintenance Cask [*Nuclear energy*]
SMCS .... Structural Mode Control System
SME .... Stalk Median Eminence [*Anatomy*]
SME .... Subject Matter Experts
SMET .... Simulated Mission Endurance Test
SMI .... Supply Management Inspection
SMIP .... Ship's 3-M Improvement Plan [*Navy*]
Smithson Contrib Anthropol ... Smithsonian Contributions to Anthropology [*A publication*]
Smithson Contrib Bot ... Smithsonian Contributions to Botany [*A publication*]
Smithson Contrib Earth Sciences ... Smithsonian Contributions to Earth Sciences [*A publication*]
Smithson Contrib Paleobiol ... Smithsonian Contributions to Paleobiology [*A publication*]
Smithson Contrib Zool ... Smithsonian Contributions to Zoology [*A publication*]
Smithson Inst Annu Rep ... Smithsonian Institution. Annual Report [*A publication*]
Smithson Misc Collect ... Smithsonian Miscellaneous Collections [*A publication*]
SMM .... Start of Manual Message
SMO .... Society of Military Otolaryngologists
SMOC .... Submodule and Operator Controller [*For sequence of telephonic operations*]
SMP .... Systems Monitoring Panel
SMR .... School of Materiel Readiness [*Army*] [*Formerly, SAM*]
SMR .... Specialized Mobile Radio
SMRT .... Single Message Rate Timing
SMS .... Stores Management System
SMS .... Student Monitoring System [*Vocational guidance*]
SMSC .... Standard Modular System Card [*Data processing*]
SMSJ .... Scott's Monthly Stamp Journal [*A publication*]
SMSV .... San Miguel Sea Lion Virus
SMT .... Sexual Medicine Today [*A publication*]
SMTI .... Sodium Mechanisms Test Installation [*Nuclear energy*]
SN .... Sign
SNAP .... Standard Network Access Protocol [*Data processing*]
SNARL ...... Suggested No Adverse Risk Levels [*Environmental Protection Agency*]
SNB .... Sierra Nevada Batholith [*Geology*]
SNM .... Square Nautical Mile
SNM .... Subject Named Member
SNN .... Shared Nearest Neighbor
SNN .... Structure-Nomenclature Notation [*Chemistry*]
SNR .... Service Not Required
SNR .... Supplier Nonconformance Report
SNY .... Sidney [*Nebraska*] [*Airport symbol*]
SOAL .... Search Optical Augmentation LASER
Soap Chem Spec ... Soap and Chemical Specialties [*Later, Soap/Cosmetics/Chemical Specialties*] [*A publication*]
SOC .... Solo [*Indonesia*] [*Airport symbol*]
SOC .... South Coast Airways [*Nederland, TX*] [*FAA designator*]

SOC .... Statement of Capability
SOC .... Strike Options Comparison
Soc Appl Bacteriol Symp Ser ... Society for Applied Bacteriology. Symposium Series [*A publication*]
Soc Appl Bacteriol Tech Ser ... Society for Applied Bacteriology. Technical Series [*A publication*]
Soc Argent Cancerol Bol Trab ... Sociedad Argentina de Cancerologia. Boletines y Trabajos [*A publication*]
Soc Argent Cir Jornadas Quir ... Sociedad Argentina de Cirujanos Jornadas Quirurgicas [*A publication*]
Soc Behav Pers ... Social Behavior and Personality [*A publication*]
Soc Biol .... Social Biology [*A publication*]
Soc Chem Ind (Lond) Monogr ... Society of Chemical Industry (London) Monograph [*A publication*]
SOCCS ..... Summary of Component Control Status
Soc Exp Biol Semin Ser ... Society for Experimental Biology. Seminar Series [*A publication*]
Soc Fauna Flora Fenn Flora Fenn ... Societas pro Fauna et Flora Fennica Flora Fennica [*A publication*]
Soc Gen Physiol Ser ... Society of General Physiologists Series [*A publication*]
Soc Ital Sci Farm Doc ... Societa Italiana di Scienze Farmaceutiche Documento [*A publication*]
Socker Handli ... Socker Handlingar [*A publication*]
Soc Malawi J ... Society of Malawi Journal [*A publication*]
Soc Nat Luxemb Bull ... Societe des Naturalistes Luxembourgeois. Bulletin [*A publication*]
Soc Nematol Spec Publ ... Society of Nematologists. Special Publication [*A publication*]
Soc Neurosci Symp ... Society for Neuroscience Symposia [*A publication*]
Soc Psychiatry ... Social Psychiatry [*A publication*]
Soc Que Prot Plant Rapp ... Societe de Quebec pour la Protection des Plantes. Rapport [*A publication*]
Soc Sci Fenn Arsb-Vuosik ... Societas Scientiarum Fennica Arsbok-Vuosikirja [*A publication*]
Soc Sci Med ... Social Science and Medicine [*A publication*]
Soc Venez Cienc Nat Bol ... Sociedad Venezolana de Ciencias Naturales. Boletin [*A publication*]
Soc Ven Sci Nat Lav ... Societa Veneziana di Scienze Naturali Lavori [*A publication*]
SOEH .... Society for Occupational and Environmental Health
SOF .... Sofia [*Bulgaria*] [*Airport symbol*]
SOG .... Sogndal [*Norway*] [*Airport symbol*]
SOI .... South Molle Island [*Australia*] [*Airport symbol*]
SOICS .... Summary of Installation Control Status
Soil Biol Biochem ... Soil Biology and Biochemistry [*A publication*]
Soil Biol Microbiol ... Soil Biology and Microbiologie [*A publication*]
Soil Sci Agron ... Soil Science and Agronomy [*A publication*]
Soil Sci Plant Nutr ... Soil Science and Plant Nutrition [*A publication*]
Soil Sci Soc Am J ... Soil Science Society of America. Journal [*A publication*]
Soil Sci Soc Am Proc ... Soil Science Society of America. Proceedings [*A publication*]
Soil Surv Invest Rep ... Soil Survey Investigations. Report [*A publication*]
SOJ .... Sorkjosen [*Norway*] [*Airport symbol*]
SOJS .... Standoff Jammer Suppression
SOK .... Semongkong [*Lesotho*] [*Airport symbol*]
SOLAR MAX ... Solar Maximum Mission Satellite
Sol Energy ... Solar Energy [*A publication*]
SOM .... Sensitivity-of-Method [*FDA*]
SOM .... Shift Operations Manager
SON .... Espiritu Santo [*Vanuata*] [*Airport symbol*]
SON .... Statement of Need
SON .... Statement of Operational Need
SOO .... Songo [*Mozambique*] [*Airport symbol*]
Soobshch Akad Nauk Gruz SSSR ... Soobshcheniya Akademii Nauk Gruzinskoi SSSR [*A publication*]
Soobshch Inst Lesa Akad Nauk SSSR ... Soobshcheniya Instituta Lesa Akademii Nauk SSSR [*A publication*]
SOP .... Pinehurst [*North Carolina*] [*Airport symbol*]
SOP .... Ship's Operational Program [*Navy*]
SOP .... Study Organization Plan
SOQ .... Sorong [*Indonesia*] [*Airport symbol*]
SORA .... Sorgento Rapido [*Reactor*]
SOS .... [*Anatoly*] Scharansky, [*Yuri*] Orlov, and [*Andrei*] Sakharov [*Organization named after dissident Soviet scientists*]

SOS........... Start of Significance [*Data processing*]
SOT........... Same Old Thing [*Slang*]
Sotilaslaak Aikak ... Sotilaslaaketieteellinen Aikakauslehti [*A publication*]
Sots Sel'sk Khoz Azerb ... Sotsialisticheskoe Sel'skoe Khozyaistvo Azerbaidzhana [*A publication*]
Sots Sel'sk Khoz Uzb ... Sotsialisticheskoe Sel'skoe Khozyaistvo Uzbekistana [*A publication*]
Sots Tvarynnytstvo ... Sotsialistychne Tvarynnytstvo [*A publication*]
SOU .... Southampton [*England*] [*Airport symbol*]
Sources Sci ... Sources of Science [*A publication*]
South Conf Gerontol Rep ... Southern Conference on Gerontology. Report [*A publication*]
South Dairy Prod J ... Southern Dairy Products Journal [*A publication*]
Southeast Geol ... Southeastern Geology [*A publication*]
South J Appl For ... Southern Journal of Applied Forestry [*A publication*]
South Lumberman ... Southern Lumberman [*A publication*]
South Med ... Southern Medicine [*A publication*]
South Med Bull ... Southern Medical Bulletin [*A publication*]
South Pac Bull ... South Pacific Bulletin [*A publication*]
South Seedsman ... Southern Seedsman [*A publication*]
Southwest Entomol ... Southwestern Entomologist [*A publication*]
Southwest J Anthropol ... Southwestern Journal of Anthropology [*A publication*]
Southwest Nat ... Southwestern Naturalist [*A publication*]
Southwest Vet ... Southwestern Veterinarian [*A publication*]
Sov Genet (Engl Transl Genetika) ... Soviet Genetics (English Translation of Genetika) [*A publication*]
Sov J Ecol (Engl Transl Ekologiya) ... Soviet Journal of Ecology (English Translation of Ekologiya) [*A publication*]
Sov Neurol Psychiatry ... Soviet Neurology and Psychiatry [*A publication*]
Sov Psychol ... Soviet Psychology [*A publication*]
Sovrem Probl Gematol Pereliv Krovi ... Sovremennye Problemy Gematologii i Perelivaniya Krovi [*A publication*]
Sovrem Probl Onkol ... Sovremennye Problemy Onkologii [*A publication*]
Sov Zdravookhr ... Sovetskoe Zdravookhranenie [*A publication*]
Sov Zdravookhr Kirg ... Sovetskoe Zdravookhranenie Kirgizii [*A publication*]
SOW .... Show Low [*Arizona*] [*Airport symbol*]
SOW .... Special Operations Wing [*Military*]
SOW .... Standoff Weapons
SOY .... Stronsay [*Scotland*] [*Airport symbol*]
Soybean Dig ... Soybean Digest [*A publication*]
Soz Kommun ... Sozialisation und Kommunikation [*A publication*]
Soz- Praeventivmed ... Sozial- und Praeventivmedizin [*A publication*]
SP .... Scientific Processor
SP .... Sensor Processor
SP .... Standard Program [*Data processing*]
SP .... Structured Programing [*Data processing*]
SP .... Surveillance Procedure
SPA .... Seaplane Pilots Association
SPA .... Spanish
SPACE ...... Society for Private and Commercial Earth Stations
SPACS ...... Sodium Purification and Characterization System
SPAL .... Simulator, Projectile, Airburst, Liquid [*Chemical defense device*] [*Military*]
SPAS .... Societatis Philosophicae Americanae Socius [*Member of the American Philosophical Society*]
SPASM ..... Self-Propelled Air-to-Surface Missile
SPB .... St. Thomas [*Virgin Islands*] Seaplane Base [*Airport symbol*]
SPBA .... Society of Professional Benefit Administrators
SPC .... Santa Cruz La Palma [*Canary Islands*] [*Airport symbol*]
SPCDS ...... Small Permanent Communications and Display Segment
SPD .... Saidpur [*Bangladesh*] [*Airport symbol*]
SPD .... Society for Pediatric Dermatology
SPEAR ...... Signal Processing, Evaluation, Alert, and Report [*Navy*]
Spec Bull Taiwan For Res Inst ... Special Bulletin of Taiwan Forestry Research Institute [*A publication*]
SPECD ...... Specification Data Base
Spec Issue Plant Cell Physiol ... Special Issue of Plant and Cell Physiology [*A publication*]
Spec Pap Palaeontol ... Special Papers in Palaeontology [*A publication*]

Spec Period Rep Aliphatic Chem ... Specialist Periodical Reports. Aliphatic Chemistry [*A publication*]
Spec Period Rep Alkaloids ... Specialist Periodical Reports. Alkaloids [*A publication*]
Spec Period Rep Biosynth ... Specialist Periodical Reports. Biosynthesis [*A publication*]
Spec Period Rep Carbohydr Chem ... Specialist Periodical Reports. Carbohydrate Chemistry [*A publication*]
Spec Period Rep Catal ... Specialist Periodical Reports. Catalysis [*A publication*]
Spec Period Rep Gen Synth Methods ... Specialist Periodical Reports. General and Synthetic Methods [*A publication*]
Spec Period Rep Terpenoids Steroids ... Specialist Periodical Reports. Terpenoids and Steroids [*A publication*]
Spec Publ Acad Nat Sci Phila ... Special Publication. Academy of Natural Sciences. Philadelphia [*A publication*]
Spec Publ Am Soc Mammal ... Special Publication. American Society of Mammalogists [*A publication*]
Speech Monogr ... Speech Monographs [*A publication*]
Sper Arch Biol Norm Patol ... Sperimentale Archivio di Biologia Normale e Patologica [*A publication*]
SPF .... Site Population Factor [*Nuclear energy*]
SPF .... Skin Protection Factor [*Medicine*]
SPF .... Standard Project Flood
SPG .... Sort Program Generator [*Data processing*]
SPG .... System Phasing Group
SPH .... Special Psychiatric Hospital [*USSR*]
SP/Hd .... Spool Piece Head
SPI .... Site Population Index [*Nuclear energy*]
SPI .... South Pacific Island Airways, Inc. [*Pago Pago, American Samoa*] [*FAA designator*]
SPI .... Soy Protein Isolate [*Food technology*]
SPI .... Springfield [*Illinois*] [*Airport symbol*]
SPIAM .... Sodium Purity In-Line Analytical Module [*Nuclear energy*]
SPINTAC .. Special Interest Aircraft
Spirt Prom-st' ... Spirtovaya Promyshlennost' [*A publication*]
Spis B'Lg Akad Nauk ... Spisanie na B'Lgarskata Akademiya na Naukite [*A publication*]
Spis B'Lg Geol Druzh ... Spisania na B'Lgarsoto Geologichesko Druzhestvo [*A publication*]
SPJ .... Sparta [*Greece*] [*Airport symbol*]
SPK .... Sapporo [*Japan*] [*Airport symbol*]
SPL .... Service Priority List
SPL .... Skin Potential Level
SPLAN ...... Support Plan
SPLANCH ... Split-Level Ranch [*House*]
SPLL .... Self-Propelled Launcher Loader
SPM .... Scratch Pad Memory
SPM .... Solar Polar Mission
SPN .... Saipan [*Mariana Islands*] [*Airport symbol*]
SPO .... Single Pickle Ordinary [*Metal industry*]
Spolia Zeylan ... Spolia Zeylanica [*A publication*]
Spolia Zool Mus Haun ... Spolia Zoologica Musei Hauniensis [*A publication*]
Sports Turf Bull ... Sports Turf Bulletin [*A publication*]
SPOTS ...... Sikorsky Program Operations Tracking System
SPOUT ...... System Peripheral Output Utility
SPP .... Menongue [*Angola*] [*Airport symbol*]
SPPF .... Solid-Phase Pressure Forming [*Shell Chemical Co.*]
SPPP .... Superior Performance Proficiency Pay
SPQ .... San Pedro [*California*] [*Airport symbol*]
SPR .... San Pedro [*Belize*] [*Airport symbol*]
SPR .... Secretary of the Air Force Program Review
SPR .... Serial Probe Recognition [*Psychometrics*]
SPR .... South Polar Region
SPS .... Scene per Second
SPS .... Self Protection System
SPS .... Shipping/Production Scheduling
SPS .... Wichita Falls [*Texas*] [*Airport symbol*]
SP/SC .... Shield Plug/Support Cylinder
SPSME ...... Spacelab Payload Standard Modular Electronics
SPSS .... Shield Plug Storage Station
SPT .... Special Purpose Tests
SPU .... Split [*Yugoslavia*] [*Airport symbol*]
SPW .... Self-Protection Weapon
SPW .... Spencer [*Iowa*] [*Airport symbol*]
SPY .... San Pedro [*Ivory Coast*] [*Airport symbol*]
SQA .... System Queue Area [*Data processing*]

SQC .... Southern Cross [*Australia*] [*Airport symbol*]
SQD .... Signal Quality Detector
SQD .... Squadron
SQH .... Ford-Aire [*Sidney, NY*] [*FAA designator*]
SQI .... Sterling/Rock Falls [*Illinois*] [*Airport symbol*]
SQM .... Sao Miguel Do Araguaia [*Brazil*] [*Airport symbol*]
SQMD .... Squadron Manning Document
SQR .... Soroako [*Indonesia*] [*Airport symbol*]
SQR .... Supplier Quality Representative
SQS .... Superquick Sensor
SQ/SD ...... Special Qualifications/Special Designation
SQX .... Sulfaquinoxaline [*or (Sulfanilamido)quinoxaline*] [*Animal antibiotic*]
SR .... Safety Rods
SR .... Savannah River Test Pile [*Nuclear energy*]
SR .... Support Reaction Load
SRA .... Shop Replaceable Assembly
SRB .... Service Request Block [*Data processing*]
SRBOC ...... Super Rapid Bloom Off Board Chaff [*Navy*]
SRC .... Spares Receiving Checklist
SRCC .... Sensor Referenced and Computer Controlled [*For remote manipulators*]
S-RD .... Shipper-Receiver Difference
SRDA .... Sodium Removal Development Apparatus [*Nuclear energy*]
SRE .... Sucre [*Bolivia*] [*Airport symbol*]
SRF .... Spacecraft Research Foundation
SRG .... Semarang [*Indonesia*] [*Airport symbol*]
SRI .... Samarinda [*Indonesia*] [*Airport symbol*]
SRI .... Selective Retention Indicators
SRI .... Standard Research Institute
SRIC .... Southwest Research and Information Center
SRJ .... San Borja [*Bolivia*] [*Airport symbol*]
SRM .... Source-Range Monitors
SRM .... System Resources Manager
SRMCASE ... Symmetry-Restricted-Multiconfiguration Annihilation of Single Excitations [*Physics*]
SRO .... Senior Reactor Operator [*Nuclear energy*]
SRO .... Specification Release Order
SRP .... Standard Review Plan
SRP .... Supply Readiness Program [*Air Force*]
Srp Arkh Tselok Lek ... Srpski Arkhiv za Tselokupno Lekarstvo [*A publication*]
SR-RSV ..... Rous Sarcoma Virus, Schmidt-Ruppin Strain
SRS .... Sodium Removal Station [*Nuclear energy*]
SRS .... Southern Railway System
SRS .... Specification Requirement Sheet
Sr Sci .... Senior Science [*A publication*]
SRSO .... Scoliosis Research Society
SRU .... Selective Reserve Unit [*Navy*]
SRV .... Stony River [*Alaska*] [*Airport symbol*]
SRX .... Sert [*Libya*] [*Airport symbol*]
SRZ .... Santa Cruz [*Bolivia*] [*Airport symbol*]
S & S .... Sense and Sensibility [*Novel by Jane Austen*]
SS .... Sessions
SS .... Special Source Materials
SSA .... Salvador [*Brazil*] [*Airport symbol*]
SSA .... Segment Search Argument [*Data processing*]
SSADC ...... Solid-State Air Data Computer
SSAR .... Site Safety Analysis Report [*Nuclear energy*]
SSAR .... Standard Safety Analysis Report [*Nuclear energy*]
SSB .... St. Croix [*Virgin Islands*] Seaplane Base [*Airport symbol*]
SSC .... Short Segmented Cask [*Nuclear energy*]
SSC .... Station Selection Code
SSC .... Sudden Storm Commencement [*Physics*]
SSC .... Systems Support Center
SSD .... Survival Support Device
SSE .... Safe Shutdown Earthquake [*Nuclear energy*]
SSE .... Squared Sum of Errors
SSEC .... Selective Sequence Electronic Calculator
SSEC .... Sound Surveillance Evaluation Center [*Navy*]
SSES .... Special Signal Exploitation Spaces
SSG .... Malabo [*Equatorial Guinea*] [*Airport symbol*]
SSG .... Stonehenge Study Group
SSGJ .... Single Strength Grapefruit Juice
SSGTG .... Ship's Service Gas Turbine Generator [*Navy*]
SSH .... Sharm E Sheikh [*Israel*] [*Airport symbol*]
SSI .... Steady-State Irradiation
SSI .... Surprise Security Inspection [*Navy*]

SSI .... System Science Institute [*IBM Corp.*]
SSIU .... Subsystem Interface Unit
SSJ .... Sandnessjoen [*Norway*] [*Airport symbol*]
SSM .... Sault Ste. Marie [*Michigan*] [*Airport symbol*]
SSMPP ...... Society for the Study of Male Psychology and Physiology
SSNAP ...... Single Seat Night Attack Program
SSN(DS) ... Submarine (Nuclear-Powered) in Direct Support [*Navy symbol*]
SSO .... Space Shuttle Orbiter [*NASA*]
SSOJ .... Single Strength Orange Juice
SSP .... Petroleum Air Transport, Inc. [*Lafayette, LA*] [*FAA designator*]
SSP .... Scientific Services Program [*Army Research Office*]
SSP .... Shortage Specialty Pay [*Navy*]
SSP .... Sodium Sampling Package [*Nuclear energy*]
SSP .... Static Sodium Pots [*Nuclear energy*]
SSPL .... Saturation Sound Pressure Level
SSR .... Site Suitability Report [*Nuclear energy*]
SSS .... Scientific Subroutine System [*Data processing*]
SSS .... Siassi [*Papua New Guinea*] [*Airport symbol*]
SSS .... Special Safety Safeguards
SSS .... Subsystem Support Service
SSSA .... Submarine SONAR Subjective Analysis
SSSA Spec Publ Ser ... SSSA [*Soil Science Society of America*] Special Publication Series [*A publication*]
SSSR .... Smallest Set of Smallest Rings [*Organic chemistry*]
SST .... Secondary Surge Tank [*Nuclear energy*]
SS/T .... Steady-State/Transient Analysis [*Nuclear energy*]
SSUS .... Spinning Solid Upper State
SSW .... Swept Square Wave
SSWLH ..... Society for the Study of Women in Legal History
SSX .... Samsun [*Turkey*] [*Airport symbol*]
SSY .... M'Banza Congo [*Angola*] [*Airport symbol*]
STA .... Stauning [*Denmark*] [*Airport symbol*]
STA .... Straight-In Approach [*Aviation*]
STABS ...... Suinn Test Anxiety Behavior Scale [*Psychology*]
Stadler Genet Symp ... Stadler Genetics Symposia [*A publication*]
STAFF .... Smart Target-Activated Fire and Forget [*Antitank weapon system*]
STAGN ...... Stagnation [*Meteorology*]
Stahlia Misc Pap ... Stahlia Miscellaneous Papers [*A publication*]
STAI .... Subtask ABEND [*Abnormal End*] Intercept [*Data processing*]
Stain Technol ... Stain Technology [*A publication*]
STALAS .... Stationary LASER Site [*NASA*]
Stal Sci Tech Anim Lab ... Stal Sciences et Techniques de l'Animal de Laboratoire [*A publication*]
Stand Methods Clin Chem ... Standard Methods of Clinical Chemistry [*A publication*]
Stanford Ichthyol Bull ... Stanford Ichthyological Bulletin [*A publication*]
Stanford Med Bull ... Stanford Medical Bulletin [*A publication*]
Stanford Stud Psychol ... Stanford Studies in Psychology [*A publication*]
Stanford Univ Publ Geol ... Stanford University Publications in the Geological Sciences [*A publication*]
Stapp Car Crash Conf Proc ... Stapp Car Crash Conference Proceedings [*A publication*]
STAR .... Self-Test Automatic Readout
STAR .... Standard Instrument Arrival [*Aviation*]
STAR .... Standard Tensioned Alongside Receiver [*Navy*]
STAS .... Short Term Analysis Services [*Scientific Services Program*] [*Army*]
STASS ...... Submarine-Towed Array Surveillance System
Stat Bull Metrop Life Insur Co ... Statistical Bulletin. Metropolitan Life Insurance Company [*A publication*]
Statens Skadedyrlab Arsberet ... Statens Skadedyrlaboratorium Arsberetning [*A publication*]
Statens Vaxtskyddsanst Medd ... Statens Vaxtskyddsanstalt Meddelanden [*A publication*]
Stat News Lett (New Delhi) ... Statistical News Letter (New Delhi) [*A publication*]
STB .... Santa Barbara [*Venezuela*] [*Airport symbol*]
STB .... Scan True Bearing
STC .... Society of Telecommunications Consultants
STC .... Subtropical Convergence [*Oceanography*]
STCA .... Sodium Trichloroacetate [*Organic chemistry*]
STCL .... Source-Term Control Loop [*Nuclear energy*]
STE .... Shield Test Experiment [*Nuclear energy*]

New Acronyms, Initialisms, & Abbreviations

STE .... Stevens Point [*Wisconsin*] [*Airport symbol*]
STEM .... Society for Teachers of Emergency Medicine
STEM .... Systems Training and Exercise Module
Steroids Lipids Res ... Steroids and Lipids Research [*A publication*]
STeZ .... South Temperate Zone
STI .... Santiago [*Dominican Republic*] [*Airport symbol*]
STIF .... Short-Term Irradiation Facility
STK .... Standard Test Key [*Data processing*]
STM .... Santarem [*Brazil*] [*Airport symbol*]
STM .... Stream [*Board on Geographic Names*]
STM .... Supersonic Tactical Missile
STN .... Stansted [*England*] [*Airport symbol*]
STNRY ...... Stationary
STO .... Stockholm [*Sweden*] [*Airport symbol*]
STOP .... Stop forced busing; Teach children, not bus them;
Operate neighborhood schools for those in the
neighborhood wishing to attend them; Put an end to
government interference in the parent-child
relationship [*In organization name, S.T.O.P. Forced
Busing*]
STOR .... Segment Table Origin Register [*Data processing*]
STORADS ... Site Tactical Optimized Range Air Defense System
STORMS ... Standardized Operation Research Management System
STP .... Systems Technology Program
STR .... Standard Training Requirements [*Navy*]
STR .... Strategic Training Range
STR .... Stuttgart [*West Germany*] [*Airport symbol*]
Strasb Med ... Strasbourg Medical [*A publication*]
Strathclyde Bioeng Semin ... Strathclyde Bioengineering Seminars
[*A publication*]
STRES ...... Store Release Evaluation System
STRESS .... Satellite Transmission Effects Simulation
STRT .... Strait [*Board on Geographic Names*]
Struct Bonding ... Structure and Bonding [*A publication*]
STRUFO .... Structural Formula [*Data processing*] [*Chemistry*]
STS .... Santa Rosa [*California*] [*Airport symbol*]
STS .... Scottish Tartans Society
STS .... Standard Technical Specifications
St Tomas J Med ... Santo Tomas Journal of Medicine [*A publication*]
STU .... Seeker Test Unit
STU .... Short Ton Unit
Stud Aliment Apa ... Studii de Alimentari cu Apa [*A publication*]
Stud Biol ... Studies in Biology [*A publication*]
Stud Biol Acad Sci Hung ... Studia Biologica. Academiae
Scientiarum Hungaricae [*A publication*]
Stud Biophys ... Studia Biophysica [*A publication*]
Stud Bot Hung ... Studia Botanica Hungarica [*A publication*]
Stud Cercet Antropol ... Studii si Cercetari de Antropologie [*A
publication*]
Stud Cercet Biochim ... Studii si Cercetari de Biochimie [*A
publication*]
Stud Cercet Biol ... Studii si Cercetari de Biologie [*A publication*]
Stud Cercet Biol Ser Bot ... Studii si Cercetari de Biologie. Seria
Botanica [*A publication*]
Stud Cercet Biol Ser Zool ... Studii si Cercetari de Biologie. Seria
Zoologie [*A publication*]
Stud Cercet Endocrinol ... Studii si Cercetari de Endocrinologie [*A
publication*]
Stud Cercet Ig Sanat Publica ... Studii si Cercetari de Igiena si
Sanatate Publica [*A publication*]
Stud Cercet Inframicrobiol ... Studii si Cercetari de
Inframicrobiologie [*A publication*]
Stud Cercet Inst Cercet Piscic ... Studii si Cercetari Institutul de
Cercetari Piscicole [*A publication*]
Stud Cercet Med (Cluj) ... Studii si Cercetari de Medicina (Cluj) [*A
publication*]
Stud Cercet Med Interna ... Studii si Cercetari de Medicina Interna [*A
publication*]
Stud Cercet Silvic ... Studii si Cercetari de Silvicultura [*A publication*]
Stud Cercet Virusol ... Studii si Cercetari de Virusologie [*A
publication*]
Stud Entomol ... Studia Entomologica [*A publication*]
Stud Epurarea Apelor ... Studii de Epurarea Apelor [*A publication*]
Stud Fam Plann ... Studies in Family Planning [*A publication*]
Stud Fauna Suriname Other Guyanas ... Studies of the Fauna of
Suriname and Other Guyanas [*A publication*]
Stud For Suec ... Studia Forestalia Suecica [*A publication*]
Stud Gen .. Studium Generale [*A publication*]
Stud Genet ... Studies in Genetics [*A publication*]

Stud Geol Pol ... Studia Geologica Polonica [*A publication*]
Stud Helminthol ... Studia Helminthologica [*A publication*]
Stud Hist Philos Sci ... Studies in History and Philosophy of Science
[*A publication*]
Stud Inst Med Res (Malaya) ... Studies from the Institute for Medical
Research (Malaya) [*A publication*]
Studi Trentini Sci Nat Sez B Biol ... Studi Trentini di Scienze Naturali.
Sezione B. Biologica [*A publication*]
Stud Med Geogr ... Studies in Medical Geography [*A publication*]
Stud Med Szegedinensia ... Studia Medica Szegedinensia [*A
publication*]
Stud Mycol ... Studies in Mycology [*A publication*]
Stud Nat Sci (Portales, NM) ... Studies in Natural Sciences (Portales,
New Mexico) [*A publication*]
Stud Neotrop Fauna ... Studies on Neotropical Fauna [*A publication*]
Stud Neotrop Fauna Environ ... Studies on Neotropical Fauna and
Environment [*A publication*]
Stud Phys Anthropol ... Studies in Physical Anthropology [*A
publication*]
Stud Pneumol Phtiseol Cech ... Studia Pneumologica et
Phtiseologica Cechoslovaca [*A publication*]
Stud Prot Epurarea Apelor ... Studii de Protectia si Epurarea Apelor
[*A publication*]
Stud Psychol (Bratisl) ... Studia Psychologica (Bratislava) [*A
publication*]
Stud Soc Sci Torun Sect D (Bot) ... Studia Societatis Scientiarum
Torunensis. Sectio D (Botanica) [*A publication*]
Stud Soc Sci Torun Sect E (Zool) ... Studia Societatis Scientiarum
Torunensis. Sectio E (Zoologia) [*A publication*]
Stud Speleol ... Studies in Speleology [*A publication*]
Stud Tokugawa Inst ... Studies from the Tokugawa Institute [*A
publication*]
Stud Trop Oceanogr (Miami) ... Studies in Tropical Oceanography
(Miami) [*A publication*]
Stud Univ Babes-Bolyai Biol ... Studia Universitatis Babes-Bolyai.
Biologia [*A publication*]
Stud Univ Babes-Bolyai Geol Geogr ... Studia Universitatis Babes-
Bolyai. Geologia-Geographia [*A publication*]
Stud VT Geol ... Studies in Vermont Geology [*A publication*]
Study Tea ... Study of Tea [*A publication*]
STURP ...... Shroud of Turin Research Project
Stuttg Beitr Naturkd ... Stuttgarter Beitraege zur Naturkunde [*A
publication*]
Stuttg Beitr Naturkd Ser A (Biol) ... Stuttgarter Beitraege zur
Naturkunde. Serie A (Biologie) [*A publication*]
STV .... Small Test Vessel
STW .... Subtropical Water
ST. WAPNIACL ... State, Treasury, War, Attorney General,
Postmaster General, Navy, Interior, Agriculture,
Commerce, Labor [*Pre-1953 mnemonic guide to
names of the departments in the President's
Cabinet, in order of creation*] [*Obsolete*]
STY .... Salto [*Uruguay*] [*Airport symbol*]
STZ .... Santa Terezinha [*Brazil*] [*Airport symbol*]
SU .... Selectable Unit
SU .... Signaling Unit
SUB .... Sunbelt Airlines [*Rome, GA*] [*FAA designator*]
SUB .... Surabaya [*Indonesia*] [*Airport symbol*]
Sub-Cell Biochem ... Sub-Cellular Biochemistry [*A publication*]
SUBRAP .... Submarine Range Prediction System [*Navy*]
Subsidia Med ... Subsidia Medica [*A publication*]
Subtrop Kul't ... Subtropicheskie Kul'tury [*A publication*]
Success Farming ... Successful Farming [*A publication*]
Sudan J Vet Sci Anim Husb ... Sudan Journal of Veterinary Science
and Animal Husbandry [*A publication*]
Sudan Notes Rec ... Sudan Notes and Records [*A publication*]
Sud-Med Ekspert ... Sudebno-Meditsinskaya Ekspertiza [*A
publication*]
Suelos Ecuat ... Suelos Ecuatoriales [*A publication*]
SUF .... Lametia-Terme [*Italy*] [*Airport symbol*]
SUG .... Surigao [*Philippines*] [*Airport symbol*]
Sugar Beet J ... Sugar Beet Journal [*A publication*]
SUJ .... Satu Mare [*Romania*] [*Airport symbol*]
SUL .... Sui [*Pakistan*] [*Airport symbol*]
SUM .... Shallow Underwater Missile
SUM .... System Check and Utility Master
Sumitomo Bull Ind Health ... Sumitomo Bulletin of Industrial Health
[*A publication*]
Summa Phytopathol ... Summa Phytopathologica [*A publication*]

SUMS........ Specialized Unit Maintenance Support
SUN........... Sun Valley [*Idaho*] [*Airport symbol*]
SUND .... Sunday
Sunshine State Agric Res Rep ... Sunshine State Agricultural Research Report [*A publication*]
Sun Work ... Sun at Work [*A publication*]
SUO .... Sun River [*Oregon*] [*Airport symbol*]
Suom Elainlaakaril ... Suomen Elainlaakarilehti [*A publication*]
Suomen Kemistil A ... Suomen Kemistilehti A [*A publication*]
Suom Hammaslaak Toimi ... Suomen Hammaslaakariseuran Toimituksia [*A publication*]
Suom Hyonteistiet Aikak ... Suomen Hyonteistieteellinen Aikakauskirja [*A publication*]
Suom Kalatalous ... Suomen Kalatalous [*A publication*]
Suom Kemistil B ... Suomen Kemistilehti B [*A publication*]
Suom Kemistiseuran Tied ... Suomen Kemistiseuran Tiedonantoja [*A publication*]
Suom Maataloustiet Seuran Julk ... Suomen Maataloustieteellisen Seuran Julkaisuja [*A publication*]
Suom Psykiatr ... Suomalaista Psykiatriaa [*A publication*]
SUPERHET ... Super Heterodyne
Suppl Ric Biol Selvaggina ... Supplemento alle Ricerche di Biologia della Selvaggina [*A publication*]
Surg Annu ... Surgery Annual [*A publication*]
Surg Clin N Am ... Surgical Clinics of North America [*A publication*]
Surg Forum ... Surgical Forum [*A publication*]
Surg Gastroenterol ... Surgical Gastroenterology [*A publication*]
Surg Gynecol Obstet ... Surgery, Gynecology, and Obstetrics [*A publication*]
Surg Neurol ... Surgical Neurology [*A publication*]
SURP......... Submerged Unmanned Recovery Platform
SURV .... Surveyor
Surv Ophthalmol ... Survey of Ophthalmology [*A publication*]
SUS........... St. Louis [*Missouri*] Spirit of St. Louis Airport [*Airport symbol*]
SUSS .... Submarine Schoolship [*Navy*]
SUSV .... Small Unit Support Vehicle [*Military*]
SUV........... Suva [*Fiji*] [*Airport symbol*]
SUX........... Sioux City [*Iowa*] [*Airport symbol*]
SUY........... Sudureyri [*Iceland*] [*Airport symbol*]
SV .... Simulated Video
SVA........... Savoonga [*Alaska*] [*Airport symbol*]
SVB........... Sambava [*Madagascar*] [*Airport symbol*]
SVC........... Silver City [*New Mexico*] [*Airport symbol*]
SVC........... Spring Viremia of Carp
SVD........... St. Vincent [*Windward Islands*] [*Airport symbol*]
SVD........... Simultaneous Voice/Data
Sven Bot Tidskr ... Svensk Botanisk Tidskrift [*A publication*]
Sven Bryggeritidskr ... Svensk Bryggeritidskrift [*A publication*]
Sven Farm Tidskr ... Svensk Farmaceutisk Tidskrift [*A publication*]
Sven Farm Tidskr Sci Ed ... Svensk Farmaceutisk Tidskrift. Scientific Edition [*A publication*]
Sven Kem Tidskr ... Svensk Kemisk Tidskrift [*A publication*]
Sven Linne-Sallsk Arsskr ... Svenska Linne-Sallskapet Arsskrift [*A publication*]
Sven Mejerition ... Svenska Mejeritioningen [*A publication*]
Sven Naturvetensk ... Svensk Naturvetenskap [*A publication*]
Sven Papperstidn ... Svensk Papperstidning [*A publication*]
Sven Skogsvardsforen Tidskr ... Svenska Skogsvardsforeningens Tidskrift [*A publication*]
Sven Tandlak Tidskr ... Svensk Tandlakare Tidskrift [*A publication*]
Sver Nat.... Sveriges Natur [*A publication*]
Sver Nat Arsb ... Sveriges Natur Arsbok [*A publication*]
Sver Skogsvardsforb Tidskr ... Sveriges Skogsvardsforbunds Tidskrift [*A publication*]
Sver Utsadesforen Tidskr ... Sveriges Utsadesforenings Tidskrift [*A publication*]
SVG........... Stavanger [*Norway*] [*Airport symbol*]
SVI............ San Vincente Del Caguan [*Colombia*] [*Airport symbol*]
SVJ........... Svolvaer [*Norway*] [*Airport symbol*]
SVL........... Savonlinna [*Finland*] [*Airport symbol*]
SVM.......... System Validation Model
SVO........... Moscow [*USSR*] Sheremetyevo Airport [*Airport symbol*]
SVP........... Bie [*Angola*] [*Airport symbol*]
SVP........... Service Processor
SVQ........... Seville [*Spain*] [*Airport symbol*]
SVRB........ Supervisor Request Block [*Data processing*]
SVS........... Stevens Village [*Alaska*] [*Airport symbol*]
SVU........... Savusavu [*Fiji*] [*Airport symbol*]

SVZ........... San Antonio [*Venezuela*] [*Airport symbol*]
SWA.......... Shantou [*China*] [*Airport symbol*]
SWAL......... Shallow Water Attack Craft, Light [*Navy symbol*]
SWAM........ Shallow Water Attack Craft, Medium [*Navy symbol*]
SWANK..... Sealed with a Nice Kiss [*Correspondence*]
SWBS........ Subcontract Work Breakdown Structure
SWC.......... Solid Wastes Cask [*Nuclear energy*]
SWC.......... Stawell [*Australia*] [*Airport symbol*]
SWDS........ Software Development System
SWECS..... Small Wind Energy Conversion Systems
Swed Dent J ... Swedish Dental Journal [*A publication*]
Swed J Agric Res ... Swedish Journal of Agricultural Research [*A publication*]
Swed Weed Conf ... Swedish Weed Conference [*A publication*]
SWF.......... Newburgh [*New York*] [*Airport symbol*]
SWF.......... Still Waters Foundation
SWI........... Sherman [*Texas*] [*Airport symbol*]
SWIFT....... Society for Worldwide Interbank Financial Transactions
SWIP......... Society for Women in Philosophy
Swiss J Hydrol ... Swiss Journal of Hydrology [*A publication*]
SWL.......... Signals Warfare Laboratory [*Army*]
SWM.......... Suia-Missu [*Brazil*] [*Airport symbol*]
SWMCCS... Standard Weather Messages Command and Control System
SWO.......... Stillwater [*Oklahoma*] [*Airport symbol*]
SWO.......... Surface Warfare Officer [*Navy*]
SWOS....... Surface Warfare Officer's School [*Navy*]
SWOSCOLCOM ... Surface Warfare Officer's School Command [*Navy*]
SWP.......... Service Water Pump [*Nuclear energy*]
SWPP........ Southwest Power Pool
SWR.......... Service Water Reservoir [*Nuclear energy*]
SWRB........ Sadler's Wells Royal Ballet [*British*]
SWS.......... Service Water System [*Nuclear energy*]
SWS.......... Swansea [*Wales*] [*Airport symbol*]
SXB........... Strasbourg [*France*] [*Airport symbol*]
SXE........... Sale [*Australia*] [*Airport symbol*]
SXF........... Berlin [*East Germany*] [*Airport symbol*]
SXG........... Senanga [*Zambia*] [*Airport symbol*]
SXH........... Sehulea [*Papua New Guinea*] [*Airport symbol*]
SXN........... Sao Jose Do Xingu [*Brazil*] [*Airport symbol*]
SXP........... Sheldon Point [*Alaska*] [*Airport symbol*]
SXR........... Srinagar [*India*] [*Airport symbol*]
SXY........... Sidney [*New York*] [*Airport symbol*]
SYA........... Shemya Island [*Alaska*] [*Airport symbol*]
SYB........... Seal Bay [*Alaska*] [*Airport symbol*]
SYCA....... Syndicat d'Etude des Centrales Atomique [*Belgium*]
SYD........... Sydney [*Australia*] [*Airport symbol*]
Sydowia Ann Mycol ... Sydowia Annales Mycologici [*A publication*]
SYE........... Sa'Dah [*Yemen Arab Republic*] [*Airport symbol*]
SYEP......... Summer Youth Employment Program [*Department of Labor*]
SYK........... Stykkisholmur [*Iceland*] [*Airport symbol*]
SYM.......... Simao [*China*] [*Airport symbol*]
Symp Angiol Sanitoriana ... Symposia Angiologica Sanitoriana [*A publication*]
Symp Biol Hung ... Symposia Biologica Hungarica [*A publication*]
Symp Bot Ups ... Symbolae Botanicae Upsalienses [*A publication*]
Symp Br Soc Parasitol ... Symposia of the British Society for Parasitology [*A publication*]
Symp Foods ... Symposium of Foods [*A publication*]
Symp Fundam Cancer Res Collect Pap ... Symposium on Fundamental Cancer Research. Collections of Papers [*A publication*]
Symp Int Soc Cell Biol ... Symposia of the International Society for Cell Biology [*A publication*]
Symp R Entomol Soc Lond ... Symposia of the Royal Entomological Society of London [*A publication*]
Symp Ser Immunobiol Stand ... Symposia Series in Immunobiological Standardization [*A publication*]
Symp Soc Dev Biol ... Symposia of the Society for Developmental Biology [*A publication*]
Symp Soc Exp Biol ... Symposia of the Society for Experimental Biology [*A publication*]
Symp Soc Gen Microbiol ... Symposium of the Society for General Microbiology [*A publication*]
Symp Soc Study Dev Growth ... Symposium of the Society for the Study of Development and Growth [*A publication*]

Symp Soc Study Hum Biol ... Symposia of the Society for the Study of Human Biology [*A publication*]

Symp Soc Study Inborn Errors Metab ... Symposium of the Society for the Study of Inborn Errors of Metabolism [*A publication*]

Symp Swed Nutr Found ... Symposia of the Swedish Nutrition Foundation [*A publication*]

Symp Zool Soc Lond ... Symposia of the Zoological Society of London [*A publication*]

Synth Commun ... Synthetic Communications [*A publication*]

Synth Methods Org Chem Yearb ... Synthetic Methods of Organic Chemistry Yearbook [*A publication*]

Syst Assoc Publ ... Systematics Association. Publication [*A publication*]

Syst Assoc Spec Vol ... Systematics Association. Special Volume [*A publication*]

SYVV .... Sowthistle Yellow Vein Virus

SYY .... Stornoway [*Scotland*] [*Airport symbol*]

SYZ .... Shiraz [*Iran*] [*Airport symbol*]

SZA .... Soyo [*Angola*] [*Airport symbol*]

SZG .... Salzburg [*Austria*] [*Airport symbol*]

SZK .... Skukuza [*South Africa*] [*Airport symbol*]

SZS .... Stewart Island [*New Zealand*] [*Airport symbol*]

SZZ .... Szczecin [*Poland*] [*Airport symbol*]

T

T .... Tactical Organization
T .... Teracycle
TAA .... Thioacetamide [*Organic chemistry*]
TAB .... Airborne Tanker, Boom
TAB .... Table
TAB .... Tobago [*Trinidad and Tobago*] [*Airport symbol*]
TABS .... Terminal Access to Batch Service [*Data processing*]
TABS .... Time Analysis and Billing System
Tabulae Biol ... Tabulae Biologicae [*A publication*]
TABWS .... Tactical Airborne Weather Stations
TAC .... Tacloban [*Philippines*] [*Airport symbol*]
TAC .... Technical Assistance Contract
TAC .... Terrain Analysis Center [*Army*]
TAC .... Time Action Calendar [*Management*]
TACCS ...... Tactical Air Command Control System
TACM .... Transit Air Cargo Manifest
TACNOTE ... Tactical Notice
TACS .... Technical Assignment Control System
TACS .... Test Assembly Conditioning Station
TAD .... Airborne Tanker, Drogue
TAD .... Trinidad [*Colorado*] [*Airport symbol*]
TADREPS ... Tactical Data Replay System
TAF .... Aerodrome Forecast [*Aviation*]
TAFIN .... Tactical Air Force Initiative
TAG .... Airborne Tanker, General
TAG .... Tactical Airlift Group
TAG .... Tagbilaran [*Philippines*] [*Army*]
TAG .... Technical Assistance Group
Tagungsber Ges Inn Med DDR ... Tagungsbericht der Gesellschaft fuer Innere Medizin der DDR [*A publication*]
TAH .... Tanna Island [*Vanuata*] [*Airport symbol*]
TAHOE ...... TOW Against Helicopter Operational Equipment
TAI .... Taiz [*Yemen Arab Republic*] [*Airport symbol*]
TAI .... Traditionally Administered Instruction
TAIS .... Tactical Air Intelligence System
Taiwan Fish Res Inst Lab Biol Rep ... Taiwan Fisheries Research Institute. Laboratory of Biology. Report [*A publication*]
Taiwan Sugar Exp Stn Annu Rep ... Taiwan Sugar Experiment Station. Annual Report [*A publication*]
Taiwan Sugar Exp Stn Res Rep ... Taiwan Sugar Experiment Station. Research Report [*A publication*]
Taiwan Sugar Res Inst Annu Rep ... Taiwan Sugar Research Institute. Annual Report [*A publication*]
TAJ .... Tadji [*Papua New Guinea*] [*Airport symbol*]
TAK .... Takamatsu [*Japan*] [*Airport symbol*]
TAL .... Tanana [*Alaska*] [*Airport symbol*]
Tall Timbers Res Stn Misc Publ ... Tall Timbers Research Station. Miscellaneous Publication [*A publication*]
TALONS .... Tactical Airborne LORAN Navigation System [*Model*]
TALT .... Tracking Altitude
TAM .... Tampico [*Mexico*] [*Airport symbol*]
TAME .... Tactical Air-to-Air Mission Evaluation
TAMM .... Tetrakis(acetoxymercuri)methane [*Organic chemistry*]
TAMP .... Tactical Armament Master Plan
TAMS .... Target Activated Munitions
TAN .... Teletype Alert Network
TANO .... Triacetoneamine Nitroxide [*Organic chemistry*]

Tanzania Silvic Res Note ... Tanzania Silviculture Research Note [*A publication*]
TAO .... Tactical Action Officer [*Navy*]
TAO .... Time and Altitude Over [*Aviation*]
TAP .... Tactical Armament Plan
TAP .... Tapachula [*Mexico*] [*Airport symbol*]
TAP .... Theater of All Possibilities [*International touring company of actor-authors*]
TAPCC ...... Technology and Pollution Control Committee [*Environmental Protection Agency*]
TAPE .... Tentative Annual Planning Estimate
TAPS .... Tarapur Atomic Power Station [*India*]
TAR .... Technical Assistance Request
TARP .... Typical Airland Resupply Profile
TAS .... Tashkent [*USSR*] [*Airport symbol*]
TAS .... Tychon's Assembler
Tasmania Dep Agric Annu Rep ... Tasmanian Department of Agriculture. Annual Report [*A publication*]
Tasmania For Comm Bull ... Tasmania Forestry Commission. Bulletin [*A publication*]
Tasmania Inland Fish Comm Rep ... Tasmania Inland Fisheries Commission. Report [*A publication*]
Tasmanian Dep Agric Pamp ... Tasmanian Department of Agriculture. Pamphlet [*A publication*]
Tasmanian Fis Res ... Tasmanian Fisheries Research [*A publication*]
Tasmanian J Agric ... Tasmanian Journal of Agriculture [*A publication*]
TASMO ..... Tactical Air Support for Maritime Operations [*Navy*]
TAT .... Tatry/Poprad [*Czechoslovakia*] [*Airport symbol*]
TAU .... Twin Agent Unit [*Fire fighting*]
TAVC .... Total Active Vitamin C [*Nutrition*]
TAWDS ..... Terminal Area Weapon Delivery Simulator
TAWS .... Tactical Area Weather Sensor
TB .... Twirly Birds [*An organization*]
TBA .... Tabibuga [*Papua New Guinea*] [*Airport symbol*]
TBA .... Taurine Bibliophiles of America
TBA .... Tertiary Butyl Alcohol [*Gasoline additive*]
TBA .... To Be Avoided [*Slang*]
TBAZFCA ... Toledo Bird Association, Zebra Finch Club of America
TBEP .... Tri(butoxyethyl) Phosphate [*Organic chemistry*]
TBF .... Tabiteuea North [*Kiribati*] [*Airport symbol*]
TBG .... Tabubil [*Papua New Guinea*] [*Airport symbol*]
TBH .... Tablas [*Philippines*] [*Airport symbol*]
TBHP .... Tertiary-Butyl Hydroperoxide [*Organic chemistry*]
TBHP .... Trihydroxybutyrophenone [*Antioxidant*] [*Organic chemistry*]
TBN .... Fort Leonard Wood [*Missouri*] [*Airport symbol*]
TBO .... Tabora [*Tanzania*] [*Airport symbol*]
TBP .... Tumbes [*Peru*] [*Airport symbol*]
TBS .... Tbilisi [*USSR*] [*Airport symbol*]
TBT .... Tabatinga [*Brazil*] [*Airport symbol*]
TBTP .... Tributyl Trithiophosphate [*Defoliant*] [*Organic chemistry*]
TBTU .... Tributylthiourea [*Organic chemistry*]
TBU .... Tongatapu [*Tonga Island*] [*Airport symbol*]
TBZ .... Tabriz [*Iran*] [*Airport symbol*]
T/C .... Tactical Coordinator
TC .... Tax Council
TC .... Terminal Computer
TC .... Terminal Controller

New Acronyms, Initialisms, & Abbreviations

T/C............ Treatment Charge [*Metallurgy*]
TCA........... Tennant Creek [*Australia*] [*Airport symbol*]
TCA........... Turbulent Contacting Absorber
TCB........... Treasure Cay [*Bahamas*] [*Airport symbol*]
TCBC........ Trichlorobenzyl Chloride [*Organic chemistry*]
TCC........... [*The*] Cola Clan [*An organization*]
TCC........... Telecommunications Consumer Coalition
TCC........... Travelers' Century Club
TCC........... Trichlorocarbanilide [*Organic chemistry*]
TCD........... Thermal Conductivity Detector [*Analytical instrumentation*]
TCE........... Tulcea [*Romania*] [*Airport symbol*]
TCH........... Tchibanga [*Gabon*] [*Airport symbol*]
TCI............ Tenerife [*Canary Islands*] [*Airport symbol*]
TCL........... Tuscaloosa [*Alabama*] [*Airport symbol*]
TC/LD....... Thermocouple/Lead Detector
TC-NBT..... Thiocarbamyl-nitro-blue Tetrazolium [*Organic chemistry*]
TCO........... Tumaco [*Colombia*] [*Airport symbol*]
TCP........... Tricalcium Phosphate [*Inorganic chemistry*]
TCP........... Trichlorophenol [*Organic chemistry*]
TCPA........ Trichlorophenylacetic Acid [*Herbicide*] [*Organic chemistry*]
TCPAM..... Tentative CNO [*Chief of Naval Operations*] Program Analysis Memorandum
TCS........... Telephone Conference Summary
TCS........... Terminal Computer System
TCS........... Two-Photon Coherent States
TCTNB...... Trichlorotrinitrobenzene [*Organic chemistry*]
TCU........... Tactical Control Unit
TCU........... Teletype Communications Unit
TD............. Tabular Data
TD............. Terminal Display
TD............. Transfer Dolly [*Bottom-loading transfer cask*] [*Nuclear energy*]
TDAS........ Thermal Decomposition Analytical System [*For study of incineration*]
TDB........... Trade Development Bank [*International banking concern*]
TDC........... Thermal Diffusion Coefficient
TDC........... Total Design Concept [*Sarcastic reference to a completely coordinated wardrobe, decorating scheme, etc.*] [*Slang*]
TDC........... Transferable Development Credit
TDCF........ Technical Directive Compliance Form
TDD........... Test Design Description
TDE........... Tactical Deception Element
TDF........... Task Deletion Form
TDG........... Test Data Generator
TDP........... Target Data Processor
TDPA........ Thiodipropionic Acid [*Organic chemistry*]
TDPAC...... Time Differential Perturbed Angular Correlation [*Physics*]
TDPP......... Traffic Data Processing Program
TDS........... Time-Division Scramble
TDT........... Thermal Death Time [*Bacteriological testing*]
TDT........... Thiodiethanethiol [*Organic chemistry*]
TDT........... Tone Decay Test [*Audiometry*]
TDT........... Toronto Dance Theatre
TDU........... Tactical Deception Unit
TDU........... Tactical Display Unit
TE.............. Test and Engineering
TE.............. Thermal Expansion Load
TEA.......... Transversely Excited Atmospheric [*LASER*]
TEA.......... Triethylamine [*Organic chemistry*]
Tea East Afr ... Tea in East Africa [*A publication*]
TEAM........ Trend Evaluation and Monitoring [*Congressional Clearinghouse on the Future*]
TEAMMATE ... Total Electronic Advanced Microprocessing Maneuvers and Tactics Equipment [*A game*]
TEAP........ Triethylammonium Phosphate [*Organic chemistry*]
Tea Q .... Tea Quarterly [*A publication*]
Tea Res Assoc Annu Sci Rep ... Tea Research Association. Annual Scientific Report [*A publication*]
Tea Res Inst Ceylon Annu Rep ... Tea Research Institute of Ceylon. Annual Report [*A publication*]
Tea Res Inst Sri Lanka Tech Rep ... Tea Research Institute of Sri Lanka. Technical Report [*A publication*]
TEBAC...... Triethylbenzylammonium Chloride [*Organic chemistry*]
TEC........... Technical Escort Center [*Army*]
Tec Agric (Catania) ... Tecnica Agricola (Catania) [*A publication*]

Tech Adv Shikoku Agric ... Technical Advances in Shikoku Agriculture [*A publication*]
Tech Biochem Biophys Morphol ... Techniques of Biochemical and Biophysical Morphology [*A publication*]
Tech Bull Fac Agric Kagawa Univ ... Technical Bulletin of Faculty of Agriculture. Kagawa University [*A publication*]
Tech Bull Fac Hortic Chiba Univ ... Technical Bulletin of Faculty of Horticulture. Chiba University [*A publication*]
Tech Bull Regist Med Technol ... Technical Bulletin of the Registry of Medical Technologists [*A publication*]
Tech Bull Taiwan Agric Res Inst ... Technical Bulletin of the Taiwan Agricultural Research Institute [*A publication*]
Technol Respir ... Technologie Respiratoire [*A publication*]
Tech Notes For Comm NSW ... Technical Notes. Forestry Commission of New South Wales [*A publication*]
Tecnol Aliment ... Tecnologia Alimentaria [*A publication*]
Tec Pecu Mex ... Tecnica Pecuaria en Mexico [*A publication*]
TEDDS...... Tactical Environmental Dissemination and Display System
TEDMA ..... Triethylene Dimethacrylate [*Organic chemistry*]
TEE .... Terminal Effects and Experimentation
TEGMA ..... Triethylene Glycol Dimethacrylate [*Organic chemistry*]
Tek Hogsk Helsingfors Vetensk Publ ... Tekniska Hogskolan i Helsingfors Vetenskapliga Publikationer [*A publication*]
Tekst Prom-st' ... Tekstil'Naya Promyshlennost' [*A publication*]
TELEMAN ... Telephone Management System
TELRY....... Telegraph Reply
TEM .... Target Engagement Message
Temas Odontol ... Temas Odontologicos [*A publication*]
TEMP .... Technique for Econometric Modeling Program
TEMPO ..... Technique for Extreme Point Optimization
Tenn Agric Exp Stn Annu Rep ... Tennessee Agricultural Experiment Station. Annual Report [*A publication*]
Tenn Agric Exp Stn Bull ... Tennessee Agricultural Experiment Station. Bulletin [*A publication*]
Tenn Farm Home Sci Prog Rep ... Tennessee Farm and Home Science Progress Report [*A publication*]
TENN-TOM ... Tennessee-Tombigbee [*Proposed waterway*]
TEOA .... Test and Evaluation Objectives Annex
Teor Prakt Fiz Kul't ... Teoriya i Praktika Fizicheskoi Kul'tury [*A publication*]
TER .... Triple Ejection Rack
Ter Arkh ... Terapevticheskii Arkhiv [*A publication*]
TERCOM... Terrain Contour Mapping
TERPS ...... Terminal Instrument Procedures
Tertiary Res Spec Pap ... Tertiary Research Special Papers [*A publication*]
TESE......... Tactical Exercise Simulator and Evaluator
TESRP ...... Test and Evaluation Support Resource Plan
TETA......... Triethylenetetramine [*Organic chemistry*]
Tethys Suppl ... Tethys. Supplement [*A publication*]
Tetrahedron Lett ... Tetrahedron Letters [*A publication*]
Tex Agric Exp Stn Bull ... Texas Agricultural Experiment Station. Bulletin [*A publication*]
Tex Agric Exp Stn Leafl ... Texas Agricultural Experiment Station. Leaflet [*A publication*]
Tex Agric Exp Stn Misc Publ ... Texas Agricultural Experiment Station. Miscellaneous Publication [*A publication*]
Tex Agric Exp Stn Prog Rep ... Texas Agricultural Experiment Station. Progress Report [*A publication*]
Tex Agric Exp Stn Tech Monogr ... Texas Agricultural Experiment Station. Technical Monograph [*A publication*]
Tex Agric Prog ... Texas Agricultural Progress [*A publication*]
Tex A M Univ Oceanogr Stud ... Texas A & M University. Oceanographic Studies [*A publication*]
Tex For Pap ... Texas Forestry Paper [*A publication*]
Tex J Sci Spec Publ ... Texas Journal of Science. Special Publication [*A publication*]
Tex Mem Mus Misc Pap ... Texas Memorial Museum. Miscellaneous Papers [*A publication*]
Tex Rep Biol Med ... Texas Reports on Biology and Medicine [*A publication*]
Tex State J Med ... Texas State Journal of Medicine [*A publication*]
TEXT......... Texas Experimental TOKAMAK [*Atomic physics*]
TFAI.......... Trifluoroacetylimidazole [*Organic chemistry*]
TFANP...... Task Force Against Nuclear Power
TFC........... United States Overseas Tax Fairness Committee
TFD........... Tactical Fighter Dispenser

TFH .... Touch for Health Foundation
TG .... Test Guaranteed
TGA .... Total Glycoalkaloids [*Analytical biochemistry*]
TGPSG ...... Tactical Global Positioning System Guidance
TGU .... Technical Guidance Unit
TGV .... Train de Grande Vitesse [*French high-speed train*]
THAA .... Tourist House Association of America
Thai J Agric Sci ... Thai Journal of Agricultural Science [*A publication*]
Thail Plant Prot Serv Tech Bull ... Thailand Plant Protection Service. Technical Bulletin [*A publication*]
Thai Natl Sci Pap Fauna Ser ... Thai National Scientific Papers. Fauna Series [*A publication*]
Thalassia Jugosl ... Thalassia Jugoslavica [*A publication*]
THAP .... Tactical High-Altitude Penetration
Theor Appl Genet ... Theoretical and Applied Genetics [*A publication*]
Theor Exp Biol ... Theoretical and Experimental Biology [*A publication*]
Theor Popul Biol ... Theoretical Population Biology [*A publication*]
Theory Exp Exobiol ... Theory and Experiment in Exobiology [*A publication*]
Ther Ggw ... Therapie der Gegenwart [*A publication*]
Ther Hung ... Therapia Hungarica [*A publication*]
Ther Umsch ... Therapeutische Umschau [*A publication*]
Theses Cathol Med Coll ... Theses of Catholic Medical College [*A publication*]
THN .... Trihydroxynaphthalene [*Organic chemistry*]
Thromb Diath Haemorrh ... Thrombosis et Diatheses Haemorrhagica [*A publication*]
THRU .... I am connecting you to another switchboard [*Communications*]
THSA .... Thomas Hardy Society of America
THTF .... Thermal Hydraulic Test Facility
THTMS...... Tetramethylthiuram Monosulfide [*Organic chemistry*] [*Also, TMTD*]
TI .... Trypsin Inhibitor [*Food technology*]
TIA .... Trypsin Inhibitor Activity [*Food technology*]
TIBA .... Triisobutylamine [*Organic chemistry*]
TIC .... Tactical Intercom Systems
TICODS .... Time Compression Display
Tidskr Dok ... Tidskrift foer Dokumentation [*A publication*]
Tidsskr Nor Laegeforen ... Tidsskrift foer den Norske Laegeforening [*A publication*]
TIEG .... Teen International Entomology Group
Tierernaehr Fuetter ... Tierernaehrung und Fuetterung [*A publication*]
TIES .... Total Information for Education System
TIF .... Task Initiation Form
Tijdschr Diergeneeskd ... Tijdschrift voor Diergeneeskunde [*A publication*]
Tijdschr Diergeneeskd Q Engl Issue ... Tijdschrift voor Diergeneeskunde. Quarterly English Issue [*A publication*]
Tijdschr Entomol ... Tijdschrift voor Entomologie [*A publication*]
Tijdschr Gastro-Enterol ... Tijdschrift voor Gastro-Enterologie [*A publication*]
Tijdschr Kindergeneeskd ... Tijdschrift voor Kindergeneeskunde [*A publication*]
Tijdschr Plantenziekten ... Tijdschrift voor Plantenziekten [*A publication*]
TIM............ Technical Information Manual
TIM............ Total Ion Scanning Mode [*Spectroscopy*]
TIMS .... Technology Integration of Missile Subsystems
TINT .... Target Intercept Timer
TIOT.......... Task Input/Output Table [*Data processing*]
TIP............. Terminal Interface Package [*Data processing*]
TIP............. Total Information Processing
TIP............. Transient [*or Traveling*] In-Core Probe [*Nuclear energy*]
TIPA .... Triisopropanolamine [*Organic chemistry*]
TIPITEF ..... Tactical Information Processing and Interpretation Total Environment Facility
TIPS .... Trends in Pharmacological Sciences [*A publication*]
TIR .... Test Incidence and Reporting System
TIS .... Tracking Instrumentation Subsystem
TISA .... Technique for Interactive Systems Analysis
TISAP........ Totalized Interface Subroutine and Post Processor [*Data processing*]
TIU .... Trypsin Inhibitory Unit [*Food analysis*]

TJ .... Terajoule [*SI unit of energy*]
TJID .... Terminal Job Identification
TL.............. Tape Library
TL.............. Task Leader
TLB .... Translation Lookaside Buffer [*Data processing*]
TLC .... Trilateral Commission [*International study group*]
TLLM........ Temperature and Liquid Level Monitor
TLP........... Telegraph Line Pair
TLP........... Top Load Pad
TLTA .... Two-Loop Test Apparatus
TM............. Tape Mark [*Data processing*]
TM............. Temperature Monitor
TMA .... Trimethylamine [*Organic chemistry*]
TMAI .... Tetramethylammonium Iodide [*Organic chemistry*]
TMAS........ Tank Main Armament Systems
TMBAC ..... Trimethylbenzylammonium Chloride [*Organic chemistry*] [*Also, BTM*]
TMC .... [*The*] Maintenance Council of the American Trucking Associations
TMC .... Terrestrial Microcosm Chamber [*For environmental studies*]
TMC .... Thick Molding Compound [*Plastics technology*]
TMCA....... Toxic Materials Control Activity [*General Motors*]
TMD .... Transient Mass Distribution Code
TMDA....... Training Media Distributors' Association
TME .... Test Marketing Exemption [*Environmental Protection Agency*]
TME .... Total Metabolizable Energy [*Nutrition*]
TME .... Trimethylolethane [*Organic chemistry*]
TMEDA...... Trimethylenediamine [*Organic chemistry*]
TMETN..... Trimethylolethane Trinitrate [*Organic chemistry*]
TMF.......... Technical Transmitter Holding Future
TMMP ...... Technical Manual Management Program [*Navy*]
TMO .... Targets Management Office [*MIRCOM*]
TMO .... Trans Mo Airlines [*Jefferson City, MO*] [*FAA designator*]
TMP.......... Temperature
TMP.......... Terminal Monitor Program
TMP.......... Thermomechanical Pulps
TMPN........ Tetramethylpiperidinol N-oxyl [*Organic chemistry*]
TMPO....... Traffic Management and Proceedings Office [*CONUS*]
TMRC....... Theoretical Maximum Residue Contribution [*to acceptable daily intake*] [*Environmental Protection Agency*]
TMS .... Telecommunications Message Switcher
TMS .... Tight Model Series
TMS .... Transaction Management System
TMU .... Transmission Message Unit
TMX .... Tandem Mirror Experiment [*Atomic fusion*]
TNA .... Tetranitroadamantane [*Explosive*] [*Organic chemistry*]
TNBA .... Tri-normal-butylamine [*Organic chemistry*]
TNBT .... Tetranitro Blue Tetrazolium [*A dye*] [*Organic chemistry*]
TNLR........ Railroad Tunnel [*Board on Geographic Names*]
TNPA........ Tri-normal-propylamine [*Organic chemistry*]
TNR .... Non-RADAR Transfer of Control Message [*Communications*]
TNS .... [*The*] Next Step [*Physics*]
TNS .... Transaction Network Service [*AT & T*]
TNV .... Tobacco Necrosis Virus
TNZ .... Thermoneutral Zone
Tob Int (NY) ... Tobacco International (New York) [*A publication*]
Tob Res Board Rhod Bull ... Tobacco Research Board of Rhodesia. Bulletin [*A publication*]
Tob Sci ..... Tobacco Science [*A publication*]
Tocklai Exp Stn Advis Bull ... Tocklai Experimental Station. Advisory Bulletin [*A publication*]
Tocklai Exp Stn Advis Leafl ... Tocklai Experimental Station. Advisory Leaflet [*A publication*]
TOD.......... Total Oxygen Demand [*Analytical chemistry*]
TODA .... Takeoff Distance Available [*Aviation*]
Tohoku J Agric Res ... Tohoku Journal of Agricultural Research [*A publication*]
Tohoku J Exp Med ... Tohoku Journal of Experimental Medicine [*A publication*]
Tohoku Med J ... Tohoku Medical Journal [*A publication*]
Tohoku Psychol Folia ... Tohoku Psychologica Folia [*A publication*]
Tokai J Exp Clin Med ... Tokai Journal of Experimental and Clinical Medicine [*A publication*]
Toko-Ginecol Pract ... Toko-Ginecologia Practica [*A publication*]

Tokushima J Exp Med ... Tokushima Journal of Experimental Medicine [*A publication*]

TOM .... Toronto, Ottawa, Montreal [*Derogatory reference to people in these cities; used by other Canadians who think people living in these cities "run things"*]

TON .... Top of the News [*A publication*]

TOP .... [*The*] Opportunity Prospector [*A publication*]

TOP .... Transient Overpower Accident [*Physics*]

TOP .... Transovarial Passage [*Virology*]

Top Appl Phys ... Topics in Applied Physics [*A publication*]

Top Curr Chem ... Topics in Current Chemistry [*A publication*]

Top Enzyme Ferment Biotechnol ... Topics in Enzyme and Fermentation Biotechnology [*A publication*]

Top Horm Chem ... Topics in Hormone Chemistry [*A publication*]

Top Hum Genet ... Topics in Human Genetics [*A publication*]

TOPLAS .... Transactions on Programing Languages and Systems

Top Med Chem ... Topics in Medicinal Chemistry [*A publication*]

TOPO .... Test Operations and Policy Office [*TECOM*]

TOPP .... Terminal-Operated Production Program

Top Phosphorus Chem ... Topics in Phosphorus Chemistry [*A publication*]

Top Photosynth ... Topics in Photosynthesis [*A publication*]

Top Probl Psychiatry Neurol ... Topical Problems in Psychiatry and Neurology [*A publication*]

Top Probl Psychother ... Topical Problems of Psychotherapy [*A publication*]

TOR .... Toronto Airways Ltd. [*Markom, ON*] [*FAA designator*]

TORA .... Takeoff Run Available [*Aviation*]

Tori Bull Ornithol Soc Jpn ... Tori. Bulletin of the Ornithological Society of Japan [*A publication*]

TOSS .... Tactical Operational Scoring System

TOSS .... Transient and/or Steady State

TOSS .... TV Ordnance Scoring System

TOT .... Texas Opera Theatre

Toxicol Annu ... Toxicology Annual [*A publication*]

Toxicol Appl Pharmacol ... Toxicology and Applied Pharmacology [*A publication*]

Toxicol Environ Chem Rev ... Toxicological and Environmental Chemistry Reviews [*A publication*]

TP .... Tape

TP .... Test Pressure

TP .... Thermoplastic [*Plastics technology*] [*Also, T*]

TPA .... Tantalum Producers Association

TPA .... Terephthalic Acid [*Organic chemistry*] [*Also, TA*]

TPA .... Triphenylamine [*Organic chemistry*]

TPD .... Time Pulse Distributor

TPLF .... Tigray People's Liberation Front

TPN .... Tetrachlorophthalodinitrile [*Organic chemistry*]

TPPGM ...... Tentative Planning and Programing Guidance Memorandum [*Navy*]

TPTA .... Tin Triphenyl [*or Triphenyltin*] Acetate [*Organic chemistry*]

TPTC .... Triphenyltin Chloride [*Organic chemistry*]

TPTH .... Triphenyltin Hydroxide [*Organic chemistry*]

TPW .... Tons per Week

TPY .... Tons per Year

TR .... Technical Review

TRA .... RADAR Transfer of Control Message [*Communications*]

TRA .... Trade Readjustment Allowance [*or Assistance*]

TRA .... Tubular Reactor Assembly [*Nuclear energy*]

Trab Compostelanos Biol ... Trabajos Compostelanos de Biologia [*A publication*]

Trab Geol ... Trabajos de Geologia [*A publication*]

Trab Inst Cajal Invest Biol ... Trabajos del Instituto Cajal de Investigaciones Biologicas [*A publication*]

Trab Inst Econ Prod Ganad Ebro ... Trabajos del Instituto de Economia y Producciones Ganaderas del Ebro [*A publication*]

Trab Inst Esp Entomol ... Trabajos del Instituto Espanol de Entomologia [*A publication*]

Trab Inst Esp Oceanogr ... Trabajos del Instituto Espanol de Oceanografia [*A publication*]

Trab Inst Oceanogr Univ Recife ... Trabalhos do Instituto Oceanografico da Universidade do Recife [*A publication*]

Trab Oceanogr Univ Fed Pernambuco ... Trabalhos Oceanograficos Universidade Federal de Pernambuco [*A publication*]

Trab Pesqui Inst Nutr Univ Bras ... Trabalhos e Pesquisas Instituto de Nutricao Universidade do Brasil [*A publication*]

TRAC .... Transaction Reporting and Control System

TRACE ...... Taxing and Routing of Aircraft Coordinating Equipment

TRADE ...... Training Devices

Traffic Saf Res Rev ... Traffic Safety Research Review [*A publication*]

Tr Akad Nauk Lit SSR Ser V ... Trudy Akademii Nauk Litovskoi SSR. Seriya V [*A publication*]

Tr Akad Nauk Tadzh SSR ... Trudy Akademii Nauk Tadzhikskoi SSR [*A publication*]

Tr Akad Nauk Turkm SSR ... Trudy Akademii Nauk Turkmenskoi SSR [*A publication*]

Tr Alma-At Med Inst ... Trudy Alma-Atinskogo Meditsinskogo Instituta [*A publication*]

Tr Alma-At Zoovet Inst ... Trudy Alma-Atinskogo Zooveterinarnogo Instituta [*A publication*]

TRAMIS .... Training Management Information System [*Air Force*]

Tr Amur S-kh Opytn Stn ... Trudy Amurskoi Sel'skokhozyaistvennoi Opytnoi Stantsii [*A publication*]

Trans All-India Inst Ment Health ... Transactions of All-India Institute of Mental Health [*A publication*]

Trans Am Clin Climatol Assoc ... Transactions of the American Clinical and Climatological Association [*A publication*]

Trans Am Entomol Soc (Phila) ... Transactions of the American Entomological Society (Philadelphia) [*A publication*]

Trans Am Fish Soc ... Transactions of the American Fisheries Society [*A publication*]

Trans Am Microsc Soc ... Transactions of the American Microscopical Society [*A publication*]

Trans Am Neurol Assoc ... Transactions of the American Neurological Association [*A publication*]

Trans Am Nucl Soc ... Transactions of the American Nuclear Society [*A publication*]

Trans Am Ophthalmol Soc ... Transactions of the American Ophthalmological Society [*A publication*]

Trans Am Philos Soc ... Transactions of the American Philosophical Society [*A publication*]

Trans Am Soc Artif Intern Organs ... Transactions of the American Society for Artificial Internal Organs [*A publication*]

Trans ASAE ... Transactions of the ASAE [*American Society of Agricultural Engineers*] [*A publication*]

Trans Bose Res Inst (Calcutta) ... Transactions of the Bose Research Institute (Calcutta) [*A publication*]

Trans Br Bryol Soc ... Transactions of the British Bryological Society [*A publication*]

Trans Br Mycol Soc ... Transactions of the British Mycological Society [*A publication*]

Trans Cardiff Nat Soc ... Transactions of the Cardiff Naturalist's Society [*A publication*]

Trans Cave Res Group GB ... Transactions of the Cave Research Group of Great Britian [*A publication*]

Trans Coll Med S Afr ... Transactions of the College of Medicine of South Africa [*A publication*]

TRANSCON ... Transcontinental

Trans Conf Cold Inj ... Transactions of the Conference on Cold Injury [*A publication*]

Trans Conf Glaucoma ... Transactions of the Conference on Glaucoma [*A publication*]

Trans Conf Group Processes ... Transactions of the Conference on Group Processes [*A publication*]

Trans Conf Neuropharmacol ... Transactions of the Conference on Neuropharmacology [*A publication*]

Trans Conf Physiol Prematurity ... Transactions of the Conference on Physiology of Prematurity [*A publication*]

Trans Conf Polysaccharides Biol ... Transactions of the Conference on Polysaccharides in Biology [*A publication*]

Trans Conn Acad Arts Sci ... Transactions. Connecticut Academy of Arts and Sciences [*A publication*]

Trans Fac Hortic Chiba Univ ... Transactions of Faculty of Horticulture. Chiba University [*A publication*]

Trans Fed-Prov Wildl Conf ... Transactions of the Federal-Provincial Wildlife Conference [*A publication*]

Trans Geol Soc Glasg ... Transactions of the Geological Society of Glasgow [*A publication*]

Trans Geol Soc S Afr ... Transactions of the Geological Society of South Africa [*A publication*]

Trans Gulf Coast Assoc Geol Soc ... Transactions of the Gulf Coast Association of Geological Societies [*A publication*]

Trans Ill State Acad Sci ... Transactions of the Illinois State Academy of Science [*A publication*]

Trans Int Conf Soil Sci ... Transactions of the International Conference of Soil Science [*A publication*]

Trans Iowa State Hortic Soc ... Transactions of the Iowa State Horticultural Society [*A publication*]

Trans Jpn Pathol Soc ... Transactions of the Japanese Pathological Society [*A publication*]

Trans Kans Acad Sci ... Transactions of the Kansas Academy of Science [*A publication*]

Trans Koll Geneeskd S-Afr ... Transaksies van die Kollege van Geneeskunde van Suid-Afrika [*A publication*]

Trans KY Acad Sci ... Transactions of the Kentucky Academy of Science [*A publication*]

Transl Beltone Inst Hear Res ... Translations of the Beltone Institute for Hearing Research [*A publication*]

Trans Linn Soc NY ... Transactions of the Linnaean Society of New York [*A publication*]

Transl Russ Game Rep ... Translations of Russian Game Reports [*A publication*]

Trans MO Acad Sci ... Transactions of the Missouri Academy of Science [*A publication*]

Trans Mycol Soc Jpn ... Transactions of the Mycological Society of Japan [*A publication*]

Trans N Am Wildl Nat Resour Conf ... Transactions of the North American Wildlife and Natural Resources Conference [*A publication*]

Trans Nat Hist Soc Northumbria ... Transactions of the Natural History Society of Northumbria [*A publication*]

Trans Nebr Acad Sci ... Transactions of the Nebraska Academy of Sciences [*A publication*]

Trans Northeast Sect Wildl Soc ... Transactions of the Northeast Section. Wildlife Society [*A publication*]

Trans NY Acad Sci ... Transactions of the New York Academy of Science [*A publication*]

Trans Ophthalmol Soc NZ ... Transactions of the Ophthalmological Society of New Zealand [*A publication*]

Trans Ophthalmol Soc UK ... Transactions of the Ophthalmological Societies of the United Kingdom [*A publication*]

Trans Peninsula Hortic Soc ... Transactions of the Peninsula Horticultural Society [*A publication*]

Transplant Bull ... Transplantation Bulletin [*A publication*]

Transplant Proc ... Transplantation Proceedings [*A publication*]

Transplant Rev ... Transplantation Reviews [*A publication*]

Trans Proc Bot Soc Edinb ... Transactions and Proceedings of the Botanical Society of Edinburgh [*A publication*]

Trans R Can Inst ... Transactions of the Royal Canadian Institute [*A publication*]

Trans R Entomol Soc Lond ... Transactions of the Royal Entomological Society of London [*A publication*]

Trans R Geol Soc Corn ... Transactions of the Royal Geological Society Cornwall [*A publication*]

Trans R Highl Agric Soc Scotl ... Transactions of the Royal Highland and Agricultural Society of Scotland [*A publication*]

Trans Rhod Sci Assoc ... Transactions of the Rhodesia Scientific Association [*A publication*]

Trans R Sch Dent Stockh Umea ... Transactions of the Royal Schools of Dentistry. Stockholm and Umea [*A publication*]

Trans R Soc Can ... Transactions of the Royal Society of Canada [*A publication*]

Trans R Soc Edinb ... Transactions of the Royal Society of Edinburgh [*A publication*]

Trans R Soc NZ ... Transactions of the Royal Society of New Zealand [*A publication*]

Trans R Soc NZ Biol Sci ... Transactions of the Royal Society of New Zealand. Biological Science [*A publication*]

Trans R Soc NZ Bot ... Transactions of the Royal Society of New Zealand. Botany [*A publication*]

Trans R Soc NZ Earth Sci ... Transactions of the Royal Society of New Zealand. Earth Science [*A publication*]

Trans R Soc NZ Gen ... Transactions of the Royal Society of New Zealand. General [*A publication*]

Trans R Soc NZ Geol ... Transactions of the Royal Society of New Zealand. Geology [*A publication*]

Trans R Soc NZ Zool ... Transactions of the Royal Society of New Zealand. Zoology [*A publication*]

Trans R Soc S Afr ... Transactions of the Royal Society of South Africa [*A publication*]

Trans R Soc S Aust ... Transactions of the Royal Society of South Australia [*A publication*]

Trans R Soc Trop Med Hyg ... Transactions of the Royal Society of Tropical Medicine and Hygiene [*A publication*]

Trans San Diego Soc Nat Hist ... Transactions of the San Diego Society of Natural History [*A publication*]

Trans Shikoku Entomol Soc ... Transactions of the Shikoku Entomological Society [*A publication*]

Trans Soc Br Entomol ... Transactions of the Society for British Entomology [*A publication*]

Trans Soc Occup Med ... Transactions of the Society of Occupational Medicine [*A publication*]

Trans St John's Hosp Dermatol Soc ... Transactions of the St. John's Hospital Dermatological Society [*A publication*]

Trans Stud Coll Physicians Phila ... Transactions and Studies of the College of Physicians of Philadelphia [*A publication*]

Trans Tottori Soc Agric Sci ... Transactions of the Tottori Society of Agricultural Sciences [*A publication*]

Transvaal Mus Bull ... Transvaal Museum Bulletin [*A publication*]

Transvaal Mus Mem ... Transvaal Museum Memoirs [*A publication*]

Transvaal Mus Rep ... Transvaal Museum Report [*A publication*]

Transvaal Nat Conserv Div Annu Rep ... Transvaal Nature Conservation Division. Annual Report [*A publication*]

Trans Wis Acad Sci Arts Lett ... Transactions of the Wisconsin Academy of Sciences, Arts, and Letters [*A publication*]

Trans Zool Soc Lond ... Transactions of the Zoological Society of London [*A publication*]

Tr Arkhang Lesotekh Inst ... Trudy Arkhangel'skogo Lesotekhnicheskogo Instituta [*A publication*]

Tr Arm Nauchno-Issled Vet Inst ... Trudy Armyanskogo Nauchno-Issledovatel'skogo Veterinarnogo Instituta [*A publication*]

Tr Arm Protivochumn Stn ... Trudy Armyanskoi Protivochumnoi Stantsii [*A publication*]

Trasfus Sangue ... Trasfusione del Sangue [*A publication*]

TRASOP.... Tax Reduction Act Stock Ownership Plan

Tr Astrakh Gos Med Inst ... Trudy Astrakhanskogo Gosudarstvennogo Meditinskogo Instituta [*A publication*]

TRAV......... Training Availability [*Navy*]

Trav Chim Aliment Hyg ... Travaux de Chimie Alimentaire et d'Hygiene [*A publication*]

Trav Doc ORSTOM ... Travaux et Documents de l'ORSTOM [*Office de la Recherche Scientifique et Technique Outre-Mer*] [*A publication*]

Trav Hum ... Travail Humain [*A publication*]

Trav Inst Sci Cherifien Ser Bot ... Travaux de l'Institut Scientifique Cherifien. Serie Botanique [*A publication*]

Trav Inst Sci Cherifien Ser Zool ... Travaux de l'Institut Scientifique Cherifien. Serie Zoologique [*A publication*]

Trav Inst Speol "Emile Racovitza" ... Travaux de l'Institut de Speologie "Emile Racovitza" [*A publication*]

Trav Jeunes Sci ... Travaux des Jeunes Scientifiques [*A publication*]

Trav Lab For Univ Toulouse ... Travaux Laboratoire Forestier Universite Toulouse [*A publication*]

Trav Lab Geol Fac Sci Grenoble ... Travaux du Laboratoire de Geologie de la Faculte des Sciences de Grenoble [*A publication*]

Trav Lab Microbiol Fac Pharm Nancy ... Travaux du Laboratoire de Microbiologie de la Faculte de Pharmacie de Nancy [*A publication*]

Trav Mus Hist Nat "Grigore Antipa" ... Travaux du Museum d'Histoire "Grigore Antipa" [*A publication*]

Trav Pech Que ... Travaux sur les Pecheries du Quebec [*A publication*]

Trav Soc Pharm Montp ... Travaux de la Societe de Pharmacie de Montpellier [*A publication*]

Tr Bashk Gos Zapov ... Trudy Bashkirskogo Gosudarstvennogo Zapovednika [*A publication*]

Tr Bashk S-kh Inst ... Trudy Bashkirskogo Sel'skokhozyaistvennogo Instituta [*A publication*]

Tr Blagoveshch Gos Med Inst ... Trudy Blagoveshchenskogo Gosudarstvennogo Meditsinskogo Instituta [*A publication*]

Tr Bot Inst Akad Nauk SSSR ... Trudy Botanicheskogo Instituta Akademii Nauk SSSR [*A publication*]

Tr Bot Sada Akad Nauk Ukr SSR ... Trudy Botanicheskogo Sada Akademii Nauk Ukrainskoi SSR [*A publication*]

Tr Briansk Lesokhoz Inst ... Trudy Brianskogo Lesokhozyaistvennogo Instituta [*A publication*]

Tr Buryat S-kh Inst ... Trudy Buryatskogo Sel'skokhozyaistvennogo Instituta [*A publication*]

TRC .... Technical Review Committee [*International Atomic Energy Agency*]

TRC .... Total Residual Chlorine [*Environmental chemistry*]

TRCO .... Technical Representative of the Contracting Officer

Tr Dagest S-kh Inst ... Trudy Dagestanskogo Sel'skokhozyaistvennogo Instituta [*A publication*]

Tr Darvinsk Gos Zapov ... Trudy Darvinskogo Gosudatstvennogo Zapovednika [*A publication*]

Tr Dnepropetr S-kh Inst ... Trudy Dnepropetrovskogo Sel'skokhozyaistvennogo Instituta [*A publication*]

TREAD ...... Troop Recognition and Detection

Treatise Collagen ... Treatise on Collagen [*A publication*]

Tree-Ring Bull ... Tree-Ring Bulletin [*A publication*]

TREES ...... Time-Resolved Europium Excitation Spectroscopy

Trees S Afr ... Trees in South Africa [*A publication*]

Trends Biochem Sci ... Trends in Biochemical Sciences [*A publication*]

Tr Erevan Med Inst ... Trudy Erevanskogo Meditsinskogo Instituta [*A publication*]

Tr Erevan Zoovet Inst ... Trudy Erevanskogo Zooveterinarnogo Instituta [*A publication*]

Tr Fiziol Lab Akad Nauk SSSR ... Trudy Fiziologicheskoi Laboratorii. Akademii Nauk SSSR [*A publication*]

TRG .... Tuned Rotor Gyro

Tr Gelmintol Lab ... Trudy Gel'mintologicheskoi Laboratorii [*A publication*]

Tr Gl Bot Sada ... Trudy Glavnogo Botanicheskogo Sada [*A publication*]

Tr Gor'k Gos Med Inst ... Trudy Gor'kovskogo Gosudarstvennogo Meditsinskogo Instituta [*A publication*]

Tr Gor'k S-kh Inst ... Trudy Gor'kovskogo Sel'skokhozyaistvennogo Instituta [*A publication*]

Tr Gos Gidrol Inst ... Trudy Gosudarstvennogo Gidrologicheskogo Instituta [*A publication*]

Tr Gruz S-kh Inst ... Trudy Gruzinskogo Sel'skokhozyaistvennogo Instituta [*A publication*]

TRIA .... Temperature Removable Instrument Assembly

Trib CEBEDEAU ... Tribune du CEBEDEAU [*Centre Belge d'Etude et de Documentation des Eaux et de l'Air*] [*A publication*]

Trib Farm (Curitiba) ... Tribuna Farmaceutica (Curitiba) [*A publication*]

TRIMM ...... Triple Missile Mount

Tr Inst Biol Bashk Univ ... Trudy Instituta Biologii Bashkirskogo Universiteta [*A publication*]

Tr Inst Eksp Klin Khir Gematol ... Trudy Instituta Eksperimental'noi i Klinicheskoi Khirurgii i Gematologii [*A publication*]

Tr Inst Fiziol Akad Nauk Kaz SSR ... Trudy Instituta Fiziologli Akademiya Nauk Kazakhskoi SSR [*A publication*]

Tr Inst Fiziol Akad Nauk SSSR ... Trudy Instituta Fiziologii Akademii Nauk SSSR [*A publication*]

Tr Inst Genet Akad Nauk SSSR ... Trudy Instituta Genetiki Akademii Nauk SSSR [*A publication*]

Tr Inst Geogr Akad Nauk SSSR ... Trudy Instituta Geografii Akademii Nauk SSSR [*A publication*]

Tr Inst Klin Eksp Kardiol ... Trudy Instituta Klinicheskoi i Eksperimental'noi Kardiologii [*A publication*]

Tr Inst Lesa Akad Nauk Gruz SSR ... Trudy Instituta Lesa Akademii Nauk Gruzinskoi SSR [*A publication*]

Tr Inst Lesa Akad Nauk SSSR ... Trudy Instituta Lesa Akademii Nauk SSSR [*A publication*]

Tr Inst Malyarii Med Parazitol ... Trudy Instituta Malyarii i Meditsinskoi Parazitologii [*A publication*]

Tr Inst Mikrobiol Akad Nauk SSSR ... Trudy Instituta Mikrobiologii Akademii Nauk SSSR [*A publication*]

Tr Inst Okeanol Akad Nauk SSSR ... Trudy Instituta Okeanologii Akademii Nauk SSSR [*A publication*]

Tr Inst Polevod Akad Nauk Gruz SSR ... Trudy Instituta Polevodstva Akademii Nauk Gruzinskoi SSR [*A publication*]

Tr Inst Zool Akad Nauk Az SSR ... Trudy Instituta Zoologii Akademii Nauk Azerbaidzhanskoi SSR [*A publication*]

Tr Inst Zool Akad Nauk Gruz SSR ... Trudy Instituta Zoologii Akademii Nauk Gruzinskoi SSR [*A publication*]

Tr Inst Zool Akad Nauk Kaz SSR ... Trudy Instituta Zoologii Akademii Nauk Kazakhskoi SSR [*A publication*]

Tr Inst Zool Akad Nauk Ukr SSR ... Trudy Instituta Zoologii Akademii Nauk Ukrainskoi SSR [*A publication*]

Tr Inst Zool Biol (Kiev) ... Trudy Instytutu Zoolohiyi ta Biolohiyi (Kiev) [*A publication*]

Tr Ivanov Med Inst ... Trudy Ivanovskogo Meditsinskogo Instituta [*A publication*]

Tr Izhevsk Med Inst ... Trudy Izhevskogo Meditsinskogo Instituta [*A publication*]

Tr Kalinin Gos Med Inst ... Trudy Kalininskogo Gosudarstvennogo Meditsinskogo Instituta [*A publication*]

Tr Karel Fil Akad Nauk SSSR ... Trudy Karel'skogo Filiala Akademii Nauk SSSR [*A publication*]

Tr Kaunas Gos Med Inst ... Trudy Kaunasskogo Gosudarstvennogo Meditsinskogo Instituta [*A publication*]

Tr Kazan Med Inst ... Trudy Kazanskogo Meditsinskogo Instituta [*A publication*]

Tr Kazan S-kh Inst ... Trudy Kazanskogo Sel'skokhozyaistvennogo Instituta [*A publication*]

Tr Kaz Nauchno-Issled Inst Tuberk ... Trudy Kazakhskogo Nauchno-Issledovatel'skogo Instituta Tuberkuleza [*A publication*]

Tr Kaz Nauchno-Issled Vet Inst ... Trudy Kazakhskogo Nauchno-Issledovatel'skogo Veterinarnogo Instituta [*A publication*]

Tr Kaz Opytn Stn Pchelovod ... Trudy Kazakhskoi Opytnoi Stantsii Pchelovodstva [*A publication*]

Tr Kaz S-kh Inst ... Trudy Kazakhskogo Sel'skokhozyaistvennogo Instituta [*A publication*]

Tr Kaz S-kh Inst Ser Agron ... Trudy Kazakhskogo Sel'skokhozyaistvennogo Instituta Seriya Agronomii [*A publication*]

Tr Khabar Med Inst ... Trudy Khabarovskogo Meditsinskogo Instituta [*A publication*]

Tr Khar'kov Med Inst ... Trudy Khar'kovskogo Meditsinskogo Instituta [*A publication*]

Tr Khar'k S-kh Inst ... Trudy Khar'kovskogo Sel'skokhozyaistvennogo Instituta [*A publication*]

Tr Kiev Vet Inst ... Trudy Kievskogo Veterinarnogo Instituta [*A publication*]

Tr Kirg Gos Med Inst ... Trudy Kirgizskogo Gosudarstvennogo Meditsinskogo Instituta [*A publication*]

Tr Kirg S-kh Inst ... Trudy Kirgizskogo Sel'skokhozyaistvennogo Instituta [*A publication*]

Tr Kirov S-kh Inst ... Trudy Kirovskogo Sel'skokhozyaistvennogo Instituta [*A publication*]

Tr Kishinev Gos Med Inst ... Trudy Kishinevskogo Gosudarstvennogo Meditsinskogo Instituta [*A publication*]

Tr Kishinev S-kh Inst ... Trudy Kishinevskogo Sel'skokhozyaistvennogo Instituta [*A publication*]

Tr Komi Fil Akad Nauk SSSR ... Trudy Komi Filiala Akademii Nauk SSSR [*A publication*]

Tr Kompleksn Eksped Dnepropetr Univ ... Trudy Kompleksnoi Ekspeditsii Dnepropetrovskogo Universiteta [*A publication*]

Tr Krasnoyarsk Med Inst ... Trudy Krasnoyarskogo Meditsinskogo Instituta [*A publication*]

Tr Krasnoyarsk S-kh Inst ... Trudy Krasnoyarskogo Sel'skokhozyaistvennogo Instituta [*A publication*]

Tr Krym S-kh Inst Im M I Kalinina ... Trudy Krymskogo Sel'skokhozyaistvennogo Instituta Imeni M I Kalinina [*A publication*]

Tr Kuban S-kh Inst ... Trudy Kubanskogo Sel'skokhozyaistvennogo Instituta [*A publication*]

Tr Kuibyshev Med Inst ... Trudy Kuibyshevskii Meditsinskii Instituta [*A publication*]

Tr Kuibyshev S-kh Inst ... Trudy Kuibyshevskogo Sel'skohozyaistvennogo Instituta [*A publication*]

Tr Kursk Med Inst ... Trudy Kurskogo Meditsinskogo Instituta [*A publication*]

Tr Latv S-kh Akad ... Trudy Latviiskoi Sel'skokhozyaistvennoi Akademii [*A publication*]

Tr Leningr Inst Epidemiol Mikrobiol ... Trudy Leningradskogo Instituta Epidemiologii i Mikrobiologii [*A publication*]

Tr Leningr Inst Usoversh Vrachei ... Trudy Leningradskogo Instituta Usovershenstvovaniya Vrachei [*A publication*]

Tr Leningr Khim-Farm Inst ... Trudy Leningradskogo Khimiko-Farmatsevticheskogo Instituta [*A publication*]

Tr Leningr O-va Estestvoispyt ... Trudy Leningradskogo Obshchestva Estestvoispytatelei [*A publication*]

Tr Leningr Pediatr Med Inst ... Trudy Leningradskogo Pediatricheskogo Meditsinskogo Instituta [*A publication*]

Tr Leningr Sanit-Gig Med Inst ... Trudy Leningradskogo Sanitarno-Gigienicheskogo Meditsinskogo Instituta [*A publication*]

Tr Lugansk S-kh Inst ... Trudy Luganskogo Sel'skokhozyaistvennoi Instituta [*A publication*]

Tr Mosk Inst Nar Khoz ... Trudy Moskovskogo Instituta Narodnogo Khozyaistva [*A publication*]

Tr Mosk Med Stomatol Inst ... Trudy Moskovskogo Meditsinskogo Stomatologichesko Instituta [*A publication*]

Tr Mosk Torf Inst ... Trudy Moskovskogo Torfyanogo Instituta [*A publication*]

Tr Mosk Vet Akad ... Trudy Moskovskoi Veterinarnoi Akademii [*A publication*]

TRMS .... Test Resource Management System [*TECOM*]

Tr Murm Morsk Biol Inst ... Trudy Murmanskogo Morskogo Biologicheskogo Instituta [*A publication*]

TRN .... Transmit

Tr Nakhich Kompleksn Zon Opytn Stn ... Trudy Nakhichevanskoi Kompleksnoi Zonal'noi Opytnoi Stantsii [*A publication*]

Tr Novocherk Vet Inst ... Trudy Novocherkasskogo Veterinarnogo Instituta [*A publication*]

Tr Novosib Gos Med Inst ... Trudy Novosibirskogo Gosudarstvennogo Meditsinskogo Instituta [*A publication*]

Tr Odess Gidrometeorol Inst ... Trudy Odesskogo Gidrometeorologicheskogo Instituta [*A publication*]

Tr Odess S-kh Inst ... Trudy Odesskogo Sel'skokhozyaistvennogo Instituta [*A publication*]

TROF .... Trough [*Meteorology*]

Tr Omsk Med Inst Im M I Kalinina ... Trudy Omskogo Meditsinskogo Instituta Imeni M I Kalinina [*A publication*]

Tromso Mus Skr ... Tromso Museums Skrifter [*A publication*]

TROP .... Tropopause [*Meteorology*]

Trop Agric ... Tropical Agriculture [*A publication*]

Trop Agric (Colombo) ... Tropical Agriculturist (Colombo) [*A publication*]

Trop Anim Health Prod ... Tropical Animal Health and Production [*A publication*]

Trop Ecol ... Tropical Ecology [*A publication*]

Tropenmed Parasitol ... Tropenmedizin und Parasitologie [*A publication*]

Trop For Notes ... Tropical Forest Notes [*A publication*]

Trop Geogr Med ... Tropical and Geographical Medicine [*A publication*]

Trop Grassl ... Tropical Grasslands [*A publication*]

Trop Med ... Tropical Medicine [*A publication*]

Trop Med Hyg News ... Tropical Medicine and Hygiene News [*A publication*]

Trop Pest Bull ... Tropical Pest Bulletin [*A publication*]

Trop Pestic Res Inst Annu Rep ... Tropical Pesticides Research Institute. Annual Report [*A publication*]

Trop Pestic Res Inst Misc Rep ... Tropical Pesticides Research Institute. Miscellaneous Report [*A publication*]

Trop Prod Inst Crop Prod Dig ... Tropical Products Institute. Crop and Product Digest [*A publication*]

Trop Prod Inst Rep ... Tropical Products Institute. Report [*A publication*]

Trop Stored Prod Inf ... Tropical Stored Products Information [*A publication*]

Trop Woods Yale Univ Sch For ... Tropical Woods. Yale University School of Forestry [*A publication*]

Tr Orenb Gos Med Inst ... Trudy Orenburgskogo Gosudarstvennogo Meditsinskogo Instituta [*A publication*]

Tr O-va Fiziol Azerb ... Trudy Obshchestva Fiziologov Azerbaidzhana [*A publication*]

Tr Paleontol Inst Akad Nauk SSSR ... Trudy Paleontologicheskogo Instituta Akademiya Nauk SSSR [*A publication*]

Tr Permsk Gos Med Inst ... Trudy Permskii Gosudarstvennyi Meditsinskii Institut [*A publication*]

Tr Permsk S-kh Inst ... Trudy Permskogo Sel'skokhozyaistvennogo Instituta [*A publication*]

TRPGDA ... Tripropylene Glycol Diacrylate [*Organic chemistry*]

Tr Prikl Bot Genet Sel ... Trudy po Prikladnoi Botanike Genetike i Selektsii USSR [*A publication*]

Tr Primorsk S-kh Inst ... Trudy Primorskogo Sel'skokhozyaistvennogo Instituta [*A publication*]

TRR .... Topical Report Request

TRR .... Topical Reports Review

TRRAPS .... Transportable Reliable Acoustic Path Sonobuoy

Tr Resp Stn Zashch Rast ... Trudy Respublikanskoi Stantsii Zashchity Rastenii [*A publication*]

Tr Ryazan Med Inst ... Trudy Ryazanskogo Meditsinskogo Instituta [*A publication*]

TRS .... Total Reduced Sulfur [*Environmental chemistry*]

TRS .... Trustees

Tr Samark Gos Univ ... Trudy Samarkanskogo Gosudarstvennogo Universiteta [*A publication*]

Tr Sarat Med Inst ... Trudy Saratovskogo Meditsinskogo Instituta [*A publication*]

Tr Sarat S-kh Inst ... Trudy Saratovskogo Sel'skokhozyaistvennogo Instituta [*A publication*]

Tr Sarat Zootekh Vet Inst ... Trudy Saratovskogo Zootekhnicheskogo Veterinarnogo Instituta [*A publication*]

Tr Sel Agrotekh Zashch Rast ... Trudy po Selektsii Agrotekhnike i Zashchite Rastenii [*A publication*]

Tr Semipalat Med Inst ... Trudy Semipalatinskogo Meditsinskogo Instituta [*A publication*]

Tr Sevansk Gidrobiol Stn ... Trudy Sevanskoi Gidrobiologicheskoi Stantsii [*A publication*]

Tr Sev-Oset Med Inst ... Trudy Severo-Osetinskogo Meditsinskogo Instituta [*A publication*]

Tr Sev-Oset S-kh Inst ... Trudy Severo-Osetinskogo Sel'skokhozyaistvennogo Instituta [*A publication*]

Tr Sib Lesotekh Inst ... Trudy Sibirskogo Lesotekhnicheskogo Instituta [*A publication*]

Tr Sikhote-Alinsk Gos Zapov ... Trudy Sikhote-Alinskogo Gosudarstvennogo Zapovednika [*A publication*]

Tr Smolensk Gos Med Inst ... Trudy Smolenskogo Gosudarstvennogo Meditsinskogo Instituta [*A publication*]

Tr Stalingr S-kh Inst ... Trudy Stalingradskogo Sel'skokhozyaistvennogo Instituta [*A publication*]

Tr Stavrop S-kh Inst ... Trudy Stavropol'skogo Sel'skokhozyaistvennogo Instituta [*A publication*]

Tr Sukhum Bot Sada ... Trudy Sukhumskogo Botanicheskogo Sada [*A publication*]

Tr Sverol Gos Med Inst ... Trudy Sverolovskogo Gosudarstvennogo Meditsinskogo Instituta [*A publication*]

Tr Sverol S-kh Inst ... Trudy Sverolovskogo Sel'skokhozyaistvennogo Instituta [*A publication*]

Tr Tadzh Med Inst ... Trudy Tadzhikskogo Meditsinskogo Instituta [*A publication*]

Tr Tashk S-kh Inst ... Trudy Tashkentskogo Sel'skokhozyaistvennogo Instituta [*A publication*]

TRTG .... Tactical RADAR Threat Generator

TRUST ...... Transportable Units and Self-Sufficient Teams

TRX .... Two-Region Physics Critical Experiment

TS .... Thermosetting [*Plastics technology*]

TSA .... Tax-Sheltered Annuity

TSA .... Time Study Analysis

TSA .... Tube Support Assemblies

TSC .... Terrestrial Science Center

TSC .... Test Shipping Cask [*Nuclear energy*]

TSC .... Time Sharing Control Task [*Data processing*]

TSCF .... Task Schedule Change Form

TSCM .... Technical Surveillance Countermeasures [*Program*] [*Air Force*]

TSD .... Thermionic Specific Detector [*Analytical instrumentation*]

TSF .... Tri-State Flite Services, Inc. [*Dubuque, IA*] [*FAA designator*]

TSIM .... (Trimethylsilyl)imidazole [*Organic chemistry*] [*Also, TMSIM*]

TSIS .... Total Specifications Information System

TSMDA ..... Test-Section Melt-Down Accident [*Nuclear energy*]

TSMNO ..... Transmitting Capability Out of Service

TSMOK ..... Transmitting Capability Returned to Service

TSP .... Tribal Sovereignty Program

TSPI .... Time-Space-Position-Information

TSR .... Thermal Shock Rig

TSR .... Total Stress Range

TSS .... Toxic Shock Syndrome [*Medicine*]

TSS .... Transtate Airways, Inc. [*Oxford, CT*] [*FAA designator*]

TSSP......... Tactical Satellite Signal Processor
TST .... Transtate Airways, Inc. [*Oxford, CT*] [*FAA designator*]
TST .... Trilogy Screening Technique
TSU........... Tarleton State University [*Texas*] [*Formerly, TSC*]
T & T .... Tanqueray [*Gin*] and Tonic
TT............. Test Temperature
TT............. Transaction Terminal
TTA .... Thenoyltrifluoroacetone [*Organic chemistry*] [*Also, TTB*]
TTA .... Triplet-Triplet Annihilation [*Spectroscopy*]
TTB .... Trifluoro(thienyl)butanedione [*Organic chemistry*] [*Also, TTA*]
TTC .... Test Transfer Cask [*Nuclear energy*]
TTCS........ Target Tracking and Control System
TTE .... Thermal Transient Equipment
TTF........... Transient Time Flowmeter
TTF & T ..... Technology Transfer, Fabrication, and Test
TTFW .... Too Tacky for Words [*Slang*]
TTHE........ Thermal Transient Histogram Equivalent
TTP .... Total Temperature Probe
TTR .... Toshiba Training Reactor [*Japan*]
TTS .... Transdermal Therapeutic System [*Medicine*]
TTSU........ Tracker Test Set Supplemental Unit
TUB .... Tubuai Island [*Austral Islands*] [*Airport symbol*]
TUC .... Tucuman [*Argentina*] [*Airport symbol*]
TUCA .... Transient Undercooling Accident [*Nuclear energy*]
TUD.......... Tambacounda [*Senegal*] [*Airport symbol*]
TUF .... Tours [*France*] [*Airport symbol*]
TUG.......... Tuguegarao [*Philippines*] [*Airport symbol*]
TUI .... Trypsin Units Inhibited [*Food technology*]
TUI .... Turaif [*Saudi Arabia*] [*Airport symbol*]
TUJ........... Tum [*Ethiopia*] [*Airport symbol*]
TUK.......... Turbat [*Pakistan*] [*Airport symbol*]
TUL .... Tulsa [*Oklahoma*] [*Airport symbol*]
TUN.......... Tunis [*Tunisia*] [*Airport symbol*]
TUO.......... Taupo [*New Zealand*] [*Airport symbol*]
TUP .... Tupelo [*Mississippi*] [*Airport symbol*]

TUR .... Tucurui [*Brazil*] [*Airport symbol*]
TUS........... Tucson [*Arizona*] [*Airport symbol*]
TUU........... Tabuk [*Saudi Arabia*] [*Airport symbol*]
TUV........... Tucupita [*Venezuela*] [*Airport symbol*]
TUY........... Tulum [*Mexico*] [*Airport symbol*]
TV............. Trans America Airlines, Inc. [*ICAO designator*]
TVA........... Morafenobe [*Madagascar*] [*Airport symbol*]
TVC.......... Traverse City [*Michigan*] [*Airport symbol*]
TVF.......... Thief River Falls [*Minnesota*] [*Airport symbol*]
TVL .... Lake Tahoe [*California*] [*Airport symbol*]
TVR .... Thermal Vapor Recompressors [*For evaporators*]
TVRP........ Television Reading Program
TVU .... Taveuni [*Fiji*] [*Airport symbol*]
TVY .... Tavoy [*Burma*] [*Airport symbol*]
TWA .... [*The*] Woman Activist, Inc.
TWAC .... Tactical Weather Analysis Center
TWB .... Toowoomba [*Australia*] [*Airport symbol*]
TWF .... Twin Falls [*Idaho*] [*Airport symbol*]
TWG......... Transfer Working Group
TWH .... Catalina Island [*California*] [*Airport symbol*]
TWMIP ..... Third World Moving Images Project
TWP .... Torwood [*Australia*] [*Airport symbol*]
TWS .... Thomas Wolfe Society
TWU .... Tawau [*Malaysia*] [*Airport symbol*]
TXK .... Texarkana [*Arkansas*] [*Airport symbol*]
TXL .... Berlin [*West Germany*] [*Airport symbol*]
TXU .... Tabou [*Ivory Coast*] [*Airport symbol*]
TYL .... Talara [*Peru*] [*Airport symbol*]
TYN........... Taiyuan [*China*] [*Airport symbol*]
TYO........... Tokyo [*Japan*] [*Airport symbol*]
TYR .... Tyler [*Texas*] [*Airport symbol*]
TYS .... Knoxville [*Tennessee*] [*Airport symbol*]
TYZ .... Taylor [*Arizona*] [*Airport symbol*]
TZ............. Transportation Zone [*Department of Transportation*]
TZN .... South Andros [*Bahamas*] [*Airport symbol*]
TZX .... Trabzon [*Turkey*] [*Airport symbol*]

U

UAC .... Universal Area Code [*Bureau of Census*]
UAH .... Ua Huka [*Marquesas Islands*] [*Airport symbol*]
UAK .... Narssarssuaq [*Greenland*] [*Airport symbol*]
UAMS .... Ukrainian Academy of Medical Sciences
UAP .... Ua Pou [*Marquesas Islands*] [*Airport symbol*]
UAQ .... San Juan [*Argentina*] [*Airport symbol*]
UA/USA .... UNESCO Association
UBA .... Uberaba [*Brazil*] [*Airport symbol*]
UBC .... Uniform Building Code
UBI .... Buin [*Papua New Guinea*] [*Airport symbol*]
UBJ .... Ube [*Japan*] [*Airport symbol*]
UBP .... Ubon Ratchathani [*Thailand*] [*Airport symbol*]
UBT .... Ubatuba [*Brazil*] [*Airport symbol*]
UCA .... Utica [*New York*] [*Airport symbol*]
UCT .... Underwater Construction Team [*Navy*]
UCW .... Unit Control Word [*Data processing*]
UDAG .... Urban Development Action Grant [*Federal program*]
UDAS .... Unified Direct Access System
UDEC .... Unitized Digital Electronic Calculator
UDI .... Uberlandia [*Brazil*] [*Airport symbol*]
UDL .... Unit Document Listing
UDMA .... United Dance Merchants of America
UDP .... United Data Processing
UDR .... Udaipur [*India*] [*Airport symbol*]
UDR .... Universal Document Reader
UE .... Urinary Energy [*Nutrition*]
UEL .... Quelimane [*Mozambique*] [*Airport symbol*]
UEO .... Kume Jima [*Japan*] [*Airport symbol*]
UET .... Quetta [*Pakistan*] [*Airport symbol*]
UFCP .... Up-Front Control Panel
UGLAS ..... Uniform General Ledger Accounting Structure
UGLE .... Universal Graphics Language Executive
UGO .... Uige [*Angola*] [*Airport symbol*]
UGT .... Underground Test
UHE .... Uherske Hradiste [*Czechoslovakia*] [*Airport symbol*]
UHF .... Ulster Historical Foundation
UHF/HF ..... Ultrahigh Frequency/High-Frequency
UHI .... Upper Head Injection
UHP .... Ultrahigh Power
UHS .... Ultimate Heat Sink
UIB .... Quibdo [*Colombia*] [*Airport symbol*]
UII .... Utila Island [*Honduras*] [*Airport symbol*]
UIN .... Quincy [*Illinois*] [*Airport symbol*]
UIO .... Quito [*Ecuador*] [*Airport symbol*]
UIP .... Quimper [*France*] [*Airport symbol*]
UIR .... Quirindi [*Australia*] [*Airport symbol*]
UJ .... Air Lanka [*Sri Lanka*] [*ICAO designator*]
UK .... Air UK Ltd. [*Great Britain*] [*ICAO designator*]
UKA .... Ulster King-at-Arms
UKADGE .... United Kingdom Air Defense Ground Environment
UKU .... Nuku [*Papua New Guinea*] [*Airport symbol*]
UL .... Urban League
ULA .... San Julian [*Argentina*] [*Airport symbol*]
ULE .... Sule [*Papua New Guinea*] [*Airport symbol*]
ULM .... New Ulm [*Minnesota*] [*Airport symbol*]
ULN .... Ulan Bator [*Mongolia*] [*Airport symbol*]
ULP .... Quilpie [*Australia*] [*Airport symbol*]
ULY .... Ulyanovsk [*USSR*] [*Airport symbol*]
UMD .... Unitized Microwave Devices

UME .... Umea [*Sweden*] [*Airport symbol*]
UMI .... Underway Material Inspection [*Navy*]
UMR .... Woomera [*Australia*] [*Airport symbol*]
UNCERT ... Uncertainty [*Standard deviation*] [*Data processing*]
UND .... Kunduz [*Afghanistan*] [*Airport symbol*]
UNE .... Qacha's Nek [*Lesotho*] [*Airport symbol*]
UNF .... Union Flights [*Sacramento, CA*] [*FAA designator*]
UNG .... Kiunga [*Papua New Guinea*] [*Airport symbol*]
UNI .... Union Island [*Windward Islands*] [*Airport symbol*]
UNIPOL ..... Universal Problem-Oriented Language [*Data processing*]
UNIV .... Universalist
UNK .... Unalakleet [*Alaska*] [*Airport symbol*]
UNT .... Unst [*Scotland*] [*Airport symbol*]
UOX .... University [*Mississippi*] [*Airport symbol*]
UPG .... Ujung Pandang [*Indonesia*] [*Airport symbol*]
UPGRADE ... User-Prompted Graphic Data Evaluation [*US Council on Environmental Quality*]
UPL .... Universal Programing Language [*Data processing*]
UPL .... Upala [*Costa Rica*] [*Airport symbol*]
UPLD .... Upland [*Plateau, highland*] [*Board on Geographic Names*]
UPM .... Universal Permissive Modules
UPP .... Upolu Point [*Hawaii*] [*Airport symbol*]
UPS .... Universities and Public Schools Battalions [*Military units*] [*British*] [*World War I*]
UPT-H .... Undergraduate Pilot Training - Helicopter [*Air Force*]
UQE .... Queen [*Alaska*] [*Airport symbol*]
URB .... Urubupunga [*Brazil*] [*Airport symbol*]
URC .... Urumqi [*China*] [*Airport symbol*]
URESA ...... Uniform Reciprocal Enforcement of Support Agreement
URG .... Uruguaiana [*Brazil*] [*Airport symbol*]
URI .... Uribe [*Colombia*] [*Airport symbol*]
URL .... Unrequited Love [*Slang*]
URM .... Uriman [*Venezuela*] [*Airport symbol*]
URN .... Uniform Random Numerator [*Data processing*]
URP .... Unmanned Recovery Platform [*Navy*]
URW .... United Racquetsports for Women
URY .... Gurayat [*Saudi Arabia*] [*Airport symbol*]
URZ .... Uroozgan [*Afghanistan*] [*Airport symbol*]
U/S .... Unsorted
USA .... Unicycling Society of America
USA .... Unsegmented Storage Analyzer [*Instrumentation*]
USAA .... United States Academy of Arms
USAAMC .. United States Army Aeromedical Center
USAAVRADCOM ... United States Army Aviation Research and Development Command
USAAVS ... United States Agency for Aviation Safety
USACC-R/FMD ... United States Army Communications Command Radio and Frequency Management Division
USACECDA ... United States Army Communications-Electronics Combat Developments Agency
USACEEIA-PAC ... United States Army Communications-Electronics Engineering Installation Agency-Pacific
USAF .... United States Aikido Federation
USAFESA-TS ... United States Army Facilities Engineering Support Agency - Technology Support Division
USAFESA-TSD ... United States Army Facilities Engineering Support Agency - Technology Support Division
USAFMD ... United States Army Frequency Management Directorate

USAFRR.... United States Air Force Resident Representative
USARFEO ... United States Army Frequency Engineering Office
USASC...... United States Army Safety Center
USCA........ United States Croquet Association
USCG-B.... United States Coast Guard Office of Boating Safety
USCG-C.... United States Coast Guard Office of Chief of Staff
USDA........ US Darting Association
USDRE...... Office of the Under Secretary of Defense for Research and Engineering
USEORD ... Use Order [*Navy*]
USF......... United Scleroderma Foundation
USFA........ US Farmers Association
USH.......... Ushuaia [*Argentina*] [*Airport symbol*]
USI........... Mabaruma [*Guyana*] [*Airport symbol*]
USL.......... Useless Loop [*Australia*] [*Airport symbol*]
USLC .... United States Locals Collectors
USM.......... Unlisted Securities Market [*London Stock Exchange*]
USMEF..... United States Meat Export Federation
USMLS...... United States Museum Librarian Society
USNA-EW ... United States Naval Academy Division of Engineering and Weapons
USNTPS.... United States Naval Test Pilot School
USPD .... US Publicity Director [*A publication*]
USRSA ...... United States Racquet Stringers Association
USSAF ...... US Sports Acrobatic Foundation
USSEA...... United States Space Education Association
USTA .... US Trivia Association
USTOA...... United States Tour Operators Association

UT .... Untested
UT .... Utah Territory [*Prior to statehood*]
UT .... Utility
UTB.......... Muttaburra [*Australia*] [*Airport symbol*]
UTH.......... Udon Thani [*Thailand*] [*Airport symbol*]
UTLAS ...... University of Toronto Library Automation Systems [*Library network*]
UTLY......... Utility
UTN.......... Upington [*South Africa*] [*Airport symbol*]
UTO.......... Utopia Creek [*Alaska*] [*Airport symbol*]
UTP .... United Teaching Profession
UTP .... Utapao [*Thailand*] [*Airport symbol*]
UTT .... Umtata [*South Africa*] [*Airport symbol*]
UTY .... Utility Air, Inc. [*Moberly, MO*] [*FAA designator*]
UU .... Unicorns Unanimous [*An organization*]
UUU.......... Manumu [*Papua New Guinea*] [*Airport symbol*]
UVCB .... Unknown or Variable Composition, Complex Reaction Products, and Biological Materials [*Chemical Abstracts Services*]
UVE .... Ouvea [*Loyalty Islands*] [*Airport symbol*]
UVF .... St. Lucia [*West Indies*] Hewanorra Airport [*Airport symbol*]
UVL .... New Valley [*Egypt*] [*Airport symbol*]
UVO.......... Uvol [*Papua New Guinea*] [*Airport symbol*]
UVV .... Upward Vertical Velocity [*Meteorology*]
UWASIS.... United Way of America Services Identification System
UX .... Lotus Airways [*Egypt*] [*ICAO designator*]
UYL .... Nyala [*Sudan*] [*Airport symbol*]

V

V .... Vehicles
VA .... End of Work [*Morse telephony*]
VA .... Vital Area
VAA .... Vaasa [*Finland*] [*Airport symbol*]
VA Agric Exp Stn Tech Bull ... Virginia Agricultural Experiment
        Station. Technical Bulletin [*A publication*]
VAB .... Variable Action Button
VAC .... Value-Added Carrier
VAD .... Vacuum Arc Degassing [*Metal technology*]
VAF .... Valence [*France*] [*Airport symbol*]
VA Fish Lab Educ Ser ... Virginia Fisheries Laboratory. Educational
        Series [*A publication*]
VAI .... Vanimo [*Papua New Guinea*] [*Airport symbol*]
VAI .... Ventilation Air Intake [*Hovercraft*]
VA Inst Mar Sci ... Virginia Institute of Marine Science [*A publication*]
VA J Sci .... Virginia Journal of Science [*A publication*]
VAK .... Chevak [*Alaska*] [*Airport symbol*]
Vakbl Biol ... Vakblad voor Biologen [*A publication*]
Valt Maatalouskoetoiminnan Julk ... Valtion Maatalouskoetoiminnan
        Julkaisuja [*A publication*]
VALT(S).... Vulnerability and Lethality Test (System)
VAM .... Medium Attack Aircraft [*Navy symbol*]
VA Med Mon ... Virginia Medical Monthly [*A publication*]
VAN .... Van [*Turkey*] [*Airport symbol*]
VA Polytech Inst Res Div Bull ... Virginia Polytechnic Institute
        Research Division. Bulletin [*A publication*]
VAR .... Varna [*Bulgaria*] [*Airport symbol*]
Vasa Suppl ... Vasa Supplementum [*A publication*]
Vasc Dis.... Vascular Diseases [*A publication*]
Vasc Surg ... Vascular Surgery [*A publication*]
VASTT ...... Variable Speed Towed Target
VAT .... Vatomandry [*Madagascar*] [*Airport symbol*]
VAT .... Voice-Activated Typewriter
VAV .... Vava'u [*Tonga Island*] [*Airport symbol*]
VAW .... Valley Airways, Inc. [*McAllen, TX*] [*FAA designator*]
VA Wildl .... Virginia Wildlife [*A publication*]
VB .... Viven and Bassiere [*Rifle grenade*]
VBI .... Vertical Blanking Interval [*Telecommunications*]
VBV .... Vanuabalavu [*Fiji*] [*Airport symbol*]
VBY .... Visby [*Sweden*] [*Airport symbol*]
VC .... Vice Commodore [*Navy*]
VCC .... Voluntary Census Committee
VCE .... Venice [*Italy*] [*Airport symbol*]
VCH .... Vichadero [*Uruguay*] [*Airport symbol*]
VCLF .... Vertical Cask-Lifting Fixture [*Nuclear energy*]
VCN .... Vinyl Cyanide [*Organic chemistry*]
VCP .... Sao Paulo [*Brazil*] Viracopos Airport [*Airport symbol*]
VCT .... Victoria [*Texas*] [*Airport symbol*]
VCT .... Voice Code Translation
VD .... Video Disk
V/D........... Voice/Data
VDE .... Valverde [*Canary Islands*] [*Airport symbol*]
VDM .... Vector Dominance Model [*Physics*]
VDM .... Viedma [*Argentina*] [*Airport symbol*]
VD/OS ...... Vacuum Distillation/Overflow Sampler
VDP .... Visual Descent Point [*Aviation*]
VDS........... Vadso [*Norway*] [*Airport symbol*]
VDS........... Vehicle Description Summary [*General Motors*]
VDZ........... Valdez [*Alaska*] [*Airport symbol*]

VE & B .... Vehicle Energy and Biotechnology
Ved Pr Cesk Zemed Muz ... Vedecke Prace Ceskoslovenskeho
        Zemedelskeho Muzea [*A publication*]
Ved Pr Lab Podoznalectva Bratisl ... Vedecke Prace Laboratoria
        Podoznalectva v Bratislave [*A publication*]
Ved Pr Ustavu Zelinarskeho Olomouci ... Vedecke Prace Ustavu
        Zelinarskeho v Olomouci [*A publication*]
Ved Pr VSCHK (Slatinany) ... Vedecke Prace VSCHK [*Vyzkumna
        Stanice pro Chov Koni*] (Slatinany) [*A publication*]
Ved Pr Vysk Ustavu Kukurice Trnave ... Vedecke Prace Vyskumneho
        Ustavu Kukurice v Trnave [*A publication*]
Ved Pr Vysk Ustavu Ovciar Trencine ... Vedecke Prace Vyskumneho
        Ustavu Ovciarskeho v Trencine [*A publication*]
VEE .... Vagina, Ectocervix, and Endocervix [*Cytopathology*]
VEE .... Venetie [*Alaska*] [*Airport symbol*]
VEG .... Maikwak [*Guyana*] [*Airport symbol*]
VEL .... Vernal [*Utah*] [*Airport symbol*]
Vema Res Ser ... Vema Research Series [*A publication*]
VENUS ...... Valuable and Effective Network Utility Services
Venus Jpn J Malacol ... Venus. The Japanese Journal of Malacology
        [*A publication*]
VEP .... Veterans Education Project
VER .... Veracruz [*Mexico*] [*Airport symbol*]
Verh Anat Ges ... Verhandlungen der Anatomischen Gesellschaft [*A
        publication*]
Verh Bot Ver Prov Brandenb ... Verhandlungen des Botanischen
        Vereins der Provinz Brandenburg [*A publication*]
Verh Dtsch Ges Exp Med ... Verhandlungen der Deutschen
        Gesellschaft fuer Experimentelle Medizin [*A
        publication*]
Verh Dtsch Ges Inn Med ... Verhandlungen der Deutschen
        Gesellschaft fuer Innere Medizin [*A publication*]
Verh Dtsch Ges Kreislaufforsch ... Verhandlungen der Deutschen
        Gesellschaft fuer Kreislaufforschung [*A publication*]
Verh Dtsch Ges Pathol ... Verhandlungen der Deutschen Gesellschaft
        fuer Pathologie [*A publication*]
Verh Dtsch Zool Ges ... Verhandlungen der Deutschen Zoologischen
        Gesellschaft [*A publication*]
Verh Geol Bundesanst ... Verhandlungen der Geologischen
        Bundesanstalt [*A publication*]
Verh Inst Praev Geneeskd ... Verhandelingen Instituut voor
        Praeventieve Geneeskunde [*A publication*]
Verh Int Psychother Kongr ... Verhandlungen des Internationalen
        Psychotherapie Kongresses [*A publication*]
Verh Naturforsch Ges Basel ... Verhandlungen der Naturforschenden
        Gesellschaft in Basel [*A publication*]
Verh Ornithol Ges Bayern ... Verhandlungen der Ornithologischen
        Gesellschaft in Bayern [*A publication*]
Verh Rikjsinst Natuurbeheer ... Verhandelingen Rijksinstituut voor
        Natuurbeheer [*A publication*]
Verh Zool-Bot Ges Wien ... Verhandlungen der Zoologisch-
        Botanischen Gesellschaft in Wien [*A publication*]
Verkehrsmed Grenzgeb ... Verkehrsmedizin und Ihre Grenzgebiete
        [*A publication*]
Veroeff Morphol Pathol ... Veroeffentlichungen aus der
        Morphologischen Pathologie [*A publication*]
Veroeff Zool Staatssamml (Muench) ... Veroeffentlichungen der
        Zoologischen Staatssammlung (Muenchen) [*A
        publication*]

Verrigtinge Kongr S-Afr Genet Ver ... Verrigtinge van die Kongres van dis Suid-Afrikaanse Genetiese Vereniging [*A publication*]
Verstaendliche Wiss ... Verstaendliche Wissenschaft [*A publication*]
Vertebr Hung ... Vertebrata Hungarica [*A publication*]
Vertebr Palasiat ... Vertebrata Palasiatica [*A publication*]
Vestn Akad Med Nauk SSSR ... Vestnik Akademii Meditsinskikh Nauk SSSR [*A publication*]
Vestn Akad Nauk Kaz SSR ... Vestnik Akademii Nauk Kazakhskoi SSR [*A publication*]
Vestn Akad Nauk SSSR ... Vestnik Akademii Nauk SSSR [*A publication*]
Vestn Beloruss Univ ... Vestnik Belorusskogo Universiteta [*A publication*]
Vestn Cesk Akad Zemed ... Vestnik Ceskoslovenske Akademie Zemedelske [*A publication*]
Vestn Cesk Akad Zemed Ved ... Vestnik Ceskoslovenske Akademie Zemedelskych Ved [*A publication*]
Vestn Cesk Spol Zool ... Vestnik Ceskoslovenske Spolecnosti Zoologicke [*A publication*]
Vestn Dermatol Venerol ... Vestnik Dermatologii i Venerologii [*A publication*]
Vestn Gos Muz Gruz ... Vestnik Gosudarstvennogo Muzeya Gruzii [*A publication*]
Vestn Khir Im I I Grekova ... Vestnik Khir Im I I Grekova [*A publication*]
Vestn Leningr Univ Biol ... Vestnik Leningradskogo Universiteta Biologiya [*A publication*]
Vestn Mosk Univ Ser V Geogr ... Vestnik Moskovskogo Universiteta. Seriya V. Geografiya [*A publication*]
Vestn Oftal'mol ... Vestnik Oftal'mologii [*A publication*]
Vestn Otorinolaringol ... Vestnik Otorinolaringologii [*A publication*]
Vestn Rentgenol Radiol ... Vestnik Rentgenologii i Radiologii [*A publication*]
Vestn S-kh Nauki (Mosc) ... Vestnik Sel'skokhozyaistvennoi Nauki (Moscow) [*A publication*]
Vestn Ustred Ustavu Geol ... Vestnik Ustredniho Ustavu Geologickeho [*A publication*]
Vestn Zool ... Vestnik Zoologii [*A publication*]
VESV .... Vesicular Exanthema Swine Virus
V & ET .... Verification and Evaluation Tests
Vet Annu ... Veterinary Annual [*A publication*]
Vet Arh ...... Veterinarski Arhiv [*A publication*]
Vet Cas (Kosice) ... Veterinarsky Casopis (Kosice) [*A publication*]
Vet Glas .... Veterinarski Glasnik [*A publication*]
Vet Ital ...... Veterinaria Italiana [*A publication*]
Vet Med Nauki ... Veterinarno Meditsinski Nauki [*A publication*]
Vet Med (Prague) ... Veterinarni Medicina (Prague) [*A publication*]
Vet Med Sci ... Veterinary Medical Science [*A publication*]
Vet Med Small Anim Clin ... Veterinary Medicine and Small Animal Clinician [*A publication*]
Vet Parasitol ... Veterinary Parasitology [*A publication*]
Vet Pathol ... Veterinary Pathology [*A publication*]
Vet Resp Mezhved Temat Nauchn Sb ... Veterinariya Respublikanskii Mezhvedomstvennyi Tematicheskii Nauchnyi Sbornik [*A publication*]
Vet Resp Mizhvid Temat Nauk Zb ... Veterinariya Respublikanskyu Mizhvidomchyi Tematychnyi Naukovyi Zbirnyk [*A publication*]
Vet Urug ... Veterinaria Uruguay [*A publication*]
VEV .... Barakoma [*Solomon Islands*] [*Airport symbol*]
VEWAA ..... Vocational Evaluation and Work Adjustment Association
VEY .... Vestmannaeyjar [*Iceland*] [*Airport symbol*]
V/F .... Voltage to Frequency [*Converter*] [*Data processing*]
VFA .... Victoria Falls [*Zimbabwe*] [*Airport symbol*]
VFCT .... Variable Frequency Carrier Tone
VFP .... Veterans for Peace
VFR .... Visiting Friends and Relatives [*Airlines*]
VFU .... Vertical Format Unit
VGA .... Vijayawada [*India*] [*Airport symbol*]
VGO .... Vigo [*Spain*] [*Airport symbol*]
VHC .... Saurimo [*Angola*] [*Airport symbol*]
VHO .... Vila Coutinho [*Mozambique*] [*Airport symbol*]
Viata Med (Buchar) ... Viata Medicala (Bucharest) [*A publication*]
VIC .... Victoria [*State in Australia*]
Victoria Mines Dep Annu Rep ... Victoria Mines Department. Annual Report [*A publication*]
Victorian Nat ... Victorian Naturalist [*A publication*]
Victoria's Resour ... Victoria's Resources [*A publication*]

VID .... Vidin [*Bulgaria*] [*Airport symbol*]
Vidensk Medd Dan Naturhist Foren ... Videnskabelige Meddelelser fra Dansk Naturhistorisk Forening [*A publication*]
VIDS/MAF ... Visual Identification System/Maintenance Action Form
VIE .... Vibration Isolation Equipment
VIE .... Vienna [*Austria*] [*Airport symbol*]
Vie Med Can Fr ... Vie Medicale au Canada Francais [*A publication*]
Vie Milieu Ser A Biol Mar ... Vie et Milieu. Serie A. Biologie Marine [*A publication*]
Vie Milieu Ser B Oceanogr ... Vie et Milieu. Serie B. Oceanographie [*A publication*]
Vie Milieu Ser C Biol Terr ... Vie et Milieu. Serie C. Biologie Terrestre [*A publication*]
Viewpoints Biol ... Viewpoints in Biology [*A publication*]
VIG .... Vigilant Identification
VIJ .... Virgin Gorda [*British Virgin Islands*] [*Airport symbol*]
Viking Fund Publ Anthropol ... Viking Fund Publication in Anthropology [*A publication*]
VIL .... Dakhla [*Mauritania*] [*Airport symbol*]
VIMS .... Vehicle Integrated Management System
Vinodel Vinograd SSSR ... Vinodelie i Vinogradarstvo SSSR [*A publication*]
VINT .... Video Integrate
VIO .... Heavy [*Used to qualify interference or static reports*] [*Communications*]
VIP .... Variable Incentive Pay [*Military*]
Virchows Arch Abt A Pathol Anat ... Virchows Archiv Abteilung. A. Pathologische Anatomie [*A publication*]
Virchows Arch Abt B Zellpathol ... Virchows Archiv Abteilung. B. Zellpathologie [*A publication*]
Virchows Arch A Pathol Anat Histol ... Virchows Archiv. A. Pathological Anatomy and Histology [*A publication*]
Virchows Arch B Cell Pathol ... Virchows Archiv. B. Cell Pathology [*A publication*]
Virol Monogr ... Virology Monographs [*A publication*]
VIS .... Virtual Information Storage
VIS .... Visalia [*California*] [*Airport symbol*]
Visindafelag Isl Rit ... Visindafelag Islendinga Rit [*A publication*]
Visn Akad Nauk Ukr RSR ... Visnyk Akademiyi Nauk Ukrayins'koyi RSR [*A publication*]
Visn Kyyiv Univ Ser Biol ... Visnyk Kyyivs'koho Universytetu. Seriya Biolohiyi [*A publication*]
Visn Sil's'kohospod Nauky ... Visnyk Sil's'kohospodarskoyi Nauky [*A publication*]
Visual Med ... Visual Medicine [*A publication*]
Visual Sonic Med ... Visual Sonic Medicine [*A publication*]
VIT .... Vitoria [*Spain*] [*Airport symbol*]
Vita Hum ... Vita Humana [*A publication*]
Vitalst Zivilisationskr ... Vitalstoffe Zivilisationskrankheiten [*A publication*]
Vitam Horm ... Vitamins and Hormones [*A publication*]
VIV .... Variable Inlet Vanes
VIV .... Vivigani [*Papua New Guinea*] [*Airport symbol*]
VIX .... Vitoria [*Brazil*] [*Airport symbol*]
VK .... Transcargo [*Compania Espanola de Carga Area SA*] [*Spain*] [*ICAO designator*]
VKO .... Moscow [*USSR*] Vnukovo Airport [*Airport symbol*]
VL .... Videlicet [*Namely*] [*Latin*]
Vlaams Diergeneeskd Tijdschr ... Vlaams Diergeneeskundig Tijdschrift [*A publication*]
VLC .... Valencia [*Spain*] [*Airport symbol*]
VLD .... Valdosta [*Georgia*] [*Airport symbol*]
VLH .... Very Lightly Hinged [*Philately*]
VLI .... Port Vila [*Vanuata*] [*Airport symbol*]
VLL .... Valladolid [*Spain*] [*Airport symbol*]
VLS .... Valesdir [*Vanuata*] [*Airport symbol*]
VLV .... Valera [*Venezuela*] [*Airport symbol*]
VME .... Villa Mercedes [*Argentina*] [*Airport symbol*]
VMS .... Visual Motion Simulator
VNO .... Vomeronasal Organ [*Anatomy*]
VNS .... Vladimir Nabokov Society
VNSP .... Vacant Nozzle Shield Plug
VOC .... Volatile Organic Compounds [*Environmental chemistry*]
VOD .... Vertical On-Board Delivery [*Navy*]
Vodn Hospod ... Vodni Hospodarstvi [*A publication*]
Voenno-Med Zh ... Voenno-Meditsinskii Zhurnal [*A publication*]
Vojen Zdrav Listy ... Vojenske Zdravotnicke Listy [*A publication*]
Vojnosanit Pregl ... Vojnosanitetski Pregled [*A publication*]

VOLMET ... Meteorological Information for Aircraft in Flight [*Aviation code*]
Vopr Antropol ... Voprosy Antropologii [*A publication*]
Vopr Filos ... Voprosy Filosofii [*A publication*]
Vopr Fiziol Rast Mikrobiol ... Voprosy Fiziologii Rastenii i Mikrobiologii [*A publication*]
Vopr Ikhtiol ... Voprosy Ikhtiologii [*A publication*]
Vopr Klin Eskp Khir ... Voprosy Klinicheskoi i Eksperimental'noi Khirurgii [*A publication*]
Vopr Kraev Patol Akad Nauk Uzb SSR ... Voprosy Kraevoi Pathologii Akademii Nauk Uzbekskoi SSR [*A publication*]
Vopr Med Khim ... Voprosy Meditsinskoi Khimii [*A publication*]
Vopr Med Virusol ... Voprosy Meditsinskoi Virusologii [*A publication*]
Vopr Neirokhir ... Voprosy Neirokhirurgii [*A publication*]
Vopr Okhr Materin Det ... Voprosy Okhrany Materinstva i Detstva [*A publication*]
Vopr Onkol (Leningr) ... Voprosy Onkologii (Leningrad) [*A publication*]
Vopr Pitan ... Voprosy Pitaniya [*A publication*]
Vopr Psikhol ... Voprosy Psikhologii [*A publication*]
Vopr Radiobiol ... Voprosy Radiobiologii [*A publication*]
Vopr Ratsion Pitan ... Voprosy Ratsional'nogo Pitaniya [*A publication*]
Vopr Revm ... Voprosy Revmatizma [*A publication*]
Vopr Sel'sk Lesn Khoz Dal'n Vost ... Voprosy Sel'skogo i Lesnogo Khozyaistva Dal'nego Vostoka [*A publication*]
Vopr Sudebno-Med Ekspert ... Voprosy Sudebno-Meditsinskoi Ekspertizy [*A publication*]
Vopr Virusol ... Voprosy Virusologii [*A publication*]
VOR ... Vestibulo-Ocular Reflex [*Neurology*]
Vortr Gesamtgeb Bot ... Vortraege aus dem Gesamtgebiet der Botanik [*A publication*]

VOSH ... Volunteer Optometric Service to Humanity
VOT ... Vorticity
Vox Sang .. Vox Sanguinis [*A publication*]
VP ... Vanuaaku Pati [*Political party*] [*New Hebrides*]
VPF ... Vertical Processing Facility
VPPD ... Vice Presidential Protective Division [*US Secret Service*]
VR ... Vulnerability Reduction [*Military*]
Vrach Delo ... Vrachebnoe Delo [*A publication*]
VRC ... Vampire Research Center
VRC ... Vertical Redundancy Check
VRDDO ... Variable Retention of Diatomic Differential [*Physics*]
VSA ... By Visual Reference to the Ground [*Aviation*]
VSEPR ... Valence Shell Electron Pair Repulsion [*Physics*]
Vses Nauchn O-vo Neirokhir ... Vsesoyuznde Nauchnoe Obshchestvo Neirokhirurgii [*A publication*]
VSM ... Virtual Storage Manager
VSR ... Vallecitos Experimental Superheat Reactor
V & T ... Vodka and Tonic
VTC ... Volunteer Training Corps [*An organization for home defense*] [*British*] [*World War I*]
VTR ... Voltage Transformation Ratio [*Physics*]
VTRB ... Variable Trim Reentry Body
V + TU ... Voice Plus Teleprinter Unit
VUA ... Virtual Unit Address
VULREP ... Vulnerability Report [*Navy*]
VVMF ... Vietnam Veterans Memorial Fund
VWGA ... Vinifera Wine Growers Association
VY ... Abelag Airways [*Belgium*] [*ICAO designator*]
Vyz Lidu ... Vyziva Lidu [*A publication*]
VZ ... Nefertiti Aviation [*Egypt*] [*ICAO designator*]
VZIG ... Varicella-Zoster Immune Globulin
VZV ... Varicella-Zoster Virus [*Also, VZ*]

W

W .... [*Alfred*] Wotquenne [*When used in identifying C. P. E. Bach's compositions, refers to cataloging of his works by musicologist Wotquenne*]

WA .... Wellness Associates [*An organization*]

WAAA .... Walleye Anglers Association of America

WAAR .... Wartime Aircraft Activity Reporting [*System*]

WABH .... Churchville, VA [*Broadcasting station call letters*]

WABK-FM ... Gardiner, ME [*Broadcasting station call letters*]

WABT........ Montgomery, AL [*Broadcasting station call letters*]

WACC ...... Washing Corrosion Control

WACQ ...... Carrville, AL [*Broadcasting station call letters*]

WACR-FM ... Columbus, MO [*Broadcasting station call letters*]

Wadley Med Bull ... Wadley Medical Bulletin [*A publication*]

WAEC .... Atlanta, GA [*Broadcasting station call letters*]

WAED .... Huntsville, AL [*Broadcasting station call letters*]

WAES........ Atlanta, GA [*Broadcasting station call letters*]

WAF .... Woman Activist Fund

WAF .... Women's Auxiliary Force [*British*] [*World War I*] [*Later, Victory Corps*]

WAF/CP.... Women and Foundations/Corporate Philanthropy [*An organization*]

WAGR .... Wald, Arnold, Goldberg, Rushton [*Test*] [*Statistics*]

WAID .... Clarksdale, MS [*Broadcasting station call letters*]

WAIM-FM ... Anderson, SC [*Broadcasting station call letters*]

WAJK .... La Salle, IL [*Broadcasting station call letters*]

WAJL .... Winter Park, FL [*Broadcasting station call letters*]

WAJX .... Titusville, FL [*Broadcasting station call letters*]

Wakayama Med Rep ... Wakayama Medical Reports [*A publication*]

Walla Walla Coll Publ ... Walla Walla College Publications [*A publication*]

Wallerstein Lab Commun ... Wallerstein Laboratories Communications [*A publication*]

WALZ........ Machias, ME [*Broadcasting station call letters*]

WAMQ....... Loretto, PA [*Broadcasting station call letters*]

WAMT .... Titusville, FL [*Broadcasting station call letters*]

WAP .... Work Analysis Program [*Data processing*]

WAQA .... Grasonville, MD [*Broadcasting station call letters*]

WAQE .... Rice Lake, WI [*Broadcasting station call letters*]

WAQX .... Manlius, NY [*Broadcasting station call letters*]

Ward's Bull ... Ward's Bulletin [*A publication*]

WARF........ Wide-Aperture Research Facility [*For hurricane detection*]

WARN .... Women of All Red Nations [*An organization*]

WAS .... War at Sea

Wash Agric Exp Stn Bull ... Washington Agricultural Experiment Station. Bulletin [*A publication*]

Wash Agric Exp Stn Tech Bull ... Washington Agricultural Experiment Station. Technical Bulletin [*A publication*]

Wash Dep Fish Annu Rep ... Washington Department of Fisheries. Annual Report [*A publication*]

Wash Dep Fish Fish Res Pap ... Washington Department of Fisheries. Fisheries Research Papers [*A publication*]

Wash Dep Fish Res Bull ... Washington Department of Fisheries. Research Bulletin [*A publication*]

Wash Dep Fish Tech Rep ... Washington Department of Fisheries. Technical Report [*A publication*]

WASM....... Saratoga Springs, NY [*Broadcasting station call letters*]

Wasmann J Biol ... Wasmann Journal of Biology [*A publication*]

Wastes Eng ... Wastes Engineering [*A publication*]

WATD........ Marshfield, MA [*Broadcasting station call letters*]

Water Air Soil Pollut ... Water, Air, and Soil Pollution [*A publication*]

Water Biol Syst ... Water in Biological Systems [*A publication*]

Water Electrolyte Metab Proc Symp ... Water and Electrolyte Metabolism. Proceedings of the Symposium [*A publication*]

Water Pollut Control ... Water Pollution Control [*A publication*]

Water Pollut Res ... Water Pollution Research (Stevenage) [*A publication*]

Water Pollut Res Can ... Water Pollution Research in Canada [*A publication*]

Water Res Found Aust Bull ... Water Research Foundation of Australia. Bulletin [*A publication*]

Water Resour Bull ... Water Resources Bulletin [*A publication*]

Water Resour Res ... Water Resources Research [*A publication*]

Water SA (Pretoria) ... Water SA (Pretoria) [*A publication*]

Water Waste Treat ... Water and Waste Treatment [*A publication*]

WAVPM..... Women Against Violence in Pornography and Media

WAVV........ Vevay, IN [*Broadcasting station call letters*]

WAVW....... Vero Beach, FL [*Broadcasting station call letters*]

WAW .... Wings Airways [*Blue Bell, PA*] [*FAA designator*]

WAXC .... St. Marys-Wapakoneta, OH [*Broadcasting station call letters*]

WAXO .... Lewisburg, TN [*Broadcasting station call letters*]

WAXX........ Eau Claire, WI [*Broadcasting station call letters*]

WAYK-FM ... Lehigh Acres, FL [*Broadcasting station call letters*]

WAZU........ Springfield, OH [*Broadcasting station call letters*]

WAZZ........ New Bern, NC [*Broadcasting station call letters*]

WB .... Wirebar [*Metal industry*]

WBAD .... Lebanon, MO [*Broadcasting station call letters*]

WBAM-FM ... Montgomery, AL [*Broadcasting station call letters*]

WBBG .... Cleveland, OH [*Broadcasting station call letters*]

WBCQ .... Bucyrus, OH [*Broadcasting station call letters*]

WBCY .... Charlotte, NC [*Broadcasting station call letters*]

WBEC-FM ... Pittsfield, MA [*Broadcasting station call letters*]

WBEK........ Cherry Hill, NJ [*Broadcasting station call letters*]

WBFJ .... Winston-Salem, NC [*Broadcasting station call letters*]

WBGP .... Waterborne Guard Post

WBIL-FM.... Tuskegee, AL [*Broadcasting station call letters*]

WBIN .... Benton, TN [*Broadcasting station call letters*]

WBIO......... Parsippany-Troy Hills, NJ [*Broadcasting station call letters*]

WBJZ .... Olean, NY [*Broadcasting station call letters*]

WBKC .... Chardon, OH [*Broadcasting station call letters*]

WBKF........ MacLenny, FL [*Broadcasting station call letters*]

WBKO .... Chardon, OH [*Broadcasting station call letters*]

WBL .... Women's Basketball League

WBLM .... Macon, GA [*Broadcasting station call letters*]

WBMI .... West Branch, MI [*Broadcasting station call letters*]

WBMI .... Women's Board of Missions of the Interior

WBMK....... Knoxville, TN [*Broadcasting station call letters*]

WBNT .... Oneida, TN [*Broadcasting station call letters*]

WBNZ........ Frankfort, MI [*Broadcasting station call letters*]

WBOZ .... San German, PR [*Broadcasting station call letters*]

WBPV-FM ... Charlton, MA [*Broadcasting station call letters*]

WBRH........ Baton Rouge, LA [*Broadcasting station call letters*]

WBSN-FM ... New Orleans, LA [*Broadcasting station call letters*]

WBTG .... Sheffield, AL [*Broadcasting station call letters*]

WBTY .... Homerville, GA [*Broadcasting station call letters*]
WBWB .... Bloomington, IN [*Broadcasting station call letters*]
WBZ-FM.... Boston, MA [*Broadcasting station call letters*]
WBZK .... York, SC [*Broadcasting station call letters*]
WC .... Whale Center
WCA .... Westair Commuter Airlines [*Santa Rosa, CA*] [*FAA designator*]
WCAR .... Garden City, MI [*Broadcasting station call letters*]
WCAZ-FM ... Carthage, IL [*Broadcasting station call letters*]
WCBR-FM ... Richmond, KY [*Broadcasting station call letters*]
WCC .... Women's Classical Caucus
WCC .... World for Christ Crusade
WCCA .... World Court Clubs Association
WCCD .... Athens, GA [*Broadcasting station call letters*]
WCCL ...... Jackson, MS [*Broadcasting station call letters*]
WCCY ...... Houghton, MI [*Broadcasting station call letters*]
WCEW .... Charleston, SC [*Broadcasting station call letters*]
WCEZ........ Jupiter, FL [*Broadcasting station call letters*]
WCGM ..... Writable Character Generation Module [*Data processing*]
WCHA .... Wooden Canoe Heritage Association
WCHY ...... Savannah, GA [*Broadcasting station call letters*]
WCIF .... Melbourne, FL [*Broadcasting station call letters*]
WCJL .... Marinette, WI [*Broadcasting station call letters*]
WCKO .... Fort Lauderdale, FL [*Broadcasting station call letters*]
WCLC .... Watch Check List Completed
WCM .... Weapon Control Module
WCM .... Writable Control Memory [*Data processing*]
WCNS .... Latrobe, PA [*Broadcasting station call letters*]
WCPQ .... Havelock, NC [*Broadcasting station call letters*]
WCQL .... Pewaukee, WI [*Broadcasting station call letters*]
WCRJ........ Jacksonville, FL [*Broadcasting station call letters*]
WCRN .... St. Thomas, VI [*Broadcasting station call letters*]
WCSO ...... Signal Mountain, TN [*Broadcasting station call letters*]
WCTD-FM ... Federalsburg, MD [*Broadcasting station call letters*]
WCTM .... Eaton, OH [*Broadcasting station call letters*]
WCU .... Weapons Control Unit
WCVC .... Tallahassee, FL [*Broadcasting station call letters*]
WCVF-FM ... Fredonia, NY [*Broadcasting station call letters*]
WCVJ........ Jefferson, OH [*Broadcasting station call letters*]
WCVY ...... Coventry, RI [*Broadcasting station call letters*]
WCXI......... Detroit, MI [*Broadcasting station call letters*]
WCYJ........ Waynesburg, PA [*Broadcasting station call letters*]
WCZY-FM ... Detroit, MI [*Broadcasting station call letters*]
WDAQ .... Danbury, CT [*Broadcasting station call letters*]
WDAT........ Ormond Beach, FL [*Broadcasting station call letters*]
WDAX-FM ... Mc Rae, GA [*Broadcasting station call letters*]
WDBK .... Springfield, TN [*Broadcasting station call letters*]
WDBY .... Duxbury, MA [*Broadcasting station call letters*]
WDC.......... Waste Disposal Cask [*Nuclear energy*]
WDCE .... Richmond, VA [*Broadcasting station call letters*]
WDCI......... Gorham, ME [*Broadcasting station call letters*]
WDDQ .... Adel, GA [*Broadcasting station call letters*]
WDDW .... Johnston City, IL [*Broadcasting station call letters*]
WDEL .... Weapons Development Effectiveness Laboratory
WDGR .... Plainfield, VT [*Broadcasting station call letters*]
WDGS .... New Albany, IN [*Broadcasting station call letters*]
WDHA .... Watery Diarrhea Hypovolemia Achlorhydria [*Medicine*]
WDIN......... Orangeburg, SC [*Broadcasting station call letters*]
WDIS......... Fort Walton Beach, FL [*Broadcasting station call letters*]
WDJD .... Jackson, MI [*Broadcasting station call letters*]
WDJQ .... Alliance, OH [*Broadcasting station call letters*]
WDJW .... Somers, CT [*Broadcasting station call letters*]
WDJX .... Xenia, OH [*Broadcasting station call letters*]
WDKB .... Auburn, IN [*Broadcasting station call letters*]
WDKN-FM ... Dickson, TN [*Broadcasting station call letters*]
WDLV .... Pinehurst, NC [*Broadcasting station call letters*]
WDLW .... Waltham, MA [*Broadcasting station call letters*]
WDNY .... Dansville, NY [*Broadcasting station call letters*]
WDOQ .... Daytona Beach, FL [*Broadcasting station call letters*]
WDOY-FM ... Fajardo, PR [*Broadcasting station call letters*]
WDRC .... Women's Defence Relief Corps [*British*] [*World War I*]
WDSPRD.... Widespread [*Meteorology*]
WDSY .... Pittsburgh, PA [*Broadcasting station call letters*]
WDWQ ...... St. George, SC [*Broadcasting station call letters*]
WDZK .... Chester, SC [*Broadcasting station call letters*]
WDZZ-FM ... Flint, MI [*Broadcasting station call letters*]
WE............. Women Entrepreneurs [*An organization*]
WEAX........ Angola, IN [*Broadcasting station call letters*]
WEC .... Women's Emergency Corps [*British*] [*World War I*]

WEEF .... Highland Park, IL [*Broadcasting station call letters*]
Wehrmed Monatsschr ... Wehrmedizinische Monatsschrift [*A publication*]
Wein-Wiss ... Wein-Wissenschaft [*A publication*]
Welsh Plant Breed Stn Bull Ser ... Welsh Plant Breeding Station. Bulletin Series [*A publication*]
WEMI .... Neenah-Menasha, WI [*Broadcasting station call letters*]
WENA .... Penuelas, PR [*Broadcasting station call letters*]
Wenner-Gren Cent Int Symp Ser ... Wenner-Gren Center. International Symposium Series [*A publication*]
WEPH........ Weapon Phenomenology
WEQC .... Kalkaska, MI [*Broadcasting station call letters*]
WEQO .... Whitley City, KY [*Broadcasting station call letters*]
WERB........ Berlin, CT [*Broadcasting station call letters*]
WERR........ Utuado, PR [*Broadcasting station call letters*]
WERU........ Champaign, IL [*Broadcasting station call letters*]
WERV........ Beaufort, SC [*Broadcasting station call letters*]
WES .... Weapons Effects Systems
WES .... Wes-Martin Aviation [*Red Bluff, CA*] [*FAA designator*]
WESD........ Schofield, WI [*Broadcasting station call letters*]
Wesley W Spink Lect Comp Med ... Wesley W. Spink Lectures on Comparative Medicine [*A publication*]
West Afr J Biol Appl Chem ... West African Journal of Biological and Applied Chemistry [*A publication*]
West Afr J Biol Chem ... West African Journal of Biological Chemistry [*A publication*]
West Afr Med J Nigerian Pract ... West African Medical Journal and Nigerian Practitioner [*A publication*]
West Afr Pharm ... West African Pharmacist [*A publication*]
West Aust Dep Agric Annu Rep ... Western Australia Department of Agriculture. Annual Report [*A publication*]
West Aust Dep Fish Fauna Rep ... Western Australia Department of Fisheries and Fauna. Report [*A publication*]
West Aust Dep Fish Wildl Rep ... Western Australia Department of Fisheries and Wildlife. Report [*A publication*]
West Aust Nat ... Western Australian Naturalist [*A publication*]
West Aust SWANS ... Western Australia SWANS [*State Wildlife Authority News Service*] [*A publication*]
West Bird Bander ... Western Bird Bander [*A publication*]
West-Eur Symp Clin Chem ... West-European Symposia on Clinical Chemistry [*A publication*]
West Feed Seed ... Western Feed and Seed [*A publication*]
West Found Vertebr Zool Occas Pap ... Western Foundation of Vertebrate Zoology. Occasional Papers [*A publication*]
West Indian Med J ... West Indian Medical Journal [*A publication*]
West Med ... Western Medicine [*A publication*]
West Resour Conf ... Western Resources Conference [*A publication*]
West Wildlands ... Western Wildlands [*A publication*]
Wet Bydraes PU CHO Reeks B Natuurwet ... Wetenskaplike Bydraes van die PU [*Potchefstroomse Universiteit*] vir CHO [*Christelike Hoere Onderwys*] Reeks B: Natuurwetenskappe [*A publication*]
Wet Meded KNNV ... Wetenschappelijke Mededeling KNNV [*Koninklijke Nederlandse Natuurhistorische Vereniging*] [*A publication*]
WEVE-FM ... Eveleth, MN [*Broadcasting station call letters*]
WEXA........ Eupora, MS [*Broadcasting station call letters*]
WEYZ........ Erie, PA [*Broadcasting station call letters*]
WEZV........ Fort Wayne, IN [*Broadcasting station call letters*]
WFAC........ Columbus, OH [*Broadcasting station call letters*]
WFB .... Wide Flange Beam [*Metal industry*]
WFBM .... Noblesville, IN [*Broadcasting station call letters*]
WFBZ .... Minocqua, WI [*Broadcasting station call letters*]
WFC .... Women's Forage Corps [*British*] [*World War I*]
WFCB .... Chillicothe, OH [*Broadcasting station call letters*]
WFCM-FM ... Orangeburg, SC [*Broadcasting station call letters*]
WFFM-FM ... Braddock, PA [*Broadcasting station call letters*]
WFFX .... Grand Rapids, MI [*Broadcasting station call letters*]
WFGS........ Milton, FL [*Broadcasting station call letters*]
WFHFF ...... World Federation of Hungarian Freedom Fighters
WFJT......... Inez, KY [*Broadcasting station call letters*]
WFL .... Work Flow Language [*Data processing*]
WFMC .... Welding Filler Material Control
WFMT .... Chicago, IL [*Broadcasting station call letters*]
WFMX .... Statesville, NC [*Broadcasting station call letters*]
WFRI .... Opelika, AL [*Broadcasting station call letters*]
WFRN .... Elkhart, IN [*Broadcasting station call letters*]
WFUM .... South Miami, FL [*Broadcasting station call letters*]

WFUN........ Ashtabula, OH [*Broadcasting station call letters*]
WFXE .... Columbus, GA [*Broadcasting station call letters*]
WFXI .... Haines City, FL [*Broadcasting station call letters*]
WFYV .... Atlantic Beach, FL [*Broadcasting station call letters*]
WG .... Air Ecosse (Charters) Ltd. [*Great Britain*] [*ICAO designator*]
WGAE .... Girard, PA [*Broadcasting station call letters*]
WGAG-FM ... Orlando, FL [*Broadcasting station call letters*]
WGBK .... Harrisonburg, VA [*Broadcasting station call letters*]
WGBQ .... Galesburg, IL [*Broadcasting station call letters*]
WGCDR..... Working Group for Community Development Reform
WGFG .... Lake City, SC [*Broadcasting station call letters*]
WGGM ...... Chester, VA [*Broadcasting station call letters*]
WGHB .... Farmville, NC [*Broadcasting station call letters*]
WGIT .... Hormigueros, PR [*Broadcasting station call letters*]
WGLO .... Pekin, IL [*Broadcasting station call letters*]
WGLR .... Lancaster, WI [*Broadcasting station call letters*]
WGMM ...... Gladwin, MI [*Broadcasting station call letters*]
WGMS-FM ... Bethesda, MD [*Broadcasting station call letters*]
WGOJ .... Conneaut, OH [*Broadcasting station call letters*]
WGSS ...... Lumberton, NC [*Broadcasting station call letters*]
WGSX .... Bayamon, PR [*Broadcasting station call letters*]
WGTR-FM ... Nantucket, MA [*Broadcasting station call letters*]
WGUS-FM ... North Augusta, SC [*Broadcasting station call letters*]
WGUY-FM ... Brewer, ME [*Broadcasting station call letters*]
WH .... City-Flug GmbH [*West Germany*] [*ICAO designator*]
WHAB .... Acton, MA [*Broadcasting station call letters*]
WHBS........ Holiday, FL [*Broadcasting station call letters*]
WHCLIS .... White House Conference on Library and Information Services
WHCOA .... White House Conference on Aging
Wheat Inf Serv ... Wheat Information Service [*A publication*]
WHEM .... Henderson, TN [*Broadcasting station call letters*]
WHFR .... Dearborn, MI [*Broadcasting station call letters*]
WHIM .... Western Humor and Irony Membership [*An organization*]
WHLA........ LaCrosse, WI [*Broadcasting station call letters*]
WHLB-FM ... Virginia, MN [*Broadcasting station call letters*]
WHLG........ Jensen Beach, FL [*Broadcasting station call letters*]
WHLP-FM ... Centerville, TN [*Broadcasting station call letters*]
WHNI......... Mebane, NC [*Broadcasting station call letters*]
WHO Food Addit Ser ... WHO [*World Health Organization*] Food Additives Series [*A publication*]
WHO Int Agency Res Cancer Annu Rep ... World Health Organization International Agency for Research on Cancer. Annual Report [*A publication*]
WHO Monogr Ser ... World Health Organization. Monograph Series [*A publication*]
WHO Offset Publ ... WHO [*World Health Organization*] Offset Publication [*A publication*]
WHO Pestic Residues Ser ... WHO [*World Health Organization*] Pesticide Residues Series [*A publication*]
WHO Tech Rep Ser ... World Health Organization. Technical Report Series [*A publication*]
WHPO .... Hopeston, IL [*Broadcasting station call letters*]
WHR .... Women and Health Roundtable [*An organization*]
WHRO .... Norfolk, VA [*Broadcasting station call letters*]
WHUE........ Boston, MA [*Broadcasting station call letters*]
WHUE-FM ... Boston, MA [*Broadcasting station call letters*]
WHWL .... Marquette, MI [*Broadcasting station call letters*]
WI.............. Air Transcontinental Airlines Ltd. [*Great Britain*] [*ICAO designator*]
WIACO ...... World Insulation and Acoustic Congress Organization
Wiad Bot ... Wiadomosci Botaniczne [*A publication*]
Wiad Ekol ... Wiadomosci Ekologiczne [*A publication*]
Wiad Lek ... Wiadomosci Lekarskie [*A publication*]
Wiad Parazytol ... Wiadomosci Parazytologiczne [*A publication*]
WIBG......... Ocean City-Somers Point, NJ [*Broadcasting station call letters*]
WIC .... Weighted Ion Concentration [*Air pollution measure*]
Wien Klin Wochenschr ... Wiener Klinische Wochenschrift [*A publication*]
Wien Klin Wochenschr Suppl ... Wiener Klinische Wochenschrift. Supplementum [*A publication*]
Wien Med Wochenschr ... Wiener Medizinische Wochenschrift [*A publication*]
Wien Med Wochenschr Suppl ... Wiener Medizinische Wochenschrift. Supplementum [*A publication*]
Wien Tieraerztl Monatsschr ... Wiener Tieraerztliche Monatsschrift [*A publication*]

Wien Z Inn Med Ihre Grenzgeb ... Wiener Zeitschrift fuer Innere Medizin und Ihre Grenzgebiete [*A publication*]
WIEZ .... Oneonta, NY [*Broadcasting station call letters*]
WIF .... Women in Film [*An organization*]
WIFE-FM ... Indianapolis, IN [*Broadcasting station call letters*]
WIGS-FM ... Gouverneur, NY [*Broadcasting station call letters*]
WIIZ........... Jacksonville, NC [*Broadcasting station call letters*]
WIKS......... Greenfield, IN [*Broadcasting station call letters*]
WIKU .... Pikesville, TN [*Broadcasting station call letters*]
Wildenowia Beih ... Wildenowia Beiheft [*A publication*]
Wildl Aust ... Wildlife Australia [*A publication*]
Wildl Dis ... Wildlife Diseases [*A publication*]
Wildl Manage Bull (Ottawa) Ser 1 ... Wildlife Management Bulletin (Ottawa) Series 1 [*A publication*]
Wildl Manage Bull (Ottawa) Ser 2 ... Wildlife Management Bulletin (Ottawa) Series 2 [*A publication*]
Wildl Monogr ... Wildlife Monographs [*A publication*]
Wildl Rev NZ Wildl Serv ... Wildlife Review. New Zealand Wildlife Service [*A publication*]
Wildl Soc Bull ... Wildlife Society Bulletin [*A publication*]
Wilhelm Roux's Arch Dev Biol ... Wilhelm Roux's Archives of Developmental Biology [*A publication*]
Wilson Bull ... Wilson Bulletin [*A publication*]
WIMG .... Trenton, NJ [*Broadcasting station call letters*]
WINB......... Western Interstate Nuclear Board
WIQX......... Millersville, PA [*Broadcasting station call letters*]
WIS .... Women in Soccer [*An organization*]
Wis Agric Exp Stn Res Bull ... Wisconsin Agricultural Experiment Station. Research Bulletin [*A publication*]
Wis Agric Exp Stn Res Rep ... Wisconsin Agricultural Experiment Station. Research Report [*A publication*]
Wis Conserv Bull ... Wisconsin Conservation Bulletin [*A publication*]
Wis Conserv Dep Tech Bull ... Wisconsin Conservation Department. Technical Bulletin [*A publication*]
Wisconsin Agric Exp Stn Bull ... Wisconsin Agricultural Experiment Station. Bulletin [*A publication*]
WISD......... Wisdom [*Old Testament book*]
Wis Dep Nat Resour Tech Bull ... Wisconsin Department of Natural Resources. Technical Bulletin [*A publication*]
Wis Geol Nat Hist Surv Bull ... Wisconsin Geological and Natural History Survey. Bulletin [*A publication*]
Wis Med J ... Wisconsin Medical Journal [*A publication*]
Wis Nat Resour Bull ... Wisconsin Natural Resources Bulletin [*A publication*]
Wiss Fortschr ... Wissenschaft und Fortschritt [*A publication*]
Wiss Taschenb ... Wissenschaftliche Taschenbuecher [*A publication*]
WITC .... Cazenovia, NY [*Broadcasting station call letters*]
WITS .... Boston, MA [*Broadcasting station call letters*]
WITS .... Worldwide Information and Trade System
WIUJ .... St. Thomas, VI [*Broadcasting station call letters*]
WIUP-FM .. Indiana, PA [*Broadcasting station call letters*]
WIVI-FM.... St. Croix, VI [*Broadcasting station call letters*]
WIYD .... Palatka, FL [*Broadcasting station call letters*]
WIZK .... Chambersburg, PA [*Broadcasting station call letters*]
WIZY .... Gordon, GA [*Broadcasting station call letters*]
WJBB-FM ... Haleyville, AL [*Broadcasting station call letters*]
WJDW .... Corydon, IN [*Broadcasting station call letters*]
WJDZ .... Levittown, PR [*Broadcasting station call letters*]
WJHR .... Jackson, TN [*Broadcasting station call letters*]
WJIB.......... Boston, MA [*Broadcasting station call letters*]
WJJB......... Hyde Park, NY [*Broadcasting station call letters*]
WJJY......... Brainerd, MN [*Broadcasting station call letters*]
WJLD .... Homewood, AL [*Broadcasting station call letters*]
WJMQ .... Norfolk, MA [*Broadcasting station call letters*]
WJMR........ Ridgeland, SC [*Broadcasting station call letters*]
WJNZ .... Greencastle, IN [*Broadcasting station call letters*]
WJRZ .... Manahawkin, NJ [*Broadcasting station call letters*]
WJSA .... Jersey Shore, PA [*Broadcasting station call letters*]
WJSQ-FM ... Athens, TN [*Broadcasting station call letters*]
WJTH .... Calhoun, GA [*Broadcasting station call letters*]
WJTP .... Newland, NC [*Broadcasting station call letters*]
WJWK .... Jamestown, NY [*Broadcasting station call letters*]
WJXL......... Jackson, AL [*Broadcasting station call letters*]
WJYE .... Buffalo, NY [*Broadcasting station call letters*]
WK .... Aerotransporte de Espana SA [*Spain*] [*ICAO designator*]
WKAD .... Canton, PA [*Broadcasting station call letters*]
WKBJ........ Wentzel-Kramers-Brillouin-Jeffreys [*Approximation or Method*] [*Physics*]
WKCK .... Dracovis, PR [*Broadcasting station call letters*]

New Acronyms, Initialisms, & Abbreviations

WKCX .... Rome, GA [*Broadcasting station call letters*]
WKDO-FM ... Liberty, KY [*Broadcasting station call letters*]
WKEA .... Scottsboro, AL [*Broadcasting station call letters*]
WKED .... Frankfort, KY [*Broadcasting station call letters*]
WKFI-FM .. Wilmington, OH [*Broadcasting station call letters*]
WKHG ...... Leitchfield, KY [*Broadcasting station call letters*]
WKHI......... Ocean City, MD [*Broadcasting station call letters*]
WKIO......... Urbana, IL [*Broadcasting station call letters*]
WKJC .... Tawas City, MI [*Broadcasting station call letters*]
WKJJ......... Louisville, KY [*Broadcasting station call letters*]
WKJJ-FM ... Louisville, KY [*Broadcasting station call letters*]
WKKL........ West Barnstable, MA [*Broadcasting station call letters*]
WKKR .... Evansville, IN [*Broadcasting station call letters*]
WKKX .... De Land, FL [*Broadcasting station call letters*]
WKKY .... Pascagoula, MS [*Broadcasting station call letters*]
WKKZ .... Dublin, GA [*Broadcasting station call letters*]
WKLX .... Plymouth, NC [*Broadcasting station call letters*]
WKNJ........ Union Township, NJ [*Broadcasting station call letters*]
WKNZ .... Collins, MS [*Broadcasting station call letters*]
WKOA-FM ... Hopkinsville, KY [*Broadcasting station call letters*]
WKOR-FM ... Starkville, MS [*Broadcasting station call letters*]
WKQE ...... Tallahassee, FL [*Broadcasting station call letters*]
WKQS .... Boca Raton, FL [*Broadcasting station call letters*]
WKQV .... Vineland, NJ [*Broadcasting station call letters*]
WKQX .... Chicago, IL [*Broadcasting station call letters*]
WKRB .... New York, NY [*Broadcasting station call letters*]
WKRP .... Dallas, GA [*Broadcasting station call letters*]
WKSD .... Huntington, WV [*Broadcasting station call letters*]
WKSJ .... Mobile, AL [*Broadcasting station call letters*]
WKTR .... Millinocket, ME [*Broadcasting station call letters*]
WKTX .... Aiken, SC [*Broadcasting station call letters*]
WKUB .... Blackshear, GA [*Broadcasting station call letters*]
WKUE .... Green Cove Springs, FL [*Broadcasting station call letters*]
WKVM-FM ... San Juan, PR [*Broadcasting station call letters*]
WKVR-FM ... Huntingdon, PA [*Broadcasting station call letters*]
WKWM...... Kentwood, MI [*Broadcasting station call letters*]
WKWQ-FM ... Batesburg, SC [*Broadcasting station call letters*]
WKXQ .... Reidsville, NC [*Broadcasting station call letters*]
WKYN .... Paducah, KY [*Broadcasting station call letters*]
WKYW....... Frankfort, KY [*Broadcasting station call letters*]
WKYZ .... Herkimer, NY [*Broadcasting station call letters*]
WKZK .... North Augusta, SC [*Broadcasting station call letters*]
WKZZ........ Lynchburg, VA [*Broadcasting station call letters*]
WL............ Women's Legion [*British*] [*World War I*]
WLAZ........ Eufaula, AL [*Broadcasting station call letters*]
WLB .... Seagoing Buoy Tender [*Coast Guard*]
WLBQ........ Morgantown, KY [*Broadcasting station call letters*]
WLBS........ Mount Clemens, MI [*Broadcasting station call letters*]
WLCB........ Hodgenville, KY [*Broadcasting station call letters*]
WLDM........ Westfield, MA [*Broadcasting station call letters*]
WLEJ........ Ellijay, GA [*Broadcasting station call letters*]
WLER .... Butler, PA [*Broadcasting station call letters*]
WLFE .... Little Falls, MN [*Broadcasting station call letters*]
WLIC .... Adamsville, TN [*Broadcasting station call letters*]
WLJY........ Marshfield, WI [*Broadcasting station call letters*]
WLKX-FM ... Forest Lake, MN [*Broadcasting station call letters*]
WLLN .... Lillington, NC [*Broadcasting station call letters*]
WLLV .... Melbourne, FL [*Broadcasting station call letters*]
WLMT .... Wilmington, IL [*Broadcasting station call letters*]
WLN .... Washington Library Network
WLNV .... Derby, CT [*Broadcasting station call letters*]
WLPA........ Lancaster, PA [*Broadcasting station call letters*]
WLPF .... William L. Patterson Foundation
WLSK........ Lebanon, KY [*Broadcasting station call letters*]
WLSN........ Lebanon, TN [*Broadcasting station call letters*]
WLTM .... Franklin, NC [*Broadcasting station call letters*]
WLUM .... Milwaukee, WI [*Broadcasting station call letters*]
WLVS........ Germantown, TN [*Broadcasting station call letters*]
WLWI .... Montgomery, AL [*Broadcasting station call letters*]
WLYN-FM ... Lynn, MA [*Broadcasting station call letters*]
WM............ Word Mark
WMAD........ Sun Prairie, WI [*Broadcasting station call letters*]
WMBR .... Cambridge, MA [*Broadcasting station call letters*]
WMCI........ Brockton, MA [*Broadcasting station call letters*]
WME .... Women and Mathematics Education [*An organization*]
WMEC....... Medium Endurance Cutter [*Coast Guard*]
WMEQ....... Menomonie, WI [*Broadcasting station call letters*]
WMFL........ Monticello, FL [*Broadcasting station call letters*]

WMIV .... Bristol Center, NY [*Broadcasting station call letters*]
WMLA .... LeRoy, IL [*Broadcasting station call letters*]
WMLM....... St. Louis, MI [*Broadcasting station call letters*]
WMMJ....... Brattleboro, VT [*Broadcasting station call letters*]
WMMQ ...... Charlotte, MI [*Broadcasting station call letters*]
WMNF .... Tampa, FL [*Broadcasting station call letters*]
WMNJ .... Madison, NJ [*Broadcasting station call letters*]
WMO Rep Mar Sci Aff ... World Meteorological Organization. Reports on Marine Science Affairs [*A publication*]
WMO Spec Environ Rep ... World Meteorological Organization. Special Environmental Report [*A publication*]
WMO Tech Note ... World Meteorological Organization. Technical Note [*A publication*]
WMRK....... Selma, AL [*Broadcasting station call letters*]
WMSK-FM ... Morganfield, KY [*Broadcasting station call letters*]
WMSQ .... Havelock, NC [*Broadcasting station call letters*]
WMUC-FM ... College Park, MD [*Broadcasting station call letters*]
WMVI .... Mechanicville, NY [*Broadcasting station call letters*]
WMVQ....... Amsterdam, NY [*Broadcasting station call letters*]
WMWV ...... Conway, NH [*Broadcasting station call letters*]
WMYD....... Wickford, RI [*Broadcasting station call letters*]
WNBY-FM ... Newbury, MI [*Broadcasting station call letters*]
WNCE-FM ... Lancaster, PA [*Broadcasting station call letters*]
WNEK-FM ... Springfield, MA [*Broadcasting station call letters*]
WNFQ .... Lake City, FL [*Broadcasting station call letters*]
WNGS .... West Palm Beach, FL [*Broadcasting station call letters*]
WNIN......... Evansville, IN [*Broadcasting station call letters*]
WNIQ......... Glens Falls, NY [*Broadcasting station call letters*]
WNIS......... Portsmouth, VA [*Broadcasting station call letters*]
WNIX......... Greenville, MS [*Broadcasting station call letters*]
WNJY .... West Palm Beach, FL [*Broadcasting station call letters*]
WNLSC ..... Women's National Land Service Corps [*British*] [*World War I*]
WNMC-FM ... Traverse City, MI [*Broadcasting station call letters*]
WNNR Spes Versl ... WNNR [*Suid-Afrikaanse Wetenskaplike en Nywerheidnavorsingsraad*] Spesiale Verslag [*A publication*]
WNOZ .... Cortland, NY [*Broadcasting station call letters*]
WNPC .... Newport, TN [*Broadcasting station call letters*]
WNSB .... Norfolk, VA [*Broadcasting station call letters*]
WNST-FM ... Milton, WV [*Broadcasting station call letters*]
WNUU .... St. Matthews, KY [*Broadcasting station call letters*]
WNV .... Wehrmachtnachrichtenverbindungen [*Armed Forces Signal Communications*] [*German military - World War II*]
WNVR........ Naugatuck, CT [*Broadcasting station call letters*]
WNWS....... Miami, FL [*Broadcasting station call letters*]
WNYE........ New York, NY [*Broadcasting station call letters*]
WNYNRC .. Western New York Nuclear Research Center Reactor
WO .... Write Only
WOAS .... Ontonagon, MI [*Broadcasting station call letters*]
WOEL-FM ... Elkton, MD [*Broadcasting station call letters*]
WOEZ-FM ... Milton, PA [*Broadcasting station call letters*]
WOF .... Warmed-Over Flavor [*Food technology*]
WOGH....... West Orange, NJ [*Broadcasting station call letters*]
WOHRC..... Women's Occupational Health Resource Center
WOKH ...... Bardstown, KY [*Broadcasting station call letters*]
WOKM ...... New Albany, MS [*Broadcasting station call letters*]
WOKV .... Hamilton, OH [*Broadcasting station call letters*]
WOMN ...... Hamden, CT [*Broadcasting station call letters*]
WONF .... With Other Natural Flavors [*Food science*]
WONX .... Evanston, IL [*Broadcasting station call letters*]
Wood Preserv ... Wood Preserving [*A publication*]
Wood Res ... Wood Research [*A publication*]
Woods Hole Oceanogr Inst Annu Rep ... Woods Hole Oceanographic Institution. Annual Report [*A publication*]
Wool Technol Sheep Breed ... Wool Technology and Sheep Breeding [*A publication*]
WOOS .... Canton, OH [*Broadcasting station call letters*]
Woo Sok Univ Med J ... Woo Sok University Medical Journal [*A publication*]
WOPP .... Opp, AL [*Broadcasting station call letters*]
WOQI .... Ponce, PR [*Broadcasting station call letters*]
WORI......... Oak Ridge, TN [*Broadcasting station call letters*]
Work-Environ-Health ... Work-Environment-Health [*A publication*]
World Anim Rev ... World Animal Review [*A publication*]
World For Ser Bull ... World Forestry Series Bulletin [*A publication*]
World Med J ... World Medical Journal [*A publication*]
World Neurol ... World Neurology [*A publication*]

World Rev Nutr Diet ... World Review of Nutrition and Dietetics [*A publication*]
World Rev Pest Control ... World Review of Pest Control [*A publication*]
World's Poult Sci J ... World's Poultry Science Journal [*A publication*]
Worldwatch Pap ... Worldwatch Paper [*A publication*]
WOSO .... San Juan, PR [*Broadcasting station call letters*]
WOWN ...... Shawano, WI [*Broadcasting station call letters*]
WP .... World Peacemakers [*An organization*]
WPA .... World Psychiatric Association
WPAK .... Farmville, VA [*Broadcasting station call letters*]
WPB .... Gunboat [*Coast Guard*]
WPBH .... Middlefield, CT [*Broadcasting station call letters*]
WPBM .... Aiken, SC [*Broadcasting station call letters*]
WPBX .... Southampton, NY [*Broadcasting station call letters*]
WPC .... World Peace Council
WPCAA .... White Park Cattle Association of America
WPCT .... Lobelville, TN [*Broadcasting station call letters*]
WPD .... World Pharmaceuticals Directory [*A publication*]
WPDZ .... Cheraw, SC [*Broadcasting station call letters*]
WPEM .... Pascagoula, MS [*Broadcasting station call letters*]
WPFL .... Winter Park, FL [*Broadcasting station call letters*]
WPFUL ...... Worshipful
WPGT .... Group Fore-Women's Pro Golf Tour
WPHP .... Wheeling, WV [*Broadcasting station call letters*]
WPIP .... Pompano Beach, FL [*Broadcasting station call letters*]
WPIQ .... Brunswick, GA [*Broadcasting station call letters*]
WPJL .... Raleigh, NC [*Broadcasting station call letters*]
WPJS .... Orangeburg, SC [*Broadcasting station call letters*]
WPKZ .... Pickens, SC [*Broadcasting station call letters*]
WPLP .... Pinellas Park, FL [*Broadcasting station call letters*]
WPLW .... Carnegie, PA [*Broadcasting station call letters*]
WPN .... Weapons Procurement, Navy
WPN .... Write Punch [*Data processing*]
WPNT .... Pittsburgh, PA [*Broadcasting station call letters*]
WPNT-FM ... Pittsburgh, PA [*Broadcasting station call letters*]
WPNX .... Columbus, GA [*Broadcasting station call letters*]
WPOE .... Greenfield, MA [*Broadcasting station call letters*]
WPOL .... Gaylord, MI [*Broadcasting station call letters*]
WPQZ .... Clarksburg, WV [*Broadcasting station call letters*]
WPRG .... Baton Rouge, LA [*Broadcasting station call letters*]
WPRV .... Rock Hill, SC [*Broadcasting station call letters*]
WPRZ .... Evanston, IL [*Broadcasting station call letters*]
WPS .... Word Processing System
WPSO ...... New Port Richey, FL [*Broadcasting station call letters*]
WPT .... Waypoint
WPTG .... Lancaster, PA [*Broadcasting station call letters*]
WPTW .... Piqua, OH [*Broadcasting station call letters*]
WPXN .... Rochester, NY [*Broadcasting station call letters*]
WPYK .... Dora, AL [*Broadcasting station call letters*]
WQAZ ...... Cleveland, MS [*Broadcasting station call letters*]
WQBA-FM ... Miami, FL [*Broadcasting station call letters*]
WQC .... Water Quality Certification
WQCC .... Charlotte, NC [*Broadcasting station call letters*]
WQEQ .... Freeland, PA [*Broadcasting station call letters*]
WQGL .... Butler, AL [*Broadcasting station call letters*]
WQGN .... Groton, CT [*Broadcasting station call letters*]
WQHK .... Fort Wayne, IN [*Broadcasting station call letters*]
WQIK .... San Juan, PR [*Broadcasting station call letters*]
WQIS .... Laurel, MS [*Broadcasting station call letters*]
WQIT-FM .. Grafton, WV [*Broadcasting station call letters*]
WQIZ-FM .. St. George, SC [*Broadcasting station call letters*]
WQKX .... Sunbury, PA [*Broadcasting station call letters*]
WQLM .... Punta Gorda, FL [*Broadcasting station call letters*]
WQMR .... Skowhegan, ME [*Broadcasting station call letters*]
WQNA .... Springfield, IL [*Broadcasting station call letters*]
WQNS ...... Waynesville, NC [*Broadcasting station call letters*]
WQRA .... Warrenton, VA [*Broadcasting station call letters*]
WQRO .... Huntington, PA [*Broadcasting station call letters*]
WQSI .... Union Springs, AL [*Broadcasting station call letters*]
WQUS .... Winchester, VA [*Broadcasting station call letters*]
WQVE .... Mechanicsburg, PA [*Broadcasting station call letters*]
WQVQ .... Highland Park, IL [*Broadcasting station call letters*]
WQVR .... Southbridge, MA [*Broadcasting station call letters*]
WQXK .... Salem, OH [*Broadcasting station call letters*]
WQXO-FM ... Munising, MI [*Broadcasting station call letters*]
WQYQ-FM ... Daytona Beach, FL [*Broadcasting station call letters*]
WQZQ .... Moyock, NC [*Broadcasting station call letters*]
WQZY .... Dublin, GA [*Broadcasting station call letters*]

WR .... Wiping Reflex [*Physiology*]
WRAM .... Water Resources Assessment Methodology [*Army Corps of Engineers*]
WRAQ .... Asheville, NC [*Broadcasting station call letters*]
WRAS .... Women's Reserve Ambulance Society [*British*] [*World War I*]
WRBH .... New Orleans, LA [*Broadcasting station call letters*]
WRDC .... Cleveland, MS [*Broadcasting station call letters*]
WREA .... Dayton, TN [*Broadcasting station call letters*]
WRED .... Monroe, GA [*Broadcasting station call letters*]
WREE .... Women for Racial and Economic Equality
WREY .... Millville, NJ [*Broadcasting station call letters*]
WRFR .... Franklin, NC [*Broadcasting station call letters*]
WRFT .... Indianapolis, IN [*Broadcasting station call letters*]
WRIQ .... Radford, VA [*Broadcasting station call letters*]
WRKA .... St. Matthews, KY [*Broadcasting station call letters*]
WRKK .... Birmingham, AL [*Broadcasting station call letters*]
WRLV .... Salyersville, KY [*Broadcasting station call letters*]
WRMF .... Palm Beach, FL [*Broadcasting station call letters*]
WRMJ .... Aledo, IL [*Broadcasting station call letters*]
WRML .... Portage, PA [*Broadcasting station call letters*]
WRMRS ..... War Reserve Materiel Rating System
WRNZ .... Wrens, GA [*Broadcasting station call letters*]
WRPS .... Rockland, MA [*Broadcasting station call letters*]
WRR .... Water Resource Region [*Water Resources Council*]
WRRD .... Minneapolis, MN [*Broadcasting station call letters*]
WRRI Auburn Univ Bull ... WRRI [*Water Resources Research Institute*] Auburn University. Bulletin [*A publication*]
WRRK .... Manistee, MI [*Broadcasting station call letters*]
WRSM .... Troy, AL [*Broadcasting station call letters*]
WRTB .... Vincennes, IN [*Broadcasting station call letters*]
WRTM .... Blountstown, FL [*Broadcasting station call letters*]
WRTR .... Two Rivers, WI [*Broadcasting station call letters*]
WRTT .... Vernon, CT [*Broadcasting station call letters*]
WRVH .... Patterson, NY [*Broadcasting station call letters*]
WRVK .... Renfro Valley, KY [*Broadcasting station call letters*]
WRVL .... Lynchburg, VA [*Broadcasting station call letters*]
WRW .... Will's Air [*Barnstable, MA*] [*FAA designator*]
WRXV .... Auburn, ME [*Broadcasting station call letters*]
WSBH .... Southhampton, NY [*Broadcasting station call letters*]
WSBV .... South Boston, VA [*Broadcasting station call letters*]
WSC .... Winston Spencer Churchill [*1874-1965*] [*British statesman and prime minister*]
WSCZ .... Greenwood, SC [*Broadcasting station call letters*]
WSD .... Working Stress Design
WSDH .... Sandwich, MA [*Broadcasting station call letters*]
WSDO .... Fort Lauderdale, FL [*Broadcasting station call letters*]
WSE .... Weapons System Evaluator
WSF .... Women's Sports Foundation
WSGL .... Naples, FL [*Broadcasting station call letters*]
WSGO .... Oswego, NY [*Broadcasting station call letters*]
WSIA .... New York, NY [*Broadcasting station call letters*]
WSJP .... Murray, KY [*Broadcasting station call letters*]
WSKS ...... Hamilton, OH [*Broadcasting station call letters*]
WSKZ .... Chattanooga, TN [*Broadcasting station call letters*]
WSMS .... Memphis, TN [*Broadcasting station call letters*]
WSOE .... Elon, NC [*Broadcasting station call letters*]
WSOM .... Weather Service Operations Manual [*National Weather Service*]
WSOX .... West Yarmouth, MA [*Broadcasting station call letters*]
WSOX-FM ... West Yarmouth, MA [*Broadcasting station call letters*]
WSR .... Weapons System Review
WSRB .... Walpole, MA [*Broadcasting station call letters*]
WSRG .... Elkton, KY [*Broadcasting station call letters*]
WSRQ .... Eden, NC [*Broadcasting station call letters*]
WSRZ .... Sarasota, FL [*Broadcasting station call letters*]
WSSD .... Chicago, IL [*Broadcasting station call letters*]
WSSF .... Weather Service Support Facility [*National Weather Service*]
WSSU .... Weather Service Support Unit [*National Weather Service*]
WSTA .... St. Thomas, VI [*Broadcasting station call letters*]
WSTCH ..... Wasatch Range [*National Weather Service*]
WSTJ .... St. Johnsbury, VT [*Broadcasting station call letters*]
WSTX .... St. Croix, VI [*Broadcasting station call letters*]
WSU .... Women on Stamps Unit
WSZE .... Saipan, Mariana Islands [*Broadcasting station call letters*]
WT .... Washington Territory [*Prior to statehood*]

WTAZ........ Morton, IL [*Broadcasting station call letters*]
WTFM .... New York, NY [*Broadcasting station call letters*]
WTGV-FM ... Sandusky, MI [*Broadcasting station call letters*]
WTJZ........ Newport News, VA [*Broadcasting station call letters*]
WTKC .... Lexington, KY [*Broadcasting station call letters*]
WTKL........ Baton Rouge, LA [*Broadcasting station call letters*]
WTKX....... Pensacola, FL [*Broadcasting station call letters*]
WTMS ...... Presque Isle, ME [*Broadcasting station call letters*]
WTNE-FM ... Trenton, TN [*Broadcasting station call letters*]
WTNR....... Kingston, TN [*Broadcasting station call letters*]
WTOH ...... Mobile, AL [*Broadcasting station call letters*]
WTRT........ Trenton, NJ [*Broadcasting station call letters*]
WTRW ...... Whitehall, MI [*Broadcasting station call letters*]
WTSU .... West Texas State University [*Formerly, WTSC*]
WTUG-FM ... Tuscaloosa, AL [*Broadcasting station call letters*]
WTWR....... Detroit, MI [*Broadcasting station call letters*]
WTXI .... Ripley, MS [*Broadcasting station call letters*]
WTXN....... Lafayette, AL [*Broadcasting station call letters*]
WTXY........ Whiteville, NC [*Broadcasting station call letters*]
WTYX........ Jackson, MS [*Broadcasting station call letters*]
WUCF-FM ... Orlando, FL [*Broadcasting station call letters*]
WUF .... Wattle-Urea-Formaldehyde [*Adhesive component*]
WUFT-FM ... Gainesville, FL [*Broadcasting station call letters*]
WUGO....... Grayson, KY [*Broadcasting station call letters*]
WUHN....... Pittsfield, MA [*Broadcasting station call letters*]
WUSB .... Stony Brook, NY [*Broadcasting station call letters*]
WUSL........ Philadelphia, PA [*Broadcasting station call letters*]
WUTZ........ Summertown, TN [*Broadcasting station call letters*]
WUVA .... Charlottesville, VA [*Broadcasting station call letters*]
WV .... Avair Ltd. [*Ireland*] [*ICAO designator*]
W Va Agric Exp Stn Circ ... West Virginia Agricultural Experiment Station. Circular [*A publication*]
W Va Agric Exp Stn Curr Rep ... West Virginia Agricultural Experiment Station. Current Report [*A publication*]
W Va Agric Exp Stn Misc Publ ... West Virginia Agricultural Experiment Station. Miscellaneous Publication [*A publication*]
W Va Agric For ... West Virginia Agriculture and Forestry [*A publication*]
W Va Agric For Exp Stn Bull ... West Virginia Agricultural and Forestry Experiment Station. Bulletin [*A publication*]
W Va For Notes ... West Virginia Forestry Notes [*A publication*]
WVCF........ Ocoee, FL [*Broadcasting station call letters*]
WVCP....... Gallatin, TN [*Broadcasting station call letters*]
WVEL .... Pekin, IL [*Broadcasting station call letters*]
WVFR....... Ridgefield, CT [*Broadcasting station call letters*]
WVHG .... Labelle, FL [*Broadcasting station call letters*]
WVIS .... St. Croix, VI [*Broadcasting station call letters*]
WVMC...... Mansfield, OH [*Broadcasting station call letters*]
WVMS ...... Appleton, WI [*Broadcasting station call letters*]
WVNP....... Wheeling, WV [*Broadcasting station call letters*]
WVOC ...... Columbus, GA [*Broadcasting station call letters*]
WVPA-FM ... Windsor, VT [*Broadcasting station call letters*]
WVPM ...... Morgantown, WV [*Broadcasting station call letters*]
WVR .... Women's Volunteer Reserve [*British*] [*World War I*]
WVRM....... Hazlet, NJ [*Broadcasting station call letters*]
WVRU....... Radford, VA [*Broadcasting station call letters*]
WVSI......... Jupiter, FL [*Broadcasting station call letters*]
WVSP........ Warrenton, NC [*Broadcasting station call letters*]
WVWI....... St. Thomas, VI [*Broadcasting station call letters*]
WWAS....... Williamsport, PA [*Broadcasting station call letters*]
WWBB....... Madison, WV [*Broadcasting station call letters*]
WWDE....... Hampton, VA [*Broadcasting station call letters*]
WWDE-FM ... Hampton, VA [*Broadcasting station call letters*]
WWDJ ...... Newark, NJ [*Broadcasting station call letters*]
WWDS....... Muncie, IN [*Broadcasting station call letters*]
WWEG....... Racine, WI [*Broadcasting station call letters*]
WWEL ...... London, KY [*Broadcasting station call letters*]
WWFC....... Worldwide Fair Play for Frogs Committee
WWHB....... Hampton Bays, NY [*Broadcasting station call letters*]
WWIMS ...... Worldwide Integrated Management of Subsistence [*Military*]
WWIW .... New Orleans, LA [*Broadcasting station call letters*]
WWJM....... New Lexington, OH [*Broadcasting station call letters*]
WWKX....... Gallatin, TN [*Broadcasting station call letters*]
WWLC....... Lynchburg, VA [*Broadcasting station call letters*]
WWLH....... Pound, VA [*Broadcasting station call letters*]
WWM .... Wings West, Inc. [*Santa Monica, CA*] [*FAA designator*]
WWMC-FM ... Mifflinburg, PA [*Broadcasting station call letters*]

WWMD ...... Hagerstown, MD [*Broadcasting station call letters*]
WWNH-FM ... Rochester, NH [*Broadcasting station call letters*]
WWNT....... Dothan, AL [*Broadcasting station call letters*]
WWOO ...... Berryville, VA [*Broadcasting station call letters*]
WWOR ...... Buffalo, NY [*Broadcasting station call letters*]
WWOZ...... New Orleans, LA [*Broadcasting station call letters*]
WWQQ ...... Wilmington, NC [*Broadcasting station call letters*]
WWQT....... Dunedin, FL [*Broadcasting station call letters*]
WWSA....... Savannah, GA [*Broadcasting station call letters*]
WWSD....... Quincy, FL [*Broadcasting station call letters*]
WWSL .... Philadelphia, MS [*Broadcasting station call letters*]
WWSU ...... Dayton, OH [*Broadcasting station call letters*]
WWUN ...... Batesville, MS [*Broadcasting station call letters*]
WWUU...... Long Branch, NJ [*Broadcasting station call letters*]
WWV .... World Wide Vermiculture [*An organization*]
WWWI .... Hyde Park, NY [*Broadcasting station call letters*]
WWWK ...... Granite City, IL [*Broadcasting station call letters*]
WWWN ...... Vienna, GA [*Broadcasting station call letters*]
WWWQ ...... Panama City, FL [*Broadcasting station call letters*]
WWWT ...... Owego, NY [*Broadcasting station call letters*]
WX .... American Eagle Airlines, Inc. [*ICAO designator*]
WXAP........ Columbia, SC [*Broadcasting station call letters*]
WXBQ .... Bristol, VA [*Broadcasting station call letters*]
WXCE........ Amery, WI [*Broadcasting station call letters*]
WXGR .... Bay St. Louis, MS [*Broadcasting station call letters*]
WXIC .... Waverly, OH [*Broadcasting station call letters*]
WXIE .... Oakland, MD [*Broadcasting station call letters*]
WXII .... Charleston, WV [*Broadcasting station call letters*]
WXIK .... Shelby, NC [*Broadcasting station call letters*]
WXIZ......... Waverly, OH [*Broadcasting station call letters*]
WXJY .... Menomonee Falls, WI [*Broadcasting station call letters*]
WXKS........ Medford, MA [*Broadcasting station call letters*]
WXKS-FM ... Medford, MA [*Broadcasting station call letters*]
WXLK........ Roanoke, VA [*Broadcasting station call letters*]
WXLN........ Louisville, KY [*Broadcasting station call letters*]
WXLP .... Moline, IL [*Broadcasting station call letters*]
WXMN...... Monticello, ME [*Broadcasting station call letters*]
WXOL........ Cicero, IL [*Broadcasting station call letters*]
WXOP....... Columbia, SC [*Broadcasting station call letters*]
WXQK....... Spring City, TN [*Broadcasting station call letters*]
WXRS........ Swainsboro, GA [*Broadcasting station call letters*]
WXTL .... Myrtle Beach, SC [*Broadcasting station call letters*]
WXTRN ...... Weak External Reference [*Data processing*]
WXVY........ Baltimore, MD [*Broadcasting station call letters*]
WXXI .... Rochester, NY [*Broadcasting station call letters*]
WXXQ .... Freeport, IL [*Broadcasting station call letters*]
WYAJ .... Sudbury, MA [*Broadcasting station call letters*]
WYAK .... Surfside Beach-Garden City, SC [*Broadcasting station call letters*]
WYBT........ Jersey Shore, PA [*Broadcasting station call letters*]
WYCB .... Washington, DC [*Broadcasting station call letters*]
WYIS .... Phoenixville, PA [*Broadcasting station call letters*]
WYNC .... Yanceyville, NC [*Broadcasting station call letters*]
WYNO ...... Nelsonville, OH [*Broadcasting station call letters*]
WYNX........ Atlanta, GA [*Broadcasting station call letters*]
Wyo Agric Exp Stn Bull ... Wyoming Agricultural Experiment Station. Bulletin [*A publication*]
Wyo Agric Exp Stn Res J ... Wyoming Agricultural Experiment Station. Research Journal [*A publication*]
Wyo Agric Exp Stn Sci Monogr ... Wyoming Agricultural Experiment Station. Science Monograph [*A publication*]
Wyo Agric Ext Serv Bull ... Wyoming Agricultural Extension Service. Bulletin [*A publication*]
Wyo Game Fish Comm Bull ... Wyoming Game and Fish Commission Bulletin [*A publication*]
WYSS........ Saegertown, PA [*Broadcasting station call letters*]
WYTK........ Washington, PA [*Broadcasting station call letters*]
WYUT........ Herkimer, NY [*Broadcasting station call letters*]
WYZD........ Dobson, NC [*Broadcasting station call letters*]
WZAL........ McDonough, GA [*Broadcasting station call letters*]
WZAR........ Ponce, PR [*Broadcasting station call letters*]
WZBR........ Amory, MS [*Broadcasting station call letters*]
WZDC ...... Soddy-Daisy, TN [*Broadcasting station call letters*]
WZDQ .... Soddy-Daisy, TN [*Broadcasting station call letters*]
WZEN........ Alton, IL [*Broadcasting station call letters*]
WZKX........ Gulfport, MS [*Broadcasting station call letters*]
WZLQ........ Tupelo, MS [*Broadcasting station call letters*]
WZLT........ Lexington, TN [*Broadcasting station call letters*]
WZNT........ San Juan, PR [*Broadcasting station call letters*]

WZUE........ Carlisle, PA [*Broadcasting station call letters*]
WZXI .... Gastonia, NC [*Broadcasting station call letters*]
WZYP........ Athens, AL [*Broadcasting station call letters*]
WZYZ........ Fairmount, NC [*Broadcasting station call letters*]
WZZB........ Centreville, MI [*Broadcasting station call letters*]

WZZC........ East Moline, IL [*Broadcasting station call letters*]
WZZI .... Madisonville, TN [*Broadcasting station call letters*]
WZZO........ Bethlehem, PA [*Broadcasting station call letters*]
WZZX .... Louisville, KY [*Broadcasting station call letters*]

X-Y-Z

X .... Mental Defects [*Used by immigration officials*] [*Obsolete*]
X (Cars) .... Designation for General Motors front-wheel-drive cars [*Citation, Omega, Phoenix, Skylark*]
XBASIC ..... Extension of BASIC [*Data processing*]
XC .... Air Routing International Corp. [*ICAO designator*]
XCP .... Except
XLPE .... Cross-Linked Polyethylene
XLS .... St. Louis [*Senegal*] [*Airport symbol*]
XM .... Christmas
XMH .... Manihi [*French Polynesia*] [*Airport symbol*]
XMI .... Masasi [*Tanzania*] [*Airport symbol*]
XML .... Minlaton [*Australia*] [*Airport symbol*]
XNN .... Xining [*China*] [*Airport symbol*]
XOFF .... Transmitter Off
XON .... Transmitter On
XPA .... Pama [*Upper Volta*] [*Airport symbol*]
XPC .... Expect
XPT .... External Page Table [*Data processing*]
X/Q .... Relative Concentration [*Symbol*]
XQP .... Quepos [*Costa Rica*] [*Airport symbol*]
XRY .... Jerez De La Frontera [*Spain*] [*Airport symbol*]
XSC .... South Caicos [*British West Indies*] [*Airport symbol*]
XSE .... Sebba [*Upper Volta*] [*Airport symbol*]
XTC .... External Transmit Clock
XTLK .... Cross Talk [*Aviation*]
XV .... Administration de Aeropuertos y Servicios Auxiliares a la Nauegacion Aerea [*AASANA*] [*Bolivia*] [*ICAO designator*]
XYA .... Yandina [*Solomon Islands*] [*Airport symbol*]
YA .... Young Adult [*Refers to books published for this market*]
YACC .... Young Adult Conservation Corps
YAF .... Asbestos Hill [*Canada*] [*Airport symbol*]
YAG .... Fort Frances [*Canada*] [*Airport symbol*]
YAG .... Young Actors Guild
YAK .... Yakutat [*Alaska*] [*Airport symbol*]
Yale J Biol Med ... Yale Journal of Biology and Medicine [*A publication*]
Yale Sci ..... Yale Scientific [*A publication*]
Yale Univ Sch For Bull ... Yale University School of Forestry Bulletin [*A publication*]
YAM .... Sault Ste. Marie [*Canada*] [*Airport symbol*]
YAO .... Yaounde [*Cameroon*] [*Airport symbol*]
YAP .... Yap [*Caroline Islands*] [*Airport symbol*]
YAP .... Younger American Playwright [*Slang*]
YAT .... Attawapiskat [*Canada*] [*Airport symbol*]
YBC .... Baie Comeau [*Canada*] [*Airport symbol*]
YBE .... Uranium City [*Canada*] [*Airport symbol*]
YBG .... Saguenay [*Canada*] [*Airport symbol*]
YBJ .... Baie Johan Beetz [*Canada*] [*Airport symbol*]
YBL .... Campbell River [*Canada*] [*Airport symbol*]
YBR .... Brandon [*Canada*] [*Airport symbol*]
YBV .... Berens River [*Canada*] [*Airport symbol*]
YBX .... Blanc Sablon [*Canada*] [*Airport symbol*]
YCB .... Cambridge Bay [*Canada*] [*Airport symbol*]
YCD .... Nanaimo [*Canada*] [*Airport symbol*]
YCG .... Castlegar [*Canada*] [*Airport symbol*]
YCH .... Chatham [*Canada*] [*Airport symbol*]
YCL .... Charlo [*Canada*] [*Airport symbol*]
YCN .... Cochrane [*Canada*] [*Airport symbol*]
YCO .... Coppermine [*Canada*] [*Airport symbol*]
YCR .... Cross Lake [*Canada*] [*Airport symbol*]
YCY .... Clyde River [*Canada*] [*Airport symbol*]
YDB .... Youth Development Bureau [*Department of Health and Human Services*]
YDF .... Deer Lake [*Canada*] [*Airport symbol*]
YDN .... Dauphin [*Canada*] [*Airport symbol*]
YDQ .... Dawson Creek [*Canada*] [*Airport symbol*]
Yearb Dermatol Syphilol ... Yearbook of Dermatology and Syphilology [*A publication*]
Yearb Med ... Yearbook of Medicine [*A publication*]
Yearb Natl Inst Sci India ... Yearbook of the National Institute of Sciences of India [*A publication*]
Year Book Indian Natl Sci Acad ... Year Book of the Indian National Science Academy [*A publication*]
Yearb Phys Anthropol ... Yearbook of Physical Anthropology [*A publication*]
YEDPA ...... Youth Employment and Demonstration Projects Act [*Department of Labor*]
YEG .... Edmonton [*Canada*] [*Airport symbol*]
YEL .... Elliot Lake [*Canada*] [*Airport symbol*]
YEV .... Inuvik [*Canada*] [*Airport symbol*]
YFA .... Fort Albany [*Canada*] [*Airport symbol*]
YFB .... Frobisher Bay [*Canada*] [*Airport symbol*]
YFC .... Fredericton [*Canada*] [*Airport symbol*]
YFO .... Flin Flon [*Canada*] [*Airport symbol*]
YFS .... Fort Simpson [*Canada*] [*Airport symbol*]
YFS .... Young Flying Service [*Harlingen, TX*] [*FAA designator*]
YGA .... Gagnon [*Canada*] [*Airport symbol*]
YGB .... Gillies Bay [*Canada*] [*Airport symbol*]
YGJ .... Yonago [*Japan*] [*Airport symbol*]
YGK .... Kingston [*Canada*] [*Airport symbol*]
YGL .... La Grande [*Canada*] [*Airport symbol*]
YGO .... Gods Narrows [*Canada*] [*Airport symbol*]
YGP .... Gaspe [*Canada*] [*Airport symbol*]
YGQ .... Geraldton [*Canada*] [*Airport symbol*]
YGR .... Iles De Madeleine [*Canada*] [*Airport symbol*]
YGW .... Great Whale [*Canada*] [*Airport symbol*]
YGX .... Gillam [*Canada*] [*Airport symbol*]
YHD .... Dryden [*Canada*] [*Airport symbol*]
YHI .... Holman Island [*Canada*] [*Airport symbol*]
YHK .... Gjoa Haven [*Canada*] [*Airport symbol*]
YHM .... Hamilton [*Canada*] [*Airport symbol*]
YHN .... Hornepayne [*Canada*] [*Airport symbol*]
YHR .... Harrington Harbour [*Canada*] [*Airport symbol*]
YHY .... Hay River [*Canada*] [*Airport symbol*]
YHZ .... Halifax [*Canada*] [*Airport symbol*]
YIB .... Atikokan [*Canada*] [*Airport symbol*]
YIEPP .... Youth Incentive Entitlement Pilot Project [*Department of Labor*]
YIF .... St. Augustin [*Canada*] [*Airport symbol*]
YIK .... Ivugivik [*Canada*] [*Airport symbol*]
YIO .... Pond Inlet [*Canada*] [*Airport symbol*]
YIV .... Island Lake [*Canada*] [*Airport symbol*]
YJT .... Stephenville [*Canada*] [*Airport symbol*]
YKA .... Kamloops [*Canada*] [*Airport symbol*]
YKL .... Schefferville [*Canada*] [*Airport symbol*]
YKM .... Yakima [*Washington*] [*Airport symbol*]
YKN .... Yankton [*South Dakota*] [*Airport symbol*]

YKQ .... Rupert House [*Canada*] [*Airport symbol*]
YKU .... Fort George [*Canada*] [*Airport symbol*]
YKX .... Kirkland Lake [*Canada*] [*Airport symbol*]
YKZ .... Toronto [*Canada*] Buttonville Airport [*Airport symbol*]
YLD .... Chapleau [*Canada*] [*Airport symbol*]
YLJ .... Meadow Lake [*Canada*] [*Airport symbol*]
YLP .... Mingan [*Canada*] [*Airport symbol*]
YLW .... Kelowna [*Canada*] [*Airport symbol*]
YM .... Yellow Man
YMM .... Fort McMurray [*Canada*] [*Airport symbol*]
YMO .... Moosonee [*Canada*] [*Airport symbol*]
YMS .... Yurimaguas [*Peru*] [*Airport symbol*]
YMT .... Chibougamau [*Canada*] [*Airport symbol*]
YMX .... Montreal [*Canada*] Mirabel International Airport [*Airport symbol*]
YNA .... Naiashquan [*Canada*] [*Airport symbol*]
YNC .... Paint Hills [*Canada*] [*Airport symbol*]
YND .... Gatineau/Hull [*Canada*] [*Airport symbol*]
YNE .... Norway House [*Canada*] [*Airport symbol*]
YNG .... Youngstown [*Ohio*] [*Airport symbol*]
YNM .... Matagami [*Canada*] [*Airport symbol*]
YOH .... Oxford House [*Canada*] [*Airport symbol*]
YOJ .... High Level [*Canada*] [*Airport symbol*]
Yokohama Med Bull ... Yokohama Medical Bulletin [*A publication*]
Yokugukai Geriatr J ... Yokugukai Geriatric Journal [*A publication*]
YOL .... Yola [*Nigeria*] [*Airport symbol*]
Yonsei J Med Sci ... Yonsei Journal of Medical Science [*A publication*]
Yonsei Med J ... Yonsei Medical Journal [*A publication*]
Yonsei Rep Trop Med ... Yonsei Reports on Tropical Medicine [*A publication*]
YOP .... Rainbow Lake [*Canada*] [*Airport symbol*]
YOW .... Ottawa [*Canada*] [*Airport symbol*]
YP .... Robex Collection Center [*ICAO designator*]
YPA .... Prince Albert [*Canada*] [*Airport symbol*]
YPD .... Parry Sound [*Canada*] [*Airport symbol*]
YPE .... Peace River [*Canada*] [*Airport symbol*]
YPH .... Port Harrison [*Canada*] [*Airport symbol*]
YPL .... Pickle Lake [*Canada*] [*Airport symbol*]
YPN .... Port Menier [*Canada*] [*Airport symbol*]
YPQ .... Peterborough [*Canada*] [*Airport symbol*]
YPR .... Prince Rupert [*Canada*] [*Airport symbol*]
YPW .... Powell River [*Canada*] [*Airport symbol*]
YPX .... Povungnituk [*Canada*] [*Airport symbol*]
YPY .... Fort Chipewyan [*Canada*] [*Airport symbol*]
YQB .... Quebec [*Canada*] [*Airport symbol*]
YQD .... The Pas [*Canada*] [*Airport symbol*]
YQF .... Red Deer [*Canada*] [*Airport symbol*]
YQG .... Windsor [*Canada*] [*Airport symbol*]
YQH .... Watson Lake [*Canada*] [*Airport symbol*]
YQI .... Yarmouth [*Canada*] [*Airport symbol*]
YQK .... Kenora [*Canada*] [*Airport symbol*]
YQL .... Lethbridge [*Canada*] [*Airport symbol*]
YQM .... Moncton [*Canada*] [*Airport symbol*]
YQQ .... Comox [*Canada*] [*Airport symbol*]
YQR .... Regina [*Canada*] [*Airport symbol*]
YQT .... Thunder Bay [*Canada*] [*Airport symbol*]
YQU .... Grande Prairie [*Canada*] [*Airport symbol*]
YQV .... Yorkton [*Canada*] [*Airport symbol*]
YQX .... Gander [*Canada*] [*Airport symbol*]
YQY .... Sydney [*Canada*] [*Airport symbol*]
YQZ .... Quesnel [*Canada*] [*Airport symbol*]
YR .... Youth Resources [*An organization*]
YRB .... Resolute [*Canada*] [*Airport symbol*]
YRF .... Yoga Research Foundation
YRI .... Riviere Du Loup [*Canada*] [*Airport symbol*]
YRJ .... Roberval [*Canada*] [*Airport symbol*]
YRL .... Red Lake [*Canada*] [*Airport symbol*]
YRT .... Rankin Inlet [*Canada*] [*Airport symbol*]
YSB .... Sudbury [*Canada*] [*Airport symbol*]
YSF .... Stoney Rapids [*Canada*] [*Airport symbol*]
YSI .... Sans Souci [*Canada*] [*Airport symbol*]
YSJ .... Saint John [*Canada*] [*Airport symbol*]
YSK .... Sanikiluaq [*Canada*] [*Airport symbol*]
YSM .... Fort Smith [*Canada*] [*Airport symbol*]
YSR .... Nanisivik [*Canada*] [*Airport symbol*]
YTA .... Pembroke [*Canada*] [*Airport symbol*]
YTE .... Cape Dorset [*Canada*] [*Airport symbol*]
YTH .... Thompson [*Canada*] [*Airport symbol*]

YTJ .... Terrace Bay [*Canada*] [*Airport symbol*]
YTL .... Big Trout Lake [*Canada*] [*Airport symbol*]
YTS .... Timmins [*Canada*] [*Airport symbol*]
YTZ .... Toronto [*Canada*] [*Airport symbol*]
YUF .... Pelly Bay [*Canada*] [*Airport symbol*]
YUL .... Montreal [*Canada*] [*Airport symbol*]
YUM .... Yuma [*Arizona*] [*Airport symbol*]
YUX .... Hall Beach [*Canada*] [*Airport symbol*]
YUY .... Rouyn-Noranda [*Canada*] [*Airport symbol*]
YVA .... Moroni [*Comoro Islands*] [*Airport symbol*]
YVB .... Bonaventure [*Canada*] [*Airport symbol*]
YVC .... Lac La Ronge [*Canada*] [*Airport symbol*]
YVM .... Broughton [*Canada*] [*Airport symbol*]
YVO .... Val D'Or [*Canada*] [*Airport symbol*]
YVP .... Fort Chimo [*Canada*] [*Airport symbol*]
YVQ .... Norman Wells [*Canada*] [*Airport symbol*]
YVR .... Vancouver [*Canada*] [*Airport symbol*]
YVT .... Buffalo Narrows [*Canada*] [*Airport symbol*]
YWG .... Winnipeg [*Canada*] [*Airport symbol*]
YWGASOYA ... You Won't Get Ahead Sitting on Your Afterdeck [*Slang*] [*Bowdlerized version*]
YWH .... Victoria [*Canada*] [*Airport symbol*]
YWK .... Wabush [*Canada*] [*Airport symbol*]
YWL .... Williams Lake [*Canada*] [*Airport symbol*]
YWN .... Winisk [*Canada*] [*Airport symbol*]
YXC .... Cranbrook [*Canada*] [*Airport symbol*]
YXD .... Edmonton [*Canada*] Municipal Airport [*Airport symbol*]
YXE .... Saskatoon [*Canada*] [*Airport symbol*]
YXH .... Medicine Hat [*Canada*] [*Airport symbol*]
YXJ .... Fort St. John [*Canada*] [*Airport symbol*]
YXK .... Rimouski [*Canada*] [*Airport symbol*]
YXL .... Sioux Lookout [*Canada*] [*Airport symbol*]
YXP .... Pangnirtung [*Canada*] [*Airport symbol*]
YXR .... Earlton [*Canada*] [*Airport symbol*]
YXS .... Prince George [*Canada*] [*Airport symbol*]
YXT .... Terrace [*Canada*] [*Airport symbol*]
YXU .... London [*Canada*] [*Airport symbol*]
YXY .... Whitehorse [*Canada*] [*Airport symbol*]
YXZ .... Wawa [*Canada*] [*Airport symbol*]
YYB .... North Bay [*Canada*] [*Airport symbol*]
YYC .... Calgary [*Canada*] [*Airport symbol*]
YYD .... Smithers [*Canada*] [*Airport symbol*]
YYE .... Fort Nelson [*Canada*] [*Airport symbol*]
YYF .... Penticton [*Canada*] [*Airport symbol*]
YYG .... Charlottetown [*Canada*] [*Airport symbol*]
YYH .... Spence Bay [*Canada*] [*Airport symbol*]
YYJ .... Victoria [*Canada*] [*Airport symbol*]
YYL .... Lynn Lake [*Canada*] [*Airport symbol*]
YYQ .... Churchill [*Canada*] [*Airport symbol*]
YYR .... Goose Bay [*Canada*] [*Airport symbol*]
YYT .... St. Johns [*Canada*] [*Airport symbol*]
YYU .... Kapuskasing [*Canada*] [*Airport symbol*]
YYY .... Mont Joli [*Canada*] [*Airport symbol*]
YYZ .... Toronto [*Canada*] [*Airport symbol*]
YZF .... Yellowknife [*Canada*] [*Airport symbol*]
YZG .... Sugluk [*Canada*] [*Airport symbol*]
YZP .... Sandspit [*Canada*] [*Airport symbol*]
YZR .... Sarnia [*Canada*] [*Airport symbol*]
YZT .... Port Hardy [*Canada*] [*Airport symbol*]
YZV .... Sept-Iles [*Canada*] [*Airport symbol*]
Z (Day) ...... Zero Day [*The date fixed for any important military operation*] [*British*]
ZAA .... Alice Arm/Kitsault [*Canada*] [*Airport symbol*]
Z Acker-Pflanzenb ... Zeitschrift fuer Acker-und Pflanzenbau [*A publication*]
ZAD .... Zadar [*Yugoslavia*] [*Airport symbol*]
Z Aerztl Fortbild ... Zeitschrift fuer Aerztliche Fortbildung [*A publication*]
ZAG .... Zagreb [*Yugoslavia*] [*Airport symbol*]
ZAH .... Zahedan [*Iran*] [*Airport symbol*]
Zahn-Mund-Kieferheilkd ... Zahn- Mund- und Kieferheilkunde [*A publication*]
Z Allg Mikrobiol ... Zeitschrift fuer Allgemeine Mikrobiologie [*A publication*]
Z Alternsforsch ... Zeitschrift fuer Alternsforschung [*A publication*]
ZAM .... Zamboanga [*Philippines*] [*Airport symbol*]
Zambia Div For Res Annu Rep ... Zambia Division of Forest Research. Annual Report [*A publication*]

Zambia For Res Bull ... Zambia Forest Research Bulletin [*A publication*]

Z Anat Entwicklungsgesch ... Zeitschrift fuer Anatomie und Entwicklungsgeschichte [*A publication*]

Z Angew Entomol ... Zeitschrift fuer Angewandte Entomologie [*A publication*]

Z Angew Zool ... Zeitschrift fuer Angewandte Zoologie [*A publication*]

Zap Khar'k S-kh Inst ... Zapiski Khar'kovskogo Sel'skokhozyaistvennogo Instituta [*A publication*]

Zap Leningr S-kh Inst ... Zapiski Leningradskogo Sel'skokhozyaistvennogo Instituta [*A publication*]

Zap Voronezh S-kh Inst ... Zapiski Voronezhskogo Sel'skokhozyaistvennogo Instituta [*A publication*]

Zap Zabaik Otd Vses Geogr O-va ... Zapiski Zabaikal'skogo Otdela Vsesoyuznogo Geograficheskogo Obshchestva [*A publication*]

Z Arbeitsgem Oesterr Entomol ... Zeitschrift der Arbeitsgemeinschaft Oesterreichischer Entomologen [*A publication*]

Zashch Rast (Mosc) ... Zashchita Rastenii (Moscow) [*A publication*]

Zashch Rast Vred Bolezn ... Zashchita Rastenii ot Vreditelei i Boleznei [*A publication*]

Zast Bilja ... Zastita Bilja [*A publication*]

ZAZ .... Zaragoza [*Spain*] [*Airport symbol*]

Zb Bioteh Fak Univ Ljublj Vet ... Zbornik Biotehniske Fakultete Univerze v Ljubljani Veterinarstvo [*A publication*]

Z Bienenforsch ... Zeitschrift fuer Bienenforschung [*A publication*]

Z Binnenfisch DDR ... Zeitschrift fuer die Binnenfischerei der DDR [*A publication*]

Z Biol .... Zeitschrift fuer Biologie [*A publication*]

Zb Nauk Pr L'viv Med Inst ... Zbirnyk Naukovykh Prats' L'viv'kyi Medychyni Instytut [*A publication*]

ZBO .... Bowen [*Australia*] [*Airport symbol*]

Z Bot .... Zeitschrift fuer Botanik [*A publication*]

Zb Pr Nauk Inst Fiziol Kyyiv Univ ... Zbirnyk Prats' Naukovodoslidnyts'koho Instytuta Fiziolohiyi Kyyivs'koho Universytetu [*A publication*]

Zb Pr Zool Muz Akad Nauk Ukr RSR ... Zbirnyk Prats' Zoolohichnoho Muzeyu Akademiyi Nauk Ukrayinskoyi RSR [*A publication*]

Zb Rad Biol Inst NR Srbye Beogr ... Zbornik Radova Bioloski Institut NR Srbye Beograd [*A publication*]

Zb Rad Poljopr Inst Osijek ... Zbornik Radova Poljoprivredni Institut Osijek [*A publication*]

Zb Slov Nar Muz Prir Vedy ... Zbornik Slovenskeho Narodneho Muzea Prirodne Vedy [*A publication*]

ZDDP .... Zinc Dialkyldithiophosphate [*Organic chemistry*]

ZDK .... Zen-Do Kai Martial Arts Association

Zdravookhr Beloruss ... Zdravookhranenie Belorussii [*A publication*]

Zdravookhr Kaz ... Zdravookhranenie Kazakhstana [*A publication*]

Zdravookhr Ross Fed ... Zdravookhranenie Rossiiskoi Federatsii [*A publication*]

Zdravookhr Sov Est Sb ... Zdravookhranenie Sovetskoi Estonii Sbornik [*A publication*]

Zdravookhr Tadzh ... Zdravookhranenie Tadzhikistana [*A publication*]

Zdravookhr Turkm ... Zdravookhranenie Turkmenistana [*A publication*]

Zdrav Vestn ... Zdravstveni Vestnik [*A publication*]

Zdrow Publiczne ... Zdrowie Publiczne [*A publication*]

Z Dtsch Geol Ges ... Zeitschrift Deutschen Geologischen Gesellschaft [*A publication*]

ZDV .... Zero Dead Volume [*Chromatography*]

Zeiss Inf .... Zeiss Information [*A publication*]

ZEL .... Bella Bella [*Canada*] [*Airport symbol*]

ZEM .... East Main [*Canada*] [*Airport symbol*]

Zemled Zhivotnovod Mold ... Zemledelie i Zhivotnovodstvo Moldavii [*A publication*]

Zemlya Vselennaya ... Zemlya i Vselennaya [*A publication*]

Zentralbl Allg Pathol Pathol Anat ... Zentralblatt fuer Allgemeine Pathologie und Pathologische Anatomie [*A publication*]

Zentralbl Arbeitsmed Arbeitsschutz ... Zentralblatt fuer Arbeitsmedizin und Arbeitsschutz [*A publication*]

Zentralbl Biol Aerosol-Forsch ... Zentralblatt fuer Biologische Aerosol-Forschung [*A publication*]

Zentralbl Gesamte Forstwes ... Zentralblatt fuer das Gesamte Forstwesen [*A publication*]

Zentralbl Gynaekol ... Zentralblatt fuer Gynaekologie [*A publication*]

Zentralbl Neurochir ... Zentralblatt fuer Neurochirurgie [*A publication*]

Zentralbl Veterinaermed ... Zentralblatt fuer Veterinaermedizin [*A publication*]

Zentralbl Veterinaermed Beih ... Zentralblatt fuer Veterinaermedizin Beiheft [*A publication*]

Zentralbl Veterinaermed Reihe A ... Zentralblatt fuer Veterinaermedizin. Reihe A [*A publication*]

Zentralbl Veterinaermed Reihe B ... Zentralblatt fuer Veterinaermedizin. Reihe B [*A publication*]

Zentralbl Veterinaermed Reihe C ... Zentralblatt fuer Veterinaermedizin. Reihe C [*A publication*]

Z Erkr Atmungsorgane ... Zeitschrift fuer Erkrankungen der Atmungsorgane [*A publication*]

Z Ernaehrungswiss ... Zeitschrift fuer Ernaehrungswissenschaft [*A publication*]

Zesz Nauk Uniw Jagiellonsk Pr Bot ... Zeszyty Naukowe Uniwersytetu Jagiellonskiego Prace Botaniczne [*A publication*]

Zesz Probl Nauki Pol ... Zeszyty Problemowe Nauki Polskiej [*A publication*]

Z Exp Chir ... Zeitschrift fuer Experimentelle Chirurgie [*A publication*]

Z Exp Chir Chir Forsch ... Zeitschrift fuer Experimentelle Chirurgie und Chirurgische Forschung [*A publication*]

Z Fisch Hilfswiss ... Zeitschrift fuer Fischerei und Deren Hilfswissenschaften [*A publication*]

ZFV .... Fort Severn [*Canada*] [*Airport symbol*]

Z Gastroenterol ... Zeitschrift fuer Gastroenterologie [*A publication*]

Z Geburtshilfe Gynaekol ... Zeitschrift fuer Geburtshilfe und Gynaekologie [*A publication*]

Z Geburtshilfe Perinatol ... Zeitschrift fuer Geburtshilfe und Perinatologie [*A publication*]

Z Gesamte Exp Med ... Zeitschrift fuer die Gesamte Experimentelle Medizin [*A publication*]

Z Gesamte Exp Med Einschl Exp Chir ... Zeitschrift fuer die Gesamte Experimentelle Medizin Einschliesslich Experimenteller Chirurgie [*A publication*]

Z Gesamte Hyg Grenzgeb ... Zeitschrift fuer die Gesamte Hygiene und Ihre Grenzgebiete [*A publication*]

Z Gesamte Inn Med Grenzgeb ... Zeitschrift fuer die Gesamte Innere Medizin und Ihre Grenzgebiete [*A publication*]

ZGF .... Grand Forks [*Canada*] [*Airport symbol*]

ZGI .... Gods River [*Canada*] [*Airport symbol*]

ZGR .... Little Grand Rapids [*Canada*] [*Airport symbol*]

ZGS .... Gethsemani [*Canada*] [*Airport symbol*]

ZHA .... Zhangjiang [*China*] [*Airport symbol*]

Z Haut-Geschlechtskr ... Zeitschrift fuer Haut- und Geschlechtskrankheiten [*A publication*]

Z Hautkr .... Zeitschrift fuer Hautkrankheiten [*A publication*]

Zh Eksp Klin Med ... Zhurnal Eksperimentalnoi i Klinicheskoi Meditsiny [*A publication*]

Zh Evol Biokhim Fiziol ... Zhurnal Evolyutsionnoi Biokhimii i Fiziologii [*A publication*]

Zh Gig Epidemiol Mikrobiol Immunol ... Zhurnal Gigieny Epidemiologii, Mikrobiologii, i Immunologii [*A publication*]

Zhivotnov'd Nauki ... Zhivotnov'dni Nauki [*A publication*]

Zh Mikrobiol Epidemiol Immunobiol ... Zhurnal Mikrobiologii Epidemiologii i Immunobiologii [*A publication*]

Zh Obshch Biol ... Zhurnal Obshchei Biologii [*A publication*]

Zh Prikl Spektrosk ... Zhurnal Prikladnoi Spektroskopii [*A publication*]

Zh Ushn Nos Gorl Bolezn ... Zhurnal Ushnykh Nosovykh i Gorlovykh Boleznei [*A publication*]

Z Hyg Infektionskr ... Zeitschrift fuer Hygiene und Infektionskrankheiten [*A publication*]

ZIF .... Zero Insertion Force [*Electronics*]

ZIG .... Ziguinchor [*Senegal*] [*Airport symbol*]

ZIH .... Zihuatanejo [*Mexico*] [*Airport symbol*]

Z Immunitaets-Allergieforsch ... Zeitschrift fuer Immunitaets-und Allergieforschung [*A publication*]

Z Immunitaetsforsch ... Zeitschrift fuer Immunitaetsforschung [*A publication*]

Z Immunitaetsforsch Exp Ther ... Zeitschrift fuer Immunitaetsforschung und Experimentelle Therapie [*A publication*]

Z Indukt Abstammungs-Vererbungsl ... Zeitschrift fuer Induktive Abstammungs- und Vererbungslehre [*A publication*]

Z Int Inst Zuckerruebenforsch ... Zeitschrift des Internationalen Institutes fuer Zuckerruebenforschung [*A publication*]

Z Jagowiss ... Zeitschrift fuer Jagowissenschaft [*A publication*]

ZKB .... Kasaba Bay [*Zambia*] [*Airport symbol*]

ZKE .... Kaschechewan [*Canada*] [*Airport symbol*]

ZKG .... Kegaska [*Canada*] [*Airport symbol*]

Z Kinderchir Grenzgeb ... Zeitschrift fuer Kinderchirurgie und Grenzgebiete [*A publication*]

Z Kinderheilkd ... Zeitschrift fuer Kinderheilkunde [*A publication*]

Z Kinder-Jugendpsychiatr ... Zeitschrift fuer Kinder- und Jugendpsychiatrie [*A publication*]

Z Klin Chem Klin Biochem ... Zeitschrift fuer Klinische Chemie und Klinische Biochemie [*A publication*]

Z Klin Med ... Zeitschrift fuer Klinische Medizin [*A publication*]

Z Klin Psychol Psychother ... Zeitschrift fuer Klinische Psychologie und Psychotherapie [*A publication*]

Z Koeln Zoo ... Zeitschrift des Koelner Zoo [*A publication*]

Z Krebsforsch ... Zeitschrift fuer Krebsforschung [*A publication*]

Z Krebsforsch Klin Onkol ... Zeitschrift fuer Krebsforschung und Klinische Onkologie [*A publication*]

Z Kreislaufforsch ... Zeitschrift fuer Kreislaufforschung [*A publication*]

Z Kulturtech Flurbereinig ... Zeitschrift fuer Kulturtechnik und Flurbereinigung [*A publication*]

Z Laryngol Rhinol Otol Grenzgeb ... Zeitschrift fuer Laryngologie, Rhinologie, Otologie, und Ihre Grenzgebiete [*A publication*]

Z Lebensm-Unters-Forsch ... Zeitschrift fuer Lebensmittel-Untersuchung und -Forschung [*A publication*]

ZLO .... Manzanillo [*Mexico*] [*Airport symbol*]

ZLT .... La Tabatiere [*Canada*] [*Airport symbol*]

ZMB .... Zinc Mercaptobenzimidazole [*Organic chemistry*]

Z Med Laboratoriumsdiagn ... Zeitschrift fuer Medizinische Laboratoriumsdiagnostik [*A publication*]

Z Med Labortech ... Zeitschrift fuer Medizinische Labortechnik [*A publication*]

Z Med Mikrobiol Immunol ... Zeitschrift fuer Medizinische Mikrobiologie und Immunologie [*A publication*]

Z Menschl Vererb-Konstitutionsl ... Zeitschrift fuer Menschliche Vererbungs- und Konstitutionslehre [*A publication*]

Z Mikrosk-Anat Forsch (Leipz) ... Zeitschrift fuer Mikroskopisch-Anatomische Forschung (Leipzig) [*A publication*]

Z Morphol Anthropol ... Zeitschrift fuer Morphologie und Anthropologie [*A publication*]

Z Morphol Oekol Tiere ... Zeitschrift fuer Morphologie und Oekologie der Tiere [*A publication*]

Z Morphol Tiere ... Zeitschrift fuer Morphologie der Tiere [*A publication*]

ZMT .... Masset [*Canada*] [*Airport symbol*]

ZNA .... Nanaimo [*Canada*] Harbour Airport [*Airport symbol*]

Z Naturforsch Sect C Biosci ... Zeitschrift fuer Naturforschung. Section C. Biosciences [*A publication*]

Z Naturwiss-Med Grundlagenforsch ... Zeitschrift fuer Naturwissenschaftlich-Medizinische Grundlagenforschung [*A publication*]

ZNE .... Newman [*Australia*] [*Airport symbol*]

Z Neurol .... Zeitschrift fuer Neurologie [*A publication*]

ZNU .... Namu [*Canada*] [*Airport symbol*]

ZNZ .... Zanzibar [*Tanzania*] [*Airport symbol*]

ZOF .... Ocean Falls [*Canada*] [*Airport symbol*]

Zooiatr Rev Med Vet Prod Pecu ... Zooiatria Revista de Medicina Veterinaria y Produccion Pecuaria [*A publication*]

Zool Abh (Dres) ... Zoologische Abhandlungen (Dresden) [*A publication*]

Zool Afr ..... Zoologica Africana [*A publication*]

Zool Anz ... Zoologischer Anzeiger [*A publication*]

Zool Beitr ... Zoologische Beitraege [*A publication*]

Zool Bidr Upps ... Zoologiska Bidrag fran Uppsala [*A publication*]

Zool Bijdr ... Zoologische Bijdragen [*A publication*]

Zool Entomol Listy ... Zoologicke a Entomologicke Listy [*A publication*]

Zool Gaert ... Zoologische Gaerten [*A publication*]

Zool J Linn Soc ... Zoological Journal of the Linnean Society [*A publication*]

Zool Listy ... Zoologicke Listy [*A publication*]

Zool Mag (Tokyo) ... Zoological Magazine (Tokyo) [*A publication*]

Zool Meded (Leiden) ... Zoologische Mededelingen (Leiden) [*A publication*]

Zool Pol ..... Zoologica Poloniae [*A publication*]

Zool Publ Victoria Univ Wellington ... Zoology Publications from Victoria University of Wellington [*A publication*]

Zool Revy ... Zoologisk Revy [*A publication*]

Zool Soc Egypt Bull ... Zoological Society of Egypt Bulletin [*A publication*]

Zool Verh (Leiden) ... Zoologische Verhandelingen (Leiden) [*A publication*]

Zool Zh ...... Zoologicheskii Zhurnal [*A publication*]

Zoonoses Res ... Zoonoses Research [*A publication*]

Zoon Suppl ... Zoon. Supplement [*A publication*]

Zoophysiol Ecol ... Zoophysiology and Ecology [*A publication*]

Zoo Rev Parque Zool Barc ... Zoo Revista del Parque Zoologico de Barcelona [*A publication*]

Zootec Nutr Anim ... Zootecnica e Nutrizione Animale [*A publication*]

Zootec Vet ... Zootecnica e Veterinaria [*A publication*]

Z Orthop Grenzgeb ... Zeitschrift fuer Orthopaedie und Ihre Grenzgebiete [*A publication*]

Z Parasitenkd ... Zeitschrift fuer Parasitenkunde [*A publication*]

Z Pflanzenernaehr Bodenkd ... Zeitschrift fuer Pflanzenernaehrung und Bodenkunde [*A publication*]

Z Pflanzenernaehr Dueng Bodenkd ... Zeitschrift fuer Pflanzenernaehrung Duengung Bodenkunde [*A publication*]

Z Pflanzenkr Pflanzenschutz ... Zeitschrift fuer Pflanzenkrankheiten und Pflanzenschutz [*A publication*]

Z Pflanzenphysiol ... Zeitschrift fuer Pflanzenphysiologie [*A publication*]

Z Pflanzenzuecht ... Zeitschrift fuer Pflanzenzuechtung [*A publication*]

Z Physiother ... Zeitschrift fuer Physiotherapie [*A publication*]

Z Pilzkd ..... Zeitschrift fuer Pilzkunde [*A publication*]

Z Praeklin Geriatr ... Zeitschrift fuer Praeklinische Geriatrie [*A publication*]

Z Praeklin Klin Geriatr ... Zeitschrift fuer Praeklinische und Klinische Geriatrie [*A publication*]

Z Praeventivmed ... Zeitschrift fuer Praeventivmedizin [*A publication*]

Z Psychol ... Zeitschrift fuer Psychologie [*A publication*]

Z Psychol Z Angew Psychol ... Zeitschrift fuer Psychologie mit Zeitschrift fuer Angewandte Psychologie [*A publication*]

Z Psychosom Med ... Zeitschrift fuer Psychosomatische Medizin [*A publication*]

Z Psychosom Med Psychoanal ... Zeitschrift fuer Psychosomatische Medizin und Psychoanalyse [*A publication*]

ZQN .... Queenstown [*New Zealand*] [*Airport symbol*]

ZRH .... Zurich [*Switzerland*] [*Airport symbol*]

Z Rheumaforsch ... Zeitschrift fuer Rheumaforschung [*A publication*]

ZRI .... Serui [*Indonesia*] [*Airport symbol*]

ZSA .... San Salvador [*Bahamas*] [*Airport symbol*]

Z Saeugetierkd ... Zeitschrift fuer Saeugetierkunde [*A publication*]

ZSS .... Sassandra [*Ivory Coast*] [*Airport symbol*]

ZST .... Stewart [*Canada*] [*Airport symbol*]

ZSW .... Prince Rupert [*Canada*]

ZTB .... Tete A La Baleine [*Canada*] [*Airport symbol*]

ZTH .... Zakinthos [*Greece*] [*Airport symbol*]

Z Tierpsychol ... Zeitschrift fuer Tierpsychologie [*A publication*]

Z Tierpsychol Beih ... Zeitschrift fuer Tierpsychologie Beiheft [*A publication*]

Z Tierz Zuechtungsbiol ... Zeitschrift fuer Tierzuechtung und Zuechtungsbiologie [*A publication*]

ZTO .... Zero Time Outage

Z Tropenmed Parasitol ... Zeitschrift fuer Tropenmedizin und Parasitologie [*A publication*]

Z Tuberkulose Erkr Thoraxogane ... Zeitschrift fuer Tuberkulose und Erkrankungen der Thoraxogane [*A publication*]

ZUM .... Churchill Falls [*Canada*] [*Airport symbol*]

Z Unfallmed Berufskr ... Zeitschrift fuer Unfallmedizin und Berufskrankheiten [*A publication*]

Z Urol Nephrol ... Zeitschrift fuer Urologie und Nephrologie [*A publication*]

ZVA .... Miandrivazo [*Madagascar*] [*Airport symbol*]

Z Vererbungsl ... Zeitschrift fuer Vererbungslehre [*A publication*]

Z Versuchstierkd ... Zeitschrift fuer Versuchstierkunde [*A publication*]

Z Vgl Physiol ... Zeitschrift fuer Vergleichende Physiologie [*A publication*]

Z Vitam-Horm-Fermentforsch ... Zeitschrift fuer Vitamin-Hormon- und Fermentforschung [*A publication*]

New Acronyms, Initialisms, & Abbreviations

ZWA .... Andapa [*Madagascar*] [*Airport symbol*]
Zwierzeta Lab ... Zwierzeta Laboratoryjne [*A publication*]
Z Wiss Mikrosk Mikrosk Tech ... Zeitschrift fuer Wissenschaftliche Mikroskopie und Mikroskopische Technik [*A publication*]
Z Wiss Zool ... Zeitschrift fuer Wissenschaftliche Zoologie [*A publication*]
ZWL .... Wollaston Lake [*Canada*] [*Airport symbol*]

ZWOK .... Zirconium-Water Oxidation Kinetics
ZYL .... Sylhet [*Bangladesh*] [*Airport symbol*]
Z Zellforsch Mikrosk Anat ... Zeitschrift fuer Zellforschung und Mikroskopische Anatomie [*A publication*]
Z Zool Syst Evolutionsforsch ... Zeitschrift fuer Zoologische Systematik und Evolutionsforschung [*A publication*]